The Caribbean Home Garden Guide

Written by Ralph Trout

LIBERTAD PUBLISHING, LLC

Copyright © 2017 by Ralph Trout
All rights reserved
This book, or parts thereof may not be reproduced in any form without permission from the publisher; exceptions are made for brief excepts used in publishing venues.

Published by
Libertad Publishing, LLC

ISBN: 10 0-9992239-0-9
ISBN 13: 987-9992239-0-1

Readers are urged to take all appropriate precautions before undertaking any how-to task. Always read and follow instructions and safety warnings for all tools and materials, and call in a professional if the task stretches your abilities too far. Neither the publisher or author are resposible for accidents, injuries, or damage incurred as a result of tasks undertaken by readers. This book is not a substitute for professional services.

Dedicated to my parents who taught me to garden before I knew I loved it.

Acknowledgements

I began composing this work several years ago after realizing there was no handbook on how to garden in a tropical climate. Initially information came from acquaintances, neighbors, and friends. Usually useful information only came when a garden disaster struck. When luck smiled and we had a good crop, we never asked questions. Our friends, the Ramcharitars from Kamp Po, provided a lot of valuable hard taught knowledge. Steven Anderson from San Souci provided much insight into plantain and banana care.

In Trinidad, I have taken several courses at the Centeno Station of the Ministry of Agriculture. These courses provided knowledge on using garden chemicals safely. I studied the grow box construction and every specific fruit and vegetable course I could attend. The Ministry of Agriculture agri-scientists at Centeno have answered many questions concerning diseases and pests. The personnel of the Agriculture Ministry Branch at Chase Village, especially the field officers, provided much help.

Clyde Sukha and Southern Chemicals demonstrated many new, and several time proven, common sense gardening techniques to get the most from garden labor. Most important, I learned to love the garden, whether in heat or mud, the process of growing my own food led me to other questions and to discover more answers.

The Internet has been the best information source for most of the crops. If you can correctly phrase the question, somewhere the Internet has the answer. Patience is the main investigative technique when working with Mr. Google. Trying to ascertain the correct name or term for a local fruit, vegetable, or root will always provide work for an earnest gardening detective. Locals have their own vocabulary, and terms may be limited to a family, village, section of the country, or an island; while the most common name is very different. Always try to first ascertain the botanical reference name of the particular fruit or vegetable. This may be difficult, but eventual success will avoid confusion.

I must give most of my Internet garden detectives credit to Purdue University Center For New Crop and Plant Products, http://www.hort.purdue.edu/newcrop/. If you can ask the food crop question with any reasonable skill, there is a very good probability this site already has someone organizing the existing research information. Several international universities are accessible for information. Deciding to deal with sources at the same latitude as the Caribbean, I have successful agricultural contacts at the University of Hawaii. There are several international web sites dedicated to tropical plants, fruits, and vegetables. These are too numerous to list.

Introduction

This garden guide does not promise gardening success. To achieve with agriculture, even in the home garden, you must invest whole hearted enthusiasm. A garden is a work of love. Love of nature, love of family, and love of good healthy food; but the garden must feel loved. Then gardening becomes an art form, and true love brings the knowledge that accompanies success.

Garden love grows as the garden matures and vegetables succeed. The garden inhales your perspiration from labor and exhales positive energy. Take the time to slow your life, enjoy being outdoors, get healthier thru exercise working in the home plot with family and friends, completely knowing the food you consume, and learning the cycles of nature.

I am adamant about a resurgence of the home garden. The modern world is separating the person from nature, from natural food, and separating the family structure. Time seems to be the main concern of everyone. Everywhere is a clock, on our phones, TV's, and microwaves; and time is quickly passing. Everyone speaks about 'quality time', spending time together, liming, or wasting time. The home garden provides all the best for time well spent.

Whether your garden space is large, or just a few containers, watching plants mature into food that feeds the human engine is a miracle of life. With gardens there are trials, and sometimes no great success, but never errors. With each attempt a lesson is learned and that is the profit. Now it appears our world is fragile, and we must as people, nations, and a species reconnect with nature and conserve what we have for future generations. The home garden is not only an investment for you and your family, but also an investment for the family and future of our world.

When the sun rises, I go to work.
When the sun goes down I take my rest,
I dig the well from which I drink,
I farm the soil which yields my food,
I share creation, Kings can do no more.
Chinese Proverb, 2500 B.C.

CONTENTS

THE GARDEN

01	Gardening Requirements
07	Container Gardens
11	Fence Gardens
15	Traditional Plot Garden
19	Water
25	Transplants
27	Fertilizers
33	Garden Chemicals
37	Pesticides in Food
41	Garden Spraying
47	Benefits of Limestone
51	Compost
53	Organic Gardening
57	Gardening with the Moon
59	How to Grow
67	Garden Tools
71	Garden Disease Prevention
75	Gardening in the Heat
79	Gardening After the Flood
83	Gardening and Good Health
89	Accounting
91	The Family Project
95	Garden Pests

HERBS AND SPICES

100	Allspice
103	Aloe Vera
106	Basil
109	Bay
112	Black Pepper
115	Cardamom
118	Cayenne Pepper
121	Chadon Benee
124	Chocolate
128	Cinnamon
131	Coriander
134	Cumin
137	Dill
140	Fennel
143	Horseradish
146	Mace
149	Marjoram
152	Mint
155	Mustard
158	Nutmeg
161	Oregano
164	Paprika
167	Parsley
170	Rosemary
173	Saffron
176	Sage
179	Tarragon
182	Thyme
185	Tonka Beans
188	Turmeric
191	Vanilla

FRUITS

196	Ackee
199	Avocado
202	Balata
204	Bananas
207	Breadfruit
210	Caimates
213	Canistele
216	Chalta
219	Chataigne
221	Chenets
223	Custard Apple
226	Dunks
229	Fat Pork
232	Grapefruit
235	Guava
238	Hog Plum
241	Jackfruit
244	Jamaican Plum
247	Lemon
250	Lime
253	Mamey Apple
255	Mango
258	Mangosteen
261	Orange
264	Papaya
267	Pewa
270	Pineapple
274	Plantain
278	Pommecythere

281	Pomegranate		**STEM AND BULB**	
284	Pomelo	404	Celery	
287	Red Banana	407	Chives	
290	Sapodilla	410	Garlic	
293	Soursop	413	Leeks	
296	Starfruit	416	Onion	
299	Sugar Apple		**VINES**	
302	Tamarind	420	Barbadine	
305	Tangelo	423	Cantaloupe	
308	West Indies Cherry	426	Carailli	
	ROOTS	429	Christophene	
312	Beets	432	Cucumber	
315	Carrots	435	Passion Fruit	
318	Cassava	438	Pumpkin	
321	Dasheen	441	Summer Squash	
324	Eddoes	444	Watermelon	
327	Ginger	447	Winter Squash	
330	Radish		**NUTS**	
333	Sweet Potato	452	Almonds	
336	Tannia	455	Brazil Nuts	
339	Toppee Tambu	458	Cashews	
342	Yam	461	Coconuts	
	VEGETABLES	464	Peanuts	
346	Bodi		**GRASSES**	
349	Broccoli	468	Marijuana	
352	Cauliflower	472	Rice	
355	Chana	475	Sugar Cane	
358	Corn	478	Tobacco	
361	Eggplant		**TREES**	
364	Green Beans	482	Calabash	
367	Hot Pepper	485	Coffee	
370	Ochro/Okra	492	Mauby	
373	Pigeon Peas	494	Noni	
376	Pimento	497	Roucou	
379	Sorrel		**APPENDICES**	
382	Sweet Peppers	501	Calorie and Nutrition Guide	
385	Tomatoes	513	Food Remedies	
	LEAFY VEGETABLES	535	Natural Remedies	
390	Cabbage	555	Glossary	
393	Lettuce	577	Sources	
396	Pak Choy			
399	Spinach			

Gardening Requirements

At one time or another most Caribbean people have come in close contact with a garden. That may sound odd, but as a culturally we have been moving away from agriculture. In just the past few years, many beautiful plots of tended crops have been replaced by roads, large homes and buildings. Perhaps, we believe we have evolved beyond the manual labor necessary to grow our own food. Yes, gardening involves some hard work, but if performed correctly, gardening can be relatively easy, belly filling, and soul fulfilling.

This type of home plot is termed, 'New Caribbean Home Gardening' because so much has changed so quickly in today's world. In a flash, food shortages are in every corner of the globe. Middlemen in the market, not farmers, are making the real profits from agriculture. Ban-dits steal garden produce where there are no watchmen. Food prices are increasing weekly. This is the new age of self-sufficiency, make your garden at home. The Caribbean is blessed with an excellent climate to grow a multitude of different crops. As nations we have plenty of fertile land, water, and energy to be a food basket for ourselves and the world. All it takes is a firm commitment to grow our own.

We've all seen photos of fields with straight rows, or neatly staked crops. Gardening is also an art form. As with blooming flowers or trimmed shrubbery in a landscaped yard, a home vegetable garden can be a rewarding and satisfying hobby. There may be some toil and expense in the initial phases, but by the end the self-satisfaction and the produce will be well worth every drop of sweat.

COMMITMENT

First and foremost, before starting any project, is the commitment.

CONDITION: Are you physically able to do the work? Almost anyone young and old can tend some type of garden. Be honest about what you can do easily without stressing yourself. Work only in the cooler mornings and evenings. Don't overdo it and drink plenty of water. In a short few weeks you'll notice as your garden begins to grow, your stamina will also increase.

MONEY: Can you afford the initial investment for tools, materials, seeds or seedlings, fertilizers, etc? A garden is an investment in both time and money. Investments take budgeting and maybe some sacrifice of fun money. With good investments there are profits. Your better health and fresh home grown food will be some of those profits.

TIME: Can you afford, or make the time necessary to daily tend your garden?

Depending on the size of your garden, the time can be minutes or hours. Even if you are financially strapped, working two jobs, you can still plant a few seasonings, peppers, or tomatoes in pots and water as you come and go. As your passion for agriculture develops, (and it will) pride of your gardening achievement will make more time for the satisfying, stress relieving gardening.

TRANSPORT: Can you find adequate and reasonable transport to get the necessary ma-terials? Surely someone you know or can hire has an appropriate vehicle and is willing to help you. This is an immense part of the gardening equation: getting the materials you need reasona-bly delivered to your site.

You need to answer these questions honestly. Do you really want to cut your home food costs, grow safer vegetables with less hazardous chemicals, get physical exercise, and share this garden project spending quality time with other family members?

SPACE: As part of your commitment, consider the size garden you and your helpers can handle. More help means the less individual work, but the produce must be shared. More help also means the commitment of every individual involved. I suggest a garden's labors be shared among family, or housemates. Sometimes the more people involved tend to cause unnecessary confusion. If you have committed to a small, perhaps eight by eight foot garden, then little extra help is needed. You also need to find adequate space for the gardening tools and supplies. Agri-chemicals need to be stored in a secure place out of reach of children and pets.

Think of everyway you can save money and time in this garden project. Simplify it as much as possible or it may beat you down before you begin. Can you borrow, or get tools from someone or a relative who is either elderly, or no longer in the mode, or mood to garden. Check house-garage sales in the newspapers for those who might have garden tools. You will need to budget some money weekly, and that's difficult in these times of inflating prices, until you have enough to begin. You may have to barter some of your future vegetable produce for tools or transport now. You will also need to budget your time, trading liming for more exercise in the garden; so every day something gets accomplished in the garden.

SPACE

How much room you have for a garden dictates the expense of time and money. There is always someplace to grow a few veggies. Start at your immediate home. Even if the entire lot is concrete you can build a partition to make a box or find suitable containers that can be filled with dirt. A corner can be barricaded or an entire wall used so materials will be less. Don't over esti-mate your energy, time, or money. Start with a small space and progress as your love for gar-dening grows. Remember it doesn't have to begin pretty, or be built of new materials.

Historically, Caribbean gardens have been away from the home separated because it was considered a work place and usually unattractive or smelly due to chemicals and fertilizers. Somehow farming in the Caribbean became considered a 'lesser '- almost

Gardening Requirements

demeaning occupation to keep hidden. However. it was farming that paid for many educations of lawyers, doctors, and engineers. Today's home plot can be productive and appealing. Even modern landscape archi-tects are building vegetable gardens as visible parts of posh estates.

You will need some basic things for your plot. Sun is ultimately necessary for all crops. Select a space that collects a minimum of six hours of direct sun every day, but ten hours is the best. The amount of sunshine will dictate what crops will grow best. Leafy veggies like lettuce, pak choy, or broccoli will survive with less sun.

Soil, or a growing medium, is the next crucial element. Soil - good old dirt - is being re-placed with other materials like bagasse (crushed sugar cane), rice husks, or compost. (More on growing mediums in Chapter 12.) Great soil is not necessary, but it must be fertile. Sand and overburden can grow some things, yet isn't the best. Hard clay or stony soil won't make a great garden. Your growing medium (soil) must be able to be softened with a fork, and or a hoe. Most important – it must drain away excess water, especially during the rainy season. If you have transport seek out good soil, but some manure, limestone, and a bit of sweat will improve almost any backyard plot.

Grow boxes, framed plots, or raised beds can be developed almost anywhere. (More on grow box farming in Chapter 2.) These raised boxes were developed to drain off excess water especially in the rainy season, and to provide a better, easier soil to work. If you are on a hillside, try terracing by staking boards across it and filling behind them with dirt or pulling a bit of the hill down. Make your rows cut across the slope like stairs.

Water is an absolute necessity, whether it is from a tap, hose, barrel, or river. The closer the water supply reduces your labor. It must also be constant. During the hot dry season, a small garden can drain a fifty-gallon barrel in a few days. A method of watering is also necessary from a watering can, bucket, sprinkler, or soaker hose. It must be adequate, and gentle so it doesn't erode the roots, knock off blossoms, or over soak the soil. Water should be applied just before the heat of the day and not later that three in the afternoon. This timing gives the plants a good drink when they need it , during the heat of the day and doesn't leave the soil damp for fungus to develop. Keeping the garden watered prop-erly is a problem we day workers have with the home garden and this means watering early in the morning before pursuing the almighty paycheck. (More on water in Chapter 5.)

Of course, the closer the garden is to your home the better. Consider driving to your gar-den, with today's traffic; you'd get there late and stressed. Build your garden close to your home and you will find it an easy satisfying hobby. Garden watching, watering,, and weeding will be come a healthy pastime. Closeness is a big plus for cooking; just walk outside and pick dinner.

Most house lots are fifty feet by one hundred feet. If you use the length for a garden three or four feet wide you will have a three to four hundred square foot garden just out-side your door. You want to make it wide enough to permit easy access to the plants at the rear without stepping into the bed. You also want to be able to pass easily along it. If you do the width of your lot, it will amount to half the size. A garden the length of your lot will feed your entire family and a lot of friends. If you don't have friends already, your garden will attract them.

Again, don't go overboard with the garden at the beginning. Four years ago I took a grow box course at an agricultural center and built a small bed – about ten by ten. That small beginner garden still feeds two families and many friends. It took two afternoons to build from old con-crete blocks in the rear corner of our lot. Christophene, sweet, hot, and seasoning peppers, let-tuce, chadon bene, chives, and several spices - plus blooming flowers are constantly being har-vested.

Drainage is necessary for water otherwise your garden will be soggy and the surrounding area will be muddy. This is not what you want. Damp soil will cause serious fungus problems. Stones or half and half placed at the very bottom beneath the soil of your garden will permit the water to drain. The garden should have good air circulation to keep fungus and disease to a mini-mum.

Security. Will yard fowl ruin your efforts? Does your dog like to sleep on the cool, tilled soil where you plant? Is your proposed plot possibly going to feed strangers who pick the fruits of your efforts in your absence? Again, keep your garden where you can see it.

PLAN FIRST TO SAVE LABOR LATER

There are few 'perfect' places for gardens, but make do. Once your space has been chosen, the next decision is what to grow. Plan first to save on labor later. Try to grow at least half of what your family needs. A kitchen garden usually contains chadon bene, let-tuce, pak choy, okra, chives, bodi, tomatoes and sweet, hot, and pimento peppers. All of these are relatively easy to grow. Make a drawing of your plot and place your veggies so they are not crowded. This will keep you from buying more plants or seeds than needed. Planting haphazard will waste time, money, energy, and deflate a positive attitude. It is important tall veggies like eggplant don't block the sun from smaller plants like pak choy or tomatoes. Tomatoes and peppers will waste energy growing to the sun rather than making the desired fruit. Also, separate crops that produce longer than others. Chadon bene leaves can be snipped with scissors and almost grow forever. Quick bearing crops, like pak choy or beans, should be the most accessible as they will need to be replanted. Allow a small area for a seedbed where you actually sprout the plants from seeds. To be the most productive, your garden should be fully planted at all times. Change the veggies you plant to confuse the insects and diseases.

An eight-foot by eight-foot garden, or slightly bigger, is a perfect size 'starter' plot for a small family. If this goes well, you can expand to a larger, or another plot with larger vegetables that need considerable space like pumpkin, squash, corn, or melons. Don't over plant or crowd your vegetables. This is counter-productive. It might seem like you should get more, but actually you will get less. The real trick is to have your seedbed working so you have new plants at the ready when a set is getting old. Good garden timing comes with practice.

Gardening Requirements

You will need some garden clothes and maybe a wide brimmed hat not only for the sun, but to get into the 'farmer look'. Depending on your career, you may require gloves for 'soft' hands. If you go into gardening in a bigger way, boots are a requirement. Not many tools are needed for a small plot. Some tools, like a fork (big or small), shovel, and wheel barrel might be borrowed for the original construction of your plot. A small hand fork, trowel, cutlass, or a hoe, a hose, water barrel, watering can, and a spray can are necessities. Don't buy cheap tools, as they won't last. Spend for quality and it will be dependable for several years. Keep your tools clean and sharpened; it will reduce your work. You will need some light rope or string and some sticks or bamboo to tie up your pepper and tomato trees to keep them off the dirt and conserve space.

As your garden expands, the need for water will increase. Irrigation is a convenience for larger plots. Piped water through a spray nozzle requires a further investment, but again drasti-cally reduces the labor of carrying heavy water buckets. Soaker hoses are now available at vari-ous agri shops and hardwares. Lay the hose between your rows of veggies. Connected to a tap it constantly provides a light spray through many tiny holes if it is turned up. Turned down it soaks where it lies. It is recommended to fill your water barrels or buckets at least eight hours before your water your garden so the chlorine will evaporate. Remember, mosquitoes lay their eggs in pools of water so keep your containers covered. Don't over water as this causes fungus and rots the roots of your vegetables.

BE CREATIVE

Part of the fun of new age gardening is scavenging or locating the materials you need to build your plot. Broken blocks, rocks, chunks of concrete, old galvanize roofing, boards, buckets, and even old auto tires can be used and tastefully arranged into a proud statement of your energy. Leaky plastic buckets, old wash tubs, or oil kegs can be filled with soil and planted. These are perfect for chives, celery, lettuce, or pak choy. With a bit of paint they'll look great. Add a few bright flowers like marigolds (ginder) or zinnias and it will look fantastic. (More on container growing in Chapter 2.)

Involve the family in the search and gaining of materials, to the actual building of the 'family plot'. Perhaps it will assist bonding the family together in these tough times. Children and elderly relatives can assist is almost every facet of the garden from planting to harvest and learning to cook with fresh vegetables. Once the plants begin to bear, everyone learns the success and failures full time farmers face every day. As much as your garden feeds your belly, it will also teach lessons valuable for an entire lifetime. Everyone will learn about the four vital ele-ments to growth; sun, wind, water, and earth. (More on the family garden in Chapter 22.)

Gardening teaches responsibility and scheduling. Plot chores like watering or weeding can be scheduled by the week to various family members. Certain plants can be assigned to indi-viduals and judged to who grows the best. Each involved learns that the plot's success depends on everyone doing their part on time and responsibly. A home garden will demonstrate where our food comes from, how dependent man as a species is to his planet, and how fragile nature has become.

THE GARDEN JOURNAL

Before starting your home garden plot acquire a notebook and begin your garden journal / diary. This seems like schoolwork, but it will take only minutes a day and save you so much time and expense in the future. Mark when you plant so you know when to expect the produce. Write the phase of the moon when you planted a specific vegetable. Many farmers swear by planting by a waning or waxing Moon. (More on the Moon and farming in Chapter 14.) Enter everything that works and doesn't. Include all expenses to later tally and see if your efforts really saved money. Keep all addresses and phone numbers of transport and material sources. Write down the garden schedule for watering, weeding, fertilizing etc.

The world is embarking on a new era of the haves and have nots. According to the news the world has much more 'nots'. With some energy and slight expense, grow a home garden and become one of the haves.

BASIC GARDEN TOOLS

Below: big fork and hand fork, hoe, cutlass, bucket, watering can, hose with spray nozzle. Spray can and sacks.

Container Gardens

Making the decision to grow at least some of your own vegetables requires organizing several items. Before you start locating tools and getting recipes, you need to decide what you can grow, and where you can grow it. Shop at home. Look around your home for what you can improvise into a garden.

Container gardens are basically raised gardens of various sizes and usually have improved soils. I've seen beautiful tomatoes grown in paint buckets, thriving celery in over-used cooking pots, house spouting filled with parsley, and amazing peppers grown in plastic bags. A lot of people fill old auto tires to grow a single vegetable. Styrotex grape boxes are fairly easy to find and work well. Cut a leaky blue plastic barrel in half. Small to large, there is something you can fill with dirt, add seeds, water, leave in a sunny spot, and grow some thing good to eat.

GROWING MEDIUMS

Potting soil, what most people call 'peat moss' is probably the best growing medium for small containers. A bale will fill a lot of pots. Some agri stores sell bags of a type of compost. If you cannot locate rich soil, the garden's growing medium will be one of the biggest expenses. The good side is, as long as you take good care of the soil, feed it and balance the acidity, it will feed you.

Dirt, soil, good old earth is the basic garden medium. Medium translates into a type of agent for growth. Different mediums for gardens are used because of different features. A truckload of good topsoil doesn't go far and is very expensive. Bagasse (mashed sugar cane) was commonly used throughout the Caribbean when sugar was king. Rice husks are priced about the same. All growing mediums have the same issue of controlling moisture, insects, and weeds. Treat the medium with a pre-emergent herbicide, and an insecticide when you are first turning it into your container or plot. It will save time and money later. In a few weeks the effects of the chemicals will be gone and the fruit of your garden shouldn't be affected by the chemicals.

SOIL PH

Measuring whether a soil medium is acid or alkaline is called soil pH (Potential Hydrogen). The soil scale ranges from 1 to 14 with 7 being neutral. Soil below 7 is acidic and above is alkaline. Before you invest time, energy and money in a big attempt at gardening it is wise to have the soil tested. An agricultural station can usually perform a soil test, or they can recommend somebody. Ask first how to obtain a sample. The best pH for a home vegetable garden is 6 to 6.5. If the soil is too acid, limestone can be added.

Where soil is often wet, as in a flood plain, it has a tendency to be acidic. Sandy soils become acidic easier than clay. You can purchase a pH tester online for a reasonable price once you have made the commitment to be a gardener.

I believe soils should be changed or rejuvenated every six months or between crops. Powdered limestone is an inexpensive soil additive. Let your fingers do the shopping as prices vary on a sack. At the producer it will be cheaper than at upscale agri shops. There are two types hydrated and unhydrated. The former is chemically calcium hydroxide and made by mixing regular or (un) limestone with water. The hydrated version is pure is more expensive (often four or fives times regular lime), white and acts on soil problems quickly. Usually effects can be seen within a week. Regular lime is gray and is takes about three months or more to change the soil pH. *(More on the benefits of limestone in Chapter 11.)*

If you have a fungus problem try mixing white, hydrated lime with water at two TBL per gallon and watering the base of the affected plants. For severe problems lightly dust the bases. Fungus and bacteria thrive on acidic soil. There are many chemical treatments, but by far white lime is successful in fighting fungus and strengthening plants. Every time we prepare ground to plant we lightly spread regular lime so months later the soil will be strong and balanced.

Soils become acidic because the natural limestone washes away either from floods or over watering/irrigation. Over fertilizing also causes a soil's pH to drop. Decay of organic materials such as chicken manure will also drop the pH. Acid soil will cause the vegetable plants roots to be stunted, under developed. This will cause the plants to need more watering and not fully accept fertilizer nutrients.

Beans corn, cucumbers, pumpkin, tomatoes, peppers and eggplant will withstand soils to 5.6pH. Lettuce, pak choy, cauliflower, spinach, okra and beets want a soil that is at least 6 or better to thrive.

Each medium needs to be fortified by adding well-rotted manure and limestone. The proportions depend on the size of the garden or container. Chicken manure is either 'bag it yourself' free, or for small money per feed sack. Horse, goat, and cow or bison manure are more expensive. If you see a horse or dairy farm, stop and ask if they'll give you manure. Sometimes it is adverted in the newspapers under 'Flowers and Plants'. Manure increases the acid content of the soil, so too much can harm young plants. Limestone lowers the acidity and fights bacteria, but use it sparingly. My soil recipe, for most vegetables grown in containers, put soil in a five-gallon bucket, add about two cups of manure and one-half cup of limestone.

FERTILIZER

Fertilizer usually is represented in three numbers like **Starter** – reddish brown 12-24-12 good until blossoms appear. Use a pinch in hole before setting young plants. **Special Green** – 15 –5 –20 –2 – great for green leafy veggies like lettuce and pak choy. **Blue** – 12-12-17-2 after blossoms begin to make the fruit come. *(More on fertilizer in Chapter 7)*

The first number in a fertilizer formula is the nitrogen content. Nitrogen is used by plants to promote leaf growth. Too much nitrogen can burn the plant. The second number is the phosphorus content. Phosphorus is used by plants to increase fruit development and to produce a strong root system. The third number is the potassium (potash) content. Potassium is important to the size and strength of the plant. For example, a 10 lb. bag of 12-24-12 converted to weight equates to 1.2 lbs. nitrogen, 2.4 lbs. phosphate, and 1.2 lbs. potash.

Bagasse, potting soil, and other mediums contain no nutrients. Manure isn't recommended for grow boxes. They require a starter mix of various nutrients, or using a stock starter fertilizer.

CONTAINERS

Nice red clay containers in all shapes and sizes can be had reasonably in most plant shops. Expensive, very lightweight, designer boxes cost a lot at various upscale hardwares, but they are tasteful.

First - plant your garden in the right place. A location that gets morning sun and afternoon shade is perfect. Each plant needs at least six hours of sun every day. But too much sun will dry out the soil. You can create some shade for your plants if you build a fence. *(More on fences in Chapter 3.)*

Plants can be started from seed in plastic or clay containers instead of directly in the garden. The containers need to be at least five inches with drain holes in the bottom. Moisten the soil before you plant the seeds. Once the seeds have sprouted they will need at least six hours of sunlight a day, but not the heat of the afternoon sun to start. Your plants will grow without a lot of labor. This is a great way to grow if you are pressed for time and space. Container gardening isn't best method to grow all kinds of vegetables. Most root crops, beans, corn, cucumbers, melons, pumpkins and squash grow better if you plant them directly in the garden.

Containers can be placed almost anywhere. Put them on the porch, along the side of your driveway or parking area. Small containers can be hung by wires from trees, or porch railings. Make certain the containers won't fall if put them on window ledges. Be careful to protect the surfaces underneath the containers from stains. The containers must have drainage holes to let out excel water. That drainage will be acid or alkaline, and that is what makes whitish stains.

A bit of paint or aluminum foil can dress up almost any container. Again, be a creative scavenger. The main requisites for container growing is that the container is durable- won't quickly rust away, has drainage holes to permit excess water to drain. All containers should have at least an inch of some rocks, broken brick, or gravel to further permit draining and give the roots something to grip. Fill with the soil medium to about an inch below the top. As the medium sinks and compacts with watering, add more. Always make certain the top roots are covered. I prefer wetting potting soil with water before putting it in the pots and planting seedlings.

There are many sites on the Internet for various types of grow systems. Most use space age materials and claim huge yields. I like dirt or bagasse because it feels good and is usually cool to the touch. Rice husks is really hot in the beginning (until it is soaked for about a week) and can shock the plants.

The most well known container and certainly well organized is Earthbox. Its website reads: *The US patented EarthBox was developed by commercial farmers and proven in the lab and on the farm. Our maintenance-free, award-winning, high-tech growing system controls soil conditions, eliminates guesswork and more than doubles the yield of a conventional garden-with less fertilizer, less water and virtually no effort.*

I saw a TV advert on the Earthbox and Googled to discover American container farming is now a state of the art, expensive commodity making big profits, but hopefully helping feed people. The Earthbox technique uses a perforated partition about an inch above the container's bottom to separate the water and soil. The plants in the soil send their roots down through the partition into the water mixed with nutrients. The water is filled through a tube extending above the soil. The water tube is kept full and you can't over fill. Earthbox provides only the plastic box and a snug box cover. They recommend potting mix, not potting soil, and recommend the type of fertilizer to purchase depending on what you intend to plant, and how many plants percontainer. It is necessary only to fertilize at the set up. The cover is cut to accept the plants and will drastically conserve water, fertilizer, and end weeding forever.

I suspect as with all container gardens, the soil must be rejuvenated at periodic intervals. The Earthbox should function well for several years. Earthboxes are 29" long, 13.5" wide, and x 11" tall, reusable, a variety of colors and cost about $60 USD. In one box they recommend sixteen beans, or six sweet pepper trees, or two tomato trees, or six cabbages, etc. (see more online)/ As far as I know there are no local agents for Earthbox in the Caribbean. The manufacturer claims this version of the container garden can double yields, with less water, fertilizer, and labor with a satisfaction money back guarantee. This is truly maintenance-free – container gardening for dummies.

A garden was the primitive prison, till man with Promethean felicity and boldness, luckily sinned himself out of it.

Charles Lamb

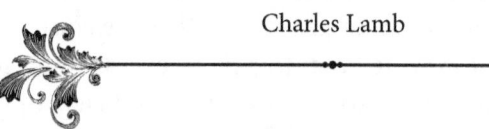

Fence Gardens

Caribbean people love to fence their property to stop encroachment and deter crime. Many 'modern style homes' decided concrete is the best and easiest landscape technique. With less visible 'dirt', no mess, and no grass to mow, the surrounding fence may be the only area available for a garden. Whether wrought iron fence, chain link, or BRC, all can support a hanging garden. Make certain the fence can take the weight of a heavy vine with fruits. If it is chain link it must have a heavy 'pull' wire near the top for support or the vine will bend it down.

Many vegetables and fruits need support of a fence, or trellis (locals call it a jamrah), to develop. A variety of plants can be easily adapted to grow on a fence. Why? Fence vegetables take less space, away from the soil with fresh air there is less chance for diseases, and ripe produce is easy to spot. A good vine like barbadine, passion fruit, christophene, or carailli, offers shade and privacy while the luscious green leaves with beautiful blossoms bear tasty fruit. Tomatoes are usually staked for support as the trees become so heavy as they mature, but they will climb a fence. Bodi needs to be away from the ground or the vines would get trampled during pickings. It is the same for christophene or seim beans. I've been successful with climbing cucumbers, pole beans, and small "sweet mama" pumpkins. Some squash can also be fence trained.

Using your fence as part of your garden will benefit other plants. The leafy fence will also provide shade for your regular flat soil plot or containers. The shade will help fight sunburn from the wilting afternoon sun of the dry season and help conserve water at the plants roots. Staking or fencing keeps the fruit away from the damp soil and reduces rot.

Plant at the bottom of the fence if there is any soil available. If not plant in a container. Either way, it only takes a few minutes a day to train the plant to grow up the fence. Once you've decided what and where to plant and have acquired the plants or the seeds, fork a spot two foot in diameter and about a foot deep. Add about a cup well-rotted manure and a half cup of limestone to each hole you are going to plant. Mark the spot you seed so you can water the roots as it grows.

Six bodi plants are enough to feed most families. Seeds can be obtained at agri shops, from friends, or go to the market and ask vendors for over ripe beans. The seeds will be very visible when bodi has been on the vine too long. Allow the beans to fully dry before shelling. My favorites are green arrow and the shorter red variety. Bodi's thin yet strong flexible vines are easy to lace through any type of fence. The long beans dangle like Christmas ornaments. Let a few beans get full so you'll have some seeds to plant back. Bodi needs just a little water and little to no fertilizer.

The seim bean is another quick climber that needs little work and is very tasty and nutritious. Find the seeds in the market or through friends. Two vines will produce plenty. I recently planted some purple seim vines on my back fence to provide shade for christophene. Seim added a nice, broad pointed, deep green leaf with purple flowers as a backdrop to my vegetable garden. Getting the tasty seim beans was a second benefit. Unless you take good care, the long seim vines will overgrow and crowd your garden. Seim is scientifically called 'the hyacinth bean or Dolichos lablab'. Pick carefully as the seim vine has a sharpness that can cut you.

The purple seim type most common in Trinidad is called Ruby Moon. Seim has purplish stems and alternate, white, pink, or purple flowers in a long bunch that produce maroon bean pods containing 3-5 green beans. When the beans dry they become black with a white streak. I pick the bean pods while the skin is smooth and the beans pushing out yet.

Passion fruit will take over and seems to grow with little attention once it is established. Plant it where it will not interfere with other vines. Occasionally toss a bit of blue fertilizer (12- 12-17-2) at its roots and hit the leaves with hose spray and it will continually produce the delicious juicy yellow fruits.

Barbadine is a sweet, good tasting fruit of a climbing vine perfect for growing on a sturdy fence. The flesh of the barbadine can be cooked as a vegetable, a dessert, or strained for the juice. Seeds from one mature fruit should produce at least ten plants, and that is a lot! Care for barbadine just as passion fruit. Passion fruit and barbadine have absolutely beautiful blossoms.

Carailli is another of the low maintenance fence vines that offers a nice light green leaf and yellow blossoms. The seeds may be difficult to locate, again go to the market and look for a fruit that has turned yellowish orange. Permit the seeds to dry before planting. Plant about four seeds per hole and space the holes at least ten feet apart. Water daily until the sprouts are about a foot long. Lay a stick or a string for the new plants to use as a ladder to the fence. Once carailli has attached there is no stopping it. Two carailli plants are plenty.

The bumpy green skinned fruit is the strangest and bitterest member of the melon family. A mature fruit should first be sliced and salted, then squeezed to remove the bitter juice before cooking. However, smaller young fruit are almost sweet. Carialli is nutritional and the bitter juice can be helpful to diabetics.

Tomatoes need to be started against the fence. I have a raised bed about a foot wide. Once the tomato tree is a foot tall I start weaving the branches carefully into the chain link. I grow tomatoes and carailli together on the fence and that permits room for sweet pepper trees in the front of the same small box. Carailli will try to take over so attention is needed so the tomato can thrive. Six tomato trees will feed most families.

Christophene needs an area to itself. The easiest method to grow this vegetable is to locate a farmer and beg a plant. Failing that, select two christophene at the market. Ask the vendor if they have any that are over ripe and budding. If not, set the christophene in a warm window, but not in direct sun. In a few days it will start to shrivel and wrinkle and soon sprout a bud. Plant the seed bud upwards in a clay pot with sandy soil. As I began growing christophene I realized that some fruit, no matter the size or age, sprout while growing on the vine. Two christophene plants are all that you will need.

After seeing jamrahs (trellis) of christophene in Lopinot, and the intense mountain cultivation on the road from Arima to Blanchisseuse, I incorrectly believed this vine needed coolness to develop. This vine loves the sun, but also needs plenty of water, yet can be grown almost anywhere. In Central Trinidad, I have a small corner of fence as a backdrop to a grow box with a sprinkler. Two christophene vines produced for over six months. In the intense heat of the dry season, I have to water it at least three times a day.

Cucumber vines will support the weight of large fruits, but this vine is fragile so be careful lacing the young vine onto a fence. Cukes will take almost the same care as christophene as they like water and special green fertilizer (15 –5 –20 –2) in small doses. Plant three cucumber vines about six feet apart and that should produce an adequate supply.

Most vines need little attention, water when necessary except for christophene. A weekly or biweekly spraying with a light insecticide like Pestac or Fastac mixed with a water soluble fertilizer like Nutrex 20-20-20 should prevent any infestation and give plenty of nourishment. It is best to spray late in the day after the heat has diminished. With Christophene, carailli and cucumber, try the spray on a small part and watch for a few days to determine if it has any burning–yellowing-side effects.

With all fence growing, be careful of the intrusion of an undesirable vine. The Caribbean has many vines as cow itch and others that will thrive with the attention given to your intended fruit or vegetable. Birds will present the biggest problem to the fruits of your fence labors.

If you don't have a fence, make a jamrah or trellis of any old PVC pipes, boards, or bamboo. Stake four posts in the earth and lace four together at the top. Make it sturdy enough and string your hammock underneath the soon to be lush vines. If this is too much work, find or buy a piece of 6 inch BRC, and stand or lean it upright for the plants to climb on.

The main reason to grow on a fence is to save space, hopefully to plant more veggies on the ground. You'll quickly see its appearance is tasteful and the vegetable or fruits are tasty. Your neighbors will surely see the value of your green thumb.

NOTES

4

The Traditional Garden Plot

Gardening is a great hobby, relaxation, and a diversion from a stressful world. For some people growing their own food is quite an accomplishment, and provides family togetherness while saving money on fresh vegetables.

GROW YOUR OWN

Home gardens are visibly transforming landscapes from the lush tropical plants and hedges to at least partial edible gardens. Vegetable gardens are no longer hidden behind the home. A vegetable garden, tastefully planned, is a living art form. The produce has the great taste of extremely fresh 'home grown'. A garden doesn't need to be unsightly and can be intermixed with flowers. Some gardeners grow hard to find, difficult to grow, or unique varieties of veggies, while the majority of us are serious growers 'for the table', doing it as easy as possible. Our gardens – large or small— are functional and attractive (at least to us!)

With proper planning, the vegetable garden can be both functional and attractive. Landscape designers today often plant flowering annuals into the vegetable gardens. This gardening philosophy, coupled with our favorable climate, can offer gardening opportunities all year long.

For a beginner gardener, don't try to plant an overly large area and don't push yourself to get it done. Constructing your own garden is not something that needs to be done instantly, unless you want to hire a crew. Make your garden a place to relax, be patient. Plan what you want to plant and make a drawing to scale if possible so you don't waste time, energy and money. Think of the garden as split into parts, one for short crops like pak choy, lettuce, spinach, bush (green) beans, celery, seasonings, and ochro arranged by height from shortest (lettuce) to the tallest (ochro). The tallest shouldn't block the sun. Prepare another section with plants like peppers, tomatoes, and cucumbers etc. Other sections can be developed as for root crops as morai and beets, a section for seasonings like chives, celery, spices, and chadon bene, or extremely tall crops like, eggplant, cassava, peas, and corn. I prefer to have the tallest at the eastern part of the garden so they get the morning sun and don't block the afternoon sun. Vines need plenty of space or they will over grow other vegetables.

SOIL

You need reasonably good soil that receives preferably eight hours of direct sun, and close to a source of water. If you can pull the soil higher into a 'raised bed' it will drain better. Drainage is very important. Once you select the area, to reduce the labor of fork ing, soak the soil at least over night. Fork the soil to eight or ten inches deep. Then let it sit in the sun for at least two full days. This is termed 'solarization' and is a method to kill some diseases. Good soil will help plants grow strong, healthy, and produce excellent fruits.

After a few days in the sun, cover the clumps of dirt with well rotted manure. Chicken manure is the most available and least expensive, but I have seen horse and bison manure for sale. Then dust with powdered limestone. If possible, wet the soil to ease breaking the clumps with a hoe. Break the soil as soft as possible into a nice mix. Pull the soil into beds bordered by drains that lead excess water away from the plants.

Mark the rows with a line or a board and cut a furrow, a two to three inch indentation into the loose soil. Space your rows about eighteen inches apart so you have room to walk after the plants mature. Space your plantings properly. It might seem that more plants per square foot will produce more, but actually crowding vegetable plants is counter productive. They need fresh air to circulate, you need to see the plants' conditions, pull weeds, and fertilize differently. Plants need watering on a regular basis, so hopefully your plot is near a water tap and you have a hose.

Dry season tip: Make a furrow four inches wide and four inches deep. Spread a one-inch thick layer of rotted manure on the bottom. Plant seeds in the furrow and cover with soil. Make certain the furrow isn't filled in to the top and will hold some water. Water the furrow daily for the first few weeks. As the plants grow mold the soil around the stems to protect the roots from the sun. Allow a bit of original furrow to remain to continue to hold the water.

TRANSPLANTS

Leave a small area, maybe two-foot square, for a seedbed to start your own plants, like tomatoes and all types of peppers, from seeds. Most seed packets and seedling dealers will tell you the mature size of the plants you are selecting. Check the seed packets to assure the seeds are fresh. Wet the seedbed to 4 inches deep, plant the seeds, and cover with dry soil. Keep soil wet to help germination. Care for the seeds until the seedlings are four to six inches tall. Then for about two weeks gradually reduce the water while increasing the exposure to sunlight to 'harden' the plants for transplanting. When pulling the seedlings, totally wet the bed to make removal easy without any damage to the seedling plant.

Transplanting is taking a plant from one soil or medium (the seedbed) to another (the garden) where plants will have more space to mature. Most plants suffer a bit of shock being transplanted. Carefully dig, remove and replant. When buying vegetable transplants, look for stocky, full plants. Their roots should be white or light tan, not brown, and they should not be root bound in their container. Transplants that have already started to fruit are not a bonus! They are stressed from being confined too long. It is best to transplant seedlings in the evening. If the transplants already have flowers or small fruits remove them to ensure more vegetative growth and adaptation to 'your garden' before fruit production begins. Keep the garden damp when transplanting.

I make a small hole for each transplant and put in just a pinch of starter (like five to ten tiny pellets) of 12-24-12 fertilizer. I pull over a bit of soil and then put in the plant. This keeps the roots away from the fertilizer until it adapts to its new setting. Then the roots hit the fertilizer and it is like getting a vitamin boost!

Direct garden planting can be done in properly wet shallow furrows. This is termed 'drilling'. This is good for lettuce, beans, etc. Place the seeds and cover them with soil, but not too deep. Seeds that are covered with too much soil may never come up. After germination, excess plants are thinned to the correct spacing. 'Hilling' or 'mounding' places several seeds in one mound with fixed spacing. Squash, pumpkins, and melons are often planted in this manner. This is also a good technique for the wet season.

Thinning seedlings to get the best spacing reduces competition for nutrients and water. It provides better conditions for growing healthier vegetables to produce higher yields. Thin the plants directly seeded to the soil when they have one or two pairs of true leaves, about 3 inches tall. In the cool evening, when the soil is damp and soft, is the best time for thinning. This is a must for leaf lettuce, beets, morai radish, and spinach.

The entire garden plot should be kept fully planted, but not over planted. Once a set of plants stops producing, pull them and replant. Try to switch plant families to confuse insects and repel some diseases. Remember, **vegetables subject to the same diseases and insects should not follow each other**. Tomatoes are cousins to all types of pepper and eggplants. Cabbage, cauliflower, broccoli are related. Cucumber, pumpkin, squash and melons are in the same family. Remove diseased plants as soon as you notice. It will be more problems and expense to cure than to replant. Do not place sick plants in a compost pile.

The biggest enemies to transplants are lack of a combination of too much sun and a lack of water. Mole crickets are the most damaging insect to new plants. They chew the stem just be low the dirt level. The best deterrent I've discovered is a mixture of insecticide with soluble Sevin's Powder. Any chemical residue is gone when the plant matures and bears fruit. Sweet peppers are really susceptible to mole cricket damage.

WATERING

Plants need about an inch of water every week. I recommend watering in the morning so the soil is not overly damp at night, which may promote fungus growth. I try to really soak the plants once a week. Water the base of the plants, slow and evenly, and try not to wet the leaves or erode the roots. Try to dampen the soil to about four inches deep. It is the roots that must receive the water. Deep watering helps strong roots develop that can find water hidden deep within the soil. *(More on watering in the next chapter.)*

FERTILIZE

Once the plants catch (become adapted and start to grow), throw just a pinch of 12-24-12 starter fertilizer abound the base. As you water it will seep to the roots. I do not recommend water soluble fertilizers as they can burn the plants unless you only spray it at the roots. The leaves absorb little water; that is the job of the roots. Soluble fertilizers often are high in nitrogen and that can delay fruit production.

As you water the soil erodes at the base of the plant. This can cause the roots to get burned by the hot sun or the fertilizer. Weekly, I carefully pull soil around the stem of the plant. This is called molding. Many gardeners over fertilize. When I mention just a pinch, it is all you can grab between two fingertips. Use the reddish brown starter fertilizer until blossoms appear, then use the blue 12-12-17-2. It is best to apply fertilizer just before a rain or watering the garden. Never permit fertilizer pellets to remain on the leaves, as it will "burn" them.

WEEDS

Weeds are undesirable in any garden since they compete for nutrients and water. Some weeds spread diseases. Start controlling weeds when you plant by pulling or hoeing. Watering just the base of the plants discourages weed growth. Work the soil properly after each deep watering to kill sprouted weeds and to leave the soil's surface loose to absorb more water.

HARVEST

Harvest is what you have worked and waited for. Remember to harvest when the fruit is ripe. Do not permit it to sit on the vine attracting damage from birds and insects. Once your garden begins to produce try to pick at least every other day. Now is the time to try new recipes and enjoy the fresh veggies. Remove the old plants immediately after harvest, cultivate, and replant. Save seeds from one of the best fruits you harvest for your seedbed. Always let the seeds completely dry before planting.

THINGS TO REMEMBER

If you have a serious gardening problem contact the professionals at a government agri station. They are garden specialists and are very busy, so don't waste their time. Don't take advice from just anyone. Other gardeners may be envious and give erroneous and spiteful advice. Agri shops want to sell you something.

Remember, dry plants are stressed plants. Too much water can damage plants by blocking oxygen to the roots or cause a fungus attack. Don't over water or over fertilize. Excess nitrogen fertilizer can cause some root-rotting fungi and bacterial growth. Stress from too much nutrient can make plants more susceptible to diseases and insect damage.

Each hour in your garden will benefit you, your family, and friends. Every year your garden skills will improve and your plants will bear more. You may never have 'the perfect garden', but who does? Disorganized, beginner gardening can be a lot of work, yet the accomplishment of growing your own will out weigh the labor. Your garden is a work of art always in progress.

Water

Water is life, and life is mostly water. All living things need water to stay alive, but plants use much more water than animals do. Plants are about 90% water, while our bodies are about 60% water. Plants absorb water and with the sun's energy transform it into food. Gardens can be compared to cities; too much, or too little water makes living difficult.

Even though water seems so plentiful, useable fresh water is very limited. Our planet is 70% water, but 96 % is saltwater. More than two thirds of the Earth's fresh water is frozen in icecaps or glaciers; thirty per cent is under the ground. Only about two thirds of one per cent, (.67%), is available for use as surface water from lakes and rivers. Trinidad is lucky to have so much fresh water, especially available for agriculture. Too many people in our world do not have access to safe drinking water.

The USA uses over three hundred billion gallons of water a day just from surface water and eighty-five billion gallons from underground resources! Forty per cent of the USA's water is used in agriculture. They are using more water than is being naturally replenished.

DID YOU KNOW?

Water (H_2O) is the most abundant molecule on Earth's surface, comprising almost 70% of the Earth's surface. In nature it exists in liquid, solid (ice), and gaseous (water vapor) states. It is in natural balance between the liquid and gaseous states at standard temperature and pressure. At room temperature, it is a nearly colorless with a hint of blue, tasteless, and odorless liquid. Drinking water is polluted by pesticides, fertilizers, sewage, and saltwater. Trinidad has about 1.2 cu miles of water, with 35% used for farming and 38% used for industrial purposes. About 90% of the population has access to pure drinking water.

The Central African countries as Congo and Cameroon have the most renewable surface and underground freshwater per national citizen. Brazil has the most freshwater with twelve percent. Russia has ten percent, China has eight percent, Canada with 300,000 lakes has six and a half percent, and the US has five percent. With the future's demand for agriculture, these water rich nations will be the important growers.

Plants absorb water at their roots and by a process called 'transpiration' trade it for carbon dioxide. It is a very complicated process, but simply, leaves have tiny pores that let water evaporate out and absorb carbon dioxide. Transpiration pulls water from the roots up the stem to the leaves. Every day a full grown vegetable plant 'transpires' three quarters of its weight in water. If humans did that, we'd have to drink more twenty-five gallons of liquids a day. Less than one percent of water pulled to the leaves is used to produce fruit growth. Most of it just evaporates.

Farmers are the biggest consumers of freshwater using more than half of the available water. Correctly used, almost all agricultural water is recycled into either surface or ground reserves. Developing countries devote most of their water supplies to agriculture. India, for instance, uses 90% of all water for agricultural purposes, with just 7% for industry, and 3% for domestic use. As more people move away from the countryside into cities, and agriculture depends more and more on irrigation, it will be difficult for cities to meet the increased demand for freshwater. In developing countries rapid urban growth often puts tremendous pressure on antiquated, inadequate water supply systems.

Plants use various amounts of water depending on age, size, type, amount of sun, temperature, etc. Correct watering is vital to growing good vegetables; enough applied properly, yet not too much. Garden vegetable plants need varying amounts of water. All watering techniques, from sprinkling can to sprinklers, are considered irrigation. It is important to get the water to the roots. The leaves absorb very little water. The soil at the roots should be moist to a depth of at least four inches. Water slowly and evenly, preferably through a sprinkler spout. Place the sprinkler spout close to the plant's stem, below the lowest leaves, and gently tilt the can. With vines like cucumber, melon or pumpkin, mark the roots when you plant and try not to get water on the leaves. This will help fight fungus. If you pour water directly, you may erode the soil at the root, which could potentially harm the plant either by sun burning the visible root,

Different soils are another water factor. Clay type soils hold water better than sandy ones. With clay it is best to hoe and roughen the soil's surface and mold around your plants weekly to keep the soil from becoming glazed. Glazed soil will cause the water to runoff rather than soak in. Organic material, like compost or well-rotted manure, worked into the garden helps hold water. Fertilizers make plants thirsty, so use as little as possible just before watering. Rough watering will knock off blossoms, or break branches bearing fruit. This happens with sweet pepper. To check how well you are watering dig a small hole at a row's end and see how deep it is moist.

It is hard to calculate the amount of rain that hits you garden unless you have a rain gauge. Just put a jar or a can in among your plants and check how much accumulates. I like to water in the early morning. I make time before I begin my day. It gives me a peaceful, cool period to check out my plants and give them a nice long drink. Watering in the heat of the day loses a lot to evaporation. Shallow or quick watering will only wet the surface and the roots may stay shallow. Deep roots that seek moisture are better and create stability.

You can make a simple sprinkling can from a gallon bleach bottle. First make certain it is clean. Then use a drill if available with a quarter inch bit or smaller and put several holes in the plastic cap. (This can also be done with a hammer and a nail.) At the top of the neck where the handle begins drill or punch one hole into the body to let out air. Once a week during the dry season, I like to give them a good soaking with a hose. This

DID YOU KNOW?

Fruit/Vegetable	Percent Water	Fruit/Vegetable	Percent Water
Bananas	74%	Broccoli	91%
Cabbage	92	Cherry	81
Cantaloupe	90	Carrots	87
Cauliflower	92	Celery	95
Cucumber	96	Eggplant	92
Grapefruit	91	Lettuce	96
Orange	87	Peppers (Sweet)	92
Pineapple	87	Spinach	92
Squash	93	Tomato	94
Watermelon	92		

is especially for eggplant, and vine crops. Tomatoes don't need much water.

The easiest method I've found is the soaker hose. I've found two types in Trinidad. One is a round black material that literally lets water soak through. The black type is fragile and breaks easily if moved. The other is a usual green and white vinyl hose that has sprinkler holes. Turned up it sprinkles, faced down it soaks. Both types are placed among the plants, and water seeps to the roots. The seeper holes in the green vinyl type clog and must be cleared with pressure one a week. They can be used on just pipe pressure.

Most sprinkler systems waste water and must be used with a pump. Drip irrigation is another method that brings water directly to the roots. This style of irrigation wastes less water, but is costly and requires regular maintenance. You can use water from the pipe, river, pond, well, or roof. I recommend collecting water in a plastic barrel so the chlorine can evaporate before the plants get it. Keep the barrel covered as a protection for children and mosquitoes.

Planting in furrows that hold water rather than in mounds where it runs off is another dry season tip. As the rains begin, mold the plants and make certain they can drain. A few crops like cassava and onions can do with minimal water. Modern agricultural science has created different strains of seeds for some vegetables that are more drought tolerant. When I plant, I soak my seeds overnight, especially corn and bodi, and get a good rate of germination.

Over watering can lead to serious garden problems, fungus, diluting, and washing out fertilizers. Make sure your garden will drain quickly and adequately after a good rain. If you are planting in a raised bed or grow box lay a first layer of stones to let the excess water pass. Keep sloped drains between the beds and rows that lead surplus water out of your garden.

Knowing when and how much water to apply at various stages of the plant is a true garden skill. Every variety of vegetable requires more water at different stages of development. In some vegetables excess water brings out the better fruit, while too much water can harm a lot of plants. Seim, bodi, passion fruit, papaya, pineapple, and cassava need little watering. Tomatoes and peppers need regular water, but not much and preferably in the morning. Beans need regular water, christophene, lettuce and leafy veggies like pak choy, take a lot several times a day. Try watering your fruit trees in the dry season at least once a month. Fill a five-gallon bucket and add some soluble 20-20-20 fertilizer for spectacular citrus. For early succulent peas, water those trees in the dry season. Good melons need plenty of water.

Trinidad is blessed with water. At times we get too much too fast. In Central we have only two seasons, fire and flood. As your garden experience grows you will learn to grow great vegetables in both the heat and the rain. Even though water is a naturally replenished resource, it is always wise to conserve by accurately and adequately watering our gardens.

Water is an essential resource to sustain life. Governments must make it a priority to deliver adequate supplies of quality water to people. Individuals must conserve and protect this precious resource in their daily lives. According to the World Water Institute, a mere 2.5 percent of the earth's ground and surface water is accessible for human use. This finite resource, maintained by the earth's natural water cycle, is used for everything from drinking water to sanitation, agriculture and industrial processes. Overuse, pollution, and inefficient infrastructure as well as natural occurrences like drought, has pushed humankind's water supply nearly to its limits. Scientists project that by 2030, almost half of the world's population will be living in areas with severe water shortages. This situation represents one of the greatest human development challenges of the new millennium. How water is conserved, used, and distributed in communities, and the quality of the water available will determine if there is enough to meet the demands of households, farms, industry, and the environment. More than 10% of people worldwide consume foods irrigated by wastewater that can contain chemicals or disease-causing organisms

If you have a garden and a library, you have everything you need.
Marcus Tullius Cicero

Water

Water methods—sprinkler, watering can, striped sprinkler hose, black soaker hose.

Watering can made from bleach bottle. Cut a notch at the base of handle with a knife. Use a hammer and nail to punch holes in lid.

NOTES

Transplants

One of the secrets to a great home garden is starting plants from seeds and knowing how and when to transplant. This is the process of changing plants' locations. This is tricky because the original location, where the plants sprout from seeds, usually is the best of all environments in either containers or a seed bed. The young plants are destined for either the usually hot, dry Caribbean weather or serious wet conditions of the rainy season.

Transplanting your own plants can save considerable expense. Sprouting seeds can acquire plants from the seeds of anyone's vegetables. Seeds from fruits of those beautiful hybrid vegetables usually won't sprout, though. Making your own plants lets you coordinate the timing of your garden plot. If you sprout the seeds before you start to fork and prepare the soil, the plants should be ready when your garden is organized. Sprouting is a chance to have well developed plants that should be able to fight off diseases. This is much better than trying to grow the plants of vegetables like tomatoes, peppers, or eggplant directly in the garden row from seeds.

To get seeds from peppers or tomatoes, let the fruit fully ripen almost to the rotting stage, clean out the seeds and let them dry in the air. A window ledge is one of the best places. Once the seeds are fully dried, plant them in a shallow small container. There are plenty of appropriate containers like styrotex cups, pie tins, etc. Specialized starting trays that can sprout one hundred and twenty seeds can be purchased. These are good for starting several different types of vegetables together at the same time. Potting soil or compost, are the best mediums to start the seeds, but good quality dirt can also be used.

One of the best things I've discovered for sprouting seeds is to save egg shells cracked in half and stored in the egg tray. Put a bit of potting soil in each half shell and set the seeds. I dampen the potting soil with a light dilution of a foliar fertilizer Powergizer 45. Put the seed into the shell, or another container, a quarter inch deep. A pencil or pen makes a good tool to place the seeds. Keep the sprouting soil damp throughout the nursery period. As the plants grow the shell can easily be cracked to let the roots out as they are put into either a larger container or the soil. The egg shell gives the baby plant some much needed calcium. Keep them in the small containers until they are two to three inches tall, perhaps three weeks or longer.

I usually go from the eggshell size to the small coffee cup, and then into the garden. While the small seedlings are in the egg crate or sprouting trays, they should be kept well watered and out of the heated direct sun. In the coffee cup or larger container, the plants are growing to about four to six inches tall. This usually takes two or three additional weeks. During this period the plants should be hardened by slowly increasing the time in the direct sun until they are able to handle a full day of dry season sun.

Healthy transplant roots should be white and developed, but not packed tight and brown. This is important if you choose to purchase young seedlings from a plant nursery.

Another way of starting seeds is directly in the soil. This is called a 'seed' or 'nursery' bed. To make a bed, fork the soil powdering all the clumps. Mix a small amount or well rotted manure. A good seedbed size is two foot square. For that size use about a cup of poultry manure. Make the bed in a location that gets the morning sun, but is shaded in the heat of the afternoon. Wet the soil until it is damp, but not soaked. Make slight indentations or rows, an inch deep with a trowel or your thumb, about six inches apart. Plant the seeds carefully about an inch apart and a half inch deep. This is good for lettuce, pak choy, and most other vegetables. Carefully dig out the plants either with a trowel of a knife. Be careful not to damage the roots.

The best time to put the young plants in the soil is in the late afternoon. Check the phases of the moon. *(More on this in Chapter 14.)* First soak where you are putting the plants. Pull all the weeds, as they might hide insects or diseases, and compete for moisture and sunlight. I usually make a hole about four inches deep - put in a literal pinch (what you can hold between your index finger and your thumb) of starter fertilizer 12-24-12 and then cover with an inch of dirt. Then place the plant and pull the soil around it to the stem level as it was in its last starting container. Make certain the ball of roots is completely covered or it will permit moisture to easily evaporate, and stunt or kill the plant.

In the garden row cabbage, cauliflower, broccoli, tomato, and pepper plants should be spaced at least a foot apart. Eggplant and ochre should be spaced every two feet, while lettuce and pak choy six inches.

During the heat of the dry season it is very important to water the transplants every morning. It usually takes about two weeks for them to 'catch' in the garden soil. A 'soaker' hose is useful to keep the garden soil moist till the roots adapt to the garden. Mulching with either dried leaves or shredded newspaper will also hold moisture and fight weeds.

Shock, either by too much sun, lack of water, or chemical, or a combination during first two weeks in the garden soil can critically stress and kill the plant. If you choose, after two weeks in the ground is the best time to spray the young plants with systemic chemical treatments for both insects and fungus.

Timing is everything with transplants. Sprout the seeds to have plants when your garden is ready. Keep sprouting plants to have a constant supply. Develop strong healthy plants that can withstand disease. Don't put them into the soil until they can take the sun. Sprouted plants, especially hard to get peppers or a special tomato, make excellent gifts for other gardeners.

Garden Fertilizers

Fertilizer is another garden chemical mystery is to be solved. They simply are food for plants, like vitamins for humans, but must be applied in the appropriate manner at the correct time to be most effective. It is possible to harm your garden with an overdose of fertilizer.

Garden vegetables need various nutrients to grow and produce. Nitrogen (N), phosphorus (P), and potassium (K) are the main elements for healthy plant growth. Others like calcium (Ca) and magnesium (Mg) are supplied by limestone, while more nutrients come from the soil, sun, water, and air. Packaged, 'man made' fertilizers usually contain two or three of these prime garden chemical elements with numbers. The numbers refer to the ratio or percentage of each element like N (nitrogen), P_2O_5 available phosphate, and K_2O available potash. Their garden duty can be easily remembered as 'N'-leaves and shoots, 'P'-stems and roots, and 'K'-flowers and fruits.

Fertilizers are created from either inorganic or organic materials and exist in many different forms. Organic or natural composts, and well-rotted manures are better substitutes than synthetic inorganic pellet mixes because they contain the same nutrients released to the vegetable, but over a longer time period. Organic fertilizers include horse, cattle, swine, or poultry manure, and fish emulsion. Compost is a mixture of decayed organic matter (plants, vegetables, weeds, etc.) used to fertilize and condition the garden soil. The organic material of compost or rotted manure will improve the soil structure, drain better, and hold nutrients longer. Manmade fertilizers come in two types, a pellet or foliar - a water soluble form sprinkled on the leaves or roots of the plant.

Both organic and inorganic provide the same essential nutrients that plants need to grow properly. Plants use nitrogen for leaf growth. Timing the application is very important. Leaf crops like lettuce, salad greens, spinach, broccoli, cauliflower, cabbage, thrive on nitrogen. Plants lacking nitrogen are stunted with yellow green leaves. Over fertilizing with nitrogen causes excessive growth of leaves at the expense of the fruit. Appling at the wrong time causes too many leaves and can delay blossoms. Too much nitrogen fertilizer can kill the plant by burning the leaves and roots. More than half of the nitrogen from synthetic fertilizers is wasted, usually washed away. All types of beans and legumes like bodi, and seime actually build soil by injecting the soil with nitrogen they take from the air. Other heavy feeding crops leaning crops like corn 'clean' the soil of nutrients. This is one of the reasons for crop rotation.

Phosphorous is necessary for blossoms and fruits. Pumpkins, squash, cucumbers, melons, tomatoes, all types of peppers, and eggplants flourish with phosphorous. Plants lacking phosphorus usually have a purple tint to the leaves. Potassium develops healthy roots and stems important to the strength of the plant to combat the weather elements and diseases. Larger roots with many root hairs have a greater capacity to absorb water and fertilizers. Onions, garlic, carrots, beets, radishes, leeks and scallions need potassium.

Fertilizers, whether inorganic or organic, usually have three numbers on the container. The numbers refer to the percentage of main nutrients nitrogen, phosphorus, and potassium in the mixture. A hundred pound sack of starter growth mix 12 –24-12 has 12 percent nitrogen, 24 percent phosphate, and 12 percent potash, or converted to weight, 12 lbs. nitrogen, 24 lbs. phosphate, and 12 lbs. potash. There are also micronutrients like boron and magnesium, but you and I both ask, what's in the other 52 pounds that I am carrying? Fillers!

The most important ingredient in a garden is soil. Garden dirt is comprised of mineral matter, sand, silt and clay or rocks with microorganisms of bacteria, and fungus, that house and feed organisms like insects and worms. Decaying compost from plants and animals provide open spaces for air and water, so roots can easily spread.

Generations of use change the character of soil. What was once fertile can be literally worked until it is dead. Fertilizing without balancing the pH can actually render soil toxic. Gardeners must respect soil as a heritage from our past to our future. Good soil conservation will assure our continued existence. We garden out of the necessity for food. The amount of fertilizer your garden needs depends on the fertility of your plot's soil. The condition of your garden's soil will determine the amount of organic matter, type of fertilizer, and the crops you intend to grow. **First get a soil test to determine your garden's nutrient deficiencies.**

SOIL TEST

Soil tests can be done at the various extensions of the Ministry of Agriculture, or at Trincarb at Waller Field. It is not free, but money well spent that will save many dollars later. The soil test examines the levels of nutrient in your plots soil and the pH of the soil. (pH means potential hydrogen.) Nutrients become unavailable to plants if the pH is above or below a certain range. Soil is based on a scale of 1 to 14 with 7 being neutral. Below 7 is acid and above alkaline. Most vegetables grow best between pH 6.0 to 6.5. This range permits the maximum intake nutrients, and particularly essential micronutrients. If the pH is too low, limestone may be necessary. Constant use of fertilizers will raise the soil's acid level. Flood, rain, and constant irrigation runoff of limestone and alkaline sources with the decaying of some organic matter will also raise the acidity.

There are several types of limestone. The most common is unhydrated lime, gray, and looks like cement. Unhydrated must be added in the initial garden planning stages after your soil test. It takes about three months to work into the soil. Hydrated lime is white and resembles flour. It is fast acting and can be used by broadcasting around the plants or can be mixed with water. Hydrated lime acts almost immediately.

Acid soil causes poor root growth. Poor roots mean the plant has difficulty taking in water or nutrients. Limestone is the most effective and least expensive method to improve your soil. To increase your soil's pH by one point more alkaline, add four ounces of lime per square meter to sandy soils, a half pound per square meter in loamy soil, and twelve ounces to clay per square meter. Plan on adding limestone every other year. A hundred pound sack of unhydrated limestone is twenty-five to fifty-five dollars depending on the vendor. *(See Chapter 11 on the benefits of limestone.)*

If available, rock sulfur may be used to reduce your soil's acidity and also fight potential fungus. Combine 1.2 oz of ground sulfur per square meter for sandy soils, or a quarter pound per square meter for all other types of soil. The sulfur should be thoroughly combined with the soil at least a week before planting. Sawdust from untreated wood, or compost will somewhat lower the pH.

Have the technician fully explain your soil test. There are trace elements like magnesium that can help or hinder your garden depending on the existing amount. If low in magnesium, dolomite (a combination of dolomite and calcium), or calcitic (calcium) limestone can be added. Calcium builds plant tissues. A lack of calcium makes plants struggle to grow in very acidic soil. Most vegetables like slightly acid soil and can be hurt by adding too much lime. Follow the soil tech's recommendations. It is necessary to determine the square footage of your plot because lime and fertilizer recommendations are based on 1,000 square feet. Measure the length and width and multiply together to get your plots size. Less than a thousand square feet, then divide your plot's square footage by a thousand and multiply the decimal result by the rates recommended for lime or fertilizer application.

SOIL TYPES

Crops grown on sandy soils usually require good doses of potassium, but crops grown on clay soils do not. Heavy clay soils can be fertilized considerably heavier at planting than sandy soils. Heavy clay soils and those high in organic matter can safely absorb and store fertilizer at three to four times the rate of sandy soils. Poor thin, sandy soils, which need fertilizer the most, unfortunately cannot be fed as heavily and still maintain plant safety. Feed poor thin sandy soils more often in smaller doses.

The main plant nutrients are nitrogen, phosphorus, and potassium. Secondary level plant nutrients are calcium, magnesium, and sulfur. Micronutrients like boron, chlorine, manganese, iron, zinc, copper, and molybdenum are all necessary for development in some veggies.

Animal manure gives the best results of all the fertilizers for it improves the quality and composition of the dirt and is usually the least expensive. A backyard garden needs about one quarter sack of well-rotted horse, cattle or chicken manure per hundred (10ft. by 10 ft.) square feet. First soak overnight and then fork the soil to a depth of about eight to ten inches apply the necessary manure and lime (if required). The following day hoe the plot breaking the clumps to as fine a powder as possible. This technique will loosen the ground and provide good drainage. This will improve your soil's ability to transfer nutrients to the roots. Adding manure will not cause fast results, but will have long lasting benefits. If stinky manure isn't you, try inorganic 5-10-10 or 12-24-12 broadcast at a rate of 2 pounds per ten by ten area. With the proper attention, as the years go by your garden's soil will become better and better.

There are many types of fertilizers as reddish brown starter 12-24-12, green for foliage and vines 15-5-20--2, bearing 12-12-17-2 soluble or dry. Almost any combination of main and secondary plus trace elements can be purchased.

Starter fertilizer at planting time is recommended to help the plants overcome shock and to ensure proper nutrients during the initial growth period. Dig the hole for the plant about two inches deeper than necessary and throw in just a pinch of 12-24-12 and with an inch of soil before putting in the plant. I do not want the transplant's roots to touch the fertilizer. As the plant adjusts to the garden soil it will send down a root and hit the food. (A pinch is exactly that – what you can hold between your thumb and index finger.)

As the veggies grow more fertilizer will be necessary, but not much. The roots of most vegetables spread to considerable distances. A fertilizer applied to the base of the plant is not always the best method although it seems better because it is closer to the plant. If too near, it will burn young plants' roots or stems. Fertilizer should be carefully placed alongside the rows and worked with a hoe into the soil.

A regimen working for me is, first while forking the soil add about a quarter feed sack of extremely rotted chicken manure and two cups of unhydrated lime per ten by ten area. I use the pinch of starter (12-24-12) at planting and another pinch about three weeks after sprouting. If it is corn or any type of peppers a mix a half-cup of white calcium nitrate to three cups of starter to get the pinch. I never use this on tomatoes. My experience with tomatoes is to only use starter throughout their life and just a little bit every three weeks. Tomatoes need little nitrogen, but plenty of phosphorus and potassium. As soon as the plants begin to blossom I hit each plant with a pinch of a mixture of 2 cups blue bearing salt (12-12-17-2) one half cup calcium nitrate and a half cup of special green (15-5-20-2). Again I toss just a pinch at the tips of the branches away from the stem. Good roots should almost reach that far. This is dry fertilizer that should be leached to the root tips by watering, rain or heavy dew. As the plants continue to grow I water twice a month with a teaspoon of calcium and a teaspoon on magnesium to two gallons of water. Every three weeks I hit them with another pinch of blue bearing salt and mixed with calcium nitrate.

The special green fertilizer (15-5-10-2) is great for leafy vegetables like pak choy and lettuce and vining vegetables like cucumbers, pumpkin and squash. Carefully place it because one pellet on a leaf means a burn spot. Try your own mixes, or use the salt straight from the sack. Corn especially needs a lot of nitrogen once it goes into tassel, but again be careful not to get it in the stalks.

Any fertilizer applied as a liquid to plant leaves is termed 'foliar'. The most basic foliar is animal manure soaked in water. Modern high tech foliar fertilizers are very concentrated mixtures of nitrogen, phosphorus and potassium and trace elements, even vitamins, chlorophyll, and growth hormones. The recommended dilution drastically reduces fertilizer burn. Dry fertilizer has to be dissolved, by watering, rain, or dew. I find it easier to overdose with liquid fertilizer than granular.

Today's modern agri-store has many fertilizer mixtures in various forms. There are single, or with trace elements like boron or magnesium, and combinations, inorganic or organic, mineral fertilizers, composts, and animal manure, to list a few.

Producing great veggies depends on available plant food in the soil. However, too much fertilizer, especially inorganic, can damage the plants causing them to not bear fruit or even die. Years of fertilizing without balancing the pH with limestone can make the soil toxic for all plants. Such small amounts of fertilizers are necessary for small home gardens. New gardeners usually apply too much too close believing 'more is better'. Burning happens when fertilizers are too close, too concentrated, or watered too soon after applying. I find it best to water about an hour before fertilizing.

Proper fertilizer use can enhance plant growth without polluting the environment. There are environmental dangers to fertilizer overuse. Fertilizer nitrogen is changed by soil bacteria into nitrates. Nitrates trickle into the groundwater or to streams and rivers. High nitrate levels in drinking water are considered to be dangerous to human health. Phosphorus can be washed into rivers and stimulate the development of algae in slow moving water. Look at the rivers. Algae plants clog many and will eventually decay reducing the oxygen from the water, killing fish and increasing the chance of floods. A good rule is to use as little fertilizer as possible. That will save you money and keep the environment safe.

REMEMBER: No fertilizer will compensate for bad soil. Be sure to give your garden plenty of compost to maintain organic matter in the soil, promote good plant growth, and retain moisture.

*Remember that children, marriages, and flower gardens
reflect the kind of care they get.*

H. Jackson Brown, Jr.

NOTES

8

Garden Chemicals

The use of chemicals in agriculture is a highly debated topic. Gardening at home gives you a chance to keep your food safe from dangerous chemicals. There are basically two perspectives to gardening, use chemicals safely, or grow organically. *(More on organic gardening in Chapter 13.)* The Caribbean's climate and soil makes large scale farming difficult without chemicals. A temperate climate, with a freezing winter kills a lot of insects and diseases so less enemies to fight.

Everything in our entire world is composed of chemicals. In agriculture there are two main types, pesticides and fertilizers. The term 'pesticide' encompasses all chemicals that kill specific things, insects, fungus, or vegetation. There seems to be a 'cide' for everything. Insecticides control insects, miticides for mites, fungicides battle fungus, and bactericides fight bacteria. Herbicides kill vegetation. It may be necessary to control pests and diseases in commercial crops for better harvests. Using chemicals is a decision that must be made concerning your garden.

In a perfect world nature's balance would protect gardens. Gardens have good insects and bad insects. If the good breeds too slowly, the good are outnumbered to combat the bad ones. Some bad have no natural enemies. Gardeners resort to their own chemical control program and all the bugs, good and bad, are exterminated. Diseased plants die, or develop abnormally. Bacteria, fungus, insects carrying viruses, or parasites can infect them. Bad soil, an extreme dry season, or lack of nutrients can also cause plant problems. Often the two different causes have similar appearances in the abnormal plants. Nature's system balances pests and controls, yet gardeners may not want to lose a quantity of their produce, so they fight nature with chemicals.

One easy control is to be certain the seeds are fresh. The 'fresh year' should be printed on the packet or can. There are disease resistant varieties of seeds. It is less expensive to purchase better seeds than to try and cure problems with chemicals.

An example of disease resistant plants is the 'Gem Pride' tomato type. It is resistant to the Gemini virus transmitted by the white fly. Once a regular tomato tree is bitten with the virus, the leaves curl up and mutate limiting fruit production. The Gem Pride resists the virus, and bears best during the hot weather of the dry season when white fly is more prevalent.

Disease prevention rather than cure is the best garden technique. Keeping weeds out of your garden is a good start. Weeds hide many insects that carry diseases. Weeds compete for water, sunlight, and nutrients. Gardening is always an education mostly learning by too many trials accompanied with twice as many errors. I put in a few extra plants in case some get sick. It is less costly to let the plant die rather than try to cure the disease. Agricultural medicines are better used as preventatives than curative. Garden chemicals aren't cheap!

Be certain you have correctly identified the plant's problems and decided it is serious, and after all non-chemical measures have been tried. Many vegetable diseases have similar appearances and the real trick is to know from experience what will be the cure. Beware of advice from other gardeners, as you may be their joke! But the real question is the cure worth the cost? If you have a half a dozen tomato, peppers, and eggplant; is it worth it to buy chemicals and a sprayer?

Each type of plant has its usual enemies. Try to keep your garden balanced. Too much nitrogen fertilizer can support fungus. Water is necessary, yet too much water can actually rot the roots. Remove sick appearing plants immediately. Harvest and then pull the old plants.

Any chemical, natural or synthetic, can be poisonous in a certain dosage. Even too much salt can kill you. Pesticides are poisonous to specific insects or diseases, and in the proper use aren't harmful to the consumer. However, there is considerably more danger is to the individual applying the poison. Used correctly, (that is the key), human-safe chemicals in the correct application and dilution should have dissipated by the time a consumer makes dinner. It is the applier who inhales the spray without a respirator, or gets it on their skin who must really worry.

Chemicals are why I decided to grow my own. I saw local farmers spraying virtually everyday and immediately bring their crop to market. Some of them spray serious poisons like lanate on pak choy and portugals. A lot of these gardeners feel chemical use is a more modern technique; yet pay little attention to the label warnings or directions. More is not necessarily better with garden chemicals; in fact it is usually increases danger to you and your garden. The three 'C's" of successful garden chemicals is correct problem identification, correct selection of the chemical, correct timing and application. All pesticides have specific instructions that reduce injury to both you and your garden plot.

Getting the correct medicine is the real trick. There are so many: synthetics, or botanicals, insect growth regulators, broad or narrow spectrum, contacts or systemics, short term vs. residual, pheromones, and many more. They are sold as sprays, dusts, lacquers, gels, baits, smokes, and powders. After you make your choice carefully read the label and use it only as directed.

If your garden has a serious problem take a few sample plants to one of the government agristations. They are extremely competent and extremely busy, so don't waste their time. With agri-shops it is best to know what you need walking in otherwise you have to trust the experience behind the counter. Remember, now your loss not only includes crop damage, but the cost of the insecticides.

After gardening for several years, I believe a balance of preventative chemicals and good garden practices is necessary to grow commercially in the Caribbean's climate. The garden chemical downsides are they are not selective in their targets and regular use can develop resistant varieties of pests. Even in a small garden, problems can be avoided by giving plants adequate distance so enough sunlight will penetrate, good air circulation, with careful fertilizing and watering. Plants that have those benefits will be more tolerant to disease than stressed plants.

When you've decided to become a sprayman, it is important to read the chemical label for instructions and warnings, and follow them explicitly. Wear rubber gloves and a respirator when using them, especially during the mixing. Wear long sleeve shirts, pants, and boots. Never spray on a windy day, and always spray late in the day after the bees have visited your veggies. Insecticides should kill the pest, but not other 'good' insects, dissipate quickly, and are nonpoisonous to humans. Bees are 'good' insects. Almost all plants need bees or other insects to pollinate to reproduce seeds and continue the species.

Wear protective clothing and glasses, and don't smoke when spraying. Take chemicals seriously. The lethal dosage rate on the label is for ingestion and does not consider what lands on your skin. Bathe after all applications. **Remember**, every stage of a pesticide's existence from production, transport, storage, use, and disposal – is dangerous to humans and our environment.

Chemical residues in food are dangerous. Check the label for the lethal dose rating of a chemical. If the number is small, the chemical is extremely poisonous. Gardeners and farmers need to be concerned with exposure limits. Many gardeners are questioning a chemical's potency from one batch to another or if the pests are becoming resilient to it.

There are botanicals, garden chemicals made from natural plants, that either kill or repel garden pests. Neem or neem oil, from the seeds of the neem tree, fights insects and fungus. Nicotine from tobacco fights aphids, whiteflies, and mites. Pyrethrum is obtained from the tropical chrysanthemum and is an excellent insecticide. Rotenone derived from the derris tree, is a contact insecticide. Botanical repellants usually cost more than synthetic varieties.

Another non-synthetic approach is insecticide soaps produced from plant oils or animal fat. These soaps must directly contact insects such as aphids, whiteflies, mealybugs, thrips, and spider mites, but no residues remain on your plants.

Sulfur is the oldest known pesticide. It can be used as a dust, or a liquid, for fungus control, and fights some insects especially on beans, tomatoes, and peas. There are several inexpensive natural ways to fight fungus and insects in your garden. A line of wood ashes or chalk (or limestone) around your garden will repel ants and especially leaf-cutter batchak. The aroma of ginder flowers (African marigolds) fends off some insects. A spray made from garlic skins with a few chopped garlic cloves mixed with two tablespoons of dishwashing soap in a gallon of water works against pests. (Try on only one plant first.)

To fight fungus, mix one kilo of cornmeal into a ten by ten area once a year. A spray can be made by combining one cup of cornmeal in a gallon of water and let sit a day before straining and using. Baking soda can prevent powdery mildew fungus, use one-tablespoon baking soda mixed with half a teaspoon dishwashing soap, in one gallon of water. Water your plants before using the mixture late in the day. (Try these remedies on one plant at first to see the effects.)

The nasturtium flower protects beans, broccoli, cabbage, cucumber, corn, and tomatoes by trapping whiteflies, aphids and red spider mites. The French marigold will fight nematodes by trapping them if placed throughout the garden.

Soap can be used as an insecticide by dissolving one pound of common laundry detergent in six gallons of water. This is good for fighting aphids. Make tobacco water by soaking a pack of broken cigarettes in gallon of water for a day. Mix a cup of this to a gallon of clean water and use as a spray.

Unless you are farming on a large scale as a livelihood, I say use chemicals as a last resort. First, try only gardening with healthy seedlings and fresh, treated seeds. Water the roots in the morning and keep the leaves dry. Watering in the evening promotes fungus growth. Use minimal fertilizer, more nitrogen will not help, but hurt the crop. Visually check your plants regularly. Occasionally use a magnifying glass to inspect stems and leaves. Pull sick plants immediately and keep the garden weed free. Rotate your vegetables. Pull the old plants quickly after the last harvest and place downwind of your garden plot.

Every time I visit an agri-shop and I'm amazed at the variety and cost of garden chemicals, and the varied types of applications. Some chemicals work on contact, some are systemic, and are natural or synthetic, etc. the list goes on with various chemical companies. Applied wrong they do harm. The Ministry of Agriculture gives free courses in garden chemical at their various stations through out Trinidad. If you choose to use chemicals it is best to learn about them first.

To this day I cannot see a bright daffodil, a proud gladiola, or a smooth eggplant without thinking of Papa. Like his plants and trees, I grew up as a part of his garden.

Leo Buscaglia

Pesticides in Food

Eating fresh vegetables and fruit, safe from most chemical contaminants is one of the main reasons to have your own home garden. Do you have any idea of the amount of pesticide still remaining on the produce you buy at the market? It may look and taste great, but do chemicals cause the nice appearance? Serious and dangerous health effects result from continuous exposure to low levels of pesticides. Continual exposure may cause cancers; damage to immune, endocrine, reproductive systems, and the nervous system. About 6000 cases of cancers per year in the USA are suspected to be pesticide related. Recent data links pesticide exposure and brain cancers and attention deficit syndrome in children. Parkinson's disease is linked to rotenone, which is the active ingredient in hundreds of pesticide products.

Some harmful things pesticides can do to us humans is to cause low birth weight, birth defects, and interfere with child development and learning abilities. Pesticides can cause neurological problems and disrupt hormone functions. They cause a variety of cancers, including leukemia, kidney cancer, brain cancer, and non-Hodgkin's lymphoma. Children and fetuses suffer more from pesticides than adults because children's bodily systems are still developing. Children systems are not developed enough to detoxify most pesticides. Pesticide effects in the unborn and infants can have lifelong effects.

In the U.S. several major organizations regulate the use of pesticide including the Environmental Protection Agency, the Food & Drug Administration, and the U.S. Department of Agriculture. There are more than 14 separate regulations governing the use of pesticides. All of these regulations are in place to help protect human health. Pesticides must be toxic to kill pests, but a pesticide can be useful only if it kills pests at a small enough dose that causes little or no harm to people, domestic animals, and wildlife. It is not easy to establish what dosage of a pesticide is "safe" for people. Despite many studies done on health effects of each pesticide, there is still uncertainty in the long-term health effects of many pesticides. It is essential pesticide exposure be minimized and the presence of pesticide residues in food be regulated and monitored.

One of the current regulations in the US requires pesticide manufacturers conduct toxicity testing before it can be permitted for use on products either directly or indirectly destined for human consumption. This includes feed for livestock. This toxicity testing determines the health effects of pesticides, and the level at which there are no toxic effects on children and the elderly, which are the most sensitive parts of the population. This **'No Toxic Effect Level'** (NOEL) is the basis of the permitted residue limit. The regulations set the permitted residue level at a level that is from 10 to 100 times lower than the NOEL.

HOW TO REDUCE THE AMOUNT OF PESTICIDE RESIDUE IN FOOD

Grow as much of your own food as possible. Wash your food with clean water (but not soap!) before it is cooked or eaten. Peeling helps reduce the levels of pesticides that may be on the surface, but some residues are absorbed into the food. Trimming excess fat from meats helps to reduce the amount of such pesticides that would be eaten. Pesticides shave been found to accumulate in animal fatty tissue. Cooking helps reduce some of the pesticide residues in food that are not removable by washing or peeling. Specific pesticides are used for specific food crops. Eat different fruits, vegetables and grains prevents eating a particular food or the pesticide residues that it may carry.

If a pesticide is tested and a NOEL can not be determined, then it is unlikely to be permitted for use on food crops. This helps ensure that if a person, child or adult, eats a larger than normal amounts of a particular food, or several different foods with the same or similar pesticide residue, they will still not reach the level of exposure required for a toxic effect to occur, even if they are more sensitive than the general population.

All of these safety precautions are used in the US, but the hazards of pesticides to human health are not distributed equally worldwide. Latin American farm workers are more than ten times more likely to suffer pesticide poisoning than US farm workers. This is because products condemned/banned by the developed countries are often sold to undeveloped nations. Farmers in the developing countries often handle extremely toxic pesticides while wearing little or no protective equipment. During the decade of the 80's more than eighty percent of all pesticide related deaths occurred in developing countries, but they only used twenty percent of the chemical pesticides. This is because of ignorance of both worker and management.

Check garden chemicals before you buy to be certain they are not banned. These are not the garden chemical names, but what makes up the toxin. Some banned pesticides include: aldrin, benezene hexachloride, cadmium compounds, chlordane, kepone, copper arsenate, DBCP, DDT, fluoroacetamide, mirex, silves, and thallium sulfate. There are many more banned chemicals and several that are severely restricted in usage such as carbofuran, daminozide, lindane, and sodium arsenate to name a few.

Everyone should be concerned about eating poison in the form of pesticides used on vegetables and fruit. Careless farmers use pesticides on their produce without allowing proper time for it to dissolve. Usually pesticides, which include insect repellants, fungicides, and weed killers take a minimum of a week to dissipate to a safe level after spraying. Most people understand organic food is a great way to reduce or eliminate exposure to pesticides in food. Totally organic growing may not be possible for everyone, or in every food choice.

Sweet bell peppers, celery, lettuce, pak choy, and carrots are the vegetables most likely to expose consumers to pesticides. In several samplings at various markets celery had the highest of percentage of samples test positive for pesticides, 94 % followed by sweet bell peppers at 81%, and carrots at 82%. Eighty per cent of the celery tested had multiple pesticides on a single vegetable, followed by sweet bell peppers with sixty two percent of the samples.

Sweet bell peppers had the most pesticides detected at 11 found on one sample. Lettuce and celery followed with samples having with nine different pesticides identified. Sweet bell peppers were the vegetable with the most pesticides overall, with 64, followed by lettuce with 57, and carrots with 40.

Vegetables least likely to be contaminated with pesticides were onions, sweet corn, asparagus, peas, eggplant, broccoli, tomatoes, and sweet potatoes. Fifty-one percent of the tomatoes tested showed no pesticide residue. Sixty-five percent of broccoli, seventy-five percent of eggplant had no detectable pesticides. Sweet corn and onions had no detectable residues on 90 percent or more of the samples. are extremely rare on any of these least contaminated vegetables. Tomatoes had the highest likelihood of multiple pesticide residues with a 14 percent chance of more than one pesticide when ready to eat. Onions and corn both had the lowest chance with zero samples containing more than one pesticide. This is because both corn and onions have a protective disposable skin.

BE CAREFUL WITH AGRICULTURAL CHEMICAL RESIDUE

Fruit and vegetables to be careful with, always wash and peel if possible before consuming: peaches, apples, sweet bell peppers, imported and local celery, local cauliflower, cabbage, and broccoli, imported carrots, strawberries, and pears.

Consume with caution: spinach, lettuce, grapes, potatoes, hot peppers, cucumbers, oranges.

Better choices: grapefruit, portugals, tomatoes, sweet potatoes, imported cauliflower, and watermelon

Best to eat: imported broccoli and cabbage, bananas, mangos, pineapple, sweet corn, onions, and avocados

NOTES

Garden Spraying

A spray can seems to be an integral part of today's garden equipment, whether it is to water, fertilize, or medicate vegetable plants. Spray cans may be either hand held in the half to two gallon size or worn as a back pack with three to five gallon capacities. Although a spray can save time and water especially in a drought, they are dangerous to the health and welfare of the user unless safety precautions are strictly followed.

First, if spraying anything but water always dress with long pants, long sleeve shirt, boots and rubber gloves, wear a respirator certified to protect against toxic chemicals. Most garden chemicals are poisonous on contact with your skin. The skin will accept the chemical into the human body just like a plant takes it in. However, instead of attacking an insect, bacteria, or a fungus; it attacks the liver. Most serious farmers who tend large gardens wrap a cloth over the respirator to avoid and contact with the spray due to a breeze. Sunglasses or safety goggles are also recommended.

Wear the respirator and gloves, especially when filling the sprayer because your face is closest to the chemical when it is filling. The chemical will either give off a cloud if it is a powder such as fungicide, or stench if it is an insecticide.

Select a sprayer that can be handled easily and the weight when filled with water isn't too heavy. You can calculate the weight you will be carrying as a liter weights 2.2 pounds. The weight of one US gallon of water is approximately 8.35 pounds. An imperial gallon (UK measurement) of water weighs 10 pounds.

Second, learn everything you can about the chemical you are about to use. Garden chemicals are expensive and dangerous. Applied incorrectly it is a dangerous waste of time and money. Teach yourself how to repair your sprayer. They are simple pumps with very few parts. Read the instruction manual and be certain before buying that repair parts are easily available. A good tip is to fill the sprayer with water to the correct level before adding the chemical. Pump it and spray. If it doesn't work or is clogged you haven't wasted any chemical and do not have to work on the sprayer while it is filled with a toxic liquid. Always clean out your sprayer when done and flush with fresh water to prevent the chemicals drying and clogging tiny orifices.

Vegetables may contain very minute remainders of the chemicals after it has grown through its life cycle. The real danger with chemicals is to the person who is applying them. Never smoke, or drink while spraying. Clean yourself immediately after spraying. Wash your hands, face and any other exposed areas with soap and water. Try to shower as soon as possible washing your hair. Gargle with clean water and clean out your nose, neck, and ears where pesticide residue may remain.

Some basic guidelines for safe garden spraying are: Never spray during a windy day. The wind may carry the chemical to vegetables that don't need it or may be harmed by it. The wind will swirl the fine spray back on to you. Use any type of spray in the early morning or the cool of evening. Try to spray after the bees have pollinated. You do not want to kill bees as they are necessary to make fruit from your vegetable plants. Target just the area you need to treat. Be careful... try not to harm the good bugs! You don't want to run off your allies. Do not spray when temps are above 80 degrees Fahrenheit! Your plants may "burn" or have a reaction to what you are using in excessive heat. Always spray only a small portion of the plant material first. Wait 24 hours to observe any negative reaction. Proceed if there is no damage. Using more of a chemical spray is not better. If you are not getting good results don't increase the strength of these remedies without testing first.

There are sprays made from combinations of relatively safe items usually found in your household. Relatively safe means anything taken over the limit will be toxic to the human body.

Warning: As a precaution always test on one plant first to check for any negative reactions. Do not proceed if there is any visible damage such as burning or discoloration.

APPLE CIDER VINEGAR FUNGICIDE is good for leaf spot, or powdery mildew Mix three tablespoons of cider vinegar (five per cent acidity) with one gallon water and spray in the morning on infested plants. Good for black spots on roses

BAKING SODA SPRAY is good for anthracnose, early tomato blight, leaf blight, powdery mildew, and as a general fungicide.

Sodium bicarbonate commonly known as baking soda has been found to posses fungicidal properties. It is recommended for plants that already have powdery mildew to use clean water to wash all infected leaves prior to spraying. This helps to dislodge as many of the spores as possibly to help you get better results. Use as prevention or treatment at first sign of any of diseases.

Mix one tablespoon baking soda, two and a half tablespoons vegetable oil with one gallon of water. Shake very thoroughly. To this mix add half teaspoon of pure Castile soap and spray.

Be sure to agitate your sprayer while you work to keep the ingredients from separating. Cover upper and lower leaf surfaces and spray some on the soil. Repeat every week as needed.

CHIVE SPRAY is good for preventing apple scab or downy mildew on cucumber, pumpkin and zucchini.

Put a bunch of chopped chives in a heat proof glass container, cover with boiling water. Let this sit until cool, strain and spray as often as two to three times a week.

COMPOST OR MANURE TEAS are an inexpensive foliar spray Many people have success with manure tea keeping blight and other pathogens away from plant. Soak the

Garden Spraying

area around plants and use as a foliar spray. Do not use on seedlings as it may encourage damping-off disease.

Fill a thirty gallon barrel with water. Let sit for a day to evaporate chlorine and other additives Add about 4 shovels worth of manure to this and cover. Let it sit for two weeks, stirring once a day. Strain and apply as needed.

NOTE: Different manures supply various nutrients when used as above. Chicken manure is rich in nitrogen and good for use for heavy feeders such as corn, tomatoes and squash. Cow manure has potash and better for root crops. Rabbit manure will promotes strong leaves and stems. Horse manure will aid in leaf development.

COMPOST TEA - Make and use just the same as you would the manure tea. This is another terrific reason to compost all those prunings, grass clippings, and kitchen wastes.

No. 1 GARLIC FUNGICIDE SPRAY is good for leaf spot and mildews.

Combine three ounces of minced garlic cloves with one ounce of mineral oil. Let soak for a day or longer. Strain. Mix one teaspoon of fish emulsion with sixteen ounces of water. Add one tablespoon of castile soap to this. Slowly add the fish emulsion water with the garlic oil. Kept in a sealed glass container this mixture will stay viable for several months.

To use: Mix two tablespoons of garlic oil with one pint of water and spray.

No. 2 GARLIC FUNGICIDE SPRAY is good for fungicide and as an insect repellent.

In a blender combine one whole head of garlic, three cups water, two tablespoons canola oil, four hot peppers and a whole lemon. Blend until finely chopped. Steep mixture overnight. Strain through fine cheesecloth. Use at a rate of four tablespoons per gallon of water. Store unused portion in the refrigerator.

HORSSERADISH TEA FUNGICIDE - The cleansing properties of horseradish have beenknown for more than a decade. This method has proved to be just as effective, and inexpensive.

Process one cup of roots in food processor till finely chopped. Combine this with sixteen ounces of water in a glass container and let soak for a day. Strain liquid, discard the solids. Now mix the liquid with two quarts of water and spray.

HYDROGEN PEROXIDE TREATMENT is used to prevent bacterial and fungal problems. Simple hydrogen peroxide that you can buy most anywhere will prevent the disease spores from adhering to the plant tissue. It causes no harm to plants or soil, however don't use on young plants.

Spray plants with undiluted three percent hydrogen peroxide. Be sure to cover tops and bottoms of leaves. Do this once a week during dry weather and twice a week in wet weather. This works as a preventative. If you already have problems use this as a direct treatment.

MILK FIGHT MILDEW - Milk's natural enzymes and simple sugar structures can be used to combat various mildews on cucumber, asters, tomato, squash and zinnia foliage. This works by changing the pH on the surface of the leaves, so they are less susceptible to powdery mildew.

Use an equal mixture of milk and water. Thoroughly spray plants every four days at first sign of mildews or use weekly as a preventative measure. Milk can also be mixed at a rate of one ounces milk to ten ounces of water and used as a spray every week to treat mosaic disease on cucumber, tomato and lettuce.

TOMATO VIRUS PROTECTIVE SPRAY— Skim milk will prevent many viruses that attack tomato plants. This protects the plant surface against disease spores. The skim milk provides the tomato plant with calcium. A calcium deficiency is common in tomato plants. Anti-transpirants are used on Christmas trees, cut flowers, newly transplanted shrubs, and in other applications to preserve and protect plants from drying out too quickly and can be purchased at most garden and cut flower shops.

Mix a half teaspoon of antitranspirant (like Cloudcover, Wiltpruf etc.) with eight ounces of skim milk, and one gallon of water. Spray plants. NOTE: an equivalent of prepared powdered milk may be substituted for the skim milk.

DAMPENING OFF DISEASE - Always use a sterile growing medium like potting soil for your seed starting as these should not contain the fungi that cause damping-off. If using regular dirt or compost try and put it in a suitable container such as old baking dishes in an oven heated to three fifty and shut off. Let stand overnight. This will kill all bacteria, fungus and most unwanted seeds. Water your seedlings with warm water that has been left to sit for an hour or more to dissipate most of the chemicals that are present in tap water. Using cold water stresses the seedlings leaving them vulnerable to harmful organisms.

CHAMOMILE SPRAY is an excellent preventative for damping-off. Use on seed starting soil, seedlings and in any humid planting area. Chamomile is a concentrated source of calcium, potash and sulfur. The sulfur is a fungus fighter. This can also be used as a seed soak prior to planting.

To make pour two cups boiling water over a quarter cup chamomile blossoms or packaged tea bags. Let steep until cool and strain into a spray bottle. Use as needed. This keeps for about a week before going rancid. Spray to prevent damping off and anytime you see any fuzzy white growth on the soil. Chamomile blossoms can be purchased at larger grocery stores.

REMEMBER

Know how and when to apply the specific mixture you are to spray. Know the amount - as drench the plant, just the roots, spray under the leaves, or give the entire plant a light spray. The amount of the mixture that hits the plant is a ratio of the dilution of the solution, the pressure you have pumped the spray tank, and the opening of the nozzle. Try to keep your spray uniform and keep it off of your skin. Wear a respirator, boots, gloves and glasses. Most chemicals are toxic.

Farming is a profession of hope.
Brian Brett

NOTES

THE BENEFITS OF LIMESTONE

If your soil is too acidic then nutrients will not be available to the plants even if they are present. The letters pH stand for Potential of Hydrogen and measures the molar concentration of hydrogen ions in the solution and as such is a measure of acidity. That may seem a bit difficult to understand for us non-chemists gardeners. The pH scale runs from 4.00, highly acidic soil, to 8.00 which is alkaline. 7 is neutral.

Various types of pH test kits are available. Simple ones require mixing a soil sample with water and comparing it to a color chart. More expensive are electronic meters, which read the soil through a metal stake. Whichever kit you use will come with instructions and will give you a reading. Never make a judgment on just one test. You may have hit a spot with particularly high or low pH. Take samples from a number of spots, and this will give you a much better general view of your soil's acidity level.

The government will come and take soil samples. This is free but it will take some time – like a few months – to get the results. You can take your own samples per their instructions, and take it to an agricultural center. This is quicker and still free. Without an accurate soil pH test, there is no way to know if lime is friend or foe.

To LOWER soil acidity you must RAISE the pH value. That always confused me. Reducing soil acidity will help deter some weeds, because they are evolved for acid soils unlike our garden plants. Opposite to what you expect, adding manure year after year will actually reduce soil fertility by making it too acid so the plants cannot access the nutrients.

Different plants require different levels of acidity. Most vegetables thrive when the soil is slightly acid at a pH level between 6.5 and 7, Potatoes tend to prefer a lower pH, a more acid soil. Members of the Brassica family – cabbage, cauliflower, broccoli - prefer a slightly alkaline soil, pH slightly higher of 7.0.

Agricultural lime or garden lime is gray and made from pulverized limestone. As well as raising the pH it will provide calcium for the crops and trace nutrients. Dolomite lime is similar to garden lime, but contains a higher percentage of magnesium.

White hydrated lime is produced by a two stage process. First rock limestone is burned in kilns. This produces quick lime, which is highly caustic and cannot be applied directly to the soil. Quicklime reacts with water to produce slaked, or hydrated, lime. Quicklime is spread in heaps to absorb rain and form slaked lime, which is then spread on the soil. Their use is prohibited by the organic standards and while fast acting, the effect is short lived in comparison to garden lime.

Garden soil needs a total of seventeen individual nutrients in the right amounts to grow. Carbon, oxygen and hydrogen are taken in as carbon dioxide and water. Although air contains vast quantities of nitrogen, most plants cannot use these. Instead plants take up nitrogen from the soil together with other nutrients such as phosphorus, potassium, calcium, magnesium, etc. These nutrients enter the roots dissolved in water.

All of the seventeen nutrients are needed for proper plant growth. No single nutrient is less important than others, but the individual nutrients are needed in different quantities. Soil typically already contains an ample supply of most micro nutrients as boron, aluminum, manganese, etc. Nutrients required in larger quantities: nitrogen, phosphorus, potassium, etc must be resupplied because a healthy garden will deplete these resources faster than nature can recreate them.

A too low pH level will make heavy metals such as aluminum and iron very mobile in the soil. That can cause the plants to get too much of these essential nutrients and actually poison them. A too high pH will tie up nutrients such as iron and phosphorus and starve the plants. The goal is to balance pH around 6.0-7.0. This can be done by liming once every year or every 2-3 years. It neutralizes soil acidity making the fertilizer more accessible to plants and is a natural source of calcium and magnesium.

Horticultural lime, not surprisingly, can be used as a soil amendment and is a blend of calcium carbonate and magnesium carbonate. The white "crusty stuff" on showerheads and faucets is largely comprised of calcium and magnesium carbonates. Calcium is necessary for cell division and healthy plant growth. Often, when soil is depleted of calcium, plant leaves may curl, yellow, and fade. When magnesium is deficient in soil, leaves yellow, vegetables lack flavor with a poor yield. When your garden is missing both calcium and magnesium, other nutrients are more quickly depleted.

Old plasterboard, or gypsum, can sometimes be found for free at home remodeling sites. Gypsum is also called hydrated calcium sulfate, and contains calcium and sulfur, two elements vital to plant growth. If you get this free and all you have to do is smash it up, it is a bonus, but I would not search it out. Gypsum will loosen clay soil and will provide better soil drainage The best time to apply limestone is just at the end of the dry season, after the first rains when the soil is easy to fork or plow. Lime usually takes three months to combine with the soil to lower acidity. The soil will be ready when the rainy season has passed. Spread the limestone evenly. Applying too much can damage your plants. When you are finished, make sure to wash your hands thoroughly. Your garden should show a great improvement.

AMOUNT OF LIME TO RAISE SOIL PH FROM ONE POINT (FROM 5.5 TO 6.5)

Soil Type	Pounds per Square Yard
Clay	1.6
Sand	1.3
Organic-cleared forest	2.0

*The first farmer was the first man.
All historic nobility rests on the possession and use of land.*

Ralph Waldo Emerson

NOTES

Compost

Compost is decayed organic matter that occurs naturally. You can make compost from a mixture of garden, home and kitchen waste. It used to fertilize and condition soil. Gardeners have been making compost since beginning to cultivate crops. Compost is well-rotted plant matter that improves fertility, structure, and water absorption. It is natural process because all plants die and decompose.

The purpose of composting plant materials is to decay it, so that it can be easily worked into the soil. By adding substance to the soil, compost improves water absorption. This is a real benefit for sandy soil. Adding compost prevents soil from packing tightly together and that aspect makes the growth and spreading of plants roots easier. It adds some nutrients and better retains fertilizers. All that translates to healthier plants. Every garden can be improved by adding compost, and it is good potting soil for houseplants or seedling trays.

Plant (organic) material decomposes at a rate depending on the size of the pieces, and exposure to elements. Nature decays plant material using microorganisms living naturally in soil. As these organisms eat, the waste becomes compost. This process creates enough heat to keep the feeders alive and kill off nearly all harmful bacteria and unwanted seeds from weeds. The internal heat is benefited by hot weather. With the best conditions it will take about six months to make compost.

Everyone has to clear bush and remove old plants. Locate your compost pile in a place convenient to your garden plot so it's not a long haul. It should be located where it gets a lot of sun. Keep it somewhat out of the way as it will tend to be unappealing and may attract some insects and perhaps rodents. An easy way to pile compost is to first get old concrete blocks, and stack them without mortar about four feet square. Start off with three or four rows high and you can easily increase if it is necessary. Keep about an inch space between the blocks. These spaces permit air to circulate so the organisms can keep feeding comfortably. Fresh air can be further increased to your pile by weekly stirring it with a fork and keeping it a moist with water. About a week after a big clean up, stick your hand into the pile and feel the generated heat.

Your pile is the place to dump all the waste from your garden and kitchen like cut bush, old plants, weeds, leaves, fruit and vegetable remains and peels, egg shells, shredded newspapers and cardboard, sawdust, wood ashes, and manure. Your sick garden plants should not be included in this pile as it may transmit the disease. To speed up the decay, get a couple of buckets of rich rotted manure and dump on your pile as the height increases every foot. This will increase the feeder organisms. Earthworms, if you can find them, also increase decay. The ideal pile height is three to four feet. The compost will be ready when it is dark brown and crumbles easily. Remove the concrete blocks, load it into a wheelbarrow, and work the compost into your home garden plot.

Compost is the end and another beginning for gardens. All gardens need to be constantly weeded and cleaned between plantings. Keep a covered bucket in the kitchen for rotted or over ripe fruits and vegetables, peelings, eggshells; and your compost will grow fast. A neat compost pile obscured from public view, will benefit your gardening efforts. Compost is another of nature's good cycles.

If you build up the soil with organic material, the plants will do just fine.
John Harrison

Organic Gardening

To most people organic gardening means simply not using synthetic fertilizers or pesticides. Yet to 'go organic' you need to adopt a philosophy that the course of nature doesn't need any changes, especially chemical-wise. An organic gardener comprehends the cycles of nature, in soil, water, sun, air, and weather, work in agreement, and tries to replenish and preserve all resources. 'Organics' try not to use synthetic fertilizers, or pesticides whose residues could harm the natural process. Since most home gardens are small, organic gardening can be a relatively easy and inexpensive alternative to chemical medicines and fertilizers. Most farmers and gardeners, who use synthetic fertilizers and pesticides, don't understand the chemical 'fix' is quick, but doesn't last. Synthetic fertilizers are never fully absorbed by the vegetable plants and the remainder stays in the soil, or is run off with rain or irrigation.

Organic gardeners believe all living things exist for one another in a natural system. Everything in nature is related. The treatment of our earth is what we leave for future generations. Organics use natural materials and methods, and avoid using chemical synthetics that may undermine our surroundings.

Soil maintenance is the most important aspect of organic gardening. The majority of garden problems are caused by poor soil. Increasing your soil's fertility is the first step. Synthetic fertilizers do not improve the soil. Soil doesn't quickly rejuvenate. It will take planning and work to change from chemicals to organic. Diseases, insects, and weeds will always need attention, but there are natural alternatives.

Compost is the best and least expensive natural fertilizer. Composting is a great habit to acquire as it takes healthy vegetative waste from the toxic landfill. Great soil has a 'fluffy' texture and easily absorbs water. Also good bacteria in the organic matter actually supplies nutrients via loose soil at the plant's roots. Household refuse as rotted fruits, vegetables, weeds, bush and non-treated sawdust, coffee grounds, shredded paper, etc. can be composted. Every time a section of your garden is replanted, the soil can recharged by forking a generous amount of compost (at least an inch) into it. Good compost will help balance the PH level.

Controlling weeds is very important to the organic gardener because they provide shelter for insects and diseases. Sick plants should be destroyed to avoid further contamination.

Growing the same crop in the same place at first seems like a good idea since you should be able to refine your gardening techniques and have a better harvest with less work. Not so, definitely not so! As you have been feeding your plants the same nutrient blend, insects and diseases have also been feeding. Your soil will be infested with insects and diseases that flourish with particular vegetable. Always rotate the different vegetable sections in your garden. This will confuse the insects and diseases, bring different nutrient combinations to the section, and discourage certain weed types. Some vegetables, like corn, consume almost all the nutrients in a section of your garden. Beans replenish nutrients, especially nitrogen. So beans should be planted in the section following corn. I recommend moving rows of beans, especially green "string' beans, to different row locations every three or four months. Green beans are tasty and they certainly revive soil. Peanuts are actually legumes or beans, and add nutrient to soil especially when the entire bushes are forked back into the soil.

Mulching is covering the spaces between your plants with materials like bamboo leaves or dead grasses. This technique conserves water, nutrients, and fights weeds. The soil around a transplant should be covered with mulch to reduce root shock from the sun and hot weather. Leaves or shredded newspapers will work to retain moisture and protect roots. Wet the garden section before and after covering it with mulch.

The location you choose for your garden can influence the health of your plants. It should get at least six to eight hours of direct sun, drain well, and have a good flow of fresh air. Choose plants that have been adapted to fight certain diseases.

Animal manures are probably the best organic fertilizer. Use manure that has rotted for several months. It should also be mixed into the compost pile. Manures vary greatly in their content of fertilizing nutrients. To recharge a ten by ten plot at least twenty-five pounds of cattle manure are need to be forked in, but only twelve pounds of chicken or sheep. This is one typical farmer complaint, so much more manure is needed versus 'synthetic' chemical fertilizer. Actually the average nutrient value of manure is ten pounds of manure provides one pound of nutrients. Your soil actually benefits more from the decayed plant matter. Synthetic fertilizers are never fully absorbed by the vegetable plants and the remainder stays in the soil or is drained off by rain or irrigation, or sinks in and makes the soil even more acidic and denser.

Another manure complaint is that it works slowly while synthetic fertilizers are faster acting. Yes, that's true, but the vegetable plants produce quicker, yet have a shorter life span. Garden soil building can be compared to body building. It takes a lot of exercise to get a person's body in shape, or you can use chemicals like steroids. You get a well built body, but it doesn't last. Your soil needs organic material so your plants will have a long healthy life.

Micronutrients are in most organic materials like compost and manure. Some are concentrated in natural materials as gypsum, which provides calcium and sulfur. Dolomite has a combination of calcium and magnesium. Limestone has calcium and reduces acidity in soil.

Pesticide is a term that includes insecticides (bug killers), fungicides (fungus killers), and herbicides (vegetation killers). One problem with using synthetic pesticides are they are usually not very selective, meaning they kill more than the pests that are hurting you veggies. There are plenty of good bugs that actually help your garden thrive, like bees. Most of the living things have a natural balance between good and bad. Sometimes the bad outnumbers the good and a crime wave takes place in your garden.

A very small percentage of insects are harmful. Beneficial insects like spiders, and wasps fight harmful insects. Bees pollinate your plants. Other good bugs assist in decaying organic matter. Bees and butterflies are needed to fertilize plants. Some ant types are nature's cleaners, while others like fire ants, leaf cutters like batchak, and tictac stinging ants can literally be a pain.

When garden pests are high, control by natural means may be very difficult. Disease and pest resistant varieties should be planted if possible. Use ten inch cardboard circles at the base of plants to fight mole cricket damage. Spade garden early so vegetation has time to rot before planting. Remove sick or infested plants immediately. Pull old plants as soon as the harvest is over. Remove weeds as they provide a habitat for insects and diseases and compete for moisture and nutrients. Water in the morning. Your plants should not be wet at night. Damp leaves cause fungus problems. Plant a few extra to allow for some damage from pests.

> *It is vitally important that we can continue to say, with absolute conviction, that organic farming delivers the highest quality, best-tasting food, produced without artificial chemicals or genetic modification, and with respect for animal welfare and the environment, while helping to maintain the landscape and rural communities.*
>
> Prince Charles

Another problem with pesticides is that insects may acquire a resistance to that particular chemical. Modern organic gardeners use the insect's own natural instincts against it. Ants can carry a poisonous, natural bait back to the nest and after a few weeks the queen and the entire nest will be dead. Borax is a good naturally occurring chemical for this. Spray aphid infested plants first with a mixture of one teaspoon dishwashing soap to a gallon of water then rinse with a spray of clean water. Another spray is a combination of one cup of soy cooking oil with a tablespoon of dishwashing soap. Combine one tablespoon of this mixture with two cups of water and spray on the plants. Keep shaking the bottle to continually combine the oil with the water.

For a more potent spray combine garlic skins with a few well chopped garlic cloves and one hot pepper in a quart of water. This will repel most insects. Be careful to try these remedies on just one plant in your garden to test the outcome before risking the entire plot.

Cornmeal worked into the soil at the rate of a kilo per hundred square feet will fight fungus. Put at the base of plants, it will fight mole crickets. A shallow bowl filled with beer, yes good old Caribe or Stag, will kill slugs and snails. They die with a smile, though.

Milk also helps a garden. A weekly spray of milk at 1 part milk to 9 parts water will reduced the severity of powdery mildew fungus infection on the plants.

To repel birds from eating peppers and tomatoes, put a stake slightly taller than the plants on each end of the row. Tie a cord between the stakes and attach pieces of used aluminum foil. As the pieces flap in the breeze, the sounds and reflections keep the birds away.

If your plants are battling for space with have pesky weeds or grass wait till a bright sunny day and carefully spray the weeds with full-strength household vinegar (acetic acid). It is a non toxic environmental friendly weed killer. Plant insect repulsing flowers throughout your garden. French marigolds will trap nematodes.

Organic gardening is not new and there are a multitude of suppliers of 'necessary organic gardening materials'. In fact there are catalogues full of every item from predator insects to biological soaps, etc. They are all labeled as 'non-toxic.' But in reality, too much of anything can be poisonous.

These are a few natural controls for pests. A garden with healthy soil will produce strong resilient plants. If an infestation occurs be certain you are killing the correct insects. If you become a full 'organic' or just partial your produce will be more nutritional than a chemically 'boosted' sample. Your garden will extend all of nature's cycles to continue human life on planet Earth. Even slightly organic gardeners realize that to work soil like a human body, must be constantly restored. Everything is part of the great life cycle.

Cultivators of the earth are the most valuable citizens. They are the most vigorous, the most independent, the most virtuous and they are tied to their country and wedded to its liberty and interests by the most lasting bands.

Thomas Jefferson

14

Gardening with the Moon

Gardening by the moon is an ancient practice that may give you a bit of an edge. Over four thousand years ago Sumerians planted by the phases of the moon as many gardeners do today. It is amazing that vastly different cultures the around the world from the ancient Chinese, Mayans, Amerindian Cherokees, Hawaiians, and Scottish Highlanders all followed the same Moon planting traditions, but each developed separately. This gives credence that there must be some substance to this way of gardening.

Many great prehistoric monuments such as Stonehenge in Great Britain, the Great Pyramid of Egypt, Machu Pichu in Peru, are oriented to certain stars and those civilizations essential activities were coordinated with the phases of the moon. Even though we are living in a futuristic, microwave, Internet world, we can still try these ancient techniques. What do we have to lose? Science has demonstrated that the Moon actually controls water tables and tides.

Our ancestors were not ignorant as they aligned their gardening with the cycles of nature. People across the globe attempt to predict when the last frost, the dry season, or the rains will occur. I keep a plant-harvest date book to report the productiveness of the Moon phase garden. One of our north coast friends who grows plenty of plantain and tannia, swears by the phases of the moon.

Everything seems to have a life cycle and the gardener's goal is to plant in harmony so their crops will flourish. The moon revolves around the earth while the Earth revolves around the Sun. Our planet's position in the great Universe is constantly changing with relation to other planets. The moon's orbit or cycle lasts 29 days and is divided into quarters. Each quarter is designated as the part of the moon we can see, new or dark of the moon when the moon is directly between the Sun and the Earth and is not able to reflect sunlight. The first quarter shows the crescent bulging to the right like the letter 'D'. The Sun's reflection on the moon increases until it reaches full moon the looks like a big 'O'. Traveling to the last quarter the bulge is to the left and looks like the letter 'C'. The days from the dark until the moon increases to full, is called the 'waxing' phase. Between the Full moon and the dark of the moon as light decreases is the 'waning' period.

Vegetables are affected differently when planted at varying moon phases. Vegetables that produce fruit above ground are best planted when the moon is filling (waxing), while root bearing vegetables are better planted when the moon is decreasing in size (waning). It is reported that it is best to repot houseplants, sow seeds for above ground plants, fertilize and graft trees during the waxing phase, by the light of the moon.

The first quarter beginning at the dark of the moon pulls the water table up towards the surface providing more sustenance and moisture. This supposedly makes seeds sprout better. This is the period that is best to plant leaf veggies like pak choy, lettuce, spinach, cabbage, celery, broccoli, or cauliflower.

During the second quarter the moon supposedly pulls less on our planet, but there is more moonlight that makes leaves develop. Tomatoes, beans, peas, and vines like cucumbers, squash and melons are best planted in this phase. This is also reported to be the best time to harvest as the fruit will have the most moisture.

In the third quarter the moon's size decreases in the waning phase. It is pulling the least on the water table and plants are supposedly growing the least. This is the best quarter to plant and prune fruit trees as less sap will come from the cuts. The plants are supposedly more compact in this phase and more oriented to their roots and this is the best time to harvest crops like cassava, eddoes, dasheen, tannia and sweet potatoes. The roots will store better.

The fourth quarter with the least moonlight is best for clearing ground, cutting grass, and weeding your garden, but little planting. It is felt that the lack of moonlight keeps the bush or grass from returning quickly as their seeds don't germinate. Before the dark of the Moon it is best to plant below ground crops, especially yams.

To add more information to this complex Universe planting guide; as our planet travels throughout its orbit the moon rises in various Zodiac signs that further increase or decrease its growing power. It is most fertile when it is in Pisces, Scorpio or Cancer. In Taurus, Libra or Capricorn it is slightly less fertile. Still less is in Aries, Sagittarius, or Aquarius and don't bother to plant at all in Gemini, Leo or Virgo. My advice is to buy McDonalds Almanac early each year to get these timetables. That little yellow book is easy to read.

Again, this is where your garden diary comes in handy. Try a few experiments, if you have enough garden space, by planting the same vegetables during different moon phases. Give them the same care and see if there is a difference in the harvest. I do give some credence to cutting bush during the dark of the moon as we cleared a new piece and it took longer before it even started to grow back. That may have been hotter sun, less rain, or the phase of the moon.

People have been planting by the moon for millenniums. Building a garden isn't easy and maybe working with the Moon can make it a bit more productive. Try it!

> *There seem to be but three ways for a nation to acquire wealth. The first is by war, as the Romans did, in plundering their conquered neighbors. This is robbery. The second by commerce, which is generally cheating. The third by agriculture, the only honest way, wherein man receives a real increase of the seed thrown into the ground, in a kind of continual miracle, wrought by the hand of God in his favor, as a reward for his innocent life and his virtuous industry.*
>
> Benjamin Franklin

15

How to Grow

It is easy to have a productive, self satisfying garden and still have an eye-catching backyard landscaped with attractive vegetables. It can be low budget elegance. A raised box garden done with staked bamboo, or planted paint buckets can look good. It all depends on effort and continual maintenance.

Every vegetable should be planted with reference to available sun, height of the mature plant, and how long to harvest. Shallow straight drains will lead the water from your garden and keep your yard from being soggy. Balance and symmetry are important so a garden doesn't become cluttered.

Try to plant with a plan, not at random. One fence line might be attractive wide leaf edible roots, while another can be cassava. Papaya and banana spaced properly can blend in beautifully. The important aspect is not to shade your main garden plot and keep everything maintained. Make a small seedling area to start your plants. A good rule is to replant when you have consumed half of the vegetable.

Keep the hammock shaded and cook pot close by.

DECORATIVE ROOTS

Tannia, eddoes, dasheen, toppee tambu, ginger, and turmeric are attractive wide leaf plants that produce tasty roots in less than a year They are virtually effortless to grow. The only danger is damaging them when cutting your yard. They do not have to be located in a traditional gardenplot. For all roots fork the soil to a foot deep and at least a foot wide.

Eddoes

Plant about a foot apart and they will grow into a clump. As they grow in two or three months and every following month, pull dirt up (mold) around the base of the stem. No fertilizer necessary except maybe a little starter 12-24-12. Water daily until they catch and then maybe twice a week. Doesn't matter if in full or partial sun. Eddoes take at least six months to grow and sometimes a year. The bulbs will protrude with their identifying brown flaky skin and the leave will wither as if they are not getting enough water. Do not water when they start to wither as they might not boil. Only harvest in the mid to late dry season, because those harvested in the rainy season won't boil. Carefully dig them using a trowel. Harvest separate bulbs. Save some for replanting and what you are going to eat dry in the sun for at least a few days. Plant at the beginning of the rainy season and it should be ready to harvest near the end of the following dry season or just let them grow.

Tannia

Tannia is a tasty root with a large leaf shaped like a spear point, which makes a great backyard landscaping plant. They can grow to three feet with at least the same distance apart. To plant fork a hole soft and free of clumps of dirt. Blend in some well-rotted chicken manure, a quarter-cup of crushed limestone, and then form mounds. If you are using a head, split it and put it in the mound split side up and cover with about five inches of lose soil. If you are planting a shoot attached to the seed, slide it in so the attached root or eye is facing up. Cover with about five inches of loose soil. If you plant shallower it will produce many small side shoots rather than one big root. Wait at least a year for this enjoyable, crunchy root.

Dasheen

Preferably plant in a damp spot of your yard or the drain edge, about 18 inches to two feet apart. If you cut the leaf for calaloo the bulb head will not develop. Same growing procedure as with eddoes. Both make nice landscaping plants when intermixed with some flowers especially as a type of 'calaloo drain hedge'.

Toppee tambu

Toppee tambu is very easy to grow and makes a nice landscaping border for gardens, a sort of edible hedge. The broad green leaves can reach five feet tall and a few will bear a white flower. The almost round root can be up to two inches in diameter and resemble 'new', first harvested small potatoes, or water chestnuts. To locate some seed roots (rhizomes) find someone selling them along a roadside. They either have some for planting or will direct you to whom they got the toppee tambu from To prepare for planting find a well drained area, fork and mix in well rotted chicken manure. Harvests will be less in clay soil than sandy. Plant the 'seeds' about a foot apart. This plant will even grow in shade, which makes it perfect for interspersing between fruit trees, cassava, or plantain. It is a long crop taking at least nine months before harvest.

Ginger

Ginger has a very different leaf and looks good in the back of a flower or spice bed. Wrap a root in damp paper until it sprouts, plant the root and wait.

Turmeric

Turmeric (saffron) is another tall green leafed root that can look good in a corner of your garden or backyard. Just find some roots and plant. Turmeric is extremely good for you and has many uses. A square foot of turmeric is a lot.

SALADS, GREENS, AND SPICES

These are best planted in a well prepared area or box that could be as small as two feet by four feet. Fork the soil eight to ten inches deep. While breaking the clumps, work in well rotted manure. All can be fertilized with either blue or green salt or a combination of the two. If you choose, a light insecticide like Pestac or Fastac could be sprayed every ten days. A good rule is to replant when you have consumed half of the vegetable. I replant as soon as blossoms come. Grow what you like to eat, and experiment. Using limestone between plantings will cut down on many green vegetable problems

Celery

Celery needs at least six hours of direct sun a day and plenty of water regularly. Use green salt, again just a pinch every week. Plant at least two dozen stalks and replant as you pick to always have a supply. Plant Three to six inches apart and harvest between so the remaining will grow and spread,

Pak Choy

Same as celery. If the leaves get wilted and have many holes it is probably web lace fungus and they need a weekly spray with Roval. Plant eight inches apart. Carefully pull out and then trim the roots off.

Lettuce

Same as pak choy. Plant eight inches apart and plant at least six.

Parsley

Same as pak choy. Plant six to eight inches apart. Depending on your usage in the kitchen plant either six or twelve at a time. When only half remain, plant again.

Spices

Spices as basil, thyme, and sage take a bit of room and grow tall. You really only need one or two of each spice, but plant them where they won't shade the shorter garden veggies.

Chadon bene

Same as the celery, but six inches apart. Doesn't need much water, but grows well when it does. Nothing kills it. Trim with scissors and it will keep regenerating tasty leaves.

Chives

Same as celery, but doesn't need any spray. Plant at least a dozen. Plant chives everywhere you have space. This is an effortless and tasty seasoning.

Garlic
Same as chives

Radish-morai
Grow like chives. They need plenty of sun and extremely well drained soil.

TREE VEGETABLES

Peppers, and tomatoes, eggplant, pimento, chilis, spinach, ochro and bush beans need well drained soil in a sunny spot. Each vegetable could be grown in a box, container or the traditional plot. Fork the soil until it is loose either in a plot or hole by hole. Work in some rotted manure and lime stone. I would put a stake of some kind, wood, bamboo, BRC or PVC pipe just as I plant so later when they are about to bear and need support I won't damage the mature roots. These should be planted according to height. Eggplant should be the tallest and fullest, which means it will make shade - so it should get the morning light first and be on the east side of your garden. You do not want to shade either the tomatoes or peppers as they will spend their energy and nutrients to get taller reaching for the sun rather than producing fruits. Tomato trees get full and tall, but you can pinch the top of the main stalk at about a month and it will spread rather than get tall. Make certain either to stake or cage your tomato trees. Pimentos, sweet peppers, and hot chilis need individual space. All can grow to two feet and bear for five months with proper care.

Tomatoes
When planting put a pinch of starter fertilizer in the hole add some dirt and then plant the tomato tree. Plant at least a foot apart with a stake two foot tall. Stake when planting so the roots aren't later damaged. After a week spray with systemic insecticide. Three or four days later drench (heavy spray) with a systemic fungicide. The three biggest enemies of tomatoes are:

1) mites and the white fly – when the leaves start to curl up,

2) fungus – when they start to wilt.

3) over fertilizing – the leaves turn brown. Use only starter fertilizer 12-24-12 sparingly.

Spray weekly with Pestac and make sure to get under the leaves where the mites live. Water daily, but never let the ground stay damp at night. Replant every two months for a constant supply. If birds peck the fruit run a string along at the top of the stakes and tie pieces of aluminum foil to it. If the end of the tomato is rotten add calcium - Calmax- 1 teaspoon to a gallon. Just add to the watering on the roots and do not touch the leaves. If you have Calmax use it before they bear fruit, in the third week for great tomatoes. I'd plant at least four and wait about a month to six weeks and plant another four to have a constant supply. My favorite types are Heatmaster for the dry season and Gem Pride for the wet months. Healthy trees can bear for six months.

Sweet Peppers

Plant with a pinch of starter fertilizer, place about a foot apart. Stake at planting. Use the starter fertilizer weekly until you see the blossoms. Then use blue salt. If you are planting on a large scale for income, after a week drench with systemic insecticide and then three or four days later a systemic fungicide. Use Pestac insecticide once a week mixed with a foliar spray like Powergizer 45. Mites are the biggest problems to peppers. Water regularly, but never soak. Always try to keep the water from the leaves. The type I like to plant is King Henry.

Pimento

Treat exactly as sweet peppers. Plant about two feet apart. Stakes are not necessary.

Hot Pepper (Chilis)

Congo-scotch bonnet, cayenne, jalapeno, ancho. Same as pimento. Needs the least water of all peppers. Use less water when the plants are bearing to make the fruit even hotter.

Eggplant

Same as sweet pepper, but at least two feet apart. Stake at planting with a stake at least a meter or better long. Water regularly but once they are bearing soak them one morning a week for excellent fruit. Spray under the leaves with Pestac mixed with miticide. Watch for white flies. You'll see tiny white dots on the underside of the leaves.

Ochro/Okra

Ochro/Okra is perfect for a hedge around a backyard garden, because the three to six foot tall plants produce beautiful blossoms that rival its cousin the hibiscus. Plant the seeds one inch deep and a foot apart. Ochro usually grows well in any good garden soil. Four or five plants produce enough ochro for most families.

Spinach

This is another very easy to grow vegetable. You might think it should be classified a leafy, but it can be grown and the leaves trimmed as needed. Red stalk spinach grows like a weed and perhaps the hardest part will be getting rid of unwanted plants. Grows to three feet or more but the main stem can be pinched so it grow out not up. Two or three good plants will provide enough.

Beans

Green, snap, string, contender types are great to rejuvenate soil. The bushes take up little space. An eight foot row should provide a lot of beans. As soon as one row blossoms, plant again so you will always have the delightful beans. Beans need little attention except for well drained soil, a little water and plenty of sun.

GROUND VINES

Cucumber, melon, squash, pumpkin. All vines need a bit of uninterrupted space and you need easy access to pick the fruit.

Pumpkin and melon will take a lot of space. Pumpkins are hearty, but need to remain undisturbed. A specialty melon like cantaloupe can be a nice treat.

Squash

Squash is separated into summer and winter types. Trinidadians are accustomed to winter squash such as the butternut. The long season, odd-shaped, hard skinned squash that store well are usually referred to as winter squash. Smaller, short season types, which are eaten before the skin and seeds begin to thicken are the summer squashes. They have a mild somewhat nutty taste that resembles corn. Summer squash, like zucchini, take up little garden space compared to butternut types. Zucchini is very tasty in stir fry.

Cucumber

Start as with the other veggies, but plant at least two feet apart. Put a stake where you plant so you will know where the roots are for water. Try not to get the water on the leaves. Use special green fertilizer weekly, but just a pinch. Spray as with other plants. Two vines are plenty, but they need about a four by four foot space each.

FENCE VINES

Bodi, seim, christophene, and carailli need little to produce well. Work the soil adding some rotted manure. Water daily till the sprouts reach up. Be patient when starting a vine to climb.

Bodi

Needs to be planted close to a fence or trellis so it can climb. You can use old eggplant or hot pepper trees. Water regularly. Spray weekly with Pestac. Doesn't need much fertilizer. Replant every two months. A family only need about 4-6 vines. There are several varieties, red, long, and short green types.

Seim Bean

This bean is now grown in almost every part of the world. It is an integral part of most Chinese back yard gardens. The purple seim type most common in Trinidad is called Ruby Moon. It is very easy to grow, resistant to most diseases, and needs little water, but does need a fence, jamrah, (trellis), or sturdy pole to climb up. Seim has purplish stems and alternate, white, pink, or purple flowers in a long bunch that produce maroon bean pods containing 3-5 green beans. When the beans dry they become black with a white streak. Pick the bean pods while the skin is smooth and the beans pushing out yet.

Christophene

Christophene is an attractive vine, but it takes a lot of attention to grow. This vine loves the sun, but also needs plenty of water and humidity, and a fence or a jammrah (trellis). The easiest method to grow this vegetable is to locate a farmer and beg a plant. Failing that, select two christophene at the market. Ask the vendor if they have any that are over ripe and budding. If not, set the christophene in a warm window, but not in direct sun. In a few days it will start to shrivel and wrinkle and soon sprout a bud. Plant the seed bud upwards in a clay pot with sandy soil. Lightly fertilize with 12 – 24 –12. Once the plant catches move it outdoors where the vine can climb. Provide it with some shade as a banana leaf or a board. Do not fully cover it. Water regularly and use 12 –12 – 17 –2 mix when it begins to blossom.

Carailli

Carailli is easy to grow from seeds. It is best planted along a fence or anywhere the vine can climb. Because carialli seeds are scarce, first visit the market and search for an over ripe fruit. Set the fruit out until it softens and then remove the seeds. Dig several small holes along a fence. Plant about four seeds per hole. Water regularly and in a few days, bright green sprouts will appear. As the vine grows carefully start it onto the fence. Carialli is a natural climber. Spray occasionally with a mild pesticide and water-soluble fertilizer. In a few weeks yellow blossoms will appear. Water every other day. Birds will be the biggest pests to your carialli.

EASY FRUIT

Papaya

Keep trees at least four feet apart. Use starter fertilizer in hole at planting. Use all the sprays, but if it gets bunchy top pull it out and replant. Over watering is biggest enemy. Once they start to blossom, use blue fertilizer weekly. I plant three trees every six months. Papaya is great for you and a healthy, refreshing desert fruit from an attractive tree. Keep away from any chlorine.

TALL

Pigeon peas, cassava, corn. These need to be on the east side of your garden so they don't block the sun from the other ground level veggies. Four pigeon pea trees will provide plenty of peas, however a mature pea tree takes up a good bit of your yard. They can be attractive nicely spaced about four feet from any property line or fence and about six feet apart. This should permit easily picking from all sides. With proper care you might get two pickings from each tree. Keep the soil well drained and fertilize every month with red (12-24-12) salt. This is along crop that takes six months to bear.

Cassava

Cassava trees could be planted along your fence line behind the peas as both grow about the same height. Cassava is another virtually effortless foodstuff. Plant it where it gets plenty of sun, in loose well drained soil. Since it is a root the softer the soil the better. Cassava can take more than a year to mature. The butterstick type has a nice red colored tree, and takes up more space because it branches. MX is drab gray usually a single stalk and makes a better hedge. After forking an area, stick two pieces of the stalk every two feet. After six months carefully brush away the soil and see how the roots are growing. Whenever you feel they are big enough, dig a root. Keep growing the others. Replant as you harvest. Occasionally apply red salt.

Corn

Corn must be planted with at least eight rows of corn for it to properly pollinate. That can be a major portion of a yard. I have seen a productive two rows along a driveway. Expect corn to six to seven feet tall, so it can dominate your garden. `

Soil Mix

Add about a half a gallon bucket –paint pail – of manure and two cups of limestone to either two five gallon buckets of dirt or fork into a small garden of eight by four. First fork soil and let sit for two days in full sun. Add manure and lime and hoe till soft. Then soak with water.

Let sit for a day and plant.

It is best to water in the morning and no later than three in the afternoon, so the ground can dry and not get fungus.

Fertilizers

Use just a pinch. Over fertilizing is a major problem of beginning gardeners. Don't push your plants and they will bear better and longer.

Red-Starter

Reddish brown 12-24-12 good until blossoms appear. Use a pinch in hole before setting young plant

Green-Starter

15 –5 –20 –2 – great for green leafy veggies like lettuce and pak choy

Blue-Starter

12-12 17-2 after blossoms begin to make the fruit.

Garden Tools

To break soil starting a basic garden you will need a few essential tools; a hoe, a fork, a bastard file, and a cutlass. These four are truly the necessities, while others like a wheel barrow will make life easier. If you are committed to growing your own, then you can get by with just these. Purchase good quality tools that will service you for many years. A saying to remember is, "Cheap things not good, and good things not cheap!"

The garden fork or digging fork has a 'T' or 'D' handle connected by a short sturdy shaft to usually four points called tines. Garden forks are different from pitchforks used for move compost, or manure. The emphasis is on sturdy, if not the tines will break or bend, or the shaft will break. It is used for loosening, and turning hard soil. Shop around if you have time and transport because sturdy doesn't have to mean heavy. A few pounds less can save a lot of sweat. You may think you can get by with a garden spade or a shovel, but either of these tools will increase your labor. The fork's tines are pushed into the ground, and not easily stopped by stones. Later when you are harvesting roots like cassava and eddoes the fork is a true labor saver. The majority are now made of steel. Ours has been working hard for six years and still going strong with help from a few repair welds.

The best method of using the fork is to stick it into the soil with the help of gravity. Don't try to thrust it. Rest your foot on the top of the tines and apply your body weight as you wiggle the shaft. This will ease the sharp tines into the soil. You decide how deep you want to go before levering out a clod of dirt. Start small to save your back from later aches. If you have had any back problems, do stretches before you start and consider wearing a back belt to share the weight with your arms and shoulders. Be careful of the tines. The more you use a garden fork the sharper the tines. Always be wary not to fork one of your feet.

Gardeners use hoes to break the clods made with the fork. Once the hoe breaks down the dirt it can be used to mix limestone and manure into the soil. After the garden is growing it's used to scrape weeds without having to bend down and pull them. Hoes haven't changed much in centuries, but they have changed. There is the basic steel hoe head cast with a ring to insert the handle. The handle must be wedged to hold the head secure. The head must be pitched, angled slightly, towards the operator. This will permit easier cutting. The next tip is to use the file, a bastard file, to keep the blade sharp. Nothing is worse than trying to work with a dull hoe.

A more modern version of the hoe has the blade attached to the handle with a piece of steel called a gooseneck. This is a shock absorber to save your back and shoulders. Again keep the blade sharp. I have seen hoes that started with a six or eight inch blade decades ago, sharpened down to three and four inches.

The cutlass is an absolute garden necessity for cutting the tropical bush before you start forking. Get a good one with some weight. I recommend a true three canal made with British steel and having a riveted wooden handle. I also recommended painting the blade a color you that makes it easy to find in the bush, like brilliant red. More sooner than later you will think you stuck it one place, and it is not there. The dull steel and wooden handle won't jump out at you from the green or dead grass.

As with everything these days there are Chinese versions of the cutlass that will not keep a sharp edge. Spend the few extra dollars and get good steel. The blade should be engraved with the maker. Again the bastard file is needed to keep it sharp, which makes your work easier. Be very careful when drawing the file across the blade. You will not be the first or the ten thousandth person to cut themselves. The best method is to place the cutlass so the blade it pointed up and run the file upwards keeping the sharp blade edge away from your tender fingers. I also recommend wrapping the cutlass handle with black vinyl electrical tape to give it less slippage in your sweaty hand.

There is also a version of the cutlass where the blade is bent and inserted into a wooden handle. This is called a brush cutter and will clear serious bush with rhythmic swinging. The blade is adhered to the handle with wraps of wire. The length of the handle depends on the height of the bush and that of the operator.

A file is a hand tool that cuts fine amounts of material from another piece of steel. It is a hardened steel bar with a series of sharp, parallel ridges, called teeth. Most files have a narrow, point at one end called a tang where you can slip on a wooden handle. It is called a bastard file because it is not classified as a 'coarse file' or as a 'second cut file', but one cut finer than coarse. Again buy wise and your file will last until you misplace it.

Buy decent gloves to save your hands, a hat to save your head, and either safety or sunglasses to save your eyes.

You will need a watering can. Get sturdy steel or make one from a plastic gallon by punching holes in the cap with a nail. You need to also cut a breather hole at the neck. Between the suns effects and the weight of the water, plastic water cans don't last. Get one that has a sprinkler nozzle that can be easily removed when it clogs. If you get a leak, whether steel or plastic, seal it with a piece of Flashband.

Hoses; buy at least 5/8 inch diameter reinforced otherwise you will spend too much time looking for water stopping kinks. Buy a simple, cheap plastic sprayer nozzle because they all break. There is a spring inside the nozzle that is supposed to force back the handle to shut off. They all rust and fail. Buy two at one time so you are not caught short.

Mechanical evolution has hit the garden. If you have the money, transport and strength, rent a gas powered rotavator or rototiller. I recommend renting this tool because it is an absolute workout. It can be a labor saver, but see if you can handle it. These are motorized cultivators that work the soil by means of rotating tines or blades. Rotary tillers are either self-propelled or you must push. Again, be careful. If you have your plot or grow box ready, a day rental should be enough time.

I feel the best recent garden innovation is the motorized string trimmer, also known as a weedeater, weedwhacker, or bushwacker. It is a powered handheld device that uses a flexible monofilament line. Some have a blade attachment for cutting thick grass and other plants. It consists of a cutting head at the opposite end from the motor separated by a long shaft with a handle or handles. Get a shoulder strap. String trimmers are usually powered by a two cycle gas engine. Some have electric motors, but don't consider them for the garden. Again good models are not inexpensive, but they do save a lot of time and labor when clearing land. Ours gets plenty of duty from initial clearing, to weeding between rows and keeping drains open and flowing. Buy the appropriate size as there are lightweight, light duty models for trimming lawns that will not stand up to serious garden chores. Get a brand name for which you can easily get parts. Ours has lasted five years and is still going strong.

That's the garden tool list. Take care of them and they will take care of you.

Why try to explain miracles to your kids when you can just have them plant a garden.

Robert Brault

NOTES

Garden Disease Prevention

Vegetable gardening can be a hobby that can become a side business, and blossom into a livelihood. Successful gardening requires attention to the environment - soil, water, sunlight, and air circulation. Your garden's environment will determine its susceptibility to plant diseases.

Just as if you get wet in the rain and sit in damp clothes; you might catch a virus if your immune system is low. Diseases attack vegetable plants when conditions are favorable. Garden damage from disease can be reduced through a combination of proven disease-prevention methods. First, select adapted, disease-resistant varieties. When you buy seeds, check if they are fresh, packaged during this year. Seedlings should look healthy and not be root bound in the growing tray. Use transplants that are supposed to be resilient to disease.

Whether you grow transplants or buy them, every transplant should be inspected for anything abnormal above and below ground, insect damage on the leaves, or insects on the lower leaf surface (especially white fly). If growing your own transplants, purchase steam-sterilized growth medium/potting soil or sterilize your own in your oven. Always disinfect seed trays with bleach, or use new containers.

Separate vegetables from the same vegetable family to various parts of the garden. Try not to plant them together because the same diseases and pests will attack all. Tomatoes, all types of peppers, and eggplants belong to the same family. A good rule is not to replant the same veggies in the same area of the garden for at least three years. However this will not prevent diseases with long-lived resting spores, such as Pythium, Fusarium, and Rhizoctonia.

Keep weeds under control as they will compete with your veggies for nutrients and may have diseases. Weeds may hide pests that can carry specific diseases. Some weeds attract insects that transmit diseases, especially viruses.

Once a plant is sick, quickly remove and destroy it before the disease spreads to more plants. Remove all plants soon after harvest. Disinfect garden tools and shears that have been used on sick plants by washing in a weak solution of bleach.

Removal of the sick plants will reduce the chance of certain diseases increasing over years. It also reduces the chance that healthy plants will become infected or infested early. Some plant diseases occur naturally with time late in the season and should not be a problem for healthy mature plants. However, these same diseases can ruin your garden if young plants catch the disease or pest from plants remaining from the last gardening season. This is a good reason not to add young plants among older ones.

Diseased plants should not be put in the compost pile. Instead it is better to put them in a specific location that can later be safely burned. I recommend burning rather than burying because some diseases as the bacterial wilt fungi can survive in the soil for many years. Prevention, rather than cure, is the best way to manage these diseases.

It may be necessary to destroy, or disinfest support structures such as wooden stakes and poles used in the garden to support diseased plants.

Keep your garden soil well fertilized and the pH properly balanced. Extremes in temperature, rainfall, nutrients, and misapplied herbicide may present similar appearances to diseased plants. However these conditions won't respond to chemicals and actually make conditions more favorable for disease development. The garden should be well drained. Wet soil encourages development of root rotting fungi. Good drainage promotes good growth of plant roots. Once a healthy root system develops the entire plant should be in good condition. Raised beds may solve the drainage problems.

Soil should be forked and left to bake in the sun at least a week. This is termed soil solarization. This either kills or reduces plant pathogens, and weed seed. It is believed that beneficial organisms are harmed less by solarization than by chemical treatment. Solarization also stimulates release of nutrients from organic matter present in the soil.

A disadvantage of solarization is the area treated must be out of production for at least a few weeks. Solarization requires the soil is free of clods and plant debris. This prevents pockets of contaminated soil. It is best to add fertilizer before beginning solarization. Dry soil should be moistened to a level that is ideal for planting. Wet soil conducts heat better than dry soil and will allow the heat to move deeper in the soil to remove diseases present.

Plants with the proper nutrients can withstand environmental stresses and plant diseases better than plants growing in poor, unbalanced soil. Powdered limestone, either hydrated or unhydrated, can help fight a lot of fungus and bacteria. Do not over fertilize. Excess nitrogen can promote some root-rotting fungi. Nutrient stress can make plants more susceptible to diseases and insect damage.

Water when the plants are dry to avoid drought stress. Excess water can lead to plant death from lack of oxygen to the roots or because of pathogen attack. Harvest produce at peak maturity. Overripe vegetables will attract insects and other pests.

No matter how hard you work to keep your garden's soil balanced, remove all weeds and diseased plants; sometimes disease still attacks. Many leaf diseases can be managed by spraying or dusting plants with an effective fungicide. Apply fungicides appropriately and in a timely manner when resistant seed or transplant varieties are not available. Most fungicides are designed to protect, not cure. They work on the plant surface and protect against infection. They do not eliminate established infections. If disease is not detected early, the plant may die and disease may spread despite fungicide treatment. Some fungicides are systemic and will move into the plant. Some of these have curative properties and will kill infections already established in the plant, but they will not remove the spots already present on the leaves.

Good luck.

> *But if each man could have his own house, a large garden to cultivate and healthy surroundings - then, I thought, there will be for them a better opportunity of a happy family life.*
>
> George Cadbury

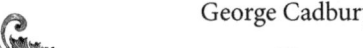

NOTES

Gardening in the Heat

The price of fresh garden vegetables is increasing due to lack of water and the constant heat. There are some simple ways the home gardener can combat most of the perils of this dry season.

First ask yourself, can you take the heat? Be honest, laboring in daily temperatures of above 33 C can be dangerous. Carry and drink plenty of fluids so you can rehydrate. Your body looses moisture through perspiration and it must be replenished. If you are going to be out in the sun for extended periods of time consume some salt to help your body retain fluids. Salt will also help to curb muscle cramps from exertion in the heat. Dress to make your own shade in long sleeve shirts, wide brimmed hats, and sunglasses. Use sunblock of SPF 30 or more. I tie a man's large handkerchief around my neck to keep it covered.

The main thing about the home garden is that it is supposed to be enjoyable. Don't over exert yourself and have a heat stroke to save the price of a few pounds of veggies. Most of us home gardeners work a regular day job, so it isn't too hard to keep our limited gardening to the cool early mornings and early evenings. Limit your labors in the heated afternoons to getting in and out of the hammock. It is said, 'only mad dogs and Englishmen go out in the midday sun'.

As the rain has ceased, our bush turns to tinder. People lacking common sense and decency for our environment set it afire without a thought to homes, gardens, or wildlife. For your protection keep a firebreak clear cut at least six feet around your garden and home. In our Central area the bush was first set on fire on Boxing Day, and four more time since. Birds and animals, which depend on the bush for food will turn toward gardens. Trapping these hungry displaced creatures is another problem of the heat wave.

Keep your garden weeded. This will drastically cut down on water consumption. Think of your garden as an adrift life boat with only a certain amount of water to survive. Don't waste water on weeds. When watering, use a sprinkler can and douse the plant so that the roots are dampened. Be careful not to pour the water hard, which will erode the soil around your plant's roots. These delicate roots will burn in the sun and stunt your plant. A soaker hose is a good thing to have. This type of hose is usually flat and has a multitude of holes on one side. Connect it to a tap and place the holes up and it is a miniature sprinkling system depending on the pressure. I recommend turning the holes down as it will soak the soil around the plants roots and zero water will be wasted. If you are really being severely pinched by WASA, collect drain water from your kitchen sink and lavatory basins. Just push the drain pipe through the wall and place it to a five gallon bucket.

I try to thoroughly soak my garden every morning and evening. A good strategy is to surround all plants and fruit trees with a circular dam about two inches high. For plants like peppers, cucumbers, and tomatoes you can make it about a foot in diameter or include several plants into one dam. This will hold all the water and it will soak down to the roots not wasting a drop. Long rows of corn, bodi, or eggplant can be dammed at the end and water is poured in between watering two rows at once. At least every other week pull some soil from within the dam back to recover the roots and mold the plant for strength.

Fruit trees need dams at least four feet in diameter. I have a five gallon bucket that I have pounded four equally spaced apart nail holes at the bottom edge. I put the nails in to fill it, and then take them out when I have the bucket at the base of the tree. This permits the water to seep out slowly and thoroughly soak the tree's roots system. A weak solution of soluble fertilizer can be added for nutrient.

Again think of the garden as a lifeboat and imagine how often you would be thirsty; all of the time. How often do you really need a drink? At least once a day, twice is best, but not during the hot afternoon. I measure out a Vienna sausage can of water to every small plant, less than eighteen inches tall, like tomatoes or peppers. The bigger plants, especially eggplants, get two full cans. As plants start to produce fruit, it is wise to give them more water. Pineapples and orange are 87 per cent water, grapefruit, broccoli, cabbage, eggplant, cauliflower, spinach, sweet potatoes, watermelon, and sweet peppers are 92%, tomatoes are 94%, and cucumbers, lettuce, celery 96%. Good, juicy vegetables take water!

Go back to the garden lifeboat again. What would make you even thirstier; eating anything salty. Don't over fertilize (salt) you garden anytime but especially during the heated season. Use the bare minimum, and I find it is best to use it mixed with water, but in a weaker than recommended solution. I do not recommend spraying soluble fertilizer directly onto the leaves in hot weather. The salt residue may burn or otherwise damage the plant. Leaves absorb very little water or nutrients. It is best sprayed or gently poured around the roots. Keep your plants molded or staked so it doesn't have to waste energy fighting to stand straight.

What would you want in your garden lifeboat; shade. A next strategy is to shade your garden. I use shade cloth on a light PVC pipe frame. 'Shade' or 'garden' cloth can be either black or green. This lets some light pass but protects the plants from the scorching afternoon sun. Price varies so shop around. Make a simple frame with four tees' and f our elbows. The tees are for the legs so place them so the frame will balance. Tie the cloth to the frame with very light wire or fishing line. A half an hour and about thirty dollars and you will cool your plants. This is especially good protection for pak choy and lettuce, but it can help sweet peppers and tomatoes withstand the dry season. The shade will permit more of the water to reach the roots and actually cool the plant.

The rainy season is a few months away, and then gardeners will be complaining about too much water and floods. Now we need to conservatively water our home gardens in the mornings and evenings, and test our hammocks during the heat of the day.

Garden shades

> *Land, then, is not merely soil; it is a fountain of energy flowing through a circuit of soils, plants, and animals.*
>
> Aldo Leopold

NOTES

Gardening After the Flood

Seems like everything can change so fast in the tropics. Months and months of scorching heat and drought, and a rain instantly transform dry river beds into roaring floods. Gardeners praying for rain get answered to the extreme. Gardens that were cared for by lugging heavy sprinkling cans must now be saved from the effects of a water overdose. The garden's enemies have switched from white fly and beetles to fungus and bacteria.

After the flood market prices sky rocket, so try a few simple steps to keep yours alive. No one thing will guarantee reviving a flooded garden, but a few simple steps will make a difference. Try to save the vegetables that take the longest to mature as peppers, sweet, bitter, and seasoning. Tomatoes don't like a lot of water, so do your best. Papayas, well on this one you better pray because this fruits biggest enemy is excess water. Most roots like eddoes and dasheen can handle the water, but a flood can make cassava rot. Ochro and eggplant need a little effort but usually pull through after a serious rain. Don't worry about short term leafy veggies like lettuce and pak choy. With any luck you can replant and have fresh again in three weeks.

Forethought from prior wet season garden experiences is always a help. The best plan is to have the garden beds raised as much as possible so moisture will seep out and the bed will dry even if thoroughly saturated. High grow boxes are the best solution. If you have a traditional plot garden you must have adequate drains at least a foot wide and deep between each garden bed. Keep those drains clean from grass and debris. The solution is to clean the drains of everything by the second week of May. Unless it is a severe drought, usually by Corpus Christi the rains have hit. If it doesn't, you still have clean drains. Run a bush whacker over each drain and wait a few days and spray the just appearing grass with a systemic herbicide. That should keep it clear for a few months.

Once the soil is wet it is as slippery as ice. A walking stick is recommended for support while maneuvering around the garden. Imagine what would happen to you if caught in a flood. You'd be tumbled in filthy water, and probably drink enough to make you very sick. Soaked to the bone until your body temperature dropped and probably catch a cold or virus. Scrapes would get infected. It would take weeks to regain your strength, if you did make a recovery.

That's what happens to garden plants. The first thing you would need is a good wash with a disinfectant and a few vitamins. That's why plants need some white hydrated powdered limestone and some magnesium. This is the least expensive and most beneficial means to revive plants after a flood. White lime is around a hundred dollars for an eighty pound sack and magnesium is small money. You should have your soil pH tested.

Ours is acidic and once the rain comes bacteria and fungus thrive. One method I use is to wait a few days till the water receded, rain isn't threatening, and the garden drains have no standing water.

If your yard was flooded you would remove the debris, before a good cleaning can begin. Likewise the first step is to weed and loosen the soil at the plants base without damaging the roots. Fungus is the big enemy and it comes in many types, but they all love damp conditions with stagnant airflow. Weeding clears some of the path so air can better flow between the plants Rough of the soil at the base of each plant – a slight rotavation with a hand fork –to make it porous and dry off some of the moisture.

> *The way I see it, if you want the rainbow, you gotta put up with the rain.*
> Dolly Parton

Once the storm is over take off all your dirty flood clothes or you get worse sickness. The same precautions apply, pull off any dead branches and leaves from tomato and pepper plants. Dispose of any dead or seriously ill plants. Trying to save an obviously seriously sick plant is a waste of effort. Do not plant back while the soil is soaked and when you do work a little white lime into each hole.

Even though the place is damp and muddy, I mix a half a Vienna sausage can of white lime to a gallon of water. Add a pinch or magnesium. I mix it well and sprinkle it, drenching each plant especially the roots. The earlier weeding and slight rotavation will permit the maglime water to access the roots. Bacteria is another enemy after a deluge. Wash all the produce your pick to protect yourself from contamination. Don't use any fertilizer salts as this will feed bad bacteria while you think it is feeding your plants. The bacteria will vigorously attack your weakened plants and that outcome is not good. Magnesium will help ward off bacteria and is an essential nutrient that is often lacking in the soil.

Hopefully there have been few slips and no falls. After all the cleaning and vitamins it is time to treat your illnesses and infections. With your garden plants that is accomplished by waiting a day and spraying with an appropriate fungicide like Allette or Acroba, and or Banrot and Rizolex. I like to use a chemical with a copper base like Cuprasan. This is an excellent chemical to get your plants healthy. This sounds like a testimonial for chemicals, but remember you have bee bruised, cut tumbling in dirty bacteria infested water that has gone down your gullet. Of course you'd take a few pills! Try to spray early and hope that it is sunny as the chemical(s) should work better. Make sure you have the nozzle adjusted for a fine mist and coat the leaves. The results of the lime and the fungicides should be visible in three or four days. Your plants will either die or spring back, but you did your best to save them.

Even though I do not recommend using fertilizer salts while the soil is moist, I do use a foliar chemical spray the third or four evening after the lime application. There are several like Powergizer, GreenStim, and Cytotkin. Use them at half dosage in the evening several days after spraying with fungicides. By this point you should either see some recovery or some have died. They will give a booster shot to the plants.

Gardening After the Flood

Even if you are a seasoned farmer, you can't fight the weather. You can prepare and give your garden your best effort at revitalization. If the flood takes it all, get out the fork and start preparing now for the next season.

Farming After the Flood ~ George Corneliussen

We must cultivate our own garden. When man was put in the garden of Eden he was put there so that he should work, which proves that man was not born to rest.

Voltaire

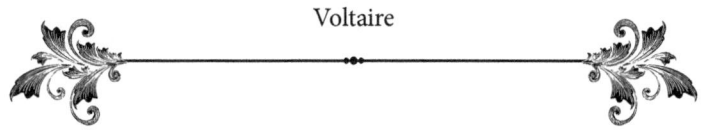

NOTES

Gardening and Good Health

Do you really want to shape up, have a healthy good looking body, and eat better? A home garden may be the best, least expensive means available with plenty of wholesome benefits.

Gardening is a great whole-body workout that leads to better physical conditioning, mental stamina, and weight loss. Digging and lifting will build muscles. Aerobic activities such as raking, cutlassing, and hoeing will burn calories while building a stronger heart and pulmonary system. A half an hour of digging, forking, weeding, or cutlassing will burn about two hundred calories. This is absolutely free – no gym membership necessary, no embarrassment about your body's weight or shape, and the perks are better homegrown foods to enjoy.

It is essential to stretch before beginning garden work. Change from forking to weeding or hoeing, to molding plants to avoid overusing specific muscles. To prevent back injuries, bend from the knees when you shovel or lift heavy objects. Use a wheel barrow to save your back. Repetitive strain injury can occur from doing one task for too long. Muscle strain, back injuries, and blisters can result from moving a greater weight than your body can handle, bending, and improper use of garden tools.

Knee muscles are the quadriceps (front of thighs) and the hamstrings (back of the thighs). To ease strain on the knees, practice strengthening exercises regularly, and stretch before starting gardening. Ask your doctor to recommend specific exercises and stretches that are appropriate. Incorrect posture while squatting can put unnecessary strain on the knees. It is best to keep feet flat with weight evenly distributed. Squatting with heels off the ground can potentially damage knee ligaments. The best posture would be having one knee on the ground, working on hands and knees using a kneeling pad, or sitting on a chair or stool.

To avoid aggravating a back injury, it is important to know how to move, sit, stand, and work in ways that will reduce strain. Use correct postures when doing garden chores. When walking keep a slight arch in the lower back, slightly tensing the abdominal muscles, and don't slouch or bend forward. Sit with feet supported and knees level or higher than hips. Always bend from the knees, never from the waist. Follow these suggestions when lifting a large or heavy object; stand the object upright, position feet shoulder-width apart, close to the object, squat or bend at the knees, tighten stomach muscles, roll the object onto bent knees and then up into arms, hold the object close to your body so that the thigh muscles are doing most of the work, and slowly lift by straightening knees. Lower loads by reversing this process.

Long-handled tools can make garden work easier by extending reach and reducing body movement necessary to complete a task. Lightweight and small-bladed tools can reduce the amount of load and resistance. Stand as close to the work area as possible, and use arms and legs to do work instead of the back.

Protect from excess sun exposure by always wearing a hat and using sunscreen of at least SPF 15. Avoid gardening between 11AM and 4PM when the sun is the strongest or garden in the shade during those hours. Wear protective clothing such as a large-brimmed hat, long sleeves, and long pants. Over-exposure to the sun can cause sunstroke, sunburn and over the long term, skin cancer.

Some good healthy gardening tips: warm up with five minutes of slow stretches. Find a comfortable posture, keep your work in front and close to you. This will avoid reaching and twisting. Use pads or a padded kneeling stool for work at ground level, and periodically change work tasks to avoid injuries from repetition. Use the right tools for the job. Use a wheelbarrow to transport earth and equipment. Work within your strength and endurance, pace yourself, and take a break when you're tired. Occupational Health Standards list safe lifting loads as 64 pounds for men and 28 pounds for women. Always wear proper equipment in the garden including proper shoes or rubber work boots, gloves, and sunglasses or safety glasses.

Always safely store all equipment out of reach of young children. Keep a close eye on children when they are in the garden. Keep them away from equipment such as brush cutters and cutlasses, fertilizers, and other chemicals, bulbs and seeds, as well as water barrels, which may be a drowning hazard.

Keep safety first and remove anything that you really don't need or want as broken tools and furniture, bush, or dead plants. Hoe around plants to break up the compacted soil. Once this is completed decide what new plants you can add. Look for those that offer long growing season, perhaps some color and fragrance. Perhaps add in some herbs such as thyme, rosemary, chives or oregano, which will be well used in recipes.

Play your favorite music while you are gardening. Nature provides its own music, but after living in today's noisy environment it may take some time to get accustomed to the birds and other natural sounds. Add the music especially with comfortable headphones is a good way to adjust to comfortable gardening.

Perspiration, or sweat, is the body's way of cooling itself, when muscles or nerves are over stimulated. As sweat evaporates from the skin's surface, it removes excess heat and cools you. All sweat does not evaporate, but rather runs off your skin. This is especially true in humid weather as the air has enough moisture and cannot acquire the body's perspiration. Each person has about two and a half million sweat glands distributed over the entire body. High sweat production occurs from exercise and or hot temperatures. Sweat cells that usually reabsorb send perspiration to the skin's surface. The chemical makeup of this hard work sweat is a concentration of sodium and chloride (salt) and potassium.

The body's largest organ is the skin, and perspiration helps the body detox and renew itself. Perspiration expels toxins and even disease from the body. Some viruses and bacteria can't live in temperatures above 98.6, so can sweating literally burns away illness. Garden work promotes perspiration, which may harden your hands while softening your skin and helping to keep pores clear and clean. After sweating though a chore, you should shower and scrub off all the toxins you have excreted.

A person who is not well acclimated to hard work in hot weather can produce is about two to three liters of perspiration per hour. Drink adequate fluids to avoid becoming dehydrated, and retreat to someplace cooler if you feel yourself getting overheated. The loss of excessive amounts of the body' salt and water can quickly dehydrate you. This can cause circulatory problems, kidney failure, and heat stroke. It is important to drink plenty of fluids during exercise or outside in high temperatures. Sports drinks contain some salts to replace those lost in the sweat. A nice homemade thirst quencher is a combination of a liter of water with one teaspoon salt, one teaspoon brown sugar or honey, and the juice of one citrus, limes or oranges. Also eat a banana every other hour to replace potassium lost through perspiration. The banana will curb muscle cramps. Dress appropriately for the garden wearing loose clothes that will contain the evaporating perspiration helping to cool you off.

Gardening is the best method to prevent osteoporosis (bones become porous from a loss of calcium) in women age 50 and older. Researchers compared gardening to bicycling, aerobics, dancing and weight training. Gardening and weight training were the only two activities shown to be significant for maintaining healthy bone mass. The best part of gardening may be the edible rewards. Home grown fruits and vegetables contain fiber that may reduce the risk for colon cancer, as well as antioxidants that reduce the risk of heart disease and some cancers. Low in fat, fruits and vegetables can help with weight loss. It is recommended adults get three to five servings of vegetables, and two to four servings of fruits each day.

HOW TO BURN CALORIES

Active for 1 Hour	*Calories Burned*	*Active for 1 Hour*	*Calories Burned*
Push ups/Sit ups	550	Take care of baby	250
House cleaning	250	Play basketball	420
Playing cricket	350	Scrubbing floors	400
Running	500	Walking	350
Swimming	400	**Farming with**	**400**
Weight lifting	300	**shovel or a hoe**	

Most people consume between fifteen hundred and two thousand calories every day.

Home gardening could also be termed 'bio-philia', which means the love of living things. A love of nature is beneficial to the human system because we are part of nature and would prefer to look at flowers and grass rather than concrete. As part of the natural world, we are connected to and regenerated by it. This natural love can lower blood pressure, boost the immune system, and reduce stress. Peace and quiet from today's hectic world can be found weeding, or watering the garden. In just a few minutes you will leave the day's stress and find yourself focused on the task at hand. It is a healthy delight to watch a tiny seed grow into a mature fruitful plant.

Watching your garden grow might keep you healthy. Simple research has discovered patients recovering from surgeries who looked out at a view of trees had significantly shorter hospital stays, fewer complaints, and took less pain medication, than those who looked out at a brick wall. Other studies have found looking at scenes of nature lowers systolic blood pressure in five minutes or less, even if the person is only looking at a photo of nature. Humans positively respond to caring human faces, nature scenes, and certain types of music. Looking at nature scenes produce positive changes in brain electrical activity, muscle tension, respiration, and shifts in emotional states, all of which may be linked to a better immune system. This will protect people from disease and help recovery if they are sick.

As you tinker in your garden listening to some nice music on your portable radio you can achieve a self styled type of meditation. You can stop thinking, obsessing, or worrying. Your senses are awakened, which brings you into dealing only with the present, not the future, or the past. This simple technique has been shown to be very effective at reducing stress. The basic question is should we spend money on drugs to medicinally calm us, or should we spend time in the garden? Having problems sleeping; work in the garden will tire you enough to get a full eight hours of delicious, sound sleep.

Don't let physical challenges keep you from gardening. Gardening will help maintain joint flexibility, range of motion, and your quality of life. Everyone and especially those suffering from arthritis will appreciate these benefits. Small garden stools or five gallon buckets with lids provide both seating and tool storage. They provide relief for the knees and reduce trips to get forgotten hand tools. If kneeling or squatting is too painful, try raising your garden to a comfortable height. The width of raised beds should be narrow enough to allow the gardener to work without straining or reaching. Containers, fence gardens, and raised beds look good while allowing those with stiff joints, back problems and other physical limitations to keep gardening. This is your garden so build it to be comfortable to you.

Pace yourself and enjoy gardening with the peppers and tomatoes. Take time to enjoy the smell of flowers and the unique beauty of nature in your home garden. A few well places placed fragrant flowers will create a soothing atmosphere in your garden and attract colorful birds and butterflies.

If you discover any work is too big or your time is limited – don't be afraid to ask for help. Gardening can also build great friendships. Working with a friend or neighbor can fill the day with work, conversation and laughter. An overwhelming task suddenly becomes a chance to spend time with new or old friends, enjoy the garden, and create new memories. After helping or being helped, end the day with a refreshment or two. Definitely take the time to admire your combined efforts. Sharing your knowledge, plant divisions or other talents like cooking or sewing may be the perfect trade for your friends' time and energy.

Planting a garden is a way of showing you believe in tomorrow. Keep yourself healthy enough to enjoy it. Remember gardening is not a race and you shouldn't have a boss to answer to. If you feel tired, it's time to take a break and rest for awhile.

> *The best six doctors anywhere*
> *And no one can deny it*
> *Are sunshine, water, rest, and air*
> *Exercise and diet.*
> *These six will gladly you attend*
> *If only you are willing*
> *Your mind they'll ease*
> *Your will they'll mend*
> *And charge you not a shilling.*

Nursery rhyme quoted by Wayne Fields, What the River Knows, 1990

NOTES

Garden Accounting

With gardening, you either love it or learn to love it. The learning part is directly related to cost. The price tag for your home garden should be hours of satisfaction enjoying quality time with family and friends, while growing quality vegetables. With all ventures that take time and money, it is wise to keep an accounting of everything to determine what it really costs.

This is another reason to keep a truthful garden diary and collect all the costs of growing your own. Before you plant anything or turn a shovel of soil, keep track on paper of the vegetables you buy, amounts and costs every week for a month with the cost of traveling. This will assist you in deciding what to grow. Also look at veggies you would like to buy, but seemingly don't want to pay the price, like cauliflower or broccoli. Both are expensive and are usually grown locally by using a lot of chemicals. Perhaps garden chemicals /pesticides create another long range expense, for health care.

During the same time frame keep track of the time you spend with family members and friends, time that is not just hi and bye. Note any projects you are involved with your children, parents, or siblings.

At the start of your garden project list every tool, chemicals, clothing, etc. you purchase and associated car fares. On a separate page keep track of your hours laboring to ready the soil. This will diminish after the first tilling. Add in limestone and manure. Keep telling yourself – it has to get easier. Once ready, add in the seeds or seedlings,

Now you have planted and every day note the time spent. Again this first garden event will become better organized; meaning it will become efficient and take considerably less time . Also note what time is spent in the garden with your close relatives and housemates. Even if they are not initially drawn to your garden plot, it will eventually become almost a magnetic force where people will gather to look, ponder, and chat.

About three months later, on a separate page in your garden diary it is time to start writing in positive outcomes, how many peppers, tomatoes, etc. Calculate what they would have cost you at the present market price including car fare and time spent. Note if the family scene seems any closer, are people actually communicating over and about the garden?

You'll undoubtedly discover home garden produce isn't inexpensive – unless you are very lucky – when you add in all the costs and hours. But you grew it yourself and that counts for a lot. You didn't have to buy a membership for a gym to get in shape, that's a plus.

Once a home garden is up and running for a few seasons and you have some experience, you will find it almost therapeutic. You didn't have to pay a psychiatrist to reduce workplace stress, or road rage. That's another plus. In the final tally, produce from your garden should save you almost two thirds of your original market bill.

I knew a full time farmer who could, or would never calculate how much he made an hour in wages. He spent every day from shortly after sunrise to sunset toiling, but his crops were good. His rational was if at the end of a crop he had money still in his pocket - it was a success. It was his rendition of the frequent credit card commercial, this and that cost so much, yet some things are priceless; like enjoyable time spend in the peaceful tranquility of the home garden.

> *The farmer is the only man in our economy who buys everything at retail, sells everything at wholesale, and pays the freight both ways.*
>
> John F. Kennedy

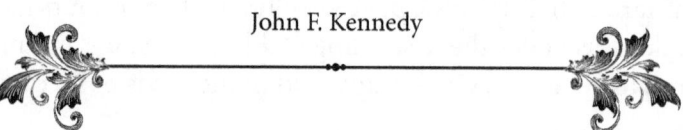

The Family Project

Gardening is an excellent opportunity to group the family together and share quality time working on a project that can satisfy every member, young or old. Today, whether it is the movies, a beach trip, a sporting event, or a meal in a restaurant, it seems to cost a lot of money just to have the family sitting side by side. That certainly doesn't mean members are communicating. Working in the home garden provides a unique occasion in today's hectic world for a totally free period for one on one communication among family members working towards a common goal, fresh food for all.

Starting a garden as a family group teaches valuable lessons in becoming dependable to others and seeing a project to its completion and reaping the benefits. Good life skills gained from family gardening are following instructions, performing step by step procedures, adhering to a schedule, and most important being responsible. Participants may learn important lessons like the ability to communicate and work with others. Love for each other, our environment, and an understanding of the cycles of nature are important ideals offered by the sharing the simple tasks of the home garden.

Every child should be encouraged to be involved in gardening. Invite children to join you among the vegetables and try to explain what you are doing, planting, weeding, watering, and why each is so important. Try not to make gardening 'work', but instead an enjoyable past time. The first perception of a young mind towards agriculture, drudgery or fun, will steer a course either among the tranquil plants, or far from your garden. Show them how much you love the garden by making quality time together among the veggies every day. Give them great garden memories.

Beginning gardening for children should involve small, easy jobs like discerning weeds from plants, or watering each plant with a sausage can, or digging in the dirt to make new rows. Children have a powerhouse of energy, but a short attention span. Many simple activity options should be readied to fight possible boredom.

My first memorable gardening experience was picking peas when I was perhaps five. My grandfather gave me my own special straw hat with red hibiscus flowers stuck in the wide brim. That, with my own picking bag, had me smiling ready every day to pick the lowest branches clean. I felt like such a 'big boy' even though I might bring home only twenty peas to shell with my granny. Had I hit a nest of wasps on one of those pea trees, I probably would never have returned to a garden again!

Planting flowers can be a great lead into gardening. Have a young preschooler actually mix the soil, fill the pot, and plant the seeds. Marigolds and zinnias are very pretty and almost always grow. A flower with a delightful scent would get better attention. This will be a great demonstration of raising something living from the soil, then take seeds from the mature plant to grow more. It will be more personal, if you actually name the plant. With several children try not to make gardening competitive, but instead cooperative.

As children age and understand some of the garden practices, try to obtain or make some kid sized tools. This will make it a more personal experience. When my mom and I planted a few tomatoes and beans, I had my own little shovel. She patiently explain that the good veggie plants can't be picked, harmed, or stepped on. The child has to understand that gardening is fun, but the garden is not a place to play.

As the child's gardening experience progresses, nature will become a reality rather than an abstract. The importance of adequate sun and water, and seasonal weather trends, teaches the cycles of life and regeneration of our valuable environment. Insects like bees and butterflies get attention when their garden role is explained. Respect for the actual fruit of their labor coupled with respect for our planet usually is difficult to comprehend.

About eight or nine, depending on the child, they should be ready to start their own small garden. Keep it small and easy, and make their private plot extremely fertile. Try not to be a 'perfectionist'. Saving all the garden and kitchen refuse for the compost pile can become another kids' garden project. The outcome will be an equally pleasant experience and truly quality shared time. Always keep in mind children have a short attention span. They can't wait weeks for seeds to sprout without forgetting what they planted. Try giving their small garden prime transplants. Beans sprout quickly and bodi climbs rapidly once it catches. Ochro and red spinach are hearty, attractive plants that will produce for many months.

Gardening provides a special chance to inject wholesome home grown, vitamin and fiber rich, vegetables into childhood diets. Spinach or ochro can be picked almost everyday and used in many dishes. Everything that is associated as a result of fun time in the garden should welcomed to the dinner table.

REMEMBER, never have dangerous chemicals or fertilizers within reach of a child. Keep all sharp tools like cutlasses or shears out of sight while children are in the garden. Large, full buckets of water can be extremely dangerous to small children. Be responsive if a child shows an allergic reaction to anything in the garden. Keep a protective eye for stinging insects like wasps, bees, or centipedes.

Teenagers with some gardening experience should participate almost equally with adults in vegetable choices, and scheduled responsibilities that do not necessarily interfere with educational or social activities. Within the garden may be one of the few quality times to communicate directly with your teenager. Gardening with the accompanying exercise, outdoor time, and the accompanying fresh veggie diet may actually make them better students.

The family garden plot must be planned to be user friendly. Non-slip paths, nothing to trip over, are necessities for the youngest and eldest gardeners. Make it comfortable with stools and maybe a hammock. If this garden experiment is a first try in a newly purchased house, plan the garden with some grafted fruit trees that will eventually shade a home comfort area.

No matter the age, family gardening provides great exercise to increase each individual's strength and flexibility. Slowly working into kneeling, carrying, weeding, forking, hoeing, are good exercises for elderly members. For those overweight, an hour of earnest gardening will burn over three hundred calories not to mention the diet change to wholesome garden produce.

Don't push yourself or anyone else, or you'll be turned off to your family plot. If you are basically inactive (behind a desk) at your job, have been retired, or been ill for awhile, stretch while looking through your garden. If you have problems with arthritis, sit on a stool or a bucket to keep above damp earth. If your knees tend to ache make a kneeling pad. Consciously try to keep your back straight while kneeling, or using garden tools like forks, hoes, and shovels. Always consider your posture and don't over do it. If necessary get a waist support belt. Don't stoop.

Break up the activities, like weeding or forking, so your muscles don't become strained. Simple cotton gloves will save hands. Always remember the garden is supposed to be fun. Don't obsess on what need to get done. There's always more time. Work during the early morning or evening. If you must be out in the heat wear a hat and sunscreen.

The family garden may present a unique chance for the elder family members to work along side younger members, doing similar chores. The elders get a chance to share experiences, tell stories, an gain a affinity rare today.

Gardening maybe an excellent way to recuperate from an illness or injury. Again start slow so you don't re-injure or regress. Know your personal time, weather, and effort limits. My good friend Doon from Pierre Road had a bypass over seven years ago. Exercise was recommended so he choose to walk along the roads in the early morning until passing traffic became too dangerous. He saw my garden and decided that his backyard wouldn't need the grass cut ever again. He slowly, a ten by ten plot at a time, created a garden that feeds his entire family, friends and rejuvenated his health and spirit.

Like so many, Doon's garden became his exercise yard, social arena, and his focal point. In his mid seventies, he awakes before the sun and is totally revitalized. His quiet garden now has two hammocks and a nice liming area to do a cook up. Doon's energy level and optimism from his garden are excellent for a man of his age. In fact since he started gardening he seems to have become twenty years younger.

My mother is eighty-four and she gardens every day, hoeing weeds, watering; and our garden is not small. She is still very flexible, with great posture. She was born to a farm and never stopped loving to grow her dinner from the dirt. Her gardening desire is a major common interest.

If something is stressing you out, the family garden may be the best avenue of therapy. Creating a beautiful garden, with your family will lead to inner contentment. Perhaps a corporate garden could help subordinates and upper level managers work jointly to create a beautiful space and relax.

A communal garden might be the path to rejuvenating the village spirit by sharing produce, saving money, while giving time. Neighbors might learn to depend on and communicate with neighbors again outside our homes sealed with bars and walls. Food is now an international priority. Isn't it time we realize we are a global family?

A simple backyard is a good start to enhance your entire family's physical condition, your table, and combined attitude.

> *A farmer travelling with his load*
> *Picked up a horseshoe on the road,*
> *And nailed if fast to his barn door,*
> *That luck might down upon him pour;*
> *That every blessing known in life*
> *Might crown his homestead and his wife,*
> *And never any kind of harm*
> *Descend upon his growing farm.*
>
> James Thomas Fields

23

Pests

A home garden is a pride, meant to be enjoyed. The backyard garden should be fun, productive, and save money while providing fresh vegetables for your family. Without proper precautions, your garden may be also be feeding, and providing a home for unwanted, very unpopular, and certainly counter-productive guests.

Household pet dogs are a joy, and almost a necessary early warning system in today's world. Your garden's soft, cool, tilled soil can be an attractive bed no matter what you have planted. Our dog seems to wait until the soil is prepared and planted before he chooses that exact place to take a snooze. Meeting crushed pepper and tomato seedlings, breeds harsh shouts and reprimands.

The stakes we later use to support the plants vertically are laid horizontal across the garden to make it uncomfortable as a doggie bed. If it is a grow box try making a fence barrier by staking pipes or sticks into the block cells. The best and safest way to keep a dog from your garden is to surround chicken wire. Hopefully they won't persist by jumping or digging.

Birds are a constant threat to gardens from planting till the picking. Every wild creature's daily goal is an easy meal. Ripe tomatoes and peppers are at the top of the menus. The seeds you plant are vulnerable from birds scratching them out of the soft soil. Usually the odor of insecticide used to ward off the even more damaging mole crickets will keep birds away. Try tying string between stakes above your plants. Wrap aluminum foil, and especially pie tins on the strings. The breeze will flip the pieces and tins causing reflections and sounds that should keep birds away. The downside of staked strings are they provide a closer perch for the more adventurous winged garden predators.

A scarecrow – a something that looks like a person is a time proven simple method. Stuff an old long sleeve shirt with grass. Fix it to a staked cross, and set a ball on top as a head with an old cap. Make it simple, and move it around the garden every few days. Try to do any repellant tricks in the evening so the bird's or dog's curiosity isn't aroused.

Rats and mice do damage especially to pumpkins. Rats, like birds, want seeds and will eat a shaft into a pumpkin and clean out the seeds overnight. If your garden is small, try to keep everything tidy. Rats and mice will take anything as string, old sacks, and coconut husk to construct a nest for breeding. Then you'll have more to deal with. Traps are recommended as pets can be harmed by misdirected poison.

Snakes are creatures that may frighten you from your garden. Always be careful and look before you put your hand anywhere dark or shaded. Non poisonous snakes might be frightening, but the little coral snakes are lethal. Tobago has no snakes, and Trinidad has four poisonous snakes. The corals are small and deadly, as are the fer'de lance and the bushmaster. Both seem to have the local name mapepire /mapapie. All four are extremely dangerous and lethal. Snakes like the same places as rats; don't leave sacks, boxes, or wood around they can use as shelter.

Mosquitoes swarm at dusk. Either leave the garden, or have repellant that works. If you have chores that can only be done as the sun sets; I recommend the old trick of burning coconut husk. Horse or deer flies are a blight in the morning. These are the big flies that can land, and you don't feel a thing until they take a bite. Best thing is a thick shirt.

There are more than twelve thousand types of ants that have colonized almost every landmass on Earth. Trinidad has too many, but there are three types that especially hinder gardening. The batchak (atta) variety is a prolific leak cutter. This type of ant is big enough to easily see, especially when toting a bigger piece of leaf. Batchaks can decimate a garden. The best time to view is either in the evening or use a torchlight at night. They follow a trail carrying your vegetables' tender leaves to their nest to grow the fungus they feed on.

The second type of ant enemy is called locally tactak. This variety of fire ants about the size of the batchak, but their bite feels like a wasp sting. The sharp pain is acute, and lingers. They are also called scorpion ants. Fire ants nest in the soil, often near moist areas, such as river banks, the edge of drains, or in an old, rotting banana stools. Usually the nest will not be visible. All ants love to make a home in the blocks used for grow boxes. Fire ant nests can be as deep as five feet. These biters makes me believe ants are really descendants of wasps.

The last type is the small biting ants, and they are the most common unwelcome garden visitor. These little ants are usually about a sixteenth of an inch, just little black dots that can inflict a bite that will immediately itch. We call them 'biting ants', or a number of other names that are not fit to print. They will swarm on you if you disturb their nest. Both the big and small biting ant attacks will swell into painful bumps, especially when stung repeatedly by several at once. The bump usually forms a white pustule, which can become infected if scratched. If left alone, nearly impossible, it will go down within a few days. If the bites become infected, they can turn into scars. Topical steroid creams as hydrocortisone, or one containing aloe vera are good to rub on the afflicted areas. Regular toothpaste can offer a quick and simple relief. A simple solution of half bleach and half water applied immediately to the area can reduce the pain, itching and, perhaps, pustule formation. Oral medicines: antihistamines.

The first step is to identify the ant enemy. Once you know what you're dealing with, your tactics will vary. A spray of recommended chemical will kill them on the spot. Ants will not cross a border around your plot of powdery wood ash. Spread a few packets of aspartame, 'Equal or Nutra Sweet', around your garden and puncture each. It's kind of scary that this sweetener kills ants. Sprinkle cornmeal around the plants the ants are feeding on. Supposedly cornmeal impedes fungus, and most ants feed on fungus. The cornmeal upsets their entire feeding structure.

Make simple inexpensive ant poison by mixing an eighth of a teaspoon of boric acid with a teaspoon of jelly and place on an ant path. Don't add more as they either won't eat it, or won't bring it back to the nest. Some ants prefer fat over sugar, use some vegetable oil in the recipe, or peanut butter. Move your bait stations every two to four days to keep it fresh, occasionally mixing up the materials you use. It may take a couple of weeks to completely kill all of the nests near your home and garden, but you should see an immediate reduction in the number of ants after only a few days. With consistency and perseverance, you can get rid of your ants permanently for only pennies compared to commercial ant bait.

Commercial baits take longer to work, but it kills the nest. Cut the neck from a plastic soda bottle and stuff half a sweet orange inside and cover with the ant bait. A worker ant comes across it and carries it back to the nest to share. When many ants do the same, the colony dies. Apply baits wherever ants are foraging and at a time when they are actively looking for food. A mature leafcutter colony can contain more than eight million ants, mostly sterile female workers. That's a lot of mouths for a garden to feed! Nests are founded by small groups of queens, or a single queen. Even if only one queen survives, within a month or so the colony can expand to thousands of individuals.

Other garden predators are the slug and snail. Both are members of the mollusk group and are similar except slugs lack the external shell. Moisture is critical to their survival and is why they are active only at night or during cloudy days. On sunny days they are hiding in moist, shady places. During hot, dry weather they seal themselves off with a membrane while attached to tree trunks, fences or walls. An infestation of these slimy critters is easy as adult snails and slugs each lay a mass of about 80-100 eggs and they may do this up to six times a year. Slugs completely ate rows of sweet pepper trees. The only way we knew what was eating the plants was to look at night with a torch light. We combated them with table salt, sprinkling it directly on them at night. The African snail is another garden villain. One trick is to place bowls of beer in the garden. The slugs and snails are attracted and drink themselves literally to their death. A barrier of oat bran will kill slugs, but that's only useful in a small plot.

The last garden villains are scorpions and centipedes. Once the plot is cleaned, scorpions are seldom seen. Centipedes like rotting wood, so that should be removed. The main deterrent to most of the garden bad guys is just to keep it clean of debris and waste. Be careful around the compost pile as that's where you want insects to do their job.

Enjoy your home garden, don't lest a few little pests take all the fun out of it.

NOTES

Herbs and Spices

Spices and herbs are common in most foods today. Herbs and spices have both been prominent throughout human history to flavor foods and some for medicinal purposes. Herbs usually come from the leafy part of a plant, and can be used fresh or dried. Spices are obtained from seeds, fruits, roots, bark, or some other vegetative substance. Spices are not necessarily as fresh. Herbs are native to many places and climates of the world, while spices are more commonly found in the Far East and tropical countries.

Traditionally, herbs were considered to be the leafy parts of low growing shrubs as parsley, oregano, coriander, rosemary, marjoram, etc. Spices are from the fruits, buds, seeds, or flowers of plants as cloves, cardamom, saffron, paprika, etc., the bark of trees as cinnamon, or even the roots like ginger. The American Spice Trade Association notes the terms have become largely interchangeable with a spice being defined as any dried plant product used to season and enhance the taste of food.

Some argue that there is no distinction between herbs and spices, considering both have similar uses. Most botanists define an herb as a plant that doesn't produce a woody stem. One of the important differences between herbs and spices is in how to use them when cooking. Herbs are usually used in larger portions than spices for flavoring foods. Spices are generally stronger tasting, and used in much smaller amounts.

Some plants are both herbs and spices. Cilantro is an herb while coriander, from the plant's seeds, is considered a spice. Dill seeds are a spice while dill weed is an herb derived from the plant's stems and leaves.

Gardening is a labor full of tranquility and satisfaction; natural and instructive, and as such contributes to the most serious contemplation, experience, health, and longevity.

John Evelyn

ALLSPICE

Allspice is the only spice commercially cultivated only in the New World. Its aroma smells like a combination of several spices, especially cinnamon, cloves, ginger, and nutmeg. That is how it acquired its name. Allspice's botanical name is pimenta dioica. It is also referred to as English spice, Jamaica pepper, clove pepper, myrtle pepper, pimenta, and pimento. (Allspice is called pimento because the early Spanish explorers thought it was black pepper, which they called pimiento.) I discovered allspice info while researching my favorite seasoning pepper, the pimento.

Allspice still grows wild in the rainforests of Central and South America. The world's best variety is cultivated in Jamaica. Historically allspice was used as an embalming agent by the Mayans. The Arawaks used allspice to preserve meats. Europeans attempted to transplant it to Asia without any profitable results. Despite a delightful and distinctive aroma, it never became as valuable as nutmeg, cinnamon, or pepper. The main purveyors were English, so it became known as English spice. Today allspice is used in men's shaving scents like Old Spice.

This spice would make an excellent shade tree for your hammock. It is an evergreen tree, with glossy, dark green leaves and gives off a refreshing scent even in a slight breeze. All it needs is well drained soil and water during the dry season. Initially feed it 12-24-12 at a rate of a cup every two months. An allspice tree reaches thirty feet tall and wide. Once it begins to blossom switch to a high nitrogen fertilizer as 12-12-17-2 at a rate of one cup every month. Small white blossoms precede green berries, which ripen to purple. Trees start to develop fruit after about five years, and will bear for decades. Allspice trees are either male or female so you need both for berries to develop, and one at each end of your hammock.

Usually handpicked, allspice berries are harvested green and dried in the sun until the two quarter inch seeds inside rattle. Allspice is a digestive aid and carminative similar to cloves. Its oil expands blood vessels; increases blood circulation, and makes the skin feel warmer. During the Napoleonic wars Russian soldiers kept allspice in their boots as a foot warmer. A poultice or steeped in a hot bath, it is a 'bush' remedy for muscles aches and arthritis.

A teaspoon of ground allspice has only six calories with some vitamin C and calcium. Allspice is a main contributor to the essence of Jamaican Jerk. Created by the Arawak Indians, the spices and peppers preserved meats just like drying them over a fire. The term 'jerk' is derived from the Spanish 'charqui', or dried meat. It is often used in European cuisine especially for pickling or marinades.

Jerk Seasoning Mix

Ingredients: two TBS dried minced onion, one TBS dried thyme, two TS ground allspice, two TS ground black pepper, one TS ground cinnamon, one TS dried cayenne pepper, half TS ground nutmeg, one TS salt, two TBS cooking oil

Method: Combine ingredients except oil in a small bowl. Coat meat with oil, and then rub seasoning onto meat. Let sit chilled for two hours. Cook meat slowly over coal, stove top, or oven.

Mango Chutney

Ingredients: twenty almost ripe mangos peeled, two large onions chopped small, six garlic cloves - minced, two cups raisins (golden preferred), half cup fresh ginger root peeled and minced, three cups distilled white vinegar, six cups white sugar, six cups brown sugar, one TS ground cinnamon, two TS ground ginger, four TS ground allspice, one TS fresh ground cloves, two TS fresh ground nutmeg, three hot peppers - seeded and minced (more to your taste), one TS salt

Method: In a large pot mix all the spice ingredients with salt, hot peppers, and vinegar. Boil for thirty minutes before adding onions, raisins, and ginger. Simmer over low stirring frequently for thirty minutes. Add mangos and simmer for another half hour. Refrigerate after cooling.

Spicy Shrimp Pasta

Ingredients: two pounds medium shrimp - peeled and deveined, half pound of pasta cooked al dente' - I like bow ties, but any will work, six cloves garlic, minced, three hot peppers seeded and minced, quarter cup chives chopped, one medium onion chopped, one TS fresh ginger root peeled and minced, one quarter cup chadon benee chopped small, three TBS oil, one green bell pepper, seeded and chopped, three large tomatoes chopped, two TS curry powder, half TS whole allspice, half cup chicken stock, two TBS soy sauce, one TBS brown sugar, one TS cornstarch

Method: Combine garlic, onion, ginger and oil in a small bowl. In another bowl, combine green pepper, tomato, chadon benee, curry powder, allspice, chicken stock, soy sauce, brown sugar, cornstarch, and hot peppers. In a large skillet heat garlic-oil mixture before

DID YOU KNOW?

Contrary to popular belief, allspice is not a blend of 'all spices'. The Caribbean Arawak Indians seasoned the meat of the wild pig with allspice and then grilled it over an allspice wood fire. Aztec Indians used allspice to flavor chocolate. Christopher Columbus confused allspice with black pepper.

add tomato mixture cook for three minutes. Stir in the shrimp, and cook for two minutes. Add pasta and stir until pasta is heated. Serve immediately.

Sweet Potato Muffins

Ingredients: four cups shredded peeled sweet potatoes, one cup brown sugar, half cup oil preferably canola, one TS vanilla extract, two eggs, two cups flour (bakers), two TS baking powder, one TS cinnamon powder (fresh grated if possible), one TS fresh grated nutmeg, one TS allspice powder, one TS salt, half cup raisins (golden preferred), half cup almonds or cashews (optional), quarter cup water

Method: In a bowl blend wet ingredients brown sugar, oil, vanilla, and eggs. In another bowl blend together the flour, baking powder, spices, salt, and sweet potatoes. Then combine both and add raisins. Add water if too lumpy. Place mixture in muffin greased tin or baking dish. Bake at 350 for half an hour. If muffins stick carefully ring each with a knife and gently tap out of the tins.

HEALTH NOTE

In the past, allspice was used to treat indigestion and gas. It was also eaten as treatment for stomachaches, vomiting, diarrhea, fever, flu, and colds. It has been used to flavor toothpastes.

The glory of gardening: hands in the dirt, head in the sun, heart with nature. To nurture a garden is to feed not just the body, but the soul.

Alfred Austin

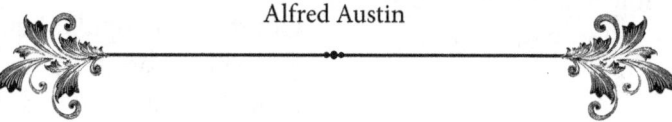

ALOE VERA

Since I was a small child my family used the aloe plant to coat cuts and especially burns. Everyone in our village simply called it aloes, but now it is probably better known in the Caribbean as medicinal aloe. Aloe vera's botanical name is *aloe barbadensis*.

Aloe vera is probably native to the area of Northern Africa, Canary Islands, and Cape Verde Islands where it gained another name - Cape Aloe. It is a short stemmed plant with thick leaves that looks like a cactus. It is considered a succulent because it retains water in its leaves fat with gel, and adapts to almost any climate or soil, even extremely dry, heated conditions. Because of its reputed medicinal qualities and being used in herbal medicine, aloe now grows worldwide in warm climates.

Aloe is considered a tropical plant, but can survive freezing air temperatures. However if the ground freezes the root dies. This plant will withstand severe heat and droughts. It will also survive floods as long as the soil eventually dries within a week after a flood. It cannot live in standing water. It resists most insect pests. Aloe is a truly basic hearty plant. Once you put it in the soil it only needs slight attention. A mature aloe plant can reach a meter tall and will spread naturally with sprouts or offshoots. The greenish gray leaves are thick and fleshy, with rough almost serrated edges. Yellow flowers are produced along a tall center spike.

I have a small cactus garden where I have planted aloe as a functional ornamental border. Small aloes sprout around the mother plant similar to the pineapple. Aloe is a perfect kitchen counter container plant. Separate the shoots and plant in well-drained sandy potting soil. Set where it will get bright sun. Just be certain it will drain adequately. Water regularly, but do not keep the potting medium wet. Potted aloe's soil medium should completely dry prior to watering. As they grow, transplant to larger containers.

Due to easy growth, many countries have large scale aloe farms supplying the cosmetics industry. Aloe is a perfect cash crop for poorer countries like Bangladesh, Cuba, the Dominican Republic, China, Mexico, India, Jamaica, Kenya and South Africa, along with the USA and Australia.

When you slice open an aloe leaf, it actually has two fluids. A bright green liquid - the sap - seeps out as soon as you scrape the surface, and this fluid is actually an irritant. When you cut the leaf open or crush it, you see the inner gel that soothes burns and

> **DID YOU KNOW?**
>
> A papyrus dating from Pharaoh Amen-Hotep's reign in 1552 BC (and found between the knees of a mummy excavated in 1858!) gave twelve different formulas for aloe vera preparations used during the preceding two thousand years.

helps healing. The latter is what is termed 'aloe juice'. Drinking aloe vera juice relieves heartburn and irritable bowel syndrome. It is common practice for cosmetic companies to add gel or other derivatives from aloe vera to products such as makeup, tissues, moisturizers, soaps, sunscreens, incense, and shampoos.

For centuries aloe vera has been used for medicinal purposes. The secret is its concentrations of nutrients and vital substances that include water, vitamins A, B, C, and E, more than 20 minerals, and fatty and amino acids. It seems scientists didn't believe aloe actually cured burns, so it was tested. Aloe is now proven to heal first and second degree burns, but it has not been proven to protect from sunburn. Drinking aloe juice improves blood glucose levels for diabetics, and patients with liver disease. Aloe juice may reduce symptoms and inflammation stomach ulcers. It will also reduce gum disease and dental plaque. Aloe vera extracts are antibiotic and fight fungus.

Aloe vera is used to treat skin ailments as insect bites, acne, sunburns, rashes, scars, blemishes, sores, eczema, and psoriasis. It is drunk to treat blood pressure, hypoglycemia, arthritis, ulcers, constipation, poor appetite, digestive disorders, diarrhea, and hemorrhoids. Aloe simply patted on the skin just once a day is sufficient to get the desired results.

Ralph's Aloe Cut and Burn Cure (Fast Healer Salve)

Combine the gel from one aloe leaf, the juice from four vitamin E capsules, and one TS benedine, iodine, or mercurochrome. Apply to cut or burn and allow to dry. Keep area from getting wet and reapply as necessary.

Drinking aloe vera helps losing weight and boosts the immune system. Many people are disciples of the aloe vera plant and have found taking the juice daily helps to maintain overall good health and provide needed energy.

Aloe Energy Punch 1

Carefully peel one long aloe leaf and combine with milk, a banana, and flesh from one mango. Blend and add honey if the taste is too tart.

Aloe Energy Punch 2

Peel and cube one apple and one banana. Combine with one cup fresh orange juice, four TBS honey and the jell from one large aloe leaf or six TBS aloe juice. Blend.

Sick Man's Punch

Combine the following and blend as smooth as possible; the juice of half a lemon or sour orange, one raw tomato sliced, one cup raw broccoli, one raw carrot sliced, one cup raw spinach, two cloves raw garlic, half cup raw almonds, one half seeded hot pepper (optional if discomfort is digestive), the jell from two large aloe leaves.

Aloe Dessert

The gel from one aloe leaf combined and blended with two cups of plain yogurt, a TS vanilla extract, a pinch cinnamon and nutmeg, and four TBS honey. Freeze over night. Blend again and refreeze before serving.

Aloe Chicken Soup

Cure for a cold or cough. Raw aloe is very slimy, more than the slimiest ochro/okra. Cooking it reduces the slime considerably, but it does still have a slippery taste. Cooking the aloe will give off a ton of liquid and the cubes will shrink and soften without losing their shape.

Ingredients: Five aloe leaves, one chicken chunked, one cup fresh grated coconut, one half seeded hot pepper, two ripe tomatoes chopped small, two cloves garlic minced, one onion chopped small, one bunch parsley chopped, salt to taste, two quarts water.

Method: Wash aloe, slice the skin and chop into chunks. Combine chicken with all ingredients, except aloe, in a suitable pot. Bring to a boil, reduce heat and simmer for two hours. Add aloe chunks. return to boil and then simmer for a half an hour.

Aloe Beauty Mask

Ingredients: One TS red clay, one TS aloe gel, one TS witch hazel (from pharmacy), two drops peppermint oil or ten mint leaves minced and crushed, enough water to make a paste.

Method: Mix with a fork or whisk and apply to clean skin and let sit for fifteen minutes. Rinse with warm water and follow with cool to close the pores. Air dry or gently blot dry.

> Four vegetables are indispensable for the well being of man;
> Wheat, the grape, the olive, and aloe. The first nourishes him,
> the second raises his spirit, The third brings him harmony,
> The fourth cures him.
>
> Christopher Columbus

BASIL – THE ROYAL HERB

Basil is one of the world's most widely grown and used herbs. It is recognized with a warm, clove-like flavor and smell. I have a few plants in my herb garden, and use it in many dishes, but especially when I experiment with Italian recipes. This herb is a relative of mint. There are over sixty varieties with various tastes and colors; with names like sweet, mammoth, dark opal, cinnamon, and licorice. The leaves used in cooking can be green, reddish, or purple. Basil is an important ingredient of Italian and Asian cuisines. Egypt is the main cultivator of basil for the world's market.

Botanists believe it originated in northeastern India. Basil is from the ancient Greek word meaning 'royal', because its medicinal properties made the herb noble and sacred. Ancient Egyptians used basil for preserving mummies. East Indians respect basil as sign of generosity, while the Italians think of it as a symbol of love.

Basil rapidly loses its taste when picked and is not well preserved by drying or refrigeration. It is very easy to grow from seed, and a great addition to any garden. Basil needs loose soil and occasional water. Once it has about eight leaves, literally pinch the top of the plant between your thumb and forefinger. This will stunt the plant's growth upward and force it to grow more leaves. The pinching will also keep the plant alive longer as it will delay the flowers. It is easily grown in pots, and if placed near a window it will deter houseflies and mosquitoes.

Basil has very few calories and is a good source of vitamins A, C, and K, magnesium, and potassium. This herb improves blood circulation by fighting bad cholesterol, while reducing the chance of irregular heartbeats. A basil leaf will relieve the pain of a mouth ulcer. Basil tea will soothe sore gums, and a good soothing remedy for arthritis or rheumatism.

Fresh basil is a requirement for most chefs especially in Italian cuisine. Its taste accents tomatoes, onions, garlic, and oregano; the basic Italian seasonings. To get the best flavor from basil add the fresh leaves towards the end of cooking. For a good sauce for fish just mix minced basil leaves with mayonnaise. It is a great addition to a stirfry, and vegetable dishes with eggplant, cabbage, or peppers. Basil ground with garlic, mixed with olive oil and cheese grated into a paste is what the Italians call 'pesto', which is usually served with pasta.

Note: One-half ounce of fresh basil leaves equals one cup chopped fresh basil. When

Herbs and Spices

substituting dried for fresh, triple the amount.

Basil, or Sweet Basil, is a common name for the culinary herb *Ocimum basilicum*, sometimes known as Saint Joseph's Wort.

Basic Pesto

Ingredients: third cup fresh basil leaves, two cloves of garlic pounded, half cup pine nuts, (Unsalted peanuts, almonds, or walnuts can be substituted.) three quarter cup grated parmesan cheese, half cup olive oil, slight salt (One leaf of chadon benee can be added to vary taste.)

> ## DID YOU KNOW?
>
> It was believed that Salome hid John the Baptist's head in a pot of basil to cover up the rotting odor. In India the basil plant is sacred to both Krishna and Vishnu, and is cherished in every Hindu house. In Italy, basil has always been a token of love. In Romania, when a boy accepts a sprig of basil from his girl, he is engaged.
>
> *A man taking basil from a woman will love her always.*
> Sir Thomas Moore

Method: Put basil leaves in blender and chop, while adding oil and garlic. Add nuts slowly until everything is a thick cream. Use it to as a pasta topping with two tablespoons of pesto per every person. Pesto can be made in volume and frozen, but only add the cheese when you are ready to prepare a meal.

Mushroom and Cabbage Pie

Ingredients: two premade pie crusts, three cups cabbage sliced thin, two cloves garlic minced, one large onion chopped fine, half pound mushrooms, one cup basil leaves chopped, half TS marjoram, half TS tarragon, quarter cup cream cheese softened, four eggs hard boiled, one egg beaten, half TS fresh dill, salt and spice to taste

Method: Coat a large frying pan with oil and sauté onions and garlic. Add cabbage and mushrooms, and simmer for about twenty minutes. Stir in basil and seasonings. Spread the soft cream cheese in bottom of pie and arrange a layer of sliced hard-boiled eggs. Cover with cooled cabbage, onion, and mushrooms. Sprinkle with dill and cover with second piecrust. Make slices to let steam escape, and brush with beaten egg. Bake at 350 degrees for half an hour. Serve cool.

Tremendous Tomatoes

Ingredients: six medium to large tomatoes, one avocado chopped, one medium onion chopped fine, one cup cheddar cheese grated, half cup fresh basil leaves chopped fine (or four TBS dried basil), quarter TS oregano

Method: Halve tomatoes and place cut side up in a baking dish. Cover with mixture of avocado, basil, onion, and cheese. Sprinkle with oregano and broil in oven or on barbecue grill (covered) for five minutes. Serve hot.

HEALTH NOTE

In ancient times, basil was used as an antidote for poison. It is an herbal remedy for diseases related to the brain, heart, lungs, bladder, and kidneys. Mixed with another herb - borage - makes a revitalizing tea tonic. An infusion of lemon-scented basil was used by Hindus to ease the symptoms of diabetes. Basil oil massaged into the skin will enhance the luster of dull looking skin as well as hair. Basil is used cosmetically as a toning body rub mixed with coarse sea salt and vegetable oil. It is also used for acne and skin infections. Basil tea is used to fight coughs, and relieve asthma, bronchitis, and sinus infections. Basil is used to suppress nervous tension, mental fatigue, melancholy, migraine headaches, and to fight depression. Basil is a good source of heart healthy magnesium, which relaxes blood vessels improving blood flow and lessening the risk of irregular heart rhythms or heart spasms.

I grow plants for many reasons: to please my eye or to please my soul, to challenge the elements or to challenge my patience, for novelty or for nostalgia, but mostly for the joy in seeing them grow.

David Hobson

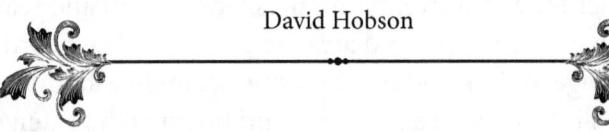

THE BAY LEAF

As a 'wannabe' chef, I use all types of spices and find those I use fresh usually have the best flavor. That's definitely not the case with the bay leaf. Its flavor intensifies when properly dried. The bay leaf is a kitchen staple the world over. Although there are a few different types of trees, each having its specific flavor, our Caribbean sweet bay trees are descendants of the Mediterranean or Turkish variety. Bay belongs to the same family as cinnamon, laurel, and avocado. East Indians call their variety 'Tej Patta' and it has more of the cinnamon flavor. Historically bay leaves adorned victorious warriors and intellectuals of both the Greek and Roman empires. This special leaf supposedly protected them against lightening and plagues. The English believed bay brought good fortune and a leaf tucked behind your ear would prevent you from getting drunk. Botanically sweet bay is *laurus nobilis*, while West Indian bay (bay rum) is *pimenta racemosa*.

Bay trees can be shaped and are a great addition to a landscaped home garden. These trees can be grown from seed if you are very, very patient as it can take up to half a year to germinate. Keep the potting soil damp, but not wet enough to rot the seeds. Try to grow several plants as few survive the first year, or buy a seedling. Bay likes sun, not too much wind or water, but don't let it dry out. Plant where it will drain and fertilize with well-rotted chicken manure twice a year. The tree can reach sixty feet, but it you trim and top it at twenty foot a bay tree will compliment any back yard. Trimming is best done during our late year rainy season and then you can make holiday gifts of the leaves. In a shaded area (so the leaves dry slowly and retain most of their flavor) arrange the fresh leaves between flat boards as plywood to prevent curling.

Put bay leaves in a damp washcloth to alleviate the pain of headaches, especially migraines. Bathing in a bath with bay leaves can treat skin rashes and pain from over sore muscles or arthritis. These same leaves hung in a wardrobe can protect your clothes from moths. Bay oil (if you can find it) increases blood circulation and is reported to prevent baldness. Bay enhances most dishes with a hearty flavor, like stews, beans, potatoes, or soups. For a different barbecue, try shish kabobs with bay leaves skewered between the fish, meat and vegetable pieces. Add the bay leaves early in the cooking or marinating as it takes a while to give off its flavor, but always remove before eating.

Chicken Stew (Not Stewed Chicken)

Ingredients: One half chicken skinned and chunked, two cups red beans cooked, two

> **DID YOU KNOW?**
>
> Bay leaves can also be crushed or ground before cooking. Crushed bay leaves impart more flavor than whole leaves, but are difficult to remove. It is best to use a muslin bag or tea infuser. In some cultures, the bay has a reputation as being a protective tree against lightning, witchcraft, and evil. A bay leaf tree is great for your yard as it is always green. Dry season, torrential rains, and hot winds do not affect it.

stalks celery, one carrot, four medium tomatoes, one medium onion, two ochro, one sweet bell pepper - all chopped small, two TBS olive oil, two cups water, two TBS ketchup or tomato paste, one bay leaf, half TS fresh thyme, one TS fresh basil, quarter hot pepper seeded (optional), salt to taste

Method: Boil chicken chunks in the two cups of water for five minutes. In a good sized pot on medium heat sauté the celery, carrot, and onion pieces in the oil for about five minutes. Pour in chicken and broth. Add everything except the beans and simmer for half an hour with an occasional stir. Add beans and cook for ten more minutes. The broth should now be thick. Remove the bay leaf and hot pepper piece. Serve hot. This is great for a rainy day lunch or dinner..

Hot Bay Bananas

This is easy and tastes great especially with fresh ingredients.

Ingredients: eight ripe bananas (firm) sliced quartered longwise, four TBS butter (prefer unsalted), two bay leaves, one cup fresh orange juice, three TBS fresh lemon juice, one cup brown sugar, four TBS brandy, cinnamon, and nutmeg to your taste, a pound cake package mix.

Method: Bake pound cake per package instructions. In a large frying pan melt butter until it bubbles and just begins to brown. Reduce heat and add bay leaves,. Then mix in the orange juice, lemon juice, brown sugar, brandy and cinnamon and nutmeg. Increase heat until everything begins to boil. Simmer stirring constantly until it has a thick, syrup consistency. Combine with banana quarters and stir gently to coat the pieces without breaking them. Once heated and coated, place bananas on sliced warm pound cake. Cover with French vanilla ice cream and enjoy.

Bay Potatoes

Ingredients: six large potatoes (or one per diner), third cup olive oil, twelve bay leaves, one TBS salt, one TBS powdered red (cayenne) pepper, herbs as sage, basil, oregano to your taste

Method: Slice the tops of each potato in a crisscross fashion without slicing through. Slide 2 bay leaves into each potato. Put potatoes in a baking dish or a bread pan. Mix oil with salt, pepper, and spices, and brush mixture onto potatoes. Cover dish with foil and bake at 350 for an hour. Uncover and put potatoes under broiler until they begin to brown. Serve hot.

Carib Bay Cabbage

Ingredients: one head cabbage cored and shredded, half pound ham, chicken, or beef chopped very fine (minced will work), six medium to large onions chopped fine, three bay leaves, half hot pepper seeded and minced (optional), one TS salt, half TS sugar, one bottle Carib beer

Method: In a large pot with a cover sauté the meat over medium heat. Then add bay leaves, onions, salt, pepper, and sugar. Cook stirring until onions lose color. Add cabbage and mix well. Cook until cabbage has wilted, usually less than five minutes. Add beer and lower the heat. Simmer covered for an hour. Remove bay leaves and serve warm.

Easy Vegetable Chili

Delicious bean dish made as spicy as you can handle it.

Ingredients: two cups soya chunks, five cups red, black, or pink beans cooked (I prefer a combination of beans), four large onions chopped small, six medium to large very ripe tomatoes chopped, quarter cup ketchup or tomato paste, three garlic cloves minced, two TBS ground cumin, three bay leaves, one hot pepper seeded whole or minced (optional), salt to your taste

Method: In a large pot with a cover mix all ingredients together. Add enough water so ingredients are covered. Bring to a boil and reduce heat. Simmer covered for at least an hour. Add more water if sauce gets too thick. Remove bay leaves and pepper before serving hot.

HEALTH NOTE

Bay leaf helps the body process insulin more efficiently, which lowers blood sugar levels. It has also been used to treat stomach ulcers. Bay leaf has anti-inflammatory, antioxidant properties, anti-fungal and anti-bacterial. Bay also treats rheumatism, and colic.

> *The Bay leaves are of as necessary use as any other in the garden or orchard, for they serve both for pleasure and profit, both for ornament and for use, both for honest civil uses and for physic, yea, both for the sick and the sound, both for the living and the dead; . . . so that from the cradle to the grave we still have use of it, we still have need of it.*
>
> Parkinson, 'Garden of Flowers' (1629)

BLACK PEPPER

With many local and exotic spices at hand, the most used is black pepper termed 'the king of spice'. Native to India it is now produced in the tropical East and West Indies, and throughout Asia. Black pepper (*Piper nigrum*) is a flowering vine whose 'heat' comes from the piperine, not capsicum found in hot peppers.

There are several types of pepper that grow on vines. Their fruit are peppercorns. Black pepper is an unripe berry that has been dried for the sharpest and hottest taste. White pepper ripens more on the vine than the more common black variety, and has a slightly less sharp taste. Green peppercorns are picked even earlier than the black or white for a fresher, less hot flavor.

Pepper has been an essence of East Indian cooking for more than four thousand years. Before petroleum, peppercorns were the original 'black gold' of trading. They were used as a form of money. Pepper was considered one of the five essential luxuries upon which foreign trade with the Roman Empire was based, the others being African ivory, Chinese silk, German amber, and Arabian incense. The term 'peppercorn rent' means small money. In the 14 and 1500's, a pound of pepper equaled a pound of gold, or up to three weeks' labor. It was the incredible value of pepper and a few other spices that led to the European efforts to find a sea route to India, and the eventual discovery of the Americas.

Many upscale markets sell whole peppercorns, and grinders can be located in various kitchen stores. Peppercorns can be ground with a simple mortar and pestle. Fresh ground pepper has a superior taste to commercial powdered pepper. Whole peppercorns hold their flavor almost indefinitely as long as they are sealed in an airtight container. Pepper is best ground directly on to food. When cooking, it is best to add pepper at the end to preserve its aroma. White pepper is used in white sauces. Green pepper is best combined with garlic and other spices as cinnamon to make fresh sauces.

The pepper vines are easy to grow in the tropics, but getting the seeds is the hard part. It is a perennial climbing vine with aerial roots like an orchid. Plants can produce for thirty years. The vine can reach thirty feet long with wide glossy green leaves. When it blooms each cluster will have about fifty small white blossoms. As the blossoms fade green peppercorn berries appear. They are green at first, maturing to a reddish. The pepper vine needs well-drained, humusrich soil and a hot wet tropical climate. Pepper is grown from cuttings or seeds cultured in a partially shaded area. Flooding or continually wet soil will kill pepper vines.

Plant in a raised grow box that can easily drain. Put large stones at the bottom, topped with smaller stones and sand. Then cover with compost material or very loose soil. The seeds or cuttings need to be watered lightly twice a day to keep the soil moist. Pepper needs poles or a trellis (jamarah) to support the vines. A long piece of cut vine - two feet or more – is tied to a pole or trellis. Rough surfaces make these vines climb better. Plant two seedlings per post. Keep all other vegetation cleared away, but keep enough trees to shade the pepper vines. Fertilize with 20-20-20 every third week.

Pepper vines should bear within three years and bear heavily for a decade. Harvest all the peppercorns as soon as one ripens to red. You want the corns to be immature and that signifies that they have the sharpest taste. The corns can be sun dried. By the fourth year each pepper vine should bear a kilo of peppercorns.

Pepper is ranked the third most added ingredient to recipes, behind water and salt. Peppercorn is the most widely traded spice in the world, making almost a quarter all spices imported. This is by monetary value not weight because a greater weight of hot peppers are traded, but they have less value. Vietnam grows a third of the world's peppercorns. Brazil grows more than ten per cent. Worldwide 350,000 tons are grown yearly. Tunisia consumes more pepper than any other country with a half a pound per person per year. Americans consume about one-quarter pound per year.

For organic gardeners, one-half teaspoon freshly ground pepper to one quart of warm water sprayed on plants can be toxic to ants and moths. Sprinkle ground black pepper in doorways and window sills to stop invading insects.

Over Dried Tomatoes

Ingredients: two pounds plum tomatoes cut in half and seeded, four TBS salt (coarse or sea preferred), fresh ground black peppercorns, one TBS dried marjoram, one TBS dried basil, two bay leaves, black peppercorns, two cloves garlic - sliced thin, two TBS olive oil

Method: Place the tomato halves, cut side up, on a baking sheet. Sprinkle with the salt, pepper, marjoram, and basil. Cover tray with foil. Bake at 300 degrees for an hour and remove foil and bake for another forty-five minutes. Cool and pack into a sealing refrigerator container. Mix in olive oil, garlic, and peppercorns. This should make a quart. These are an excellent addition to any salad and will keep for several months refrigerated.

Pepper Steak

Ingredients: one pound thick strip steak, two TBS whole peppercorns, one TS allspice, salt, one TS cooking oil (canola preferred), one TBS butter or margarine, The sauce: one small onion chopped small, two TBS chive minced, two TBS brandy or red wine, half cup beef stock, one TBS soft butter or margarine, two TBS parsley chopped

Method: Trim the steak of any fat and slice in half and salt. Smash peppercorns using a rolling pin or mortar and pestle and roll the steaks on it until covered. In a large frying pan over high, heat the oil and the butter. When the skillet is very hot, place the peppered steaks and fry each side for about two minutes. (Longer if you detest rare or medium rare meat as I do.)

Making the pan sauce: Add onion and chives to the pan and fry for about a minute continually stirring. Add the brandy carefully as it should flame up and burn off the alcohol. Fry for a few minutes before adding the beef stock. Bring to a boil and stir in the soft butter. Pour sauce over the steaks and garnish with chopped parsley.

HEALTH NOTE

Medicinally black pepper is considered good for the digestive system and fights bacteria. Pepper soothes nausea and increases body temperature to fight fevers and chills. Its spicy hot flavor makes the nose and throat produce (water) a lubricating secretion, and assists anyone who needs to cough up and clear their lungs. Pepper was also used as an ointment to relieve skin afflictions and hives. However, coarsely ground black pepper does irritate the intestines.

The disparity between a restaurant's price and food quality rises in direct proportion to the size of the pepper mill.

Bryan Miller

CARDAMOM

My spice garden enlarged as my research progressed. I've added cardamom after reading about its qualities. Cardamom isn't difficult to locate as a spice, but locating quality seeds is another quest. Cardamom is also called Guinea grains, or grains of paradise.

Cardamom is one of the world's most ancient spices. It is native to southern India where it grows wild. Ancient Egyptians chewed cardamom seeds for clean teeth and fresh breath. Cleopatra was so enticed by the scent that her palace pleasantly smelled of cardamom smoke when Marc Anthony arrived. Ancient Greeks and Romans cooked with cardamom, and used it in medicines and perfumes. Ancient Indians used cardamom medicinally as a stimulant, to relieve indigestion, and as a cure for obesity, flatulence, and headaches. The Arabs attributed aphrodisiac qualities to it. It is a traditional flavoring in coffees and teas, essential in Arabic coffee. Freshly ground seeds are steeped with the coffee, or a few whole pods are put in the coffeepot. Only saffron and vanilla are more expensive spices.

Cardamom is often misspelled as *cardamon*. It is native to India and southeastern Asia. True cardamom has large leaves, white flowers with blue stripes and yellow edges, and grows eight to twelve feet high. The fruit is a small pod with up to twenty dark brown seeds. It is the seeds that are used as a spice. Most commonly used for cooking purposes is the true green cardamom, botanically *Elettaria cardamomum*. It has a strong pungent aromatic smell, and is a spice as well as medicinal herb. There are counterfeit cardamoms available today, which do not have all the culinary and medicinal properties. Java, Siam, and Nepal all grow 'bastard' cardamom. Cardamom is grown under the shade of tall forest trees. Numerous flavorful little cardamom seeds are encased within a single cardamom pod which is green in color when fresh. Fruits are picked by hand before fully ripe, over a period of several months.

Cardamom is highly aromatic and most commonly used in Asian, Indian, Arabic, and some Scandinavian dishes. Its complex flavor; slightly sweet, floral, spicy, slightly citrusy, and savory allows it to enhance sea food, sauces, meats, poultry, vegetables and even desserts, pastries, and other baked goods. Its aftertaste is a warm, very clean sensation similar to eucalyptus.

Cardamom can be grown from seeds, but the most familiar fashion is similar to growing ginger, by spreading the roots. To try your luck, the easiest least expensive way is to locate some brown seeds, not green; or find the pods. The roots are separated into single pieces and planted. Seeds or root pieces should be sown in deep rich soil prepared with well-rotted manure. Since cardamom requires plenty of rain, it is best planted in raised beds and kept moist. The cardamom plant likes an acidic soil with a pH that ranges 5.0 to 6.5. Get your irrigation ready as cardamom requires a hundred and fifty inches of rain yearly and an average temperature of seventy-five degrees. The cardamom root pieces or seeds begin to germinate around six weeks. They are ready to be transplanted at a height of a foot, after sprouting a couple of leaves. The cardamom plant grows best among trees in shady areas with just moderate sunshine.

Once the plants are started from either seeds or roots, they are best transplanted as they send up 6 to 8 foot leafy shoots. Mature plants send up flower spikes, which produce the green cardamom capsules. The flower spikes produce white or pale green flowers that produce green pod capsules, one to two inches long, containing the seeds. The seeds are in three double rows with about six seeds to the row. The larger cardamom plant is known as 'black' cardamom even though it is actually dark brown. The smaller cardamom is green. These seeds are small black and sticky. The best quality cardamom seeds are ripe, hard, and dark brown in color.

The premium green cardamom pods have been picked while still immature and sun dried to preserve the bright green color. White cardamom has been bleached of color, or lack of it. It is often used in baking and some desserts that want to remain all white. Black cardamom is not a suitable substitute for the real thing.

Cardamom seeds are available in some local markets, but it is better to buy the entire pods, as they will last longer, and storage is far easier. When buying cardamom make sure it looks fresh and smells with a strong aroma. To avoid spreading their aroma to other spices, cardamom should be stored separately in airtight containers in their pods until it is time to use. Put dry paper in the cardamom jar to absorb any moisture. If not, the cardamom will lose a lot of its aroma and will have less of an effect on the food. Pods should keep their aroma for a year. Keep in mind that when the spice is pre-ground its flavor and aroma are quickly lost. Ten pods are the equivalent of one and a half teaspoons of ground cardamom.

A medicinal, perhaps aphrodisiac, drink can be made by steeping seeds in hot water, or you can just suck a cardamom seed. This is good for the throat, respiratory tract, teeth, breath, and stomach. Green cardamom is used to treat tooth and gum infections (just like cloves), treat throat problems, lung congestion, and also digestive disorders. Cardamom is an ingredient in curry powders, and used to flavor sweets, liqueurs like Aquavit, and chewing gums.

Generally there are two ways people prepare cardamom. You can either use it as a whole pod, or remove the seeds and throw away the pod. Spices such as cardamoms can quickly over flavor the dish. Therefore, you need to be very careful when you add this spice; put in the exact amount in the right form as well. Cardamom is available in green and white pods with about 20 small black sticky seeds. You can either bruise them and toss them into your pot, or peel the skin off and use the seeds whole or ground. If you cannot find whole pods use the ground cardamom.

Nutritionally per hundred grams cardamom has three hundred calories, seventy grams of carbohydrates, ten grams of protein, and seven grams of fat, with twelve grams of fiber. It is high in calcium, iron, magnesium, phosphorus, and potassium. It also has vitamin C, B, thiamin, niacin, and folate.

Cardamom Blended Spices

Ingredients: two TBS fresh ground cardamom, one TBS ground turmeric, one TBS chili powder, one TBS ground cinnamon

Method: Heat the mixture of all spices in frying pan over medium heat stirring until the mix just begins to smoke. Allow to cool before storing in an airtight container. Use within two months and in the following recipe.

Cardamom Carrot Soup

Ingredients: one TBS cardamom spice blend, two TBS oil, two large chicken thighs, two quarts of water, one onion chopped, four TBS fresh ginger peeled and chopped fine, six carrots peeled, one sweet bell pepper seeded, one potato peeled brown sugar, one half cup fresh lime juice, one quarter cup parsley chopped, four TBS butter or margarine, salt and pepper to your taste

Method: Simmer two chicken thighs in two quarts of water for forty five minutes until a nice broth is formed. In a large skillet heat the oil over medium and add onion, ginger, carrots, sweet pepper, and potato pieces. Stir in spice blend and cook for twenty minutes. Put vegetables into chicken broth, add sugar. Boil then simmer for half an hour. Add lime juice, butter, parsley, salt and pepper. Cook for another twenty minutes.

HEALTH NOTE

Cardamom oil is popularly used in massages and is known to relieve mental stress and ease muscle tension. Tea blended with the powdered seeds of this herb helps fight depression. Herbalists also use cardamom seed extracts in treating sexual dysfunctions such as impotency. Cardamom in small quantities fights asthma or bronchitis.

THE SPECTACULAR CAYENNE PEPPER

Islanders with 'hot mouths' love our spicy foods, and we owe it all to hot peppers. We know a variety of hot peppers by name, yet the world clumps them together under 'chilis', which was the Aztec term. Cayenne peppers are supposedly named after the Tupi Amerindian term for the Cayenne area of French Guiana. The botanical name is *capsicum frutescens*. These peppers are another of the foods from South and Central America that have been grown for almost seven thousand years. According to some agronomists, hot peppers are crossbreed of the potato and tomato families. Since the seeds stay fertile, peppers were easy to extend to the Caribbean chain. Columbus carried them to Europe as a replacement for black pepper. Magellan spread the hot pepper to Africa and Asia. Cayenne peppers are now grown on every continent except Antarctica. China, Turkey, Spain and Mexico are the largest commercial cayenne pepper growers.

Peppers add a unique flavor to cuisines with a certain amount of 'heat'. The heat is caused by capsaicin, thus the hotter the pepper the more capsaicin. The hottest are our seven pot, the habañero, congo, and Scotch bonnet as well as cayenne peppers, and jalapenos. Cayenne pepper is a specific type of pepper, about five inches long, tapered, and slim, ranging from deep green to bright red when ripe. It is a larger variation of our difficult to grow 'bird' pepper. But cayenne pepper has become a term to mean any pepper ground into a fine dusty powder. The powder is red to red-brown, and some of the hotter versions include the seeds.

Cayenne peppers are some of the easiest to grow and bear the longest. I start them from seeds in trays. Four plants are plenty for any household with many to give to friends. They should sprout in ten days. Plant the seedlings about two feet apart and place a stick to later tie it to when it gets heavy with peppers. They will mature in about seventy days. Some trees bear for over six months with very little attention except an occasional watering. Their only enemy is too much water. Pick when the peppers are about five inches long and turn red. The green ones are also very potent. To dry the peppers, be careful not to get them on your bare skin. The easiest way is to pull the whole plant out when filled with peppers and hang in a shaded breezy spot. To reduce to powder, carefully use a mortar and pistil, or a blender. I recommended wearing long sleeves, full pants, rubber gloves, and simple dust mask to prevent skin or nasal irritation.

Back to Eden written by Jethro Kloss concerns herbal remedies. Of all the herbs listed cayenne pepper seemed to cause the most spectacular cures. I grew it and offered some to our friend, a roadside vendor, to sell. He said Trinis wanted only congo peppers, as that's what was usual. I offered to just give them away. Within days he wanted more, amazed that so many people had told him of the pepper's health benefits.

Cayenne is a food spice, but it also has been used as a miracle herb for the digestive and circulatory system. Peppers like cayenne have reputation for causing stomach problems including ulcers. That is unfounded because hot peppers actually may help prevent problems by killing bacteria you may have eaten, and stimulates the stomach to secrete a natural protective coating that prevents ulcers. Cayenne also helps the body secrete hydrochloric acid necessary for digestion. Once you have good digestion all the other organs of the body get the proper nutrients. Consumed as a tea or in a capsule, cayenne pepper lowers the effects of asthma, and clears congestion. Rubbed on the skin, mixed with a skin cream as a paste, will reduce the pain of arthritis or stop an itch. Studies have demonstrated if you consume a lot of 'pepper' you chances of having a heart attack or stroke are lowered. Cayenne reduces cholesterol. Gargling with cayenne pepper tea will help relieve a sore throat.

Two teaspoons of cayenne pepper has about ten calories. It is a good source of vitamins A and C, has the complete B complexes, and is very rich in calcium, manganese, and potassium. Cayenne pepper is typically used in cooking almost anything from seafood, to eggs, meat and cheeses. It can be used in baking or barbecues. It makes stews, casseroles and sauces tangy. It is an ingredient of English (Worcestershire) sauce. Cayenne will spice up any stir fry and where would our delicious curries be without pepper? For something entirely different add some to cocoa tea. Cayenne peppers combined with the juice of a lemon will enhance the flavor of simple cooked greens as spinach or pak choy.

Cayenne Ointment

Good for aches and sore muscles

Ingredients: one cayenne pepper chopped very fine, half cup vegetable oil, two TBS natural beeswax grated. (Get this from a beekeeper or a hair dresser who waxes).

Method: Heat oil on medium heat in a small sauce pan. Add minced pepper. Cook without boiling for five minutes. Remove from heat and pour through a strainer to remove pepper and seeds. Add beeswax and reheat until wax melts. Pour into suitable container or small jar and cool. Try on your next muscle ache.

Jump Up Juice

More spike than coffee without caffeine

Ingredients: two TBS apple cider vinegar, eighth TS (a pinch) of baking soda, quarter TS cayenne pepper powder, one glass of hot water

Method: First, turn your head away as you add the cayenne powder to the vinegar and water so you don't inhale it as the vinegar (acid) bubbles with the baking soda (alkaline). Sip slowly. It is a real energy boost, especially when I am hungry and tired in the afternoon.

Mexicana Kettle Corn

Ingredients: six cups popped corn or two microwave bags, quarter cup butter or margarine, third cup finely grated cheddar cheese, one TS cayenne red pepper powder or one or two dried peppers crushed, half TS ground cumin

Method: Melt butter in a saucepan. Add all ingredients to the butter and mix well before pouring over popped corn. Mix well, cover with foil and let sit for five minutes, and serve.

Spiced Lentils

Ingredients: two cups brown lentils, five cups water, one TS turmeric, two cloves garlic minced, two TBS butter, one large onion chopped small, one small sweet pepper preferably red color chopped small, one medium tomato chopped small, one TS ground cayenne pepper or one cayenne pepper seeded and minced, one TS coriander, one TS fresh ginger minced, one TS garam masala

Method: After washing lentils, combine them in a large pot with water, garlic, and turmeric. Simmer covered for half an hour. Remove cover, add remaining ingredients and increase heat stirring constantly to reduce the liquid. Cook for five minutes. Serve warm with rice or pasta.

HEALTH NOTE

Cayenne cleans the arteries, great for circulation, can rebuild blood cells, lowers cholesterol, and improves overall heart health. It rapidly equalizes blood pressure in your system, shrinks hemorrhoids, and heals the gall bladder. It has been reported a teaspoon of cayenne could bring a patient out of a heart attack. It is also reported to kill cancer cells in the prostate, lungs, and pancreas. Cayenne is great for the stomach and the intestinal tract.

*A garden requires patient labor and attention.
Plants do not grow merely to satisfy ambitions or to fulfill good intentions.
They thrive because someone expended effort on them.*

Liberty Hyde Bailey

CHADON BENEE OR CULANTRO

Like me, you probably thought our favorite kitchen herb was spelled shadow benee, or chado benee. I write it as chadon benee and use quite a bit in my cooking. The East Indian word for this green leaf is dhania. Our favorite seasoning is really named culantro, and its botanical name is *Eryngium foetidum L., Apiaceae*. It is a biennial herb, which means it is a plant that lives only two years. It sprouts from seed the first season, but usually does not flower or fruit until the second year after which it dies. Chadon benee is native to the Central American tropics and the Caribbean Islands. Although widely used in cooking throughout the Caribbean, Central America, and the Far East, it is not well known in the United States and Europe. It is often misnamed for its close relative cilantro or coriander. Some of its common names are spiny coriander, shado beni and bhandhania (locally in Trinidad and Tobago), chadron benee in Dominica, coulante in Haiti, recao in Puerto Rico, and fit weed in Guyana.

However you say or spell this great tasting leaf, it is one of the most used plants in Trinidad and throughout the Caribbean. Chadon benee is actually part of the carrot family and is more commonly known as culantro, or Chinese parsley. The entire plant, including the leaves, seeds, and roots are edible. The older plants usually have stronger flavor. Trinidad grows the most potent variety in the world.

Fresh chadon benee will keep extremely well if wrapped in paper towels and then put in a plastic bag before storing in the fridge. Another method of keeping this herb fresh is to place it in a cup of water, uncovered in the refrigerator.

Chadon benee grows almost anywhere, especially in full sun. The plant should be watered and well drained. Replanting every three weeks should keep your kitchen supplied with the fresh spice. A small four-foot by two-foot bed produces more than one kitchen can use. A well cared for plant should have leaves of eight to ten inches. If you want to save seeds for future planting, wait until the leaves and flowers turn brown. To quicken the germination, wash the seeds in dish soap and only slightly dry before planting one inch deep and one inch apart. Make rows fifteen inches apart. The easiest way to get chadon benee growing is to cut the root from stalks bought from the market. Plant the roots in wet soil and keep damp. You can trim the leaves with scissors and the plant will continue producing. Although chadon benee grows well in full sun most commercial plantings are partially shaded. This produces large plants with greener leaves, more marketable because of their better appearance and higher pungent aroma.

Other than taste, chadon benee has slight food value. A quarter cup of leaves has only four calories, with virtually no fat, fiber, cholesterol, or carbohydrates and only one mg of vitamin C. The plant is reportedly rich in calcium, iron, carotene, and riboflavin. In Trinidad chadon benee leaves are used in seasoning pickles, barbecue sauce, curries, and chutneys. In Mexico and Central America it is used from salsas and salads, to burritos or meat dishes.

> **DID YOU KNOW?**
>
> Bay leaves can also be crushed or ground before cooking. Crushed bay leaves impart more flavor than whole leaves, but are difficult to remove. It is best to use a muslin bag or tea infuser. In some cultures, the bay has a reputation as being a protective tree against lightning, witchcraft, and evil. A bay leaf tree is great for your yard as it is always green. Dry season, torrential rains, and hot winds do not affect it.

Traditional Green Sauce

Add to almost any cooking

Ingredients: twelve leaves chadon benee, one head garlic, one full grown stalk celery, two leaves Spanish thyme, quarter cup vinegar.

Method: Mince it all together with a blender and store in bottle. Use to marinate.

Chadon Benee Oyster Stew

Ingredients: half cup chadon benee, four dozen large fresh oysters (use more if small), one cup white wine, quarter pound butter, half cup chopped chives, one cup oyster juice (water poured off fresh oysters), one quart cream, one quart water, salt and pepper to taste

Method: Boil wine in a large frying pan until only about two tablespoons remain. Add butter and lightly cook the green onions. Add the oyster water, water and milk and simmer as you blend in the chadon benee. Add salt and pepper levels to your taste. Add the oysters to the soup and cook for five minutes. Serve in bowls with rice. Serves six. (Add a variety of garden vegetables to your taste)

Chadon Benee Carbecue Sauce

Ingredients: three cups chadon benee, two heads garlic, one cup parsley, half cup lemon juice, two TBS olive oil, salt and pepper to taste

Method: Wrap garlic in foil and bake in 400-degree oven for 45 minutes. Cool and squeeze the garlic into a food processor or blender. Add the remaining ingredients and blend. It is best to marinate the chicken, lamb, fish or pork in this sauce overnight. While grilling keep applying this sauce. You can also use this sauce over pasta, rice, or grilled vegetables.

HEALTH NOTE

Chadon benee is used in traditional medicines for fevers and chills, vomiting, diarrhea. Jamaicans use it to alleviate colds and convulsions in children. Bush medicine recommends the leaves and roots boiled and the water drunk for pneumonia, flu, diabetes, constipation, and malaria fever. The root can be eaten raw for scorpion stings. East Indians reportedly use this root to stop stomach pains.

*A garden is a grand teacher. It teaches patience and careful watchfulness;
it teaches industry and thrift; above all it teaches entire trust.*

Gertrude Jekyll

CHOCOLATE

I love chocolate, and I'm proud Trinidad grows what the world market considers to be the best. Few of us, consumers of countless candy bars, understand what it takes to make that creamy sweet brown concoction called chocolate.

Cocoa is the drink commonly known as hot chocolate or cocoa tea. It can also mean cocoa powder; the dry powder made by grinding cocoa seeds and removing the cocoa butter from the dark, bitter cocoa solids. It may also be the combination of both cocoa powder and cocoa butter together. It is not the plant that produces cocaine.

All those delicious sweet, mouth watering chocolate candies begin with the cocoa bean from the oblong cacao pod, mostly shell and pulp. Cocoa is really the dried and fully fermented fatty seed of the cacao tree. Each pod may have from thirty to fifty seeds/beans.

The cacao tree is native to the Amazon in the lower Andes Mountains. The ancient Mayas may have brought it to Central America where it was cultivated by the Olmecs, and the Toltecs. Both were conquered by the Aztecs. Cocoa beans were a type of currency before the Europeans arrived. The Aztecs were such powerful rulers they received annual tribute of 980 loads of cocoa beans, Each load was exactly 8000 beans. The buying power of quality beans was such that 80-100 beans could buy a new robe.

Columbus encountered cocoa in 1502, when they captured a canoe off of what is now Honduras containing a quantity of mysterious-looking nuts. In1519. Cortez witnessed Montezuma, the Aztec chief, drink enormous quantities of their variety of cocoa tea. Montezuma drank only chocolate from a gold goblet and eaten with a gold spoon. It was flavored with vanilla and spices, and then whipped into a froth that dissolved in the mouth. The Spanish conquistadors reported the Aztec chief enjoyed fifty servings of chocolate every day.

The Spanish carried chocolate to Europe and by the mid 1600s it was a popular beverage. The Spanish also began cocoa plantations throughout the West Indies and the Philippines. The cacao plant was first given its botanical name by Swedish natural scientist Carolus Linnaeus who called it Theobroma, 'the food of the gods' or 'cacao', or *theobroma cacao.*

Cocoa requires a humid tropical climate with regular rainfall and good soil. It grows best with some overhead shade. There are three main types of beans used to make cocoa and chocolate. The most rare and expensive is the Criollo, the cocoa bean used by the

Maya. Only 10% of chocolate is made from Criollo, which tastes sweeter and smells better. The most popular bean is the Forastero, which is used to make 80% of chocolate. Forastero trees grow well in dryer African climates and produce cheaper beans. The Trinitario tree created in 1939 is a cross of the Criollo and Forastero, grown in Trinidad and Grenada, it is used in about 10% of chocolate.

Trinidad has the best soil and climate to grow the best cocoa beans. It grows best on a sandy clay soil. Once planted cocoa trees require good drainage and regular weeding. They are topped to around twenty feet tall to make harvesting easier. Local superstition says 'Never prune a cocoa tree under a full moon or an evil spirit / jumbie will live in that tree.' Although labor costs have taken a cut into Trinidad's cocoa production, Grenada has more than 6000 small cocoa growers. Cocoa trees bear at four or five years. A mature tree might have thousands of blossoms and only make about 20 pods. Ten pods, 300-600 beans, produce one kilogram of cocoa paste.

Here's where the labor problem arises. As the pods ripen, they are harvested with a curved knife on a long pole. The best pods are ready for harvest when green. Red, purple, or orange pods are considered of a lesser quality because their flavors and aromas are poorer; these are used for industrial chocolate. The seeds extracted and carried to a place to ferment, known locally as 'sweating' for six or seven days, and then dried. This is really important to increase the quality of the beans, which naturally have a strong, bitter taste. If the fermentation is too short the cocoa may be ruined.

Once fully fermented, the cocoa beans are sun dried by spreading them out over a large surface and constantly raking them. Sun drying permits no other tastes, such as smoke or oil, to taint the flavor. The beans are shuffled or 'danced' and clay mixed with water is sprinkled over the beans to obtain a finer color, polish, and protection against molds during shipment.

The beans are ground into a thick creamy paste, known as chocolate liquor, or cocoa paste. This "liquor" is then further processed into chocolate by mixing in cocoa butter and sugar. Liquor makes unsweetened chocolate. The dried beans can also be separated into cocoa powder and cocoa butter using a hydraulic press, or the Broma process. This process produces around half cocoa butter and half cocoa powder. Standard cocoa powder has a fat content of 10–12 percent. Cocoa butter is used in chocolate bars, other confectionery, soaps, and cosmetics. Plain chocolate is made of cocoa powder, chocolate liquor, cocoa butter, and sugar. Milk chocolate has milk added. White chocolate is made of cocoa butter, milk, and sugar.

Dutch processed cocoa powder is less acidic, darker, and smoother in flavor because they add an alkaline base. Another process that helps develop the flavor is roasting. Roasting can be done on the whole bean before shelling or on the nib after shelling. Low temperature roasting produces a more acidic, aromatic flavor; while a high temperature roasting produces a more bitter flavor. After the ingredients are mixed, the product is further refined to create chocolate suitable for solid bars and pieces. It's mixed, heated, and cooled very precisely in methods called 'conching' and 'tempering'. These processes can take up to a week for the finest chocolates.

Cocoa beans, cocoa butter, and cocoa powder are traded on two world exchanges: London and New York. The London market is based on West African cocoa and New York on cocoa predominantly comes from South East Asia. Cocoa is the world's smallest soft commodity market. Cacao production has more than doubled in the last twenty years to 3.5 million tons in 2003 - 2004, an increase due to the expansion of the plantations rather than increased productivity.

Cocoa powder is actually good for you! At 12 calories a tablespoon it has nearly twice the antioxidants of red wine, and three times the antioxidants in green tea. Cocoa contains magnesium, iron, chromium, vitamin C, zinc, and other minerals. In moderation, it reduces blood pressure. Men over fifty who eat a small bit of dark unsweetened chocolate every day live longer!

Too Easy Chocolate Bar Pie

Ingredients: six milk chocolate candy bars with almonds, seventy-five miniature marshmallows, quarter cup milk, one pint whipping cream, pre made pie crust

Method: Melt candy bars and marshmallows with milk in saucepan over medium heat. A double boiler would be better. Cool for an hour before folding in half of the stiff whipped cream. Pour mixture into pie crust. Chill for at least six hours. Cover top with remaining whipped cream.

Chocolate Cream Pie

Ingredients: quarter cup cornstarch, one cup white sugar, quarter TS salt, two cups scalded milk, three TBS butter, half TS vanilla, one ounce of unsweetened chocolate shaved thin, three egg yolks, prebaked pie crust, spices like cinnamon and nutmeg, and nut pieces may be added.

Method: Combine cornstarch, sugar and salt. Add milk and chocolate shavings. Cook over moderate heat, stirring constantly, until mixture thickens and boils - about two minutes. Remove from heat. Whisk egg yolks into hot mixture. Return to heat and cook for one minute, stirring constantly. Whisk in butter, vanilla. Set aside to cool. Pour in baked pie crust. Bake at 350 degrees, for twenty minutes.

The Best Cocoa Tea Mix

Enough for a big family.

Ingredients: two pounds instant chocolate drink, one pound non-dairy creamer (flavored if possible as Hazelnut or French Vanilla), one cup sugar (powdered if possible because it dissolves better), eight cups nonfat dry milk, one TS salt

Method: Combine ingredients well and seal in an air tight container. Refrigerate if possible. Add hot water to quarter cup of this mixture for one cup of the best tasting cocoa tea.

Chocolate Lovers Fudge

Ingredients: three cups semi-sweet chocolate chips, one can sweetened condensed milk, half TS salt, two TS vanilla extract, one cup chopped almonds or cashews (optional)

Method: In a medium pot melt the chocolate chips with sweetened condensed milk and salt in over low heat stirring constantly. Remove from heat; stir in nuts and vanilla. Get a square eight inch pan and line with waxed paper and spread mixture evenly into it. Refrigerate for at least three hours. Cut into squares and enjoy.

Brownies

Ingredients: two ounces unsweetened chocolate shaved thin, six TBS butter, one TS vanilla, one cup granulated white sugar, two large eggs, one cup all-purpose flour, half TS baking powder half TS salt, half cup chopped almonds or cashews

Method: In a suitable pan combine chocolate and butter over low heat stirring constantly. Remove from heat and allow to cool. Whisk in vanilla and sugar. Add eggs one at a time whisking continually. In a bowl combine flour, baking powder and salt. Combine the flour mixture into the chocolate. Add nuts. Pour into a well greased baking dish and bake at 350 degrees for twenty five minutes.

Chocolate Biscuits

Ingredients: two cups flour, half cup unsweetened baking cocoa, quarter TS baking soda, quarter cup brown sugar, two TS baking powder, half cup soft cooking margarine, one TS vanilla, half cup milk

Method: in a suitable bowl mix all dry ingredients, blend in margarine with a fork until flour mixture gets a crumb texture. Add vanilla and milk. Mixture should becomes a soft dough. Roll dough and cut into circles or squares. Bake at 450 for fifteen minutes.

HEALTH NOTE

Chocolate contains flavonoids, which act as antioxidants. Some protect from aging caused by free radicals, which can lead to heart disease. Dark chocolate contains a number of antioxidants. Studies show consuming a small bar of dark chocolate everyday can reduce blood pressure in individuals with hypertension. Dark chocolate has also been shown to reduce LDL cholesterol (the bad cholesterol) by up to 10 percent. Chocolate stimulates endorphin production, which gives a feeling of pleasure. It also contains caffeine and other substances which are stimulants. Dark chocolate has 65 percent or higher cocoa content.

UNIQUE CINNAMON

As kids, we used cinnamon to make sweet rice during Divali. The cinnamon came in strips of bark rolled one in another, called 'quills'. We would grate it and measure it for our recipes. I love the fresh sweet fragrance of cinnamon.

Cinnamon is the inner bark of a tropical evergreen tree and one of the oldest spices. There are at least fifty different varieties and the very best type is still grown in Sri Lanka (previously Ceylon) along the coast near Columbo. The Queen of Sheba gave cinnamon as a gift to King Solomon. The Chinese have used it as an herbal medicine for over four thousand years. In ancient Egypt It was used as a drink, medicine, a preservative for embalming, and could be considered more valuable to the Pharaohs than gold. Portuguese conquered Sri Lanka in 1536 to control the world's cinnamon supply. A century later the Dutch took control of Sri Lanka and started the planned cultivation of the spice that still exists. Instead of permitting the trees to just grow tall the Dutch transformed the tree by continually cropping and topping, into almost a bush. The Dutch fought to control the valuable cinnamon monopoly for two hundred years until the English traveled cinnamon farming to South America and the Caribbean.

A trimmed cinnamon tree will grow from ten to twenty-five feet with a thick, very scabby rough bark. Cinnamon grows better in sandy, well-drained soil with good, constant moisture. The leaves are shiny, and blooms small pale yellow flowers that become dark purple berries. Trees can be obtained from plant shops or from woodsmen who hike and find them in the wild mountain bush. The few people we know who make cinnamon, skin fresh branch shoots of the tree and the inner bark is left to dry and curl into the spice.

Medicinally cinnamon is considered a mild tranquilizer and relieves nausea, gas, and diarrhea. It is an antibiotic that fights some fungi and bacteria better than over the counter medication. One-half teaspoon of cinnamon each day may reduce blood sugar and cholesterol in Type II diabetes sufferers. Consuming cinnamon daily may increase insulin resistance, can help to control weight gain, and lower cholesterol, as well as to decrease the risk of heart disease. A tea of cinnamon and ginger is great for fighting a cold or flu and indigestion. Several studies have shown improved insulin sensitivity and blood glucose control by taking as little as half teaspoon of cinnamon per day.

One tablespoon of cinnamon has seventeen calories with only one calorie from fat and five from carbohydrates. It is a source of manganese, calcium, and iron. Cinnamon should smell sweet when you buy it, and will stay fresh in a sealed container.

Cinnamon is essential in my kitchen. I use it in cakes, cookies, puddings, drinks, and curries. On cold rainy days make a tasty drink of warmed milk with cinnamon and honey, or add it to coffee with cocoa powder. It pleasantly changes the 'usual taste' of bean and eggplant dishes. Toasted buttered bread spread with sugar and cinnamon is an easy treat.

There is an ancient fable of the Cinnamon Bird that supposedly lived in Arabia and used cinnamon to build its nests. Greeks wrote that these birds flew to an unknown land and collected cinnamon and carried it to Arabia. The Arabians got the cinnamon by tempting the birds with pieces of raw meat. The birds carried the large pieces of meat back to their nests, which caused the nests to fall. This destroyed the nests made from cinnamon. As the nest fell the people collected the cinnamon.

Easy Papaya Bread

Ingredients: one package yellow cake mix, one cup mashed papaya, three eggs beaten, third cup vegetable oil, half cup of sour cream, quarter cup water, half cup applesauce, half TS ground cinnamon, half TS ground ginger, one cup raisins (preferably soaked in hot water), quarter cup grated coconut (optional)

Method: Combine cake mix, eggs, oil, sour cream, applesauce, cinnamon, ginger and water in a large bowl. Beat as smooth as possible before adding the papaya, raisins, and coconut. Pour into a greased, floured bread pan and bake for half an hour at 350 degrees. Insert a knife to see if it is baked through the center. If knife doesn't stick and comes out clean, it is baked. If not continue baking for ten more minutes.

Sweet Potato Casserole

Ingredients: three sweet potatoes, peeled, boiled, and mashed, two thirds cup all purpose flour, one cup sugar, half cup butter, one TS ground cinnamon, two TBS orange juice, a pinch of grated ginger, quarter TS ground nutmeg, quarter cup milk, one TS vanilla extract, two eggs beaten.

Method: In a small mixing bowl combine half of the flour with the brown sugar. Blend in half of the butter until mixture is flaky. In second - larger bowl combine the remaining ingredients. Pour sweet potato mixture into a greased baking dish and sprinkle the top evenly with the flour/sugar/butter mixture. Bake about 40 minutes at 350 degrees.

Cinnamon Chicken

Ingredients: four chicken breasts boned and chunked small, one large sweet pepper cut into strips, one small pineapple cored and chunked, half TS fresh ginger root minced, half TS hot pepper seeded and minced (optional), two leaves of chadon benee chopped fine, half TS ground cinnamon, two TBS butter, half cup water

Method: In a frying pan cook chicken pieces in one tablespoon of the butter until browned. Remove from frying pan. In the same pan with the other tablespoon of butter quickly cook the sweet pepper. Add pineapple and water and remaining ingredients except chadon benee. Simmer for fifteen minutes. Add chicken, heat, sprinkle with chadon benee, serve with rice or pasta.

HEALTH NOTE

Cinnamon has many health benefits. It has shown promise in the treatment of diabetes, arthritis, high cholesterol, memory function, and even leukemia and lymphoma. It helps in removing blood impurities, effective on external as well as internal infections, and is recommended for acne. It helps in destroying germs in the gall bladder and bacteria in staph infections. Cinnamon is also anti inflammatory, relieving pain and stiffness of muscle and joints. Cinnamon is recommended for arthritis. It is used in chewing gums because it is a good mouth freshener. Cinnamon is very effective for indigestion, nausea, vomiting, upset stomach, diarrhea, and flatulence. Cinnamon is a good brain tonic, boosts brain activity, helps remove nervous tension and memory loss.

"Cinnamon bites and kisses simultaneously."
Vanna Bonta

CORIANDER—CILANTRO

So you have never heard of coriander? The bulk of most curry powder is ground coriander. To harvest coriander you must plant cilantro, which is similar to one of our favorite seasonings chadon benee - also known as culantro. In fact, our chadon benee is known otherwise as long, saw tooth, or black benee coriander. At maturity, cilantro seeds full and dried become coriander. Immature cilantro seeds do not have a pleasant odor, so the Greeks called the seeds bugs, 'koros' in Greek. Cilantro is part of the parsley family, often called Chinese parsley. Coriander's botanical name is *coriandrum sativum*.

Cilantro's seeds are tiny, around an eighth of an inch, little balls slightly out of round. They stink if you work with them too soon. Wait till they are dried light brown. Coriander is available both whole and ground.

Coriander is a very old spice referred to in the Bible's Exodus. It is native to the Middle East, but has been grown in all parts of Asia for thousands of years. It grows wild in Egypt and in England where it was transplanted by the Romans.

I've tried this in my spice garden and it grows well in slightly moist soil planted where it gets the morning light until about eleven or noon. Partial shade from a banana will also work. If cilantro gets a daily dose of tropical sun it will be bitter. In proper conditions this plant grows like a weed. Make two plantings so you can have one for fresh cilantro leaves, the other will mature in about three months into coriander seed. You will know when the seeds smell good they are ready to harvest. To grow plant the seeds about half an inch deep and about six inches apart and water regularly. This can also be grown indoors, but need to get four to six hours of sunlight.

Coriander seeds have a nice smell when they ripen, like a bit of orange peel. East Indian, Mexican, and Middle Eastern cuisines depend on this herb. Its main producers are North Africa, South America, and Russia.

Coriander seed, and especially the oil, is an appetite stimulator and will sooth a gaseous tummy, headaches, and arthritis. The cilantro plant can be used as a poultice against wound infections.

Whole coriander seed is easy to pound in a mortar. This will provide better flavor and aroma to your dishes. Whole seeds keep indefinitely and light roasting will enhance their taste. Cilantro leaves can be chopped or minced before use and definitely lose taste if dried.

This is one spice that has a wide variety of use. Coriander is an ingredient in garam masala, pickling spice, and is used in cakes, breads, and other baked goods. Cilantro leaves are should be used fresh in sauces, soups and curries and sprinkled like parsley on cooked dishes. Even the cilantro root is used to spice meat and curries dishes.

Four grams of coriander has only one calorie with some vitamins A and C.

> **DID YOU KNOW?**
>
> Coriander is one of the oldest cultivated herbs. It is mentioned in the Bible and found in tombs of Egyptian pharaohs. It is also the stuff of dreams; "while visions of sugarplums danced in their head". Sugarplums originally were sugar coated coriander, a treat that initially tasted sweet with a spicy flavor after taste. That recipe later included small bits of fruit and became the sugarplum sweet we sing of today.

Coriander Carrot Soup

Good for a cold, rainy day.

Ingredients: one pound of carrots chopped small, one large onion chopped small, one bunch fresh cilantro leaves stripped from the stems and chopped – stems dumped, one TS ground coriander, two veggie stock bouillon cubes, two TBS oil, salt and black pepper to taste, one quart of water, cup cooked rice or small noodles

Method: In an appropriate sized pot heat the oil over medium and add the onion and carrots. Cook for five minutes until the carrots soften. Add ground coriander and cook for a few more minutes. Add salt and pepper and water. Reduce heat to low and stir in the veggie cubes. Simmer for a half an hour stirring occasionally. Add rice or noodles. Adjust salt and pepper to your taste. Stir in fresh cilantro leaves and serve with toasted bread.

Coriander Beef or Pork

Ingredients: two pounds beef steak (clod) or pork sliced into half inch wide strips, one cup water, one quarter cup cider vinegar, two TBS fresh lemon juice, a quarter cup canola oil, two TS ground coriander, one half hot pepper seeded and minced (optional), one TS salt, two TBS cream (optional)

Method: Combine water, cider vinegar, half of the oil, pepper, salt, and coriander. Put the meat slices in a suitable dish, cover with mixture and let sit overnight. Heat the rest of the oil in a large skillet with a cover and brown meat. Pour in the marinade and bring to a boil. Cover and simmer for about half an hour. If you choose add the heavy cream to the juices remaining in the skillet and pour over meat before serving.

Simple Curry Powder

Ingredients: two TBS ground coriander, two TBS ground ginger, two TBS ground cardamom, four TBS cayenne powder, four TBS ground turmeric.

Method: Mix well and store in a tightly sealed jar or refrigerate.

Where life is colorful and varied, religion can be austere or unimportant. Where life is appallingly monotonous, religion must be emotional, dramatic and intense. Without the curry, boiled rice can be very dull.

C. Northcote Parkinson

CUMIN

Cumin (jeera) is something readily available in the markets, yet still should be planted in your spice garden. It has sharp, almost overpowering, slightly bitter taste. Dishes cooked with it have a warm, spicy-sweet smell. East Indian and Mexican cuisines require cumin. To the unknowing, cumin's flavor is often confused for caraway. Some think there are dark seed and light seed cumin, but there is only light. The dark is from a totally different plant, the 'love in the mist flower'. Cumin is native to the areas surrounding the Mediterranean and Egypt.

This is a spice that grows like a weed in the tropics. Cumin is a cousin of parsley and can grow a foot tall, and will usually bend under the weight of the seeds. As the flower matures two seeds form in the head. The quarter inch or smaller seeds are shaped like a boat and slightly fuzzy. Cumin doesn't require much in your spice garden except for regular watering and full sunlight. In well worked soil plant the seeds about a half inch deep and an inch apart. Don't permit the soil to dry out. The seeds usually mature in four months. Cumin plants will not all ripen at once, so wait until the first seeds are dry enough to crack when you pinch the pod between your fingers. Then cut the plant and hang over a clean cloth. After the pods thoroughly dry, put them in an old pillow case. This will be used later to thresh them. Keep adding as they ripen and dry. Bang the case or bag against the floor to bust loose the seeds. Sift to remove parts of the pods. Keep in a sealed container in a dark place, or refrigerate until ready to grind.

Cumin stimulates your appetite while helping the stomach to relieve gas. It will reduce nausea during pregnancy. Cumin could be called the 'breast spice' because it supposedly increases both lactation and size.

This spice should be used minimally because its flavor can overpower other flavors in most dishes. A teaspoon is enough in a dish for four. Cumin is used to highly spice a food. East Indian, Middle Eastern, Mexican, Portuguese, and Spanish cooks love it. Most curry powders and many savory spice mixtures have it as an ingredient. A pinch of cumin will invigorate plain rice, beans, and casseroles. It is a pickling ingredient for cabbage to make sauerkraut, and is used in chutneys. Six grams of cumin has about twenty calories of which half are from fat. It also has some iron and calcium.

DID YOU KNOW?

Cumin is the second most popular spice in the world. Black pepper is number one. A Middle Age superstition was that cumin kept yard fowl and lovers from wandering. It was also believed happiness would bless any bride and groom who carried cumin seeds at their wedding. Cumin's botanical name is *cuminum cyminum*.

Latin Chicken (or Turkey) Soup

Ingredients: one TBS oil, one large onion chopped small, two stalks celery chopped small, three cloves garlic minced, two TS chili powder, one TS cumin for full flavor - half is adequate, one TS oregano, one quart water, four large tomatoes diced, four cups shredded cooked chicken or turkey, two TBS fresh parsley, three chicken bouillon cubes, two cups or one large can black or red beans, two cups fresh corn cut from the cob or frozen corn, half cup sour cream optional, two TBS chadon benee chopped

Method: In a large skillet heat oil, add onion and cook till soft and clear. Add garlic, chili powder, cumin, and oregano and stir for about a minute. Add water, diced tomatoes, celery, shredded chicken or turkey, parsley, and bouillon cubes. Bring to a boil, then simmer. Stir until the bouillon cubes dissolve. Add beans, corn, sour cream and chadon benee. Simmer for half an hour.

Pepper - Squash Stew

Ingredients: one cup lentils, one large onion chopped small, four stalks celery chopped small, two squash (Could be yellow, crookneck, zucchini) chopped, three large sweet pepper chopped small, one cup parsley chopped, two large tomatoes chopped, one can tomato paste or a quarter cup of ketchup, one hot pepper seeded and minced (optional), three bay leaves, four garlic cloves minced, three TBS oil, one Spanish thyme leaf chopped, one TS each of ground cinnamon, ground cumin, and ground coriander, one can channa/chick peas, one half cup plain yogurt (optional)

Method: Put water in a large two quart pot and bring to a boil. Add lentils, bay leaves, and half of the garlic. Simmer lentils about ten minutes. Drain and place lentils in a bowl. Retain this water, but remove bay leaves. Toss with oil, thyme, and remainder of minced garlic. In a large skillet heat one tablespoon of oil and stir in spices. Add garlic, onion, celery, sweet peppers, and squash; simmer for five minutes. Add lentils, tomatoes, and paste, chick peas/garbanzo beans/channa, two to four cups of remaining lentil/ vegetable stock water. First add two cups and continue to add until you get the consistency of stew you desire from thick to runny. Bring stew to a boil; then reduce to simmer and cover for about half an hour. Stir occasionally. Add the chopped parsley. Serve in bowls topped with a spoon of plain yogurt, sour cream, or grated cheese.

Cuban Black Bean Burgers

Ingredients: two cups cooked black beans, one sweet pepper chopped very small, one small onion chopped very small, three cloves garlic minced, two stalks celery chopped very small, one egg, one TBS chili powder, one TBS cumin, one TS hot pepper sauce, one cup bread crumbs

Method: Mash black beans in a bowl with a fork or spoon. Add sweet pepper, onion, garlic, and celery. In a cup mix the egg with the spices and add to the bean paste. Add bread crumbs until the bean mixture holds together. Make four patties. Put a tablespoon of oil in a skillet and fry the veggie burgers about ten minutes on each side. If grilling, place patties on foil, and grill about 8 minutes on each side. If baking, place patties on baking sheet, and bake about 10 minutes on each side.

HEALTH NOTE

Cumin is a stimulant as well as a great herb for digestive disorders as flatulence, indigestion, diarrhea, nausea, and morning sickness. A good recipe for one dose is one teaspoon of seeds boiled in one glass water with a pinch of salt and a teaspoon of coriander or chadon benee leaf juice The seeds are rich in iron and stimulate the secretion of enzymes from the pancreas which can help absorb nutrients into the system. It also boosts the liver's ability to detoxify the human body.

As a spice, cumin's mellow enough to play nice with others, personable enough to show distinction, earthy enough to feel well grounded, and exotic enough to render mundane ingredients sultry and seductive.

Jo Marshall

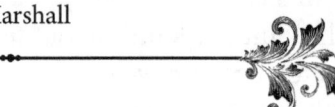

DILL

Dill is not a traditional tropical spice, but it is delicious. I keep four stalks growing and use it fresh when cooking fish fillets. Dill is another plant that is best used fresh as an herb - dill weed's wispy leaves; while dill seed is considered a spice. Yes, it is actually called a weed and it can grow that easily, perfect for a spice garden. Dill leaves have a crisp clean taste that is excellent with vegetable dishes, cucumber salads, and makes especially tasty potatoes.

Dill seeds have a much more potent flavor, like a blend of anise and celery. The seeds are eighth inch ovals. Both seeds and leaves are used for pickling.

Dill, botanically anethum graveolens, originated around the fertile crescent in the Middle East. It was mentioned in Egyptian medical texts about five thousand years ago. Dill branches were found in Egyptian tombs. Roman soldiers burned dill seeds directly on to their wounds to promote healing. Dill is a favorite spice of northern Europe, particularly Germany and Russia.

Dill is a perennial and self seeding herb; one planting can last several years. Dill requires full sun, good drainage, and rich soil. Keep it weeded, occasionally water, and it will mature in about two months. Spread the seed over well worked soil and cover with a half inch of damp sand (Not beach sand.). Sprouts emerge in about two weeks, and should be thinned to six inches apart. Dill attracts beneficial insects who feed on aphids making it a good plant to protect your roses. Snip what you need with scissors, and leave the remainder of the plant to keep growing.

Dill seed is harvested by snipping off the flat, yellow flower head as it ripens. Put the flowers in a brown paper bag and dry in the sun. Shake the bag a few times to separate the seeds. Store in a cool dark shelf, or refrigerate. These seeds can be used whole, or crushed in a mill or coffee grinder. These seed heads, combined with vinegar, garlic, sugar, salt, and pepper produce dilled pickles, or can be used in breads, stews, and rice dishes.

Dill tea is recommended to overcome insomnia. In foods it will relieve that gassy feeling, stop hiccups, and ease digestion for children. It is rich in vitamin C and one tablespoon contains more calcium than in a third cup of milk.

Fresh or dried, dill's leaves and seeds are great additions to fish, lamb, potatoes and pea dishes. Always add dill at the end of cooking, otherwise the heat will destroy most of its flavor. Use it sparingly or it will overwhelm other flavors.

Dilled Fish in Foil

Ingredients: one pound fresh fish fillets - salmon, grouper, or king steaks preferred, a quarter cup lemon juice, one TS fresh dill weed - leaves crushed, one medium onion chopped very small, two TBS butter or margarine, one TBS fresh chopped parsley, one TS salt

Method: Smear one TBS butter on four squares of heavy-duty aluminum foil, then put fish on each piece of foil. Melt the other TBS butter in a small sauté pan and add lemon juice, parsley, dill weed, and salt. Pour over fish. Top with onion. Fold foil so it doesn't leak and put the four pieces in another baking dish. Bake at 350 for twenty minutes or longer depending on the thickness of the fillets.

Plenty Beans Stew

Ingredients: One large onion and the following chopped, two cloves garlic, two stalks of celery, one cup carrots, two cups potatoes, a half cup of the following beans - pinto, kidney, black, and lentils, one bay leaf, one TS fresh dill leaves crushed, one TBS oil, one TS salt

Method: Sauté onion, garlic in oil. Combine ingredients except dill in a large slow cooker, crock pot, or large covered pot, bring to a boil and simmer for about 4 hours. Add dill before serving.

Cabbage and Mushroom Pie

Absolutely delicious.

Ingredients: Pie Crust: three cups flour, one TBS baking powder, a pinch of salt and pepper, a third cup plus one TBS vegetable shortening, six large eggs beaten.

Filling: three cups cabbage shredded, one large onion chopped, two TBS oil, half pound fresh mushrooms, one TS fresh basil chopped, one TS dried marjoram, quarter TS dried tarragon, four ounces cream cheese at room temperature, four hard boiled eggs sliced, one TS fresh chopped dill, one egg - beaten, salt and pepper to taste

Method: Pie dough: Blend flour, baking powder, salt, and pepper. Whisk in shortening until mixture forms coarse crumbs. Beat in eggs until a soft, easy to work with dough forms. Cover and refrigerate while cooking the filling.

Filling: In a large skillet heat oil over medium heat. Add cabbage, onion, and mushrooms. Cook until cabbage is wilted and tender, about twenty minutes. Stir often. Add basil, marjoram, tarragon, along with salt and pepper.

On a lightly floured board cut dough in half and roll out a top and bottom crust. Place bottom crust in a 10-inch deep dish pie pan. Spread bottom with softened cream cheese and cover with a layer of the sliced hard-boiled eggs. Top with the cooled cabbage and mushroom filling. Sprinkle lightly with dill. Apply top crust, crimping and sealing edges. Cut four small slits in the center of the top crust in a decorative pattern to allow steam to escape. Brush lightly with the beaten egg. Bake at 350 for 30 minutes until crust is golden. Let sit twenty minutes before serving.

Cheesey Dill Biscuit Bread

Ingredients: two cups bakers flour, a third cup whole milk, three quarter cup cheddar cheese grated, six TBS cold butter or margarine chopped (must be cold), two TBS baking powder, half TS salt, one TS sugar, half TS baking soda, three quarter cup plain yogurt, one and a half TBS sliced fresh dill (or one TS dried)

Method: In a suitable bowl whisk together all dry ingredients. Add cold butter pieces and continue to blend until the mixture is coarse. Add cheese and dill. Combine yogurt and milk into the flour-cheese mixture. On an ungreased cookie sheet, divide dough into quarter cup mounds and keep about two inches apart. Bake at 400 for about fifteen minutes or until pale golden brown. Best to use the middle oven rack to keep bottoms from over hardening and burning.

HEALTH NOTE

Dill weed contains carvone, which has a calming effect and aids digestion by relieving intestinal gas. Dill seeds are high in calcium, one tablespoon equals a quarter cup of milk. Dill is believed to increase lactation in nursing mothers and is used in a weak tea for babies to ease colic, encourage sleep, and get rid of hiccups. Crushed dill seeds, mixed with water, are used to strengthen fingernails. Chewed dill seeds can cure bad breath.

*Gardens are not made by singing 'Oh, how beautiful,'
and sitting in the shade.*

Rudyard Kipling

FENNEL

Fennel is a herb that isn't used much throughout the Caribbean because of its limited availability. I found my plant at a nursery, and it is a very attractive addition to my herb garden and spice shelf. Fennel is another plant considered both an herb and a spice. It has a thick, perennial root system and can grow to five feet tall. This herb is an erect cylinder of vivid green, smooth polished leaves. Fennel blooms with bright golden flowers. It has an almost aniseed flavor and is often used to season fish and broths. Every part of fennel is edible. The leaves can be used as a garnish. The swollen leaf base is eaten, and the seeds are used for flavoring.

Fennel originated around the Mediterranean, and was well known to the ancient Greeks who used it as a digestive remedy. It is now grown worldwide where climate permits. Fennel prefers hot dry, sunny conditions, yet can adapt to partial shade. Since fennel grows so tall and truly can survive for years, plan your garden and place it where it will not shade or interfere with your other plants. A few plants about twenty inches apart are all that's necessary. Plant seeds an inch and a half deep in well worked soil. Fennel doesn't require much attention or water. A warning, fennel will cross pollinate with dill weed; do not plant these two herbs close together as both of their tastes will be dulled. After about four months collect the flowers before the seeds ripen. When dry shake the seeds on to a white cloth. Pick fresh leaves as needed and harvest the bulb for salads.

Fennel is used as an eye wash and once believed to increase breast milk. Fennel is thought to curb eating and great for dieters. It will reduce gas and stomach cramps. In medieval times this herb was hung over doors to ward off evil spirits. It is reputed to stimulate strength and courage, and increase the eater's life span.

As a herb, fennel leaves are used by French and Italian cooks in fish sauces and in mayonnaise. It is one of the best herbs for fish dishes. Three grams of fennel is about three calories. Fennel is an ingredient of Chinese Five Spices and of some curry powders. Fennel contains manganese, calcium, potassium, magnesium, phosphorus, and

vitamin C.

Baked Fennel - Potato

Ingredients: four TBS margarine or butter, two pounds Irish potatoes washed clean, one fennel bulb, pinch grated fresh nutmeg, salt to taste, half hot pepper seeded and minced (optional), one cup milk, one half cup grated cheddar cheese.

Method: Slice fennel bulb and potatoes very thin. Place half of the slices in a grease oven proof dish and give a dash of nutmeg, salt and pepper if you choose. Cover with milk. Place more slices on top and cover with grated cheese. Cover dish with foil and bake at 350 for forty-five minutes. Uncover and bake fifteen minutes longer.

Rice and Fennel Cake

Ingredients: Two fennel bulbs peeled and chopped small, two cups milk, one cup cooked rice, four eggs, half cup brown sugar, one TBS butter or margarine, two to three TBS bakers flour

Method: In a suitable pot boil the milk and stir in the rice and fennel pieces. Simmer for half an hour before stirring in the sugar. Mix in one egg at a time. Slowly stir in the flour. Spoon mixture into a greased cake pan and bake covered at 350 for forty-five minutes. Uncover and bake ten more minutes. Cool before serving.

Roast Garlic and Fennel

Ingredients, three heads garlic peeled, two fennel bulbs sliced, one bunch chives chopped, one TBS oil (prefer canola), one half hot pepper seeded and minced (optional), pinch of salt

Method: Place peeled garlic bulbs and sliced fennel on a piece of foil and add chives, pepper, salt, and oil. Wrap tightly and put in another oven proof dish. Bake at 350 for half an hour. Serve as a spread for roti or bread.

Roasted Fennel

Ingredients: two fennel bulbs (just use the base of plant) sliced, one to two TBS oil (canola preferred), one TBS Balsamic or another flavored vinegar

Method: In a bowl stir fennel slices with oil and vinegar until they are coated. Transfer to an oven dish and bake uncovered for fifteen minutes at 400 degrees. Serve warm.

HEALTH NOTE

Fennel is in mouth fresheners, toothpastes, desserts, and antacids. It fights anemia, indigestion, flatulence, constipation, colic, diarrhea, respiratory disorders, menstrual disorders, and promotes eye care. With carrot juice, fennel is a very good treatment for night blindness or to strengthen the optic nerve. Add beet juice to make a remedy for anemia resulting from menstruation. Fennel juice assists convalescence. The French use it for migraine and dizziness. Boiling fennel leaves and inhaling the steam can relieve asthma and bronchitis. Fennel is used after cancer radiation and chemotherapy treatments to help rebuild the digestive system. Ground fennel seed tea is believed to be good for snake bites, insect bites, or food poisoning. It increases the flow of urine.

It is not really an exaggeration to say that peace and happiness begin, geographically, where garlic is used in cooking

X. Marcel Boulestin

HORSERADISH

Living in the tropics we usually get our hot mouth through pepper sauces. At a friend's insistence, and perhaps humor, I tried horseradish in cocktail sauce. I loved its sharp bite and the different type of 'heat' that shoots up your nose and makes your eyes water. Horseradish is a root that can be bought fresh and easily cultivated in your herb garden.

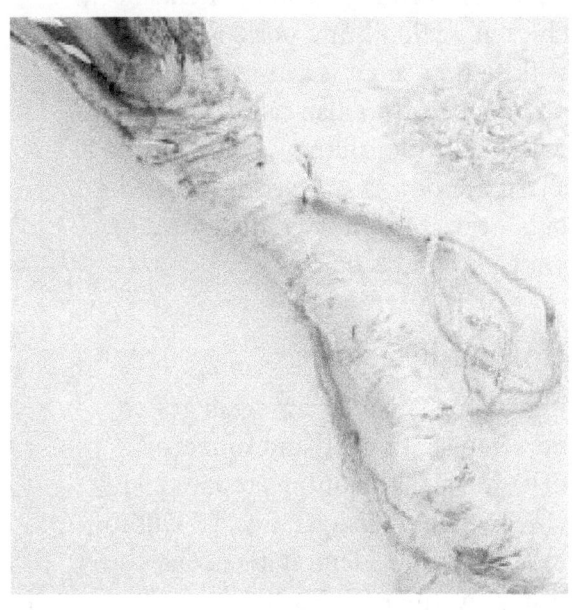

Botanically horseradish is *A. rusticana*. Related to the mustard family, it is believed to be native to Russia or Hungary. The Egyptians seasoned food with it while the pyramids were being built. The 'horse' name may refer to the size of the root and its pungency. Horseradish was referred to as 'German mustard'.

Horseradish is a long whitish root, and looks a lot like morai / daikon radish. Thick roots are best. You can buy fresh, but it is usually available grated, preserved in vinegar. Some are purple from beet root juice added. Horseradish's 'heat' comes from isothiocyanate, a volatile compound when combined with air and saliva generates the sinus clearing tang. Dried or powdered horseradish is more pungent than the vinegar preserved. I have three roots growing in my garden. Horseradish is a perennial, which means it will just continue to grow. In fact if you aren't careful it will take over like a weed. When you see the large, long leaves you will know it is a cousin to mustard. The leaves can be cooked like spinach and have a nice, uniquely spicy taste. It grows best in a place that gets only the morning sun. Sections of the roots are planted in soft well worked soil about ten inches apart. Look for an 'eye' where a shoot is starting to form. As a beginner about four roots should be enough. After about four months carefully whisk away the soil from under the leaves to reveal the top of the root. If it is two inches wide of better it is time to carefully dig it out. Save an 'eye' of the root to replant.

Horseradish is a gastric stimulant that will help you digest rich foods. It is richer in vitamin C than an orange and works as an antiseptic. It has long been valued for its medicinal properties to help relieve respiratory congestion, and as a poultice to reduce aches from arthritis or rheumatism. Horseradish has only two calories per teaspoon.

Before you grate fresh horseradish, the root should first be washed trimmed, and peeled. Grate as you would a cabbage or a carrot. The outside layer has the most pungent taste. Whole root can be refrigerated for a few weeks. Grated horseradish may be kept in white vinegar or frozen in a sealed container.

This root's main use is in horseradish sauces, made most simply by mixing the grated root with sugar, spices, and vinegar. As a sauce, horseradish complements beef, chicken, seafood, and pork. Mixed with sour cream it is a great on baked potatoes. Horseradish can be blended with butter for grilling. It is famous as a sharp 'seafood sauce' for shrimp cocktails. Served hot, horseradish loses its pungency and is quite mild.

Horseradish Sauce

Ingredients: quarter cup fresh grated horseradish, drained and squeezed dry (or a half cup of the prepared with vinegar), half TS sugar, two TS Dijon mustard, one TS lemon juice, one cup heavy cream, half TS salt

Method: Combine horseradish, sugar, mustard, salt, and whisk until smooth. Gently fold in cream. Chill two hours

> **DID YOU KNOW?**
>
> In 1597 John Gerarde published a book of herbal medicinal plants and mentioned horseradish. Horseradish doesn't interest horses and it is not a a member of the radish family. It is really a mustard. Germans called it 'meerrettich', or 'sea radish'. 'Meer' in German came out 'mare' in English. Perhaps 'mareradish' eventually became horseradish. The plant was known as in England as 'redcole' and as 'stingnose' in some parts of the U.S. Germans still brew horseradish schnapps and some also add it to their beer. Horseradish was rubbed on the forehead to relieve headaches. This root is still planted and harvested mostly by hand.

Horseradish Dip

Ingredients: one and half TBS fresh grated horseradish drained and dried, half cup plain yogurt, half cup sour cream, one bunch chives chopped, quarter cup cucumber chopped fine, salt and pepper to taste

Method: Combine all ingredients in a small bowl. Chill dip overnight. Serve with raw vegetables or cooked shrimp.

Horseradish Applesauce Dip

Ingredients: half cup applesauce, quarter cup yogurt, three TBS fresh grated horseradish or prepared horseradish, one TS white vinegar, salt and pepper to taste.

Method: Combine all ingredients in a bowl and chill.

Spicy Herbal Pate

Appetizer, snack, or protein main dish.

Ingredients: one cup ground sunflower seeds, half cup cornmeal, half cup nutritional (brewers) yeast, one TBS parsley, one TBS basil, one TS thyme, half TS salt (sea salt preferred), half TS sage, one cup potato - finely grated, one and a third cup water, quarter cup sunflower oil, two TBS soy, one TBS prepared horseradish

Method: In a bowl combine ground sunflower seeds, cornmeal, yeast, parsley, basil, thyme, salt, sage, and together. Grate potato and rinse, squeeze, and drain to remove excess starch. Add water, oil, soy, and horseradish; add potato last. Mix well. Grease an oven pan and spoon in mixture. Bake at 350 for 45 minutes until brown. Let cool before serving with crackers or sada roti.

HEALTH NOTE

Horseradish dates back 3,000 years. It has been used for an aphrodisiac, a treatment for tuberculosis, a rub for low back pain, headaches, and a bitter condiment. Horseradish is rich in vitamin C, also high in calcium, sulfur, and potassium. Horse radish has been used to treat diabetes and circulatory problems. Consuming horseradish can relieve the symptoms of a sinus infection. Eating horseradish can cure water retention.

Life begins the day you start a garden.
Chinese Proverb

MACE

The nutmeg tree is the only tree that grows two spices. Mace is similar to nutmeg with a slightly better aroma. Mace covers the nutmeg in its shell. It is used to flavor baked goods, meat and fish dishes, sauces and vegetables, and in preserving and pickling spice mixtures.

It is hard to find anything more purely red than fresh mace. When I carefully crack open a yellow-green nutmeg, see the red mace and get a faint whiff of nutmeg; it just exhilarates me. Considering the universal popularity of these two spices historically, a lot of Europeans must have felt the same way. Arab traders brought mace to Europe in the sixth century A.D. In England during the 1500's one pound of mace was worth three sheep. High quality mace retains an orangish-red color, but some types dry to light tan.

Nutmeg grows throughout the tropics, but in Grenada it is cultivated in estates. Driving across from St. Georges to Grenville on the east coast there are several government nutmeg buying and processing stations. On most driveways mace is drying on cardboard. Mace has several levels of quality. Grenada is second to Indonesia for production of mace.

A whole dried mace is termed a blade. Preserved blades are preferred rather than ground mace, since fresh dried can be ground as needed. The flavor of an intact blade is much better than the powdered version. The flavor of mace is very delicate, so it should be carefully stored in a cool dry place and used quickly to maximize the flavor.

Mace is a bright red lacy skin removed by hand after the nutmeg is harvested. Then it is left to dry flat in the sun. While it cures its intense aroma develops while its color fades.

Nutmeg trees are native to Indonesia's Moluccan Islands. It is large tropical evergreen that can reach 60 feet. The trees are either male or female, and both are needed for pollination. Small, light yellow blossoms precede the pale yellow fruit. As it ripens it splits to expel the seed. Nutmegs are grown from seeds, and after about six months they are ready to be transplanted. If you see trees during your island drives look for sprouted seeds. After five years the trees flower, and then can be sexed. The males are thinned to one male for every ten females. They bear after seven years, but reach full productivity at fifteen. Nutmeg trees continue to bear fruit for about fifty years. A single mature tree can produce two thousand nutmegs per year. A pile of fruit large enough to make one hundred pounds of nutmeg produces a single pound of mace. This naturally makes mace more valuable than nutmeg.

Dried mace pieces are not easy to crush. Ready-ground mace is easier to use, but the flavor and aroma will fade quicker. A trick is to dip the mace blade in a tiny bit of hot water. The blade and the liquid can be used in the recipe. One mace blade will season a dish for four. Mace should be added at the end of the cooking process, and the mace blade should be removed before serving. Obviously in baked goods and roasted meat recipes, mace is added at the beginning with the other ingredients.

> **DID YOU KNOW?**
> One productive acre will yield 500 pounds of nutmeg, yet only 75 pounds of mace. This makes mace more valuable than nutmeg. Records show that in fourteenth century England one pound of mace was worth three sheep. Nutmeg has been cultivated for 1000 yrs.

Mace is used to flavor white sauces, lasagna, meat and vegetable stews, pastries, and some East Indian desserts. Add some to potatoes or sweet potatoes for something new. Hot chocolate drinks and tropical punches improve by adding a little mace. It is high in calcium, phosphorus, and magnesium. Five grams of mace has about twenty five calories.

Chocolate Cherry Pieces

Ingredients: one cup seeded dried cherries minced, half cup butter - softened, half cup brown sugar, quarter cup granulated sugar, one egg, one TS vanilla extract, one cup all purpose flour, quarter cup cocoa powder, half TS baking powder, half TS ground mace, one and a half cups rolled oats, half cup chocolate chips, a pinch of salt

Method: In a large mixing bowl blend the butter and sugars until fluffy. Whip in the egg and vanilla extract, add flour, cocoa, baking powder, mace and salt. Whip until smooth before stirring in the oats, chocolate chips, and cherries. The final mixture will be very stiff. Drop tablespoons of dough onto greased or non stick baking trays about an inch apart. Bake 10-12 minutes at 375 or until the tops appear dry, yet not browned. Remove and allow to cool.

Coconut Muffins

Ingredients: one cup grated coconut, three cups all purpose flour, three quarter cup brown sugar, one and a half TS baking powder, one TS baking soda, half TS salt, quarter TS ground mace, one egg, one cup milk, quarter cup orange juice, third cup vegetable oil

Method: In a large bowl combine flour, sugar, grated coconut, baking powder, baking soda, salt, and mace. In a next small bowl beat the egg and combine with milk, vegetable oil, and orange juice. Slowly stir in flour mixture until dry ingredients are just moistened. Don't worry about the lumps. Spoon into greased muffin cups two-thirds full. Bake for 20 to 25 minutes at 425.

All Day Yam Bread

This takes awhile and is worth the time and effort.

Ingredients: one cup cooked yam mashed, two packages dry yeast, one and a half cups very warm water, 6 cups unbleached white flour, one TBS salt, one TBS brown sugar, a pinch of ground allspice, half TS mace, two TBS soft butter, one egg for glaze. Sweet potatoes may be substituted for the yams.

Method: Dissolve yeast in the warm water. In a large bowl combine flour, salt, sugar, allspice, and mace. Stir in the yeast mixture. Add butter and mashed yam puree. The dough should now be moist and ready to knead for ten minutes by hand. Then put in a greased bowl, cover with a damp towel, and let rise in a warm place until doubled. Punch dough down and let rise again about 45 minutes. Punch down and shape into one large round loaf or divide. Let rise once more for another 45 minutes. Beat egg with a teaspoon of water and use as glaze for top of bread. Bake at 425 degrees for 45 minutes or until the loaf sounds hollow when tapped.

Spice Cabinet Mix

We love our seasoning and this is easy. Just mix together what dry spices you have on your shelf with salt. This can also be done with crushed fresh spices if available. For best quality and freshness, both versions must be refrigerated in a sealed container.

Ingredients: one TBS ground cayenne pepper, one TBS garlic powder, one TBS onion powder, one TS dried basil, one TS dried oregano, one TS dried thyme, one TS dried parsley flakes, one TS dried savory, one TS ground mace, one TS black pepper, one TS dried sage, one TS dried marjoram, one TS ground dried grated lemon peel

Method: Combine everything, store in a sealed container and refrigerate.

HEALTH NOTE

Mace and nutmeg are very similar in culinary and medicinal properties. Both spices are efficient in treating digestive and stomach problems, relive intestinal gas and flatulence. It can reduce vomiting, nausea and general stomach uneasiness. Nutmeg and mace are botanically referred to as myristica fragrans.

MARJORAM – THE HERB OF HAPPINESS

Marjoram is oregano's sweet sister. Oregano is basically a Mediterranean spice with a zesty lemon-peppery flavor, while sweet marjoram is more delicate and fragrant. These two spices are almost interchangeable. They look almost identical except marjoram is usually a bright green and oregano a duller green. Both herbs are members of the mint family. Sweet marjoram is botanically known as *origanum majorana*, while oregano is *origanum vulgare*. Wild marjoram is better known as oregano, so think of marjoram as 'tame' oregano.

The only way to discern the intricate differences between oregano and marjoram is to have a plant of each and take leaves; crush marjoram in your right hand while doing the same with oregano in your left. Oregano's aroma is a sharp pine smell of a commercial air freshener. Marjoram is more like a refined perfume with a clean, flavor. Sweet marjoram is a perennial, but to keep it from becoming woody, replant some every year. Oregano is also a perennial that keeps growing with reasonable trimming.

Marjoram is native to North Africa and western Asia, the Mediterranean area, and was known to the Greeks and Romans, who looked on it as a symbol of happiness. It was said that if marjoram grew on the grave of a dead person, he would enjoy eternal bliss. Egyptians used marjoram with other fragrant spices in their embalming process. To the ancient Greeks marjoram was the herb of a happy marriage. Thought to be a favorite of the goddess of love, it was woven into wreaths that brides and grooms wore on their heads. Also according to ancient folklore, sleeping with marjoram under your pillow was supposed to promote dreams of true love.

Marjoram is easy to grow from seed. This herb prefers well-drained soil, full sun, and room to spread. Marjoram prefers the soil slightly moist. Cut the plant back if it becomes woody and it will re-grow. Its flowers run pink to purple. It can be used fresh, or dried by spreading in a cool, well-ventilated place. This herb will grow to about a foot tall and needs to be spaced about eighteen inches apart from other plants in your herb garden. This plant's flavor usually peaks just before the flower buds forms. To harvest cut the whole plant back by two-thirds its size.

Oregano and marjoram have a high amount of antioxidants, especially used fresh. It's often used to season meats and fish, and works best when it's added near the end of the cooking period. As with most herbs, fresh is best, but dried this herb holds its lovely fragrance and flavor much better than many other dried herbs. One tablespoon fresh

> ### DID YOU KNOW?
> Oregano is often confused with marjoram, mainly because oregano actually translates to marjoram in Spanish. The tops and leaves of this herb are distilled to produce an essential oil. It has many components; one is camphor.

equals one teaspoon dried.

A tea brewed from marjoram leaves may help with indigestion, headache, or stress. Externally dried leaves and flowers may be applied as poultices to reduce the pain of rheumatism. Marjoram is a natural with meat dishes, cooked or raw vegetables, fish, and chicken. It is especially good along with other herbs in beef stew. Marjoram also is good on fresh tomato sandwiches, and it pairs well with eggs or cheese. A light sprinkling adds flavor to cream-based sauces or soups, especially potato soup. When growing this herb use the flowers to make a herbal vinegar. Marjoram is also used in body care products, including skin creams, lotion, body wash, and shaving gels.

Marjoram Pasta

Ingredients: a quarter pound of your favorite type of pasta, two cloves of garlic quartered, three cups fresh broccoli chopped small, one firm large tomato chopped small, four ounces softened cream cheese, one half TS salt, one half TS black pepper, one TBS fresh marjoram leaves chopped small or one TS dried, one cup grated cheddar cheese,

Method: Bring a large pot of water to boil over medium heat. Add garlic and pasta. Just before the pasta is fully cooked add the broccoli. Remove from heat and drain keeping the pasta and broccoli in the pot. Add the cream cheese, salt, pepper, and marjoram. Stir to combine all the ingredients. Top with cheddar cheese and chopped fresh tomatoes.

Easy 'Homemade' Tomato Sauce

Ingredients: one pound leanest minced beef (minced chicken or lamb could be substituted), two cloves garlic minced, one large onion chopped small, two eight ounce cans tomato sauce, one TS dried oregano, one half TS dried marjoram, one TS basil, one TS sugar, salt to taste

Method: In a large skillet on medium heat, brown and crumble the meat. As the meat begins to produce a liquid add the garlic and onion. When the meat is fully cooked and crumbled, drain off excess liquid. Add remaining ingredients. If you are using fresh herbs chop them just before adding. Return to heat. Bring to a boil and then simmer stirring for ten minutes. Serve over pasta or rice.

Lemon Marjoram Roast Chicken

Ingredients: One whole chicken, one lemon halved, one TBS fresh marjoram, one TS black pepper, one TS salt.

Method: Wash chicken and rub inside thoroughly with salt and pepper. Gently squeeze the juice of the halves of the lemon into the chicken's cavity. Put the lemon halves inside and add the marjoram. Put the chicken in a baking or roasting dish and cover with foil. Cook at 350 degrees for an hour. Uncover and continue to cook for fifteen more minutes.

Tomato Marjoram Chicken

Ingredients: One chicken cut into pieces, three large tomatoes (about four cups) chopped, one quarter cup oil (prefer olive or canola), four cloves of garlic minced, one half hot pepper seeded and minced, two TBS fresh marjoram chopped small, one TS salt

Method: Combine the tomatoes with the oil, garlic, minced pepper, salt, and one tablespoon marjoram in large bowl. Place chicken in a baking dish. Pour tomato mixture over chicken. Bake chicken at 450 degrees for forty minutes. Uncover and continue to bake chicken for fifteen more minutes. Sprinkle with remaining tablespoon marjoram just before serving.

HEALTH NOTE

Marjoram is considered the most fragrant essential oil among all herbs used in aromatherapy. It is also a warming and soothing message oil for muscle aches. It fights asthma, headaches, and soothes digestion. Marjoram is used to loosen phlegm and is a decongestant used to fight bronchitis, and sinus headaches. It is useful as a tonic for the nervous system. Marjoram may be more calming than oregano, to soothe the nerves, reduce tension and stress. One component in marjoram is flavonoids, which relieve insomnia, tension headaches, and migraines.

The hum of bees is the voice of the garden.

Elizabeth Lawrence

MINT

Consider how many things we eat that contain mint, and that doesn't include menthol cigarettes, or toothpaste. There's spearmint chewing gum and Peppermint Patties. There are many varieties of mint, each has a distinct taste and smell. Penny royal is probably the most commonly used in the kitchen. Spearmint is a sweet flavor that seems to cool the mouth. Peppermint has a stronger mentholated taste, while pennyroyal has a strong almost medicine flavor.

I grow my mint in a window box by the door so that anyone, especially my dogs, brushes against, it will produce the delightful smell. Mint is a great fragrance that symbolizes hospitality. Ancient Greeks and Romans rubbed tables with mint before their guests arrived. The Japanese learned to distill peppermint oil to produce menthol. Mint smell keeps mice and rats away and pennyroyal is an effective insect repellant for fleas and aphids.

Mint probably originated along the Mediterranean, but is now grown everywhere in the world. Spearmint is an attractive perennial that can grow a meter tall with grayish green leaves and clusters of small blue spiked flowers. Peppermint has purple spiked flowers on red tinged leaves. Pennyroyal is the smaller mint that grows close to the ground with pink flowers. Mints thrive in cool and moist places, but will grow almost anywhere. The best way is to divide growing plants, seeds take forever.

There are over a hundred different types of mint. Bowles has the best flavor for cooking or drinks. Spearmint plants have full flavor, apple mint has the best taste for fruit salads, while pennyroyal has the strongest flavor. Mint grows easily in either shade or sun with very little maintenance. It takes about ninety days for seedlings to mature. If not trimmed they will rapidly take over your garden. Just snip the necessary leaves when needed. Mint is another perfect plant to be grown indoors in pots. Don't overwater, or let mint dry out.

Mint combines well with many vegetables such as potatoes, tomatoes, or carrots. A few chopped leaves enhance salads and dressings. Peppermint is usually used in desserts like fruit salads, sorbets, and sherbets. Spearmint is used with grilled meats, stuffed vegetables and rice. East Indians make fresh mint chutney. A mint julep is an American classic drink of bourbon whiskey and mint. Two mint leaves have little calories with some calcium and potassium.

Herbs and Spices

Mint Topped Eggplant

Ingredients: three eggplants or about two pounds, one TBS sesame oil, three TBS fresh lime juice, two TBS water, two TBS sugar, one TS garlic minced, one hot pepper seeded and minced, one TBS fresh mint chopped

> ### DID YOU KNOW?
> Peppermint is a hybrid cross between water mint and spearmint. Spearmint results from a cross between apple mint and wild water mint. The common garden mint is spearmint, not peppermint as most people assume. In Mexico mint is known as yerba buena, the good herb. Botanically apple mint is *mentha suaveolens*, spearmint *mentha spicata*, and peppermint is *mentha piperata*.

Method: First prick each eggplant all around with a fork or a knife so it won't burst as it roasts. Place the eggplants on a hot grill or rotate over a stove burner. Roast until it is fairly soft and blisters, about 3 minutes. Cool and peel under cool running water. Chop the eggplants into big pieces and place in a bowl. In another bowl combine the sesame oil, lime juice, water, and sugar. Add garlic and the hot pepper. Pour over eggplant and sprinkle top with chopped mint and chives. Serve cool.

Mint Mango Salsa

Ingredients: two ripe mangos peeled and chopped, one bunch chives chopped, half cup chopped mint, two TBS fresh lime juice, half hot pepper seeded and minced, salt to taste

Method: All ingredients should be chopped as small as possible. Combine all ingredients. Let stand at least an hour.

Mint Julip Cocktail

Ingredients: four sprigs of mint, one TS powdered sugar, two TS water, three ounces Kentucky Bourbon Whiskey

Method: Combine everything in a shaker glass with a top. Fill with ice and shake. Add a sprig of mint to the glass. Enjoy.

Mustard Mint Sauce

Ingredients: one TBS white vinegar, one TBS brown mustard preferably Dijon, pinch of salt, quarter cup vegetable oil, two TBS fresh mint leaves finely minced

Method: Blend together vinegar, mustard, salt. Whisk while pouring oil in a thin steady stream. Add mint leaves.

Alcohol-Free Mint Julip

Excellent on a hot day

Ingredients: quarter cup water, quarter cup white sugar, one TBS fresh mint leaves chopped, half cup of prepared frozen lemonade, crushed ice

Method: Dissolve sugar into boiling hot water. Add mint and remove from heat. Cover and cool. Strain mint leaves. Fill two glasses with ice. Pour half of the lemonade into each glass stir in a tablespoon of the mint sugar syrup. Garnish with a sprig of mint.

Frozen Mint

Ingredients: two-eight ounce packages of cream cheese softened, half cup sugar, divided, one package lime flavor gelatin, one TBS lime zest, quarter cup fresh lime juice, one-eight ounce tub whipped topping, two TBS fresh mint chopped fine, one and a half cups pretzels finely crushed, six TBS melted butter or margarine

Method: In a suitable bowl combine cream cheese, quarter cup sugar until blended. Add dry gelatin mix, zest and juice. Blend until creamy smooth and add whipped topping and mint. Pour into a 9-inch round pan lined with plastic wrap. Ends must hang over pan. Sprinkle a mixture of pretzel crumbs, remaining sugar and melted butter over the pudding mixture. Slightly stir it into the pudding. Cover dessert with ends of plastic wrap. Freeze until firm about four hours. Place frozen desert upside down on a serving plate and remove plastic wrap and dish. Let soften for a bout ten minutes before serving.

HEALTH NOTE

Peppermint is one of the oldest and best tasting home remedies for indigestion, headache, and rheumatism. After dinner mints are used to improve bad breath, ease gas, and aid digestion. Peppermint lessens the amount of time food spends in the stomach by stimulating the gastric lining to produce enzymes that aid digestion. It relaxes muscles lessening stress, has antiviral and anti-bactericidal qualities, which clears congestion related to colds and allergies, and eases intestinal cramping.

Plants give us oxygen for the lungs and for the soul.
Terri Guillemets

MUSTARD

Mustard is one very unique plant. Mustard is considered a fresh leafy herb and its seeds are a spice, and it makes some of the world's most used condiments. Of the many greens (bhaggis) sold in the markets, mustards have the spiciest flavor of all the cooking leaves. They have a peppery flavor. I grow it because it is another excellent source of iron. Like its cousin spinach, it is extremely easy to grow. Mustard greens are high in vitamins A and C.

Mustard is native to the Himalayan region of northern India more than five millenniums ago. Mustard is one of the oldest spices and one of the most widely used. The Ancient Greeks and the Chinese began using it thousands of years ago. Romans used it as a condiment and pickling spice. The usually yellow, sometimes brown, condiment was made by grinding mustard seeds into a paste and combining it with an unfermented wine called 'must'. Thus it is named mustard. Mustard greens are common in Chinese, African, and Caribbean recipes.

To grow plant seeds half an inch deep in well worked soil. Once they sprout, thin plants to six inches apart. With regular water and plenty of sun, mustard should grow non-stop. Cut the young and tender leaves and cook them first. As time progresses the leaf flavor will become stronger. Let the plants go to seed and cut off the seed pods before they burst. Put in a pillowcase and beat against the floor to separate the seeds. Then try making your own mustard sauce.

Mustard is a member of the Brassica family that includes broccoli, cabbage, cauliflower, turnips and radishes. The mustard family also includes plants grown for their leaves, like pak choy, as well as mustard greens. Three related species of mustard are grown for their seeds. Most mustard plants will reach a meter tall.

Brassica alba or white mustard has bright yellow flowers that produce a round, light tan, very hard seed with a mild flavor. It is a good preservative and most commonly used in yellow mustard. In India, whole seeds are fried in ghee until the seed pops, producing a soft nut taste used to season some Indian dishes. White seeds are the base of yellow American style mustard that has sugar, vinegar and is colored by adding turmeric.

Brassica nigra or black mustard can grow to six feet tall and matures with a very fragile pod that produces a smaller round, dark seed, with a more pungent taste. Classic French Dijon mustard is made from these husked black seeds blended with wine, salt, and spices. Brassica juncea or brown mustard is the middle of the road seed with a sharper taste than the white, yet not as sharp as the black. Brown seeds are pounded and blended with other spices to create come curry powders. Mustard seeds are in most pickling spices.

Mustard oil is made from the brown seeds. It is used in India the same as ghee. Compared with other cooking oils, mustard is considered a low fat variety and its use may actually lower cholesterol. However culinary use of mustard oil is banned in some countries. This oil is used in India as fuel for the diyas during Divali. It is also excellent as a massage oil. It is believed to rejuvenate hair growth when rubbed into the scalp. It is antibiotic and antifungal.

Mustard powder is used to flavor barbecue sauces, baked beans, many meat and fish dishes, deviled eggs, and beets. Mustard powder is made from white mustard seeds. It has no taste when dry, yet once combined with cool water (not warm) its sharp taste is created after about a ten minute wait. A chemical reaction occurs and warm or hot water can interfere. Once the strong taste has formed, other ingredients may be combined to further enhance the taste.

There are many commercial mustards with tastes from mild and sweet to sharp and strong. They can be smooth or coarse and flavored with a wide variety of herbs, spices and liquids. Today, our world consumes more than two hundred thousand tons of mustard yearly!

Mustard was always important in medicine. Mustard oil can be so irritable that it can burn the skin. Diluted, it is used as a liniment for sore muscles. Powdered mustard is used in mustard plasters to fight bad coughs and colds. Various cultures have used mustard for snake bites, bruises, stiff neck, rheumatism, and respiratory troubles. It is delightful in bath water or as a foot bath to ease aches and pains.

A cup of cooked mustard greens has only twenty calories with vitamins K, A, E, and C, potassium, calcium, and iron.

Simple Cooked Mustard Greens

Ingredients: one bunch, about two pounds of greens, one large onion chopped small, two cloves of garlic sliced very thin, three TBS oil (canola preferred), salt to taste

Method: Steam greens in a large covered pot with about two inches of water for about five to eight minutes. Remove from heat, drain, and leave covered. In a skillet brown the onion and garlic. Pour on the greens and stir.

Mustard and Pasta

Ingredients: one bunch, about two pounds, mustard greens sliced into one inch pieces, one pound pasta like elbow, springs or bow ties, one large onion chopped, one green sweet pepper seeded and chopped, four cloves of garlic sliced thin, four TBS oil (canola or olive oil preferred), one hot pepper seeded and minced, two TBS vinegar, salt to taste

Method: Boil mustard green pieces in salted water for about ten minutes to your desired consistency. Remove from heat, drain, and leave covered. Cook pasta, drain and keep covered. In a frying pan heat the oil and fry the onion, garlic, and pepper till soft about 2-3 minutes. Add hot pepper and vinegar. Combine everything. Season to your taste. Serve warm.

Stir Fried Beef and Mustard Greens

Ingredients: one pound of boneless beef sliced thin, two TBS sesame oil, half TS mustard seeds, one pound mustard greens, washed - stems removed sliced to inch wide pieces,

two TBS chives finely chopped, two cloves of garlic minced, one TBS fresh ginger peeled and sliced very thin, one cup beef broth, two TBS cornstarch or arrowroot, two TBS teriyaki sauce, one TS sugar, three cups cooked rice

Method: In a covered skillet heat one tablespoon oil and add mustard seeds. Cover and heat until seeds pop. Add sliced mustard greens and stir fry for three to four minutes. Remove from heat to a bowl. In the same skillet heat another tablespoon of oil. Add beef, chives, ginger, and garlic. Stir fry until meat is well browned, about 3 minutes. Remove to bowl with mustard greens. In the same skillet combine broth, cornstarch, teriyaki sauce and sugar and cook, stirring until thickened. Stir in beef mixture and greens; heat to boiling. Serve with rice.

Mustard the Condiment

To make your own special tasting mustard all you need to do is either grind mustard seeds into a powder or mix prepared mustard powder with cold water. Wait about ten minutes and you have simple mustard. You can add wine or hearty beer, spiced vinegars, or fruit juices for a truly unique flavor. Add spices to your taste. Salt, garlic, or onion powder, ginger, allspice, pepper, nutmeg, basil, and/or rosemary. Any herb-spice combo can make your mustard special.

*Courage, not cleverness; not even inspiration,
is the grain of mustard that grows up to be a great tree.*

Ludwig Wittgenstein

NUTMEG – THE SPICE THAT STARTED WARS

We have located several nutmeg trees along the road to Matlot. As with bay and several other spices, one drive fills my small spice bottles for another month. A few nutmegs go a long way. It makes a good combo with cinnamon, especially in hot beverages like cocoa, tea, or coffee. Nutmeg makes a nice backyard tree that is easy to trim and shape.

Nutmeg is an evergreen tree that originated in tropical Southeast Asia on Banda, the largest of Indonesia's spice islands. It is important to the world's spice cabinet for two spices derived from the seeds, nutmeg and mace

The fruit is light yellow resembling a small tennis ball. Nutmeg refers to the actual egg shaped seed. Its reddish membrane covering is called mace. Nutmeg has a sweeter taste than mace. Mace has a more delicate flavor, like a mix of cinnamon with pepper. Indonesia and Grenada produce a combined 12,000 tons per year.

Find a mature tree, search the surrounding area, and you should find some sprouted seeds. Carefully plant and coddle these shoots. The small trees do not take well to direct heat and sun. Plant with at least twenty feet of space on all sides from other trees, buildings or fences. Make sure the soil drains, and give the sprouting nutmeg tree 12-24-12 starting-rooting fertilizer every four months. Start with broadcasting a quarter cup around its roots when it is about three feet tall. As it grows increase to a cup. Be patient as it takes at least seven years before the first spice harvest. When it starts to bear fertilize three times a year by broadcasting a cup of 12-12-17 fertilizer. Water during the dry season. As the fruit ripens, the outer covering splits showing the seed covered with red mace membranes. The nut must dry for at least two months.

In the sixth century, Arab traders cameled nutmeg to Constantinople. In the 1300's, half a kilo of nutmeg was as valuable as a cow. The Dutch fought to control the nutmeg trade, including the extermination of the native people of Banda Island. By the mid 1700's the Dutch kept the price high by reducing the supply by burning supplies. The Dutch controlled Indonesia's spice islands until the 1940's. The British East India Company transported nutmeg trees to Singapore, India, Sri Lanka, throughout the West Indies, especially Grenada, where it is the nation's symbol.

Nutmeg was so important because of the purported medicinal properties of its seeds. It is an astringent and stimulant, as well as an aphrodisiac. At the height of its value in Europe, nutmeg was carried to demonstrate wealth. Ground nutmeg is also smoked in India. Nutmeg oil is used in perfume, toothpastes, and cough medicines and in pharmaceutical drugs. The oil is used externally for rheumatism and gargled for bad breath and toothaches. Nutmeg oil is believed to have aphrodisiac qualities if topically applied to certain body areas. East Indians have long used nutmeg as a treatment for fever, asthma and heart disease. Arabs used it for digestive disorders, and kidney diseases.

If at all possible grate fresh nutmeg for you recipes and add it at the end of cooking since heat reduces the flavor. These spices should be kept in a sealed jar in a shaded corner or shelf of your kitchen. Mace is used in cheese, chicken, and fish entrees and especially chocolate or cherry desserts. Nutmeg works well with stewed fruit, custards, potato dishes, and is especially tasty with spinach. A single nutmeg grated yields 2 to 3 teaspoons of ground nutmeg that has about three calories. For all its great culinary and medicinal value, nutmeg has no notable vitamins or mineral content. Nutmeg and mace are botanically referred to as *myristica fragrans*.

Nutmeg Ice Cream

Ingredients: two cups milk, two cups heavy cream, four eggs, one cup sugar, one TBS fresh grated nutmeg, one TS vanilla extract, a pinch of salt

Method: Combine milk and cream in a suitable pot, bring to a boil, and remove from heat. Combine eggs, sugar, salt, vanilla, and nutmeg in a bowl. Add to the milk mixture and cook over medium heat with constant stirring. Put in an ice cream machine and crank. If a traditional ice cream machine is not available, put in a freezer until ice begins to form. Put in a blender and then refreeze.

Sweet Shepherd's Pie

Ingredients: two pounds minced beef or chicken, five large sweet potatoes peeled, boiled, and mashed, one medium onion chopped small, two cloves of garlic minced, half hot pepper seeded and minced, quarter cup all purpose flour, one cup broth from the meat, two eggs beaten, half cup butter or margarine, four eggs hard boiled, one bundle fresh spinach or pak choy chopped small, one TS rosemary, one TS salt, one TS nutmeg

Method: In a large skillet brown the meat and add enough water to produce a cup of broth, Remove meat to a bowl. Ina small skillet butter, and sauté onions and garlic. Remove from heat and stir in flour slowly adding the broth. Bring to a boil, stirring constantly as it thickens add the beaten eggs. Pour this over the meat adding the spices and pepper. Press the mashed sweet potatoes into greased baking dish forming a shell. Layer in the chopped spinach. Slice the hardboiled eggs and arrange on top of the greens. Cover with the meat mixture. Bake at 350 for forty-five minutes.

Low-Budget Cappucino Mix

Ingredients: three quarters cup instant coffee, one cup powdered cocoa tea mix, half cup sugar (less to your taste), one cup powdered nondairy creamer (splurge and try hazelnut flavor), one TS ground cinnamon, half TS ground nutmeg

Method: Mix all ingredients together and store in a sealed container. Refrigerate if possible. Use two tablespoons per cup of hot water.

Banana-Pumpkin Spice Bread

Ingredients: four cups bakers flour, two TS baking powder, two TS baking soda, two TS ground cinnamon, two TS ground nutmeg, one TS ground ginger, half TS salt, one and a half cup pumpkin cooked and mashed, one and a half cup very ripe bananas mashed, one cup plain yogurt, half cup cooking oil, four large eggs, one cup brown sugar, one cup grated coconut

Method: Combine flour, baking powder and soda, spices and salt in a large bowl. In a second bowl mix pumpkin, bananas, yogurt, oil, eggs, and sugar until it is creamy. Slowly blend in flour mixture. Add half of the coconut. Pour into two greased bread pans and cover top with remaining coconut. Bake at 350 for forty-five minutes. Test center firmness with a toothpick.

HEALTH NOTE

Nutmeg oil stimulates the brain reducing mental exhaustion and stress. It improves the quality of your dreams, making them more intense and colorful. It is a good remedy for anxiety as well as depression. Nutmeg oil treats muscular and joint pain and it is an excellent sedative. Nutmeg's relaxing aroma comforts the body, and increases blood circulation.

> *The voyage had proved a human and financial disaster. Of the 198 men who rounded the Cape, only 25 returned alive. Worse still, two of the three ships had been lost and the one that did manage to limp into port was carrying not spices but scurvy. Lancaster had proved--if proof was needed-- that the spice trade involved risks that London's merchants could ill afford. It was not until they learned that the Dutch had entered the spice race, and achieved a remarkable success, that they would consider financing a new expedition to the islands of the East Indies.*
>
> Giles Milton, *Nathaniel's Nutmeg: How One Man's Courage Changed the Course of History*

OREGANO

If you like well spiced Italian cuisine, you like oregano. All of our favorite garden vegetables take on a new personality when cooked with oregano. Eggplant becomes eggplant parmesan, and please don't forget spaghetti sauce or pizza.

Oregano is a member of the mint family and another of the many confusing spices. It could be oregano or marjoram. According to my internet research all marjorams are oreganos, yet all oreganos are not marjorams. Oregano is the genus of which sweet marjoram is only one variety. The confusion continues as the herb called 'wild marjoram' is in fact common oregano. Crush a leaf of oregano and its robust, almost peppery smell jolts your nose. When a leaf of marjoram is crushed, it releases a pleasant flowery perfume aroma. It is better to say oregano is an herbal flavor, rather than a particular herb. Oregano is best used as a dried herb, and sweet or knotted marjoram is best used as a fresh herb with the leaves snipped as needed.

Oregano and marjoram probably developed from the same plant grown in various areas of the Mediterranean having different climates. They basically evolved into three varieties, common oregano (wild marjoram), pot marjoram, and sweet (knotted) marjoram. All probably originated in Greece where newlyweds would be crowned with wreaths of oregano. The French used oregano to scent soap, the English made oregano snuff, while Germans seasoned sausage with it.

Oregano is a hardy perennial while marjoram is also a perennial, but marjoram is usually grown as an annual. Both want full sun and soft well drained soil. Both need large 10 to 12 inch pots and plenty of sun to grow indoors. Like most herbs they need little attention except occasional water. It is best not to fertilize herbs as it seems to dull their taste. Since oregano is a perennial it is wise to divide and restart the plant every few years.

With oregano it is better to harvest the leaves for drying before the plants makes flowers as the latter will make for a bitter taste. Snip the leaves on a dry day and place them in a paper bag and put in a dark, warm place (I use a closet shelf.) until they have thoroughly dried. Store in a sealed container whole or crumbled. Oregano leaves will hold their flavor for three months or until you have more leaves to snip

Oregano is very good for you, helping with digestion by increasing the flow of bile. Studies have shown oregano fights viruses, fungus, and bacteria. The French oregano soaps may have been the first to really be antibacterial. This is a great herb to drink as a tea whenever you have a cold or fever.

Oregano's pungent taste is reduced by cooking, so it is best added to any dish just shortly before serving it. Three grams or a tablespoon of oregano has nine calories of with some protein. It is high in vitamins A, C, E, and K, and minerals as iron, calcium, iron, magnesium, phosphorus, and potassium.

> **DID YOU KNOW?**
>
> Oregano probably originated in Greece as oregano translates in Greek as 'joy of the mountain.' The ancient Greeks believed cows produced tastier meat when they grazed in pastures of oregano.

Garden Stew

Ingredients: six ounces cubed beef stew meat, one large onion chopped, three cloves garlic minced, two large squash chunked, half hot pepper seeded and minced (optional), four large tomatoes chopped, one TS chili powder, one TS cumin, one TS dried oregano, one TS Italian seasoning, three cups water, two beef bouillon cubes, two TBS cream or milk, one cup whole kernel corn sliced from the cob or canned, salt and spice to taste.

Method: Cook beef in a large pot over medium heat until fully browned. Stir in onion, garlic, zucchini, squash, and tomatoes. Cook for five minutes. Add hot pepper, chili powder, cumin, oregano, Italian seasoning, and pepper. Add water, bouillon, salt, and cream. Cover, reduce heat to low, and simmer two hours. Add corn. Cover and simmer for 45 minutes. If the stew becomes too thick, stir in a little water. If too thin add sifted flour to reach the desired consistency.

Spaghetti Sauce

Ingredients: one large can of stewed tomatoes, one large can crushed tomatoes, one pound minced beef - leaner the better, two large onions, two sweet peppers, five cloves garlic - all chopped small, two TBS white sugar, one TBS oil, one TBS dried basil, one TBS dried oregano, quarter cup fresh parsley chopped small, two Bay leaves, salt and pepper to taste

Method: In a blender combine the stewed tomatoes and crushed tomatoes. In a large pot heat the oil and brown the ground beef with the onions, peppers, and garlic. Add tomatoes, and reduce heat. Add sugar, basil, bay leaves and oregano, and simmer about 40 minutes. Remove bay leaves and season with salt and pepper before serving.

Tuna Fish Pasta Casserole

Ingredients: a half pound of cooked pasta (elbow, bow tie, or springs), one can tuna fish (save liquid), two large tomatoes chopped, one small onion chopped, a quarter pound cheddar cheese grated, one TBS parsley chopped, three garlic cloves crushed, two TBS water, salt and pepper to taste, two TBS sugar, one TBS vinegar, one TBS oregano, one

TBS oil (prefer olive), four TBS mayonnaise,

Method: In a frying pan at low heat, add the oil and cook the onion until clear. Add the garlic and oregano and continue to cook. Turn up the heat and add vinegar, tuna, and tuna liquid, reduce until almost completely evaporated. Reduce to a low heat. Add the chopped tomatoes and water. Quickly stir. Add salt, black pepper, and sugar. Combine the tuna, mayonnaise, and cooked pasta in an oven dish and top with grated cheese and parsley. Bake for twenty minutes at 250.

HEALTH NOTE

The ancient Greeks applied poultices of oregano leaves to treat sores and muscle aches. Chinese herbal doctors used oregano to lower fevers, fight vomiting, diarrhea, jaundice, and itchy skin. Europeans use this herb for improved digestion and to soothe coughs. Germans produce oregano based cough syrups. Oregano fights the bacterial disease known as giardia amoeba, common throughout the world. It can cause serious illness and oregano proved to be more effective as treatment than the prescription drug.

Oregano is such an antioxidant-rich herb that researchers decided to see if it could reduce the DNA-damaging effects of radiation.

Michael Greger

PAPRIKA

Don't be frightened by the name as most thick flesh sweet red peppers can be dried to make paprika. Paprika is a spice that doesn't get the acclaim it deserves in Caribbean cuisine. I became acquainted with its special taste and aroma through some Eastern European visitors. After enjoying it, I am slowly progressing to dry and smoke my own peppers - both sweet and bitter. Paprika is the nice crimson powder internationally used that originated in Central and South America. Originally this pepper variety was tropical, but over time it was adapted to temperate European climates and lost most of its heat. Present day Hungary is famous for growing and processing the world's best paprika. Botanically paprika is *capsicum annuum*.

The pepper paprika is ground from is 3-4 inches long and 2 inches wide. It is a narrow pepper fully ripened to a brilliant red. It is bigger and much milder than the local red scotch bonnet, hot congo, or habanero. Paprika is made from the same red peppers used to stuff pitted olives. Paprika powder can vary from bright red to rusty brown. Its main purpose is to add color. Paprika is listed as 'natural color' in most red food items, like processed cheeses and meats, tomato sauces, chili powders and soups.

Paprika isn't difficult to grow when you find the seeds. You don't have to grow peppers termed 'paprika', but you can grow bell peppers that turn red, and also cayennes to make the dry powder spicy. Even if you intend to smoke and grind your own peppers you shouldn't need more than a dozen plants. However, paprika pepper plants can grow to four feet tall so allow plenty of space and make stakes. Sprout the seeds and transplant at about five inches to a well drained sunny area. A week after planting give them a pinch of 12-24-12 and regular water. Once blossoms come, use a pinch of 12-12-17-2. The fruit is green when unripe and may ripen to red, brown, or purple. Only red fruit is used for paprika. European farmers sun dry the selected peppers for two weeks; then finish with a smoke dry to produce the special paprika flavor.

Red peppers, from which paprika is ground, have much more vitamin C than oranges. The high heat of commercial processing destroys much of the vitamin C in paprika so look for the sun dried variety. Paprika is a good source for beta carotene, and is considered both a stimulant and a blood pressure regulator. It fights bacteria and aids digestion. Try substituting at least part of the salt you use on cooked food with paprika and you will be pleasantly surprised.

Smoked paprika has received the world's culinary attention only within the last thirty years. There are three flavors, sweet, bittersweet, and hot. I use the sweet smoked pepper with other spices in a mayonnaise mix to completely revive any traditional sandwich. Paprika gives any dish color. Use it as a last sprinkle garnish on eggs, soups, stews, casseroles, and vegetables. When you are dipping chicken or fish parts in flour for frying, baking, or broiling, add some paprika. Paprika will help blend oil and vinegar to make a smooth salad dressings.

Paprika has only six calories per teaspoon with a good bit of calcium and potassium.

> ### DID YOU KNOW?
> Budapest Hungary's national paprika Internet site says paprika was brought by the Turks as late as the 1700's. A Hungarian scientist, Szent-Györgyi, designed large-scale extraction of vitamin C from peppers. He won the Nobel Prize for his research on the vitamin content of paprika. Pound for pound, it has a higher content of Vitamin C than citrus fruit. Almost all of the international spice trade is in whole spices. Paprika is only ground spice sold in any significant quantities. Originally paprika peppers were hot. Over time, they have evolved to the milder varieties. In Hungary there are six classes or types of paprika ranging from delicate to hot. Orange colored paprika is usually the hottest.

Mexican Spice

Use on beef, pork, fish, chicken, eggs, rice, potatoes, etc.

Ingredients: half cup chili powder, quarter cup paprika (sweet or smoked), two TBS ground cumin, one TBS garlic powder, one TBS onion powder, two TBS ground red hot pepper, one TBS dried oregano, two TS salt.

Method: Combine all ingredients. Store in a tight sealing container and preferably refrigerate.

Spicey Mushrooms

Ingredients: one pound fresh mushrooms sliced a quarter inch thick, one onion chopped small, one clove garlic minced, one red bell pepper chopped small, quarter cup oil, one TS paprika (prefer smoked), one TS ground cumin, one TS dried thyme, quarter TS cayenne pepper, salt and pepper to taste

Method: Sauté onion and garlic in oil until they just start to brown. At medium heat stir in all spices and mushroom pieces. Cook for five to ten minutes. Any firm vegetable can be substituted for mushrooms.

Twwice-Spiced Shrimp

Ingredients: two pounds large shrimp peeled and cleaned, two cloves garlic minced, one medium onion chopped small, one sweet bell pepper preferably red chopped small, two TS paprika, juice of a lemon, two TBS lemon zest, two to three TBS oil, quarter cup apple cider vinegar, two TBS fresh dill weed, two TS paprika, two TS brown mustard, one TBS honey, one TS salt

Method: Combine onion, garlic, lemon juice, vinegar, one TS paprika, and add peeled shrimp. Add water if necessary so liquid will cover shrimp. Refrigerate overnight. Strain, separating the liquid from the onions and garlic. Heat oil in skillet and fry onion and garlic a few minutes before adding the shrimp. Cook for about five minutes and add pepper, one TS paprika, and two tablespoons of the vinegar - lemon marinade water. Cook for five more minutes or until the shrimp start turning pink. Serve with rice or oriental noodles.

Caribbean Paprika Chicken

Ingredients: One chicken cut up, one TS paprika, half TS sugar, one hot pepper minced, salt

Method: Wash chicken pieces and arrange in a baking dish. Combine ingredients and sprinkle over chicken. Cover and bake at 400 for half an hour. Uncover, turn pieces, and continue to bake for twenty minutes. Serve with rice or pasta.

DID YOU KNOW?

Begin the paprika process by getting the proper pepper seeds. Common paprika varieties are Hungarian or Spanish in origin. Pick peppers when ripe to a deep red. Wash before drying. Peppers can be air dried, but it is easier to use your kitchen oven set at 200 degrees F. Place whole peppers on a baking sheet and turn until dried. This should take several hours. Remove stem and halve the peppers open to finish drying interior. If you want it spicy, leave in the seeds. Grind dried peppers into powder using the "pulse" feature of an electric blender. Do not blend steady for several minutes without permitting blender to cool. Extended blending can cause a burned taste.

A garden is always a series of losses set against a few triumphs, like life itself.

May Sarton

PARSLEY

Parsley is the main ingredient of my homemade green seasoning. Parsley is a unique, bright green plant with a vibrant taste and fresh aroma. Even though parsley has a great taste, it may also be used as a medicinal herb. Originating along the Mediterranean Sea in Southern Spain, Italy, and Greece, parsley has been cultivated for over two millenniums. Originally parsley was grown for its medicinal properties to the extent the Greeks considered parsley to be a sacred gift from their gods. The queen of the Greek gods, Juno, grazed her horses in fields of parsley to keep them high-spirited. During the Middle Ages, the French popularized parsley as a kitchen herb. Parsley was introduced to England in the 1500's and brought to the Americas before 1800.

Trinidad grows the two most common types of parsley, the curly fern leafed and the flat. We love the sharp smell and almost sweet taste of the flat leafed variety. It is not difficult to grow from seedlings, yet very difficult to sprout directly in the garden from seeds. Work the dirt of a row until it is fine. Carefully plant the seeds every two inches. Carefully cover with about a half-inch of dirt. Water carefully so not to wash away the seeds. Patience and constant watering is necessary as parsley seeds germinate so slowly it is said, 'Parsley goes to Hell and back again nine times before it comes up.'

Parsley has lots of vitamin C. It also has a good amount of potassium. To obtain the maximum food value from parsley it should be eaten raw. Heat from cooking greatly reduces the vitamin content and the taste. If you are including parsley in cooked recipes use the flat leaf type, and add it towards the end so it will retain most of its taste, color, and food value. In most upscale restaurants sprigs of parsley accompany the dinner entrée as a garnish. Don't push it aside, enjoy eating it, as it is not only tasty and cures bad breathe, but can be very healthy for you. Two tablespoons of parsley contain about three calories with anti-oxidants such as vitamin C, betacarotene, and folic acid. These anti-oxidants fight many diseases such as

DID YOU KNOW?

Parsley is has three varieties: curly, Italian flat leaf, and Hamburg. It can be bought fresh or dried. Curly is used as a garnish due to its appearance and bitter taste while Italian flat leaf packs more flavor, thus adding more to a dish. Hamburg is not common and the root is the part used rather than the leaves. Parsley's botanical name is *petroselinum crispum*.

arthritis, asthma, diabetes, colon cancer, heart attacks, and strokes.

Parsley is a natural diuretic and can be used by women to alleviate irregular menstrual cycles. Parsley eaten raw or as tea may ease the bloating that occurs during menstruation. Chewing parsley will help with bad breath from food odors such as garlic or onions. A tea made from parsley will stimulate as much as a cup of coffee, but watch out as parsley has been reported to be an aphrodisiac. A poultice of its leaves can be used for insect bites or stings. Parsley is fragile so wash it carefully in a colander or by swishing it in a bowl of water. Parsley makes an excellent addition to soups, salads, and baking.

Taboulah-Parsley Salad

Ingredients: three quarters cup wheat bulgur, oats, or cooked rice, two cups cold water, two cups chopped parsley, quarter cup chopped mint leaves, half cup chopped onions, two medium ripe tomatoes chopped, quarter cup olive oil, two TBS lemon juice, salt and spice to taste.

Method: Soak oats or bulgur in a bowl with the cold water for a half hour. Drain and mix grain with chopped onions. If substituting cooked rice just mix with chopped onions. Add parsley and mint. Mix lemon juice, oil, and spices then add to grain-parsley mixture. Add chopped tomatoes and chill for at least an hour before serving on a bed of lettuce. Serves six.

Parsley and Potato Soup

Ingredients: one cup chopped potatoes, half cup chopped parsley, one bunch chopped chives, one medium onion chopped, four cups chicken stock or vegetable bullion, salt and spice to taste

Method: Combine all ingredients except spices and parsley in a large pot and bring to a boil. Lower the cooking heat and simmer for an hour. Stir in salt and spices to taste. Just before serving add the chopped parsley.

Parsley Fish Cakes

Ingredients: two cups mashed potatoes, half pound skinned salmon fillet, half pound skinned king or carite fillet, one ounce melted butter, quarter cup chopped parsley, quarter cup chopped chives, one medium onion chopped, one egg beaten, quarter cup crushed biscuits (Crix) or bread crumbs, two TBS oil for frying, salt and spice to taste

Method: Mix mashed potatoes with butter and spices. Cover the bottom of a medium fry pan with a half-inch of water and poach the fish fillets until just tender and then flake the fish apart with a fork. In a suitable bowl mix the fish and potatoes together with the onion, parsley and chives. First roll mixture into balls and then flatten with a spatula or spoon. Place beaten egg in one small bowl and biscuit/bread crumbs in another. Dip fish/potato cakes first in the egg and then coat with the crumbs. Heat the canola oil in a skillet and fry the cakes until crisp. Drain on paper and serve with your favorite dressing.

Parsley Rice

Ingredients: two cups boiling water, two cups rice (prefer brown rice), quarter cup chopped parsley, two chives chopped, salt and spice to taste

Method: Using a large pot, bring water to a boil, and then add rice and spices. Seal pot with foil, reduce heat, and simmer until rice is cooked. Stir in parsley and chives before serving.

Parsley Cookies for the Puppies

Does your pooch have bad breath???

Ingredients: three cups chopped parsley, quarter cup chopped carrots, two TBS vegetable oil, three cups flour (prefer whole wheat), quarter cup wheat bran, three TBS baking powder, half cup of water, more water may be necessary to get the correct consistency.

Method: Mix parsley, carrots, flour, bran and baking powder with a half cup of water. Mix and knead. Add more water if mixture feels too dry. Roll dough into half inch thick logs. Cut the logs according to the size of your dog. A big dog should get four-inch pieces while small pompeks get only one-inch pieces. Bake pieces on a cookie sheet at 350 degrees for thirty minutes. This should make three-dozen dog biscuits. Store in a sealed container after they have cooled.

HEALTH NOTE

Two tablespoons of parsley contain more than of the recommended daily dose of Vitamin K. Parsley contains more vitamin C than lemon, orange, or any other fruit. To make a parsley face tonic steep a quarter cup of fresh parsley in two cups of hot water for two hours. Then pass through a sieve. Drink before meals. Parsley's supply of vitamin A benefits skin tone and its vitamin E fights wrinkles. Parsley fortifies the immune system, and benefits liver, spleen, digestive and endocrine organs.

One of the most delightful things about a garden is the anticipation it provides.

W.E. Johns

ROSEMARY

Rosemary and I are still getting acquainted, Rosemary, the herb, that is. It is one of the most attractive plants in my herb garden, but I'm still learning to enjoy its unique flavor. It has needle leaves like a pine tree. Its taste is like a piney and sweet-mint with a gingerish tang. Rosemary is native to the Mediterranean and is mostly used when roasting meats, fish, or poultry.

Rosemary is easy to grow. It is a perennial, which means it continues to grow year after year without replanting. It can grow to five feet or more, so make adequate room in full sun, and you'll have it around for a couple decades. There are many different types of rosemary so be certain what type you are planting. It is slightly difficult to grow from seeds so cuttings from another mature plant is a suggestion. Seeds may take two to three months to germinate. Rosemary likes slightly alkaline, sandy soil. Be careful not to let this herb dry out, or to over water it. It adapts well to indoor container growing. Once or twice a year give it some fertilizer like special green and it should be content to flavor many dishes for you.

In ancient Greece students wore rosemary head wreaths to improve their memory. During the Middle Ages people believed rosemary could ward off evil, so they slept with pieces of rosemary under their pillows. Rosemary symbolizes friendship and love and all brides carried it during wedding ceremonies. It was a main ingredient in various love potions.

Rosemary stimulates the circulatory and nervous systems while it also calms indigestion. It will help fight severe headaches. Rosemary's essential oil will ease muscle strains and aches. It is a usual ingredient in shampoos and hair conditioners that fight dandruff and (if you believe it) hair loss. It is thought that adding rosemary to your diet may reduce the chances of having a stroke or contracting Alzheimer's. Rosemary is a good herb to use as a mouth wash because it soothes sore throats and freshens breath. When put in a drawer or closet with clothes it will repel moths.

Rosemary leaves look like miniature pine tree branches. This herb has very few calories and nutrients. The fresh, flavorful needles are chopped. A little rosemary goes a long way in most dishes. Try using it the next time you roast a piece of pork or a chicken. It improves the flavor of many vegetable dishes, especially tomatoes, squash, and spinach. It is a great addition to most marinades and light flavored soups like potato or cauliflower. Rosemary keep extremely well when frozen in a sealed container. Rosemary has about three calories per teaspoon.

Herbs and Spices

Bouquet Garni

This classic herb combination is secured in a cheesecloth pouch and used to flavor meat and vegetable dishes.

Ingredients: quarter cup dried parsley, two TBS dried thyme, two dried bay leaves, two TBS dried rosemary

Method: Combine all ingredients. Store in a well sealed container. Refrigerate. Cut a circle of cheesecloth about six inches in diameter. Fill with two tablespoons of herb combination. Tie tightly with string. Use in recommended dishes and remove intact after cooking.

Lemon Rosemary Infused Oil

Ingredients: two cups cooking oil (prefer either canola or olive), one sprig fresh rosemary, one bunch of fresh lemon grass, a fresh sprig of thyme, one clove of garlic, one TS black peppercorns, one TS salt

Method: combine all ingredients. Put in a sealed bottle and refrigerate for two weeks before using. Great on salads or fried vegetable dishes.

Rosemary Chicken and Potatoes

Ingredients: one chicken, one lemon quartered, four sprigs of fresh rosemary, six medium potatoes chunked, three TBS butter or margarine, three TBS oil (prefer canola), two TS dried rosemary, one TS dried thyme, salt and pepper to taste, one quarter cup water

Method: Rub chicken with lemon inside and out. Leave one quarter of the lemon with 2 sprigs of rosemary in the cavity and the other sprigs under the chicken's loose skin where ever you can place it. Put whole chicken in a suitable roasting pan and surround with potato chunks. Pour in water. Smear chicken and potatoes with butter, then cover with dried rosemary and thyme. Roast covered at 350 for an hour. Uncover and continue to roast for fifteen more minutes.

DID YOU KNOW?

Greek students braided rosemary into their hair to improve their exams. Of the mint family, rosemary is not named after roses or a woman named Mary, but from the Latin rosmarinus, which translates to 'dew of the sea.' Botanically rosemary is rosmarinus officinalis. Chinese combine it with borax to treat baldness. Rub your pets with powdered rosemary leaves as a natural flea and tick repellent due to its antimicrobial properties.

Rosemary Hair Rinse
Boil ten sprigs fresh rosemary in two cups water for thirty minutes. Cool and store in a tightly sealed container. Refrigerate. Once a week combine one half cup rosemary water with a cup of warm water and work through your hair. You will be amazed at the luster.

Rosemary Steamed Shrimp

Ingredients: two pounds fresh shrimp, shelled and deveined, one bottle Carib beer, four sprigs fresh rosemary, salt and pepper to taste

Method: Place beer and rosemary in a steamer. Boil and steam shrimp for five minutes until pink. Add salt and pepper to your taste.

Rosemary Cornbread

Ingredients: three TBS fresh rosemary chopped fine, one medium onion chopped very small, one cup cornmeal, one cup bakers flour, two TS baking powder, one TS baking soda, one TS salt, one TS cayenne pepper, one cup milk, one half cup melted butter or margarine, two eggs, one TBS butter or margarine

Method: In a small skillet fry onion in one tablespoon of butter until it becomes clear and soft. In a bowl combine all dry ingredients, rosemary, and cooked onions. In another bowl combine milk, melted butter and eggs. Combine both wet and dry ingredients in a loaf pan. Bake at 400 for forty to fifty minutes. Cool before cutting.

Refreshing Rosemary Lemonade

Ingredients: three sprigs of fresh rosemary, two cups fresh lemon juice, two TBS grated lemon skin, half cup sugar (more to your taste), two quarts of water, pinch of salt

Method: Stir the sugar, one cup water, grated lemon, rosemary, salt, in a pot and boil until sugar dissolves, about fifteen minutes. Cool the sugar mixture. Add it to the fresh lemon juice and the water. Serve chilled.

HEALTH NOTE

Rosemary treats stomach upsets, digestive disorders, and headaches. Research has shown its ability to help prevent cancer and age-related skin damage, boost the functioning of the liver and act as a mild diuretic to help reduce swelling.

In order to live off a garden, you practically have to live in it.
Frank McKinney Hubbard

REAL SAFFRON

Real saffron is probably the world's most expensive spice. What most people know as saffron is really turmeric. Saffron comes from the dried stigmas of the saffron crocus flower, Crocus sativus Linneaus. The stigmas are the female part of the flower. In a good year, each saffron crocus plant might produce several flowers. Each flower contains three stigmas, which are the only part of the saffron responsible for its therapeutic properties.

An acre of saffron flowers will yield only ten pounds of spice. It takes 75,000 blossoms or 225,000 hand-picked stigmas to make a single pound! One ounce of saffron threads is one hundred and fifty USD an ounce, or ten USD a gram. There are four to five hundred saffron stigmas to the gram. The stigma are also called threads, strings, pieces, or strands. One gram equals two teaspoons whole, one teaspoon crumbled, or a half teaspoon powdered. It is not wise to buy pre-powdered saffron as it loses flavor quickly. Saffron powder is usually cut with turmeric.

The saffron crocus flower grows in warm climates. It grows to about a foot tall and has long thin leaves. The blue-violet flowers contain the precious stigmas. They are delicate threads, each measuring about an inch. Superior saffron is a bright orange-red color. Inferior saffron with white streaks or light patches is usually adulterated. Good saffron should have a strong honey-like smell and taste. Saffron is the most frequently adulterated spice throughout history. Low grade saffron has even been treated with urine to give it an orange tint. Most often dried marigold is used to 'cut' this spice.

According to a Greek myth, a handsome mortal named Krocos fell in love with a beautiful wood nymph named Smilax. But Krocus' affection was not returned by Smilax. Some versions tell that the Gods turned Krocus into a beautiful purple crocus flower, and other say Smilax did it to keep him close. The name is from the Arabic word 'zafaran', which means 'yellow'. Saffron was used to scent the baths and public halls of Imperial Rome. The Romans initially brought saffron to England, but it was lost to them during the Dark Ages. It is claimed today's English saffron comes from a 14th century pilgrim who smuggled one crocus bulb from the Holy Land.

Saffron is native to Western Asia, most likely Persia where Iran and Iraq are today. The crocus was cultivated in ancient Europe. The Mongols took saffron from Persia to India. In ancient time saffron was used medicinally, as well as for food and as a dye. It was cultivated in Spain around 700 AD. Spain now rivals Kashmir for the best saffron. Saffron is also cultivated in India, Turkey, China, and Iran. Saffron is prized for its taste and the way it colors food. In India, saffron orange is considered the most beautiful color and is the official color of Buddhist robes.

Saffron crocus becomes commercial saffron when cured properly. Each red stigma has complex chemicals that create the unique aroma, flavor, and yellow dye. Crocus sativus linneaus contains crocin, the source of its strong coloring property, and bitter-crocin, the cause of the distinctive aroma, taste, and essential oils.

The very best saffron usually produced in Spain is termed coupe. It is the least produced, thus the most valuable. It is almost impossible to purchase. Mancha is what the best, most available is termed. Mancha's stigmas are deep red. Other types termed Rio and Sierra have stigmas that are lighter yellow.

Commercially grown saffron is produced from corms or bulbs because the plants are sterile and don't produce seeds. The plant dies back once it has flowered. Each crocus bulb produces two to nine flowers per season, and each flower has three long red-orange stigma branches, attached together at the base. The stigma are hand harvested during the short season.

To grow saffron first you have to locate the necessary bulbs from a supplier usually though the Internet. One bulb costs five USD; plan on buying at least ten. Prepare a spot in your garden protected from strong winds. Work the soil until it easily crumbles. Add sand and rotted compost. Plant the saffron bulbs four inches deep and six inches apart. Cover with cut vegetation. During the early months of the following year the bulbs will sprout. Only the female stigmas of the flowers are used for the saffron spice. The stigmas are the three bright orange appendages attached to the center of the flower. You need to dry the stigmas in an airy spot away from direct sunlight. When the stigmas crumble easily when crushed, they are adequately dried for storage. Store in cool dark place in airtight containers.

Be particularly careful when buying powdered saffron as it can be 'cut' or diluted with turmeric or other additives. Saffron should be kept in an airtight container in the fridge. Due to its expense, unique taste, and strong dying properties, very little saffron is required for cooking. The trick is to mix the tiny bit of saffron evenly throughout the prepared dish. If too much is used it will over power the dish and have a medicine taste. Saffron can be crushed to a fine powder in a mortar and pestle. One method is to soak or steep the threads in water, or white wine and then add to the dish. The threads may be toasted in a heavy cast iron skillet over medium heat and then ground with a mortar and pestle before adding to the dish. With soups, or salad dressings crumble the threads and add directly to the dish. Soaking, even for a few minutes works better, provides better distribution of color and a more robust flavor.

The easiest way to get it thoroughly combined in your recipe is to steep the saffron in hot water. Use only a pinch to a cup for good taste. Real saffron will expand in the hot water. A steeped cup should flavor a pound of rice. Saffron is used in Mediterranean and Asian dishes. Good yellow rice is made with saffron, not turmeric. It flavors and colors fish and seafood, especially the Spanish paella.

Large dosages of saffron can be fatal. It is considered an excellent stomach tonic and helps digestion and increases appetite. It is also relieves tension and fights depression. It is a fact since antiquity, crocus was attributed to have aphrodisiac properties. Many writers along with Greek mythology sources associate crocus with fertility. Crocus in general is an excellent stimulant. One quarter teaspoon has only one calorie and some potassium.

Saffron Scalloped Potatoes

Ingredients: one half TS saffron threads, one half cup whipping cream, one cup whole milk, three TBS butter, one tablespoon oil, two large onions sliced thin then chopped small, two cloves of garlic minced, six large white potatoes sliced thin, one cup cheddar cheese grated

Method: In a suitable pot combine milk and cream and heat. Remove from heat and add saffron. Allow to steep for twenty minutes. In a frying pan with the butter and oil sauté onion and garlic until clear. In a baking dish layer potatoes, onion and garlic. Cover with milk - saffron mixture. Cover with foil and bake at 350 for an hour. Uncover and bake another fifteen minutes.

Indian Saffron Rice

Ingredients: pinch powdered saffron, two cups boiling water-divided, two TBS butter, one cup uncooked long-grain white rice - not rinsed, one teaspoon salt

Method: Steep the saffron in one half cup boiling water. In a covered frying pan melt the butter over medium heat. Stir in the rice and salt. Cook, stirring constantly, until the rice begins to absorb the butter and becomes opaque. Do not brown the rice. Add one and a half cups boiling water along with the saffron water. Cover tightly and simmer for twenty minutes until all of the liquid is absorbed. Try not to peak or remove the lid while the rice is cooking.

God Almighty first planted a garden.
And indeed, it is the purest of human pleasures.

Francis Bacon

SAGE

I never really used a lot of sage until I stuffed a holiday turkey for some visiting stateside friends. Poultry seasoning is almost impossible to locate in Trinidad so I mixed my own from fresh sage and thyme. Now, I use sage in soups, and especially with chicken. I have three plants in my garden, so I'm never without. Aromatic sage belongs to the mint family. It should be used fresh for the best flavor.

Sage is native to countries surrounding the Mediterranean Sea and has been consumed in these regions for thousands of years. Botanically sage is known as Sage salvia officinalis. In medicinal lore, sage has one of the longest histories of use of any herb. The Greeks and Romans highly prized the healing properties of sage. The Romans treated it as sacred and created a special ceremony for gathering sage. Both cultures used it as a preservative for meat, a tradition that continued until the beginning of refrigeration.

Arab physicians in the 10th century believed that it extended life, while 14th century Europeans used it to protect from witches. Sage was in much demand in China during the 1600's, because Chinese yearned for sage to make tea. Dutch traders profited when the Chinese would trade three chests of their China tea for one chest of sage leaves.

Sage is easy to grow in almost any well-drained soil or window pot in full sun. It can reach three feet tall, but trimming can keep it small. Two or three plants will keep you and friend s supplied with this herb. Sage doesn't need much except sun and just enough water, don't overwater. It is a perennial, but I trim mine every year and sprout one or two of the cuttings to keep the flavor fresh. It can be grown from seed, but buy a plant when you can find it. Sage is great for your indoor spice garden. Never cut more than a quarter of a sage plant. Old leaves are strong flavored, and are best for cooking; younger leaves have a lighter taste and good with egg or cheese dishes.

Medicinally, smoking sage helps relieve asthma, and sage tea will help fight a fever or a sore throat. Sage is a good source of vitamins A and C. Sage contains six calories in two grams with some calcium and iron.

When cooking, sage should be used in moderation as its flavor can overtake a dish. Sage combines well with rosemary, oregano, and thyme. Sage is a very powerful spice. It is sometimes combined with garlic and green pepper for frying meat. Because of its strong taste, combination of sage with more delicate herbs does not make much sense.

When preparing any batter for frying for onion rings, chicken, or fish add two table spoons of fresh sage for a unique and delicious taste. Sage goes with eggplant, pumpkin, tomato choka, and bodi.

Fresh Herb Biscuits

Ingredients: Two cups bakers flour, quarter cup mayonnaise, one TBS fresh sage minced, one TBS fresh thyme minced, one cup milk, half TS salt

Method: In a large bowl combine all ingredients. Use a large spoon, and carefully place spoonfuls on a greased baking sheet. Bake fifteen minutes at 400 degrees.

Squash Soup

Ingredients: four pounds squash - peeled, seeded, and cubed, one medium onion chopped, two cloves garlic minced, half hot pepper seeded and minced, one TBS butter, six nice sage leaves minced or two TBS ground sage, one TBS brown sugar, four cups chicken broth, one TS salt

Method: In a large pot brown the onion and garlic in the butter. Add sugar, squash cubes, sage, salt and the pepper. Add the chicken broth, bring to a boil and simmer for forty-five minutes.

Sage Pesto

This is a great flavor to just blend with noodles, potato, or rice dishes.

Ingredients: two cups sage leaves minced, two cups shelled walnuts, half cup oil (prefer olive oil), two cloves garlic minced, one bunch chives chopped extremely small, half hot pepper seeded and minced (optional), half TS salt

Method: Place all ingredients in a blender and puree. Use a tablespoon with noodles or rice to your taste. Slowly add more to increase sharpness.

Easy Pumpkin Soup

Ingredients: one small pumpkin peeled and cubed, three cups chicken stock, quarter TS ground nutmeg, half TS ground sage, salt and spice to taste

Method: In a suitable pot, add pumpkin to chicken broth and bring to a boil. Add remaining ingredients and simmer, stirring occasionally until pumpkin is tender and most water boils away. Four tablespoons more water may be added to change consistency.

> **DID YOU KNOW?**
>
> To hide gray hair put one half cup of dried sage in two cups of water and simmer for half an hour. Cover and allow the sage water to steep over night. Over a basin, pour the rinse over your hair at least ten times catching and reusing the same sage water. On the last rinsing, leave the sage water dry on the hair before rinsing with fresh water. Repeat every week until your hair is the desired shade. Then rinse every month to retain your hair color.
> (from Pioneer Thinking)

HEALTH NOTE

Sage has the longest history of medicinal use of any herb. The Romans named this herb salvere, meaning to save or cure. Modern studies support its effects as an antibiotic, antifungal, and an astringent. Recent tests have confirmed sage is an outstanding memory enhancer. Sage has been studied to be effective in the management of mild to moderate Alzheimer's disease. Sage is effective as a food preservative because it inhibits the growth of bacteria.

Over two millenniums ago, the Chinese were using sage tea as a mild tonic to invigorate the nervous system. Sage stimulates the central nervous system, while reducing excess nervous energy. This mild tonic quiets the nerves, and helps induce sleep. Sage will fight depression, mental exhaustion, trembling, and nervousness.

Sage helps the nerves and by its powerful might palsy is cured and fever put to flight. ~ French saying. If one consults enough herbals...every sickness known to humanity will be listed as being cured by sage.

Varro Taylor, Ph.D. (herb expert)

The desire of sage is to render man immortal," instructs a late medieval treatise. Indeed, the sage plant has been praised highly throughout history and on many continents for its power of longevity.

TARRAGON

Tarragon is a small shrub, a perennial herb from the same family as sunflowers. Two types are grown, the French variety with glossy sharp licorice smelling leaves and the much blander Russian type. Most dried tarragon comes from French tarragon. Only the leaves are edible. This herb is excellent with seafood, fruits, poultry, eggs, and most vegetables, as well as sauces - particularly béarnaise sauce.

Native to remote areas of China and Russia, tarragon is believed to have been brought to Europe the by invading Mongols in the 13th century. Today its primary producer is France. Tarragon is relatively new on the world's herbal scene. Unlike many herbs, it was not used by ancient peoples. Tarragon's name is from the French *esdragon*, which means 'little dragon' because of its winding root system. The tangled roots will strangle the plant if not often divided. Botanically tarragon is *artemisia dracunculu*.

When planting be absolutely certain it is French tarragon, not inferior Russian tarragon, which is a completely different species. French tarragon rarely, if ever makes seed, and so it must be grown from cuttings. This herb can grow to two feet across. To grow indoors it needs a goodsized deep pot because its roots need plenty of room. It is best planted in sandy soil, to have the best possible drainage. Clay soils are very bad for tarragon. Put gravel at the bottom of the pot before adding the soil to facilitate drainage.

Keep this herb pruned so the plant is open to the breeze and try not to let it touch any other plant. Harvest tarragon when ready to cook with it. Cut about a third of a branch, then chop the leaves fine, to fully release the full flavor.

Tarragon was considered 'the banishing herb'. Burn dried leaves while writing on paper what you want to banish from your life (bad habits or people). Then burn the paper with the remaining smoldering herb. It was also known to put guests at ease and make them feel welcome. It was carried in packet charms or sachets for love, peace, and good luck.

DID YOU KNOW?

Tarragon increases appetite, improves circulation of blood, and helps in the proper distribution of nutrients, oxygen, hormones, and enzymes throughout the body. It stimulates the brain, nervous, digestive, circulatory, and endocrine systems. This in turn stimulates the whole metabolic system and as a result, growth and immunity are stimulated.

Tarragon makes an excellent flavored vinegar, and an excellent herb butter, alone or in combination with other fines herbs. Tarragon vinegar is easy to make. Put fresh tarragon sprigs into a sterilized bottle of distilled white vinegar. Taste after a few days. Continue steeping until it suits your taste. Once the taste is strong enough remove the sprigs. Tarragon is also a good herb to use in infused oils. Heat greatly intensifies the flavor of tarragon, both fresh and dried. Care should be taken when using tarragon or it will overpower other flavors.

Tarragon is the main ingredient in Béarnaise Sauce and the French favorite herb mixture, 'fines herbes'. It is used with chicken, fish, and egg dishes. Tarragon flavors a popular carbonated soft drink in the eastern European countries of Armenia, Georgia, Russia, and Ukraine. The drink is made from sweetened tarragon concentrate and colored bright green.

One teaspoon of ground tarragon has 14 calories with plenty of potassium. A half ounce of fresh tarragon equals a third of a cup. One tablespoon of fresh tarragon equals one teaspoon of dried.

Herb or Spice Infused Oil

Ingredients: Favorite herbs and/or spices, prefer sunflower, safflower, or extra-virgin olive oil

Method: Wash and dry your choice of herb branches and lightly bruise them to release flavor. Place them in a clean glass container that seals tightly. Cover with warm oil, and seal. Leave in a cool, dark place for ten days or longer. If not strong enough for your taste add more herbs and remain sealed. If you do not strain the herbs out, the flavor will become stronger the longer it sits. If you infuse olive oil keep it refrigerated. Consider combinations with onion and garlic and a variety of herbs as rosemary, thyme, basil, tarragon, summer savory, oregano, chadon benee, marjoram, chives, dill, mint, parsley, and bay leaf. Use within two months and keep refrigerated.

Tarragon Salad Dressing

Ingredients: two TBS fresh tarragon chopped fine or one TS dried, two TBS finely chopped parsley, one clove of garlic minced, one half cup sour cream, one half cup mayonnaise, one TBS fresh lemon juice, salt to taste

Method: In a bowl combine tarragon, parsley, and garlic. Add sour cream, mayonnaise, lemon juice, and salt. Blend thoroughly.

Fine Herbs Mix

Ingredients: One TBS tarragon chopped, one TBS chives chopped, one TBS parsley chopped, one TBS chervil chopped

Method: Fresh Herbs: Combine tarragon, chervil, chives, and parsley. Add this mix at the end of the cooking process of any recipe to preserve their flavor.

Dried Herbs: Combine the herbs. Place in a glass jar and seal tightly. Refrigerate.

Herb Mustard Sauce

Ingredients: quarter cup unsweetened evaporated milk (must be chilled in freezer for ten minutes), one quarter cup tarragon vinegar, two TBS grainy Dijon mustard, one half cup vegetable or olive oil, two TBS fresh tarragon chopped, one bunch chives chopped fine, salt to taste

Method: Use a blender to combine tarragon, vinegar, and Dijon mustard. Add chilled evaporated milk. Blender running, slowly pour in oil. Add chopped fresh tarragon, chives, and salt. Blend.

Refried Potatoes

Ingredients: Two cups Irish potatoes cubed, oil for frying, four TBS butter or margarine, one TS tarragon leaves minced, one clove garlic minced, salt to taste

Method: Fry potatoes in oil until color just begins to brown. Then melt butter in another skillet and add garlic and tarragon. Then refry the potato cubes until golden brown. Serve hot.

HEALTH NOTE

Tarragon is a delicate, green herb with long, thin pointy leaves with a unique, distinct flavor with just a hint of anise. The French call French tarragon the 'King of Herbs'. Tarragon is a perennial herb with aromatic leaves rich in iodine, minerals, and vitamins A and C, and was used to prevent scurvy. It is also used as an appetite stimulant and digestive tonic, while commercially as a fragrance component in soaps and cosmetics. French and the Russian tarragon are both well known to herbalists for their curative properties.

It pleases me to take amateur photographs of my garden, and it pleases my garden to make my photographs look professional.

Robert Brault

THYME

Fresh thyme is constantly used in my kitchen to flavor to soups, stews, and casseroles. I use it with most meat and fish dishes. Thyme has a sharp smell that is spicy, but also very earthy. It has a warm flavor that remains after the meal and seems to freshen the breath with a faint clove aftertaste. It ranks as one of the fine herbs of French cuisine.

This is another herb first cultivated around the Mediterranean Sea. The Egyptians used it to embalm their mummies, and the Greeks used it smoldering to chase insects from their residences. In fact, that is where the name thyme originates, In Greek 'thymon' translates 'to fumigate'. The Romans used thyme to make alcohol. The botanical name is *thymus vulgaris*.

Although there are over 100 varieties of thyme, only common garden thyme and lemon thyme are used in cooking. The remainder are used as ornamental plants. It is known locally as Spanish thyme. Garden thyme is a small perennial - once planted it is there as long as you care for it. Its appearance depends on soil type, care, and amount of sun, and water. Usually thyme is stiff and bushy with many thin, erect stalks covered with pairs of small, narrow dull green leaves. The blossoms are usually pale pink and loved by honey bees. Lemon thyme is smaller with bright green leaves that have a slight lemony taste.

Thyme will grow almost anywhere with little effort as long as it is planted in well drained soil with at least six hours of sun. It is usually planted from a piece of a mature plant stuck in a pot of damp soil, but you can grow it from seeds. As long as you don't over water or allow it to dry out, thyme should catch in two to three weeks. Once it is about six inches tall it can be transplanted to your herb garden or to a larger pot. Thyme seems to be almost dry when picked. I treat thyme like sage, oregano, and rosemary. I put it in a brown paper bag in indirect sunlight for a week. Then I force it through a strainer and store in a sealed bottle in the fridge. It is preferable to strip the leaves from the stems for your recipes when using either dry or fresh thyme because sometimes the stems can be woody.

Thyme is traditional in bouquet garni combined with marjoram, parsley, and bay. Thyme works well with lamb, beef, poultry, fish, stews, soups, and bean and lentil casseroles. Use it with tomatoes, onions, cucumbers, carrots, eggplant, parsnips, leeks, mushrooms, asparagus, green beans, broccoli, sweet peppers, potatoes, spinach, corn, peas, cheese, eggs, and rice. Its flavor blends well with those of lemon, garlic, and basil.

Herbs and Spices

Store fresh thyme in a plastic bag in the vegetable crisper drawer of your refrigerator or stand sprigs in a glass of water on the refrigerator shelf. When cooking with thyme, be aware that one fresh sprig equals the flavoring power of one-half teaspoon of dried thyme. As with most leafy dried herbs, be sure to crush the leaves between your hands before adding them to your recipe. Dried thyme should be stored in a cool, dark place, in an airtight container for no more than six months. One gram of thyme has three calories with calcium, vitamin A and iron.

Caribbean Special Shrimp Stew

Ingredients: two pounds fresh medium shrimp - peeled, cleaned, and boiled - save the water, one pound white potatoes - peeled and cubed, one pound sweet potatoes - peeled and cubed, three cups of chopped onion, a cup of chopped chives, quarter cup celery chopped, four medium ripe tomatoes chopped, four chadon benee leaves chopped, six cloves of garlic minced, half cup vegetable oil, half cup flour, two TS salt, one hot pepper seeded and minced (optional), two TS fresh or dried thyme, three bay leaves, one TS fresh lemon juice

Method: In a large pot heat the oil and whisk in a little flour at a time until all becomes a rich light brown color. Add chopped onion, chives, chadon benee, celery, and garlic. Keep stirring over low heat for ten minutes. Add salt, pepper, bay leaves, and thyme. Mix well. Add the chopped tomatoes, two cups of the shrimp water, and lemon juice. Simmer for one hour with regular stirrings. Add the cubed potatoes and simmer for ten minutes longer. Add the shrimp, cover, and simmer for half an hour. Serve warm with roti or fresh, crusty bread.

Tropical Bird

Ingredients: two pounds turkey chopped or chicken, one medium onion chopped small, one half hot pepper seeded and minced (optional), juice from one fresh orange, one TBS corn starch, two TBS butter or margarine, one cup bread crumbs, one TS fresh or dried sage, one TS fresh or dried thyme crushed, salt to taste, two cups brown sugar

Method: Combine bread crumbs, sage, thyme, onion, salt, and pepper. Roll turkey or chicken pieces in crumbs. Place in baking dish and cook in oven at 400 degrees for forty-five minutes. Combine orange juice and cornstarch and set aside. In a frying pan melt butter and stir in brown sugar until it melts. Stir in orange juice/cornstarch. Pour over baked poultry pieces. Serve with boiled banana.

French Creole Spice Mix

Ingredients: a third cup sweet paprika, third cup dried basil, third cup dried thyme, three TBS cayenne pepper, two TBS chili powder

Method: Combine paprika, basil, thyme, cayenne, and chili powder in a glass sealable container. Shake until well-combined. Best stored in fridge.

Green Beans and Fresh Herbs

Ingredients: two pounds fresh, canned or frozen green beans, one medium onion chopped small, one TS fresh parsley chopped, one TS fresh thyme leaves chopped, one TS fresh lemon juice, quarter cup butter, salt to taste

Method: Wash beans and chop into half inch pieces. Steam beans about a quarter hour and drain. In a skillet melt the butter and add the onion, lemon juice, parsley, thyme, and salt. Simmer for 5 minutes, stir in the green bean pieces. Serve warm.

Thyme Refresher

Ingredients: two cups water, one TS fresh thyme leaves (lemon preferred), one TS honey, one TS fresh lemon juice

Method: Boil water. Add thyme leaves and steep for five minutes. Strain and add honey and lemon juice. Relax and enjoy.

HEALTH NOTE

Nightmares were treated with thyme tea. Thyme oil was used during World War I to treat infection and to help relieve pain. Small amounts of this herb are sedative, but larger amounts are stimulant. Thyme is used against hookworm, roundworms, and threadworms. Thyme also warms and stimulates the lungs, expels mucus, and relieves congestion such as asthma. It also helps deter bacterial, fungal, and viral infections. Thyme has always been used as a poultice for wounds, insect bites, and stings. It is a good wash for sore eyes, and a hair rinse to fight dandruff.

Give me odorous at sunrise a garden of
beautiful flowers where I can walk undisturbed.

Walt Whitman

TONKA BEAN

I grew up sucking tonka (or tanka) beans because they had such a strong, spicy taste. The seed is shiny black and smooth when fresh, but dries wrinkled. It is an oblong pod, three inch by one inch. It has a smooth brown interior that has a weird type of fiber almost like mango, under a thin skin. The hair is what we sucked to get a type of almost sweet, chocolaty flavor. The smell is an excellent blend of spices like vanilla with cinnamon and cloves. Inside the hair covered pod is the actual tonka bean. These are true unique American fruits probably native to Venezuela and Guyana. The name 'tonka' is from the Carib and Tupi Amerindians. Like so many spices it grows in estates along the north coast road. Botanically tonka bean is *dipteryx odorata*.

It is a true bean as it is a member of the pulse or legume family. This can be backyard tree if it is topped at about fifteen feet as it will grow to over a hundred feet. All it needs is well drained soil. Tonka trees can be grown from seeds. If you remember where one was, check around underneath it to locate sprouted beans. It bears after five years and the beans can be harvested after they have matured for about a year. Tonka bean trees have been carbon dated to prove they are one of only four species of trees that live over a thousand years!

DID YOU KNOW?

There are perhaps one or two tonka bean trees in a hectare (2.47 acres) of forest. The size and long life of the tree have given it a local significance akin to the baobab tree in Africa and Madagascar. This tree can grow for a millennium. These beans add fragrance to salves, creams, and oils, and for direct scenting of botanicals. Its use in the cosmetics industry is increasing because the seeds are so aromatic. After years of use in perfumes, the tonka bean is also now beginning to make an appearance as a dessert flavoring in fine-dining menus.

The Tupi Indian name for the tonka bean tree is 'kumaru' which foretells the tonka beans main ingredient courmarin, lethal in large doses. If it wasn't for courmarin, tonka beans might be as commercial as cocoa. Coumarin is a toxin that can cause liver damage in dosages as little as a gram. That is a lot of seeds, so don't worry about sucking one once in awhile! For this reason its use in food is banned in the US and UK. It prevents blood coagulation and was used in rat poisons. To extract courmarin, tonka beans are dried after a day soaking in alcohol. The toxic courmarin crystals can be removed by scraping off the dried pod and washing the bean.

Tonka beans were used to flavor cigarettes and pipe tobacco, but the courmarin issue has stopped that, at least in the US and UK. They are still used in other less developed countries as a substitute for vanilla beans. The unique tonka scent is used to imitate musk in some perfumes. The dense wood is excellent for furniture and boat building.

Since tonka beans have Amerindian influence, they are used in local supernatural potions to bolster courage, attract good luck with money, and in finding love. In fact it is known as the love wishing bean. Supposedly if you wish and throw seven tonka beans into a river, your wish will come true.

Tonka beans are not harmful unless many are consumed. I keep a few of them soaking in rum in the fridge for special occasions. The rum is also spiced with cloves, cinnamon, and nutmeg. For occasional baking needs I'll dry a bean and use it to flavor my favorite pineapple upside down cake recipe. Tonka beans create a unique flavor for homemade ice cream. Usually one bean will flavor an entire dessert. I use it as an flavoring addition to a simple sugar syrup that can be mixed into store bought vanilla ice cream or dripped on cake or cookies. Hard to believe, but tomato pasta sauce made with the usual spices of oregano, basil, garlic etc., becomes a work of art when one tonka bean is added. Tonka beans are a quarter fat with a large percentage of starch.

Tonka Pineapple Cake

Ingredients: One yellow or white package cake mix, one half cup brown sugar, one quarter cup water, one quarter cup pineapple juice, one half tonka bean grated, six rings of fresh pineapple

Method: In a small pot combine water and sugar and bring to a boil stirring until it is a syrup. Add grated tonka bean and cook for ten minutes. Set aside and cool. Make package cake substituting the pineapple juice for part of the water required. Put pineapple rings on the bottom of a greased round or square cake pan. Pour in cake batter. Drizzle tonka bean syrup through the cake batter. Do not stir it in as it should stay as distinct flavor lines. Follow baking directions and permit to cool thoroughly before turning cake over to remove pan.

Tonka Delight

Ingredients: a quarter pound of bitter cocoa powder, two pounds of confectioner's or powdered sugar, one quart of water, one liter of clear rum, peels from two oranges, three tonka beans

Method: In a big pot heat water, dissolve sugar, and boil for fifteen minutes stirring constantly. This will produce a thick syrup. Cool slightly before stirring in the cocoa powder a little at a time to avoil any lumps, add orange peels and bring to a boil stirring constantly so it doesn't stick and burn. That would ruin the taste. Boil for twenty minutes and then add the tonka beans and boil for fifteen more minutes. When the syrup has cooled stir in the alcohol. Strain as you funnel it into sterlized bottles. Store in a dark place or refrigerate. This makes an excellent holiday gift.

Tonka Rice Pudding

Ingredients: two cups cooked rice, one half cup brown sugar, two egg whites, two cups milk, one half tonka bean grated.

Method: Combine all ingredients and bake at 350 covered for forty minutes. Uncover and bake for ten minutes or until top starts to brown.

Tonka Mango Cake

Ingredients: a quarter pound soft butter, two cups cake flour, half TS baking soda, half TS baking powder, one TS freshly grated tonka bean, pinch salt, two cups sugar, three large eggs, one TS vanilla extract, one cup sour cream, three to four mangos not soft ripe- peeled, seeded and sliced.

Method: Combine all dry ingredients. Beat in one egg at a time, and slowly add the sour cream until all are mixed into a smooth batter. Pour into greased cake pan and add mango pieces. Bake at 350 for half an hour.

HEALTH NOTE

Extracts of tonka bean plant have been used in bush medicine as a tonic, and used to treat cramps and nausea. It has also been fabled to have aphrodisiac and occult properties. Cured seeds are used chiefly for scenting tobacco and snuff. Tonka beans are used for all forms of financial good luck, love, health, or anything else. They can also help fight depression during difficult times.

Creating your own urban farm is as simple as planting your flowerbeds with edibles.

Greg Peterson

TURMERIC

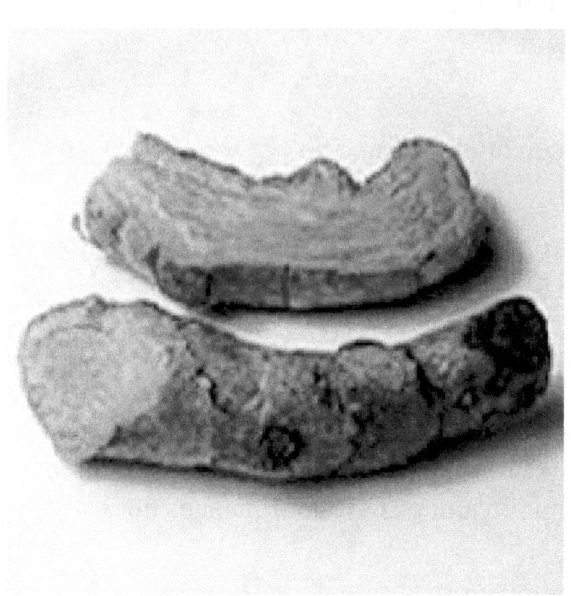

I confused turmeric with saffron until I discovered the expense of real saffron. What we have is called 'Indian saffron' and grows wild in the bush around our house in Central. After some research, I realized I'd been enjoying turmeric all my life in curries. Several friends reported they had serious ailments cured by using this common root. Other local farmers washed and boiled their own before pounding it into a paste.

Turmeric is also known as curcumin, and native to Southern Asia. It is a close relative to ginger. For more than 5,000 years, this root was used as a dye and a cooking spice in India. In medieval Europe, turmeric became known as 'Indian saffron' and used as an inexpensive substitute for real crocus saffron. Turmeric is one of the key ingredients in many curries, providing them both color and flavor. The root and rhizome (underground stem) of the turmeric plant are used medicinally. Turmeric's scientific name is *curcuma longa*.

I believe turmeric is such an important herb I have transplanted a row of turmeric along the fence in the backyard. It is easy to grow after you find some seed roots. Just plant it where it won't be too damp and leave it alone except for an occasional weeding. When the leaves start to wither dig the roots and replant some of the small 'knobs' attached. An attractive plant, ours grows to about two feet tall, and turmeric has a large yellow and white flower spike surrounded by long leaves. The roots form bulbs and seed - rhizomes.

Turmeric is famous for its roots' color, pale tan to yellow on the outside, but bright orange on the inside. It is used to color and flavor mustard, cheese, butter, pickles, relish, chutneys, rice, and an important ingredient in curry powder.

Turmeric's flavor resembles a combination of ginger and pepper. Turmeric is a powerful coloring agent. Occasionally shredded and used fresh, turmeric is more often dried and powdered for use. The roots are boiled for hours, dried for days or weeks, then ground into powder. Turmeric removes accumulation of cholesterol in the liver and promotes a healthy circulatory system. It is also a great stomach tonic for gas

DID YOU KNOW?

As early as 3000 B.C. the turmeric plants were cultivated by a civilization in Punjab Pakistan. Kunkuma is a red powder made of turmeric and lime and worn by Hindus as the pottu, dot, at the point of the third eye on the forehead.

or indigestion. East Indian women with lovely, velvety skin often attribute it to consuming turmeric. It contains manganese, vitamin B6, and iron with about four calories to a gram.

Remedies

To make a tea from turmeric, pour 8 ounces of boiling water over a half-teaspoon grated or powdered, and let sit covered for 5 minutes, then strain, if necessary. Drink two or three cups daily, as desired.

Mix turmeric powder with cooking oil to make a thick paste. Put on the skin over wounds, bites, bruises, etc. Cover with bandage and leave on several hours. It washes off and the color disappears quickly. If you have a toothache, paint this on your face over the toothache.

Easy-Easy Trini Veggie Stew

Ingredients: one squash seeded - peeled and chunked, two cups eggplant chunked with or without skin, one cup ochro, two large tomatoes chopped small, two potatoes peeled and chopped small, quarter cup ketchup or tomato paste, one large onion chopped small, one carrot chopped small, three cloves garlic minced, one cup water, one whole hot pepper seeded (optional), one TS turmeric powder, half TS cumin powder, quarter TS cinnamon powder, salt and spices to taste

Method: In a large pot with a cover, combine all ingredients. Simmer for at least four hours. A slow cooker or crock pot is perfect for this dish. Serve with rice or pasta.

Yellow Veggie Cakes

Ingredients: one carrot chopped small, half cup pigeon peas, one stalk celery chopped small, one and a half cups potatoes - peeled, boiled, and mashed, quarter cup all purpose flour, one hot pepper seeded and minced (optional), two leaves chadon benee chopped small, one TS ginger root minced, one TS turmeric powder, half TS salt, oil for frying

Method: Mix all ingredients together and roll into balls, about an inch to two inches in diameter. The bigger will take longer to fry. Drop into hot oil and fry till brown. Eat with spicy sauce.

Pomatoes

Ingredients: four nice potatoes peeled and chopped small, one stalk celery chopped, one medium onion chopped small, two medium ripe tomatoes chopped small, two cloves garlic minced, quarter cup oil, half hot pepper seeded and minced (optional), one TS turmeric powder, half TS cumin powder, half TS salt

Method: In a frying pan with a cover brown the onion and garlic in oil. Blend in all the spices, celery, and then add potato cubes. Cook for ten to fifteen minutes stirring intermittently. Add tomatoes and cook for another ten minutes. Serve with sada or rice.

Yellow Scrambled Eggs and Potatoes

Ingredients: two large potatoes either baked or boiled - peeled and cubed, four eggs, one small onion minced, two TBS evaporated milk, half hot pepper seeded and minced, one TS turmeric powder, half TS cumin powder, salt and other spices to your taste, oil, butter or margarine for frying

Method: In a skillet heat two TBS butter or oil, lightly brown onion and fry potato cubes. Add all spices Blend eggs and milk together. Add egg mixture and scramble. Serve with sada or toasted hops.

Trini Tomato Chicken

Ingredients: one whole chicken chunked (skinned if you like it so), four large tomatoes chopped small, one large onion chopped small, three cloves garlic minced, half hot pepper seeded and minced, quarter TS ginger root minced, one TBS oil, one TS turmeric powder, two TS cumin powder, quarter cup water, two bay leaves, half TS cinnamon powder, quarter TS nutmeg, salt and other spices to your taste.

Method: Heat oil in a large frying pan with a cover and brown onion and garlic. Add spices including turmeric and cook for about two minutes. Add chicken chunks and cover with spiceonion mixture. Add tomato pieces and quarter cup of water. Lower heat and simmer covered for up to two hours or until chicken is extremely tender. For thicker sauce uncover for last half hour.

HEALTH NOTE

Turmeric keeps viruses from replicating, kills staphylococcus, and salmonella. It aids the digestive system. It is a blood purifier and regulates blood sugar. It corrects anemia and restores poor circulation. Turmeric removes oxidized cholesterol to help prevent heart attacks. It keeps muscles and joints flexible and strong.

*Gardens always mean something else,
man absolutely uses one thing to say another.*

Robert Harbison

VANILLA

I fancy orchids, tasty desserts, and ice cream. Thus, I must love vanilla! Vanilla is the only edible fruit of the orchid family, the largest family of flowering plants in the world. It's a tropical orchid, *Vanilla planifolia* (also known as fragrans) originally cultivated around the Vera Cruz area of Mexico. This orchid produces ninety-nine per cent of the world's vanilla. It also grows throughout the Caribbean, including Trinidad. Another genus, the *Vanilla tahitensis*, cultivated in Tahiti, produces beans with stronger aroma, but less flavor.

Only saffron and cardamom, are more expensive as spices than vanilla. Vanilla beans retail in some specialty shops for $2-3 US each. Like oil, the prices of valuable spices fluctuate. Bad weather and political rebellions pushed vanilla to US$500 per kilo in 2004. A good crop, coupled with decreased demand caused by the production of imitation vanilla, the market price dropped to the $40 per kilo range in the middle of 2005.

Vanilla is so valuable that in Madagascar vanilla theft was a major problem. Growers marked their beans with pin pricks before harvest for identification. Vanilla is expensive because it is the world's most labor-intensive agricultural crop. It takes three years after the vines are planted before the first flowers appear. The fruits, which resemble big green beans, mature on the vine for nine months. The fruit is not permitted to fully-ripen, which would cause the beans to split, and reduce value. The pods must be picked by hand four to six months after the fruit appears on the vines. The green beans are then soaked in hot water, rolled in blankets to 'sweat' evaporating the water. Then they are stored in a ventilated room to slowly ferment and produce their unique aroma and flavor. They develop flavor and fragrance during this curing process.

Then the beans are sorted for size and quality. Then they rest for a month or two to finish developing their full flavor and fragrance. By the time they are shipped around the world, their aroma is quite remarkable! The delicious flavor comes from the seed pod, or the 'bean' of the vanilla plant. The prepared beans are very dark brown, and slender, about 8 inches long. All beans contain thousands of tiny black seeds.

Vanilla is native to Mexico (where it is still grown commercially), originally cultivated by the Totonaca tribe. They and vanilla were conquered by the Aztecs who in turn were conquered by the Spanish. Vanilla hit the big time when Cortez returned to Spain. It was valuable for both its fragrance and flavor. The term French vanilla is not a type of vanilla, but is often used to designate preparations that have a strong vanilla aroma and contain vanilla grains.

Growing vanilla beans is time consuming and expensive. The first problem is to locate the proper orchid cuttings. Forget about trying from seeds. The flowers are quite large and attractive with white, green, greenish yellow or cream colors. Vanilla blossoms grow in bunches and open one by one, and only last about a day. Each flower opens in the morning and closes late in the afternoon on the same day, never to re-open. It is then time to hand pollinate and to be scientific. Open the lip of the flower, take the pollen from the anther and place it in the nectar, which is located in the stigma. (Look for a labeled illustration before beginning.) Be careful because the white sap emitted by the plant can irritate your skin. After pollination, long green pods will begin growing. Vanilla flowers can only be naturally pollinated by a specific bee found only in Mexico. This very rare bee graced Mexico with a three century monopoly on vanilla production. In 1841, a teenaged French slave on Reunion Island discovered the plant could be hand pollinated with a thin piece of bamboo replicating the bees. This opened a global vanilla industry.

Vanilla orchids are grown in tropic climates, primarily Mexico, Tahiti, Madagascar, Reunion, Mauritius, Comoro, Indonesia, Uganda, and Tongo, with three-fourths of the world's supply coming from Madagascar. Quality and aroma varies with location. The resulting dark brown vanilla bean is usually 7-9 inches long, weighs about 5 grams and yields about half a teaspoon of seeds. The current annual demand for natural vanilla is 2200 tons. The biggest buyer of vanilla is the United States. Vanilla is also a fragrance. Because vanilla is so much in demand, and because it's so expensive, 97% of vanilla used is synthetic. The dairy industry uses a large percentage of the world's vanilla in ice creams, yogurt, and other flavored dairy products.

One-quarter teaspoon should be enough to flavor a recipe for 4 to 5 persons. Pure vanilla extract should have no sugar added and will last forever, aging like fine liquor. Vanilla extract is made by percolating alcohol and water through chopped, cured beans, somewhat like making coffee. Pure vanilla extract must contain 13.35 ounces of vanilla beans per gallon during extraction and 35 percent alcohol. Imitation vanilla is made from artificial flavorings, most of which come from wood byproducts and often contain chemicals. Twice as much imitation vanilla flavoring is required to match the strength of pure vanilla extract. The best rule for substitutions is one teaspoon of vanilla extract equals one inch of a vanilla bean. Nutritionally vanilla has nothing except great taste and aroma.

Choose nice fat vanilla beans with a thin skin and you will get the most seeds. The pods should be dark brown, and just soft enough to wrap around your finger without breaking. To use the vanilla bean first split it lengthwise with a sharp knife. Scrape the seeds from the pod. A good way to store whole vanilla beans is to bury them in sugar. Use a jar with a tight-fitting lid that will hold about a pound of sugar, bury the beans so no light can reach it. After two weeks the sugar will take the taste of the vanilla beans. This can flavor coffee and deserts. The beans can be removed and returned to the sugar jar. Keep refilling the sugar.

Herbs and Spices

Homemade Vanilla Extract

Ingredients: two vanilla beans sliced open, one bottle Kentucky bourbon whiskey

Method: Place the beans in a one cup jar with a glass sealing top. Fill with bourbon whiskey. Seal and put in a dark spot for two weeks. Replace what you use with more bourbon until the beans are expired. Vodka can be used for a clearer vanilla flavor.

Vanilla Pudding

Ingredients: one third cup sugar, three TBS cornstarch, quarter TS salt, two and a half cups milk, one and a half TS vanilla extract

Method: Combine sugar, cornstarch and salt; then blend in milk. Cook over medium heat, stirring constantly, till mixture thickens. Cook 2 or 3 minutes more. Add vanilla. Pour into suitable bowls and chill until firm.

Instant Rich Vanilla Coffee

Ingredients: a third cup instant coffee, one cup instant dry milk powder, half cup powdered coffee creamer, one quarter cup brown sugar, one quarter cup instant vanilla pudding mix

Method: Combine all ingredients in a suitable bowl. Store in a resealing airtight container. Place quarter cup of dry rich vanilla coffee mix into a coffee cup. Fill cup with hot water and stir.

Vanilla Rice

Ingredients: two cups water, half TS salt, one TS sugar, half TS powdered cayenne pepper, one cup long-grain rice, half tsp vanilla extract.

Method: Boil water in a suitable pan. Add the salt, sugar, cayenne pepper, and rice, and stir. Simmer until the rice is tender and the liquid has been absorbed. Remove from heat, sprinkle with the vanilla and fluff the rice with a fork to separate the grains.

A garden is a delight to the eye and a solace for the soul.
Sadi

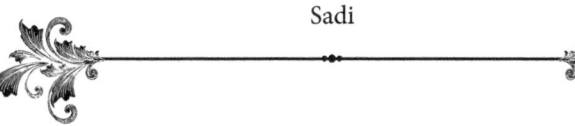

NOTES

Fruits

What determines if something is classified a fruit, vegetable, or nut? This question has been debated by botanists, chefs, and gardeners for centuries.

Fruits are the ripened ovaries containing the reproductive seeds of a plant. The plant produces flowers. The flowers are pollinated. Once pollinated, the flesh around the seeds often expands, and becomes edible. Fruits are the means by which flowering plants disseminate seeds. In cuisine, when discussing fruit as food, the term usually refers to just those plant fruits that are sweet and fleshy, as plums, apples, and oranges. The 'ovary' definition also includes many common vegetables, as well as nuts and grains. They are the fruit carrying the seeds of their plant species. The enormous variety among plant fruit makes a precise definition impossible.

The differences between fruits and vegetables are confusing since many fruits are classified as vegetables by the general public. A professional cook might determine a 'fruit' is sweet and a vegetable is not. Vegetables are the stalks, leaves, flowers, and roots of edible plants. Vegetables are drab in color - mostly green or brown; while fruits are bright vivid yellows, oranges, reds, and purples. A vegetable is a plant cultivated for the edible part. It can be a bulb, root, seeds, or the fruit itself. They are not sweet and many have to be cooked to be edible. Fruits are not cooked in most cases, and almost all fruits can be consumed raw.

The fruit of a plant contains the seeds of the plant. Vegetables consist of virtually every part; seeds (peas and beans), stems (asparagus, celery), leaves (lettuce, pak choy, and spinach), flowers (broccoli and cauliflower), and roots (carrots, eddoes, dasheen, tannia, and potatoes). Nuts are tree seeds. Peanuts are a variety of beans. Peas and beans are vegetables, but peas in the pod are fruit. String beans, the green bean pod and the beans inside, are fruit. Tomatoes, cucumbers, watermelon, and squash are fruit. Some fruit, however, does not contain real seeds. Few modern varieties of bananas contain seeds. Strawberries have the seeds on the outside.

Finally vegetables grow faster, while fruits are slower. A tree can takes years to bear fruits. Vegetable plants grow quickly, and within months vegetables are ready to be harvested. The US Supreme Court ruled on fruits versus vegetables in 1893 with the Nix vs. Hedden case. Fruits and vegetables were taxed differently, and Nix who was a tomato importer wanted it to be a fruit, and Hedden, the tax collector, wanted it to be a vegetable. The Supreme Court ruled that because tomatoes were served with dinner, not with dessert, they were vegetables.

ACKEE

Ackee is a very strange fruit, almost a mistake of nature. It is delicious, nutritious, yet can be poisonous if not picked when perfectly ripe. It is so plentiful in Jamaica it could be considered their national food dish fried with salt fish. I've been lucky to locate a few trees in Trinidad and find the correctly ripened fruit at Pricemart. Blighia sapida is the botanical name of the ackee.

Captain Bligh, of 'Mutiny on the Bounty', can be blamed for importing this tree from West Africa in the late seventeen hundreds. Ackee was a perfect food for the sugar plantations as it was cheap and nutritious. It is a distant relative of the lychee. Ackees must be properly picked and cooked. Ackee fruit or pods must fully ripen naturally and split open while on the tree. The ackee flesh must be cleaned, washed, and boiled. This water must be dumped and cannot be used again for cooking. The base membrane must be removed.

Even though this fruit can be life threatening, the ackee fruit is a major Jamaican export of more than a half a billion dollars a year! The US did not permit ackee imports until 2005 because so many people died from eating unripe ackee. Now Haiti is canning fully ripened fruits and exporting to the American market.

How can a tree with poison fruit be Jamaica's national food? Picked before ripe, ackee contains an alkaloid toxin that blocks the liver from releasing the natural supply of glucose to your body. We use glucose or blood sugar constantly for energy and maintaining body functions. Every few hours our body needs another burst of natural sugar to keep our blood sugar normal.

The illness resulting from eating bad ackee is known as the 'vomiting sickness of Jamaica'. About two hours after eating unripe ackee fruit nausea begins followed by vomiting, dizziness, fever, convulsions, coma, and even death. This is caused by the lack of blood sugar or hypoglycemia, which can be corrected by an IV of glucose. Most cases of poisoning are young children of very poor families.

Ackee grows throughout the Caribbean, and Central and South America as an ornamental, but only Jamaica considers it an edible fruit. Ackee could make an excellent backyard tree to shade your hammock. It is a tropical evergreen, which will grow in most well drained soils and loves plenty of sun. Leave plenty of space as it gets to thirty feet both high and wide. The pale green blossoms have a nice aroma. To me, the fruit resembles a cashew. As the ackee ripens it becomes red or orange. Mature fruit split open to reveal three black seeds in a creamy flesh. A good sized ackee is about a half pound.

Please don't be frightened away from this fruit. When properly prepared, the ackee is delicious, rich in vitamin A, zinc, iron, potassium, and calcium. A good sized fruit usually has a hundred and fifty calories. Ackee provides enough protein that it can be the center of a meal. It can be consumed fresh, baked, boiled in milk, or in soup. They are absolutely delicious fried with onions, tomatoes, peppers, and saltfish. Ackee can be cooked with fish pork, or chicken. If you have your own tree it will be free.

When you buy fresh ackee, take the ackee out of the skin, remove the black seeds, and with a small knife remove the little pinkish - purple string membrane. This is the poisonous part of the ackee. Always drain the ackee after boiling. If you are timid, buy canned ackee.

Ackee Cheesecake

Ingredients: The filling—a half dozen ripe ackee chopped small, a quart of French vanilla ice cream, two packages of cream cheese softened, eight whole eggs

The shell: an eight ounce package of vanilla wafers or graham crackers smashed into small crumbs, a quarter pound of soft butter

Method: Mix softened butter and biscuit crumbs. Press mixture evenly into a suitable pie pan. Combine sugar and cream cheese, add eggs and ice cream. Then mix in the chopped ackee. Pour this over the crushed crackers and bake at 350 for half an hour. Remove from oven, allow to cool before freezing. Serve direct from the freezer.

Simple Ackee and Saltfish

Ingredients: ten ackees cleaned and boiled, one onion chopped, one sweet pepper chopped, four tomatoes diced, two stalks of celery chopped, two cloves of garlic minced, one sprig of thyme, one hot pepper seeded and minced, one TS curry powder, two TBS cooking oil, one pound of saltfish washed, boiled, and flaked apart

Method: In a large frying pan heat oil. Add curry, onion, thyme, and garlic stirring constantly. Then mix in remaining vegetables. Add the ackee last. Keep stirring and add saltfish. Cook covered for two minutes. Add dumplings, ochro, or plantain pieces if desired.

Ackee with Ochro

Ingredients: twelve ackee cleaned, eight okra chopped (best if left to dry a few hours in the sun before preparation begins), one onion chopped, two medium tomatoes chopped, one bunch chives chopped, one sprig of thyme, one hot pepper seeded and minced, one clove of garlic minced, one TS oregano, salt to taste, four TBS cooking oil.

When cleaned put the ackee in a pot with water and salt and boil it for ten minutes until the ackee is almost soft. In another pot add the oil and sauté the onion, tomato, okra, garlic, chives and hot pepper. Add about two tablespoons of water and the remaining ingredients. Cook until okra is tender. Add ackee to the vegetables and simmer stirring for two minutes.

Ackee Soup

Ingredients: four cups of cleaned boiled ackee, two cups chicken broth or vegetable stock, two large tomatoes cubed, one bunch chives chopped, one medium onion chopped, one clove garlic minced, one half hot pepper seeded and minced (optional), salt to taste

Method: In a pot combine ackees, chicken broth, and all ingredients. Simmer half an hour.

HEALTH NOTE

The fruit of the ackee is not edible. Only the fleshy arils around the seeds are edible. The remainder of the fruit, including the seeds are POISONOUS. This fruit should be picked only after the fruit has opened naturally. The ackee cannot be overripe. Immature and overripe ackee are also POISONOUS!

A society grows great when old men plant trees whose shade they know they shall never sit in.

Old Greek proverb

AVOCADO - ZABOCA

A firm sliced avocado (or zaboca) alone or with fish or chicken on a sandwich with salt and slight pepper is a personal favorite. Avocado is a very nutritional tree fruit, an elder member of the laurel family that has been growing in Central and South America an estimated ten thousand years. Spanish explorers rediscovered the tree with long, egg shaped leaves and greenish flowers without petals. It's name, avocado, is derived from the Spanish aguacate, but originally was known in the Mexican Aztec word, ahuacatl, which translates as 'testicle tree'. Branch grafting has been the best method of cultivating this type of tree since the beginning of the twentieth century. Now avocados are grown throughout the world in temperate and tropical climates.

The fruit can be round or oval, with green, purple, or black skin. Avocados are usually one to two pounds, but can grow to double that size. The fruits' flesh is yellowish green around a single large seed. Avocados provide vitamin A, thiamine, and riboflavin. They contain the most protein of any fruit and more potassium than a banana.

Avocado trees are usually bought at nurseries. They grow to sixty feet with a spread of twenty feet, so they need ample space. A nice project for a young person or a newlywed couple is to sprout your own tree from seed. Select a seed from a specific tree; a purple Pollock avocado is my favorite. Use the fruit, saving the seed. In a glass or cup of water, suspend the seed by toothpicks so only half of the seed is submersed. Watch as the seed sprouts roots.

Transplant the seed when the roots are about two inches long to a plant pot with soft soil and keep it moist. Increase pot size as the tree grows and plant in a well worked two by two foot hole when it is two years old or thirty inches tall. Avocado trees need well drained soil and scheduled watering especially in the dry months. Monthly broadcast a half cup of 12-24-12 for excellent root development. Once the tree blossoms broadcast a cup of 12-12-17-2 every other month, To keep the tree short – cut the top when it reaches about twenty feet, best done during the full moon. This will cause the tree to spread out and make picking this delicate fruit easier.

This fruit bruise easily, sit it should not hit the ground. A pole picker or 'kali'-a stiff wire hoop with a net - both knocks the fruit loose and catches it. Another method is for the picker to climb and throw or drop the fruits to a catcher with a large net usually made of a feed bag and two long straight branches, one for each hand.

Although high in calories, eating avocado is good for the heart. They contain oleic acid, which helps lower cholesterol, potassium to lower blood pressure, and folate to lower the risk of heart attacks. One cup of avocado has 236 calories, but is also rich in vitamin K, B-6, C, and copper. Avocado contains a high percentage of lutein, an important nutrient for healthy eyes.

Avocados are used in salads, spread on sandwiches, and in soups. The most common use of avocado is 'guacamole', where the soft fruit is blended with various spices and used as a spread or as a dip.

DID YOU KNOW?

Avocado is also called the 'alligator pear' because of its skin texture and pear shape. One tree can produce between 150 and 500 avocados per year. The average avocado contains 300 calories and 30 grams of healthy polyunsaturated and monounsaturated fat. Second only to the olive, the avocado is comprised of about a quarter of oil. Mexico produces the most avocados, with California coming in second with 7,000 avocado groves. The Dominican Republic, Brazil, and Colombia also are top avocado producers. Once picked, an avocado takes at least a week to fully ripen. The refrigerator will slow ripening, but putting it in a paper bag with a ripe apple will speed up the process. Avocado's botanical name is *persea americana*.

Hot Scorpion Guacamole

Ingredients: two ripe avocados, half cup tofu, half an onion chopped fine, one clove of garlic minced, one TBS lemon juice, one TS English Sauce (Worcestershire), one hot pepper seeded and minced, juice of one lemon or lime, salt to taste

Method: Blend tofu with a blender in a food processor or blender until smooth and then mash avocados. Mix together all ingredients. Place in covered bowl and the lemon juioce should prevent darkening. Chill and serve.

Chilled Avocado Oyster Soup

Ingredients: two ripe avocados, juice of one lemon and one lime, half bunch chadon benee, two cups chicken broth, half TS English Sauce (Worcestershire), salt and pepper to taste, two dozen nice sized, well cleaned oysters

Method: Peel seeded avocados and then mix with all ingredients except the oysters in a blender. Add oysters to the mix, chill the soup and serve. Serves four.

Fettuccine Pasta with Walnuts and Avocados

Ingredients: two TBS oil (olive or canola preferred), half cup firm tomato diced, quarter cup wine vinegar, two TBS chopped walnuts, half cup fresh or dried basil, one avocado diced, two TBS chives chopped, one pound dried fettuccine noodles, quarter cup sweet pepper diced, half hot pepper seeded and minced (optional), and salt to taste.

Method: Cook the fettuccine pasta for three minutes and drain. In a large bowl combine all other ingredients with half the avocado. Combine with hot noodles and top with remaining diced avocado. Serve while the noodles are warm as a dinner entre' or chill for a salad.

Avocado - Banana Bread

Ingredients: one ripe avocado-peeled and seeded, half cup rolled oats, one cup all purpose flour, one TS each baking powder and baking soda, half TS salt, one TS cinnamon, quarter cup oil-canola preferred, one cup brown sugar, two eggs, two very ripe bananas, half cup chopped walnuts, almonds, or cashews, quarter cup sour cream

Method: In a large bowl mash the avocado. Add oil and brown sugar and mix –preferably with an electric mixer but a whisk will do – until creamy. Beat the eggs one at a time into the mixture. Add nuts and peeled bananas. Combine all dry ingredients in another bowl - oats, flour, baking powder, baking soda, salt and cinnamon – and add to avocado mixture. Stir in sour cream. Pour mixture into a greased nine inch loaf pan and bake at 350 for one hour and fifteen minutes. Do the toothpick or knife test to see if the center is fully baked.

HEALTH NOTE

Avocados are excellent for moisturizing and nourishing mature skin. This fruit will help prevent wrinkles when used as a mask. Avocados contain at least 14 minerals with vitamins A and E essential for skincare as we get age. Gently scrub your face before applying the avocado mask. Combine half a good sized avocado with one egg yolk and a tablespoon of honey preferably in a blender. Apply mixture immediately to your face, neck, shoulders and hands. Relax in a cool, shaded place with the mask for half an hour. Rinse with warm water and apply a moisturizer.

Green fingers are the extension of a verdant heart.
Russell Page

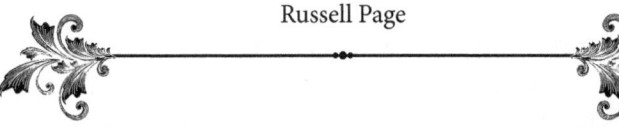

BALATA

We Trinis know the balata by its tasty, sweet fruit with too little flesh, and too much seed. However, this tree is famous elsewhere for its wood. In its native Puerto Rico, balata (or ausubo as it is know in PR) is that island's most valued tree for lumber. From research it seems the tree is called the ausubo, and the fruit ausubo fruit. Balata's botanical name is manilkara bidentata. Only the sap is known as balata. Puerto Rican balata trees have reached four hundred years. That age is relatively incredible since strong storms, floods, and hurricanes often hit Puerto Rico. That is possible because the balata tree is a slow grower, very tolerant of shade especially in the rain forest. This develops strong, deep roots that can withstand powerful winds. Since it grows so slowly, it is often consumed by grazing animals or wild fires.

Balata trees are plentiful throughout the Caribbean chain, northern South America, Brazil, Peru, and Mexico. This tree is best grown from the seeds, and we balata lovers know how many seeds are in one fruiting season. Be very patient as the seeds may take a year to sprout. It grows well in all types of soil, hillsides, floodplains, or along the sea. Balata only requires adequately drained soil. We found the biggest and juiciest balata variety along Trinidad's northern range.

First and foremost, if you plan to grow a balata tree make certain you have enough space. These trees grow to more than seventy feet and about thirty feet in diameter. Once the tree is three years old give it starter fertilizer (12-24-12) mixed equally with calcium nitrate at one cup every three months. Balata grows slow, but needs water so irrigate monthly in the dry season. Wrap the trunk with aluminum foil so the whip string of a bushwhacker can't damage it.

The main use of the tree outside Trinidad is as commercial wood. Balata timber is used for railroad ties under the rails, heavy construction, furniture, and even pool cues. This wood can be bent in a steam box for boat frames and other curved pieces. Balata resembles mahogany and is resistant to the dry wood termites because the wood is deadly poisonous. If working with balata lumber be sure to wear a dust mask.

Mature trees are tapped for balata gum, which is similar to gutta-percha, a not very elastic rubber. Sap has been harvested from some trees for more than two decades. Originally the latex was thickened by fire or dried in the sun, and souvenirs or novelties were fabricated. Now the latex is used for a non-elastic rubber needed for golf-ball skins, and machine belts. It is very waterproof and excellent for insulating underwater and underground electric cables and connections. Legends report the sap is so creamy it could be substituted for cow's milk. However, over indulging the sap will 'bind' you.

The delicious fruits are most often eaten fresh. A hundred grams of balatas, about a big handful, have sixty-two calories with two and a half grams of protein and ten grams of fat.

Balata Ice

Work a quantity of balata fruits through a mesh strainer or a colander into a bowl to catch the juice. Put about six ice cubes in a blender with the juice, a literal pinch of cinnamon and nutmeg. Put the blender on chop until you gain the correct consistency for a snow cone. Be certain your blender is able to chop ice.

Balata Sherbert

Ingredients: juice from five pounds of balata fruits, half can sweetened condensed milk, one package unflavored gelatin, three cups water.

> ## DID YOU KNOW?
> Balata translates to 'sap' in Spanish.
>
> It is also called the 'cow tree' because of its latex sap. This may be folk lore. The sap from some of the species can be used to substitute cow's milk. The latex has the consistency and taste of cream, but overindulgence in it can result in severe constipation.
>
> Balatá was often used in the production of high-quality golf balls.
>
> Balata is the tree Manikara bidentata and it produces a natural non elastic rubber obtained from the latex sap.
>
> Some trees have been tapped for sap for more than 25 years.
>
> It is often called 'bulletwood' since it is extremely hard. Balata wood is so dense it does not float in water. It must be pre drilled to drive nail.

Method: Juice the balata fruit by forcing it through a mesh strainer and collect the juice in a bowl. You need at least two cups of juice. In a pot on low, heat the water while stirring in the powdered gelatin. Stir in the milk. Once this is thoroughly mixed add the balata juice. Mix well. Allow to cool on the kitchen counter covered. Put in a covered container and freeze. After about three hours remove from freezer and blend to break up the ice crystals. Refreeze. This can also be made without milk as a tasty sorbet.

DID YOU KNOW?

The balata is a true rainforest tree. It is very tall, spreading when mature. Its long life is due to excellent root development and tolerance of shade. This enables balata trees to exist for three to four centuries. Inexperienced, and perhaps greedy foresters can kill this tree by slashing its bark to obtain sap. Some actually cut down the tree to obtain the latex.

BANANAS

Bananas aren't trees, fruits, or vegetables, but a flower, part of the palm and lily family. Bananas grow the tallest of any flower on earth, some varieties to 40 feet, without a woody stem. Researchers believe bananas originated in Malaysia. India has cultivated the banana for at least 4,000 years. The earliest written reference is a Sanskrit text from around 600 BC. Alexander the Great discovered bananas in his conquest of India in 327 B.C. Nomadic Arabs cameled bananas to Palestine, Egypt, and Africa. The word 'banana' is derived from the Arabic word 'banan' meaning 'finger'. During the Crusades of the Middle Ages, both Moslems and Christians believed the banana was the forbidden fruit of paradise.

The Portuguese discovered bananas on the Atlantic coast of Africa and carried them to the Canary Islands. From there in 1516, a Spanish missionary, Friar Tomas de Berlanga, carried the plants to tropical parts of the Western Hemisphere. Since bananas multiply quickly, it became an essential food in many parts of the world. Bananas reached the United States from Cuba in 1804. At the cost of one tenth of a dollar, foil wrapped bananas were the hit of the Philadelphia Centennial Exhibition in 1876.

Bananas not only taste good, but also are a healthy, quick energy food packed with vitamins, two grams of protein, and four grams of fiber. Bananas are rich in potassium, vitamins A, C, and the B complex. One banana is about 99.5% fat free with usually 90 calories comprised of 75% water, 20% starch and 1% sugar. Compared to apples, bananas have less water, fifty percent more food energy, four times the protein, half the fat, twice the carbohydrate, almost three times the phosphorus, nearly five times the vitamin A and iron, and at least twice the other vitamins and minerals as in an apple.

Although there are approximately 500 species of bananas, only 20 varieties are commercially cultivated. There are two main varieties of bananas, the sweet banana and the plantain. The fruit banana is eaten raw while the plantain is usually cooked. Plantains have lower water content, making them drier and starchier than fruit bananas. Trinidad grows silk fig, Gros Michelle, pink and white mataborro, French, giant, and horse plantain, sucrier, giant fig, long fig, lacatang, mysore, governor, and moka.

Bananas thrive in the hot tropics, with an average a humid 80 degrees Fahrenheit (27 degrees Celsius), and a minimum of 3 1/2 inches (75 mm) of rainfall a month. Brazil, China, India, and Thailand grow them as a local food source and export very few. The major exporters include Ecuador, Costa Rica, Colombia, Honduras, the Philippines,

Panama, and Guatemala. Surprisingly, 80% of the bananas grown throughout the world are of the plantain or cooking variety. Trinidad imports a million kilograms of bananas a year at a cost of $2.8 million TTD, while exporting only twenty-seven thousand kilos for fifty thousand TTD.

All varieties of bananas require rich soil with good drainage. Bananas do not grow simply from seed. Farmers start a crop by cutting growths (suckers, slips, pups, or ratoons) from the underground stems of mature banana plants. These suckers are replanted and sprout three to four weeks later. In about nine months the plants mature to a height of about 15 to 30 feet. A 16 – 8 – 24 fertilizer mix is excellent for bananas and plantains. When the banana bears fruit a large bud rises from center of the bundle of leaves. The bud consists of small purple leaves called bracts. As the stem grows, the purple pulls back to reveal clusters of small flowers, which become tiny green bananas. Exactly how bananas ripen is a scientific mystery. Little bananas grow downward. Double rows develop vertically around the stem. As the sun ripens, they begin to turn upward against the natural force of gravity!

Bananas ripen three months after flowering. Harvested too early, instead of a sweet flavor, you get a floury pulp. Every bunch has many 'hands' or rows of bananas; while each bunch will yield about 200 'fingers', or individual bananas. An average bunch of bananas can weigh between 80 and 125 pounds (35 to 50 kilograms). Bananas are not just green and yellow; some bananas, like the mataburro, are red. Banana's botanical name is *musa paradisiacal*.

A banana's skin indicates the degree of ripeness. Green bananas can used in soups and stews. When green bananas turn yellow, the starch becomes sugar. Partially ripe, yellow with green tips, may be broiled, baked, or fried. Ripe, all yellow, are eaten raw or in puddings, cakes, or pies. Full-ripe yellow with brown freckles again may be raw. Over ripe, all brown, are still good if the flesh is firm. When they are the color you need, bananas can be refrigerated.

Banana Ice Cream

Makes a quart overnight.

Ingredients: Four or more ripe bananas, two TBS coconut (either grated or powder), quarter cup milk, quarter cup of sweetened condensed milk.

Method: Mash bananas with a fork and mix everything together in a small pot. Slowly bring to a boil while continuously stirring. Once cooled, pour into suitable freezing containers. Reusable ice cream containers are perfect. Add sliced bananas and nuts if desired. Freeze. Check after a few hours and whip again with a fork. This will remove most of the ice crystals. Freeze solid.

Banana Bread

Ingredients: two cups all-purpose flour, two TBS baking powder, one quarter TS soda, three quarter TS salt, one third cup shortening, two thirds cup sugar, two eggs, one cup mashed, very ripe bananas

Method: Blend flour with baking powder, soda, and salt. Cream shortening and sugar until light and. Add eggs one at a time and beat well after each addition. Add bananas and mix. It will be easier to add the flour in four portions and beat until smooth after adding each portion. Turn into well-greased pan (8x4x2-1/2 inches) and bake in moderate oven (350 degrees F) for 50 minutes, or until bread tests done in the center with a knife or toothpick. Cool on rack before slicing. Yield: 1 loaf

Vegetable and Banana Bake

Ingredients: two carrots, two green bananas, ten mushrooms (optional), one medium onion, one sweet green pepper, (optional one christophene, cucumber, or any other veggie you like), one cup water, four slices stale or toasted bread crumbled, spices to taste - perhaps curry, or oregano and basil, or garlic (tomatoes, nuts – add what you like)

Method: Chop vegetables and mix together with the water and spices and place into baking dish. Cover with breadcrumbs and bake at 350 for 35 minutes. Add meat, fish – fresh or salted, or cheese if desired to make this a one dish main course.

Banana Fritters

Ingredients: one and a half cups flour, one TS baking powder, quarter TS baking soda, quarter TS salt, three quarters cup water, four firm bananas, five cups vegetable oil (for frying)

Method: In a large bowl combine one cup of flour, baking powder, soda and salt. Gradually blend in the water and beat with whisk until smooth. Cut each banana crosswise into 3 pieces. You should have 12 pieces altogether. Coat bananas with remaining half cup of flour. Heat oil in a large skillet over high heat. Dip banana pieces in flour water mixture, coating well. Cook 4-6 pieces at a time until golden brown, about 3-5 minutes. Drain on paper towels.

HEALTH NOTE

The New England Journal of Medicine reported a banana a day can decrease the risk of death from strokes by as much as forty percent in certain cases. Bananas have many medicinal uses. Because they are very high in iron they are great for treating anemia. The high potassium and low salt help reduce blood pressure. The high fiber can overcome constipation. Bananas naturally contain tryptophan, which the body converts into serotonin – known to improve your mood and generally make you feel happier, fighting depression. The banana neutralizes burning stomach acid.

BREADFRUIT

Breadfruit originated in the Micronesia area of the Pacific Ocean. It is the fruit of a beautiful tree that grows to a hundred feet. The Caribbean's mix of ethnic populations appreciates both the seeded and seedless varieties. The tree acquired its name because explorers found the fruit could be eaten before it is ripe; tasting and feeling like fresh bread. Polynesian sailors spread the fruit far and wide, bringing it to Hawaii around 1100 AD. European explorers first encountered breadfruit about 1600 and quickly realized its nutritional value to cost effectively feed the enslaved labor. Breadfruit's botanical name is *artocarpus altilis* of the mulberry family.

Although credit for the breadfruit trees in the Caribbean is given to the famous Captain Bligh; a French sailor, Sonnerat, first brought seeds from the Philippines to Martinique in 1772. Bligh failed on his first attempt to carry a thousand breadfruit trees from Tahiti in 1787. Six years later, Bligh delivered two thousand trees of five different types to Jamaica. The real cause of the famous Mutiny on the HMS Bounty wasn't just the beautiful Tahitian women, but breadfruit! The sailors didn't enjoy the thought of living thirsty while the breadfruit trees got watered. After all the problems, when the trees finally reached the Caribbean Islands the slaves didn't like the taste and refused to consume it! It took decades until their descendants learned delicious recipes, and now appreciate the breadfruit.

Breadfruit needs space to grow and deep fertile well drained soil. However breadfruit has adapted to various climate and soil conditions throughout the world. Some Pacific island varieties grow along rivers while others thrive on sandy coral soils. One variety is tolerant of the salty seawater environment. Transplant a sucker of the seedless breadfruit variety. It should be partially shaded and watered daily. These sucker trees should bear fruit in about five years. Mealy bugs and ants are enemies of these trees. Breadfruit is fragile and easily bruised. The fruit must be used within a week of picking. One means of preserving is to keep excess fruit underwater until they are desired. All parts of the breadfruit tree including the fruit are rich in milky latex. Jamaicans partially roast their breadfruit to congeal or thicken the latex for export markets.

Breadfruit may be consumed before it ripens. Generally unripe fruits are green, turning yellowish green as it ripens. When it is fully ripe the fruit is a yellow brown. Unripe breadfruit can be chunked and boiled with seasonings and other vegetables as a type of chowder. Breadfruit can be steamed, boiled, roasted, or fried. Ripe fruits may be quartered and steamed with seasonings or it may be rolled in flour and fried. The pulp from ripe breadfruits can be mixed with coconut milk, salt and sugar to create a pudding. In Barbados, breadfruit has been dried and made into flour as a substitute for wheat. Soft overripe fruit is best for frying as chips.

Nutritionally a breadfruit has about a hundred calories of which two grams are protein with less than one gram of fat. It has twenty-five grams of carbs. Breadfruit is a good source of Vitamin B and there is more Vitamin C in the riper fruits. It contains calcium, phosphorus and iron.

Simple Breadfruit Dessert

Ingredients: one well ripened breadfruit mashed, two TBS butter, two eggs beaten, quarter cup brown sugar, spices as cinnamon, nutmeg, and cloves to your taste, two TBS brandy (optional)

Method: Boil all ingredients and blend well. Serve warm or cold.

Two-Day Breadfruit Chips

Ingredients: one green breadfruit, ice cubes, vegetable oil for frying, salt and spices to taste

Method: Scrub, peel and core the fruit. Put pieces in ice water in the fridge overnight. Slice breadfruit pieces as thin as possible and replace in ice water. Heat the oil and fry until golden brown. Drain and spice as you like it.

Candied Breadfruit

Ingredients: one large ripe breadfruit, one cup water, one TS canola oil, half cup brown sugar, four TBS butter or margarine, quarter cup lemon juice

Method: Peel breadfruit and simmer one hour in a pot with water. Slice the fruit in half, core it, and slice half inch thick. Grease a baking dish with the canola oil. Place the slices in layers coating each layer with sugar, butter, and lemon juice. Place in a 350-degree oven for half an hour.

Breadfruit Tuna Cakes

Ingredients: half a soft breadfruit, cooked and mashed, one pound fresh tuna or two cans, one beaten egg, one large chopped onion, two cloves of garlic minced, salt and spice to taste, one cup bread crumbs, and oil for frying.

Method: Mix all ingredients (except the oil and breadcrumbs) into ten four inch cakes. Dip in breadcrumbs and fry until light brown on both sides.

Baked Stuffed Breadfruit

Ingredients: one whole breadfruit, one pound minced beef, chicken, or fish, one large onion chopped, one tomato chopped, two cloves garlic minced, one bunch chives, one TBS butter or margarine, salt and spices to taste

Method: Boil the breadfruit for ten minutes in salted water. It will not be fully cooked. Fry onions, garlic, chives, and minced meat, then add tomato and spices. Peel and core the breadfruit. Then stuff the fruit with the minced meat mixture. Brush the outside of the fruit with butter or canola oil. Bake in a 350-degree oven for forty minutes. Every ten minutes brush the fruit with butter or oil. Serve hot.

Cheesey Breadfruit

Ingredients: one breadfruit, peeled, cored, and chunked, quarter cup butter or margarine, two onions chopped small, one clove garlic minced, two cups whole milk, two TBS flour, one cup cheddar cheese grated or sliced very thin, half a hot pepper seeded and minced (optional), salt to taste

Method: Cook breadfruit chunks in salted water until tender. In a skillet heat the butter and sauté the onions and then add the minced garlic. Add flour and milk stirring constantly. Remove from heat and place breadfruit chunks in an oven proof dish or pan. Add milk/onion/flour mixture. Stir in the grated cheese and minced hot pepper. Bake for half an hour at 350. Serve hot or cold.

DID YOU KNOW?

Botanists classify breadfruit as a vegetable and it is related to the fig. In the St. Vincent Botanical Gardens there still exists a breadfruit tree planted by Captain Bligh. Not only are Pacific breadfruit trees prized for their fruits, but the wood is also highly valued. In Hawaii, the first long surfboards were made from breadfruit wood. It was also used to produce canoes, and drums. In the Pacific islands of Guam and Samoa, the bark of the breadfruit trees was pounded and used for making tapa cloth. A decoction of breadfruit leaves is believed to lower blood pressure, and is also said to relieve asthma. The leaf juice is employed as ear-drops. Ashes of burned leaves are used on skin infections.

Everything that slows us down and forces patience,
everything that sets us back into the slow circles of nature, is a help.
Gardening is an instrument of grace.

May Sarton

CAIMATE

The caimate is another unique tropical fruit grown throughout the Caribbean. As kids our mouths were often sticky when the caimates were ripe. The green or purple fruit has a soft sweet, milky pulp with flat seeds. It is also called the West Indian star apple because when cut, the seed groups radiate from the core like a many-pointed star. The skin shouldn't be eaten; enjoy the pulp only after cutting this fruit either in half, or better quartered. For the best flavor don't let any of the harsh tasting sap of the skin contact the milky flesh.

Spanish explorers in Peru first recorded caimate in the mid 1500's. It is common on most of the Caribbean Islands and throughout the world's tropical countries. Botanists believe the caimate actually originated in the West Indies. It is a nice tree for the garden as its leaves are two toned with a shiny blue green upper side and a coppery under side. It can be topped and trimmed to stay at about twenty feet tall. Caimates will grow in almost any soil as long as it is well drained. These trees are easy to start from seeds or cuttings from mature trees, but they may take five years to bear. Grafted varieties have been known to bear fruit the first year after being planted. Young caimate trees need regular watering and once a month a half cup of starter 12–24 –12 fertilizer. After the trees blossom use a foliar spray, combined with an insecticide-miticide once a month, and a cup of bearing fertilizer 12-12-17-2. Leave caimates on the tree until they are fully ripe. It is best to pick caimates leaving the stem in the fruit so they keep fresh longer.

Caimate is seldom used as lumber although it is an attractive and durable wood. The bark is rich in tannin used to tan leather, and is thought to fight cancer. A drink made from the boiled bark is used as a stimulant tonic. Cooked caimate is used to reduce a fever. The leaves are grated and applied to cuts to reduce infection. The leaves may be boiled and the resulting liquid drank to combat hypoglycemia.

Caimates are usually eaten fresh, best when chilled, and may also be used as an ingredient of ice cream and sherbet. Caimate mixes extremely well with coconut. A hundred grams of caimate has sixty calories with calcium and phosphorous. In Jamaica the flesh of the caimate is mixed with sour orange or lemon juice and the mixture is called 'matrimony'. The flesh is also combined with regular orange juice, a pinch of sugar, nutmeg, and eaten as a dessert called 'strawberries and cream'. However, too much caimate can cause constipation.

Fruits

Frozen Fruit Mix

Ingredients: the seeded pulp of six caimates, one cup chopped pineapple, two mangos skinned seeded, and chopped, half cup shaved coconut, half cup currants or raisins, half cup shaved almonds, two cups coconut water.

Method: Mix, freeze. After four hours remove and stir or blend again to remove ice crystals. Freeze.

Sticky Rice Pudding

Ingredients: seeded pulp of six caimates, a pinch of cinnamon and nutmeg, one cup milk, two cups cooked rice

Method: Mix all ingredients in a pot. Bring to a boil carefully stirring to avoid sticking and burning. Cool and refrigerate.

Caimate Shakes

Ingredients: seeded pulp of two caimates, one TBS brown sugar, half TS vanilla, ice

Method: Combine ingredients in a blender. The amount of ice and duration of blending will determine the thickness of the shake.

Caimate Chicken

Ingredients: six to eight nice size caimates the riper the better, one chicken—cut up and steamed -fully cooked, four cups cooked rice, two TBS cooking oil, half cup sweet pepper chopped small, two bunches of chives chopped small, two cloves of garlic minced, half cup condensed milk (optional), two TBS chadon benee chopped, salt and spices to taste

Method: Heat in a large frying pan. Simmer sweet pepper, chives, garlic, and caimates until tender, maybe ten minutes. Add condensed milk and seasonings. Continue to simmer and stir so it doesn't stick for another ten minutes. Put chicken and rice in a suitable over proof dish and cover with caimate –milk mixture. Bake at 350 for half an hour.

DID YOU KNOW?

The caimate is also known cainito, caimito, star apple, golden leaf tree, abiaba, pomme du lait, estrella, milk fruit, and milky apple. Caimate's botanical name is chrysophyllum cainito. A caimate's skin contains an unpleasant sticky latex. Do not bite directly into one because the white sappy latex is will make your lips very sticky.

HEALTH NOTE

In addition to having tasty fruits, the caimate has varied uses in bush medicine. A regimen of drinking tea made from the golden leaves steeped in boiling water is believed to cure diabetes, rheumatoid arthritis, and prevents cancer. A tea made from caimate bark is used to alleviate coughs. It is also considered a total physical tonic. All bush remedies must be properly prepared and used in the proper dosage only after consulting a doctor.

In almost every garden, the land is made better and so is the gardener.
Robert Rodale

CANISTEL

The canistel is a rare, delectable tropical fruit often called the egg-fruit, or yellow sapote. This evergreen tree is usually short, seldom higher than eight meters, with fragrant blossoms. I've only enjoyed canistel a few times when I was in the Rio Claro, San Pedro area. Scientists believe that the canistel is native to Mexico's Yucatan area.

Because of its rarity and small size this tree is another good one for the backyard. It will grow in most soils and usually will do well where other citrus trees won't. Canistel can be planted from seeds, but may take four to five months to germinate. Cuttings take long to root. Grafted trees will produce fruit quicker. Combine mulching with a half cup of 12-12-24 fertilizer every other month for the first year to promote root growth. After two years and the tree begins to blossom use a cup of a bearing blend of fertilizer like 12-12-17-2 every four months. Water regularly, especially in the dry season. Canistel trees have few pests, but a regular spray of an insecticide such as Fastac mixed with a foliar spray at two or three month intervals will produce better fruit.

This fruit is usually almost round, but can be slightly oval. As it ripens its smooth, glossy skin turns yellowish. The yellow flesh is firm, but the center is softer and pasty. It has been often likened in texture to the yolk of a hard-boiled egg. The flavor is sweet like a baked sweet potato.

The sweet musky flavor and the unique texture of canistel flesh have turned a few away. It is an individual taste. A hundred grams of canistel has 140 calories, with 35 grams of carbs, one gram of protein and plenty of calcium, phosphorus, iron, niacin, carotene, and vitamin C. Canistels are usually enjoyed raw and plain. Some locals eat them with salt and pepper with a sprinkling of lime juice. I have a friend who slightly cooks them smeared with mayonnaise on a barbecue grill.

DID YOU KNOW?

Canistel's botanical name is Pouteria campechiana. This delicious fruit has many names including egg-fruit, ti-es, yellow sapote, siguapa, zapotillo custiczapotl fruta de huevo, zapote amarillo, kaniste, limoncillo, mamee ciruela, zapotillo de Montana, huevo vegeta, mammee sapota, and many more.

Canistel Smoothie

In a blender mix the skinned, seeded pulp of six canistels with two cups of whole milk, two TBS brown sugar, one TS vanilla extract, half TS cinnamon, and half TS nutmeg. Fill blender with ice cubes and blend.

Canistel Pie

Ingredients: two cups mashed canistel pulp, one half cup sugar or honey, one half TS salt, a quarter TS nutmeg, one TS vanilla, one TS lime juice, two beaten eggs, two cups evaporated milk and one ready- made pie crust.

Method: Blend ingredients and pour into pie crust and bake for one hour at 300° F. Let cool for at least an hour before serving.

Canistel Spread

Ingredients: two cups canistel skinned seedless pulp, one TBS brown sugar, one TS lemon zest (grated lemon peel), and one TS lemon juice.

Method: Mix pulp and sugar in an electric blender. Then cook in a covered pot over medium heat stirring constantly. Add lemon juice and zest. Remove from heat and refrigerate in suitable container. Use for topping on toast, ice cream, or pancakes.

Baked Canistel Custard

Ingredients: two cups mashed canistel pulp, one cup sugar, quarter TS salt, three eggs, one TS vanilla, two cups whole milk

Method: Combine dry ingredients in a small bowl. In a bigger bowl whisk the eggs and add dry mix. Whisk in canistel pulp, milk and vanilla. Pour mixture into a suitable oven baking dish and bake at 350 degrees for forty-five minutes or until firm. Test with a toothpick. Cool and serve.

Canistel Coconut Bread

Ingredients: two cups ripe canistels skinned and mashed - seeds removed, two cups flour, half TS baking soda, half cup soft butter or margarine, one cup sugar, one cup whole milk, half TS vanilla extract, two eggs, one cup grated fresh coconut, a pinch of the following - salt, ground cloves and cinnamon

Method: Combine in a suitable bowl flour, salt, baking soda and spices. In another bowl blend butter and sugar, slowly stirring in the eggs. Whisk in milk, vanilla and canistel before combining with the flour mixture. Finally add the grated coconut. Pour into a greased bread pan and bake at 350 for forty-five minutes. Check with a toothpick before removing from oven. This is best if baked on the center oven rack.

Canistel Chicken Soup

Ingredients: one and a half cups canistel seeded, one package chicken soup mix, one onion chopped small, one clove of garlic minced, one TBS butter or margarine, two cups condensed milk, two cups steamed chicken pieces, two cups of the water the chicken was steamed in, half hot pepper seeded and minced, one bundle chives minced, salt to taste

Method: In a frying pan melt the butter before adding onion and garlic. Fry until onion is tender. Add canistel, milk, chicken, chicken stock, soup mix, chives, pepper and salt. Cook for 15 minutes, stirring constantly.

Baked Canistel

Easy and different.

Cut four fruit in half and scoop out the flesh removing the seeds. In a bowl combine flesh with two TBS onion chopped small. Add half a hot pepper seeded and minced (to taste), one TBS mayonnaise, and one TBS lemon juice. Return mixture to fruit shells and bake in suitable oven ware at 300 for fifteen minutes. Cool and enjoy.

HEALTH NOTE

Almost all parts of canistel trees are used for medicinal properties. The oil from the seeds is used as a hair dressing, thought to prevent hair loss. The seed kernel oil is also used to treat indigestion, ulcers, toothache, eye and ear diseases, and as a skin ointment. The residue remaining after oil extraction is applied to treat painful skin afflictions. A decoction of the bark can also help to heal skin disease, and taken to reduce fever. The leaves are reported to be anti-inflammatory. Fungus infections, as athlete's foot, can be treated by applying the latex.

My garden is my favorite teacher.
Betsy Cañas Garmon

CHALTA - THE ELEPHANT APPLE

Chalta, or chulta, has the botanical name dillenia indica, and is one of the strangest fruits Trinidad has to offer. It is both unique and unattractive, yet tasty. Chalta may be called elephant apple or the wood-apple, monkey fruit, or curd fruit. It is common to India and throughout Southeast Asia, and a favorite fruit of elephants as well as the Hindu God Lord Vinayaka. I learned to pick ripe chlata by climbing the tree and dropping the tough skinned fruit. Ripe elephant apples don't bounce.

Chalta, the elephant apple, is usually four to five inches in diameter, with a hard, woody, light grey skin, a quarter inch thick. The inner brown pulp has a weird grainy texture, with almost a sour smell and plenty of small, whitish seeds. Depending on the ripeness, chalta tastes run from sweet to acidic if too ripe. There seem to be two types of chalta. One has large sweeter fruits; the other has smaller more acidic fruits.

The elephant apple tree prefers full sun or very light shade. It has dark green, toothed, leathery leaves and grows up to 25 feet tall. The elephant apple tree has a standing core reaching up with long drooping branches returning to the earth. The bark is scaly. The flowers of the tree are white to pale red in color and have a distinctive very pleasant odor.

Chalta trees need plenty of rain, but also require a distinct dry season. It grows best in light soils. Trees grown from seeds usually don't bear fruit for ten years or more. Grafted dwarf chalta trees bear within five years. Hearty trees, chalta needs little, only a half cup of starter fertilizer (12-24-12) every other month until the tree bears. A cup of bearing fertilizer (12-12-17-2) twice a year there after.

When picking chalta first check its outer husk. Shake it gently to see whether the fruit has become dislodged, which will indicate it is ripe. When you open the fruit, the pulp should be a rich brown. The skin or husk can be cracked with a hammer. Chalta pulp is a third carbohydrate with a small bit of protein. One fruit has about fifty calories with beta-carotene, thiamine and riboflavin.

This tree has many names other than chalta, which is Bengalese. It is outenga in Assamese, wood-apple, chalita, elephant apple, monkey fruit, curd fruit, bael fruit, matoom, Bengal quince, golden apple, holy fruit, stone apple, velakkaya, and kath bel. In India, chalta is consumed as a tonic for liver and heart. Consumed unripe, it will cure diarrhea and hiccough, sore throat, and gum diseases. A poultice of the pulp is used on insect bites. Dried leaves are used as a sandpaper substitute to polish ivory.

To discern the ripeness of a chalta sniff for a sweet smell. If they are not ripe enough set them in hot sun for a day or two days till they ripen. If these fruit are not ripe the pulp will not come out of the shell when scooped, and it will taste slightly bitter

> **DID YOU KNOW?**
>
> Chalta fruit pulp is also used for glue; mixed with lime and plaster it is used as a sealant; and added to watercolor paints. In the cosmetic industry limonene is extracted from the rind as a rich oil used to scent hair products. The husk makes a yellow dye. The seed pulp is also used as a household glue.

Chalta-Dahl One

Ingredients: a half pound of pigeon-peas, a half dozen chalta slices, three green (not ripe) hot peppers seeded and minced, one whole red congo pepper, one cup water, one TBS mustard powder, three TS mustard oil, one TS ghee or butter, one TS salt, one TS sugar (more to taste), one TS cumin, two bay leaves.

Method: Slice chalta and mash. Boil pigeon peas over medium heat. After a few minutes, add salt, green hot peppers, and sugar - according to taste. After boiling remove surface foam. In a large skillet fry red hot pepper, cumin, mustard, mashed chalta slices, and bay leaves in the ghee/butter. Add water and boil. Pour boiled peas in the mixture. Cook two to three minutes. Remove from heat.

Chalta-Dahl Two

Ingredients: one chalta, three green unripe hot peppers, one TS cumin seeds, one TBS salt, a pinch of powdered turmeric, one TS oil for seasoning, one TS each of urad dahl, sugar, mustard seeds, cumin seeds, channa dahl, fenugreek seeds, and dried red peppers.

Method: Remove chalta pulp. Combine by grinding together pulp with cumin seeds, turmeric, salt, and green peppers to a paste. In a skillet heat the oil and add seasoning ingredients. Add the paste to the seasoning and simmer for two minutes. Serve with rice or sada roti.

Chalta Chutney

Ingredients: one chalta, one half cup brown sugar, three TBS anchar masala, one entire head of garlic minced or grated, one TS salt, two TBS oil, one hot pepper (optional), quarter cup water

Method: Break the shell of the chalta and empty the flesh content into a bowl. Chop chalta into one inch chunks and boil till tender. Heat oil in a frying pan and add garlic, anchar masala, sugar, pepper, and salt and pound. When everything is cooked a few minutes add water and bring to a boil. Add chalta pieces and mix thoroughly. Cover and simmer for about five minutes. Serve warm or cold.

Chalta Sweet

Remove the flesh of four chaltas to a bowl and combine with one cup coconut, half cup grated coconut, a pinch of nutmeg and cinnamon. Add sugar to taste. Blend and drink on ice or freeze to make a sorbet.

HEALTH NOTE

A tea made from chalta leaves helps avoid repeated colds and related respiratory conditions, cures a sore throat and treats chronic coughs. Fifty milligrams of chalta juice mixed with warm water and sugar will assist blood purification. Regular consumption of chalta is recommended for people with kidney problems. Scientists believe an extract of chalta fruits may fight types of human leukemia. Chalta is a high energy food as 100 grams produces a hundred and forty calories, and it benefits digestion. All parts of the chalta tree are used to heal snake bites. Tea made from the flowers is used to cleanse eye infections.

The love of gardening is a seed once sown that never dies.

Gertrude Jekyll

CHATAIGNE - THE GREEN CHESTNUT

Chataigne is a food that really fools you by its appearance, closely resembling its cousin, the always sort of bland breadfruit. Chataigne looks as if a breadfruit received an serious electric shock. The seeds and husk make chataigne a unique flavorful, East Indian wedding dinner delicacy. I grew up with chataigne; my grandfather had five nice trees. This is a dish you seldom find in any restaurant and must be prepared differently depending on this fruits' ripeness.

Researching chataigne was difficult, as I didn't know its recognized name, the breadnut is also a name for the breadfruit. Breadnut is also a tree that existed in Central America and bears one inch fruits, and was cultivated by the pre-Columbian Maya Amerindians. Our chataigne / breadnut botanically is artocarpus camansi. Chataigne in French translates to chestnut, and it is very close to the same tree named chatiagnier of French Guiana. Chataigne-breadnut trees originated in Southeast Asia, probably New Guinea, and believed to be brought to the Caribbean with the breadfruit trees by Captain Bligh in 1793.

Trinidad's chataigne trees are beautiful and eventually grow tall and full. A chataigne tree makes a great addition to any garden or liming area. Find someone that has a healthy tree and check the roots for shoots, or try your luck with seeds. Leave about twenty-foot radius clear and plant this tree where it is well drained, away from septic tanks as the roots will travel.

This tree is also best planted where it doesn't get sunshine the entire day and will get occasional moist soil. Plant in a hole worked about a foot and a half deep. Water weekly during the dry months, and every two months broadcast some 12-24-12 fertilizer. The chataigne shoot can also first be potted and used both indoors and outdoors, treated like a large shrub. A chataigne tree is very adaptable. Given the right conditions the chataigne tree can reach a spreading sixty feet tall.

Chataigne fruit is a bright green pod usually 5 to 8 inches in diameter. Unless picked the seeds -nuts will continue to grow until the fruit bursts open for the birds to enjoy. One ounce has about 100 calories, of which 5% is

DID YOU KNOW?

Chataigne / Breadnut is thought to be the wild ancestor of breadfruit. It is mainly native to New Guinea and possibly the Moluccas and the Philippines. The seeds comprise half the weight of the fruit!

protein, 1% fat, 45% carbs, 17% fiber, with vitamins C, B6, thiamin, folate, and niacin. A tea can be made of the young leaves to lower blood pressure and fight diabetes.

The easiest way to enjoy chatiagne is to buy the seeds already cleaned in the market or from a roadside vendor. Then boil in salted water for about forty minutes. Peel and eat. For something different peel the boiled seeds, chop, and sauté with butter, garlic, and chadon benee. Eat over spring or bow tie pasta.

> **DID YOU KNOW?**
>
> Chatiagne / Breadnut is grown for its seeds; which are a good source of protein and low in fat compared to other nuts such as almond, brazil nut, and macadamia nut. The fat extracted from the seed is a light yellow, viscous liquid at room temperature with a characteristic odor similar to that of peanuts. It has physical properties similar to those of olive oil. Its seeds are a good source of minerals and contain more niacin than most other nuts.

Red Chataigne

Ingredients: one cup chatiagne seeds - boiled, peeled, and chopped, one cup onion chopped small, two cloves garlic minced, three cups tomatoes chopped, two cups cooked channa, one hot pepper seeded and chopped small, one bunch chadon benee chopped small, one TS lemon juice, one TBS oil peanut preferred, one TBS garam masala, quarter TS more or less of each of the following - depending on your taste - cumin, mustard seeds, turmeric, and salt

Method: In a large frying pan heat the oil, with the cumin and mustard seeds until they start to pop open. Add the onion and fry till brown. Add the chopped tomatoes and simmer until it becomes a thin paste. Add chadon benee, pepper, chatiagne, the channa, with the garam massala, the other spices, and two cups water. Amount of water depends on the consistency you desire, less for thick, more for thin. Simmer for a half an hour. Serve with rice or roti. For an Italian flavor to this dish use olive oil and substitute oregano, basil, and thyme for the herbs, and add more garlic. Eat over pasta.

Tanty's Chataigne

Ingredients: one good size chataigne, one cup coconut milk, one half medium onion chopped, four cloves garlic minced, two TBS oil, one TBS curry powder, one half TS anchar masala, one half TS roasted geera/cumin, one half TS salt

Method: Half chataigne, remove core, cut into one-inch strips, and peel. Remove seeds and peel them. Strip the surrounding husk into thin pieces. Wash and set aside. In a good sized pot heat the oil, add curry powder and anchar masala. As the powder starts to sizzle add a half cup of water and stir until it thickens. Add garlic and onions, and simmer until it becomes a thin paste. Add chataigne husk, seeds, and salt. Lower heat and cover. Cook until mixture just begins to stick. Add coconut milk with one cup of water and increase heat until it boils. Reduce heat and cover. Simmer for half an hour till the seeds are soft. Cook off all extra liquid. Add geera/cumin and cook 5 more minutes. Cool and serve.

CHENETS - GENIPS

Come on, admit it, you can't wait for the chenets to ripen. Sucking on these unique tasty fruits always returns you to pleasant memories of your childhood days. They look like a lime, yet grow in bunches like cherries or plums. Inside the fruit's leathery skin is a pinkish pulp that is succulent and tasty, like pink lemonade. The fruit is almost all seed, yet only a few know these seeds can be roasted and eaten like nuts.

This fruit is related to the lychee and classed as a drupe. A genip - chenet fruit has a tight and thin, yet rigid layer of skin that experienced eaters crack with their teeth. Inside the skin is the tart and tangy, but creamy fruit pulp. It is sucked by putting the whole fruit inside the mouth. The fruits seed is big so the flesh layer is only about a quarter inch thick. Be careful to lean forward when you are indulging in genips as the juice stains a dark brown color.

This fruit is usually started from cuttings. First find the one tree that produces the biggest fruit. Some chenets are as small as three quarters of an inch while others are an inch and a half wide. Snip about three or four young branch tips and dip in a rooting compound. This will 'almost' guarantee your tree will bear fruit like its parent. Plant in the soil at a place where it can spread to a thirty foot dianeter. The area needs to drain off water during the rainy season. Keep the weeds pulled from around this young tree. Water during dry spells. Chenet trees will become large, up to seventy feet tall and forty feet wide, if not topped and pruned. Use a half cup of starter 12-24-12 fertilizer every other month until the tree is about three years old. Then apply a cup of bearing fertilizer 12-12-17-2 every other month. Once it starts to flower increase the fertilizer to every month.

DID YOU KNOW?

This fruit has a variety of names common to various cultures and locales. Its botanical name is melicoccus bijugatus. It is known as mamoncillo chenet, chenettes, gnep, ginep, genip, guinep, kinnip, quenepa, Spanish lime, or limoncillo. This tree's leaves when spread on a floor of a stable or fowl pen are reputed to attract and kill flies.

The chenet is botanically *melicoccus bijugatus* and native to the Western Hemisphere. It seems chenets grow everywhere in the Caribbean and everyone calls them a different name; Spanish limes, limoncillos, genips, and mamoncillo among others.

For the few who have never

experienced the joy of eating a chenet, the skin is cracked opened and the pulp-coated seed is popped into your mouth. The delightful juice is sucked from the pulp until there is nothing left of it except the seed. Be careful and don't choke on a seed! Chenet juice stains clothes, so eat neat.

If you are lucky to find a tree with extra large chenets, you can scrape the pulp from the seeds to make marmalade or jelly, but this is a lot of scraping. Peeled fruits can be boiled and juice is a fantastic cold drink and especially for daiquiris. Colombia and Venezuela sell canned chenet juice.

According to Caribbean tales, girls learn the art of kissing by eating the sweet flesh of this fruit. Chenets have about sixty calories per quarter pound with some calcium, phosphorus and iron. One hundred grams of chenets has sixty calories with some calcium, iron and niacin.

Kiss of the sun for pardon. Song of the birds for mirth. You're closer to God's heart in the garden than any place else on earth.
Dorothy Frances Gurney

Kicking Genip Sherbert

Ingredients: two cups genip/chenet juice (probably will take about three gallons of genips!), four TBS ginger water, one package unflavored gelatin, two TBS rum (optional), one cup ginger beer, one egg white

Method: Wash ginger root and slice thin. Put in a small pot and add just enough water to cover pieces and boil for five minutes. In a bowl add one TBS genip juice to unflavored gelatin before adding the hot ginger water. Combine and whisk all ingredients except egg white. Put into a suitable container and put in freezer until it just starts to freeze. Blend and add egg white. Fully freeze in a sealed container.

Genip Water

Perfect for a hot afternoon.

Peel a pound of genips, avoid staining any clothes with the juice. Put in a large pitcher and let sit for an hour in the shade. Pour into ice filled glasses. Add sugar as desired. This raw unsweetened juice will curb your thirst and cool you off.

HEALTH NOTE

In Venezuela, roasted chenet seeds are smashed, combined with honey to curb diarrhea. An astringent decoction of chenet leaves is taken as an enema for intestinal complaints.

CUSTARD APPLE

Once a year I beg my north coast friend, Bam Bam, for a few of the delicious custard apples that grow near his new house. This year he gave me a newly sprouted tree. To me, spooning into a chilled custard apple is a true delight of nature. It is a heart shaped fruit, usually yellow-tan with edges of pinkish brown. The mild, creamy insides are as close to real custard as Mother Nature can make. A really sweet apple feels like it has hard sugar inside because the creamy flesh crunches as you eat it.

I've seen only a few trees that are wide with large leaves, usually about twenty feet tall. The leaves hang over the delicate fruit to protect it from burning in the tropical sun. The pale yellowish slightly fragrant blossoms hang in clusters, but never seem to fully open. This fruit is usually about four inches in diameter and irregular shaped like a heart, almost round or oval with a depression at the base. The skin is thin, but tough. It can be yellowish brown with a brownish-red tint when ripe. The custard apples usually have more than fifty seeds, but there are varieties that have a single seed or as many as seventy. It has a thick, white creamy, somewhat grainy flesh. The flavor is sweet and agreeable though without the sugary sweetness of the cherimoya, sugar apple.

Scientists believe the custard apple originated in the Caribbean before explorers carried the seeds throughout the tropical world. Custard apple's botanical name is *annona cherimola*.

A custard apple tree grows from seeds or from grafts. These trees grow best in rich soil especially along rivers. It matures quickly especially if it is mulched, fertilized, and watered regularly. The first two years use a starter-rooting fertilizer mix such as 12-24-12, a half cup bi monthly. After blossoming begins, use the same amount, but switch to a bearing fertilizer mix as 12-12-17-2. Prune to shape the tree to your yard. The chalcid fly is the custard apple's insect enemy. Spray monthly with an insecticide as Fastac or Pestac combined with a soluble foliar fertilizer. Bats also will damage these fruits.

DID YOU KNOW?

Custard apples are also called cherimoyas, bullock's heart, or bull's heart; all due to its shape and reddish tint. The skin color is reflected in the Bolivian name, chirimoya roia. This fruit is juicy with a creamy white flesh and large, black seeds, and tastes like a combination of pineapple, mango, papaya, and vanilla.

Crushed leaves or a paste of the fruit's flesh may be applied to boils, abscesses, and ulcers. The bark is very astringent and when boiled in water, it is drunk for a tonic and a remedy for diarrhea and dysentery. Pieces of the skin of the tree's roots will relieve a toothache when put against the bad tooth.

Check the ripeness of a custard apple just as an avocado, when you gently squeeze, it gives under your finger tips. Custard apples can be purchased ready to eat, or hard to the touch— to ripen in a few days. They should never be black or pulpy. Fully ripe it is soft to the touch; and the stem and attached core can be pulled out. Custard apples are only eaten when soft, and only the flesh is eaten. To eat, simply cut in half and scoop out the white flesh. The custard apple should be moist with a pleasant sweet aroma. They are absolutely the best when chilled.

One hundred grams of custard apple has about a hundred calories with good amounts of calcium, phosphorus, and vitamin C. Custard apples are a well-balanced food having protein, fiber, minerals, vitamins, energy, and little fat. They are a good source of dietary fiber, vitamin B6, magnesium, potassium, with some B2 and complex carbohydrate.

Creamed Custard Apple

Ingredients: the pulp of two seeded, pureed custard apples, one TS lemon juice, two cups cream or one cup whole milk, three TBS clear gelatin, one package softened cream cheese, one half cup powdered sugar, one quarter cup boiling water

Method: Dissolve gelatin into boiling water. In a bowl whisk the soft cream cheese gradually adding the gelatin mix, lemon juice, powdered sugar, and cream. Add custard apple and whisk as smooth as possible. Chill and serve with cake or pastry.

Custard Apple Sorbet

Ingredients: the pulp of six custard apples - peeled and seeded, one half cup powdered sugar, one cup boiling water

Method: Dissolve powdered sugar in boiling water stirring until a syrup forms. Let cool before blending in the custard apple pulp. You can combine both in a blender or food processor. Freeze until it is a stiff slush. Blend again and refreeze.

Custard Apple Sauce

Different for the grill especially for fish steaks and fillets.

Ingredients: one custard apple - skinned, seeded, and pureed, one bunch chives chopped as small as possible, two cloves of garlic minced, one TBS butter or margarine, one half cup fish or chicken stock, one half cup white wine, one half hot pepper seeded and minced (optional), salt and spices to your taste

Method: Cook chives and garlic in butter. Add wine and simmer until it thickens before adding the stock. Simmer and add custard apple. Add spices and salt. Apply to fish steaks while they are either baking or grilling.

Custard Apple Cake

Ingredients: four ripe custard apples peeled, seeded and minced, one quarter pound butter, three quarters cup powdered sugar, three eggs, one TS vanilla extract, two cups self rising flour, one TS cinnamon, one half TS nutmeg

Method: With a whisk or electric mixer beat a half cup powdered sugar and vanilla into the butter in a medium bowl. Add eggs one at a time. Beat until mixture is pale and creamy. Add custard apple puree to mixture. Mix till totally combined. Divide flour in half and carefully fold into mixture so not to get any lumps. When flour is fully added and mixture is smooth pour into a greased oven pan. Sprinkle remaining sugar, cinnamon, and nutmeg over mixture. Bake for one hour at 350 degrees. Let cool and serve.

HEALTH NOTE

Central Americans roast and smash a few seeds, then combine with water or raw milk to induce vomiting, or the removal of waste from the body. This was used for poisonings. This same roasted seed powder is mixed with cooking grease or oil to kill skin parasites as lice. A tea made from custard apple skin is used to fight pneumonia.

Trees and plants always look like the people they live with, somehow.

Zora Neale Hurston

DUNKS—INDIAN JUJUBE

I never thought an apple could be grown in the tropics until my neighbor, Rambo, showed me his dunks. The green fruit was about the size, shape, and color of a small green Granny Smith apple, but the dunks taste is very tart and bitter sharp. As I talked to elders, and did my research, I realized the grafted dunk tree is rare. The fruit is usually very small, and it is more often called Indian Jujube. This fruit is believed to have originated in China.

The dunk tree can grow to about forty feet. It will adapt to almost any soil or climate condition, and is very drought resistant. The dunk should be grown in full sun. It grows quick because its tap root descends to locate water and nutrients. The yellow, five petal blossoms are selfpollinating and produce varied sizes of fruit. Most dunk fruit is small, about a inch in diameter.

A well cared for grafted tree, as my neighbor's, produces three inch diameter fruit. Dunk fruit can be round or oblong with thin skin. Just like an apple it ripens from a yellow green to a full red. The flesh is white and crisp and even smells almost like an apple before it fully ripens. It is slightly acidic and perfect for making chow. Ripe dunk flesh is less firm and pulpy. Overripe fruits have wrinkled skin, and are soft to the touch.

Dunks are easily grown from seeds of fruits that fully ripened on the tree. Each fruit has a center pit with two seeds. A trick for sprouting the seeds is to put them into water. Discard those that float. Of the rest carefully try to delicately split the shell. If you are careful and successful the seeds should germinate within two weeks. Grafting produces a better fruit. With warm temperatures and direct sun dunks will thrive. Regular watering and fertilizing can not only increase the size of the fruit, but triple the harvest. Fruit flies are dunks main pest that can be controlled by a regular spray of insecticides mixed with a foliar mixture containing zinc and boron.

Dunks have more vitamins A and C than apples. In fact dunks have twice the vitamin C than citrus and are used

DID YOU KNOW?

There are two types of jujube trees farmed for their fruit, the Indian jujube and the Chinese jujube. There are 700 varieties of the Chinese jujube, and 90 varieties of the Indian jujube. The Chinese jujube has been cultivated for 4,000 years. In Jamaica dunks are called coolie plums or crabapples. Dunks' botanical name is *zizyphus mauritiana*.

as a tea to cure sore throats. Dunks are used to calm digestive and intestinal ailments. A tea of the bark will help fight diarrhea. It is believed that a diet of dunks will cure baldness. Beware and don't eat too many raw fruits as they have a laxative quality.

Fruit is eaten fresh or dried, and also used for pickling like chow or anchar.

Dunk Water

In a clean gallon bucket mash a dozen dunks. Fill with water and cover for four hours. Strain and chill. This is very refreshing over ice.

Dunk Butter

Wash, seed, and quarter about thirty ripe dunks. Put in a large pot and cover with water. Add three to six cups of sugar depending on your sweet tooth, a TBS each cinnamon and nutmeg, and one TBS cornstarch. Simmer uncovered for two hours. Let stand overnight. Eat on bread, or biscuits.

Dunk Bread

Ingredients: two cups minced fully ripened dunks, one cup brown sugar, one half cup butter or margarine, one cup water, two cups whole wheat flour, one TBS baking soda, and a half TS salt, and a TS cinnamon.

Method: In a large frying pan bring combine the dunks, water, sugar, and butter and bring to a boil. Once thoroughly blended remove from heat and allow to cool. Then add the dry ingredients till it is a stiff mixture. Spoon into greased ovenware and bake for one hour at 350 degrees. Check with a toothpick before removing from oven.

Dunk Cake

Ingredients: one cup sugar. one half cup butter, two cups minced dunks seeded (peeled or not), one cup water, two cups bakers flour, one TS baking soda, one half TS salt

Method: In a sizable pot combine the water sugar, butter and mined dunks. Bring to a boil, cover a remove from heat. Sift all dry ingredients together and combine with liquid mixture. Pour mixture into a greased cake or bread pan. Bake at 350 degrees for forty minutes.

Spiced Dunk Pieces

Ingredients: three pounds of dunks - quartered seeds removed, four cups brown sugar, five cups of water, one TBS cornstarch, one TS nutmeg, one TBS cinnamon, one TBS salt

Method: Wash dunks; drain and prick each several times with a fork. In a kettle bring to a boil water, sugar, spices, and corn starch. Add dunk pieces and simmer, uncovered, stirring occasionally, for half an hour. Remove from heat, cover, and chill overnight. The following day bring syrup and jujubes to a boil and simmer, uncovered, for half an hour. With a slotted spoon lift jujubes from syrup and place slightly apart on cookie sheets or trays suitable for the oven. Dry in oven at 250 for two hours. Check fruit pieces frequently and turn fruit occasionally. Turn oven off, but do not remove dunk pieces. Remove from oven the next morning and store in the refrigerator.

HEALTH NOTE

Dunks have been used by Chinese and Indians for millennia, there are many medicinal uses. Often used to sooth sore throats, dunks have many medicinal purposes. This fruit improves stamina and strength, stimulates the immune system, helps liver functions, is sedating, and serves as an all purpose tonic. Raw dunks are wrapped or poulticed over cuts and ulcers. They are used against blood circulation ailments and fevers. Combined with salt and hot peppers they ease indigestion and gas. Dried ripe fruit is a mild laxative. Dunk seeds are sedative and are taken, sometimes with whole milk, to halt nausea, vomiting, and abdominal pains especially during pregnancy. Pulverized roasted seeds combined with cooking oil are rubbed to relieve rheumatic areas. Dunk leaves are applied as poultices to assist liver ailments, asthma, and fevers. A decoction of the bitter, astringent bark will fight diarrhea and dysentery, and relieve gingivitis. A paste made from the boiled bark is applied on sores. Dunk root decoction will make a good purge. Powdered root is dusted on wounds. Juice of the root bark is said to alleviate gout and rheumatism. **BEWARE** -Strong doses of the bark or root may be toxic. An infusion of the flowers serves as an eye lotion.

It is only the farmer who faithfully plants seeds in the Spring, who reaps a harvest in the Autumn.

B.C. Forbes

FAT PORK – ICACOS PLUM

Why does every tropical fruit that is considered a 'plum' have too many names? Another Trinidad specialty fruit is the icacos plum; or as it is locally known, 'fat pork'. Its scientific name is Chrysobalanus icaco. This tree is also known elsewhere as the coco plum, bears what we call 'fat pork fruit or apple'. The fat pork is usually found wild, and seldom cultivated throughout Trinidad.

I only know of one fat pork tree along the north coast not far from Toco. This almost unknown, small pinkish fruit is about the size of a big plum. My research presented it better known as the coco-plum, the cotton plum, icaco, icaque ponne, pork-fat-apple, or zicate. Fat pork fruit is usually a flushed pink color, but they can be white or purple. The flesh is never crisp, but spongy, whitish, and slightly sweet, but usually tasteless when ripe. This tree's availability of water determines the thickness of the fruit's flesh.

References to the icacos plum usually refer to it as a small shrub growing to ten feet. The fat pork tree I know of is at least thirty feet and usually bears fruit twice a year. The icacos plum is native to Mexico, Central America and South America, to Ecuador and northern Brazil, and throughout the Caribbean chain. This is a good tree for a river bank, or to stop soil erosion close to a beach. Fat pork can survive wind storms, salt spray, and floods. Shade is its biggest enemy. It can be cultivated from seeds and is a relatively slow growing tree. Thus its area must be cleaned of weeds at least monthly. Once this tree is six feet tall it can withstand damp soil or very dry conditions.

Fat pork is one of the very few fruits we Trinis don't really crave. The fruits are edible raw and can be made into

DID YOU KNOW?

Triniview.com reports that Icacos Point in the southwestern tip of Trinidad is actually named after the fat pork or 'port' tree. A British surveyor in 1797 named the area "Marsh of Icaque". The fat pork plum-like fruit shrub covered the land. Trini view reports the 'the icaco is a velvety fruit that is bluish-red in color and is commonly called "fat port" in Trinidad and Tobago.' These fruits can be white yellow red or purple. The name originated from Haiti where the Taino Amerindians called it icaco. It was considered a subsistence food, only if you are starving. Fat pork, Icacos, coco plum; all I know is the fat pork fruit I've eaten is a flushed pink.

preserves. I never tried to make chow with unripe fruits. Why call it was named fat pork? I believe the name 'fat pork' comes from a successful pig farmer who was lucky to have a couple of these trees close to his pens. When this fruit dropped to the ground, his pigs got fat. Fat pork is a rich fruit with the consistency close to that of an ackee. Another name 'cotton plum' is derived from someone referring to the consistency and taste of the fruit as 'sweetened cotton'.

A tea made from the leaves is reported to help control type II diabetes. A combination of fruits, bark and leaves boiled in water will produce a tea that will help fight severe diarrhea. A tea made only from the bark may help kidney ailments.

Fat pork seeds have a lot of edible oil. These fruits are so rich that a quarter pound has fifty calories with some calcium and phosphorus. To get a better taste of these bland fruits is to cover them in sugar water over night before using them in any recipe.

Fat Pork Sherbert

Ingredients: thirty ripe fat pork plums halved with seeds removed,, one half cup sugar, one quarter cup water, one cup fresh orange juice, one half cup corn syrup, two TBS grated orange peel, one teaspoon fresh lemon juice, one TS vanilla extract, one teaspoon salt, one cup whipping cream.

Method: Combine fat pork plums, sugar, and a quarter cup of water in large skillet. Bring to a boil and then reduce hit to a simmer always stirring until fat pork starts to fall apart, usually about ten minutes. Set aside until cool. Pour into a blender and puree until smooth. Add remaining ingredients and blend. Freeze for three hours and then blend again to break down ice crystals.

Fat Pork Stuffing

For a unique chicken dinner.

Ingredients: one whole roasting chicken - four to five pounds, a dozen fat pork fruits -seeded and peeled, one clove of garlic minced, one small onion chopped very small, one TS salt, two TBS brown sugar, two bay leaves, a pinch of cinnamon, and or nutmeg optional.

Method: Rub the cavity of the chicken with salt. Combine remaining ingredients and fill the chicken. For a more nutty taste use the cinnamon and nutmeg. Cover with foil and bake for an hour at 300 degrees. Remove foil and continue to bake for thirty minutes more or until skin has started to brown. Cool slightly before serving.

Fat Pork Potatoes

Ingredients: two dozen fat pork fruits seeded and peeled, three large potatoes boiled and chunked, one bunch chives - chopped small, two chadon benee leaves minced, one TS salt, two stalks celery chopped small, one half a small onion chopped small, and one cup grated cheddar cheese.

Method: In a suitable greased baking dish or bread pan, combine all the ingredients except cheese. Cover with foil. Bake at 250 degrees for thirty minutes. Uncover and spread cheese on top. Continue to bake for fifteen more minutes. Allow to cool slightly before serving.

Fat Pork and Raisin Compote

Ingredients: two pounds of fat pork fruits (about sixty) peeled and seeded, one half cup raisins, one half cup brown sugar, one TBS fresh lemon juice, one half TS salt, one cup water, a TS cinnamon, and a pinch of nutmeg

Method: Boil the water in a medium sized pot. Add sugar and stir until a syrup begins to form. Mix in the fat pork pieces, raisins, and salt. Reduce heat and simmer for about ten minutes. Add lemon juice, cinnamon and nutmeg. Stir over heat for two minutes. Remove from the heat and add cover. Cool to rum temperature. Eat over ice cream or cake.

HEALTH NOTE

The chemical features of the icacos plum/fat pork include flavonoids, terpenoids, steroids, and tannins. Scientific medical interest in flavonoids has increased because many of them exhibit healthful attributes including anti-inflammatory, antiviral, antibacterial, as well as anticancer.

My garden is my most beautiful masterpiece.
Claude Monet

GRAPEFRUIT

My grandfather had a nice citrus orchard with navel oranges, Portugals, and grapefruit. As kids we loved to eat grapefruit, and to drink the semi-sweet juice.

The grapefruit is a large citrus fruit related to the orange, lemon, and pummelo. Grapefruits are categorized as white, pink, or ruby - the color of their flesh. Historically, it is a very young fruit. The grapefruit hasn't even existed 300 years as of yet. In Jamaica it was accidentally crossed between a fruit called the pummelo and the orange. The Trinidadian name, 'shaddock', comes from the seafarer Captain Shaddock who carried the pummelo seeds from Indonesia to the West Indies in 1793. The grapefruit has many names including the 'forbidden fruit' in Barbados and the 'chadique' in Haiti. The Dutch call it 'pampelmoose', which translates to pumpkin sized citrus. Grapefruit's botanical name is *citrus paradise*.

At first the grapefruit was too bitter to be enjoyed, but cross-pollination (again in Jamaica) between the grapefruit and the tangerine, created the 'ugli fruit'. Correctly named, the ugli has wrinkled skin and a flat bottom. Most people didn't care for the thick-skinned, sour fruits. The name grapefruit comes from how the fruits grow in clusters like grapes. The grapefruit was first commercially cultivated in the US in the 1880's. Presently the United States grows over forty per cent of the world's grapefruit.

The grapefruit may cure many of the world's ills. It is claimed that the fruit's enzymes will burn body fat. Grapefruits' essential oil has a stimulating trait. A diet including half a grapefruit or a large glass of grapefruit juice should melt away ten pounds in twelve days. (Wouldn't that be great!) The grapefruit industry created special 'grapefruit knives and spoons' to easier eat the juicy fruit. Most of the commercial grapefruit production is aimed at canning the juice, yet very little of the fruit is wasted. A cooking oil is pressed from the seeds. Farmers revitalize their soils by using the seed hulls. The pulp is dried and fed to cattle. Seed extract is used as a remedy for foot fungus, and a concoction prepared from the blossoms is used as a blood tonic and as a cure for sleeplessness.

Grapefruit lowers some cholesterol, helps digestion, and reduces gas. It is also a treatment for water retention, urinary, liver, kidney, and gall bladder problems. Grapefruit can be rubbed directly on the skin to alleviate pimples and greasiness. The leaves have antibiotic properties.

Fruits

To grow a tree, first find either a tree vendor or a fruit you like and sprout the seeds. Trees should grow to twenty feet and bear fruit in five years. Grapefruit will develop in most soils, but requires regular watering. A little high nitrogen fertilizer mix should be applied monthly. A single tree can bear over a thousand pounds of fruit yearly. Ripe fruits may be stored for two to three months on the tree permitting extra growth.

One grapefruit has 80 calories with one gram of protein, eighteen grams of carbohydrates, and three grams of fiber. It is an excellent source for Vitamins A and C, most B vitamins with folic acid, pectin, calcium, potassium, and magnesium.

Grapefruit is more than a fruit or a juice. It can be used in a multitude of recipes. Grapefruit sections chopped with chadon benee, sweet onions, sweet peppers, and half a hot pepper makes an excellent salsa. To make a great salad, mix grapefruit sections with cooked shrimp and chopped avocado placed on a bed of lettuce. Mix the juice with club soda and perhaps your favorite liquor. Grapefruit Ice can be easily prepared by mixing grapefruit juice with some pulp and freezing. After two hours machine blend it or stir well, and return to the freezer.

Grilled Citrus Fish

Ingredients: two pounds king, carite, or salmon, one lemon, one orange, one grapefruit, half cup olive oil, one TS thyme, two cloves minced garlic, one small minced onion, salt and spice to taste

Method: Season the fish. Light your grill. Section the fruit and place in a small skillet with the olive oil, thyme, salt and spices, onion and garlic. Bring to a boil and simmer for about three minutes. Grill the fish until well done. Cover with the citrus sauce and let stand for five minutes before serving.

Citrus Shrimp Stew

Ingredients: two pounds medium or large shrimp peeled and deveined, two cups each of orange and grapefruit juice, half cup chopped onion, one orange and one grapefruit peeled and cut into sections without membrane, one seeded hot pepper well minced, three bunches of chadon benee chopped, two TBS brown sugar, two medium tomatoes chopped, three potatoes boiled and cubed small, one nice eddo sliced, one small dasheen boiled and chopped, two green cooking bananas chopped, one bunch celery chopped, salt and spices to taste

Method: In a small skillet combine juices, onion, two bunches chopped chadon benee, sugar, half minced hot pepper, and bring to a boil, then simmer for ten minutes. Use half of this citrus mixture to marinade the shrimp for two hours in the fridge. (The longer you marinade the shrimp the better - up to two days.) In a large pot bring remaining citrus marinade to a boil before adding potatoes, tomato, celery, eddo, dasheen and banana, one bunched chopped chadon benee and remaining mined hot pepper. Cook for half an hour. Add shrimp and cook for fifteen more minutes. Serve with rice.

Cuban Black Bean Grapefruit Ensalada

Ingredients: two grapefruits-peeled, seeded, and sliced thin, half cup grapefruit juice, one bunch chadon benee chopped, , one pound boiled or canned black beans, one nice cucumber sliced, one cup papaya seeded, peeled and cubed, quarter pound cheddar cheese grated, one head of lettuce, half TS ground cumin, two TBS honey, salt and spice to taste

Method: Cover four salad plates neatly with lettuce and border each with grapefruit slices. Then spoon each plate with equal amounts of the beans, cucumber slices, and papaya cubes. Cover with grated cheese. Mix the grapefruit juice with chadon benee, cumin, honey, salt and spices. Pour mix over salads.

HEALTH NOTE

Check with a qualified doctor or pharmacist before drinking grapefruit juice if you're taking pharmaceutical medicines. Certain medicines when combined with grapefruit juice become more potent. Compounds in grapefruit juice slow the normal detoxification and metabolism processes in the intestines and liver, which hinders the body's ability to breakdown and eliminate these drugs.

Garden as though you will live forever.
William Kent

GUAVA

As kid I would love to sit on a guava branch, pick the fruit, and with some salt eat a belly full. I would have to hide from Mama, because she knew guavas would bind me up for days. Guava is another fruit native to the Western Hemisphere that has over a hundred species. Guavas grow in many forms and colors; pear-shaped, round, or oval; with yellow to green skins, and creamy or grainy yellow, pink or red flesh. The botanical name psidium guajava refers to the most common type, the apple guava.

All guavas have rows of small hard seeds with a strong aroma and taste. Guava is used green or ripe in punches, syrups, jams, chutneys, ice creams, and a paste called 'guava cheese'. Scientists believe the guava was first cultivated in the mountains of Peru thousands of years ago, but man and birds have spread the seeds though all the tropics and the Caribbean. The European voyagers carried the guava from the West Indies to the East Indies, Asia, Africa, and Egypt. India now invests over a hundred thousand acres in guavas producing over twenty-five thousand tons of fruit annually.

The guava is usually a small tree growing to thirty feet, but new grafted types seldom reach fifteen feet. It is a type of evergreen with smooth brown bark. These trees can be grown from seeds, but better results are delivered from the grafting-budding process. Guavas prefer full sun and can grow in almost any soil type. They flourish in well-drained soil with a pH of 6. Mature guava trees need a half-pound of nitrogen rich urea a year, but should also be fertilized monthly with an quarter cup of the mix 10 – 4 – 10 plus 5 per cent magnesium. Pruning will increase blossoms and larger fruit. Red alga is a parasitic problem especially in Trinidad's high humidity. Spraying with a copper based algaecide at the first appearance should control this problem. Mealybugs and fruit flies can also be problems. Where fruit flies are a problem, the immature fruit is covered with paper bags for protection to assure prime quality produce for the markets.

Fine-grained guava wood is valued in India for carvings. It is also a good wood for charcoal. Guava bark and leaves are almost twenty-five per cent tannin, which is necessary to process animal hides. Asians use the leaves as a dye for cotton garments. The guava tree leaves are also a natural astringent that are used to stop diarrhea. They can be pounded into a poultice for wounds, boils, and aches. In fact, guava leaves can be chewed to relieve a toothache. Amazon Indians use a tea of the leaves as a remedy for sore throats, nausea, and to regulate menstrual periods. Tender leaves are chewed for bleeding gums and bad breath. If chewed before drinking alcohol, it is said to prevent hangovers. A poultice of guava blossoms is reported to relieve sun strain, conjunctivitis, or eye injuries.

Guavas are high in vitamins A and C, phosphorus, and niacin. Some types of guavas have four times the Vitamin C of an orange. A quarter pound of guavas has only 60 calories. They can be eaten raw, but I like slicing them chilled and seeded. The most common way of preparing guavas is to remove the center pulp and stew them in the shells. Cooking will usually reduce the strong odor associated with guavas. Guavas can be used in jams, jellies, and paste, canned or frozen. Straining the liquid after boiling seeded guavas makes guava juice, one of the main ingredients of Hawaiian Punch.

Guava Sauce

A great addition for fish, pork, duck or chicken.

Ingredients: a quarter pound guavas, two cups orange juice, sugar, and spices to taste

Method: Place guavas in a large pot, cover with orange juice and simmer until cooked. Strain and add sugar and or spices.

Guava Bread Pudding

Ingredients: a dozen small guavas, or three large guavas – boiled and strained or a half package guava paste, four cups scalded milk, two cups bread cubes, four beaten eggs, half cup sugar, one TS vanilla extract, half TS nutmeg, half TS cinnamon, salt to taste

Method: Soak bread cubes in scalded milk for five minutes. Mix in sugar, salt, vanilla and eggs. Pour into baking dish. Cut paste into half inch cubes and spread out evenly through the dish. Sprinkle top with cinnamon and nutmeg. Bake at 350 for one hour

Guava Pastry

Ingredients: one and a half pound guava paste sliced a quarter inch thick, three quarter cup vegetable shortening, two cups bakers flour, four TBS butter, one cup sugar, three large eggs, one large egg yolk, three TS baking powder, one TS salt, three TBS dark rum (optional)

Method: Melt butter and shortening in a medium skillet. Combine all other ingredients (except egg yolk, guava slices and rum) in a large bowl adding melted shortening. Work dough with your hands until everything is mixed well. Cut dough in half. Place one half of the dough in a greased baking dish – 9x12. Cover with guava slices and sprinkle with rum. Cover with remaining dough and brush with egg yolk. Bake for 40 minutes at 350.

Guava Cake

Ingredients: a dozen small or three large guavas boiled and strained or a half pound guava paste sliced a quarter inch thick, three quarters cup butter, one cup sugar, two eggs, two cups bakers flour, one TS baking powder, one TS vanilla extract, a quarter TS salt

Method: In a medium skillet melt butter and slowly mix in sugar. Add eggs individually and vanilla. Separately combine flour, baking powder, and salt. Then combine the flour and melted butter/eggs mix. Pour half the mix into an eight-inch baking pan. Cover with guava slices, cover with remaining batter. Bake at 350 for an hour.

Poached Guava

Ingredients: eight very ripe guavas—peeled, seeded, and halved (save seeds and pulp), one and a half cup water, four cups sugar, three TBS lemon juice

Method: Slice the guavas into quarter inch strips. Place seeds and pulp in a skillet with the water and boil for five minutes. Use a wire mesh strainer to strain the liquid to another saucepan. Add sugar, guava strips, and lemon juice. Boil for three minutes or until fruit strips are soft. Serve as a topping for cakes or ice cream.

HEALTH NOTE

Guava is one of the best sources of dietary fiber. Its seeds are excellent laxatives. Guava fights diabetes, protects the prostrate, and reduces the risk of cancer. Guavas are rich in vitamins, proteins and minerals, but with no cholesterol, and easily satisfies appetite.

Everything that slows us down and forces patience, everything that sets us back into the slow circles of nature, is a help. Gardening is an instrument of grace.

May Sarton

HOG PLUM—YELLOW MOMBIN

I am easily confused by the array of Caribbean plums. All are tasty, but many have the same names. 'Mombins' are tropical plums. There is the red mombin native to tropical America. It can also be called the Chili (Chile) plum, the Spanish plum, the governor plum, the Jamaican plum, or purple mombin. What Trinidadians call hog plum is the yellow mombin. It is native from southern Mexico to Peru and Brazil. In Jamaica, our hog plum is also known as Spanish plum, or gully plum. Net research showed the red mombin as *spondias purpurea*, the purple mombin as *spondias purpurea L*, while the hog plum is *spondias lutea* or *s.mombin*. I've also seen it referred to as *spondees monsoon*.

The yellowish hog plum is related to the mango, cashew, and pommecythere. (Beware, some call the pommecythere hog plum.) Yellow mombin is the fruit of a fairly large tree that can grow to about twenty meters tall and almost a meter thick. This is twice as large as the red mombin tree. It has pale yellow blossoms that produce oval, bright yellow fruit, which are the size of a small plum. The hog plum has an acidic-sweet tangy mushy pulp around a large, fibrous pit/seed much like a small pommecythere. The fruit hang along the branches in numerous clusters of a dozen or more.

Because the taste is just so-so, and the seed so big, very few people cultivate these trees. Most of the trees I know of are wild usually near a river. When they bear the surrounding ground is littered with yellow fruit. It is one of the few trees that Trinis don't rush. The reason this is named the hog plum is that it is excellent feed for pigs. This fruit is also excellent to cook with pork.

A tree may be started from seed. First, find a wild hog plum tree and search for some sprouted seeds. If you are not successful then plant some seeds or take some cuttings from young branches. These will root quickly in loose soil kept moderately moist. Once the cutting has rooted, probably six months, transplant to an area where it can spread as it matures. The hog plum needs about six meters on all sides. The tree is fast-growing in full sun and well drained soil, but needs plenty of water during the dry season. This can be a great shade tree.

The yellow mombin is less desirable than the purple mombin, and usually eaten out-of-hand, or stewed with sugar. The juice can be mixed with other citrus to make a tasty punch, or used to flavor ice creams and sorbets. The immature green hog plums can be pickled as chow and eaten with salt and pepper sauce, same as the chili plum.

A quarter pound of hog plums has about forty calories with a lot of carotene, calcium, and thiamine. Eating too many ripe hog plums can cause diarrhea. A tea can be made with the blossoms and leaves for relieve from stomachache and inflammation of the throat. The juice of crushed leaves and the powder of dried leaves are used as poultices on wounds and inflammations.

Stewed Hog Plums

Ingredients: two pound fresh ripe hog plums (about fifty), one half cup sugar, one cup water, a quarter TS salt, one TBS fresh lemon juice, one cinnamon stick

Method: Wash and cut plums in half and remove seeds. In a medium pot, combine sugar, water, salt, lemon juice, and add cinnamon stick. Bring to a boil stirring constantly. Place plum pieces in the boiling syrup. Continue boiling for five minutes. Remove from heat and refrigerate.

Hog Plum Sorbet

Ingredients: three cups of washed sliced plums, pits removed, a quarter cup and two TBS sugar, one TS fresh lemon juice, a quarter TS salt, two TBS orange juice

Method: Blend the sliced plums, sugar, lemon juice, and salt at purée speed until it becomes very smooth. Then force this puree through a fine mesh sieve to remove the hog plum skin. Add the orange juice and blend well again. Freeze in a suitable container. After three hours in the freezer, take out and blend again to break down the ice crystals. Freeze and serve.

Hog Plum Marmalade

Since hog plum trees bear so heavily there is always an abundance of fruit.

Ingredients: four pounds of hog plums, washed with the seeds, one pound golden raisins, two cups water, four cups brown sugar, sugar, juice of two fresh lemons, and the grated peel of one lemon

Method: Put the hog plums, water, sugar, raisins, and salt in a large heavy skillet, cast iron preferred. Bring to a boil, stirring for twenty minutes or until the seeds float. Remove from heat and spoon out the seeds. Grate the peel one of the lemons and add with the lemon juice. Simmer uncovered for about an hour stirring frequently so it does not stick to the bottom of the pan and burn. Remove marmalade from heat and put one tablespoon of marmalade on a chilled plate. If the plum marmalade makes a crinkly track the marmalade has set. When cooled pour into warm, sterilized jars and seal the jars with wax. Store in a cool dark place.

HEALTH NOTE

The hog plum tree is very therapeutic in bush medicine. Boiling the bark in water is drank to cure ailments of reproductive system, a remedy for diarrhea, and hemorrhoids. The plant leaves reportedly contain antiviral and antibacterial qualities, and a tea of the leaves is used to rid the body of parasitic worms. The leaves are fed to pregnant domesticated animals to hasten littering or to expel placenta after successful littering.

When your back stops aching and your hands begin to harden...
You will find yourself a partner in the Glory of the Garden.
Gardens are not made by sitting in the shade.

Rudyard Kipling

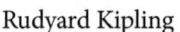

JACKFRUIT - KATAHAR

Friends recently gave me a very big, strange fruit that looked like a cross of a breadfruit and a soursop. They called it katahar, but it is better known as 'jackfruit'. The green, oblong, four-pound odd flesh is seedy like a chatiagne, but with a sort of a sweet custardy taste. A few minutes after we sliced it, a sweet pleasant aroma filled the kitchen. The white katahar pulp tastes strange, yet the pale yellow pulp around the seeds taste good, like a pineapple smoothie. The seeds also have tasty insides. Every part is sticky. Jackfruit must be an acquired taste.

By the name, katahar has East Indian origins back at least three millenniums. Supposedly the way the fruit got known in English as 'jack' is from the Portuguese 'jaca', from the Malay 'chakka', from the Indian 'Katah'. This fruit was well traveled early in history. Presently it is Bangladesh's and Indonesia's the national fruit. I went to see our friend's tree in Cunupia and found the big fruits growing directly from the trunk of the small fifteenfoot tree. Their tree was at least forty years old. They had other younger trees grown from this tree's seeds, and all took about three years to bring fruit. The biggest fruit they had seen was about thirty pounds!

DID YOU KNOW?

Jackfruit/katahar is the largest of all tree grown fruits. This unique fruit is rough skinned and oval-shaped, and can be three feet long and eighteen inches wide. One can weigh up to a hundred pounds, but the average is forty to fifty pounds. Jackfruit / katahar is a cousin to the breadfruit in the mulberry family, *Moraceae*. Its botanical name is *Artocarpus heterophyllus*. Similar to the pineapple, jackfruit is made up of fused individual fruitlets. Archeological discoveries in India reveal jackfruit was cultivated in India 3000 years ago.

The jackfruit bears the world's largest fruit, often more than sixty pounds with the world's record jackfruit over a hundred pounds. When it's ripe it should thump hollow, just as a melon.

The bright green skin is tough with rough points all over it. The cut open katahar has large seeds encased in tasty flesh surrounded by white 'stuff'. It is high in pectin and has white latex goo used in India and Southeast Asia as glue. Some believe jackfruit goo is the secret base for the flavor of Juicy Fruit chewing gum.

Katahar can be eaten green or ripe; raw or prepared. It is a staple food boiled or curried. In many countries it is considered a 'poor man's food'. There may be a hundred or more seeds. The nut-sized

> ## DID YOU KNOW?
>
> Jackfruit mature eight months after flowering and contain as many as five hundred one-inch seeds that can be boiled or roasted, and used for seasoning. The seeds are valued more than the pulp. The flavor of this fruit's flesh tastes like melon, mango, papaya, and banana combined. This fruit is only viable for a few days. Sticky latex accumulates on utensils so dip everything in cooking oil first.

seeds are wrapped in a tasty skin. Inside they are crisp like a nut and can be fried, or boiled for five minutes, then roasted. The younger the jackfruit, the milder the flavor. Ripe jackfruit is used mostly for desserts.

A one-cup serving of raw jackfruit has about one hundred and fifty calories, with four grams of fat and two grams of protein. It provides one-tenth the daily requirement of vitamin A and twenty per cent of vitamin C with calcium, iron, zinc, and phosphorus. The benefits of the antioxidant seeds fight cancer, hypertension, ageing, and ulcers. Powder ground from the seeds relieves indigestion.

Before beginning any katahar or jackfruit recipe wipe your knife and cutting board with cooking oil because the fruit will drain a white, very sticky milky latex goo. Always remove the skin.

Curried Katahar

Ingredients: one large katahar fruit, two large onions chopped, half garlic clove minced, one large hot pepper, one TBS ground garam masala, one TS ground geera/cumin, two TBS curry powder, two TBS salt, one TBS vegetable oil, one cup coconut milk

Method: Slice well washed peeled katahar flesh and seeds into pieces. Sautee onions and garlic with garam massala, geera/cumin, curry powder, and salt. Heat oil in a large frying pan with the massala mixture and the katahar seeds four five minutes. Then add the flesh and fry for three more minutes. Add pepper, cover, and cook another couple of minutes before adding the coconut milk. Simmer for another twenty minutes. Remove hot pepper ands serve with rice.

Jackfruit Delight

Sweeten to taste.

Ingredients: one katahar peeled and cut into small pieces, two cups grated coconut, one to two cups powdered sugar, quarter cup small pieces of coconut, one cup milk, two to four TBS brown sugar, one TS cinnamon, three TBS butter, ten chopped cashews

Method: Fry katahar pieces in two TBS of butter for six minutes. Boil grated coconut and powdered sugar in two cups of water for ten minutes before adding the fried katahar pieces. Continue boiling for two minutes. Fry the cashews and coconut pieces in a tablespoon of butter. As they brown add sugar and cinnamon. Mix with jackfruit and add milk. Simmer till everything is warm. This can also be served chilled.

Katahar Chicken

Ingredients: one chicken cut up, two pounds katahar, five large tomatoes chopped, one medium onion chopped, one TS minced garlic, one TS minced ginger, one TBS minced thyme leaves, two TBS chadon benee, five bay leaves, seven TBS curry powder, three TBS cooking oil, one to two cups water

Method: Cut jackfruit into one-inch cubes. Keep in ice water to reduce browning. Heat three tablespoons of oil in a large frying pan. Add chicken chunks and fry till brown. Add onions, garlic, ginger, thyme, and tomatoes. Add water if mixture gets too thick and starts to burn. Add jackfruit chunks. Stir before adding the curry powder, bay leaves, chadon benee, and one cup of water. Cover and simmer for at least a half an hour. Remove bay leaves before serving.

Jackfruit Ice

Ingredients: one jackfruit peel, trimmed and seeded, two cups sweetened condensed milk, two TBS lemon juice, sugar to taste

Method: Blend all ingredients and freeze until it starts becoming icy. Blend again and refreeze. Grated coconut and the fried jackfruit deeds may be added with cinnamon and nutmeg for a different variation.

*A person cannot love a plant after he has pruned it,
then he has either done a poor job or is devoid of emotion.*

Liberty Hyde Bailey

JAMAICAN PLUM

We islanders love strange things, things that seem strange to outsiders anyway, like the Jamaican plum. We eat it before they ripen with salt and some pepper. I love plum season so much, I know where every tree is close to my house. They are also called Governor or the Jamaican Jew/June plum. I eat them green, but Jamaican plums turn a gorgeous deep red or burgundy color, with a beautifully contrasting yellow juiciness inside and are very juicy when ripe. Few make it to be fully ripe between the birds and Trinis sucking the plum pit.

Trinidad's plums are one of my many favorite fruits. Researching the different types governor, Jamaican, and Chili (Chile), has driven me up the proverbial wall. A friend at the agricultural ministry says there are three distinct types of plums in Trinidad. A friend a Brichlen Castle provided delicious yellow plums he designated as Jamaican. North Coast friends provided red plums they said were governor. I still haven't found the chilies! Other than the color, the taste seems almost the same. I decided if they are not yet ripe they must be called chili. I'm certain someone out there can differentiate. There is also the hog plum, but that is definitely different.

One reference confirmed my theory. From the horticultural website of Perdue University:

One of the most popular small fruits of the American tropics, the purple mombin, Spondias Purpurea L., has acquired many other colloquial names: in English, red mombin, Spanish plum, hog plum, scarlet plum; purple plum in the Virgin Islands; Jamaica plum in Trinidad; Chile plum in Barbados; wild plum in Costa Rica and Panama; red plum.

There are three main types of plums, the Japanese, the west Asian, and the European. There are thousands of varieties of plums and all are family to the rose. Jamaican plums are native to Central and South America. Jamaican plums have large seeds compared to its thin flesh. The flesh is sour, but sweetens if you add salt. I believe we eat them green just to beat the birds to the tree.

The Assyrians first cultivated wild plums over 2,000 years ago. The Chinese also cultivated plums, and guess who developed the Japanese plum. The Crusaders are credited with bringing plums to Europe in 1369. Jamaican plums are native to Central and South America.

The Jamaican plum is an attractive small tree. Grafted varieties are usually without

> ## NAME CONFUSION
>
> The common name for the ramontchi in India is governor's plum. The ramontchi is native to tropical Africa, Madagascar, India, parts of Malaya and Southeast Asia, and much of Malaysia including the Philippines. It has been planted in Florida, Puerto Rico, Trinidad, Guatemala, Honduras and Venezuela. The fruit is round, half to one inch thick, smooth, glossy, dark red-purple, with light-brown, acid to sweet, astringent, slightly bitter, flesh, with six to ten small, flat seeds. Ramontchi is not what Trinis call governor plum.

thorns or pickers, self-pollinating, and easy to grow. Plants grow rapidly, often five feet a year, and produce large quantities of fruits about one inch in diameter, which are red to purple to blackish at maturity. Trees prefer full sun for best growth. The Jamaican plum is tolerant of a wide range of soil conditions, and also will tolerate some light salt spray. Plants generally need pruning at least once or twice a year to keep from becoming too overgrown. Make sure the area where you plant this tree is well drained. Every other month for the first two years broadcast a cup starter fertilizer 12-24-12 around the tree. Water if there is a long drought.

Jamaican plums are a good source of vitamins A and C and potassium, they have very little protein and only a trace of fat, but they do contain more antioxidants than any other fruit.

I could sit and eat green plums with salt and hot sauce for hours, or at least until my belly aches. Here a few recipes for those who can find some ripe plums the birds haven't hit.

Spicy Plum Jam

Ingredients: five pounds ripe plums, a half cup water, a half cup fresh lemon juice, one TS ground cloves, one TS ground cinnamon, five cups sugar, a half bottle Certo

Method: Remove seeds from plums. In a small pot combine water, cinnamon, cloves, and lemon juice. Cover and simmer on low for five minutes. Add sugar (more for sweeter) and bring to a boil for one minute stirring constantly. Remove from heat and add Certo stirring for five minutes. Spoon into sterilized - boiled - jars to a quarter inch from the top and seal with melted paraffin. Should make about eight pints.

Jamaican Plum Wine

Ingredients: five pounds ripe plums, four pounds of sugar, four liters of boiled water (boiling should remove all impurities), one package dry yeast.

Method: First wash all plums and then mash the pulp in a very clean five gallon bucket with a top. Pour in water, mix in sugar and stir until dissolved. In a cup of warm water, dissolve the yeast and pour into plum mixture. Cover and let sit in a cool place for a week stirring once each day. Using organdy or cheesecloth strain and place in a next very clean bucket with a cover. Check daily to see if fermentation bubbling has finished. Strain again with cheesecloth and funnel into sterilized (boiled) preferably brown bottles. Seal caps with melted wax-paraffin. Store in a dark place for at least six months. Makes five liters.

Plum Crisp

Ingredients: one cup very ripe plum pulp - skinned, peeled and seeded, one cup flour, one cup brown sugar, a half cup butter or margarine, one TS ground cinnamon, a half TS ground cloves, one TS ground nutmeg, one TBS Cornstarch, a half TS salt

Method: Combine the flour with half of the sugar and the spices. Blend in the butter until flour mixture is flaky. Mix the plum pulp with the remaining sugar and cloves and put in a greased baking dish or bread pan. Cover with flour mixture. Bake for one hour at 350.

Plum Dumplings

This is something different, but delectable as a unique dessert or appetizer!

Ingredients: two cups ripe plums peeled and seeded, two cups flour, three large potatoes peeled boiled and mashed, two TBS butter or margarine, one TS salt,

Method: Mix all ingredients together, except plums, into a dough about a half-inch thick. Slice dough into three- inch squares. Place one spoonful of plums in the center of each square. Pull up the corners to cover the plums and pinch shut. Carefully drop in boiling water and cook for fifteen minutes. Adding sugar or slight pepper sauce to the plums will obviously change the flavor and intention of these dumplings.

HEALTH NOTE

This plum is used as to increase urination and to relieve stomach spasms. A decoction made from the plums is used to bathe wounds and heal mouth sores. Syrup prepared from these plums is taken to stop chronic diarrhea. A bark decoction is a remedy for mange, ulcers, dysentery and for bloating caused by intestinal gas in infants. The gum-resin of the tree is blended with pineapple or soursop juice for treating jaundice.

Despite the gardener's best intentions, Nature will improvise.
Michael P. Garofalo

THE AMAZING LEMON

We have an old lemon tree that provides nice shade in the afternoon. It is too thorny for me to climb to pick so I knock the fruit with a long bamboo. Before I researched the lemon, I only used lemons to wash chicken and fish before beginning to prepare a meal. I did not know the real health value of the versatile lemon. Lemon's botanical name is *citrus limonum*.

The lemon is one of the world's oldest fruits and was probably first grown in Assam in northwestern India. By 200 A.D. the lemon had reached southern Italy, and spread to Iraq, Egypt and China during the next five centuries. Columbus brought lemon seeds to Hispanola in 1493. The Spaniards planted the first lemon trees in Florida near St. Augustine. Today the biggest lemon producers are India, Argentina, Iran, and Brazil.

In Trinidad we have the 'rough' lemon with bumps over its round fruit. Lemon trees are easy to grow from seed and will do well in most soils. The very thorny tree can grow large and should be pruned at after about two years to keep it less than fifteen feet tall for easy picking. The lemon is used for a rootstock to graft most citrus such as sweet orange and grapefruit. Plant where water will not be a problem during the rainy season as lemon trees are subject to root rot. Spray every tree monthly with an insecticide to controls mites mixed with a soluble nutrient and throw a cup of 12-12-17-2 (blue) fertilizer. This practice and regular watering in the dry season will produce large juicy fruit. In Mexico and India, fine-grained lemon tree wood is used for carving toys and other small articles.

A sprinkling of lemon juice on sliced apples, bananas, and avocados, acts as short-term preservative and keeps them from turning brown. The sour juice has been used for bleaching freckles, lightening hair, and is used in some facial cleansing creams. Use a slice of lemon dipped in salt to clean the copper bottoms of scorched cooking pots and pans. It will remove the dried soap and stains in the shower and washbasin. Cut a lemon in half and dip in baking soda for scrubbing dishes and stained surfaces. Oil from the lemon peel is used in furniture polish or make your own by mixing a cup of olive oil with a cup and a half of lemon juice. This is great on hardwood floors. Its 'clean' scent is widely used in soaps, shampoos and perfumes. Mixed with water the juice will help potted plants (except chrysanthemums) to hold their flowers longer.

It was the juice of the lemon originally picked in the Mediterranean countries, not limes, which were first used aboard British sailing ships to prevent scurvy. After planting limes through out the Caribbean chain as a preventive measure the sailors became known as 'limeys'. A lemon has only 25 calories with one gram of protein, eight grams of carbs with calcium, iron, potassium, and phosphorous. One hundred ml of lemon juice has 50 ml of vitamin C (ascorbic acid).

The average lemon contains approximately three tablespoons of juice. Although not antiseptic, lemon juice will clean most meats and fish of anything on their surface. If left in the tart juice, beef or lamb gets tender. Lemons, with or without oranges, are used to make marmalade. Lemon zest is the grated rind used to flavor many dishes. Try something new and stuff lemon slices inside a whole chicken and bake for a unique flavor. Lemons juice squeezed on vegetables while steaming will keep the colors bright. Rice cooked with lemon juice will be fluffier.

Lemonade

Lemonade may have originated in medieval Egypt, but still not very popular in the Caribbean. Mix the juice of one lemon with three cups pure water per every two glasses of beverage desired. Add sugar to taste. Serve over ice.

Lemon Chicken

Ingredients: one chicken cut up, half cup olive or canola oil, the juice of two lemons, two cups white wine (optional), two TS minced garlic, ten green olives chopped, one medium onion minced, quarter TS nutmeg, quarter TS saffron, salt and seasoning to your taste

Method: Mix oil, lemon juice, garlic, and saffron preferably in a blender and coat chicken pieces. Place in a frying pan and add onion and nutmeg. Cover and simmer for half an hour. Add salt and pepper to taste.

Lemon Ochro Soup

Ingredients: one chicken cut up, juice of two lemons, two cups sliced ochros, six cups water, one large onion chopped, four medium tomatoes chopped, quarter cup tomato paste (or ketchup), third cup uncooked rice (prefer brown), two TS salt, one TS turmeric, pepper, and other seasonings to taste

Method: Rub chicken parts with lemon. Put chicken and lemon juice in large pot and add water. Bring to a boil and then simmer covered for fifteen minutes. Add all other ingredients and cook for a half an hour or until chicken is tender and rice is ready.

Mediterranean Potatoes

Ingredients: seven medium potatoes peeled and quartered, quarter cup olive or canola oil, two TBS ketchup or tomato paste, the juice of two lemons, one and a half cup chicken broth, one TBS oregano

Method: Bake, microwave, or boil potato pieces until tender. Mix oil, tomato paste and all other ingredients in a saucepan and simmer for five minutes stirring so it doesn't burn or stick. Pour mixture over potatoes and let stand for at least a quarter of an hour before placing uncovered in an over at 350 for twenty minutes.

Rice Salad

Ingredients: three cups cooked rice (brown preferred), juice of two lemons, three chives chopped

fine, quarter cup parsley - minced, two medium tomatoes chopped, three stalks celery chopped, half cup peas, half TS salt, quarter cup olive oil, pepper, and spices to your taste

Method: Mix lemon juice and rice. Stir in the vegetables, salt, seasonings and oil. Chill in fridge at least one hour before serving.

Lemon Sorbet Dessert

Ingredients: two cups water, half cup sugar, two cups lemon juice, zest of six lemons

Method: Heat water enough to completely dissolve the sugar and pour into a bowl over the lemon zest. This will enhance the lemony flavor. If you have an ice cream maker use it or just put into a freezer until it just begins to freeze. Then put into a blender to smooth and reduce the ice crystals. Return and fully freeze. Adjust the amount of sugar used according to your family's sweet tooth and add any type of other citrus available.

HEALTH NOTE

Lemons, rich in vitamin C, strengthen the body's immune system as an antioxidant, protecting cells from damage. For a cough, sore throat, or cold; make a syrup by heating one tablespoon lemon juice with two tablespoons honey. Try lemon juice mixed with salt and ginger as a tonic for a cold. The aroma of lemon oil has been tested to reduce stress in aromatherapy. Lemon juice mixed with water will aid sdigestion, and pat an insect bite with raw lemon to stop the itch and reduce swelling. Lemons help cleanse the body through perspiration and as a natural diuretic. Lemon juice is believed to actually cleanse the liver of toxins.

Many things grow in the garden that were never sown there.

Thomas Fuller

THE SWEET AND TART LIME

I love the smell of a fresh cut squeezed lime and the thirst quenching taste of tart limeade. We have a small grafted seedless lime tree that grows tennis ball size juicy limes, which I use to 'wash' my chicken and fish. Like most of the other citrus fruits, the juicy lime, originated in Southern Asia. Arab traders carried the lime from India to the Middle East where the twelfth century crusaders carried this tart fruit to the Mediterranean. Supposedly Columbus planted the first limes in Hispaniola. Spanish explorers sailed the lime to Florida spawning the 'Key Lime'.

There are three basic types of limes with various names. The West Indian, Key, or Mexican lime has many seeds and is smaller than the big seedless Tahiti variety. The Tahitian may be a genetic hybrid between the true lime and citron that arrived in California around 1850 with fruit imported from Tahiti. There is also a Southeastern Asia variety called the Kaffir lime, which is similar to Trinidad's rough skinned lemon. 'Kaffir' is a strange name because in Arabic it means unbeliever, but is derogatory in other meanings.

The lime was medicine for the ancient peoples. During the Middle Ages fragrant limes were used to ward moths from hanging clothes just as today's mothballs. Sailors loved the lime since it prevented the weakening disease of scurvy. Picking limes ashore was considered the best duty of the British sailors, who became known as 'limeys'. 'Limin'' or hanging out is derived from sailors' lime picking, which always included resting, and gossip under the lime tree.

A perfect addition to any yard is a grafted or budded lime tree that bears in three to four years. Thorny, wild, West Indian lime trees grown from seeds may reach twenty feet and take at least six years to bear. These trees need good, well-drained soil, and planted in full sun. When planting, carefully place the tree and water after refilling half the soil in the hole. Pile the second half of the soil higher to prevent puddles after rains that could cause root rot. About two feet around the high soil at the tree's trunk create a three-inch high water ring. This will hold water for the fine outer roots during the dry season. Water every few days for the first month, then weekly for the next four months if it is the dry season. Pull or gently hoe all weeds and lawn grass from inside the water ring so the young tree doesn't have to compete for water. Do not use herbicide.

Wrap the tree's trunk with aluminum foil so it is not damaged by a brushcutter. A half cup of urea sprinkled is the recommended fertilizer every three months. After the tree starts to blossom, alternate between urea and 12 –12 17 –2 every two months. Limes are sturdy trees that have few natural enemies, so little chemical spraying is necessary. Fruit that ripens to yellow on the tree will soon turn brown at one end. Brazil and Mexico lead the world's lime production with a combined 1.2 million metric tons.

One lime has only twenty calories with absolutely no fat, sugar, or cholesterol. Citrate of lime and citric acid are also derived from this fruit. One lime contains a third of the daily requirement of Vitamin C as ascorbic acid. Limes also have some fiber and potassium.

Caribbean people use the lime in pepper sauce and chutneys. Throughout the Caribbean and Central and South America limejuice is used in marinades, salad vinaigrettes, fish dishes, cocktails, and ceviche (pronounced sa-vi'-chee or sa-vich'). In ceviche style cooking, lime juice mixed with chopped hot and sweet peppers, tomatoes, chadon benee, and onions not only flavors fish or seafood; its acid actually cooks the flesh firm and opaque.

> **DID YOU KNOW?**
>
> Key limes (*Citrus aurantifolia*) that predominate the world are smaller, yellower in color, seedy, sourer, and grow on thorny trees than the large, green, seedless limes. The Persian or Tahiti Lime (*Citrus latifolia*) is a hybrid developed in the early 20th century. The fruit is larger than the Key Lime, more resistant to disease and pests, and has a thicker rind. They are picked slightly immature, while still green in color because they turn yellow when fully ripe, and might be confused with lemons.

Ceviche Shrimp

Ingredients: one pound large shrimp, six limes (the juice from four and two sliced thin), one large ripe tomato chopped, one medium sweet onion, one hot pepper minced, quarter cup fresh orange juice, one bunch chadon benee chopped fine, salt and spice to taste

Method: Bring a two-quart pot of water to a boil. Turn off and then add shrimp for only one and a half minutes, then remove from water, drain and place in a glass bowl. Add all chopped vegetables, the minced hot pepper, lime and orange juices, and lime slices to the shrimp. Let sit covered in fridge for at least four hours. Serve on biscuits, sada roti, or warm garlic bread.

Grilled Lime Chicken

Ingredients: three limes, four large chicken breasts, three TBS canola oil, one medium onion minced, six garlic cloves minced, half hot pepper minced (optional), one leaf chadon benee - chopped fine, salt and spices to taste

Method: In a bowl mix oil, lime juice, chadon benee, and hot pepper. Add chicken. Let marinate in the fridge four hours. Grill over hot coals for twenty minutes basting chicken with marinade.

Lime Biscuits

Ingredients: three TBS lime juice, half pound baker's flour, one TS baking powder, one stick (four ounces) butter or margarine, quarter TS salt, one egg plus one egg yolk, two TS grated lime peel, quarter cup brown sugar

Method: In a suitable bowl combine flour, baking soda, and salt. In another smaller bowl mix butter with the sugar until creamy, before adding the egg and yolk, limejuice and grated lime peel. Combine flour mix with the creamed butter mix into a soft dough. Form the dough into one half-inch balls and place on cookie sheets. Bake at 180 degrees for twelve to fifteen minutes until golden brown. Sprinkle with sugar if a sweet taste is desired.

Lime Balls

Ingredients: The juice of three limes, grated peel of one lime, two cups grated green papaya, half cup water, one cup brown sugar

Method: Boil grated papaya, cool, and strain. Press papaya to remove all excess liquid. Place sugar and a half-cup of water in a saucepan and bring to a boil. Stir until thick before adding grated papaya, lime juice, and grated lime peel. Boil for two minutes stirring constantly. Remove from heat and slightly cool before rolling spoonfuls into balls. Allow to dry on a wax paper.

The Easiest Lime Pie

Ingredients: half cup lime juice, two egg yolks beaten, one can sweetened condensed milk, one pre-made pie shell.

Method: Bake pie shell in a 350 degree oven for ten minutes. Blend egg yolks and milk in a bowl. Mix in lemon juice. Boil mixture in a double boiler stirring constantly until it thickens, or it will stick and burn. Pour into pie crust and put in fridge for at least an hour before serving.

HEALTH NOTE

Lime oil smells sweet and blends well with citronella, lavender, or rosemary. It also increases blood circulation, relieves arthritis, reduces high blood pressure, and fights colds and flu. It can be rubbed on areas to reduce acne, and take the pain from the stings of insects.

MAMEY APPLE

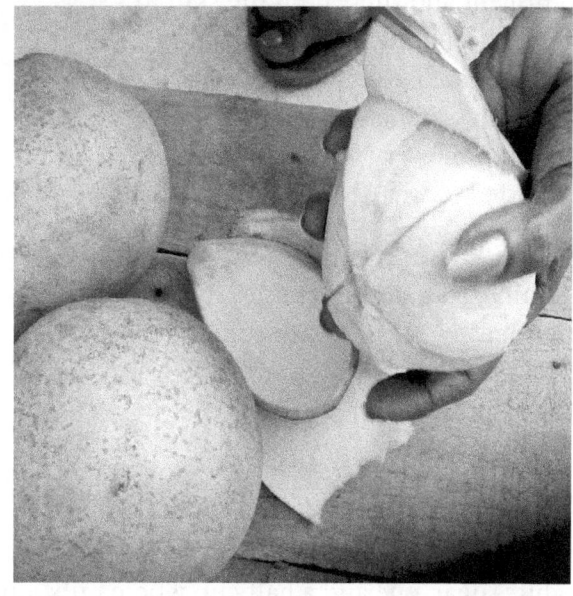

The mamey, or mamey apple, is another delicious tropical fruit seldom seen in the local markets. The nearly round fruit is about six inches in diameter. The leathery, thick skin is light gray-brown, and bitter. The peel must be sliced with a knife and pulled back. This will expose orange flesh usually wrapped in a white membrane. This membrane, called 'rag', is very bitter and must be removed from the flesh. The juicy flesh can be golden or orange, depending on the tree. It has a sweet aroma and taste usually without any acidity. Remove the seeds from the flesh and enjoy. Often this fruit is confused with the mamey sapote, which is not round, but oblong.

The mamey is native to the Caribbean and northern South America. It is seldom cultivated, but grown individually as a shade tree. Costa Rica, Columbia, and Venezuela are reported to have mamey orchards. The mamey tree grows well in deep, rich, well-drained soil, but can adapt to the sand and limestone of the Bahamas and southeastern Florida.

If you are lucky enough to find a mature tree locally, search under it for seedlings. Most mamey apple trees are grown from seeds. Placed in moist soil, the seeds should germinate within sixty days. However you could be unlucky and get a sterile male tree. Mamey trees take up to ten years to bear fruit. Grafted trees are available if you can find one.

The best way to determine if a mamey apple is ripe is to use your thumb nail to scratch the skin. If green shows, it is not ripe. Wait until it shows yellow, or golden orange. Be careful picking as these fruits easily bruise.

I got some mamey apples from a friend near Toco who knows of a tree far in the bush. I wonder how an exotic tree was planted where there are no homes? After carefully scoring the peel with a knife I pulled back the skin. The juicy flesh is delicious raw. I'm told Jamaicans steep peeled mamey apples over night in wine and sugar, or in just lightly salted water. Sliced mamey flesh may also be stewed with sugar and some lemon juice and then used to fill pies or tarts. Stewed mameys can be seasoned with cinnamon, nutmeg, and or ginger. When cooking the flesh for any purpose, one is advised to skim off any foam that forms on the surface of the water, as this is usually bitter.

In the French West Indies, an aromatic liqueur called Creole Water or Creole Cream, is distilled from the flowers and described as a tonic, or digestive remedy. In Venezuela, powdered seeds are made into a pasty ointment and rubbed on the skin to treat skin parasites. For mosquito fevers Brazilians boil mamey apple leaves in water and give the patient a teaspoon every four hours. It is reported to work when quinine has failed.

A hundred grams of mamey apple pulp has only 45 calories with some calcium, phosphorus, iron, Vitamin A & B, and thiamine.

> **DID YOU KNOW?**
>
> Commonly known as the mammee, mamey, or mammee apple is botanically *mammea americana*. This fruit is also known as the Santo Domingo apricot or South American apricot. The mamey is unique in remaining virtually static in the past 40 years, receiving little attention at home or abroad. Trees and their fruit remain rare, delicious finds throughout the Caribbean.

Mamey Muffins

Ingredients: two cups mamey, peeled, seeded and pureed, two eggs, one and a half cup white sugar, one and a half cup whole milk, one and a half cup bakers flour, one TS baking soda, one TS cinnamon, one TS nutmeg, one half TS ginger, one quarter cup grated coconut, one quarter cup soft butter, one half cup brown sugar

Method: In a suitable bowl blend eggs and white sugar, then add mamey and milk. In another bowl combine flour, soda and spices and add to mamey mixture. In a separate bowl, combine coconut, butter and sugar. Spoon mamey batter into a greased muffin tin and top each with a teaspoon of coconut mixture. Bake at 350 for twenty –five minutes

Mamey Apple Colada

Ingredients: two cups mamey, peeled, seeded and pureed, one cup low fat milk, one cup fresh orange juice, four ice cubes.

Method: Put everything in a blender and give it a whirl.

Mamey Sherbert

Ingredients: two cups of chilled peeled and pitted mamey pulp, one cup white sugar, one TS powdered cinnamon

Method: Slowly combine the sugar and mamey apple by stirring. Add cinnamon. Pour into an ice cube tray and freeze.

Mamey Ade

Ingredients: two mameys seeded and peeled, six cups water; one half cup sugar, one TS fresh lemon juice

Method: Boil mamey pulp for five minutes. Add lemon juice and sugar. Let stand preferably over night. Serve chilled.

Fruits

MANGO

What could taste better than biting into the first Julie mango of the season? When I was a kid as soon as the mangos started to get full everybody was making chow. Now I anxiously watch our tree for the first fruits to change color. A chilled, juicy mango is my favorite treat while watching night-time television.

About four thousand years ago the delicious mango originated in East India in the foothills of the Himalayan Mountains. Mangos were one of the first fruits humans farmed. Asian kings had vast orchards of trees. An Emperor of Delhi, Akbar (1556 to 1606), had a hundred thousand hectares of mango trees. The word 'mango' is derived from the Tamil East Indian dialect word, man-kay, which Portuguese explorers changed to manga. India is still the largest producer of mangos with very little exported. Mangos traveled to the Caribbean in the mid 1700's. More mangos are eaten throughout the world than any other fruit. There are over 20 million metric tons of mangos grown yearly. Mango's botanical reference is *mangifera indica*.

Mango is a true 'comfort food' because, like papaya, mango contains a stomach-soothing enzyme. Mangos not only make you feel good, they are great health wise because they contain plenty of fiber, vitamins A and C, and potassium. One large mango has about a hundred calories with no cholesterol and half of the necessary daily fiber.

There are over a thousand varieties of mangos throughout the world. Trinidad has starch, rose, Julie, calabash, doodoo, turpentine, Graham, ten-pound, spice, grafted and others. My personal favorites are doodoo and calabash. Green mango can be prepared into kutchela, chutney, preserves, takari, anchar. Choose your favorite type and seek out a tree vendor. Unless you choose a dwarf grafted mango, allow at least a circumference of fifty feet for the tree. It should bear about the third year. Plant in an area that drains well to avoid root rot. Keep adequately watered. In the dry season use the hose water for at least and hour a month for excellent fruit. Tend with a cup of high nitrogen fertilizer mix monthly, and watch for pests. Your tree should give you a lifetime of shade and delicious fruit.

Mango Pie

Ingredients: three cups of sliced peeled mangos, two TBS quick tapioca, three quarter cup brown sugar, quarter TS salt, one TBS butter or margarine melted, two nine inch pie crusts

Method: Combine all ingredients except pastry and let stand for fifteen minutes. Fill one pie shell with fruit mix and cover with the other shell. Wet your fingers and press edges of both shells together. Using a fork neatly pierce the top several times. Bake at 400 degrees for one hour. Let stand till cool before serving.

Method: In a bowl combine dry ingredients. Create a pond in the center and add everything else. Mix with a big spoon. Place in a greased and floured bread pan. Let the mixture sit for half an hour before baking at 350 degrees for one hour.

Mango Crisp

Ingredients: five cups ripe mangos peeled and sliced, half cup brown sugar, half cup flour, half cup soft butter/margarine, one TBS lemon juice, quarter TS nutmeg, one and a half TS cinnamon

> **DID YOU KNOW?**
>
> Everybody loves the mango. So much that it is known by the same name in various languages. This luscious fruit is mango in English and Spanish, and only slight different in French (mangot, mangue, manguier), Portuguese (manga, mangueira), and Dutch (manja). In some parts of Africa it is called mangou, or mangoro. India produces more than half of the world's mango crop nearly a billion tons on two and a half million acres. There are more than five hundred different varieties of mango in India. Supposedly a French ship, from an Indian ocean island named Isle de Bourbon with several varieties of mango were shipped to Martinique, but were seized as a prize of war by Admiral Rodney. These mangoes eventually found themselves on all the islands.

Method: Mix mangos, nutmeg, one TS cinnamon, and lemon juice and place in a greased ten by ten baking dish. Blend flour, brown sugar, a half TS cinnamon with butter until mixture is crumbly. Drop the flour mix over the mango. Place in a 350 degree oven for thirty five minutes.

Mango Salsa

Ingredients: one cup diced mangos, half cup diced red sweet peppers, half cup red Spanish onion, one small hot pepper minced, one TBS fresh lime juice

Method: Combine all ingredients and chill. Use as a accompanying sauce or marinade with meat, chicken, or fish dishes. Eat with sada roti, or chips.

Mango Chicken

Ingredients: two very ripe mangos - peeled, halved, and pitted, one small hot pepper minced, two chadon benee leaves chopped fine, one medium onion chopped, one whole chicken

Method: Mix all ingredients and stuff in the chicken. Place in a baking dish and cover.

Fruits

Bake at 350 degrees for an hour. Uncover and bake for another fifteen minutes.

Mango Chow

Wash and slice two just ripening mangoes into thin strips. Place in a bowl with a pinch of salt, one hot pepper— seeded and minced, one TS black pepper, two chadon benee leaves. Let sit for an hour and enjoy.

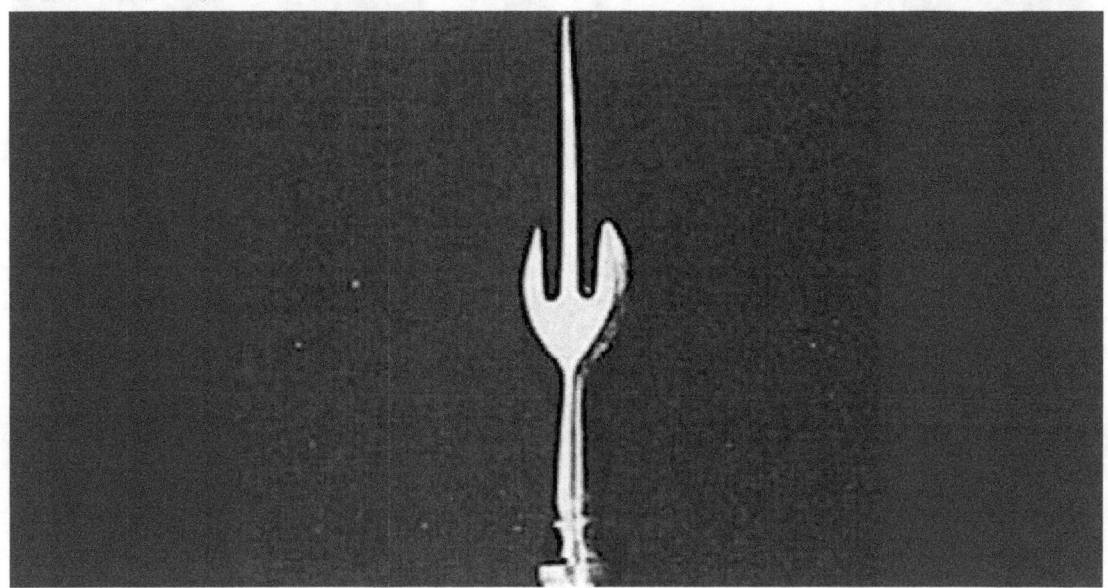

The long center tine of the mango fork is designed to pierce a mango through the seed. With the peel removed, the most flavorful flesh around the seed can be enjoyed like a lollipop.

A king asked a sage to explain the Truth. In response the sage asked the king how he would convey the taste of a mango to someone who had never eaten anything sweet. No matter how hard the king tried, he could not adequately describe the flavor of the fruit, and, in frustration, he demanded of the sage "Tell me then, how would you describe it?" The sage picked up a mango and handed it to the king saying "This is very sweet. Try eating it!"

Hindu Teaching

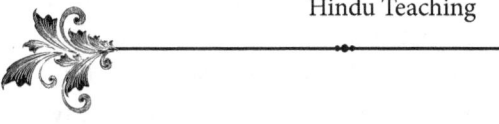

MANGOSTEEN

Widely cultivated in the Asian tropics, the mangosteen is no relation to the mango. The mangosteen is a tropical evergreen tree with an aril fruit, native to Indonesia. I stumbled upon a mangosteen tree or I might never have the chance to sample its luscious taste. The tree is almost twice the size of the usual orange. The ripe fruit is deeper, more reddish purple than the canistel. The segmented white flesh has a nice fresh aroma. The taste is a non acidic orange and peach flavor. Mangosteen's botanical name is *garcinia mangostana*.

You will be lucky to find one of these trees in the wild. Try for them with the grafted tree vendors. It can be grown from seed, but do multiple plantings as the success rate is low. Keep the seed moist until it is planted. In damp potting soil, seeds should sprout within a month. This tree has a long, fragile taproot and that makes transplanting difficult. It is advised to transplant this tree before it gets more than a foot and a half tall. This will keep the tap root at a manageable length. It may take two years to grow this size.

Be certain to dig an exceptionally deep hole, thirty inches, and have someone suspend the mangosteen seedling while crumbled earth is gently put around the long root. The mangosteen tree is a very slow growing. It does well in deep rich, sandy soil. Keep the surrounding area weeded. It needs good drainage, but can handle and may thrive in damp soils. It does not do well in area that has sea blast. The mangosteen needs about twenty feet on all sides. Every other month sprinkle a cup bearing fertilizer 12 –12-17-2. The tree may bear fruit within five to seven years, or longer. Keep this tree watered! Mangosteen trees, with the roots almost constantly wet, as around a pond or along a stream, bear the most fruit. To combat the dry season use a mulch of coconut husks or palm fronds around the base of the tree to help hold moisture. Spray with an insecticide combined with a foliar fertilizer once a month. Keep ants away from this tree as they will decimate the tender leaves.

The exquisite taste of mangosteen's juicy, snow-white, soft flesh is well worth the effort and wait. The fruit may be seedless or have multiple seeds that cling to the flesh. The flesh is slightly acidic, but exquisitely delicious. Young mangosteen are pale light green. Ripe mangosteen are bright purple and just slightly soft. These fruits must be harvested by hand and not be allowed to damage with a fall. One taste and you know why they call mangosteen, 'The Queen's Fruit'. There is a legend Queen Victoria offered a sizeable reward to anyone who would bring her a mangosteen.

> **DID YOU KNOW?**
> Mangosteen is perhaps the finest flavored of all of the fruit in the world, hence the nickname 'Queen of Fruits'. It is called 'Food of the Gods' on some French Caribbean islands. Many compare the taste to combination of strawberries and oranges.

To open a mangosteen use a knife to score the peel. Grab the fruit with both hands. Be careful not to get any of the juice on your clothes as it will stain. Twist gently along the score with the thumbs until the rind cracks. Pull the halves apart along the crack and remove the fruit. Mangosteens are dried to use medicinally throughout Asia. The powder is made into an ointment for skin disorders. A piece of this fruits peel put into boiled water and soaked overnight is a bush remedy for chronic diarrhea. Mangosteen have sixty calories per hundred grams of flesh with calcium, phosphorus and iron.

Mangosteen Sorbet

Ingredients: One cup mangosteen chopped as small as possible, one cup sparkling grape juice, one egg white, one half cup white sugar, six slices of peeled firm limes, six slices of a firm peeled orange

Method: Put mangosteen pieces in a bowl and add the grape juice. Stir the effervescent fruit juice into the puree. Whip the egg white until it thickens adding the sugar. Combine this with the mangosteen and grape juice. Gently stir in the lime and orange pieces. Freeze.

Mangosteen Cocktail

Ingredients: Two ounces mangosteen juice (squeeze one fruit), a splash of fresh lime, orange, or lemon juice or a combination, three ounces of either vodka or light rum, one twenty ounce soda.

Method: Combine ingredients and pour into two glasses with ice. Top off with soda.

Mangosteen Pudding

Ingredients: Two cups mangosteen segments chopped small, two cups milk, two cups whipping cream, one quarter cup white sugar, a quarter cup hot water, two tablespoons gelatin

Method: In a coffee cup dissolve gelatin in hot water. In a two quart pot combine the sugar and mangosteen. Constantly stirring, bring mixture to a boil over low heat. Stir in milk, whipping cream. Bring this mixture to a boil again stirring constantly over low heat. Add gelatin and leave it until this boils one more time. Remove from heat and pour into a suitable container. Cool in the fridge until it congeals.

HEALTH NOTE

Mangosteen's peel contains the highest level of nutrients, while the actual fruit pulp is one of the world's best tasting fruits. Mangosteen has compounds that have antioxidant, anti-bacterial, anti-fungal, and anti-tumor activity. It also has anti-histamine and antiinflammatory properties.

You ain't old yet but when you get old, all the women in the village start to look down on you when they find out you want to do something other than sweep the kitchen or cut up vegetables. Had this big starch mango tree when I was small. Anytime I set myself to climb it, there was always a woman passing by to yell at me and tell me to get down. Asked me why I leaving my poor mother to do all the housework. I never got to the top. It was like God was always watching, ready to send another hag to tell me down.
Then, one day, they cut down the tree.

K. Jared Hosein

ORANGE

On a hot day, very few fruits taste better than a peeled, fresh orange The orange was first cultivated in the area between Southern China and northeastern India thousands of years ago. This fruit slowly migrated to the Middle East about 800 AD, and made the trip to Europe seven centuries later. The fantastic, healthy, great tasting, sweet orange was brought to the Caribbean by Christopher Columbus on his second voyage and planted in what is now the Dominican Republic. The world famous Florida oranges were first planted around St. Augustine before 1600, but it took two more  centuries to travel across the United States to California. Outside of the tropics, oranges were considered a 'holiday' treat because of their cost. Efficient steamship transport brought the orange to everyone at a reasonable price. Brazil leads a list of the worlds orange growers including the US, Mexico, Spain, and Israel. Botanically sweet orange is *citrus sinensis*.

Perfect, name brand, brilliant orange fruits are injected with a dye – citrus red #2 – into the skins (not the pulp). Also the oranges grown in the temperate climate of Florida tend to become more orange than their tropical cousins. Partially green oranges or even those with brown rusty spots may be as delicious. Oranges with smooth textured skins, firm and heavy are the better choice. Small, heavy oranges with thinner skins are usually the best for juice.

Oranges have both sweet and bitter varieties. Most of the oranges grown are round like king, osbeck, or dansi. The Mediterranean naval orange actually has a second fruit set in the blossom end. More varieties of the orange are sweet 'Parson Brown', seedless 'Hamlin', 'Marrs', and the pineapple orange. The thin-peel, seedless Jaffa was developed in Palestine, while the very desirable, large seedless Valencia came from Spain, and the smaller mandarin came from China. Other members of the orange family are the everhard, kumquat, calamondin, and some tangelos. The tangerine is a type of mandarin first grown in Tangiers Morocco in 1841. Bitter oranges are used to make marmalade and liquors as Triple Sec, Grand Marnier, and Cointreau.

To grow oranges first select the variety you love. You can try planting seeds, but usually this will usually have disappointing and time wasting results. This is because the bitter orange is often used as rootstock for grafting. It is better to buy a tree created by budding. All types prefer well-drained loamy soil with a pH between 6 to 8. Continually damp or dense clay soil will result in poor growth, low production, and a short life for the tree. Oranges need full sunlight for the growth and production. They should be

DID YOU KNOW?

The sour -Seville orange is bitter, rarely eaten fresh, cultivated for marmalade and grafting rootstock. The sweet orange was introduced in the 15th century. The bergamot orange is not as sour as lemon, but not as sweet as grapefruit, grown for cosmetic oils and flavoring. The smaller mandarin oranges or portugals/tangerines have loose skins and are cold and drought hardy. Only 20 per cent of all oranges are sold as whole fruit; the rest used for orange juice, extracts, and preserves. The orange is subtropical, not tropical and the most commonly grown fruit tree in the world. Brazil grows the most oranges.

planted at least ten feet from buildings, driveways, walkways, and fences. Keep trees twenty feet apart. When planting orange trees do not leave any indentation where water can settle and cause root rot. The soil around the tree should be higher with an outside ring of soil constructed to make efficient watering. Inside the ring should be barren of grass. The orange tree should be watered daily when planted, then weekly. A good way to protect the new orange tree is to wrap some aluminum foil around the young trunk. The foil will protect against herbicide spray and bushwhacker damage.

Fertilize infant orange trees with a cup of ammonium sulfate (urea 21 – 0 – 0) every three months during the first year. Increase to two cups the second year and three cups the third. Once the tree begins to blossom add 12 – 12 –17 –2 at the rate of two cups every three months per tree plus the ammonium sulfate. Always keep the grass away from the tree. Leafminers are a problem, but indiscriminate spraying of pesticides will destroy the natural predators. If you feel spraying chemicals is the answer, first identify the problem by speaking with someone at an agricultural center, and then select the appropriate chemical. Apply it properly and at the appropriate time to control the pest while minimizing the amount of chemical used.

Cooking with oranges is easy. Sauté onions and ginger slices in butter and then pour in orange juice. This is a great sauce for fish or chicken. Mix peeled and seeded orange pieces with beet root slices for a tasty salad. Sweet potatoes or squash can be simmered in orange juice for a wonderful taste.

Sun Soup

Ingredients: one cup orange juice, one medium onion chopped, one cup 'soaked' red lentils, one cup pumpkin boiled and mashed, juice of half a lemon, one sweet red pepper-chopped, half cup sliced mushrooms, one and a half cups vegetable broth, one TBS butter or margarine, one TBS grated ginger, two TBS sugar, half TS cumin, half TS coriander, one TS cinnamon, half TS salt

Method: In a soup pot brown the onions in the butter adding the sweet pepper and mushrooms. Slowly add vegetable broth with lentils with spices. Stir in pumpkin, then add lemon juice. Bring to a boil, add orange juice, and simmer until lentils are tender.

Sweet and Sour Cabbage

Ingredients: one cup orange juice, four cups shredded cabbage, one cup shredded carrots, four pimentos seeded and chopped small, one TBS cornstarch, one TBS vinegar, one TBS brown sugar, salt and spices to taste

Method: Mix brown sugar, vinegar, cornstarch, and a pinch of salt. In a large pot heat orange juice until it begins to boil before adding cabbage, carrots, and pimentos. Mix in sugar cornstarch combination. Cook for fifteen minutes stirring to keep from sticking.

Orange Sweet Potatoes

Ingredients: half cup orange juice, one pound sweet potatoes-peeled and boiled, one TBS brown sugar, one TBS butter or margarine, half TS cinnamon, half TS nutmeg, salt to taste.

Method: Combine orange juice, sugar, and spices. Pour over sweet potatoes and boil uncovered for five minutes. You may have to add a few tablespoons of water if mix gets too low. Stir occasionally.

Orange Pie

Ingredients: one and a half cups orange juice, two oranges-peeled, seeded and sectioned with no membrane, one cup milk, two egg yolks, half cup sugar, three TBS cornstarch, one pack unflavored gelatin (orange flavor may be substituted), one prepared or packaged pie crust

Method: In a skillet mix orange juice with milk, egg yolks, sugar, cornstarch, and gelatin. Cook over medium heat until it just starts to boil. Pour mixture into pie crust and chill until almost firm. Carefully stir in orange segments and chill again until firm.

HEALTH NOTE

Each orange has about sixty calories packed with vitamins C, and B-1, fiber, and folate. One orange contains about 50mg. vitamin C; or two-thirds of our daily need. Remember how our grannies had dried orange peels hanging for use in flavoring tea? Seems they knew more then than we do today. Orange peels contain compounds known as 'polymethoxylates (PMF)', which has been tested to lower cholesterol significantly – as much as some prescription drugs! Just dry the peel and add to tea or boiling water. Chinese use dried mandarin peel to regulate their chi or flow of energy.

PAPAYA

A papaya a day should keep the doctor away. Many people swear to good health from consuming this fruit, usually with the seeds. Papaya is native to the tropics of the Americas. Explorers carried this revered fruit to Asia, Africa, and India. Columbus called papaya 'the fruit of the angels'. The pear shaped, orange papayas can grow to twenty pounds with a soft sweet flesh and great for your health. The seeds can be eaten, but they have a peppery taste. Each orange fruit is a rich source of nutrients such as vitamins C, A and E, plus fiber, folate, and potassium. Basically there are two types of papayas, Hawaiian and Mexican. The Hawaiian varieties are pear-shaped fruit generally weigh about 3 pounds and have yellow skin when ripe. The flesh is bright orange or pinkish, and are easier to harvest because the plants seldom grow taller than 8 feet. Mexican papayas are much larger and may weigh up to 10 pounds and be more than 15 inches long. The flesh may be yellow, orange, or pink. Locally the most common type is Red Lady which produces a succulent fruit in seven to eight months. Papaya's botanical name is *carica papaya*.

Papaya trees like sunshine and reflected heat, so the hottest place, against the house where nothing else will grow is a perfect location. Papayas dislike wind, but can withstand some stiff breezes. Papayas can be grown from dried seeds. Papayas do not handle transplanting well. For the best results start them in large containers, such as a gallon paint pail, so they only have to be transplanted once. Do not damage the root ball when planting in the soil. Papaya trees are either male or female. The female has flower blossoms close to the trunk and males have blossoms on branches. Males are not necessary for pollination. Pant at least six plants to insure of having females.

In a well-drained area, fork a two foot by two foot hole a foot deep. I add a shovel full of rotten manure and then add a layer of dirt building a mound before placing in the new tree. It is necessary to water often during the early weeks. Almost all transplants enter a 'shock period' as they become accustomed to their environment. Too much rain is the biggest enemy of the papaya. In the rainy season with hard winds these trees may need to be propped or staked with ropes to keep the roots from pulling out of the soil. In the rainy season with hard winds these trees may need to be propped or staked with ropes to keep the roots from pulling out of the soil. If you are planning to grow papaya commercially, plow the land so it drains well. Too much rain and water soaked land is the biggest enemy of the papaya. Use a 12 – 24 –12 fertilizer for the first two to four months switching to 12 –12 –17 –2. Papaya trees can bear fruit two years or longer. Papayas do not need to be pruned, but some growers pinch the seedlings or cut back established plants to encourage multiple trunks.

Bunching is a disease where the top leaves do not spread, and black spot rot is another disease that occurs on the fruit. Papayas are ready to pick when the skin is yellow-green. Bring inside to protect against bird damage and store at room temperature for two or three days until they are almost fully yellow and slightly soft to the touch. If you want to speed this process, place them in a paper bag with a banana or ripe apple. Ripe papayas should be stored in the refrigerator and consumed within one or two days, so you can enjoy their maximum flavor.

Dark green fruit will not ripen properly off the tree, even though it may turn yellow on the outside. Papayas are often sliced and eaten alone. They can also be cooked to make chutney or various desserts. Green papayas should not be eaten raw because of the latex they contain, although they are frequently boiled and eaten as a vegetable. In the West Indies, young leaves are cooked and eaten like spinach. In India, seeds are sometimes used as black pepper.

> **DID YOU KNOW?**
>
> Papayas have 33% more vitamin C and 50% more potassium than oranges with fewer calories, 13 times more vitamin C and more than twice the potassium than apples, and four times more vitamin E than both apples and oranges. Tea made from papaya leaves is consumed in some countries as protection against malaria. Papaya leaves are steamed and eaten in parts of Asia. The bark of the papaya tree is often used to make rope. Modern research has confirmed that unripe papaya does indeed work as a natural contraceptive and can induce abortion when eaten in large quantities.

The most common use for papaya is to aid digestion. Papayas are the only natural source of papain, an effective natural digestive aid, which breaks down protein and cleanses the digestive track. This means less food settles into the metabolism and becomes fat, making papayas' natural digestive properties an advantage to people trying to lose weight. Eating papayas helps to prevent diabetic heart disease. Nutrients in papayas prevent cholesterol from clogging arteries reducing the possibility of strokes. Papaya may lower cholesterol, prevent against colon cancer, and reduce inflammation caused by rheumatoid arthritis. Researchers believe papaya may be great for your sense of sight. The high vitamin A (300 percent of the daily need) content of papaya will help smokers prevent emphysema or lung inflammation from second hand smoke. A cup of papaya has 120 calories with good doses of vitamins A, E, and C, folic acid, potassium and fiber.

Papaya Pie

Ingredients: one medium papaya – about two cups fresh papaya cut into one inch cubes, half cup brown sugar, one egg beaten, and one premade graham cracker pie crust, one TS ground cinnamon, half TS ground nutmeg, pinch of salt

Method: Combine sugar and papaya chunks and let sit for ten minutes. Place in a saucepan and simmer for ten minutes. Stir in cinnamon, nutmeg and salt. Simmer until fruit is soft, but hasn't totally dissolved. Remove papaya mixture from the heat and let cool until lukewarm. Stir in beaten egg with a large fork until well-combined, but the fruit in chunks should remain. Pour papaya filling into graham cracker pie crust. Bake for about 45 minutes at 350. Let papaya pie cool before serving. Best to refrigerate for a few hours.

Papaya Stuffed with Shrimp

A great lunch.

Ingredients: two ripe papayas cut in half lengthwise and seeded, half pound cooked shrimp cleaned and cut into one inch pieces, two limes, one small onion minced, one stalk celery minced, half cup mayonnaise, pinch curry powder, salt and pepper to taste

Method: Combine mayonnaise with juice of one lime, curry powder, salt, and pepper. Add shrimp, onion and celery. Mix and chill for one hour. Spoon shrimp salad into the papaya halves. Cut remaining lime into wedges and use as garnish.

Papaya Coconut Pudding

Ingredients: two medium ripe papayas, two TBS quick-cooking tapioca, one cup unsweetened coconut milk, three quarter cup milk, three TBS sugar, half TS vanilla extract

Method: In a medium pot, combine coconut milk, milk, sugar, and tapioca, and bring to a boil over high heat. Reduce the heat to simmer, stirring for five minutes, until the tapioca becomes almost clear and slightly thick. Do not overcook; the mixture will continue to set as it cools. Add vanilla extract. Let the tapioca cool, cover, and refrigerate at least an hour. Slice the papayas in half and remove the seeds, scoop out the flesh and dice very small or place it in a blender or food processor to a puree. This should make about 2 cups of puree. Cover and refrigerate at least an hour. Combine the tapioca pudding and the papaya puree just before serving.

The garden suggests there might be a place where we can meet nature halfway.

Michael Pollan

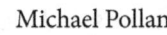

PEWA – PEACH PALM

I don't find the fruit of the peach palm sweet or overly tasty, but I sill crave it. Like the chenet, and governor plum—it is the peeling, salt, and sucking that make eating pewa enjoyable.

Pewa grows on a type of palm called the peach palm. There are more than 200 names for the species of palm scientists label as bactris gasipaes. In Trinidad it is pewa. In Costa Rica it is 'pejibaye', and 'macana' in Venezuela. Pewa's relatives are the gru gru and gri gri.

This palm can grow to about fifty feet, but it is usually shorter as most pewa can be picked without a ladder. Peach palm originated in the Western Hemisphere, probably native to the Amazon rainforest, and is presently grown from Nicaragua and Honduras to northern Bolivia. This type of palm thrives at low altitudes, especially at sea level. Once you find a tree, carefully free a shoot form the parent palm. This must be done with a broad sharp chisel or a sharp luchette, as the parent's roots can be tough. The only concern is to plant in soil that doesn't hold water. However, it will do fine in the rich soil along drains or rivers as long as the roots don't constantly stay wet. Dampness is one of the peach palms main enemies. Loosen the soil about a foot in diameter and a foot deep, but only cover the roots of the shoot. Weeds are another enemy, so clear the area around the palm three or four times a year. I recommend wrapping aluminium foil around the trunk so a bushwhacker doesn't damage the trunk.

Although this palm is not so bushy, it needs about ten feet spacing from other trees and walls. It will take about five years before developing shoots at the base of the fronds, which form a clump of pewa. A peach palm tree can live sixty or more years. Pewa is a fragile fruit that lasts only four or five days, so only pick what you can use. Various colors of pewa indicate different varieties of the peach palm. Many species of birds feed on this palm, especially parrots and parakeets. Once the fruit is ripening I put pieces of aluminium foil or pie plates on the palm leaves to chase the birds. A great cluster has a hundred or more pewa, and will weigh up to ten kilos.

Pewa cannot be eaten raw, it must be boiled with salt and spices, and eaten only after the skin is peeled off. The red pewa contains high amounts of carotene, iron, calcium, phosphorus, and are especially high in vitamins A and C. A hundred grams, or about four ounces of pewa have a hundred and fifty calories. We boil pewa in salt water, often with salt beef or fish for seasoning. The fruit is peeled the seed removed and eaten plain or with a dip of mayonnaise and pepper sauce. The pewa flesh can be deep-fried or roasted. Agro scientists are breeding spineless trees that bear seedless fruit with a higher carotene

DID YOU KNOW?

Pewa fruit contain carotene, calcium, phosphorus, and ascorbic acid, vitamin A, and nicotinic acid. Fruit should be boiled within 2 to 4 days of picking. They are eaten boiled in salty water, often with salt pork for seasoning. The fruit is then peeled, and the seed remove. Flavor varies with the carotenoid content and may be bland or have a strong nutty taste. Boiled pewa is eaten plain or with a dip of mayonnaise or cheese, or deep-fried, or roasted. It may be ground into meal, mixed with egg and milk and fried as tortillas. Raw fruits may be kept for several weeks in a cool, dry place and cooked fruits may be held in the refrigerator for 5 or 6 days.

content. Pewa is recommended as a remedy for headache and a bellyache.

Although we don't do it in Trinidad yet, the peach palm can be harvested for heart of palm. This has good commercial farming potential as the first harvest can be from 18 to 24 months after planting. In Brazil heart of palm is a big agri-business. There is a growing demand for heart of palm internationally for gourmet salads and dishes.

Don't toss the seeds, as they are rich in protein and fiber. They make good food for ducks and swine. Like other palms, the seed is rich in saturated fatty acids, and could be used to manufacture cosmetics and soap.

The following recipes might seem like a lot of work for us pewa lovers who just want to peel and suck. Try them, they are absolutely delicious.

Creamed Pewa

Ingredients: four pounds pewa shelled and seeded, two medium onions chopped small, three TBS cornmeal, two thirds cup milk, one TBS butter, half TS fresh grated nutmeg, salt and other spices to your taste

Method: In a skillet fry the onion in the butter and add the pewa flesh. Increase the heat and sauté quickly. Add milk and thicken with cornmeal and season to your taste. Serve on rice with grated nutmeg.

Fried Pewa Number One

Ingredients: three pounds of pewa cleaned and seeded, quarter cup all purpose flour, two TS baking powder, quarter cup milk, one egg separated, oil for frying, half TS salt, peppers, and spice to taste

Method: In a bowl combine flour, salt, and baking powder. Mix egg yolk with the milk and gradually add this mixture to the dry ingredients. When mixture is stiff blend in egg white and add pewa flesh. Carefully drop spoonfuls of this mixture into hot oil. Fry on both sides and eat while hot.

Fruits

Fried Pewa Number Two

Ingredients: a dozen pewa shelled and seeded pounded flat, breadcrumbs, three TBS flour, one TS English / Worcestershire sauce, two eggs beaten, one cup milk, butter or oil for frying, salt and spices to taste

Method: take the flat pewa and dip first in English sauce, then roll in flour, dip into the egg, salt, spice and milk mixture, and roll in the breadcrumbs. Fry quickly and serve hot with a spicy dip.

To forget how to dig the earth and to tend the soil is to forget ourselves.
Mahatma Gandhi

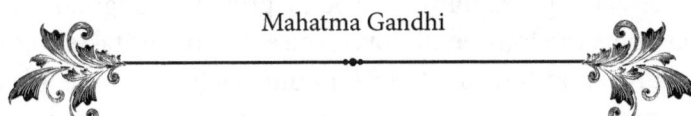

PINEAPPLE

Pineapple is one of God's best tasting, and strangest creations. We saved our cut off tops and planted them above the front yard drain. After a year we had sweet pine with very little effort. Although it looks like a cactus the pineapple, botanically ananas comosus, is the fruit of hundreds of individual flowers that cluster on the barb of the plant. When mature, all the pineapple's fleshy tissues swell with juice. The pineapple does not grow on a tree or a cactus, but on a 'bromeliad' with stiff leathery leaves around a center spike, which we call the core. Pineapples are usually four to nine pounds, but the Giant Kew type can be more than twenty pounds.

The pineapple originated in South America where Indians named the fruit 'anana' meaning excellent fruit. These Amerindians planted pineapples with their sharp picker leaves surrounding their villages to keep out intruders. In 1493 Columbus discovered the Carib Indians growing pineapples on the island of Guadeloupe. His sailors created the present name because the exterior appeared as a pinecone, yet the core tasted as an apple. By the mid 1500's pineapples were being grown in the West Indies for export to Britain. Two centuries later, pineapples were being grown throughout the Caribbean chain. French King Louis the fourteenth loved the sweet fruits' taste so much he forgot his manners and cut his mouth trying to bite an unpeeled pineapple. He treasured the fruit so much glass 'greenhouses' were created to grow them. Pineapples became a status symbol as a party decoration and as a dessert.

Captain Cook sailed the pineapple to Hawaii in 1790. It took another century and the efficiency of steamship transport to make commercial production feasible. Pineapples were made available to the world when Dole began canning them in 1903. Hawaii produces 10% of the world's pineapple, and it is the third most canned fruit after applesauce and peaches. Thailand is the presently world's largest producer of pineapples.

Pineapples rarely have seeds, but are grown from cuttings, which are either the tops or the suckers that appear close to the base of the fruit. The soil must be worked a foot wide and deep. Some rotted manure can be placed deep in the hole before returning the soil. Plant at least two feet apart, water regularly and fertilize monthly with a high nitrogen mix. Harvest when they turn a bright gold and can be easily twisted from the plant. If you are buying, a ripe pineapple should be firm, smell sweet with fresh green leaves. A pineapple is ripe if one of its top leaves can easily be pulled out. To reduce the acid content, permit the pineapple to sit for three days before using. To increase its sweetness, salt and let sit before eating.

Pineapple is another fruit that not only tastes good, but also is good for you. Pineapple juice is chemically close to our stomach juices. Consumed moderately pineapple aids digestion. It has plenty of fiber and helps the body relieve fluids, especially mucus from nasal passages. Never consume an unripe pineapple, as it can be poisonous causing throat irritations and diarrhea. The juice is an excellent cooking marinade tenderizing the meats while adding a tropical flavor. Two slices of a regular sized pineapple should be about a hundred grams and has sixty calories with no fat or cholesterol. Pineapple is a good source of vitamin C.

> **DID YOU KNOW?**
>
> Next to bananas, pineapple is the second most popular tropical fruit. In 2004 over 200,000 tons of pineapple were grown in Hawaii. Canned pineapple wasn't financially feasible until Henry Ginaca, an engineer, invented a machine in 1911 that could remove the outer shell, inner core and both ends of 100 pineapples in less than a minute.

Stewed Pineapple

Ingredients: one medium pineapple peeled, quarter cup dark rum, half cup sultana raisins, two TBS butter or margarine, quarter cup brown sugar

Method: Cut pineapple in half. One half chunked into half-inch pieces. The other half should be juiced, or canned juice may be substituted. Heat rum in a saucepan for one minute. Add raisins and stir before removing from heat. In a large skillet melt one TBS of butter. Add pineapple chunks and cook until sides are golden brown – about two minutes a side. Remove pineapple and clean skillet before melting the other TBS butter. Stir in sugar until it melts, add juice and boil for five minutes. Add raisins, rum, and pineapple chunks and heat for two minutes. Serve warm.

Scalloped Pineapple

Ingredients: one medium pineapple peeled and cut into half inch chunks, one cup butter or margarine, two cups sugar, four beaten eggs, quarter cup milk, one TS vanilla essence, four cups white bread cut into cubes (Sugar may be reduced to taste.)

Method: In a frying pan over medium heat; blend butter, sugar, and eggs into a cream then add remaining ingredients. Pour into a greased baking dish and bake at 350 degrees for an hour.

Pineapple Stuffed Pumpkin

Ingredients: one small whole pumpkin (2-4lbs), two apples cored, peeled, and chunked, half regular pineapple peeled and chunked, half cup peanuts (walnuts, cashews, or almonds may be used) one TS cinnamon, one TS nutmeg, half TS cloves, quarter cup grated coconut

Method: Neatly remove top of pumpkin (save) and remove seeds and membrane. Mix all ingredients and place in the pumpkin. Cover with top. Bake at 400 degrees for one hour.

Pineapple Pie

Ingredients: one pineapple peeled and crushed, one can sweetened condensed milk, half cup fresh lemon juice, one prepared pie crust, one container (half pound) non dairy whipped topping

Method: Mix sweet condensed milk with lemon juice. Add pineapple and whipped topping. Pour into pie crust. Chill at least four hours before serving.

Pineapple Rice

Ingredients: one fresh pineapple, two TBS canola oil, two cups cooked rice, one cup medium shrimp peeled and cooked, one chicken breast cooked and cubed, two bunches chives chopped, quarter cup carrots chopped, quarter cup peas (canned peas and carrots are fine)

Method: Cut pineapple in half and clean out the shell. Place shell under broiler or on grill until thoroughly heated. Chop a half cup of the pineapple flesh as small as possible. In a large skillet heat oil and stir in rice cooking for two minutes. Stir in remaining ingredients including the chopped pineapple. Spoon into heated pineapple shells.

Spicey Pine Fritters

Ingredients: one fresh peeled pineapple chunked small as possible, one hot pepper seeded and minced, two bunches chives minced, one medium onion chopped as small as possible, two cloves of garlic minced, half TS turmeric, one and a half cup flour, half cup milk, two beaten eggs, half cup canola oil for frying, salt and spices to taste

Method: Mix flour, milk, eggs, salt and spices until smooth. Refrigerate covered for 4 hours. Mix together with pineapple, pepper, chives, onion and garlic and blend into batter. Drop batter from a large spoon into a skillet with hot oil and fry about 3 minutes a side. Remove fritters and drain.

HEALTH NOTE

Pineapple contains micro-nutrients believed to prevent cancer and also break up blood clots. Pineapple juice kills intestinal worms, relieves intestinal disorders, and soothes the bile. The juice also stimulates the kidneys and aids in removing toxic elements in the body. Pineapple contains a mixture of enzymes called bromelain that helps reduce swelling by arthritis, gout, sore throat, and acute sinusitis. This also helps accelerate the healing of wounds due to injury or surgery. For the medicinal benefits eat pineapple between meals. Eaten with meals the enzymes are used digesting food.

Be a pineapple: Stand tall, wear a crown, and be sweet on the inside.
Katherine Gaskin

PLANTAINS

At most fruit stands there usually are very large bananas in varying stages of ripeness. They might be green, yellow, or black. I'm certain you wondered who would buy such under or over ripe fruit from the vendor. I would because the fruit isn't bananas, but instead plantains.

Plantains are in the genus *Musa*, and likely native to Malaysia and what is now the Indonesian islands. Plantain was brought to Madagascar from Malaysia and India through trading with Asian merchants. Alexander the Great's army carried plantains to southern Europe during his world conquest. The history of banana and plantain in the Caribbean has been traced to a Portuguese Franciscan Monk who brought them to Hispaniola from Canary Islands in 1516.

I know of three types of plantain, but there are probably others, or different names. The smallest, most curved plantain is the French. Horse plantain is bigger, but the giant are the biggest. To grow, first you must locate some healthy suckers. You do not need anything but a small grapefruit ball termed, the eye. I thought you had to carry out the big plants. The bigger the banana tree you attempt to plant will have less success. The big ones will die and then sprout. In plantains and bananas, small suckers adapt best. Experience has taught the eye, a small ball attached to the root is all that's necessary. Carefully chop off enough of the 'eye' that will grow without hurting the parent plant. This can be done best with a sharp tool called a luchette. It is recommended to soak the shoots for an hour in a pesticide solution like Malathion to kill any worms. Dig a hole about two foot deep and break up the compacted soil as loose as possible. Old heads recommend putting a piece of pitch in the hole before placing the eye. Make sure that the eye has a bit exposed to the air. Water, use 12-24-12 fertilizer at the base, and watch it grow.

Plantains mature in a year or less. They should be spaced about six to ten feet apart. Air must circulate, so don't crowd, and keep them trimmed. Plantains can grow to twenty feet tall are excellent garden shade and attractive landscaping. They take little work except for trimming, watering during the dry spells, and bi monthly broadcast a half cup of bearing, high potassium fertilizer around the base. Once the plant sends out the flag that announces it is ready to bear, feed it with a half cup of high potassium fertilizer, and keep it watered for bigger fruit. If the weight of the bunch gets too heavy and the tree starts to tilt, carefully prop or tie it for support. Once the bunch begins to form it may take two months to develop. Keep the birds away from the ripening plantains. Pick before they ripen and store in a breezy location, don't refrigerate.

Fruits

The only downside is that plantains and bananas are perennials, they are there until you remove them, always making in more shoots, which must be trimmed or within a few years they will crowd themselves into producing smaller bunches.

> ## DID YOU KNOW?
> The plantain averages about 65% moisture content and the banana averages about 83%. Compared to the banana, plantains have twenty times the vitamin A, about three times the vitamin C, double the magnesium, and almost twice the potassium.

Presently Southeast Asia produces 35 million tons annually, India produces 11 million, Africa 7.7 million tons, Central America 8 million, and South America 16 million tons. The plantain is a banana which is eaten cooked rather than raw. The fruit banana is eaten raw when it turns yellow. The plantain, also called air potatoes or cooking bananas, are drier with lower water content, making them starchier than fruit bananas. They are a staple crop in much of South and Central America, Africa, and the Caribbean.

Plantains are belly fillers, not for the dieters, as they are mostly carbohydrate, approximately 40 grams per half banana with180 calories, very high in potassium approximately 500 milligrams per serving. Plantains can be cooked at varying stages of ripeness.

Green plantain is starchy like a potato and can be fried or boiled.

Boiled Green Plantains

Side dish

Ingredients: three green plantains, half cup diced onion, third cup olive oil, one TBS vinegar, one TBS salt, half cup grated white cheese

Method: Peel the plantains. Beware green plantains have a slimy goop when they are peeled. A trick is to let dishwashing detergent dry on your hands. After peeling the plantains, the slime should easily rinse from your hands. Rinse any soap from the plantains before cutting them into one inch pieces. Boil for ten minutes in salted water or until tender. Sauté the onion in oil and vinegar. Mash the plantain pieces with an potato masher or a sturdy fork and fold in the sautéed onions. Cover with grated cheese. To make this into a casserole; add pieces of cooked carrots, green beans, beef or chicken, and bake for twenty minutes at 300.

Fried Green Plantains (Tostones)

Appetizer

Ingredients: four green plantains peeled and cut into one inch pieces, four cloves of garlic smashed, one TBS salt, one quart water, oil for frying

Traditional Method: smash garlic with salt to a paste and mix into water. Soak plantains pieces in garlic water for an hour. Drain and fry pieces in vegetable oil until golden brown. Be careful of the oil splatter. Flatten fried plantain pieces by pressing them with a large spoon on wax paper, and return to hot oil for two minutes. Great served warm with hot sauce and cold beers.

Green Plantain Balls

Appetizer or side dish

Ingredients: two green plantains peeled and grated, half cup flour, one medium onion chopped small, two cloves garlic minced, two chadon benee leaves chopped as small as possible, salt and pepper to taste, two cups oil for frying

Method: In a dish mix the grated plantains, onion, garlic, chadon benee, and flour with salt and pepper. In a deep pot, heat the oil. Squeeze the excess water from the plantain mixture between two large spoons, and form into small balls. Carefully drop into the hot oil. Cook a few minutes until golden brown. Remove and drain oil on a paper towel or newspaper. Eat with spicy sauce.

Yellow plantains are just beginning to ripen and are slightly sweet.

Ripe Plantain Baked

Breakfast or dessert

Ingredients: four ripe plantains, half cup apple juice, two TBS molasses or honey, one TS ground cinnamon, half TS ground nutmeg, half TS ground ginger

Method: Peel the ripe plantains, halve, and split. Place round side up in a baking dish. Mix other ingredients and pour over plantain pieces. Bake covered for 45 minutes at 300.

Poinonos

Venezuelan traditional dish

Ingredients: ripe yellow plantains peeled and cut into four long slices, two thirds cup of grated cheddar cheese, two eggs, a pinch salt, one TBS flour, one TBS water, oil for frying, toothpicks

Method: In a frying pan or wok, lightly fry the plantain slices on each side until slices are pliable, not brittle. Remove the slices and drain on paper towels until cool enough to handle. Form each slice into a ring, with ends overlapping about an inch. Secure with toothpicks. Stuff each ring with cheddar cheese. Squeeze the cheese together slightly so that it will not fall apart. In a bowl combine eggs, salt, flour and water. Cover the cheese centers with the flour and egg mix. Fry each side until it is sealed and golden.

Over ripe plantains are fully black. Once it turns black, the plantain is at it's sweetest, used for dessert or any recipe where a sweet taste is desirable. You may purchase yellow plantains and store them in a paper bag until they turn black.

Fried Ripe Plantain

Side dish or dessert

Ingredients: four black skinned plantains, half cup butter or margarine, one TS ground cloves, one TS ground cinnamon, two TBS brown sugar

Method: Peel the firm sweet smelling plantains. Heat butter or margarine and spices. Fry over medium heat until browned about 10 minutes. Sprinkle with brown sugar.

To forget how to dig the earth and to tend the soil is to forget ourselves.
Mahatma Gandhi

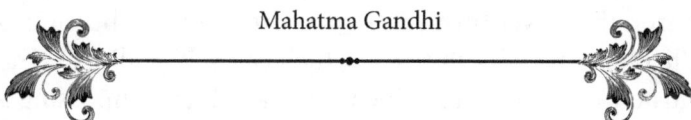

POMMECYTHERE

Soaked pommecythere (pronounced pom-sit-tey) is a personal favorite. The oblong, yellow-orange pommecythere tastes like a cross breed of a mango and a pineapple. It is believed to have originated in Tahiti and is native to Polynesia and Malaysia. Pommecythere was first brought to Jamaica in 1782. This plum shaped fruit is very popular in Asia, and eaten at all stages of ripeness. Pommecythere's main distinguishing feature is its spiny seed. These spines harden when the fruit matures, so the fully ripe fruit should be carefully sucked from the seed to avoid to an unwanted pieced lip or tongue.

Pommecythere trees thrive in all types of well-drained soil. The trees can be grown from seeds, which take a month to sprout. After a few months, the sprouts can be planted in holes bedded with well-rotted manure. It is best to have the small trees at least partially shaded by mature bananas. They should be spaced at least fifteen feet apart and from fences or buildings. Pommecythere trees can grow as much as six feet a year. The trees should be topped to keep to a reasonable height, otherwise they will grow rapidly to forty feet or more, which makes the fruit difficult to harvest, and susceptible to damage from high winds. These trees should bear in three to four years. Dwarf types bear in one to two years at a height of less than six feet.

During the dry season the leaves turn yellow and drop. Just as the rains begin, clusters form of small white blossoms of both sexes, which can self-pollinate. The fruit will appear in green clusters of ten or more ripening to a golden skin. Using a half cup of high nitrogen fertilizer mix once a month with regular watering, a mature tree should annually bear about two hundred pounds. Sri Lanka is the world's biggest producer for export of 250 metric tons each year.

Pommecythere leaves smell great, but are slightly sour and are used for flavoring, particularly curries. Indonesians make a dish with steamed leaves, salt fish, and rice. This tree's wood is adequate to make fishing floats or boats. Tree sap can be used for medicinal poultices. A tea made from the bark is a supposed remedy for diarrhea. The fruit is good source of vitamin C, potassium, carbohydrates, and fiber. The juice can be used to relieve diabetes, heart ailments, and urinary problems.

Pommecythere has suffered by comparison with the taste and desirable appearance of the mango. However, if the pommecythere is picked at the correct time, while still firm, it yields a delicious juice for cold beverages. As the pommecythere ripens the flesh changes from yellow to orange and becomes sweet with a sort of pineapple flavor. It can be frozen to make a delicious ice. Stewing the ripe flesh with a little water and sugar and then straining produces a rich appletype sauce. By adding cinnamon or cloves, this sauce can be slowly cooked to a thick preserve similar to apple butter. Unripe fruits can be made into chutney or pickled. Pommecythere is a good flavor ingredient for sauces and soups, and can be used like papaya as a meat tenderizer. Pommecythere fruit have 160 calories for 100 grams because 10% is sugar, 85% is water, which is why it is great for juice.

> **DID YOU KNOW?**
>
> Botanically this fruit is named *Spondias dulcis*. Pommecythere is the French name, but it has other callings such as ambarella, golden apple, Tahitian or Polynesian plum, Jew or Jamaican plum, mango jojo, or Tahitian quince. The name of the city of Bangkok, Thailand is derived from makok, the Thai name for pommecythere. Captain Bligh brought pommecythere to Jamaica in 1792 from Hawaii.

Pommecythere Chutney with Raisins

Ingredients: Two pounds pommecythere fruit half ripe, half pound golden raisins, two cloves garlic minced, two TBS fresh ginger grated, three cups clear vinegar, two cups sugar, two TBS salt, five hot peppers cleaned of seeds, stems and membranes (more can be added to taste), one TBS or one stick cinnamon, five whole cloves

Method: After thoroughly washing, slice fruit into sections and combine with all other ingredients in a stainless steel or cast iron skillet. Aluminum will blacken the chutney. Bring to a boil and then simmer for an hour and a half until thick. Stir often to keep chutney from sticking to the skillet and burning. Fill jars, which have been sterilized by immersing in boiling water. It is best to use containers that do not have metal lids.

Pommecythere Fruit Sauce

Ingredients: five pounds fruit peeled with seeds removed, half cup water, two TBS cinnamon, cloves, and other spices to taste

Method: Bring all ingredients to a boil and simmer for one hour with continuous stirring to mash up the fruit. Strain if the consistency is too thick. Continue cooking if the consistency is too thin. Serve hot or cold as a side for beef or chicken main dishes.

Pommecythere Conserve

Ingredients: one pound pommecythere, one cup brown sugar, one cup water, one stick cinnamon, six drops bitters

Method: Wash fruit and make many pricks with a fork. Combine water and sugar in a saucepan and boil. Add pommecythere, cinnamon and boil stirring constantly until fruit becomes clear, in thick syrup. Stir in bitters. Store in hot sterile jars or refrigerate.

Ralph's Soaked Pommecythere

Ingredients: About a dozen full but not ripe pommecythere. (The amount depends on the size of the container you are planning to fill.), half cup white vinegar, one TBS salt, half TS black pepper, five big cloves of garlic minced, half hot pepper to your taste

Method: Fill half of your container, jar or bowl, with water. Add remaining ingredients. Peel and make cuts into the pommecythere flesh. Put into container and let sit for at least two days.

Pommecythere Kuchela

Ingredients: a dozen green pommecythere grated, four cloves of garlic minced, one hot pepper seeded and minced, one TBS salt, quarter cup anchar masala, four TBS oil

Method: In a frying pan on low—heat oil, add garlic and pepper, pommecythere, anchar masala, and salt. Keep stirring until everything is evenly mixed. Remove from heat and put into sterilized bottles.

DID YOU KNOW?

The pommecythere is plum shaped, sweet-sour and eaten at all stages of ripeness. Its distinguishing feature is it's unique spiny seed. The spines harden as the fruit ages, so be careful eating almost-ripe fruit. The sweet flesh hides a tough fiber. Unripe, green pommecythere chow is made by peeling with a knife and sliced. Then add in bitter pepper and salt. Ripe fruit are yellow to orange, fragrant, and sweet with a taste like pineapple.

There is no gardening without humility. Nature is constantly sending even its oldest scholars to the bottom of the class for some egregious blunder.

Alfred Austin

THE POMEGRANATE

The pomegranate is another passionate fruit. Like the sugar apple, you must passionately want to enjoy its unique flavor, to deal with the seeds. The round, usually reddish-maroon three inch fruit has a distinctive royal crown at the blossom end. The pomegranate is technically a big, tough-skinned berry with many seeds in juicy, transparent, jellied membrane compartments.

If you do not like seeds, this fruit is not for you. A juicer or food processor can be used to extract the juice from the pulp. The juice can be strained to remove any seed sediment. Seeds are more than half of the weight of this fruit.

The pomegranate has every reason to wear a crown. It is an ancient fruit native to an area in the Himalayas north of India, but has been cultivated throughout the entire Mediterranean region since ancient times. Greek mythology explained the four seasons with pomegranates. Demeter, who was the goddess of the harvest, had a daughter Persephone who was kidnapped by Hades, the lord of the underworld. Demeter refused to permit anything to grow on earth until Persephone was returned. Zeus, the lord over all the lesser gods, ordered her to be reunited with her mother, but she had eaten four pomegranate seeds. The rule was if you ate anything while in the underworld you were forced to spend eternity there. Each seed equaled one barren month on earth, or winter.

The Moors brought the pomegranate to Spain where it is the national emblem. The Spanish city of Granada is named for it. Kandahar in Afghanistan is famous for quality pomegranates The unique pomegranate is a perfect backyard tree. It grows to between fifteen and thirty feet. The pomegranate will grow in any well drained soil, even rocky. For a small tree, it has almost as many branches as seeds. Some trees at France's Versailles Gardens have lived for two hundred years. Every three months feed young, not yet bearing trees, a half cup of 12-24-12 starter fertilizer around the roots and water during dry season. Once it bears change to a cup 12-12-17-2 or another bearing salt twice a year.

Pomegranate will develop suckers at the roots. These can be used to plant, or trees can be raised from seeds. The tree can be evergreen or deciduous. Pomegranate seeds sprout easily, but better trees are developed from cuttings. The pomegranate may begin to bear in a year after planting, but two to three years is more common. The fruits ripen six months after blossoms appear. Too much sun exposure will dull the usual reddish skin to a burnt brown and toughen the skin. The pomegranate is equal to the apple in having a long storage life of more than six months if refrigerated. This fruit improves with time

> ## DID YOU KNOW?
>
> Pomegranate is called granada in Spanish and grenade in French. Botanically is punica granatum. Buddhists believe the pomegranate to be a blessed fruit, and some scholars believe the pomegranate, not the apple, was the forbidden fruit in the Garden of Eden. A pomegranate tree may live for more than a century. Once the pomegranate fruit is picked it stops ripening, but will become more flavorful after being in storage.

as it gains juice and flavor. In northern India, pomegranate seed sacs are dried in the sun for two weeks and sold as a spice.

How to eat a pomegranate without mess: cut out the crown blossom end, and remove some of the white membrane while trying not to break the red pulp around the seeds. The entire seed is consumed raw, though the juice is the tasty part. With a sharp knife cut slits in the fruit's skin making quarters. Break the pomegranate apart on the slits and bend back the skin to remove the seeds. It is also possible to freeze the whole fruit, making the red arils easy to separate from the white pulp membranes. Avoid using aluminum cooking pots or carbon steel knives with pomegranates as they can turn the juice bitter.

Pomegranate juice has been used as a natural dye in many countries and will stain fingers and clothes. Ink can be made by steeping the leaves in vinegar. The Japanese make an insecticide from the bark. The pale-yellow wood is very hard and makes excellent walking canes.

Pomegranate adds a distinctive flavor to sorbets, icings, salad dressings, soups, and puddings. The juice provides a fresh, unique flavor to marinade fish, chicken, pork, and beef. Grenadine is a thick red syrup made from pomegranates and often used in cocktails such as the Tequila Sunrise. An ordinary home kitchen orange-juice squeezer can extract the juice.

Pomegranate juice has also been shown to lower blood pressure, inhibit viral infections, and may destroy dental plaque. A hundred 100 grams of pomegranate has seventy calories with plenty of potassium, vitamins C and B5. Pomegranates are considered one of the best fruits for fighting illnesses due to its high levels of vitamins, minerals, and antioxidants.

Pomegranate Chutney

Seeds in the following recipes include the juicy membrane.

Ingredients: one cup pomegranate seeds, half cup red currant jelly, third cup chives including tops chopped fine , one TBS fresh ginger minced, one TBS hot pepper seeded and minced, one TS ground coriander, one TBS fresh lemon juice, salt to taste

Method: Remove pomegranate seeds the night before and chill seeds in an airtight container. Soften currant jelly in the sun or in sauté pan on high for about a minute. Add chives, pomegranate seeds, ginger, hot pepper, coriander, and lemon juice. Add salt to taste. Let stand about 15 minutes before serving.

Pomegranate Vinegar

Ingredients: one cup fresh pomegranate seeds, two cups white vinegar

Method: Place pomegranate seeds in a clean wide mouthed bottle with a lid. Rough the seeds up with a spoon then cover with vinegar and seal tightly. Place jar in a window in full sunlight and let steep for two weeks. Use through a strainer or strain vinegar through a cloth.

Pomegranate Roast Chicken

Ingredients: quarter cup cooking oil, two cloves of garlic minced, one medium chicken-quartered, one pomegranate-halved, juice of a lemon, half TS cinnamon, one TBS brown sugar, salt to taste

Method: Mix oil and garlic and coat chicken pieces. Put pieces in a baking dish with any garlic oil that remains. Bake at 375 degrees for thirty minutes. Then combine pomegranate lemon, cinnamon, sugar, and salt and baste the pieces. Return to the oven for another twenty minutes until skin is browned. Serve with the juices.

Pomegranate Cake

Ingredients: seeds from one large pomegranate, three quarters cup sugar, six TBS margarine, two large eggs, one large egg white, three quarters cup milk, one TS lemon zest, two TS vanilla extract, one TS baking soda, three cups bakers flour, half TS salt

Method: Blend sugar and butter until creamy – ten minutes of whisking. Add eggs and egg whites one at a time and continue to blend. Combine milk, lemon zest, vanilla, and baking soda. Combine flour and salt, with milk-butter mixture. Add pomegranate seeds. Spoon into a greased bread loaf pan, and bake for an hour at 350 degrees. Cool before slicing.

> *Wilt thou be gone? It is not yet near day. It was the nightingale, and not the lark, that pierced the fearful hollow of thine ear. Nightly she sings on yon pomegranate tree. Believe me, love, it was the nightingale.*
>
> Juliet, Romeo and Juliet Act 3 Scene 5

POMELO - SHADDOCK

The pomelo is the largest citrus fruit and the ancestor of the grapefruit. Unfortunately the majority of a pomelo fruit is a spongy rind with white inedible pulp. It took a lot of evolution to produce the relatively thin skinned grapefruit. The pomelo is a delicious fruit with a reddish core with succulent tangy sweet juice. These fruits can reach two kilos in weight and almost the size of a volley ball. The largest shaddock on record weighed twenty-two pounds!

The name is Dutch, but in Trinidad it is usually called Shaddock after the ship captain who brought this fruit from Indonesia. Like so many tropical fruits this one has numerous names pummelo, pommelo, Chinese grapefruit, Lusho Fruit, jabong, pompelmous, and shaddock.

The pomelo is native to southeastern Asia and all of Malaysia, Indonesia, New Guinea and Tahiti. The first seeds were brought to the Western Hemisphere in the 1600's by Captain Shaddock who stopped at Barbados on his way to England. By 1696, the fruit was being cultivated in Barbados and Jamaica. The original trees were grown from seeds, but today they are grafted. The fruit's flesh may be white or red.

You can try to start a tree from seeds, but I recommend finding a garden shop that has grafted trees. A tree sprouted from grafted seeds may produce the root stock rather than the graft. Plant it in an area that gets full sun and is well drained. These trees will not survive any standing water, or seriously damp soil. Give it a cup of 12 -24-12 starter fertilizer every three months for the first two years. Once you see blossoms give it a cup of 12-12-17 -2 bearing fertilizer every six months. In the dry season give this tree plenty of water, five gallons, every week. This will produce succulent fruit. Twice a year spray the tree with an insecticide like Fastac mixed with a foliar mix with trace minerals. Watch your tree for damage to the new leaves from ants. A grafted pomelo is a nice backyard tree. It doesn't have a lot of small branches so it doesn't make deep shade. After five years our grafted tree is still only six foot tall and seems to be always bearing. It began to bear huge fruits after the second year. These trees are unique sights with bunch of big fruits hanging on a small tree.

The pomelo-shaddock is eaten by peeling it, skinning the segments, and enjoying the juicy pulp. Because the fruits are so large, usually about ten inches in diameter and the flesh center much smaller – about four inches across – it is difficult to determine when the fruit is ripe. If the fruit stays too long on the tree the pulp dries out. The fruit rarely changes from its green color as it matures, but some do become slightly yellow.

Pieces of the pulp can be segmented for salads and desserts, or just eaten raw. The juice is delicious. The pomelo tastes like a sweet, mild grapefruit with little of the bitterness common among grapefruit. The peel can be candied. Be careful if you have to peel a lot of pomelos because there are chemicals in the peel that can irritate skin.

One cup of pomelo has only seventy calories and is very high in potassium. The Chinese believe that a bath with water from boiling pomelo husks will cleanse a person and repel evil.

> ## DID YOU KNOW?
> It is the largest fruit identified as *Citrus maxima Merr.*, (*C. grandis Osbeck*; *C. decumana L.*). The common name is derived from the Dutch pompelmoes, which is rendered pompelmus or pampelmus in German, pamplemousse in French. Alternate names include, shaddock, limau abong, limau betawi, limau bali, limau besar, limau bol, limau jambua, Bali lemon, and pomelo.

Pomelo Chicken Salad

Ingredients: one pomelo - peeled, seeded, and broken into pieces, one cooked chicken breast shredded, one cup cooked medium shrimp cleaned and deveined, one teaspoon chopped hot red pepper seeded and minced, one teaspoon sugar, juice from one lime, one tablespoon chopped fresh chadon benee, small head red leaf lettuce. Garnish with one quarter cup roasted peanuts, and julienned fresh red sweet pepper.

Method: Add shredded chicken and shrimp with the pomelo. In another bowl combine the chopped red chili, sugar, lime juice and chadon benee. Mix with the pomelo chicken and shrimp. Spoon this over the lettuce. Top with peanuts and garnish with sweet red pepper slivers.

Pomelo Ice

Ingredients: one pomelo peeled, an ice cube tray and fresh pure water.

Method: Peel and core the fruits over a bowl and squeeze to catch the juice. Combine with water and pour into the ice cube tray. Freeze overnight in the freezer.

Pomelo Fish

Ingredients: one cup of pomelo juice, one pomelo peeled and sliced a half inch thick, two pounds of fish steaks or fillets like king, tuna or salmon. One small onion chopped small, one clove garlic minced, one TBS chadon benee

Method: Combine juice, onion, and garlic and chadon benee. Marinate fish for at least an hour, but four hours will be better. Save marinate. Line a baking dish with the pomelo pieces. Lay the fish on the pomelo and pour the marinade over the fish. Cover tightly with foil. Bake at 350 degrees for thirty minutes. Uncover and bake another five minutes.

Chicken Pomelo

Ingredients: one whole chicken, two pomelos—one quartered and one juiced, one half hot pepper seeded and minced (optional), salt and seasoning to taste.

Method: Season inside of chicken cavity with salt and hot pepper. Place pomelo quarters halves inside chicken. Place chicken in a pan. Pour half of the pomelo juice into cavity and the remainder on the chicken. Cover with foil and bake at 400 degrees for forty five minutes. Remove foil and continue to bake for ten to fifteen minutes till brown.

Fried Pomelo

Ingredients: two or more pomelos seeded and halved, two TBS butter or margarine, two TBS brown sugar, cinnamon and nutmeg to taste

Method: Heat a large frying pan and melt butter over medium heat. Put pomelos face down and cover. Fry for four minutes. Remove and sprinkle with sugar, cinnamon and nutmeg.

Broiled Pomelo Crisp

Ingredients: one pomelo seeded and halved, quarter cup old-fashioned oats, one TBS brown sugar, quarter TS ground cinnamon, pinch of salt, two TBS butter

Method: In a bowl combine oats, sugar and cinnamon. Put pomelo halves on an tray and cover with oat mixture. Put under broiler for eight to ten minutes. Serve warm.

HEALTH NOTE

Pomelo is loaded with vitamins, rich in vitamins C and B complex, and beta-carotene. It is a great source of folic acid which is especially good during pregnancy. It contains a lot of heart friendly potassium. It fights atherosclerosis and helps regulate blood pressure. Pomelo is great for dieting because it quenches your appetite and has only thirty five calories per hundred grams. Limonoids found in pomelo are being studied for their cancer fighting properties. Eating a pomelo is invigorating and increases stamina and lifts your spirit.

RED BANANAS

For some strange reason, the red banana has locally acquired a bad, and unwarranted reputation. Trinidadians named the red banana mataboro, donkey stones, and even go so far as to call it 'the man killer.' There is a superstition that eating red banana when drinking rum is a lethal combination. It is definitely an old wives tale and red bananas are harmless, although heavy doses of rum can make almost anything deadly.

It is amazing how few people have tried or even seen red bananas, a variety with a reddish-purple skin. They are smaller and plumper, more like the local silk fig. The ripe banana flesh is creamy yellowish and even pink when fully ripe, but they are certainly sweet. They taste sweetest when fully ripe. The redder a fruit, usually means it contains more carotene. Perhaps the red banana is actually nutritionally better than the usual yellow varieties.

Red bananas are also known as Jamaican bananas, Red Spanish, Red Cuban, Colorado, Macaboo, or Klue Nak. In India where it may have originated, red bananas are 'Lal Kela'. Since Alexander the Great found a liking for red bananas in 327BC they are grown the world over. They are a strain of the Cavendish banana.

The red banana plant is large and is highly resistant to disease. The entire plant is elegant for a productive landscape theme as it is almost all maroon. As the bunch evolves it goes from deep maroon to a bright orangish-red when fully ripened. As the fingers are small the bunch may be large and the tree will probably need to be propped in the latter stages of growth. These bananas have a thick peel, but not as thick as a plantain. The flesh is firm and has a nice aroma and flavor quite different from other bananas. This tree is uniquely red maroon with nice stature and is a great addition in a backyard landscape.

First find someone who has red bananas and get some suckers. Soak in a recommended mixture of a mild insecticide such as Malathion and water for an hour before planting to rid it of any worms. Dig a deep hole and refill as your crumble and soften the earth. Plant the sucker so a bit is exposed. This will be a bigger than usual tree, and needs a space of eight to ten feet from any neighbor or building. Water regularly, and every other month hit it with a quarter cup of some high potassium fertilizer. When it shoots up the signal leaf indicating it is about to bear, keep it moist and broadcast a cup of high potassium salt around the base. This tree should bear in sixteen to eighteen months, but it may take two years to make a bunch. This strain of banana appears to be more resistant to the diseases prevalent today.

DID YOU KNOW?

Red bananas are often used to make dried banana chips. Dried bananas contain have five times more calories than fresh. Bananas are fermented to make beer in east Africa. India grows the most bananas. Wild banana varieties carry much bigger seeds that would make it difficult to eat, but necessary for the plant's reproduction. The definition of fruit is 'a mature ovary containing seeds'. In fact, a banana is more precisely referred to as a berry! The modern banana is cultivated to be seedless. The yellow bananas that we eat (Actinidia deliciosa) do have seeds, but they're so small they're not functional, meaning they are not useful for the plant's reproduction.

I have had these trees for years since they were recommended by a friend who had eaten them in Mexico. Once they start bearing you should have a bunch every three months from the same stool. The bunch bears about six nice hands, the fruits are thick, about six inches long. They are beautiful to look at and delightful to eat, especially fried for breakfast. I have been told there is also a white variety of mataboro, but that seems to be silly. Why would you want a white version of a red banana?

Red bananas are eaten in the same way as yellow bananas, by peeling the fruit before eating. They are most frequently eaten whole raw, or chopped and added to desserts or fruit salads. They can also be baked, fried, or toasted. Red bananas are one of the varieties commonly used for store-bought dried bananas.

According to banana giant Dole, Americans eat thirty-three pounds of bananas annually. Red bananas are excellent as an energy snack. High in potassium, they can help reduce cramping after exercise or stress.

Ideally, red bananas should be eaten when they are soft, not mushy. They will ripen in a few days at room temperature, and refrigeration is generally not advised because it can make them extremely mushy. A red banana will also emit ethylene gas, that quickly ripens other fruits.

Every red banana has about 115 calories with 400 mg potassium and 15% of your daily requirements for vitamins C and B6 and one gram of protein.

Red Bananas with Cardamom

Ingredients: six red bananas peeled and cut long ways, quarter cup butter, half cup brown sugar, two TBS fresh lime juice, half TS fresh cardamom seeds ground, a quart vanilla ice cream

Method: Melt butter in sauté pan over medium heat. Add brown sugar and stir until dissolved. Add bananas, lime juice, and ground cardamom. Cover and simmer for five minutes, stirring occasionally, until bananas are tender. Spoon bananas with sauce over ice cream.

Fruits

Friend Red Bananas with Fruit Salsa

Ingredients: six red bananas-peeled and sliced long ways, two TBS butter for frying, two TBS brown sugar, two portugals or tangelos,-peeled, one grapefruit or shaddock, and two mangoes-all fruit peeled, seeded and chopped as small as possible, two TBS honey, one TS vanilla extract, two TBS grated fresh coconut

Method: In a sauté pan brown the red banana slices in the butter over medium heat. After turning the slices twice sprinkle the brown sugar in the pan and stir until the slices are covered. Remove from heat. In a bowl combine all fruit pieces, vanilla, and honey. Let stand in the fridge for an hour or until chilled. Put banana slices in bowls and cover with fruit salsa. Sprinkle each bowl with fresh coconut and serve.

HEALTH NOTE

Bananas are said to contain everything a human body needs including all eight amino acids, which our bodies can't self produce. Bananas are a good source of fiber and potassium. Red bananas have more vitamin C than the usual yellow types. The redder the fruit the more nutritious. Eat at least one banana a day. It comes in truly germ proof package, because its thick peel is an excellent protection against bacteria and other contamination.

Man is like a banana: when he leaves the bunch, he gets skinned.
Proverb

SAPODILLA

My primary school was renovated and grafted sapodilla trees were a welcomed addition to the landscape. Three years later, all the standard four students played marble pitch for the sweet fruits. The sapodilla is round, about three inches in diameter, with a flat base and a thin brown leathery skin. It resembles a small potato. It is about 2-4 inches in diameter. The flesh varies from yellow to reddish-brown, and usually has a grainy texture. Sapodilla tastes sweet, like a pear dipped in crunchy cinnamon-brown sugar. Fruits usually have from 3 to 12 hard, black, shiny flattened seeds about 3/4 inch long at the center of the fruit. Ripe sapodillas have a great aroma. This fruit is believed to have originated in Southeast Mexico. Sweet-toothed Amerindian tribes as the Mayans and Aztecs, and the European explorers spread sapodillas throughout the tropical Americas to southern Florida and the West Indies.

Sapodillas are most commonly grown from seeds and take at least five years to bear fruit. It is wise to use the seeds from the largest sweetest sapodillas you are lucky to locate. A grafted tree will bear fruit in about three years. This tree will grow easily in most well drained soils. Every month fertilize with an 8-4-8 mix for the best results. Once the tree blossoms it takes about five months for the fruit to ripen. Sapodillas are difficult to decide when they are ripe enough to harvest. When the fruit is brown and pulls easily from the stem without leaking any of the latex, it is fully mature yet should be kept at room temperature for few days to soften. Wash off the sandy scruff before setting the fruit aside to ripen. It should be eaten when they just start to get soft, before it gets mushy. It is an ideal dessert fruit as the skin (not to be consumed) serves as a 'shell'. Do not accidentally swallow a seed, because the protruding hook can cause you to choke erasing all the enjoyment from this delicious fruit. Ripe, firm sapodillas can be stored for several days in your refrigerator. Frozen fruits can be kept perfectly for a month.

The sapodilla produces strong and long-lasting timber. This type of wood is so strong and durable that the timbers used as beams in ancient Mayan temples have been found intact in the ruins. It has also been used for railway crossties, floor planks, carts, and handles. The wood's reddish core makes archers' bows, furniture, railings, and intricate cabinets. Due to the latex content, sapodilla sawdust irritates the nostrils.

The sap of the sapodilla tree is called chicle. Containing 15% rubber, chicle is harmless and tasteless. It was dried and chewed by the Mayans as a primitive chewing gum to ward off hunger. The Mexican General Santa Ana introduced chewing chicle to America in the mid 1800's beginning the chewing gum industry. The demand for sap became so great that it was 'tapped' from sapodilla trees throughout Central America delivering over seven tons a year.

Medicinally young sapodilla fruits can be boiled and eaten as a bush remedy for diarrhea. A tea made from the old, yellowed leaves is a reputed remedy for coughs and colds. Eating crushed seeds are claimed to help heal the bladder and expel kidney stones. The liquid essence of the crushed seeds is used throughout the Yucatan as a tranquilizer. The seeds can be crushed into a paste to sooth insect bites. Chicle is used in Central America as a primitive dental filling.

A raw sapodilla has about 120 calories with calcium, potassium, vitamins A and C, and folate. Most often sapodillas are eaten raw, but a sauce can be prepared from peeled seeded fruit forced through a strainer, and then mixed with orange juice and heavy cream. The fruits' flesh can be mixed with egg and cream to make delicious custard. Crushed boiled fruits can be strained to create sweet syrup. Mashed sapodillas can be added to a batter to make dessert fritters. If you add sugar when cooking sapodillas the flesh will turn red.

> ## DID YOU KNOW?
> Sapodilla is a distant relative of the canistel and starfruit. Many believe the flavor bears a striking resemblance to caramel. Others think it tastes like a combination cinnamon, apple, and pear. An excellent backyard tree, the sapodilla usually bears fruit twice a year, but may have blossoms year round. It is a good source of vitamins A and C, calcium, and phosphorus. There are several vari eties of sapodillas including the brown sugar with grainy flesh, prolific with pinkish flesh, the early ripening Tikal, and the large Russel, which can grow to five inches in diameter.

Simple Sapodilla Pie

Ingredients: two cups sapodillas - peeled, seeded, chunked, half cup golden raisins, half cup lemon or lime juice, half cup brown sugar, one pie crust

Method: Fill pie crust with sapodilla pieces, then top with raisins. Pour the limejuice over the pie to prevent the sapodilla from becoming chewy. Sprinkle sugar over the pie and cover with top crust with plenty of fork holes to release the steam. Bake at 350 degrees for 45 minutes.

Easy Sapodilla Rice

Ingredients: two cups cooked rice, two sapodillas - peeled, seeded and chunked, one TBS lemon zest, one TBS ginger peeled and minced

Method: Mix everything into the warm cooked rice. Let sit for fifteen minutes covered and serve.

Sapodilla Custard

Ingredients: one and a half cup sapodilla - peeled, seeded, and mashed, one and a half cup milk, four eggs whisked slightly, one ripe banana sliced, four TBS brown sugar, slight salt

> **DID YOU KNOW?**
>
> The sapodilla's botanical name is *manilkara zapota*, but is known as Chico in Mexico and the Philippines, Chikuu in India, and Chicozapote in Venezuela.

Method: Bring milk to a boil in a medium pot and turn off before adding all ingredients. Pour into a well-greased (with butter) baking dish. Bake at 350 degrees for half an hour. Top with fresh banana slices before serving.

Sapodilla Soufflé

Ingredients: one cup sapodilla - peeled, seeded, and mashed, half cup heavy cream, quarter cup milk, one TS cinnamon powder, one TS lemon juice, two TBS brown sugar, one TS salt, four whipped egg whites, quarter cup melted butter

Method: In a skillet combine sapodilla, milk, and cream. Simmer for ten minutes constantly stirring. Add lemon juice, sugar, cinnamon, and salt. Remove from heat and cool for two hours. Then when it has reached room temperature, fold in the egg whites. Carefully fill small ovenproof bowls and bake at 300 degrees for half an hour. Brush tops with melted butter. Serve without delay.

Sapodilla Colada

Ingredients: half cup sapodilla peeled and seeded, half cup milk, one TBS honey or brown sugar, two TBS brandy or dark rum (optional), four cups ice

Method: Put everything in a blender or processor until smooth. Sit back, relax, and enjoy.

> *I like gardening — it's a place where I find myself when I need to lose myself.*
>
> Alice Sebold

SOURSOP

I can remember plenty of soursop trees in my village when I was growing up. Then the mealy bug hit and destroyed most of them. Occasionally I'll see one in the market, but soursop is no longer plentiful as it once was. It is another unglamorous, yet very tasty fruit that originated in the Western Hemisphere. It is native to northern South America. Spanish explorers carried the soursop across the world. It is 'guanábana' in Spanish-speaking countries.

Soursop has a weird irregular shape with a greenish skin covered with short stubs that look like pickers. Its skin almost makes you afraid to touch it until you taste the delicious flesh. A ripe soursop feels soft to the touch. The foot long prickly green fruit can weigh up to five pounds. The thick, inedible skin hides a white pulp that is a bit fibrous, grainy, with a exceptional taste - like a combination of pineapple and strawberries, or coconut and banana. Soursops may have a few seeds, or over a hundred. Soursop is usually juiced rather than eaten directly. Eating it raw is a bit difficult because of the many large seeds, and the sections of soft pulp are held by fibers.

The soursop tree is perfect for a back yard garden. There are many classifications of these fruit from sweet to acidic taste, small to big, round, oblong and angular shapes, juicy to dry. The soursop is usually grown from seeds, so choose a tasty variety. They should be sown in containers and kept moist and shaded. Germination takes from 15 to 30 days. Soursop will grow almost anywhere in the tropics. It grows best in rich, deep, well-drained soil. Most are bushy evergreens with low-branches and only mature to twenty feet tall.

Mealybugs, moths, and wasps are the main pests and can be prevented with a regular spraying of an insecticide like Fastac or Pestac. Use a cup of starter fertilizer like 12-24-12 every other month until it blossoms then switch to 15-15-20. Water regularly, especially

DID YOU KNOW?

The soursop, also known as the prickly custard apple, was one of the first fruit trees carried from the Americas to the tropical Far East. It is popular from southeastern China to Australia, throughout lowland Africa, and Malaysia. The tastes of soursops are divided into three classifications, sweet, slightly acidic, and acidic. Then they are classed by shapes as round, heart shaped, oblong, and angular. Finally they are classed by flesh texture from soft and juicy, to firm and comparatively dry.

in dry spells. Don't expect a big crop as most soursop trees only produce less than two dozen fruits.

Soursops should be picked when firm, just slightly soft, and starting to yellow. If permitted to tree ripen either the bats or birds will get more than you, or they can fall and smash on the ground. A bruised soursop will blacken like a banana, and should be refrigerated.

Enjoying a soursop is not only about excellent tastes and aromas, but consuming this fruit can better your mood. Soursop juice will fight fevers, and supposedly increases mother's milk after childbirth. Crushed seeds can be pounded and the result used as a body wash to against ticks and lice. The leaves are considered to be a sedative, helping to reduce hypoglycemia and hypertension.

Soursop is usually pressed through a colander or strainer to extract the juice from the pulp. Do not consume the seeds. The juice can be blended with milk or water. A hundred grams of soursop has sixty calories with good amounts of calcium, phosphorus and amino acids. The fruit also contains significant amounts of vitamin C, vitamin B1, and vitamin B2.

Basic Soursop Juice

Remove the seeds from a nice soft soursop and strain the pulp. Blend the juice with sweetened condensed milk. Chill and enjoy.

Soursop Freeze

Take the soursop juice combined with sweetened evaporated milk and pour into a suitable container or ice cube tray. Stir a few times while it is freezing to break up the ice crystals.

Soursop Juice Extrordinare

Ingredients: two cups soursop pulp and juice, two TBS lime juice, one TS vanilla extract, one large can of sweetened condensed milk (or two small)

Method: Combine soursop with the other ingredients. It is best to use a blender. Pour into a suitable container and freeze till slushy and blend again. Refreeze.

Soursop Cheesecake

Ingredients: two cups vanilla wafers crumble, four TBS butter melted, one eight ounce package of cream cheese softened, one small can of sweetened condensed milk, one quarter cup fresh lemon juice, one and a half cup soursop pulp blended or whipped, three TS plain gelatin dissolved in quarter cup hot water, two TS fresh mint chopped

Method: In a pie pan combine melted butter with crumbled vanilla wafers. In a suitable bowl combine remaining ingredients whipping until smooth. Pour into crumb lined pie pan and chill for four hours before serving. Sprinkle with mint and enjoy.

HEALTH NOTE

Soursop, botanically *Annona Montana*, gained attention in the 1970's as a natural cancer cell killer. In the few laboratory studies that have been performed, extracts from soursop can kill some types of liver and breast cancer cells usually resistant to particular chemotherapy drugs. One study conducted by the Catholic University of South Korea found that soursop was 10,000 times more effective at killing colon cancer cells than chemotherapy. It is its anti tumor effect that is of most interest. But there haven't been any large scale studies in humans, so there is no conclusive proof it can work as a cancer treatment. However some tests did discover that in some people, soursop can cause nerve damage that is similar to Parkinson's Disease. Soursop also fights bacteria and fungus infections, is effective against internal parasites, and lowers high blood pressure. The flesh and juice fights depression, stress and nervous disorders. It is reported crushed soursop leaves mixed with water and the juice of two limes will sober a dunk when rubbed on his head. A tea made from this tree's leaves will have a calming effect. A poultice of mashed leaves will fight skin problems as eczema, and soothe rheumatism. Chewed leaves combined with saliva put on bad cuts will prevent scarring. A compress soaked with a decoction of leaves will reduce inflammation and swollen feet. This same decoction will kill head lice and bedbugs.

The root bark is used as an antidote for poisoning. The juice of the fruit can be taken orally as a remedy for liver ailments A decoction of the young shoots or leaves is regarded as a remedy for gall bladder trouble, as well as coughs, catarrh, diarrhea, dysentery, fever and indigestion. To speed the healing of wounds, the flesh of the soursop is applied as a poultice unchanged for 3 days. The seeds have emetic properties, and treat vomiting.

STARFRUIT—FIVE FINGERS—CARAMBOLAS

I love juicy starfruit. It has different regional names. Starfruit comes from the fivepointed star that appears when you slice it across the width. Some areas also call it five fingers because it also looks like a hand, with the fingers extended. Averrhoa carambola is the botanical name. Carambola in Spanish translates as by accident or luck; and discovering this fruit ripe certainly is good luck. It also translates as an exclamation, and a bank shot in billiards where the cue ball hits an object ball and then the other ball. I guess you could drink the juice, while playing billiards, and scream when you make a good shot.

The starfruit is believed to have originated in Sri Lanka (Ceylon) and was cultivated for centuries before Spanish explorers brought trees to the Caribbean and the Americas.

There are two varieties of starfruit, sour and sweet. The fruits with narrow spaced fingers or ribs are less sweet than the fruit with thick fingers. This fruit starts out green, and yellows as it ripens, though it can be eaten in both stages. I love making five-finger chow from the slightly ripe fruit. Fully ripe fruit makes great juice and tasty five fingers wine.

The starfruit is all about its shape. They can grow to about a foot long always with five triangular sectioned ribs. Slices cut in cross-section become star shaped. It has a thin skin from pale to dark yellow with a usually a waxy smooth texture. The flesh is paler yellow to almost clear. A great starfruit is crisp and very juicy, without any fiber. It has a sharp acidic aroma from the oxalic acid. The taste ranges from lip clenching tart to almost sweet. Even the sweet variety seldom has more than 4% sugar. Usually a starfruit has ten to twelve flat, half inch long brown seeds. The color of starfruit slightly intensifies as they ripen, but it is best check for ripeness by eating one.

To grow a tree from seeds is difficult since the seeds become infertile in a few days after removing them from the fruit; so have your potting soil ready. Nice fat seeds should sprout in a week to ten days. Grafted trees can be purchased at garden shops. A star fruit tree is perfect for a garden as they seldom grow more than fifteen to twenty feet tall. Keep them at least twenty feet apart and away from walls. Young trees should be sheltered from a full wind. Only light pruning is ever required. Make certain the area you plant is drained, as water is this tree's biggest enemy. However star fruit must be watered regularly during the dry season to produce a juicy crop. Run a hose for a half an hour every week during a dry spell. Spray with a pesticide-miticide and foliar fertilizer once a month. Sprinkle about a half-cup of 12-12-17-2 every month around the base. Starfruit should flower a few times a year, with the best crop during the heated dry season.

One nice starfruit has about twenty calories and is high in carbohydrates, calcium, phosphorus, vitamins A, B, and C, plus amino acids. Starfruit is a good source of dietary fiber and can help to reduce blood pressure and cholesterol. Ripe starfruit are great eaten just picked and washed, and of course the green or slightly ripe make excellent chow. They can be stewed with cloves and raisins. Star fruit cooked or raw are a great accompaniment for seafood.

> ### DID YOU KNOW?
> Star fruit juice will clean brass and silver. It will also remove rust stains from white clothes.

Individuals with kidney problems shouldn't eat starfruit because of oxalic acid. Juice made from starfruit is very dangerous because this acid is concentrated.

Starfruit Chow

Ingredients: four to six nice sized starfruit sliced about a quarter inch thick seeds removed, two chadon benee leaves minced, one to two cloves of garlic minced, one hot pepper seeded and minced, pinch of salt

Method: Combine all ingredients in a bowl. Let sit for at least two hours before serving. Best if chilled.

Starfruit Bread

Ingredients: four medium starfruit washed and minced, half cup sugar, three quarters cup milk, one egg, one cup whole wheat flour, a cup white baker's flour, three quarters TS salt, one TS baking powder, one TS baking soda, one TS powder ginger, half TS cinnamon, one quarter cup currants or raisins (increase sugar if you have a sweet tooth)

Method: Combine the fruit, sugar, egg, and milk in a large bowl. In another bowl mix the remaining ingredients and then slowly add to the fruit combination and mix until all the flour is moist. Don't over blend. Pour into greased bread pans and bake at 350 for forty-five minutes.

Star Chicken

Ingredients: one chicken chunked, four starfruit cut to quarter inch star slices, one large sweet onion sliced thin as possible, quarter cup olive oil, two TBS honey, quarter cup fresh lime juice, two TBS lime zest (grated lime peel), one bunch chadon benee chopped fine, one TBS fresh ginger minced, half cup raw almonds (cashews or peanuts may be substituted), half hot pepper seeded minced, salt and spices to your taste

Method: Combine chicken, honey, limejuice and zest, onions, ginger and pepper in a large bowl preferably with a tight cover. Refrigerate for a day or two, stirring occasionally. Put chicken mixture in a baking dish and cover with the nuts. Cover with foil and bake at 375 for about half an hour. Then uncover and bake for another twenty minutes. Add chadon benee just before serving.

Starfruit Sauce

Great on fish, pork, or chicken and on cake, or ice cream.

Ingredients: four ripe starfruit, two cups either orange, passion fruit, or guava juice, two cups sugar, two TBS fresh ginger grated, two bay leaves best boiled in a cheesecloth bag, one stick of cinnamon or one TBS powdered, half TS nutmeg, a half cup of apple, or cranberry sauce or a quarter cup of orange marmalade may be added for a taste twist, one TS cornstarch to thicken.

Method: Remove seeds before dicing three starfruit. In a two quart pot combine the sugar, juice, and corn starch, bring to a boil stirring constantly. Reduce heat and simmer for five minutes with occasional stirring. Add diced starfruit, other fruit sauces if desired, bay leaves, cinnamon and nutmeg. Simmer for ten minutes and cool before serving.

HEALTH NOTE

In bush medicine, the starfruit tree is a virtual pharmacy. In India, ripe starfruit is used to halt hemorrhages and to relieve a bleeding hemorrhoid. Dried fruit, or the juice may be taken to fight a fever. A heated or cooked version of this fruit will fight intestinal gas, diarrhea, and is believed to relieve an alcohol hangover. A salve made of starfruit will aid eye afflictions. Starfruit is used by Brazilians to fight kidney and bladder problems. It is also used to treat eczema. A decoction made from the fruit will overcome severe nausea and vomiting. Starfruit tree leaves can be plastered on the temples to soothe headaches. A poultice of crushed leaves will eradicate ringworm. This tree's roots, combined with sugar are believed to be an antidote for poison. Hydrocyanic acid has been detected in the leaves, stems, and roots. Powdered seeds serve as a sedative in cases of asthma and colic.

NOTE: Individuals with kidney problems shouldn't eat starfruit because of oxalic acid. Juice made from starfruit is very dangerous because this acid is concentrated.

SUGAR APPLE

The sugar apple is what I call a 'busy fruit'. They keep you occupied sorting and spitting out the seeds. I love them, the creamier the better. When I was a child, there was a tree close to our school. You never forget the location of a good sugar apple tree. This popular fruit originated in Central or South America and is now grown in the tropics around the world. Sugar apple seeds keep extremely well, up to four years. The Spanish Conquistadors were able to carry seeds to transplant this fruit to the Philippines, and it spread throughout Asia. The Portuguese supposedly brought the sugar apple to India in the late 1500's.

Sugar apples are widely cultivated in southern China, Queensland-Australia, Polynesia, Hawaii, tropical Africa, Egypt, and even the lowlands of Palestine. India probably grows the most sugar apples. It is one of the most important fruits of the interior of Brazil. Cuba developed a seedless variety in the 1940's.

Sugar apple trees are nice for the small backyard garden as they seldom get taller than twenty feet and are extremely easy to grow from a seed. The seeds germinate better after being dried for at least a week after removal from the fruit than when perfectly fresh. They usually take four years to bear, but grafted trees will bear sooner. The blossoms are very fragrant. The main enemy is too much water and associated fungus. Plant it in well drained soil at a breezy spot. It should be planted at least ten feet away from other trees or walls. For spectacular fruit, monthly spray with a pesticide that also works for mites mixed with a foliar booster. Young trees to two years old should get a half-cup of 12-24-12. Older trees should get a half-cup of 12-12-17-2. When the blossoms appear water the tree every other week. Fruits ripen in about four months.

DID YOU KNOW?

This fruit's scientific name is annona squamosa, but it is called chirimoya throughout South America. The name originates from the Andes mountain Indian language word 'chirimuya', which means "cold seeds", because the seeds will germinate and the plant grows at higher altitudes. It is named pomme cannelle in Guadeloupe, French Guiana, and French West Africa. It is rinon in Venezuela, and sweetsop in Jamaica and the Bahamas. It is known as sitaphal, custard apple, or scaly custard apple in India.

A big sugar apple is a cone about four inches long with a thick, knobby, segmented grayish green skin. Once you pull it apart the creamy white flesh smells as sweet as it tastes, like a prepared sherbet. The flesh can be pressed through a sieve to eliminate the seeds, and then added to ice cream, or blended with milk to make a tasty 'colada' drink. Ripe sugar apples can be frozen and eaten like ice cream. They are best served chilled, cut in half, or quartered; and eaten with a spoon.

A tea made of sugar apple leaves is considered an excellent tonic, especially for colds and diarrhea. A bath in the leaves relieves severe arthritis and rheumatism. A medium sized fruit is about eighty calories with a little protein, but one gram of fat. They contain good amounts of phosphorous and calcium. A luscious, perfectly ripe sugar apple is worth the effort.

Sugar Apple Chicken

Ingredients: one cup seeded and pureed sugar apple, one cup plain yogurt, one chicken quartered or chunked, three medium onions (prefer white) sliced thin, three cloves of garlic minced, one half cup of chicken broth, oil for frying

Method: combine puree, yogurt and let sit. Brown the chicken pieces in a large frying pan with two tablespoons oil and remove. In the same oil sauté the onions and garlic, then add the chicken, the broth, and cover. Cook at medium heat until the chicken is tender. Drain the liquid from the pan with a half-cup remaining. Lower heat and stir in the sugar apple puree and yogurt. Stir briskly for three minutes and remove from heat. Serve warm.

Sugar Apple Custard

Ingredients: two sugar apples seeded and pureed, one pound of softened cream cheese, two TBS sugar, three quarters cup cream, one third cup boiling water, three TS gelatin (plain preferred, but flavored will slightly alter the taste)

Method: Dissolve the gelatin in a third cup boiling water. Whip the cream cheese adding the gelatin and water, sugar and cream. Add the sugar apple puree and beat until smooth. Refrigerate for four hours before serving.

Sugar Apple Cake

Ingredients: two ripe sugar apples seeded and pureed. half cup sugar, one TS vanilla, two eggs, quarter cup of soft butter or margarine, one and a half cup of bakers flour, two TS baking powder, two eggs, half TS ground cinnamon, half TS nutmeg

Method: Whip the butter, sugar, and vanilla until creamy. Add eggs one at a time to mixture, then sugar apple puree, and spices. Continue to whip while adding the flour. Pour into a greased bread pan and bake at 350 for an hour. Check consistency with a toothpick. Cool and serve.

Fruits

Decadent Sugar Apple Pie

Ingredients: two cups sugar apples seeded and pureed, one pack of cookies of your choice smashed to crumbs, half cup strawberry jam or chocolate syrup, one large banana sliced thin, half pint whipping cream, one TS lemon or lime juice

Method: Layer the bottom of a pie dish, or medium sized bowl with the cookie crumbs. This is kind of sticky so you might want to keep your fingers moist. Pour into this crust just enough of the sugar apple puree and then carefully stir in swirls of the jam or syrup. Mix banana slices with the lemon /lime juice and top the pie with the slices. Repeat this until the pan is filled. Refrigerate for at least an hour. Top with whipped cream when serving.

HEALTH NOTE

Sugar apple seeds are poisonous. Powdered seeds are used as fish poison and as insecticide in India. Powdered seeds made into a paste will kill head lice, but must be kept away from the eyes as it is highly irritant and can cause blindness.

*I love spring anywhere, but if I could choose
I would always greet it in a garden.*

Ruth Stout

TAMARIND

When my granny curried fish, she always added tamarind. I can still taste it. In those days almost every family had a tall tamarind tree. We played a lot of marbles in their shade.

Tamarind fruit is one of the weirdest. Can you say why you love the flavor, or even describe the flavor as sour or sweet? But you just love them! The six-inch pods can have as much as twelve seeds in a sticky brown paste. The shells are brittle and break easily when the pods are fully ripe. The pulp is actually good for you as it is high in calcium and vitamin B. I can't think of any other fruit than tamarind that can just stay ripe on the tree for months.

The tamarind is considered the only spice to have originated in Africa, although India also tries to claim the delicious fruit. Tamarind's botanical name is tamarindus indica. The word 'tamarind' translates as 'Indian date', and India is the world's largest producer harvesting 300,000 tons every year.

Tamarind trees are slow to mature to the grandeur of seventy-foot height and thirty-foot width; so give it a lot of space. It's a hearty tree that can adapt to most conditions, and only needs well-drained soil. Enjoy the shade. To get the best results in both number of pods and amount of pulp, fertilize young trees to three years old with a cup of 6-6-3, about three times a year. Bearing trees should get 8-3-9, at a cup for every five years of age at the same intervals.

Tamarinds may be left on the tree for as long as 6 months after maturity, which will reduce the moisture content. East Indians shake the branches to make ripe fruits fall. Pickers should not use long sticks to knock the fruits because this could damage both the fruits and tree.

Green pods can be used as a seasoning, boiled with rice. The tamarind pulp is used in a variety of sauces including Worcestershire (English Sauce). Tamarind balls are probably the most common way of eating the pulp. To separate the pulp from the seeds, work the goo on a colander and keep adding powdered sugar. Shape what is strained into balls and roll in sugar. It is messy to make, yet delicious to savor. Tamarind water is another easy treat. Put as many shelled fruits as you choose (more will make a stronger flavor) in a bottle of water overnight. Cloves, ginger, and even a hot pepper may be added to enhance the flavor. Add sugar to your taste. In Thailand they grind the dry tamarind seeds to make a coffee substitute. These seeds have a property that makes things gel better than pectin, and are used as a stabilizer for ice creams.

Tamarind pulp has only fifty calories in two ounces with some protein and fiber. Tamarind is high in calcium, phosphorus, and potassium. Fresh pulp can be applied directly on inflammations and used as a rinse for a sore throat. Pets infested with fleas or tick can be washed and then rinsed with strong tamarind water. Let it dry on them as a repellant. A tea from the tree's bark makes an excellent tonic. Hard tamarind heart wood makes the best hoe handles, also mortars, and pestles.

Tamarind-ade is a popular tropical drink and is now bottled carbonated in Guatemala, Mexico, and Puerto Rico. The easiest method of preparing this drink is to first shell the fruits, and put six in a bottle of water. Let stand overnight before adding a tablespoonful of sugar. Shake vigorously. For a stronger drink cover about thirty tamarinds with hot sugar syrup. Add spices of your choice such as cloves, cinnamon, allspice, ginger, pepper, and-or lime slices. Let stand in a dark place for several days before straining. Dilute this with water and chill before serving.

> **DID YOU KNOW?**
>
> There is a superstition it is harmful to sleep or to tie a horse under a tamarind tree. Some African tribes regard this tree as sacred. Burmese believe the tamarind tree is the house of the rain god. Hindus marry a tamarind tree to a mango tree before enjoying the mango fruit. In central Africa corn soaked with tamarind bark is fed to domestic fowl; if they stray, or are stolen they will always return home. Malaysians combine tamarind and coconut milk and feed it to infants at birth to hopefully make them wise.

Tamarind Paste

Shell one pound or more of tamarind and remove stems, fibers, etc. Put into a pot and cover with boiling water to soften the pulp. Push softened mixture thru a sieve. Place in pot with one and a half cups of apple cider vinegar, a half cup of brown sugar, plus spices you may choose. Boil until a thick paste. Push thru a sieve again. Cool before freezing.

Tamarind Black Beans

Ingredients: two cups soaked black beans, quarter cup tamarind paste, third cup oil, two onions chopped, one tomato-chopped small, two TBS grated ginger, two TBS minced garlic, one hot pepper-seeded and minced (optional), one TS roasted ground cumin, half TSP turmeric, two TS roasted cumin seeds, one TS garam masala, two bundles chadon benee chopped, salt to taste

Method: Soak tamarind paste in two cups of hot water for an hour. When it has cooled work the paste between your hands to produce a strong juice. In a large skillet heat oil and sauté the onions until they brown. Add garlic and ginger and cook for five minutes. Stir constantly or it will stick. Add the hot pepper, cumin, and turmeric; cook for a half a minute and remove from the heat. Stir in the tomato, the beans and two cups of water,

Cook covered until beans are tender. Add water as necessary to provide a good sauce. Stir in the tamarind paste and simmer for ten minutes. Add the roasted cumin seeds, garam massala, and chadon benee. Cook for five minutes and remove from heat; let sit for ten minutes before serving.

Tamarind Chutney

Ingredients: quarter cup tamarind paste, three quarter cup water, third cup seedless raisins, one TBS sugar, one TS roasted ground cumin seeds, one TS lemon juice, one hot pepper seeded and minced, salt to your taste

Method: Bring water to a boil before adding tamarind paste and raisins. Remove from heat and soak for an hour. Work the tamarind paste to a creamy juice while adding the spices, pepper, and lemon juice. Blend it very smooth. Cover and let stand at room temperature overnight.

Tastey Tamarind Veggies

A different stir fry

Ingredients: third cup tamarind paste, two cups water, one onion sliced, three cloves garlicminced, one hot pepper-seeded and minced (optional), one large sweet pepper-seeded and chunked, two cups cauliflower, quarter cup mushrooms sliced, one carrot chunked, one bunch bodi chopped into one inch pieces, two TBS curry, two TS finely chopped ginger root, one TBS curry powder one cup coconut milk, three TBS oil, two cups channa, three TBS chadon benee

Method: Boil one cup of water and add the tamarind paste. Let it sit for an hour and then work it soft. In a large frying pan with a cover heat the oil, cook the onion, garlic, ginger, hot pepper for five minutes and then add the curry powder. Cook three minutes. Add vegetables and mushrooms. Simmer covered for five minutes. Increase the heat and add a third of a cup of the softened tamarind paste and bring to a boil. Reduce heat and simmer for twenty minutes. Add the channa and simmer until they are tender. Sprinkle with chadon benee.

HEALTH NOTE

A hundred tons of tamarind are imported yearly by US drug companies. Tamarind preparations are known as coolants for fevers, and as laxatives. Tamarind leaves and flowers, dried or boiled, as poultices will relieve swollen joints, sprains, and boils. A thick tea made of the fruit or leaves is used in cases of gingivitis, asthma, and eye inflammations.

TANGELO

Okay, so you thought you knew of every type of citrus grown in the Caribbean, but you never heard of a tangelo? If that's the case, then you have missed one of the best tastes. I discovered tangelos by accident one day at a roadside market. I frequent one that usually has a variety of fruit like canistels and caimates. The vendor offered me a quarter of a unique fruit, which I thought was a miniature grapefruit, until I tasted it. The tangelo is very sweet without the usual acidic bite of typical citrus with a slight spicy aftertaste.

The most common citrus fruits are lemons, limes, grapefruits, oranges, and portugals. Most of these have varieties that have adapted over time to a variety of climates, altitudes, and regional elements. The tangelo is a cross of two plants, the tangerine, more commonly known as the mandarin orange, and the grapefruit, a relative of the pomelo. Tangelos are believed to have originated in Southeast Asia some 3,000 years ago.

A tangelo is the size of an orange, yet oblong instead of perfectly round. Some tangelos have a neck on them much like the mandarin orange. A ripe tangelo is very juicy and tastes like a sweet, orangish shaddock. The peel is fairly loose, and easily removed like a portugal.

Even though this hybrid already existed naturally, scientists didn't quit manipulating the tangelo until they did nature one better. The two main types of commercial tangelos are the Minneola tangelo, which was created in 1931, and the Orlando tangelo, created in 1911. Each of these 'breeds' is the hybrid of one specific type of tangerine and one specific type of grapefruit. Minneola tangelos are a Duncan grapefruit crossed with a danci tangerine.

Our tree is a grafted variety purchased from a local garden shop. The tangelo needs plenty of sun and well drained soil. Every second month we sprinkle a cup of bearing fertilizer, 12-12 -17-2, around the base. In the dry season it gets a good drenching every other week. On the full moon we check every grafted tree and trim unwanted branches from the original root stock. They are easy to tell because those branches should be the only ones that have thorns (pickers) and they usually grow straight up. Our tangelo tree began to bear fruit in its second year.

The tangelo is excellent for eating fresh or adding to fruit or vegetable salads. Its segments will liven up coleslaw or tuna salad. It is excellent as a dessert fruit.

Tangelos have about a hundred calories per fruit with plenty of potassium and of course

Vitamin C.

Tangelo Sorbet

Ingredients: four cups fresh tangelo juice from about ten fruits, one cup sugar, one cup water

Method: In a sauce pan combine water and sugar, bring to a boil and then simmer. Add grated rind (zest) of one tangelo. Simmer for ten minutes stirring frequently. Add four cups of the strained tangelo juice. Remove from heat to a bowl. Cool before putting in the freezer. After two hours in the freezer, remove and put into blender, or vigorously beat with a slotted spoon. This is to break up the ice crystals. Refreeze. For very smooth sorbet wait another two hours and blend again before freezing solid.

DID YOU KNOW?

Natural occurring tangelos are most likely the result of insect cross pollination of the Mandarin orange and the pomelo, the ancestor of the grapefruit. They are so unlike other citrus fruits that they have been set aside in a class by themselves designated *Citrus X tangelo J*. Tangerines are deliberate or accidental hybrids of the mandarin (*Citrus reticulata*) and the sweet orange. The Jamaican 'Ugli' fruit is believed to be a chance hybrid between a mandarin orange and grapefruit. UGLI® is the registered trade mark under which Cabel Hall Citrus Ltd. markets its brand of tangelos from Jamaica.

Tangelo Rice Special

Ingredients: one cup rice - prefer brown whole grain, three cups vegetable stock, one half cup fresh squeezed tangelo juice, one quarter TS salt, one half cup shelled pigeon peas, one TS grated tangelo rind (zest), one quarter tangelo peeled and chopped small, one TS ground coriander, two TS chopped raw almonds, peanuts, or cashews.

Method: In a suitable pot combine rice, salt, vegetable stock, and tangelo juice. Boil, cover and simmer, occasionally stirring, for a half an hour. Add peas, tangelo rind, and coriander. Stir thoroughly and cover again, let simmer another twenty minutes until the rice is cooked to a nice texture. Remove from heat and let stand, covered, for five minutes. Uncover, stir in chopped nuts, and serve immediately.

Tangelo Dessert

A bit of work, but the taste is worth it.

Ingredients: two tangelos (grate zest before juicing), half cup butter-softened, three quarter cup powdered sugar, three eggs separated, half cup bakers' flour-sifted, one and a half cups milk

Method: With an egg beater, mixer, or blender beat butter, sugar, zest, and yolks until light and creamy, then fold in the flour. Add one third cup tangelo juice and the milk. Beat egg whites to form soft peaks before adding to batter. Pour batter into a greased baking dish. It is important to set this batter dish in another larger baking pan. Fill the outer baking pan half with water. Bake for forty-five minutes at 200 degrees. Allow to cool before serving.

Tangelo Apple Salad

Ingredients: four tangelos - two peeled and sectioned and two juiced, six apples peeled, cored and sliced, one cup yogurt plain or orange flavored

Method: In a bowl combine all ingredients. Chill and serve.

Tangelo Cake

Ingredients: quarter cup butter or margarine, three quarter cup baker's flour, half cup milk, zest and juice from one tangelo, half cup powdered sugar, two eggs, two TBS brown sugar

Method: Combine butter, milk, flour, and sugar. Beat with a mixer or whisk for five minutes. Pour batter into a cake pan and bake at 350 for forty minutes. In a sauce pan on medium heat combine brown sugar, tangelo zest, and juice until a thin syrup forms. Remove from heat and pour over cake.

All gardeners know better than other gardeners.
Chinese proverb

THE WEST INDIAN CHERRY

The most popular tropical cherry is the acerola cherry also known as the Barbados cherry. It is a relatively small fruit tree and may be trimmed to a convenient sized shrub.

The acerola has recently become famous since it has the highest vitamin C content of all fruits, and is now cultivated for medicinal purposes. A hundred grams of cherry flesh usually has about 2,000 mg of Vitamin C. It is amazing that immature green cherries actually have twice the vitamin C than the fully grown red.

Botanists believe this fruit tree originated in Mexico's Yucatan Peninsula. Acerola cherries can be found in all of Central America, throughout the Caribbean, and parts of South America and Southeast Asia. The acerola- Barbados cherry is relatively common to the Lesser Antilles from St. Croix to Trinidad, also Curacao, Margarita, and neighboring northern South America as far south as Brazil.

The acerola cherry is grown from seed, cuttings, or grafts. It can adapt to most environments found in tropical regions and is able to withstand even a severe drought. Its shallow root system can be uprooted by strong winds. For the tree to produce abundant fruit regular watering is necessary with adequate drainage. This tree can also be grown in sizable pots where it will get sun. The pots should have good drain holes and the potting soil kept slightly alkaline. The acerola is an attractive tree with dark green leaves and pink or white blossoms. It will grow to about fifteen feet and can be shaped by pruning. Keep the tree to a height that can be easily picked. Otherwise the birds and bats will get most of the cherries. It is self pollinating and loves the sun.

Acerola fruit are brilliant red and juicy with a slightly sweet taste. They mature from blossoms in about one month. Fertilize immature trees every three months with 12-24-12 and water regularly. Once blossoms appear use 12-12-17-2 and increase water until the fruits appear. For a better harvest, lime the soil once a year.

Nematodes are a problem for immature trees. Spray the trees monthly with an insecticide such as Fastac combined with a foliar mix containing boron. This is an excellent backyard tree because with proper fertilizing and watering, an acerola cherry tree can bear in its third year. At five or six it will fruit three times a year, and can bear fruit for twenty years.

Acerola cherries' high vitamin C content has been used to treat dysentery, severe colds, and fever. These cherries can also reduce joint inflammation from arthritis and prevent infections. One hundred grams has 32 calories and is high in vitamin C, potassium, and iron.

The juice is tasty diluted with water with added sugar. Add another favorite juice such as orange, pineapple, or a banana. Add ice and blend until smooth. Pitted cherry pulp can be frozen with additional sweeteners and blended into a sorbet. Milk may be added to either make a shake or to refreeze into ice cream.

> **DID YOU KNOW?**
>
> *M. Punicifolia L.* is generally accepted as the correct botanical name for the acerola-Barbados cherry, which is also called West Indian cherry, sweet, Puerto Rican, Jamaican, the native cherry, garden cherry, or French cherry. In Spanish it is named acerola, cereza, or cereza colorada. The wood is surprisingly hard and heavy, and won't ignite even when treated with flammable fluid unless perfectly dried.

Cherry Juice

Strain seeded cherries until you have two cups of juice. Mix with an equal amount of water. It is slightly acidic so add sugar to taste. Pour over ice and enjoy.

Cherry Concentrate

Strain seeded cherries until you have two cups. Put into an uncovered pot over medium heat. Stir constantly as half of the liquid evaporates. Remove from heat and cool before pouring into containers for freezing. Keep as a cold remedy or as flavorings for drinks, cakes, and frozen desserts.

Tropical Frozen Blend

Strain seeded cherries until you have a cup of juice. Mix in a blender with a cup of orange juice, a quarter cup of pineapple, and two ripe bananas. Add ice to the blender's capacity. Cover and blend until smooth. Guava and apple are also good combinations with acerola cherries.

Cherry Sorbet

Get two cups of seeded cherry pulp. Add two tablespoons of sugar, one teaspoon of lime juice, and blend with a tray of ice cubes. Freeze until slushy, blend again and refreeze. A cup of milk may be added, but the amount of ice should be reduced by half.

Exquisite Cherry Ginger Bread

Ingredients: one cup cherry pulp, one cup milk, three TBS butter, three TS active dry yeast, quarter cup firmly packed brown sugar, quarter cup fresh lime juice, quarter cup fresh cherry juice, one TS salt, four cups baker's flour - divided, one cup toasted coconut, one TS grated lemon peel, one TBS minced fresh ginger

Method: Combine milk and butter in a small pan and heat just until butter melts. Remove from heat, pour into a large bowl and stir in yeast. Let sit for five minutes before adding brown sugar, lemon and cherry juices, salt, and two cups of the flour. Combine thoroughly, electric mixer preferred. Add remaining two cups of flour and mix until the dough doesn't stick to the bowl. Add tablespoons of water if too dry. Blend in cherry pulp, a quarter cup coconut, grated lemon peel, and ginger. Knead dough until it is elastic and let sit in a warm place until it doubles in size - usually about an hour. Punch it down and place in a greased baking pan and let it sit for another hour. Rub grated coconut into the top. Bake at 350 for an hour or until a toothpick or knife pulls out without sticking.

HEALTH NOTE

In 1945 the West Indian cherry was found to be extremely high in ascorbic acid. A single cherry has 81 milligrams, 25 percent more than the recommended daily allowance. The fruits are beneficial for patients with liver ailments, diarrhea and dysentery as well as those with coughs or colds. The juice may be gargled to relieve sore throat.

But always, to her, red and green cabbages were to be jade and burgundy, chrysoprase and prophyry. Life has no weapons against a woman like that.

Edna Ferber

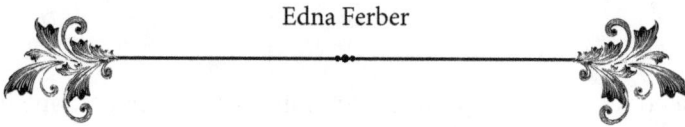

Roots

The root is the part of the plant usually below the soil's surface. Roots, which are edible for humans are 'enlarged' roots that store food for the plant, and from which the above ground plant grows. The major functions of roots are to absorb water and nutrients to keep the plant alive. Roots also anchor the plant's body to the ground and store food and nutrients. In some cases they are a means of asexual reproduction.

Beets, carrots, and radishes, are examples of true root vegetables. They are actually the taproot of the plant, which is formed as the very first root from the seed. However 'roots' also include corms, rhizomes, and tubers. Tubers are underground stems. They grow in thickness instead of length. Irish and sweet potatoes, cassava, tannia, and yams are tubers. Corms are the underground swollen base of the stems that grow vertically and store starch for the plant. Roots are on the bottom of the corms. A corm is a mass of solid tissue of stored water and nutrients to feed the plant. They do not have separate fleshy scales as in a bulb, although there is usually a dry papery covering that are really modified leaves. Eddoes and toppetambu are corms.

Rhizomes are knobby underground stems relished for their pungent and flavorful flesh. Rhizomes are stems that grow horizontally underground. A rhizome is similar to a corm, but new rhizomes are not produced annually. Instead, the older parts die off and the tips of the rhizome grow longer. The plants grow rhizomes, and rhizomes grow roots plus the above ground parts of the plant. A rhizome may be propagated by division, when these resting buds will grow and produce leaves for a new plant. Ginger and turmeric are rhizomes.

Confused: Peanuts are 'technically root vegetables', because they are tubers that grow off a rhizome underground, but they are treated as a nut.

> *Any garden demands as much of its maker as he has to give. But I do not need to tell you, if you are a gardener, that no other undertaking will give as great a return for the amount of effort put into it.*
>
> Elizabeth Lawrence

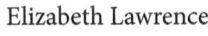

BEET ROOT

Beet root as a side dish never excited me when I was a kid. My grandmother served curried beets and roti. I began to love beets when I had them baked with spicy mustard. Eating beet roots dates back to prehistoric times. Ancient civilizations along the shores of the Mediterranean Sea first cultivated beets for medicine. Later, as the cultivated root grew plumper and more succulent, they were desired for its pleasant taste and texture. French chefs in the 1800's made the beet tasty and popular before this root's esteemed taste migrated to Germany. Beet root cultivation eventually crossed the English Channel and to more fertile terrain in the Americas.

Although both the root and leaves are eaten, dried beet powder is used as a coloring agent for many foods. Some frozen pizzas are colored by using beet powder added to the tomato sauce. The most common garden beet is a deep ruby red in color, but yellow, white, and even candystriped (with red and white) are farmed. Beets to botanists are *beta vulgaris*.

To plant beets you must work the soil with a fork until it is loose to about ten inches deep. This is necessary for the beetroot to form to a good size. Plant seeds about a half inch deep and one inch apart. Keep a foot between rows. It may take ten to fourteen days for the beets to sprout. If the seeds are planted too deep, or the soil gets hard after a heavy rain, the beets will sprout irregularly. Placing a board or a piece of plastic as a cover over the row of beet seeds may help keep the moisture in, and protect from damage from hard rains. Remove any cover as soon as sprouts appear. The sprouts should be thinned to about two inches apart.

Clean the beet rows of weeds often, but do it by hand. This is because using a hoe may damage the beets' shallow roots. Beets will not develop if they are overcrowded or are forced to compete with weeds. About a month after the beets sprout carefully mold, pulling soil up to the leaves. Every month give the beets a light sprinkle with a 12 – 24 – 12 fertilizer mix. Keep the soil moist for the best results.

In about two months the beets should be about two inches in diameter and harvesting can begin. With proper thinning, light fertilizer and water, local beets can grow to three inches. Larger beets have a tendency to taste woody. Planting a row of beets every month will keep you supplied with this healthy food.

Beets are rich in folic acid, which fights heart disease and anemia. Beets are high in fiber. Fiber is good for the intestines and helps regulate blood sugar and cholesterol. One cup of fresh cooked beets has only seventy-five calories of which one and a half grams are fiber, with the same amount of protein, and eight grams of carbohydrates. Beets also contain vitamin A, potassium, and phosphorus.

When preparing, always wash beets, and leave on the skin to contain the nutrients. Be careful because beet juice will stain anything it contacts. Beets can be microwaved, steamed, boiled, pickled, roasted, or eaten raw. Beets are delicious roasted in a hot oven. They are done when easily pricked with a fork. Raw beets also can be grated, diced, or sliced. Beets pickled in salt-vinegar brine are a tasty addition to salads.

> **DID YOU KNOW?**
>
> The Romans considered beet juice an aphrodisiac and grew beets throughout their Empire. Australians put pickled beets on hamburgers. Homemade wine can be made from beets. Beet greens are even better for you than beet roots.

Borscht - Beet Soup

Ingredients: five nice sized beets, one TBS vegetable oil, half carrot chopped, two cloves garlic, one small head of cabbage, eight cups chicken broth, two large potatoes, one large onion and two leaves of chadon benee, salt and pepper to taste

Method: Steam beets until skins pull off. Chop beets and potatoes into small cubes. Chop garlic, chadon benee, and onion, then sauté in oil. Add beets and carrot and stir constantly. In a large pot heat the chicken broth, add the potatoes and cabbage, and cook for ten minutes. Add the beetgarlic-onion mixture. Simmer for twenty minutes. Add salt and pepper to taste. Lemon juice may also be added if you like tart soups. Serves six.

Trinidad Spicy Shredded Beets

Ingredients: three nice beets washed, peeled and grated, half cup grated onion, three TBS margarine, half cup water, two TBS lemon juice, a quarter TS each of cinnamon and nutmeg, salt and pepper to taste

Method: In a covered pan cook all ingredients over low heat for half an hour. Beets should be tender. Do not stir mixture often. Serves four.

Roasted Beets

Ingredients: Five nice sized beets, four TBS olive oil, one TBS Dijon Mustard, juice from one orange, and one TBS vinegar, one clove of garlic.

Method: Place cleaned beets in a large bowl and mix with one-tablespoon olive oil, salt, garlic, and pepper. Place in oven ware into a 400 degree oven for forty-five minutes. While beets are roasting, in a bowl mix mustard, orange juice, three tablespoons olive oil and vinegar. Remove beets and cool. Rub off the beet skins and slice or cube. Mix with dressing. Serves six.

Curried Beets

Ingredients: six nice beets - cooked and chopped small, one large potato chopped small, half cup pigeon peas, quarter cup onion chopped, three TBS butter, half TS cumin seeds, one bay leaf, half hot pepper - seeded and minced, half TS garam masala, salt and spices to taste

Method: In a suitable frying pan heat butter and fry cumin seeds, bay leaf, spiced onion, pepper, and garam masala for one minute. Add potato, peas and beets. Cook stirring for two minutes. Add salt, spices and a little water. Cook gently until the potato is tender. Serve over rice or with sada roti.

HEALTH NOTE

Beet juice is considered to one of the best vegetable juices. It is a rich source of natural sugar. It contains sodium, potassium, phosphorus, calcium, sulfur, chlorine, iodine, iron, copper, vitamins B1, B2, C, and P. This juice is rich in easily digestible carbohydrates, but the calorie content is low. Red beet juice is high in iron, and it regenerates and reactivates the red blood cells, supplies fresh oxygen to the body. It is useful in treating anemia. Beet juice is a good treatment for jaundice, hepatitis, and nausea. Add a teaspoonful of lime juice to increase its medicinal value. Fresh beet juice mixed with a tablespoonful of honey taken every morning before breakfast will help heal a gastric ulcer. The beet juice combined with carrot and cucumber juices, is one of the finest cleansing agents for the kidneys and gall bladder. Beet juice acts as a natural tonic for the dry tired skin. Blend one beet root with a half cup of cabbage, set some juice aside. Add one tablespoon of mayonnaise or olive oil with beets and cabbage that remains after juicing, and apply to your face. Mix the beet juice with water and freeze to ice cubes. Use one cube to cleanse and tone your skin every morning and evening.

CARROT

We seem to take the delicious, crunchy carrot for granted in the Caribbean. There never seems to be any shortage even though most are imported. My favorite is to pickle firm carrot pieces with hot peppers. The carrot, botanically daucus carota, is one of the world's most popular vegetables grown for the thickened orange root.

Carrots originated some 5000 years ago in the hills of Punjab and Kashmir in India and slowly spread into the Mediterranean area. The first carrots were white, purple, red, yellow, green, or black - not orange and its roots were thin. Ancient Egyptians highly regarded the medicinal properties of carrots. Drawings containing information about carrots used in medicinal treatments and even carrot seeds were found in pharaoh tombs.

Carrots are rich in beta-carotene, which the human body converts to vitamin A. Beta-carotene fights some forms of cancer, especially lung cancer. Eating carrots may also protect against stroke and heart disease. A half cup serving of cooked carrots contains four times the recommended daily intake of vitamin A, with only 35 calories, one gram protein, eight grams of carbohydrates, with two grams of fiber. Carrot is rich in alkaline elements that cleanse and rejuvenate the blood. Carrots also supply the human body with vitamin C, calcium, phosphorus, sodium, sulfur, and chlorine with traces of iodine. The mineral contents in carrots lie very close to the skin and should not be peeled or scrapped off. A good washing is always necessary.

Carrot juice strengthens the eyes and is a great treatment when rubbed on dry skin. Carrot juice drank daily may cure colic, colitis, and peptic ulcers. Raw carrots are good for fertility. Eaten after a meal, a raw carrot destroys germs in the mouth and prevents bleeding of the gums and tooth decay. Carrots speed up digestion, and when eaten regularly prevent gastric ulcer and other digestive disorders. Carrot soup is a natural remedy for diarrhea. Carrots fight all body parasites including intestinal worms.

Always reasonable in the market, carrots are a challenge to grow locally, but it can be done. Although carrots will endure some heat, they grow best planted in a shaded, cool area with sandy soil. The soil should be prepared to a depth of ten inches with clumps smashed completely so the carrots can fully development. Two or three seeds should be planted every inch, at a half inch deep, with rows 12 to 18 inches apart. Thin the seedlings when they are one inch tall to one seedling per 1 to 2 inches. It is essential to keep weeds under control for the first few weeks. Carefully pull loose dirt up and mold the rows when the carrot roots begin to enlarge usually forty days after planting. Fertilize with a higher phosphorus mix when the plants are about a month old. Carrots can be harvested when the root tops are at least three-quarter inch in diameter, about 60 to 70 days after planting. Dig to remove the roots without damage. They may be harvested over a 3 to 4 week period. Big, overgrown carrots are less tasty. Stored properly carrots keep 4 to 6 months.

Always wash carrots first. Raw carrots are naturally sweet, yet slightly cooked carrots may be sweeter. Carrots lose very little vitamins and minerals during cooking. Carrots are a versatile veggie, and can be shredded, chopped, juiced, or cooked whole. They are delicious roasted, boiled, steamed, stir-fried, grilled, and they team up beautifully with almost any vegetable companion. Carrots boost the nutritional value of soups, stews, and salads.

Fresh Herbs with Braised Carrots

A tasty side dish.

Ingredients: one pound carrots chopped three inches long one, cup canned or fresh beef broth, one TS honey, one TBS butter or margarine, two TBS fresh parsley, chopped (or one TBS dried)

Method: In a medium saucepan bring beef broth to a boil, add carrots, honey, butter. and parsley. Cover and simmer for ten minutes. Serves four.

Marinated Carrots

This is a great healthy salad or snack.

Ingredients: one pound carrots, two TBS lime juice, half TS brown mustard, quarter cup olive oil, two chives chopped, one TBS chopped parsley, one clove garlic crushed, salt

Method: Scrub and peel carrots. Cut into half inch wide strips. Boil carrots for 3 minutes or until tender, but still crispy. Drain. In a small bowl, stir together the lemon juice and mustard. Using a fork mix in olive oil a little at a time. Add chives, parsley and garlic. Pour over warm carrots. Season to your taste with salt and pepper. Refrigerate 6 to 8 hours or overnight. Makes 3 cups.

Healthy Carrot Dessert

Ingredients: three cups carrots grated, half cup wheat germ, one cup dried fruit - raisins, or dates (seeded), one cup chopped nuts or grated coconut, half cup honey, one TS cinnamon, half TS nutmeg

Method: Mix all ingredients together. Press into a bowl and chill. Turn and tap out onto a plate. Serve with plain or vanilla yogurt.

Carrot-Pineapple Cake

Ingredients: two cups shredded carrots, three cups flour, one small pineapple chopped and mashed saving the juice, (You can use a 8 oz. can of pineapple drained.) one and a half cups brown sugar, three large eggs beaten, one and a half cups canola oil, one cup chopped walnuts (or coconut), two TS cinnamon, three TS baking powder, one TS baking soda, one TS vanilla extract, one TS salt

Method: Mix flour, sugar, baking soda, baking powder, cinnamon, and salt in a large bowl. In a separate bowl beat eggs and stir in oil and vanilla extract. Add this and the crushed pineapple, shredded carrots, and nuts to the flour and stir until the mixture becomes moist. Stir egg mixture, shredded carrots, nuts and crushed pineapple into flour mixture until flour is moistened. This will make a large cake or can be halved. Pour into greased and floured pans. Bake fifty minutes to an hour at 350 degrees. Use the toothpick method to tell when done in the center. Cool completely before serving.

> **DID YOU KNOW?**
>
> Carrots are a distant cousin of chadon benee. Ancient Greeks believed eating carrots made both men and women more amorous and recommended women eat carrot seeds to prevent pregnancy. Dutch carrot growers cross bred pale yellow carrots with red carrots and created today's orange carrot to honor of the House of Orange, the Dutch Royal Family. China is the world's top carrot grower, producing 35 percent of the world's carrots. Carrots are about 87% water. The longest carrot ever recorded was almost seventeen feet long and the largest carrot ever recorded weighed eighteen pounds. Unlike most other vegetables, carrots are more nutritious when eaten cooked than eaten raw. Carrot greens are high in vitamin K, which is lacking in the carrot root and its skin contain ten percent of all nutrients found in carrots.

Baked Carrots

Ingredients: two cups carrots sliced thin, three TBS butter, half TS nutmeg, one TBS brown sugar, quarter cup water, salt and spices to taste

Method: In suitable oven ware combine nutmeg, sugar, salt and your spices with water. Add carrots and dot top with butter. Bake at 350 for twenty minutes. Let sit ten minute before serving.

CASSAVA

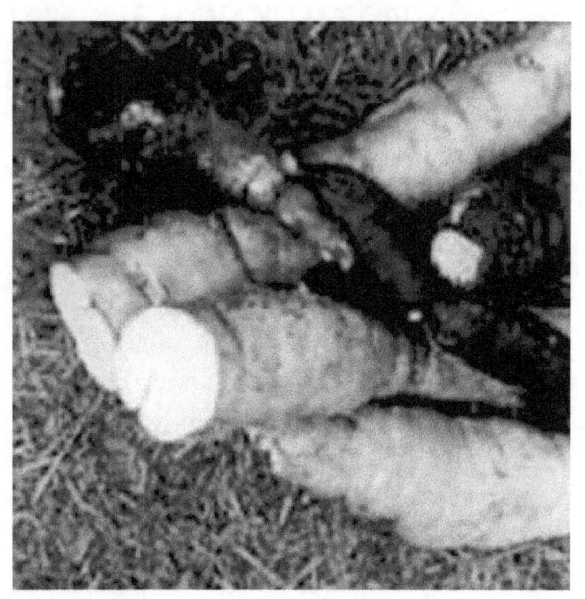

Cassava must be one of God's greatest gifts to this earth. It takes little effort to plant; this root grows easily, and tastes so great. Cassava is a perennial bush with an edible root. The root is a tasty food and a great source of carbohydrates. Scientists rate cassava after rice and wheat in importance of feeding the world. The root is the main source of nutrition for about five hundred million people. It is also called yucca or manioc. Cassava originated in Brazil, along the Amazon River, and has been cultivated for at least five thousand years. Cassava's botanical name is *manihot esculenta*.

It is reputed Columbus was introduced to cassava when he first visited the Island of Hispaniola. The native Arawak Indians fed the explorer a type of fried cake prepared from the root. Portuguese and Spanish sailors brought cassava to Europe, Africa, and Asia – mainly as a food source for slaves. In 2000, worldwide cassava production was more than 175 million tons, with more than half grown in Africa. Cassava is also used for animal feed, laundry starch, has become a source for ethanol fuel production.

Cassava is an important food source because it is easily grown in almost any type of soil with a pH that may vary from 5 to 9. Cassava can withstand almost any conditions from infertile soil to droughts. Only twenty inches of annual rain is necessary for the crop to mature. Cassava bush grows to six to eight feet with large green reddish veined leaves. The stalk has bumpy nodes from which new plants are grown. Cassava plants may be bitter or sweet. The wild purple type is bitter, but the white, butter root, and the new MX are very sweet tasting. The roots grow in clusters and can be up to five inches thick and over eighteen inches long covered with a thin brown bark. Since the bark may contain toxins, it must be removed before cooking.

For such an important edible plant, some varieties of cassava can be quite poisonous without proper preparation. The poison is linamarin, which is chemically similar to sugar. However when eaten raw, the human digestive system changes it to cyanide poison. It only takes two cassava roots to contain a fatal dose of poison. This cyanide is actually a natural protection for the roots as it repels most bugs and borers. Primitive cultures grind the roots into a paste, which releases any poisons. The paste is placed in a wicker tube (called a tipitipi), stretched on a frame. The juice containing the poison drains from the paste. The paste is made into loaves and dried in the sun for better storage.

To plant cassava first you need to locate a suitable variety already growing, preferably butter stick or MX. Cut the stem of the growing plants into one foot long pieces. Dig a two-foot circle about a foot deep with a fork, and then hoe the clumps until the soil is smooth. Insert the stems – root side down – about four inches. This is the most important aspect of growing cassava. The thicker end of the stem must be planted as it produces the root. Cassava is a long crop taking eight to ten months. Some new varieties mature in less than six months. Watering every other day is necessary in the beginning, but can be reduced to once a week after the new leaves have sprouted. Water heavily twice a month during the dry season. Cassava's main enemy is too much water, which will rot the roots. Use a high potassium fertilizer once a month. The only problem with cassava is that it spoils relatively quickly. Stored properly in a cool dark place, the roots should last three weeks. Uncovering the cassava roots takes time and patience, or the roots will be damaged. To harvest, carefully clear the soil from around the tree to determine where the roots run. Carefully fork and gently pry until the tree is free enough to shake. Continue working the roots loose. If a root is pierced with a fork or broken it must be cooked, otherwise it will spoil and rot. Digging cassava is a lot like unwrapping a gift; you never know what you are going to get!

Cassava can be processed into flour, pastes, and granules, or fermented. Some African countries boil cassava leaves as a vegetable. In Central and South America cassava is boiled, fried, or made into cassava flour bread. Cassava is a great addition to soups and stews.

Cassava is such an important food because it is high in starch, which produces energy. A half pound of cassava has 215 calories, of which a quarter is carbohydrates, with one gram of fat, and three grams of protein. It also has vitamin C.

Cassava Cake

Ingredients: two cassava roots and one dried coconut– both grated, one cup milk, one egg, one cup sweetened-condensed milk.

Method: Mix cassava, coconut, and milk and place in a greased baking dish. Bake in a 350 degree oven for half an hour. Remove. Beat the egg into the condensed milk. Spread this mixture over the cassava cake and replace it in the oven for twenty minutes. Let cool before slicing.

Cassava Pone

Ingredients: four pounds cassava, two pounds pumpkin, one dry coconut, one small can evaporated milk, one TBS vanilla, one and a quarter pound margarine or butter, Cinnamon and nutmeg to taste.

Method: Grate cassava, pumpkin and coconut meat mix well with other ingredients. Pour into a well-greased baking dish and bake at 350 degrees for one hour.

Astounding Cassava

Ingredients: two pounds boiled, mashed cassava, one egg, quarter cup flour, one pound minced beef, chicken, or fish, one bunch chives, one bunch celery, salt and spices to taste, oil for frying

Method: Spice the minced meat to your taste and fry till brown. Mix the egg, some salt, into the mashed cassava with the flour. Flatten this mixture and divide into two parts. On one part place the minced meat, celery and chives. Cover with the other part. Cut into squares and pinch the ends. Fry until golden brown. This could also be baked in a casserole dish at 350 for an hour.

Cassava Banana Cake

Ingredients: two TBS sugar, sixteen ounces of coconut cream (canned Coco Loco), eight ripe bananas mashed, four pounds fresh cassava-peeled and grated

Method: Place sugar and coconut cream in a large bowl and mix until all sugar is dissolved. Stir in mashed bananas. Blend the grated cassava into the mixture and mix to fairly smooth. Pour the mixture into the greased cake pan and bake at 250F for 30-40 minutes until golden brown.

Cassava Pudding

Ingredients: two pounds fresh cassava - peeled and grated, three ounces shredded coconut, one TBS freshly grated ginger root, a half pound of sugar, four cloves, lightly crushed

Method: In a large bowl combine all ingredients and blend well. Divide the mixture in four and place each portion in the centre of four pieces of foil or traditionally on banana leaves. Wrap into parcels and steam for 40 minutes. Serve hot.

HEALTH NOTE

Cassava leaves and roots have been a folk remedy for tumors and cancers, which may be due to the B17 content, also known as laetrile. Vitamin B17 is also found in some seeds like apricots, peaches, and apples. B17 stimulates hemoglobin red blood cell count. The bitter cassava variety is used to treat diarrhea and malaria. The leaves are used to treat hypertension, headache, and pain. Cubans commonly use cassava to treat irritable bowel syndrome, the paste eaten in excess during treatment.

DASHEEN

Never a big eater, I grew up hating ground provision. I finally realized the leaf of the same boiled root made my favorite callaloo soup. Dasheen, often called callaloo, is a true favorite of Caribbean people. It is a fast growing tropical plant grown for the broad heart-shaped leaves called dasheen bush, and the roots. Dasheen leaves can easily be confused with eddoes, but the dasheen stem attaches to the center of the leaf and does not touch the 'heart notch'. Dasheen bush is not very tasty until cooked and drained to remove oxalic acid.

Dasheen roots consist of one or more large central heads sometimes called a 'mammy', which may grow to eight pounds. Around the dasheen head is a cluster of smaller roots, usually two to four ounces in size. The growing season for dasheen roots is about seven months. Trinidadians grow dasheen to use the starchy roots like potatoes, yet sweeter, to thicken soups and stews. The leaves are cooked as greens similar to spinach. The stock or leaf stem can be peeled and boiled to a taste akin to asparagus. Also the blanched young shoots obtained by growing in heavy shade (usually under bananas) supply a tender vegetable having a flavor somewhat like that of mushrooms. I grow a few plants along the front drain to gain a tropical landscaping effect and contribute to dinner.

Dasheen roots left in the ground usually stay in good condition until they begin to sprout again. First fork the soil to a foot deep and wide. Add either a phosphate fertilizer or rotted manure to the bottom of the forked ditch. Dasheen roots or suckers of small roots are planted whole, three inches deep, about two feet apart in rows spaced four feet apart. Dasheen requires moist soil. Along an irrigation or drainage ditch is perfect. Every two months use a pound of rich phosphate fertilizer mix as 12-24-12 for every hundred square feet. Dasheen does not compete well against weeds before its big leaf canopy is formed. The best method of controlling weeds is to pull them by hand. This should not be too difficult as the soil should be moist. Water is the key ingredient to making dasheen bush produce. Using insecticides as Pestac can control most insect pests, such as leafhopper and aphids. Ants may attack the roots. Malathion should stop them.

Dasheen is ready to harvest when the leaves turn yellowish and the roots protrude from the ground. This may be in six or eight months depending on location, soil fertility, and wetness.

Dasheen is a belly filling starch with 250 calories to a cup full. It has low fat, no cholesterol, one gram of fiber, but 60 grams of carbohydrates with healthy Palmitic, oleic and linoleic acids and adequate levels of the other essential amino acids. Dasheen is low in protein, but contain moderate quantities of calcium, phosphorus, and magnesium. Dasheen roots can be boiled, steamed, or baked, and may be fried to make chips.

Dasheen Gnocchi

(gnocchi is the Italian version of potato dumplings)

Ingredients: two pounds dasheen peeled and chunked, one medium onion chopped very fine, two TBS olive oil, two TBS fresh basil herb, two cloves of garlic minced, one bunch chadon benee chopped small, one cup dry white wine, two medium ripe tomatoes chopped small, half cup prepared spaghetti sauce, two large eggs beaten, one cup bakers flour, half TS nutmeg, one cup grated Parmesan or cheddar cheese.

Method: Boil dasheen pieces in salted water until tender approximately 30 minutes. To make the sauce use a large skillet, heat the oil adding basil, chadon benee, garlic, and onions and cook for about three minutes. Next lower heat before adding the white wine, tomatoes, and marinara sauce. Simmer for one minute. Then season with salt and pepper to your taste. To make the gnocchi, drain the dasheen before passing them though a ricer or sieve into a large bowl. Add eggs and nutmeg. Season to taste. Slowly add flour evenly, stirring constantly to prevent lumps. Bring a pot of slightly salted water to boil. Carefully spoon the dasheen mixture into as neat as possible balls before dropping into the boiling water. Cook these dasheen gnocchi balls until they float for five minutes. Drain and add to the skillet with the sauce. Serve warm with grated Parmesan or cheddar cheese.

Dasheen Chips

Ingredients: one pound raw dasheen peeled and sliced about an eighth inch thick, oil for frying, salt and spices

Method: Place dasheen slices in a large strainer or colander and blanche them with hot water. Drain and dry with towels. Sprinkle with onion, pepper, or garlic salts and cook in hot oil until golden brown. Drain and eat warm.

> **DID YOU KNOW?**
>
> Dasheen is also known as callaloo, elephant ears, taro, tropic potato, malanga, cocoyam, or blue food. Botanically it is *Colocasia esculenta*. Dasheen was probably first native to the lowland marshes of Malaysia and was cultivated in India before 5000 B.C. There is much confusion with eddoes because both have similar leaves. Dasheen thrives in moist soil, but eddoes like a drier growing medium. When a white dasheen root is peeled and boiled it will gain a bluish tint while eddoes remain white and makes its own gravy.

Dasheen Salad

Ingredients: three pounds dasheen peeled, boiled, and diced, one cup mayonnaise, three TBS vegetable oil, six pimentos preferably red chopped thin, three bunches of parsley, two bunches of chives chopped, two medium onions chopped, two cloves of garlic minced, three TBS white vinegar, a dozen green or black olives sliced thin

Method: Combine onions, garlic, parsley, chives, and all seasonings with the oil and vinegar. Add dasheen cubes, olive slices, and mayonnaise. Cool and serve

Dasheen Puffs

Ingredients: two pounds peeled, cooked, and mashed dasheen, quarter cup milk, two TBS butter or margarine, one egg beaten, four TBS bread crumbs, quarter cup all purpose flour, one cup oil for frying, salt and spice to taste

Method: Combine mashed dasheen, butter, milk, and the egg into a soft mix. On a smooth flat surface mix breadcrumbs and flour. With your hands, form balls of the dasheen mixture and roll in the flour and breadcrumbs. Fry in hot oil until golden brown. Serve hot.

Scalloped Dasheen

Ingredients: two pounds peeled, cooked, and sliced dasheen, half pound grated cheddar cheese, one and a half cup milk, one medium onions sliced fine, one leaf chadon benee chopped small, one bunch chives chopped small, one egg, salt and spice to taste

Method: Layer sliced dasheen in a greased baking pan. Cover with onion, chadon benee, cheese, and chives Repeat alternating layer of sliced dasheen with the onions, chadon benee, cheese, and chives. The top layer should be dasheen slices. Mix egg, milk, salt and spices and pour over the dish. Top with grated cheese. Bake at 350 degrees for 45 minutes until top is golden brown.

The love of gardening is a seed once sown that never dies.

Gertrude Jekyl

EDDOES

Our friend Rudy says that you just can't make a suitable broth without eddoes. Like dasheen, eddoes will grow almost anywhere, but will they boil when you buy them in the market?

Eddo is a perennial root crop grown for its edible roots throughout the tropics. Once planted, eddoes can be harvested every six months. It is a starch with a hairy outer coating similar to a cross between an old red onion and a hairy coconut that can be used instead of potatoes. Eddoes are also known as 'taro root' in Hawaii. They are the main ingredient of the Hawaiian dish 'poi', which is made from steaming or boiling eddoes before mashing it into a paste. The starch molecules in eddoes are among the smallest in the plant world and easy to digest.

Eddoes are a very old food, cultivated longer than wheat. First grown in Southeast Asia, eddo was first recorded by the Chinese about the time of Christ. Eddoes or taro root is mentioned on one of the bamboo slips found in the two thousand year old tomb of the Lady Tai. Eddoes were grown around the Mediterranean long before the potato. Researching Purdue Horticultire Education's web site, both dasheen and eddoes are referred botanically as colocasia esculenta. There must be a further distinction, but as of yet these valuable roots appear to have not been properly researched.

Eddoes flourish easily in moist soil. Clusters of smaller brown hairy roots surround the central 'head' eddo root. It is the smaller roots, which are harvested. This is what makes eddo different from the single-root dasheen. The flesh is usually white; but this root can also be yellow, pink, or orange, and can weigh up to five pounds. The taste is similar to an Irish potato, but with a pleasant, slightly nutty flavor. Raw eddoes should never be eaten as all varieties contain calcium xilate crystals. These crystals can cause you considerable discomfort, but disappear during cooking. If you are a new to eddoes, wear gloves when peeling as it can irritate the skin.

Growing eddoes is very easy. First locate some eddoes to plant. For a nice sized row you need a gallon bucket of starter eddoes. Fork the row about twelve inches deep and the same wide. Pull dirt up so the row is about eight inches high. Plant the starter eddoes so the green stem points upward. Space the roots about six to nine inches apart. Keep eddoes watered and they should sprout new stems in two weeks. For a small vegetable plot, or even a flower garden, eddoes make a nice border, but initially will take daily watering. A soaker hose is a useful tool to get the eddoes growing. Eddoes grow up, not down as most roots, so dirt must be carefully pulled around the protruding roots.

This molding will cause the eddoes to start more of the small clusters. Once a month fertilize with diamonium sulfate and phosphorus. Eddoes must be harvested in the dry season when the leaves yellow, wilt, and disappear. This is usually a five to six month cycle depending on the occurrence of rain. Use a fork and carefully pry the soil from the clusters. Then wash and store in the sun to dry. Once dry, remove to a cool dry place and eddoes will last for a few months.

The only problem with planting eddoes is getting rid of them. In the United States ddoes are considered a pest plant. Left alone, eddoes will naturally multiply especially if the area is often wet.

> **DID YOU KNOW?**
>
> Cultivated for 6,000 years, eddoes has traveled all around the world. The botanical name for eddoes is *Colocasia esculenta*. Researchers believe it originated in the East Indies. Traders are credited with taking taro root to Japan, China and the Mediterranean over 2,500 years ago. Historians say it reached the South Pacific around the time of Christ. It was many centuries later when New Zealand and Hawaii received eddoes. This root is a staple in Asia, the Pacific Islands, Africa, the Caribbean, and parts of South America. Its most familiar use is in poi, traditionally served in Hawaii.

Eddoes have a creamy, nut-like flavor. They can be fried, baked, roasted, boiled, or steamed. Eddoes absorb large quantities of liquid while cooking adding bulk and flavor. Casseroles, soups and stews benefit from these roots. Select tubers that are firm, hairy, with no wrinkling. Purchase smooth bulbs that attach to the head root. Store the roots for up to one week in a cool and dry location, making sure that the roots do not dry out. Eddoes provide a good dietary fiber at 110 calories per adult serving with no cholesterol, but two grams of protein. These roots contain some vitamin C, B6 and E.

Eddo Garlic Pie

Ingredients: one pound boiled and mashed eddoes, two medium onions chopped, six cloves fresh garlic minced, quarter cup grated cheese (prefer Parmesan, but cheddar will work), quarter cup flour, quarter cup bread crumbs, three TBS butter or margarine, one cup milk, salt and spice to taste

Method: Mix mashed eddoes with onions, garlic, flour, salt, spices and milk. Place into a greased oven baking dish or pie pan. Cover with butter slices and cheese. Bake or 45 minutes at 375 degrees. Remove and cover with bread crumbs. Return to oven for 10 minutes. Serves four. Sliced mushrooms, shredded carrots, or other vegetables may be added. Eddo pie firms as it cools.

Cream of Eddo Soup

Ingredients: two pounds eddoes-peeled and diced, quarter cup celery chopped, four cups chicken broth, two cloves garlic minced, one medium onion chopped, two TBS butter or margarine, one bunch chadon benee chopped, salt and spices to taste.

Method: In a large pot on low heat, melt butter, stir in onion, garlic, and celery, add eddoes. Cover for fifteen minutes. Add chicken broth and boil until eddoes are soft. Add chadon benee. This maybe served it as it is or pureed in a blender.

Eddo Shoestrings

Ingredients: two pounds eddoes, salt and spice to taste, oil for deep frying (3-4 cups)

Method: Peel and slice eddoes into thin strips (an eighth inch thick), Place strips in ice water for half an hour then towel dry. Drop into heated oil and fry until golden brown. Turn carefully with a wire skimmer. Drain on newspaper or paper towels. Sprinkle with salt and seasonings.

Eddo Cakes

Ingredients: one pound eddoes grated, two chadon benee leaves chopped fine, one medium onion chopped, one medium sweet pepper chopped, three TBS butter or margarine, two TBS flour, salt and seasoning to taste.

Method: Cook onion, pepper, in butter until browning. Blend grated eddoes, flour, and chadon benee. Spice to your taste. Drop large spoonfuls into the hot skillet on the onions and peppers. Cook until golden brown. Cake should be about three inches in diameter and less than one inch thick. Carefully turn with a spatula.

Gardens are an autobiography, and yet still a friend you can visit anytime.
Unknown

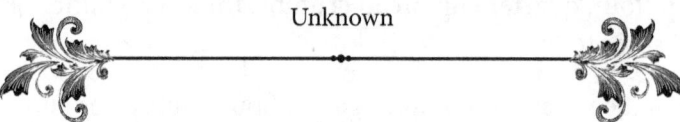

GINGER

Maybe I was sixteen before I tasted ginger beer during the Christmas holidays. My uncles were mixing rum with it. At first I coughed and almost choked at the ginger beer's bite, but now I look forward to making it each season.

The strange looking, brown, knobby ginger root is both a unique, sharp tasting flavoring and medicinal herb. Ginger originated in Asia and belongs to the same spice family as cardamom and turmeric. The Greeks and Romans used the root for medicine, yet its use almost disappeared. Ginger was rediscovered by the Italian adventurer Marco Polo in far eastern Asia where it had been growing for 5000 years. The name 'ginger' means horned root in Sanskrit. Botanically it is zingiber officinale. Ginger is used medicinally because it stimulates and strengthens the stomach, breaks colds and coughs, diarrhea, rheumatism, and especially for nausea. The root can be boiled and pounded into a paste applied to the forehead to ease headaches or made into a poultice to sooth arthritis. As a flavoring, ginger is well used for beverages as ginger beer, and for ginger bread. Although Queen Elizabeth I is reputed to have invented gingerbread for Christmas; it was actually created by the ancient Greeks to aid digestion.

Ginger is easily grown locally, usually to harvest for the Christmas holidays. First, at the market, purchase some fat ginger roots with many buds or fingers. Wrap these roots in damp paper towels and place in your fridge's vegetable drawer, or cool shade, until sprouts appear. Fork a row about ten inches deep and wide. Create a raised bed that will drain otherwise the ginger root will rot. Carefully separate the root 'eyes'. Plant the ginger root pieces eight inches apart and two inches deep with the buds or fingers turned upward. Water regularly and fertilize with 12-24-12. It takes approximately nine months for ginger to mature. Ginger is ready to harvest after the tops begin to wilt. Break up the clumps of roots and wash extremely well, and completely dry in the sun before storage.

Ginger is available fresh, dried, preserved by pickling, tinctures from distillation, or candied. Dried ginger can be ground into a powder. Ginger tea is a safe remedy for motion sickness and the nausea of morning sickness during pregnancy. It is also very helpful in reducing the nausea from chemotherapy. Ginger slows the feedback from the stomach to the brain to prevent the feeling of nausea. Ginger may inhibit blood clotting and reduce heart attacks. Ginger tea may also relieve the pain of your arthritis and cure the common cold. To prepare the tea just slice some thin slivers off the root and boil. Let stand for ten minutes before drinking. Scientists suggest that only a gram a day of ginger should be ingested. Always check with your physician before using any herbal remedies.

Nutritionally ginger doesn't have much. Two grams of ginger have eight calories, only thirty milligrams of carbs, four milligrams of fiber, and just three milligrams of protein with no noticeable vitamins or minerals.

To candy ginger thinly slice peeled ginger root and place in a pot with just enough water to cover. Boil for half an hour until tender. Drain and place ginger slices in a saucepan with an equal amount of brown sugar and three tablespoons of water. Cook over low heat stirring continuously until all liquid is gone. Sprinkle ginger pieces with additional brown sugar.

Ginger Rice

Ingredients: one piece of peeled ginger root, two cups chicken broth, two TBS soy sauce, two TBS olive (or any) oil, one and a half cups rice, two cloves of garlic minced, salt and spice to taste.

Method: On a cutting board thinly slice peeled ginger and smash slices as best as possible in a spoon. Scrape all pieces and juice into a medium size saucepan with the broth and soy sauce. In a skillet heat oil and add rice and garlic. Stir until rice begins to brown in about five minutes. Remove from heat and dump rice into a covered casserole dish adding ginger broth. Place in 400-degree oven until all liquid is dissolved in about twenty-five minutes.

Easy Ginger Ale

Ingredients: two cups peeled ginger chopped as small as possible, four cups water, three four-inch strips of fresh lemon peel, half cup sugar, three liters of club soda

Method: In a large pot mix water, ginger, and lemon. Boil uncovered for ten minutes. Add sugar and boil again for fifteen more minutes. Pour mixture through a fine wire strainer. (Note: This ginger may be reused to flavor baking or ice cream.) Cover and cool the liquid at least two hours. Add one cup of the ginger syrup to a liter of club soda or moderate to your specific taste.

Spicey Ginger Fish

Ingredients: two pounds of filleted kingfish, tuna, salmon, or dolphin, half hot pepper - seeded and minced, one ripe pineapple chopped, one TBS fresh ginger chopped small, quarter cup chicken broth, half cup diced sweet pepper, two TBS chadon benee, salt and spice to taste

Method: Season the fish fillets with salt, hot pepper, and any other spices you like; then sauté for three minutes on each side. In another skillet on high heat, cook pineapple slices, sweet pepper, and ginger until brown. Add chadon benee and the chicken broth, then scrape the pan clean of pineapple and pepper pieces. Place the fish on individual's plates and cover with the gingerpineapple sauce.

Roots

Ginger Pumpkin Cakes

Ingredients: half cup brown sugar, two cups all purpose flower, two and a half TS baking powder, one TS cinnamon, half TS salt, five TBS butter or margarine, one egg, half cup boiled - mashed pumpkin, four TBS minced ginger, quarter cup sour cream

Method: Mix all ingredients (except one TBS of butter) until a soft dough forms. Then roll out on a floured surface. Knead at least ten times. Using a rolling pin, make dough into a ten by five rectangle. Cut dough into five two inch sections then cut these diagonally. Place these ten triangles on an ungreased baking sheet. Brush triangles with melted remaining tablespoon of butter. If desired sprinkle with reserve sugar. Bake 15 minutes at 400 degrees or until golden brown. Cool for 10 minutes.

HEALTH NOTE

For thousands of years Chinese medicine has used ginger to help cure and prevent several health problems. It is known to promote energy, blood circulation in the body while positively increasing the body's metabolic rate. Ginger is good for your health and has been said by some to be a plant directly from the Garden of Eden. It is also reported consuming ginger before taking a plane flight can prevent any kind of motion sickness. It can make good tea, or you can use it as a spicy addition to almost any recipe. antiemetic/anti-nausea, anti-clotting agent, anti-spasmodic, anti-fungal, anti-inflammatory, antiseptic, antibacterial, antiviral, analgesic, circulatory stimulant, carminative, expectorant, increases blood flow, promotes sweating, and relaxes peripheral blood vessels. Ginger does it all. Ginger is a very good addition to your diet.

A garden is never so good as it will be next year.

Thomas Cooper

RADISH

I didn't know anything about radish until I looked at a seed catalogue. I would see them in the supermarket, but we just called them 'white carrots'. My grandparents would only use morai for pepper sauce.

Radish isn't very common in the Caribbean unless they are imported. The most commonly grown radish throughout the islands is the morai. This spicy radish is easy to grow, very tasty, and nutritional. It is a Japanese favorite. Thousands of years ago radishes were first cultivated in China. Along the Mediterranean the Greeks grew a primitive type of radish, but the Egyptians farmed radishes to a great extent for the Pharaoh's tables. The radish did not reach Europe or Britian until the mid 1500s. Radish gets its name from the Latin 'radix' meaning root.

Morai is the word daikon, which means 'great root' in Japanese. In cool shaded area, morai will grow rapidly. A mature morai radish can weigh 5 or 6 pounds. There are several varieties of radishes. Some are red, white, or black, thin, and long, while others are short and round. All radish greens are edible.

Radishes can be grown wherever there is sun and moist, fertile soil, even on the smallest backyard garden. Create a raised bed (4 inches) because radishes need loose soil that drains well to develop the root. Fork the soil a foot deep and remove all stones from the radish bed. Spread a cup of 10-20-10 fertilizer mix for every ten feet of row, or add a five gallon pail of well-rotted chicken manure. Spread two tablespoons of Sevin Powder throughout each row. The more the soil is worked, the easier the radishes will grow. The following day wet the bed thoroughly and carefully plant radish seeds half inch deep and one inch apart. Within a week you should see radish sprouts. Water regularly, but do not soak the bed. Some radish types are ready to harvest within a month. To insure a continuous supply, make successive plantings of short rows every 10 to 14 days. Radishes may be planted in spaces between vegetables peppers or tomatoes.

Morai is considered a 'winter radish' while the red 'globe' (seldom found in the Caribbean unless at an upscale grocery) is a summer type. All radishes are very flavorful and low in calories. A half cup has only 12 calories with a good balance of fiber, potassium, and folate. A half cup of morai daily will help prevent kidney or gall stones.

Red radishes are usually eaten raw. Always wash radishes. There is no need to peel or remove the skin from red radishes except at the top and root end. Radishes may be sliced, diced, shredded, or served whole. However, morai radishes should be peeled , just wash. Those smaller than six inches can be eaten raw, but the longer ones are excellent when added to stirfry, or cut up and simmered in stews and soups. Morai aids in digestion of fatty fried foods.

> **DID YOU KNOW?**
>
> Radish's botanical name is *raphanus*. There are two types; the spring usually red (*R. sativus*) commonly in salads, and the Oriental or winter white radish (*R. sativus variety longipinnatus*).

Grated Radish Salad

Ingredients: four large red radishes or one large morai white radish grated, one carrot grated, two big stalks of celery chopped like small matchsticks, four bunches of chives chopped into one inch pieces, one head of lettuce chopped small, quarter cup rice vinegar, quarter cup olive or canola oil, half TS celery seed, salt and spice to taste

Method: Wash all vegetables, then mix together in a large bowl. In a small bowl mix remaining ingredients and pour over vegetables and mix well.

Pasta with Radishes

Ingredients: two dozen red radishes or four morai white radishes with green tops, two TBS olive oil, one onion chopped small, one pound pasta cooked (shells, springs or elbows) - keep a quarter of the cooking water, quarter cup grated parmesan cheese or cheddar, salt and pepper to taste

Method: Wash radishes and greens several times before separating tops. Slice radishes very thin. In a large frying pan heat the oil. Fry onions two minutes until soft. Add radish slices and greens. Cover and cook for five minutes until the greens have wilted. Season and cool before adding drained pasta. Add remaining water from cooking pasta stirring while adding grated cheese.

Hot and Sour Spinach Radish Soup

Ingredients: five cups chicken broth, quarter cup rice wine vinegar, two TBS sugar, quarter hot pepper seeded and minced, one peeled and minced ginger, one pound peeled shrimp, one and a half cup sliced radish, one and a half cup shredded spinach leaves, two third cup chopped chives.

Method: In a large skillet bring chicken broth to a boil. Add rice vinegar, sugar, hot pepper, and ginger. Then add shrimp and cook a few minutes until they become pink. Mix in radish, spinach, and chives. Cover and let sit for five minutes before serving.

Chinese Radish Salad

Ingredients: one large morai white radish – sliced into large match sticks, two TBS rice or clear vinegar, one TBS soy sauce, one TS sugar, two TS sesame oil, two cloves garlic minced

Method: Mix all ingredients in a large bowl.

Morai Match Salad

Ingredients: one pound morai radish washed and cut into two inch long thin strips, three TBS brown spicy or Dijon type mustard, three TBS hot water, four TBS olive oil, one TS rice wine vinegar (white vinegar may substitute), quarter cup parsley chopped fine, salt and spice to taste

Method: In a large bowl mix mustard with hot water. Slowly add the oil stirring constantly (Use a whisk if you have one). Then mix in vinegar and spices. Add morai strips and parsley.

Radish Slaw

Ingredients: two cups morai radish coarsely grated, three cups shredded cabbage, three carrots grated coarse, one red Spanish onion sliced thin—chopped small, two TBS fresh lemon juice, half TS sugar, two TBS olive oil, two TBS fresh chadon bene chopped.

Method: Place morai, carrots and cabbage in a large bowl. In a smaller bowl mix all other ingredients. Mix everything together in the large bowl.

Morai Salsa

Great on grilled fish, pork or beef. Use it on scrambled eggs or as a chip dip.

Ingredients: a dozen red radishes or two morai radishes, two medium ripe tomatoes, one medium onion, one bunch chadon benee, one clove garlic minced, juice from one lemon, hot pepper seeded and minced, salt and spices to taste

Method: Chop all ingredients fine and mix. Place in fridge for at least an hour to let the flavors mix before serving.

HEALTH NOTE

Radishes and their green tops are an excellent source of vitamin C. The leaves contain six times the vitamin C content of their root, and are also a good source of calcium. Red radishes provide the trace mineral molybdenum and a good source of potassium. Morai provides a very good source of potassium and copper. Historically radishes were used as a medicinal food for liver disorders. They contain a variety of sulfur-based chemicals to increase the flow of bile, which helps to maintain a healthy gallbladder and liver, and improve digestion.

SWEET POTATO

When I grew up, everybody in my family loved roasted or boiled sweet potato, or sweet potato chips. My grandfather grew them, so we had a fairly constant supply.

Sweet potato is a local staple vegetable that requires a long growing season to produce mature roots. Sweet potatoes are often confused with yams, however yams are very different. While the sweet potato, ipomoea batatas, is native to Peru, yams originated in Africa. Yams are not very sweet, and grow as large as 100 pounds. Before Europeans landed in the Western Hemisphere the sweet potato was already well traveled. This root had already passed through South America, Mexico, carried by boat to far away Pacific islands and farther on to New Zealand. In many countries of the Pacific, the sweet potato is a prime food source especially if the rice crop fails. China grows most of the world's crop.

Columbus brought back to Spain many new foods he discovered during his first voyage in 1492. Sweet potatoes were among Columbus' treasures. The Spanish immediately loved sweet potatoes and began cultivation. Soon Spain exported the sweet root to their rival England. France acquired a taste for the root when Napoleon's wife, French Empress Josephine, who was born in Martinique, craved the sweet potato. The Portuguese seafarers carried them to Africa and Asia.

Caribbean people love sweet potatoes and they are grown profitably on almost every island. Sweet potatoes grow best in sandy soil from what are called 'slips' or fertile branches of the parent bush. Plant the slips two inches deep and a foot apart. The row should be molded at least eight inches high. Add another inch of cover sand when the slip begins to grow. Keep three feet between rows, as healthy plants will vine. The rows must be kept wet in the development stage. Carefully pull out any weeds. Once the vines are mature water sparingly, perhaps once a week. Sweet potatoes prefer hot dry weather, but will need occasional watering. If too arid the bushes will die or produce small roots. A heavy rain, or over watering will cause the roots not to form properly. To harvest dig them carefully with a fork and dry in a shady, cool spot for a week.

The sweet potato is very nutritious. A half-cup of cooked sweet potato supplies two grams of protein, four grams of fiber, vitamins A and C, calcium, beta-carotene, manganese, and folic acid. Sweet potatoes may be shredded raw and added to salads or to top soups. Sweet potatoes can also be juiced.

Over 95 percent of the global sweet potato crop is produced in developing countries. It ranks as the world's seventh most important food crop—after wheat, rice, maize, potato, barley, and cassava. More than 133 million tons are produced globally per year. China grows 90 percent of worldwide sweet potato production.

Sliced Baked Sweet Potato

Slice peeled sweet potatoes a quarter inch thick. Place on a piece of foil or baking sheet and brush with vegetable oil. Bake at 400 degrees for half an hour.

Fried Sweet Potato Cakes

Ingredients: three nice size sweet potatoes, two eggs, half cup flour, two TBS cooking oil, salt and pepper to taste

Method: Grate peeled raw sweet potatoes. Mix in eggs and flour. Season to taste. Form into cakes about an inch thick. Heat oil in skillet and place cakes. Cover and fry till cooked through and the cake breaks easily. Uncover and brown. Serves four.

> **DID YOU KNOW?**
>
> Botanists believe that sweet potato was domesticated more than 5000 years ago. Despite its name, the sweet potato really doesn't belong to the same family as the potato, not even close. Potatoes are tubers, sweet potatoes are roots. George Washington Carver who discovered three hundred uses for peanuts, worked extensively with the sweet potato. The list of sweet potato inventions compiled from Carver's records includes 73 dyes, 17 wood fillers, 14 candies, 5 library pastes, 5 breakfast foods, 4 starches, 4 flours, and 3 types of molasses. Carver's research also demonstrated the value of soil regeneration by planting sweet potatoes as a rotation crop.

Sweet Potato Soup

Ingredients: four large sweet potatoes peeled and chopped into one inch pieces, one large onion cut into one inch pieces, four cups of water, an additional three cups of water later, salt and seasoning to taste.

Method: In a large stockpot put water, potatoes. and onion. Boil until potato is soft. Put pieces and liquid into a food processor and blend and puree, or force through a sieve. Return pureed mixture to stockpot and add additional three cups of water. Heat and add seasonings. Serves six.

Spicy Sweet Potatoes

Makes a great side dish or a unique appetizer.

Ingredients: three large sweet potatoes, two TBS butter or margarine, quarter cup chopped or sliced almonds (Other nuts - even coconut - can be substituted), half cup of flour, a pinch (to taste) of salt, pepper, cloves and cinnamon, two cups vegetable oil for frying

Method: Peel and mash boiled sweet potatoes, then add nuts and spices. Blend until sweet potatoes can be rolled into small balls. Carefully roll the balls into flour. Deep fry until golden brown and serve hot.

Sweet Potato Casserole

Ingredients: four medium sweet potatoes – boiled and mashed, four ripe bananas – mashed, half cup chopped nuts, six TBS butter or margarine, half cup brown sugar (or less to taste), half cup coconut, one cup crushed corn flakes

Method: In an appropriate pot or bowl combine mashed sweet potatoes with nuts, 4 tablespoons butter, a quarter cup of sugar, and coconut. Pour half of this mixture into an oven casserole dish. Spread mashed bananas and cover with remaining sweet potato mixture. Cover top with crushed corn flakes remaining butter and sugar. Bake at 350 degrees for fifteen minutes. Uncover and bake for another ten till top is browned and crunchy.

HEALTH NOTE

Center for Science in the Public Interest (CSPI) ranked sweet potatoes number one in nutrition of all vegetables. With a score of 184, the sweet potato outscored the next highest vegetable (broccoli) by more than 100 points. Points were given for content of dietary fiber, naturally occurring sugars and complex carbohydrates, protein, vitamins A and C, iron and calcium. Points were deducted for fat content (especially saturated fat), sodium, cholesterol, added refined sugars, and caffeine. The higher the score, the more nutritious the food. Sweet potato is a good food for people involved in heavy muscular work, since this food is high in vitamins and minerals. Sweet potatoes are rich in vitamin Abetacarotene, and C. Both are powerful antioxidants that work in the body to remove free radicals, which are chemicals that damage cells. They are good for stomach ulcers and inflamed conditions of the colon and beneficial for lower blood pressure. They also are a good food for diabetics to help stabilize blood sugar levels. Sweet potatoes contain an enzyme to convert most of its starches into sugars as the potato matures. This sweetness increases during storage and when they are cooked.

TANNIA

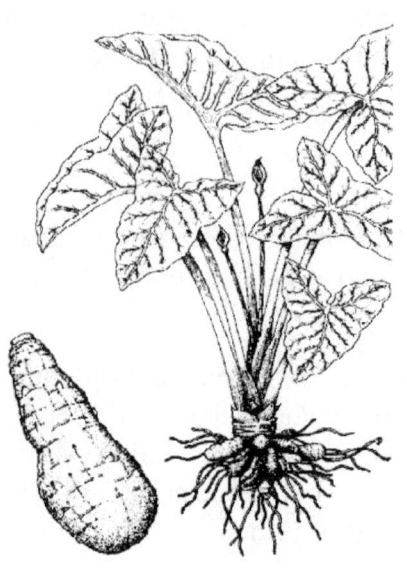

Tannia is a tasty root with a large leaf shaped like a spear point. We found some small tannia plants while driving along the north coast and two years later they are huge. Tannia is also known as yautia, malanga, or cocoyam tanier. Botanically it is *xanthosoma sagittifolium*.

Tannia is one of the roots that originated in tropical Central and South America. English and Spanish explorers found it cultivated through out the Caribbean chain of islands. They carried tannia to Africa where it became a major food source. Tannia's flavor and texture is considered superior to cassava, potatoes, and yams. It is a perennial, so once you have it, it will remain.

As with everything you want to grow, first you must find some tannia seeds to plant. Trinidad has a few types of tannia, just as there are several types of cassava. We like the one that has a faint red line along the leaf stem. It seems to be the tastiest. As with eddoes, tannia forms both heads and seeds (cormels). We have a few friends who farm in the northern mountains and they recommend to use a piece of the tannia head with a few of the seeds attached. Tannia grows best in open sun, but needs consistent water. Don't bother to plant if your soil is all clay.

To plant tannia first work the ground well with a fork so that it is soft and free of clumps of hard dirt. Blend in some well-rotted chicken manure, a quarter-cup of crushed limestone, and then form mounds. If you are using a head, split it and put it in the mound split side up and cover with about five inches of lose soil. If you are planting a shoot attached to the seed, slide it in so the attached root is facing up. Again cover with about five inches of loose soil. If you plant shallower it will produce many small side shoots rather than one big root. Tannia's big leaves don't like neighbors so plant about a meter or further apart. After two weeks use 12-24-12 fertilizer at about an eighth cup per plant and again every time you remold, or every two months. Keep weeds down until the leaves develop. Fungus and bacteria are tannia's main enemies, so spray monthly with Ban Rot or Rizolex. Tannia is a long crop and can take from eight to twelve months. In the sixth month fertilize with 13-13-21 mixture. Keeping tannia well drained during the rainy season is the best solution. During the severe part of the dry season try to water tannia heavily once a week. The roots should take about a year to develop and you can harvest carefully with a garden fork. It is wise to wash the roots clean of dirt and rinse with a mild disinfectant if you wish to store for later use. Save the small seeds, or cormels, to replant. There is a tannia virus, but as of yet it hasn't found its way here.

North coast Steven is one of the few tannia farmers we've met. He swears by planting tannia with the moon, He plants in the ascending moon and gets long fat tannia, but if he plants in the descending moon he gets long thin roots. Tannia is in demand because of its taste, and unlike eddoes it always will boil. West Africa, Cuba, Puerto Rico and the Dominican Republic are the biggest producers of tannia.

Tannia like most roots is about a third starch, with a small amount of protein. Tannia chips are gaining international fame. One cup of cooked tannia has about a hundred calories, mostly water and carbohydrates with a little protein and virtually no fat. Tannia is a great source of calcium, phosphorous and iron. These roots also supply vitamin A, thiamin, and riboflavin.

> **DID YOU KNOW?**
>
> Tannia's botanical name is *xanthosoma sagittifolium*. It is also known in English as tannia; yautia. new cocoyam, tanier, arrowwleaf, and elephant ear. The Spanish Caribbean call it yautía or malanga. In Yucatan, Mexico it is macal, Honduras – quiscamote, Costa Rica - tiquisque, Panama – otó, Venezuela - okumo, Peru - uncucha, Bolivia - gualuza, Colombia – malangay. Among Brazil's Portuguese it is taioba, mangareto, mangarito, mangarás. On the French Caribbean islands it is chou caribe. There are two types of tannia, white and yellow. West Africa is now the major tannia producer.

Tannia makes a great backyard landscaping plant. It is very tropical looking and will grow to a meter tall with full sun and plenty of water. The best thing is that it can be closely groomed so there are no weedy areas, just lush tall tannia that look like they belong in Jurassic Park. If you plan your backyard landscaping, tannia will not shade a large area.

Tannia Fritters

Ingredients: one pound tannia - peeled and grated, two stalks of celery chopped, one medium onion minced, four TBS flour, half TS cayenne pepper, one TS salt, one TS lime juice, one egg, two TBS milk, spices to your taste

Method: Combine everything in a bowl. Beat the egg in well. Carefully drop spoonfuls of this tannia mixture into hot oil until both sides are brown. Drain and serve hot.

Tannia Pie

Ingredients: one pound tannia - peeled, boiled, and mashed, one pound cooked minced meat seasoned to your taste, one medium onion chopped, two cloves garlic minced, one medium sweet pepper chopped small, half hot pepper seeded and well minced, half cup cheddar cheese grated, quarter cup milk, two TBS flour, one TBS butter, salt and seasonings to your taste

Method: Mash tannia with milk, butter, your seasonings, and flour into a pie shell.

Combine the minced meat (lamb, beef, or chicken) with onion, garlic, and pepper. Bake at 350 for a half hour and then cover top with grated cheese. Bake for another half hour. Serve hot.

Tannia Soup

Ingredients: one pound tannias - peeled and chunked, two cups vegetable stock, one medium onion chopped fine, two bunches chives chopped, two cloves garlic minced, two TBS butter or margarine, half cup milk, salt and spices to your taste

Method: Lightly brown tannia pieces with the onion and garlic in a large pot with the butter. Add stock and spices, and boil for five minutes. Simmer for twenty minutes. Then blend in the milk and chives and serve.

Tannia - Provision Pot

Ingredients: equal amounts, two pounds of each tannia, sweet potato, yam, dasheen, green banana, one large onion sliced, three cloves garlic sliced thin, two TBS oil, salt and spice to taste

Method: Wash and peel all provision and banana. Chop into chunks. Boil till soft. In a good sized frying pan heat oil before adding garlic and onion pieces. Slowly add provision and banana. Cover and reduce heat. Stir in salt and spices to your taste. Serve warm or cold.

One who plants a garden, plants happiness.
Unknown

TOPPEE TAMBU – GUINEA ARROWROOT

(Left) Toppee tambu not yet cleaned and still attached to the leaves and stems. (Right) cleaned toppee tambu roots

My grandfather grew toppee tambu on the borders of his garden. He'd bring the brown, round roots home and we'd scrub, boil, and peel them. Crunching would be all you'd hear around the table. Toppee tambu has many names, topiambour, or sweet corn root. It is probably best known as Guinea arrowroot, which is not the thickening agent - arrowroot from St. Vincent.

Toppee tambu is very easy to grow and makes a nice landscaping border for gardens, another edible hedge. The broad green leaves can reach five feet tall and a few will bear white flowers. The almost round root can be up to two inches in diameter and resemble 'new', first harvested small potatoes, or water chestnuts. Toppee tambu is seldom affected by any insects or worms, and only needs watering in a drought. To locate some seed roots (rhizomes) find someone selling them along a roadside. They either have some for planting, or will direct you to whom they boought the toppee tambu. To prepare for planting find a well drained area, fork and mix in well-rotted chicken manure. Harvests will be less in clay soil than sandy. Plant the 'seeds' about a foot apart. This plant will even grow in shade, which makes it perfect for interspersing between fruit trees, cassava, or plantain. It is a long crop taking about nine months to harvest.

Toppee tambu roots are usually boiled for 15 to 20 minutes and can then be fried, grilled, or mashed; and especially are great for stirfry. Its flavor is similar to that of cooked young corn. Toppee tambu remains crisp long after cooking. Tender new leaves can be boiled in soups and stews. Flour made from the dried roots contain 15% starch and 6.6% protein.

Nutritionally toppee tambu is actually more than a starchy, belly filler. Per 100 grams nutrition the roots have sixty calories, nine grams of carbs, a half gram of protein, with calcium, phosphorus, and some vitamin C. It is good food for a non-irritating recuperation diet, and for infants as a replacement of breast milk. It can eaten in the form of jelly seasoned with sugar, lemon-juice, or fruit jellies. Medicinally the leaves are also used in a broth as a diuretic and in the treatment of cystitis.

Toppee tambu may have a future as a starch as the world searches for new food sources, This root isn't cultivated on a large scale in most countries. However, in the few plantations where it is grown, no pest attacks or diseases have caused significant damage during the last 15 years. With the impact of so many fungus and pests, considering the escalating costs of preventative garden treatments, toppee tambu may be a crop that can make a considerable profit.

> ## DID YOU KNOW?
> Toppee tambu is also called Guiana arrowroot. During research I became confused with the arrow root thickener grown mostly in St. Vincent, and the Guiana arrowroot. Toppee tambu botanically is *calathea allouia*, while the thickener arrowroot is *maranta arundinacea*. The English say either Guinea arrowroot, or sweet corn root. Caribbean islanders call it topee tampo, topi-tamboo, or topinambour. In Spanish it is dale dale, especially in Peru. It is agua bendita, cocurito in Venezuela. Lerenes in Puerto Rico. Brazilians say it in Portuguese as ariá, or láirem. French say touple nambours particularly in Santa Lucía, but in the French islands it is alléluia. curcuma d'Amérique.

Toppee tambu roots are unique because after they are cooked their texture remains crisp. It is best to cook the toppee tambu before using them in any recipes. As well as being eaten on its own, toppee tambu can used in salads, soups, and fish dishes.

Toppee Tambu Stew

Ingredients: two to four pounds fresh toppee tambu washed, depending on the size chunk them if they are bigger than a spoon can hold. One sweet green pepper seeded and sliced, three tomatoes quartered, one large onion sliced thin, two cloves of garlic minced, two TBS oil for frying, a pound of stew beef, chicken, or pork (if not keep it vegetarian), a pound of cooked red beans, three cups water, two leaves chadon benee minced, salt and spices to taste

Method: In a deep skillet or big pot fry the onion in the oil till it becomes clear, add meat (if using), cook till no red remains inside. Add beans and remaining vegetables then water. Cover and simmer for two hours. Add chadon benee and cook for ten more minutes.

Toppee Tambu French Style—Creamed

Ingredients: two pounds toppee tambu boiled and skin removed, then sliced a quarter inch thick. One onion sliced thin, one clove garlic minced, two TBS oil for frying, one cup evaporated milk, three leaves chadon benee or quarter cup parsley, salt and spices to taste

Method: Sauté onion and garlic in the oil in a frying pan, Add toppee tambu and brown a bit before adding condensed milk. Simmer and stir frequently so milk doesn't burn. Add chadon benee or parsley at end of cooking—about fifteen minutes. Great as a side dish with chicken or fish.

Scalloped Toppee Tambu

Ingredients: two pounds toppee tambu, boiled and skinned, one onion sliced thin, one clove garlic minced, one cup evaporated milk, one cup cheddar cheese grated, half TBS nutmeg, salt and spices to taste.

Method: Combine all ingredients in an oven ware pan. Bake at 350 for forty minutes.

Toppeee Shish Kabob

Ingredients: six metal skewers, two pounds toppee tambu boiled and peeled, two medium onions quartered, two sweet peppers quartered, three medium tomatoes quartered, two ripe plantains skinned and cut into two inch pieces, curry powder or jeera (cumin), salt and spices to taste

Method: Put all ingredients on to metal skewers, roll or dust with either curry or jeera. Cook over a coal pot or gas grill until all veggies just start to brown. Serve with pasta or rice.

As the garden grows, so grows the gardener.
Unknown

THE YUMMY YAM

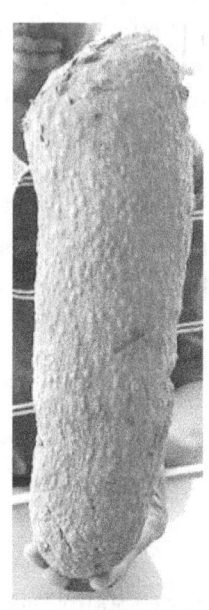

Yam is not a pretty food, yet without it I find a good provision soup or casserole is incomplete. Traditionally Caribbean people call root crops 'provisions' or 'ground food'. This term came from sugar plantation days when food for the workers was scarce. Ground food was a reliable source since these roots could survive extreme dry spells and the wrath of tropical storms.

Also roots such as yam, dasheen, and cassava could be grown inconspicuously within the cane crop. The nice part about yams and other roots is that you only dig what you need for a meal and leave the remainder in the ground staying fresh. The yam is a staple food in many of the Caribbean Islands, Africa, and South America.

The origin of yams is uncertain, but definitely they are one of the world's oldest foods. Traces found in caves in Asia and Africa have been carbon dated to over fifty thousand years ago! The yellow yam is native to Asia, while the white yam is from Africa. Africa grows almost ninety-per cent of the world's yams. Yams grow on all continents and most tropical islands.

In the 1600's Portuguese explorers saw African tribesmen digging yams and asked what the root was called. The African tribesmen did not understand and merely answered , 'it was something to eat' or 'nyami' in Guinea. The Portuguese changed the word to 'Inhame'. The French called the root 'igname', and the English derived it to yam. In Hindi, yams are 'suar alu'. Even today there is considerable confusion in determining the name of the specific root yam, or sweet potato. The sweet potato is a member of the Morning Glory family and is not a yam, but in the southern US sweet potatoes are termed yams. *Dioscorea alata L* is the greater yam, *D. cayenensis Lam.*, the yellow yam, and *D. rotundata Poir.*, the white yam. True yams generally grow only in the Caribbean, Africa, Asia, and Mexico. The US imports yams from at least fourteen different countries.

Root crops of the tropics appear slightly similar, but each is very different as is their name from that island or country. Yams contain more natural sugar than sweet potatoes and have higher moisture content. Yam's shape is long and cylindrical and their skin is rough and scaly almost like a tree's bark. There are nearly two hundred varieties of yams with brown, black, white, or pink skin, having white, yellow, or purple flesh. Yams taste more like an Irish potato than any other tropical tuber and can grow up to seven feet and weigh two hundred pounds!

We have a friend on the north coast who is one of the few people we know who actually cultivates yam. Most others are what we would call yam hunters. They walk the fields searching for yams growing naturally. To cultivate, first you have to locate some small yam roots by seeking the brilliant green vines. After digging the small yams and taking them to your garden, dig a hole big enough - a two foot cube, throw in a chubby cap full of 12-24-12 fertilizer and cover with a layer of dirt. Then drop in the small yam stem side up, and fill to about eight inches from the top. Finish filling the hole with organic materials like cut grass, or garden compost. This will decompose and feed the yam. Water regularly – soak them once a week in the dry season. As the organic compost rots, add more on top of the yam. After six or seven months, cut the vines and carefully use a fork to remove the now large root. Use the old vines as compost for your next yam planting. Control the yam vines or they will take over.

When buying yams, look for solid, hard roots, no soft shrunken spots, cracks, or mold. Pick the best by pricking through the skin with a fingernail. The flesh should be crisp and juicy. Store yams in a cool, well-ventilated place and use, before they get soft. They keep for a week.

Yam flesh is poisonous raw, but cooking makes it safe and edible. One cup of cooked yam contains 150 calories with five grams of fiber, vitamins C and B6, potassium, and manganese. Potassium helps lower blood pressure. Wild Asian yam has traditionally been used in herbal medicine to treat organ system function, especially the kidneys and the female endocrine system. Diosgenin, a natural occurring steroid, in yam makes it an herbal remedy for arthritis, asthma, eczema, carbuncles, diarrhea, menstrual disorders, and certain inflammatory conditions, and may help reduce the risk of osteoporosis. Yam extracts are used as a natural alternative to hormonal replacement in women who have reached the age of menopause. Yams' vitamin B6 has been used as a natural herbal supplement for premenstrual syndrome (PMS) in women, especially with the accompanied depression.

Yams' sugars and complex carbohydrates are absorbed into the bloodstream slowly and because yams are high in fiber, yams fill you up without filling out your hips and waistline. Manganese in yams helps to slow the carbohydrate metabolism and is important in energy production.

Wear gloves when peeling yams since they secrete an acrid juice that can irritate skin. Yams can be boiled, mashed with milk, butter and cheese to make yam pie. Or yams can be just mashed with plenty of butter and seasoned to compliment meat, chicken or fish dishes. Yams can be finely sliced into chips or simply baked in their skins. My favorite is king fish broth rich in onion and butter, with slices of yam. Cold boiled yam can be made into a type of potato salad by mixing it with mayonnaise, onion, and celery. Yam chunks can be added to stir fry or pan of roasted vegetables. Roasted yams, fennel, onions, and mushrooms are a delicious combination.

Healthy Yammy Chips

Ingredients: two pounds of scrubbed yams sliced as thin as possible, two TBS lemon juice, three TBS canola oil, salt and seasoning to taste

Method: Rinse yam slices in cold water mixed with the lemon juice to keep the flesh from turning gray. Lay slices on a baking sheet, sprinkle with oil and toss so both sides of the chips are coated with oil. Sprinkle chips with salt and pepper for spicy chips or use nutmeg cinnamon and sugar for something different.

Stuffed Yams

Ingredients: three nice yam pieces (about a pound each) washed peeled, cut lengthwise, one pound medium shrimp boiled, vein removed, and peeled, four chives, one medium onion, two cloves garlic minced, half cup milk, two TBS butter or margarine, salt, spice to taste

Method: Boil yam in salt water careful to avoid breaking. Scoop out center of yam halves so that only an inch of the shell remains. Mash the scooped out yam. Sauté onion, chive, shrimp, and garlic in butter. Mix in the mashed yam and the milk. Fill yam hollows with mixture and broil until brown.

Gingered Chicked and Yams

Ingredients: one pound yams sliced and chopped into matchstick sized pieces, half a chicken chopped into small pieces, one red onion chopped, two TBS olive oil, two TBS ginger root minced. four chives chopped, three TBS soy sauce, three TBS water, one TBS brown sugar, one TBS cornstarch, salt and spices to taste

Method: In a large frying pan on medium heat add one TBS oil, yam sticks, and onion. Cook for five minutes stirring frequently. Spoon off into a sealed bowl, but keep warm. Increase heat to high and add the other one TBS of oil, chicken, and ginger. Cook for five minutes till chicken is no longer pink inside. Add the vegetables to the chicken and mix in the rema ining ingredients. Bring to a boil for three to five minutes. Remove from heat and serve with rice or pasta.

Vegetables

The term vegetable usually means that the leaf, stem, or root of a plant that is edible for humans. This word does not apply to any rule of botany and is subjective. Vegetable is not a scientific or botanical term, and is based on regional food and cultural customs. Most vegetables are annual plants, meaning they must be replanted yearly.

There is no clear distinction between vegetables and fruits. Most vegetables consist largely of water, making them low in calories. They are excellent sources of fiber, vitamins A and C, potassium, calcium, and iron. All the amino acids needed to synthesize protein are available in vegetables. Fresh vegetables quickly age and spoil, but their storage life can be extended by such preservation methods as dehydration, canning, freezing, fermenting, and pickling.

Botanists define most vegetables developed from plant blossoms as fruits. However, at the market everyone knows the difference between a fruit and a veggie. Eggplants, bell peppers, and tomatoes are botanically fruits, as are most grains, and even some spices like black and red pepper. Some vegetables are variable as corn; considered a vegetable only when fresh before it is dried, and then becoming a grain.

Garden: One of a vast number of free outdoor restaurants operated by charity-minded amateurs in an effort to provide healthful, balanced meals for insects, birds, and animals.

Henry Beard and Roy McKie, Gardener's Dictionary

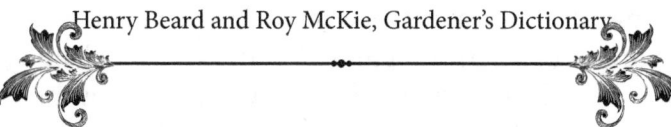

BODI

We have had success growing bodi, yet not green or bush beans. Bodi seems to be more tolerant to the climatic conditions, diseases, and pests of the tropics. Done right, bodi can be an attractive and tasty addition to any home garden. Done without planning, the vines that produce this long bean easily can take over a back yard. Bodi cannot be allowed just to rest on the ground. It needs to be up on a fence, or jamrah / trellis otherwise it bears poorly.

Bodi is a pencil-thin bean that resembles a green bean although not as crisp, and grows up to about 3 feet long. It's usually harvested at 18 inches or less. Bodi is an annual climbing plant with white, yellow, or pale purple flowers. Bodi is also called asparagus bean, Chinese long bean, snake bean, or yard bean and belongs to the same family as the black-eyed pea and pigeon pea. Beans have been cultivated for at least 7000 years, and there are more than 12,000 species of beans through out the world. Bodi, botanically *vigna unguiculat*, is native to Southeast Asia. Bodi comes in different varieties from the more common pale green pod variety, to the more slender darker green one, to a deep brownish red variety. These beans are rich in vitamins A and C. Bodi is very nutritious. A hundred gram serving gives four grams of protein, 110 mg calcium, 5 mg iron, 2 mg vitamin A, 35 mg vitamin C, and calcium.

Bodi grows quickly in Caribbean's tropical climate. In fact it grows so well that Trinidad produced nine million kilos of bodi in 2003. Bodi prefers a light, well-drained soil with a pH of 5.5 to 6.8, enriched with compost, or rotted chicken manure and grows to maturity in less than sixty days. Being a climbing plant, bodi provides extra work for the gardener. Plant seeds an inch deep, at least eight inches apart with raised rows separated at least three feet. Soak the seeds in water before sowing, for better germination.

The distance between rows is necessary because sticks need to be placed every six to eight feet along the rows. Some farmers put in the sticks before planting so not to later irritate the roots of young plants. Strings are then pulled at two or three levels, one, two, and four feet, between the sticks. Then carefully weave the bodi vines between these strings. Bodi is perfect for the home gardener who has a chain link fence for it to climb. Bodi can also vine on dead eggplant or hot pepper trees. In a small garden plot it is best to plant bodi at the rear so it does not shade the other vegetables. Care must be taken to ensure the sprawling vines are controlled and do not interfere with other veggies. In the early growth stages use a 12-24-12 fertilizer m ix and 12-12-17-2 mix when flowering begins. Bodi requires water. If it is an extremely dry season the beans will be short, tough, and stringy. Fruits grow from open flower to marketable length of 18 to 30 inches in about nine days.

Flowering will occur five weeks after sowing. Fruits will grow from open flower to suitable length in about two weeks. Pick the pods at the tender stage at maximum length, before the seeds mature, or swell. Bodi beans may grow up to 24inch long, but it is better to pick them at 12 to 18 inches.

Urea or a high nitrogen fertilizer works well on all beans. Beans are hungry and deplete

> **DID YOU KNOW?**
>
> Most types of beans have the ability to pump nitrogen from the environment into your soil -- making a more nitrogen-rich soil. This is done through nodules on their fine roots. It is wise to plant beans/bodi where the heavy nitrogen feeding veggies, like corn, were planted the year before.

the soil of nutrients, so it is wise to rotate planting areas. Mole crickets love young bodi. Aphids are drawn to the pods of this plant. Thrips tend to be a pest early in the season. Spider mites can be a problem, producing a silver speckled appearance on leaves. Ringing, where the beans actually turn into a spiral, is one of the most common diseases and this may be also caused by mites.

Bodi is susceptible to nematodes and mosaic virus. A chemical spray of an insecticide like Fastac is beneficial. Be careful to spray chemicals at least two weeks before harvest.

Bodi can be prepared in various ways: stewed with tomato sauce; boiled and drained, then seasoned with lemon juice and oil; or simmered in butter or oil and garlic. The pale green bean is meatier and sweeter than the dark green bean, which has a less delicate taste.

Long Bean Stir Fry

Ingredients: one pound bodi, one pound pak choy, one TBS sesame seeds, two TS peanut oil, half TS sesame oil, two TBS soy sauce. Salt and pepper to taste.

Method: Cut off stems from the pak choy, trim ends before slicing into long strips. Blanch the pak choy in hot water, remove and set aside. First steam the bodi until bright green (about four minutes), and then combine with pak choy. Heat peanut oil and sesame oil in a hot frying pan. Add the vegetables and pepper to taste. Stir-fry for 2 minutes. Add and soy sauce and sesame seeds. Season with salt and pepper. Makes four servings

Simple Chinese Bodi

Ingredients: one pound cooked bodi, three cloves garlic chopped small as possible, half cup balsamic vinegar

Method: Mix all ingredients in a bowl and serve at room temperature. Serves four.

Chinese Bodi Salad

Ingredients: one cup bodi cut into two inch pieces, one cup bean sprouts, one sweet bell pepper (prefer red) seeded and sliced into thin strips, one medium cucumber sliced thin, one red onion, one TBS balsamic vinegar

Dressing: third cup white vinegar, one TBS olive oil, two TBS sugar, one TBS herbs such as basil and or thyme chopped, two garlic cloves minced , salt to taste

Method: In a large frying pan mix bodi, onion, and vinegar. Cook two minutes with constant stirring. Take off heat and allow cooling. Mix in remaining ingredients. Then mix in dressing. Chill for two hours before serving. Serves six.

Saute Bodi

Ingredients: half pound bodi, half cup chopped onion, half cup deveined shrimp, half cup pork cut into thin strips (Chicken, beef, or boneless fish chunks may be substituted.), two ripe tomatoes, two TBS minced garlic, two TBS vegetable oil, salt and pepper to taste

Method: Heat oil, garlic, and onion. Add tomatoes and cook until soft, stir in pork and shrimp. Simmer stirring occasionally. Add bodi and cook until tender. Serve hot. Serves four.

Peanuts, Bodi and Shrimp

Ingredients: one pound bodi cut into one inch pieces, one pound or more shrimp-medium or large, one medium onion chopped small, one hot pepper seeded and minced (optional), one bunch chives chopped small, half cup shelled peanuts, one TBS crunchy peanut butter, one TBS sugar, four TBS peanut oil, three cloves garlic coarsely chopped, two TBS lime juice, two TBS water, salt and spices to taste

Method: In a large frying pan heat oil and add onion and garlic and fry a few minutes till they become clear. Reduce heat to lowest possible and add shrimp. Cover and cook for ten minutes. Add remaining ingredients and cook for twenty minutes stirring frequently so peanut butter doesn't stick. Serve with rice or pasta.

BROCCOLI, HEALTHY BROCCOLI

Broccoli could possibly be the healthiest food you can grow and eat. It contains vitamins C, A, K, B1, B2, B3, and B5. With soluble fiber and many nutrients, broccoli has been researched to provide the human immune system with anti-virus, anti-infection, and anti-cancer capacities. All for only twenty-two calories a serving!

Broccoli is derived from the Italian word 'broccolo' for branch, stem, or stalk; and is usually considered an Italian vegetable. The botanical name is brassica olerace. Broccoli is actually the flower head of the plant. If broccoli is not harvested and left 'to go to seed', the familiar green florets transform into yellow flowers. The florets are healthier in vitamins than the stalk. Broccoli's leaves can also be cooked, and contain more vitamin A than the florets.

Until recently broccoli was considered a cool weather crop that would not grow in the tropics. Now, through considerable agri-science manipulation, broccoli is an excellent and profitable Caribbean crop. There are two types, curding and sprouting. Curding grows white or purple heads similar to cauliflower. Sprouting is the most familiar type with numerous small headed, green shoots.

It takes an average of sixty days to mature, but can produce for a few weeks longer as smaller side heads will develop after the large, central head is removed. To grow broccoli work plenty of well-rotted chicken manure into the plot. It is best to layout your plot in an area that does not get the direct heat of the midday sub. If you are earnest about growing broccoli consider growing it under a mesh roof. Broccoli plants can grow to two feet tall. It is important to plant seedlings at least a foot apart, (Two feet apart will be better and reduce fungus problems.) and two feet between rows. A high nitrogen fertilizer may be applied when the plants five weeks old.

Broccoli needs constant water to cool the leaves for the heads to fully develop, but be careful they do not become water logged. This requires excellent drainage. They also need space between the plants for air to circulate.

The part of broccoli we eat is the stem and its bunch of unopened flower buds. The green buds develop first in one large central head and later in several smaller side shoots. Serious growers recommend cutting the central head leaving two or three inches of stem. This is done after the head is fully developed, but before it spreads out into individual florets. This stimulates the side shoots to develop for later pickings. This permits a continued harvest of broccoli for several weeks.

DID YOU KNOW?

Broccoli helps fight cancer, especially breast, colon, and lung. It boosts the immune system. It also contains antioxidants and a substance called sulforaphane, a powerful cancer fighter and preventative. Broccoli may reduce the risk of heart disease. It is an antioxidant and helps with stress. To retain the nutrients in broccoli, either steam it, stir-fry it, or boil it in a very small amount of water. Most other methods will cause a nutrient loss of about 25 to 35 percent. Broccoli that has been cooked still has 15 percent more vitamin C than an orange and as much calcium as milk. To eliminate the smell of broccoli, add a slice of bread to the pot.

Broccoli suffers the same pests as cabbage and cauliflower. Aphids and the cabbage worm from the diamond back moth are the main enemies. Fungus is always a potential problem.

A half cup of steamed or boiled broccoli has twenty-two calories, two and a half grams of both protein and fiber with a tiny bit of fat, and no cholesterol. The same small portion of broccoli has one and a half times the daily amount of vitamin C, plus vitamin A, niacin, thiamin, iron, folate, selenium, phosphorus, potassium, zinc, and magnesium. For those who are lactose intolerant, broccoli is a good source of calcium necessary for controlling high blood pressure, and in prevention of colon cancer.

Researchers have discovered a compound in broccoli that fights the bacteria that causes peptic ulcers much better than modern antibiotic drugs. This same broccoli compound protects against stomach cancer, currently the second most common type of cancer. Broccoli has been found to lower the risk of prostrate and lung cancers.

Broccoli is appearing in markets all over the Caribbean. When purchasing, the better broccoli tops will be a darker green than the stems, closed with no yellowing, and should feel crisp. If stored properly in the fridge, unwashed, dry, in a plastic bag, broccoli will keep up to two weeks. However, like most fruits and veggies, it is best eaten fresh to gain the most nutrients.

Before preparing, broccoli should be washed quickly and never left to sit in water. Steam it for only three to four minutes. Overcooking makes broccoli soft, and again loses vitamins and minerals. This vegetable is great eaten raw, steamed, or stir-fried.

Broccoli Pasta

Ingredients: three cups chopped broccoli florets and stems, one cup carrots peeled and sliced about a quarter inch thick, one clove of garlic minced, one medium onion chopped small, onehalf cup whole milk, one-quarter cup grated cheddar cheese, three cups boiled noodles (elbows, bowtie, or spaghetti), two cups chicken broth, one half cup boned chicken. (Chicken pieces may also be used.), salt and spices to taste.

Method: Boil chicken pieces in suitable pot for ten minutes and retain the remaining broth. Remove chicken bones if you desire. Boil noodles. Combine all ingredients in a suitable baking dish, cover, and bake at 350 degrees for thirty minutes.

Broccoli Stir Fry

Ingredients: three cups chopped broccoli florets and stems, one medium onion chopped large and separated, one clove garlic minced, two peeled carrots sliced thin, one medium Irish potato cubed, one yellow crook neck squash sliced, one sweet pepper sliced, two TBS oil (prefer olive) salt and spices to your taste.

Method: In a large, hot frying pan or wok put oil, and onion, sweet pepper, and garlic. Cook for two or three minutes, add remaining veggies and spices. Cook for eight to ten minutes. Serve warm.

Cheese Broccoli

Ingredients: two cups chopped broccoli stems and florets, one-half cup sliced peeled carrots, one cup cooked rice, one clove of garlic minced, one large onion chopped small, one-half cup water, one cup milk, one-half cup grated cheddar cheese, salt and spices to taste.

Method: In a large frying pan heat the water before adding broccoli, garlic, onion, carrots, and seasonings. Cook for five minutes before adding remaining ingredients. Cook for ten minutes stirring frequently as it will stick and burn.

Almond Broccoli

Ingredients: one head of broccoli - stem and florets sliced a quarter inch thick, half cup almonds, two TBS oil, juice from one-half fresh lemon, salt and spices to your taste.

Method: Steam broccoli pieces for ten minutes, remove and cool. Heat oil in a frying pan and cook almonds for three minutes while adding spices. Remove from heat and add broccoli and lemon juice. Stir and serve.

CAULIFLOWER

Cauliflower is another of the veggies that makes one wonder how it evolved. It is a bit difficult to grow, but easy to cook in a variety of tasty dishes. Cauliflower is a delicious standard for stirfry, great crispy raw in salads, creamed, or curried.

Cauliflower's Latin reference is *brassica oleracea var. botrytis*. It is one of the Caribbean's most popular vegetables. It is part of the cabbage family and believed to have originated in Asia Minor. For 2500 years, cauliflower has been a part of the diet in Turkey. Early traders brought it to Europe. The Italians became famous for spicy cauliflower salads while the French chefs created creamy cauliflower soups. Asians mix vegetables and curry to make a cauliflower stew. Trinidad enjoyed over three hundred thousand kilos of cauliflower last year.

Cauliflower has a white head, which consists of unformed flower buds that average six inches in diameter. The head is called a 'curd'. The curd forms off of a stalk. As the curd is pulled apart, the cauliflower looks like a small tree enclosed in stiff green leaves, which provide protection from the sun. This leaf protection slows or stops the development of chlorophyll, which contributes to the head being white. Raw cauliflower is firm and slightly bitter in flavor.

Cauliflower is very fragile. To offset pests, heat, and drought that may easily damage it, what is grown locally is often sprayed with too much agricultural chemicals. If chemical spray worries you, as it does me, try growing your own. The most successful method of starting cauliflower is in seed trays. Spray with starter fertilizer and systemic pesticide such as Admire before and after transplanting. Seedlings should be at least four inches tall before transplanting. They should be spaced in the rows at least a foot apart. Cauliflower is best planted in raised beds so the soil can easily drain. Any interruption in the growing cycle of cauliflower, such as intense heat, drought, or hard rain, may stunt the development of the edible head. Cauliflower needs constant water, and fertilizer high in nitrogen. If cauliflower is kept too wet the curd or head will turn brown from mildew. Cabbageworms and black rot are cauliflower's most common enemy.

Several types of cauliflower are self-blanching. This means the leaves naturally pull back as the head forms. If this does not happen, when two to three inches of the white head shows, tie the outer leaves together over the center of the plant to protect the head from sunburn and to keep it from turning green giving it a sour flavor. With the proper high nitrogen fertilizer mix and enough water, the head should grow rapidly until it is six to eight inches in diameter. This will happen one to two weeks after blanching. A perfect head of cauliflower has white, firm and tight flowers. Cut the head off at the stem leaving a few leaves attached for protection of the flowers. The flowers will separate and become coarse with a strong taste, if you wait too long to harvest. Extremely hot weather will also cause flower separation.

When buying always seek clean tight white cauliflower heads with no spots. In cauliflower, size has no relation to quality. Uncooked heads are best kept in the fridge stem side down in a paper or plastic bag with a few holes poked in it. This should prevent moisture and mildew from developing, and keep up to seven days.

> **DID YOU KNOW?**
> Cauliflower may yellow when in alkaline water. For whiter cauliflower, add a tablespoon of milk, or lemon juice to the water. Do not cook cauliflower in an aluminum or cast iron pot. The chemical compounds in cauliflower will react with the aluminum and turn the vegetable yellow. While in an iron pot, it will turn a brown or blue-green color.

Cauliflower is very nutritional especially when eaten raw. One cup of raw cauliflower has only twenty-five calories. It is very rich in vitamins K, and C. One cup has more than the daily requirement of B6, B5, B3, folate, biotin, magnesium, iron, manganese, and molybdenum.

Again, the best cauliflower is organically grown as agricultural chemicals may offset all of cauliflower's nutritional value. Cauliflower and other members of the cabbage family have compounds that activate enzymes, which may disable and eliminate cancer-causing agents.

Too Hot Cauliflower

Ingredients: three cups steamed cauliflower well drained, one TBS flour, three quarters cup of milk, one TBS chopped hot pepper, half TS margarine, half cup shredded cheddar cheese, quarter cup bread crumbs, salt and spice to taste

Method: In a saucepan melt the margarine over a medium flame. Combine flour, spices, and milk in a sealed container and shake vigorously. Add this mixture to the saucepan of margarine stirring constantly. Keep stirring as you add the cheese, then the chopped hot pepper. Place the cauliflower in a baking dish and cover with the mixture. Cover with bread or biscuit crumbs. Put in an oven preheated to 350 degrees for 15 minutes.

Cauliflower Soup

Ingredients: one nice sized head of cauliflower chopped, one TS olive oil, one small onion, one clove of garlic, one large potato chopped into small pieces, one cup chicken broth, one cup water, one TBS chopped chives, salt and pepper to taste

Method: Heat oil in skillet and cook onion and garlic until soft; add potato, chicken broth, water, and cauliflower. Boil, then simmer covered for ten minutes until vegetables are soft. Season to taste. Top with a sprinkle of chives. Note: This may also be put into a blender and liquefied.

Cheesey Veggie Casserole

Ingredients: half pound cheddar cheese, half cup margarine, half cup chopped of each of carrots, cauliflower, pak choy, sweet green pepper, one cup crushed biscuits (crackers), salt and pepper to taste (Almost any vegetable can be added.)

Method: Cube cheese small and place in saucepan with quarter cup margarine. Melt over medium heat. Stir constantly or it will stick and burn. Place vegetables in an oven dish and cover with cheese mixture. Stir and sprinkle the top with the crushed crackers mixed with the remaining quarter cup of melted margarine. Bake uncovered at 350 degrees for twenty-five minutes.

Braised Cauliflower

Ingredients: one medium head cauliflower (about two pounds), one TS sesame oil, salt, pepper and seasonings to taste

Method: Cut cauliflower into quarters and slice again into quarter inch thick pieces. Mix slices, oil, and seasonings in a large bowl. Spread on a non stick baking sheet. Bake twenty-five minutes at four hundred degrees. Turn the cauliflower every ten minutes until cauliflower is browned.

HEALTH NOTE

Cauliflower contains allicin to improve heart health and reduce the risk of strokes, and also selenium, which with vitamin C strengthens the immune system. Cauliflower assists to maintain a healthy cholesterol level. It has folate, a B vitamin needed for cell growth. and replication. Cauliflower is recommended to women who are pregnant to help properly develop unborn children. Cauliflower is an excellent source of fiber to improve colon health and prevent cancer. It is also a blood and liver detoxifier. Cauliflower with turmeric may prevent or inhibit the spread of established prostate cancer.

ENCHANTING CHANA

Where would we be without the main ingredient of doubles, chana? This bean is better known throughout the world as chick-peas in English, or garbanzos in Central and South American countries. Chana has been grown around the Mediterranean for eight thousand years. The Latin term for chana, *cicer arietinum*, means 'small ram' referring to this bean's ram's head shape. Chana is also known as Bengal grams, Hommes, Hamaz, and Egyptian peas.

This high protein legume was probably cultivated first in the Middle East and then traveled to the ancient Egyptians, Greeks, and Romans. In the 1500's Spanish and Portuguese explorers brought this bean to other subtropical regions of the world. Today, the main commercial producers of chana are India, Burma, Pakistan, Turkey, Ethiopia, and Mexico.

Chana has been domesticated into many varieties. Types are suited for tropical, subtropical, and temperate regions. There are two main types of chana: the Desi originally in India, and Kabuli initially from the Mediterranean and Middle Eastern regions and now grown in Canada. The difference between the two main types of chana are 'Kabuli' type beans generally have the largest seeds, and grow well in cooler regions under irrigation. Desi chickpeas have smaller seeds, and yield better in India and other dry climate conditions.

Chana is the cassava of beans. It takes little work, will grow about anywhere and with little water. Chana is inexpensive, but try and grow some as an experiment. If you've only ever eaten dried or canned channa, fresh home grown ones are so much tastier.

The chana plant has branches near the ground and will grow to two feet high. Rain usually provides enough water, but chana will thrive with irrigation. In India, chana is grown in sugarcane fields. Although usually considered a dry-land crop, chana develop well on rice lands. To grow chana get raw seeds at the market and wrap in a slightly moist paper towel for a few days until they begin to sprout. Have a nice patch of soil well prepared with few clumps. Plant the sprouting seeds two inches deep, about a foot part. Chana requires occasional weeding and slight fertilizing with 12-24-12 and will tolerate long dry stretches, but try to regularly water it. It is ready to harvest in four months. These dry pods are more difficult to shell than pigeon peas because they are sticky and cave in rather than split apart. Cows, goats, or sheep will enjoy these plants for forage.

Chana is a very versatile vegetable; consumed as a fresh green vegetable, dried, fried, roasted, or boiled; as a main course, snack food, a sweet, or a condiment. Chana is ground into flour; and used for soup, dhal, and to make bread. Chana has a nutty flavor, yet the overall taste is like starchy butter. We usually see beige chana, but there are black, green, red, and brown varieties. One cup of chana provides two hundred and sixty calories, and is a great source of protein (25%), fiber, manganese, molybdenum, copper, phosphorus, and iron. Eating chana as sprouts will increase its' food value. Chana provides slow burning carbohydrates, manganese, and iron needed for a long energy supply while its fiber stabilizes your blood sugar. Unlike hard to digest meat, chana is low in calories and virtually fat-free. However chana contains 'purine' and individuals with kidney problems or gout may want to avoid these beans. Research has found that a seven day diet (one meal a day) of chana cooked with onions and turmeric powder will drastically reduce your overall cholesterol.

Chana should be dry, intact - not cracked, without any insect damage. In an airtight container, chana should keep for a year. Once cooked, it will keep two or three days in the fridge. Channa has about the same nutritional value canned or dry. Like rice, it is best to inspect chana before cooking to remove stones, and damaged beans by rinsing them in a strainer.

Chana varieties are used in Middle Eastern, Indian, Spanish, Italian, Greek, Asian and North African cooking. Add chana to penne pasta mixed with olive oil, feta cheese, and fresh oregano for a unique tasty lunch, or just add chana to simple mixed vegetable soup to enhance its taste, texture, and nutrition.

Hummus

Ingredients: one pound well cooked chick peas, two cloves garlic, quarter cup fresh lemon juice, quarter cup water, one TS salt, half cup sesame tahini spread (optional), two TBS olive oil, pepper and spices to your taste

Method: put everything in a blender or food processor and blend until smooth. Serve with sada roti or crackers (biscuits)

Roasted Chana

Ingredients: one pound of well-cooked chana, two TBS olive oil, one TS soy sauce, spices to your taste

Method: Mix ingredients in a bowl and place on a baking sheet. Bake at 450 degrees for half an hour or until brown and crunchy.

Falafel

Ingredients: one pound of cooked chana, one large onion chopped fine, four cloves of garlic minced, two TBS chopped parsley, one TS coriander, one TS cumin. Half TS salt, two TBS flour, spices to your taste, and oil for frying

Method: Combine all ingredients in a bowl or food processor, mashing the chana. It should become a thick paste which forms into the size of small, slightly flattened, ping pong balls. Fry on high in two inches of oil for a few minutes until golden brown.

Chana Burgers

Ingredients: one pound of well cooked chana, three bunches of chives chopped, one small onion chopped, two cloves of garlic minced, two TBS olive oil, one cup diced sweet pepper, half hot pepper (optional), one medium tomato chopped, two TBS chadon benee chopped, one TBS parsley chopped, a third cup bread crumbs, two TBS flour, one TS chili powder, one TS chopped fresh or dried oregano, salt and spices to your taste

Method: Sauté onions, garlic, peppers, tomato, and spices in one TBS of oil, until liquid is gone – about four minutes. In a blender or food processor mix this sautéed mixture with chana, parsley, chadon benee, and breadcrumbs. Press resulting mixture into four burger shapes. In the same frying pan fry these paddies about five minutes a side. Pile on the condiments and enjoy.

Chana Sprouts

Wash and soak chana over night and then drain the water. Put the chana in a cheesecloth or just a light cotton kitchen towel. Roll it up, place in cool, sunny spot and don't let it dry out. They should sprout in two to three days. The sprouts can be steamed, stir fried, or eaten raw.

Algerian Chana

(To prepare this you must first combine the following spices: three TBS ground coriander, three TBS paprika, two TBS cumin, one TBS dried thyme, two TS cayenne pepper, one TS cinnamon)

Ingredients: two pounds well cooked chana, two cloves garlic minced, one TBS of above spice mix, one large ripe tomato chopped, one medium onion minced, one TBS olive oil, two TBS fresh mint, quarter cup fresh parsley chopped, two TBS chadon benee chopped, salt and spices to your taste

Method: In a frying pan on medium heat the oil and add onion, garlic, and spices. Cook for five minutes. Add chana and cook for another seven minutes. Reduce heat and add tomatoes, parsley and chadon benee and cook for another five minutes. Serve warm with rice or pasta.

CORN

Roasted corn is a great part of any summer Sunday drive. One of my first memories is of Nani boiling young, seasoned ears on the fireside while roasting the more mature ears in the coals. Nothing was wasted from our homegrown corn as the yard fowl would peck the cobs clean, before our dogs crunched the cobs, and the cows got the green stalks.

The Western Hemisphere's primary grain was maize, now called corn in some countries, before the Europeans intruded. Around 6000BC the inhabitants of Mexico probably first grew corn! Corn is unique from other grains since scientists do not know how the plant evolved. In the Old World such as Egypt or Greece, no evidence exists of maize in archaeological remains, and no mention of it is made in ancient writings. It is believed to have evolved only in the West. Explorers carried corn to many parts of the world and use it nearly everywhere today, often as feed grain for animals. Corn is a European word, which means kernel. Botanically it is *zea mays*.

Caribbean islanders love corn to the extent two and a half million ears were grown in Trinidad last year. Pioneer is the most common type of corn grown in the Caribbean. Pioneer is what Americans would call 'cow corn' since it is not sweet. For some reason the Customs Department seizes any sweet corn seed imported into the islands as it must be 'quarantined'. This causes any available sweet corn seed to be a bit stale. Try to secure corn seed that says 'sweet' in its name, harvest early before the kernels have a chance to harden. A local superstition is that once one earn is picked, all remaining ears will quickly ripen. Fresh corn on the cob may be blanched by boiling for a few minutes, and plunged into iced water. Allow to cool before storing in sealing freezer bags and frozen. Frozen ears may last six months.

Corn can be grown easily in any garden with sufficient light, fertile soil, and enough space. It is especially popular with home gardeners, because it tastes better when it is harvested and eaten fresh. Corn is best grown in full sun, with a soil level of pH 6. Plant two seeds, one inch deep, every 12 inches. Rows should be about 24 inches apart. To insure proper pollination and formation of the ears, plant at least four rows of corn in the garden. For smaller gardens, try planting in a 4 feet by 4 feet block. Corn is a heavy feeder, use rotted chicken manure, a 12-24-12 mix, or two parts urea mixed with one part of potash when the plants are 12 to 18 inches tall. Fertilize corn every eight days until ripe. Each cornstalk should produce at least one large ear. Using this method, you should harvest 16 to 24 ears from a small garden area.

Vegetables

Corn regularly requires water. Hot, dry conditions during pollination result in missing kernels, small ears, and poor development of the tips of the ears. Harvest after the kernels are full and milky when pinched. This will occur in 12 to 18 days after the silk first shows. Corn earworms are a constant problem laying eggs on the developing silks or on the leaves near the ear. Tiny caterpillars follow the silks down into the ear, where they feed on the tip. Only one corn earworm will be found per ear because they are cannibalistic, with the largest devouring all others. Once the worm is inside the protective husk covering, there is no effective control. The corn borer can be somewhat controlled by the regular spraying of Malathion or Fastac.

Eating corn is good for you. Corn is high in fiber, niacin, folate, and some vitamin A. Folate has been found to prevent some birth defects and to reduce the risk of heart disease and stroke. Fiber keeps the intestinal track running smoothly. One ear yellow corn has only 80 calories, 2.5 grams protein, 20 grams carbohydrates, 2 grams dietary fiber, potassium, vitamin A, niacin, and folate.

> **DID YOU KNOW?**
>
> Evidence has been found for the earliest domestication corn in Mexico about nine thousand years ago! By volume of production, corn is the third most important food crop of the world behind wheat and rice. Farmers grow corn on every continent except Antarctica. An ear of corn has an average of 800 kernels, arranged in 12 to 16 rows. There is one piece of silk for each kernel. The corncob or ear is part of the corn plant's flower. A pound of corn consists of approximately 1,300 kernels. Each tassel on a corn plant releases as many as 5 million grains of pollen. Corn is an ingredient in more than 3,000 grocery products. One bushel of corn will sweeten more than 400 cans of Coca-Cola, produce 32 pounds of starch, or 2 1/2 gallons of ethanol fuel. The main ingredient in most dry pet food is corn.

Boiled Corn on the Cob

Drop washed, corn into a pot of rapidly boiling water. Boil for four minutes. The cooking time will vary depending on the size and age of the corn. Do not over cook the corn or it will toughen.

Corn Pudding

Ingredients: two cans whole corn or shave the kernels off four large ears, one cup biscuit crumbs (Crix), two third cup flour, three cups milk, four eggs, quarter cup cooking butter, two TBS sugar, a pinch of nutmeg, salt and pepper to taste.

Method: In a large bowl, mix together the corn, cracker crumbs and milk. Beat the eggs fairly well and add to the corn mixture. Add salt, pepper, and nutmeg to your taste; stir well. Pour into a pudding pan or large baking dish and dot with bits of butter. Bake slowly in a 300° oven for about an hour.

Savory Corncakes

Ingredients: three quarters cup all-purpose flour, quarter cup yellow cornmeal, half TS baking powder, quarter TS pepper sauce, one cup canned creamed corn, one egg lightly beaten, half cup milk, one TBS vegetable oil, one large ear of corn - kernels cut off-the cob (two third cup), two third cup minced onion

Method: Sift together dry ingredients. Whip the creamed corn, egg, milk and oil, and stir into the dry mixture. Do not overmix. Let the batter rest in the refrigerator for an hour or more. Then stir in the corn kernels and the minced onion. Cook the batter in batches, dropping tablespoonfuls onto a greased griddle over medium heat. Cook 2 minutes per side, or until golden. Keep warm in a 200 degee F. oven while finishing. Makes 24 small corncakes.

Corn Pepper Stir Fry

Ingredients: four cups corn kernels about five ears, one TBS vegetable oil, one TBS cooking butter, two sweet bell peppers -diced, one small onion - diced, one TS ground cumin, salt and black pepper to taste, two TS chopped chadon benee

Method: Heat oil in a large frying pan; add corn, peppers, and onion. Once everything is cooked add spices and butter. Serves four.

CRUSTY CORN CASSEROLE

Ingredients: one 16 oz can creamed corn, the kernels sliced off four ears of fresh corn, (or one 16 oz can whole corn), two beaten eggs, half cup sour cream, two cups corn-meal, two TS baking powder, two TBS brown sugar, one stick of butter or margarine, one small onion, one TBS finely chopped green pepper, half small hot pepper (optional)

Method: Preheat over to 350F. Melt butter in an 8X12 inch glass-baking dish in the oven. Mix all ingredients and pour into the hot buttered pan. Bake one hour until a crust forms.

When planning for a year, plant corn.
When planning for a decade, plant trees.
When planning for a lifetime, train, and educate people.
Chinese proverb

Vegetables

EGGPLANT OR MELOGENE

My grandfather, Nana, grew eggplant (bigan or melongen) by the acre. Now roasted bigan for choka is one of the smells that truly makes my mouth water.

Eggplant or melogene ranks among the world's most popular edible vegetables. Native to India and what is now Pakistan, eggplant was first domesticated over 4000 years ago. In its home region, the eggplant is used in many local dishes and carries a wide range of names. Eggplant, solanum melongen, is derived from its ancient Sanskrit name.

Related to the tomato, potato, and the pepper, eggplant is the only member of the deadly nightshade family to originate in the Eastern Hemisphere. As tomatoes were first believed to be poisonous, eggplant was believed to cause mental illness, and became known as the 'Mad Apple'. The Spanish explorers believed its fruit to be a powerful aphrodisiac. When a variety with egg shaped white fruit were grown in Germany around 1600, the English gave the name 'eggplant'. The Spanish introduced eggplant to Brazil before 1650.

Eggplant is grown in many shapes, sizes, and colors. When selected, grown, and prepared properly, anyone will become a true eggplant fan. Local farmers produced three and a half million kilos of eggplant last year. Two or three plants will yield enough for most families. Eggplant is best started from transplants spaced 18 to 24 inches apart. Eggplant prefers a well drained, sunny location for the best results. Use starter fertilizer for transplanting and a high nitrogen fertilizer when the plants are half grown and again immediately after harvest of the first fruits. Water the plants regularly and add a potassium rich fertilizer with each watering when the eggplant fruits begin to swell.

Verticillium wilt causes yellowing, wilting, and death of the plants. Flea beetles cause tiny holes in the leaves. Damage can be severe on young plants, but can be controlled by applying a suitable insecticide. White flies love the shade of eggplants broad leaves. Inspect the underside of the leaves regularly. White fly infestation could ruin an entire garden. If you see white specs get the appropriate chemical pesticide and treat the plants without hesitation.

To test if the fruit is ripe, hold it in your palm and gently press it with your thumb. If the flesh presses in, but bounces back; it is ready. If the flesh is hard and does not give, the eggplant is too young. Eggplants bruise easily, so harvest gently and cut the eggplant with the cap and some of the stem attached.

Eating eggplant is good for you. It can help reduce high cholesterol. One cup of cooked eggplant has 27 calories, 1 gram of protein, 6 grams of carbohydrates (two grams of fiber if eaten with the skin), phosphorus, potassium, and folate. Eggplant has an agreeable texture and slightly bitter taste. Cooked eggplant soaks up a lot of oil, so to remedy this, salt and press the air and water out before cooking. To peel or not to peel the eggplant, depends on its use in the recipe. Eggplant can be baked, grilled, steamed, or sautéed. It is versatile and works well with tomatoes, onions, garlic, and cheese. My puppy loves raw eggplant.

Popular dishes include eggplant Parmigianino. ratatouille, mousakka, stuffed with minced meat, pickled, baked with onions and chopped tomatoes, sliced and grilled, and curried.

Easiest Eggplant

Ingredients: Two eggplant, two TBS vegetable oil, jerk seasoning mix, cumin (geera), or curry spice, hot pepper to taste, quarter cup grated cheese.

Method: Wash and slice the eggplant making circles, but the leaving skin on. Put in baking pan and coat with oil. Then sprinkle spice of your choice. Bake for twenty to thirty minutes turning once with a spatula. Sprinkle with cheese and shut oven off. Keep in oven ten more minutes until cheese melts. Serves four.

Eggplant Casserole

Ingredients: One large eggplant, one TS grated onion, pinch, hot pepper to taste, four TBS cooking butter, four TBS flour, one and a quarter cups milk, one green pepper chopped, three quarter cup grated cheese, two eggs-separated and beaten separately

Method: In a pot cook peeled eggplant in boiling water with onion, salt, and pepper until tender. Drain. Next melt butter and blend in flour. Add milk gradually stirring. Add chopped sweet pepper, cheese, slightly beaten egg yolks, hot pepper, and eggplant. Fold in stiffly beaten egg whites. Bake in greased oven dish 40 minutes at 350°. Serves 6.

Ratatouille

A great vegetable stew served hot or cold.

Ingredients: two TBS olive oil, two cloves garlic, crushed, one large onion thinly chopped, one eggplant cubed, two green peppers chopped, four large tomatoes chopped, three potatoes sliced quarter inch, one TS dried basil, half TS dried oregano, half TS dried thyme, two TBS chopped fresh parsley (or use two TBS Italian seasoning).

Method: In a 4 quart pot heat oil. Add garlic and onions and cook until soft. Stir in eggplant until coated with oil then add peppers. Cover pot and cook over medium heat for 10 minutes, stirring occasionally to keep the vegetables from sticking. Add tomatoes, potatoes, and herbs; mix well. Cover and simmer about 15 to 20 minutes. The eggplant should be tender, but not mushy. Serve hot or chilled.

Vegetables

Baganoush

To roast stab eggplant with a knife and place garlic cloves and spices in the wounds, before carefully turning above an open flame. With a sturdy fork blend roasted eggplant, two minced or pressed garlic cloves, juice of half a fresh lemon, and one TBS olive oil. Use as a dip or as a sandwich spread. Great on sada roti.

Stuffed Eggplant Creole Style

One pot meal

Ingredients: two eggplants, about one pound each, quarter cup olive oil, three TBS butter, one small onion, chopped, two green chives chopped, two cloves garlic minced, one cup peeled and chopped ripe tomatoes, half TS dried thyme, hot pepper to taste, half pound cooked minced meat (ham or beef), two cups fresh bread crumbs, two TBS chopped parsley

Method: Half the eggplants lengthwise and make a 1/2-inch thick, scooped-out shell by spooning out the pulp. Chop pulp and set aside. Heat the olive oil in a large frying pan and gently cook the eggplant shells, cut side down, for 5 minutes. Put shells in a shallow baking dish. Add butter to frying pan, with any remaining oil, and sauté onions and garlic for 2 minutes. Add pulp, tomatoes, thyme, and hot pepper and cook until most of the liquid has evaporated leaving a thick mixture. Remove from heat and mix in ham, breadcrumbs and parsley. Fill the eggplant shells and bake in a preheated 400° oven for fifteen minutes until slightly browned.

Fried Parmesan Eggplant

Ingredients: one eggplant, one TS salt, three quarter cup cornmeal, hot pepper to taste, two cloves minced garlic, vegetable oil, quarter cup grated cheese (Parmesan if you can find it)

Method: Peel and cut eggplant into inch strips; sprinkle with salt, and let stand 30 minutes. Pat dry. Combine cornmeal, pepper, and garlic powder. Dredge eggplant in cornmeal mixture, and fry in deep, hot oil (375°) until brown, cooking only a few at a time. Sprinkle with cheese.

HEALTH NOTE

An Australian study found eggplant absorbs more fat in cooking than any other vegetable. One serving deep fried absorbed 83 grams of fat in just 70 seconds, four times as much as an equal portion of potatoes and added more than 700 calories.

GREEN BEANS

I loved tender green beans the first time I tried them and now always have a few bean bushes in the garden. It doesn't take many; maybe five plants, to provide a constant supply of the tender beans. Green beans are descended from a bean ancestor that originated in Peru thousands of years ago. Migrating Indian tribes spread this vegetable through South and Central America before the Spanish Conquistadors took them around the world after 1700. Although green beans are not yet a big commercial crop throughout the Caribbean more farmers are cultivating them now. The largest growers include the United States, China, Japan, Spain, Italy and France.

There are basically two bean categories: edible pod beans and shell beans. Green beans, *phaseolus vulgaris*, also known as snap or string beans, are the most popular edible pod bean. These beans are often called string beans because years ago a fibrous string ran along the seam of the bean. The string was noticeable when you snapped off the ends. Somehow that trademark has been bred out bean of the modern varieties. The snapping noise is the reason for its other nickname. Green beans are actually picked while still immature and the inner bean is just beginning to form. The variety may vary in size, but average about four inches in length, deep emerald green, and come to a slight point at either end. They contain tiny seeds within their thin pods.

Green beans are easy to grow and well worth the effort. They will adapt to almost any loose soil with a pH of 6 or higher. To make a few green bean rows, fork a well drained area ten foot by four foot mixing in some well rotted chicken manure and a few shovels of limestone. Plant the seeds about an inch deep and four inches apart while keeping the rows separated by a foot to 18 inches. When the sprouts are about six inches tall, carefully mold around the base and add about a soda bottle cap of 12-24-12 fertilizer to the base of each bush. Green beans don't need much water; in fact too much water can be an enemy. Water once a week until they flower and start to bear, and then water three times a week. Replant every two weeks to have a constant supply of these tasty beans. If bugs are eating the leaves, spray once with a light pesticide as Malathion or Pestac. Beans actually nourish the soil by producing much needed nitrogen. Green beans are an excellent crop to plant in a field after a heavy eater like corn, which takes many nutrients from the soil.

Green beans, have only 45 calories per cup, yet are loaded with many potent nutrients. They are an great source of vitamins A, C, and K. Green beans are a good source of dietary fiber, potassium, folate, iron, magnesium, manganese, thiamin, riboflavin, copper, calcium, phosphorous, protein, omega-3 fatty acids, and niacin.

Eating these delicious beans help lower high blood pressure and their fiber may also help prevent colon cancer. Green beans reduce the severity of diseases such as asthma, arthritis, and rheumatoid arthritis. Green beans are a good source of riboflavin, which has been shown to help reduce the frequency of migraine attacks. These beans are a very good source of iron. Compared to red meat, green beans provide iron for a lot less calories and are totally fat-free. Iron is an integral component of hemoglobin, which transports oxygen from the lungs to all body cells, and is also part of key enzyme systems for energy production and metabolism. If you're menstruating, pregnant, or lactating, you need iron!

When purchasing string beans they should be fairly stiff, and should snap sharply, with a spray of juice from the seam. If soft, they've been around too long and will taste disappointing. Avoid beans with obvious seed bumps pressing up through the pods as they were picked too late and will tend to be tough.

I prefer to steam green beans as these beans will continue to cook after you take them out of boiling water. A good rule is to cook green beans as little as possible using the smallest amount of water possible.

Simple Green Bean and Tuna Salad

Ingredients: one pound green beans, tips trimmed and steamed, two cans of processed tuna fish crumbled, juice of one lemon, olive oil, salt and spice to taste

Method: In a large bowl combine all the ingredients, chill, and serve.

Beef and Green Bean Stew

Ingredients: two pounds stew beef cubed, two pounds green beans tips removed, two carrots peeled and cut into rounds, one large onion chopped, two cloves of garlic minced, one cup tomato sauce or ketchup, quarter cup olive oil, four cups water, one TBS English (Worcestershire Sauce), salt and spice to taste

Method: Heat oil in a large pot and add the chopped onions and garlic. Cook for a few minutes then add the meat, and continue cooking. Add everything except green beans and simmer for an hour stirring often so tomato sauce doesn't burn. Add green beans and cook for another thirty minutes. Serve with rice or pasta.

Lemon-Walnut Green Beans

Ingredients: three pounds green beans, one third cup butter or margarine, six chives chopped, two thirds cup chopped walnuts, (peanuts or almonds can be substituted), two TBS chopped fresh or crushed dried rosemary, three TBS fresh lemon juice, one TBS grated lemon rind

Method: Steam green beans for ten minutes. In a large pot with a cover melt butter. Add chives and cook until tender. Add green beans, walnuts/peanuts/almonds, rosemary, and lemon juice; cook, stirring constantly, until thoroughly heated. Sprinkle with lemon rind. Serve immediately.

Green Bean Supreme

Ingredients: two pounds green beans, one medium onion chopped, one clove garlic minced, one green sweet pepper chopped, four chopped pimentos, two TBS butter or margarine, one can cream of mushroom soup, quarter cup cheddar cheese sliced thin, one TS English (Worcestershire) Sauce, one cup biscuits (Crix) crushed

Method: In a large saucepan simmer green beans, garlic, and onion long enough to cook bacon and season beans; remove from heat. Drain bean mixture and place into an ungreased two-quart oven dish. Then in the same saucepan sauté the bell pepper and pimiento in butter or margarine. Add mushroom soup, cheese, and English sauce. Cook, stirring occasionally, until cheese is melted and mixture is thick. Remove from heat and pour over beans. Sprinkle with crushed Crix biscuits. Bake, uncovered for a half an hour at 350 until top is golden brown and thoroughly heated. Remove from oven and serve.

Hot Pepper Green Beans

Ingredients: one pound green beans-tips removed, four cloves of garlic minced, one medium onion chopped, one hot pepper-seeds removed and minced as fine as possible, three TBS vinegar, two TBS brown sugar, two TBS soy sauce, one and a half TS cornstarch, three TBS sesame oil, salt and spices to taste

Method: Steam green beans for five minutes. In one bowl combine onion, peppers, garlic and green beans. In another bowl combine vinegar, soy, cornstarch, and sugar. In a large frying pan heat the oil and add the bean bowl mixture and stir fry for two minutes. Add the remaining bowl of ingredients and stir fry until beans are coated.

Nothing is more the child of art than a garden.
Sir Walter Scott

HOT PEPPERS – CHILIS

My first experience with hot pepper was when Mama put it on my fingers to stop me from sucking them. I guess that's how I got such a hot mouth!

The hot pepper originated in tropical Americas about 3000 years before Christ. The Incas and Aztecs cultivated the hot pepper, but they mainly used it for medicines. The hot chili pepper is the spicy side of the *Capsicum* family, which also produces the sweet green bell pepper. The Caribbean's passion for hot peppers can be traced directly to Christopher Columbus. The explorer was searching for spices of the Far East, especially black pepper; when he stumbled upon the potent hot pepper. Five centuries later, hot peppers are grown everywhere the climate permits and are the biggest hit of the modern spice market. By mid 1500 England was growing peppers. A century later the pepper had won over Europe and the spice paprika was born. By 1600 Portuguese sailors planted peppers in Asia and India. All peppers in India are called 'chilis' (from the South American country) even though their America origin is forgotten.

Due to various climates and soils, nature has produced an assortment of hot pepper types. Trinidad grows the Scotch Bonnet/Congo, the bird pepper, the fiery seven pot (habenero), the long red Cayenne chili (from Guyana), and the jalapeno. These pepper types vary in size, shape and color. The hottest peppers usually mature to fiery red. Dried peppers are even hotter than fresh. The seeds and membrane are the hottest part of the pepper. All types of hot peppers emit oil that can burn eyes or skin when handled.

Black pepper has nothing in common with hot peppers. Black pepper, one of the world's most common tabletop condiments, is ground from the seeds of a vine grown in Asia. Black pepper actually is bad for digestion as it's coarseness can irritate the stomach's lining.

Peppers are easy to grow. I suggest starting them in trays from seeds. When four to six inches tall, transplant to a well-forked bed. Plant about a foot apart and water regularly. Use a fungicide such as ban rot in the first weeks and then use a light pesticide as Pestac sparingly. Peppers thrive on light doses of 20-20-20 fertilizer mix every three weeks. If you are light on the fertilizer, a good pepper tree can produce for almost a year. Once the trees start to flower use 12-12-17-2 mix. Water is the biggest enemy to pepper cultivation. The plants must be well drained. Harvest when the green fruit changes to yellow or red. Be careful as if the peppers are pungent; your hands and eyes may suffer.

Why does the world have a hot mouth? It seems 'capsaicin', the active ingredient of hot peppers, fools the body into experiencing pain. Capsaicin causes the brain to produce natural pleasure chemicals called 'endorphins'. These pleasure chemicals remain after the pain of the pepper. The brain remembers the pleasure and forgets the spicy pain.

Hot peppers contain high levels of vitamins A, C, E and some B's. They can be eaten fresh, dried, or pickled. Supposedly the first hot pepper sauce was made from the Tabasco pepper and took its name.

DID YOU KNOW?

If the pepper is too hot do not drink water because the heat - capsaicin - is an oil, and will spread to more parts of the mouth. One teaspoon of hot sauce can provide the daily requirement of vitamin A. The Mayans rubbed hot peppers on their gums to stop toothaches. The smaller the pepper, the hotter it will be. All the world's most potent peppers are less than three inches long. Hot peppers are considered fruits, not vegetables. The Incas believed eyesight was improved by eating hot peppers.

Mango Heat

Ingredients: two starch or rose mangos, one hot pepper without seeds, one small green - about to ripen papaya, one TS ginger root grated, one TS honey, salt and spice to taste

Method: Slice peeled mangos from the seed, spoon mango flesh into a blender. Slice seeded peeled papaya and add to blender with pepper and spices. Pour blended mixture into a small pot and cook over low heat for ten minutes. Serve with chicken, beef, or fish dishes.

Smoking Pepper Soup

Could be too hot!

Ingredients: six Congo peppers, one medium onion chopped, two cloves garlic minced, two cups chicken broth, one cup boneless chicken cubes, salt and spice to taste, one TBS olive oil, three TBS butter or margarine, one brown paper bag, two TBS flour, two cups milk, one cup cooked pasta may be added.

Method: In a frying pan place one TBS oil on high heat. Put in peppers turning until all sides are blistered and browned. Place them in a clean brown bag and seal until they cool. This is done so none of the taste evaporates as they cool. Then remove stems and seeds. Sauté onion and garlic in a small skillet with olive oil. Put peppers in a blender with onions, garlic, chicken broth and spices and blend until smooth. In a pot heat the milk, with the butter and flour. Mix in the pepper blend. Add pasta and cubed chicken. Cook on low heat stirring constantly for 30 minutes.

Vegetables

Three Pot Pepper Soup

Ingredients: one and a half pounds cubed beef, one pound spinach chopped, two medium onions chopped, four cloves of garlic minced, one hot pepper seeded, two TBS butter or margarine, quarter pound ochro sliced, salt and spice to taste

Method: Cover beef cubes in a pot with water and boil. Then simmer for one hour. In another pot boil the spinach and simmer for ten minutes. Drain and blend spinach. To the beef and broth, add pepper, onions, garlic, spices, and spinach. Bring to a boil and simmer for 15 minutes. In a third pot, fry ochro in butter until browned. Add to beef mix. Let sit for ten minutes so the flavors can combine before serving.

Chili Pepper Poppers

Ingredients: Two dozen jalapeno peppers with the tops removed and seeded, one medium onion finely chopped, one clove garlic minced, quarter cup bread crumbs, quarter cup grated cheddar cheese

Method: Mix all ingredients except pepper. Then stuff peppers. Place in a covered oven dish and bake in a 350 degree oven for twenty minutes. Make sure there is plenty to quench your thirst.

Simple Pepper Sauce

Ingredients: four Congo peppers, two cayenne peppers, two jalapeno (or can all be the same), one and a half cups white vinegar, two TBS ketchup, three cloves of garlic minced, half small unripe papaya - peeled, seeded, and cubed, one TBS fresh lemon juice, two TBS olive oil

Method: Lightly fry peppers and garlic in olive oil. Add ketchup and half the vinegar. Boil while adding remaining ingredients. Simmer five minutes. This can be blended or bottled just as it is.

HEALTH NOTE

If you are a smoker, you will benefit by eating hot peppers every day. Studies have shown that red peppers contain carotenoid, a Beta-cryptoxanthin, that helps to promote healthy lung function. Peppers improve digestion and can increase your metabolic rate by up to 25%, which makes you less hungry. Hot peppers can make some food safer because they reduce harmful bacteria on food. Low in calories, hot peppers, especially red, contain more vitamin A than carrots and make it easier to stick to a healthy diet since the food has more flavor.

OCHRO - OKRA

We always had a few ochro trees growing around our kitchen. Mama fried it with aloo (potato), chopped it in soups and of course callaloo. Our ochro is okra in the USA.

Ochro is a tall growing vegetable from the same family as the hibiscus. Ochro or okra is also related to , and originated in Ethiopia before spreading to North Africa and the Middle East and reaching the Americas. The name 'ochro' itself is of African origin. This green pod is best known as a key ingredient in the thick spicy stew named 'gumbo', which is Swahili for ochro.

Ochro types vary from shades of green to white, fat or slender shapes, with either a ribbed or smooth surface. Green, ribbed pods are the most common.

Ochro is rarely cooked unaccompanied except when it is fried. Usually a little of it is added with other vegetables into rice, soups, and stews. Ochro alone is generally too 'gooey'. This veggie has a unique flavor and texture, and the juice will thicken any liquid to which it is added. With a taste somewhere between that of eggplant and asparagus, ochro mixes well with other vegetables, particularly tomatoes, peppers, and corn. Ochro is easily dried for later use. A little dried okra in prepared dishes produces much the same result as the fresh vegetable.

In some lands ochro is grown just for the seeds. Ripe seeds produce an edible cooking oil. The ripe seeds of ochro are sometimes roasted and ground as a substitute for coffee.

Ochro is perfect for a hedge around a backyard garden, because the three to six foot tall plants produce beautiful blossoms that rival its cousin the hibiscus. Plant the seeds one inch deep and a foot apart. Ochro usually grows well in any good garden soil. Four or five plants produce enough ochro for most families. Trinidad produces five and a half million pods every year.

Pods should be cut (not picked) while they are still immature and tender at two to three inches long. This vegetable must be picked at least every other day. Ochro has short hairs that can irritate bare skin so it is wise to wear gloves and long sleeves when harvesting. A sharp knife will cut the pods and should not harm the plant. When the stem is difficult to cut, the pod is probably too old to use. The large pods rapidly become tough and woody.

Ochro has many valuable nutrients. It is a prime source of soluble fiber in the form of gums and pectins. Soluble fiber lowers cholesterol and reduces the risk of heart disease. The other half is insoluble fiber, which keeps the intestinal tract healthy, decreasing the risk of some forms of cancer, especially colon-rectal cancer. A half-cup of cooked ochro has only 25 calories; 2 grams of fiber, 1.5 grams protein, vitamin A and C, calcium, potassium, and manganese. Nearly 10% of the recommended levels of vitamin B6 and folic acid are also present.

Don't wash ochro until just before you cook it; moisture will cause the pods to become slimy. Store untrimmed, uncut ochro in a paper or plastic bag in the refrigerator crisper for no longer than three or four days or it will turn to mush.

> ## DID YOU KNOW?
> Ochro, *abelmoschus esculentus*, is also known as Lady's Fingers, gombo, gumbo, quingombo, okro, ochro, bamia, bamie, quiabo. In Spanish okra is quibombo; the French word is gombo, bamia or bamya, in India it is bhindi, and in the eastern Mediterranean and Arab countries bamies. Ochro is a member of the Mallow family, related to cotton and hibiscus.

Never prepare ochro in a cast iron or aluminum pot, or the vegetable will darken. The discoloration is harmless, but makes the okra look rather unappetizing. To remove some of the stickiness from ochro, soak the pods in vinegar for half an hour. I slice my ochro early in the morning and let dry in the sun for hours before frying.

When serving ochro as a side dish, cook the whole pods rapidly until crisp-tender, or just tender to minimize the thickening juices. Try the same quick cooking when you are adding ochro to any cooked dish in which you want to retain its crisp, fresh quality. Add the vegetable during the last 10 minutes of cooking time. On the other hand, when ochro is to be used in a soup, stew, or casserole like callaloo or coo coo that requires long cooking, it should be cut up and allowed to thicken with its juices.

Ochro Melee

This can be from your backyard garden.

Ingredients: two TBS cooking oil (prefer health-wise canola), one large onion sliced, two cloves of garlic chopped, two bay leaves, half TS of thyme and basil, one sweet bell pepper chopped, three large ripe tomatoes chopped, corn kernels cut from four ears, two cups small ochro pods chopped quarter inch thick, half cup chicken broth, salt and pepper to taste.

Method: In a large frying pan, heat oil and add onions, garlic, and spices until onions are limp add bell pepper and continue cooking until onions are clear. Add tomatoes, ochro, broth, salt and pepper. Reduce heat and simmer uncovered for 15 minutes, stirring occasionally. Add corn and cook five more minutes longer. Season to taste. Serves six.

Ochro and Bodi

Ingredients: one pound of whole ochro pods, four TBS olive oil, one onion chopped, two cloves of garlic chopped, two pounds bodi, two ripe tomatoes chopped (or quarter cup ketchup), one cup water, salt and pepper to taste

Method: Wash and rinse ochro pods with the caps still on. Chop bodi into two inch pieces. In a saucepan combine water, tomatoes, olive oil, onion, and garlic, bring to a boil stirring frequently. Add ochro and bodi. Water may be added to cover vegetables. Lower heat and simmer for half an hour or until the beans just become tender. Serves six.

Ochro Soup

Simple or to your taste.

Ingredients: one pound young ochro pods sliced into quarter inch rounds, two large tomatoes chopped small, one cup corn, one medium onion chopped, two cups water, one lemon, one hot pepper seeded and minced (optional), pinch of the following to your taste, salt, cumin (jeera)

Method: Place all the ingredients in a saucepan and bring to the boil. Reduce the heat and simmer for about 15 minutes, until the ochro is tender.

HEALTH NOTE

Ochro is recommended for pregnant women because it is rich in folic acid. The mucilage and fiber found in ochro helps adjust blood sugar by regulating its absorption in the small intestine. Ochro helps grow good bacteria (similar to the ones fed by yoghurt) in the small intestine and helps the body absorb vitamin B complex. For adding bounce your hair boil horizontally sliced ochro till the brew becomes totally slimy. Cool it and add a few drops of fresh lemon juice, then use as the last hair rinse. Your hair will spring back to youthfulness. Ochro is an excellent laxative and treats irritable bowels, heals ulcers, and sooths the gastro-intestinal track. Protein and oil contained in the seeds of ochro are a source of first-rate vegetable protein. It is enriched with amino acids like of tryptophan, cystine, and other sulfur amino acids.

PIGEON PEAS

Carnival usually means pigeon peas by the vanload. Caribbean people love the nutlike taste of fresh picked peas. Peas make a lot of peleau to satisfy the hunger of revelers. India produces the largest amount of peas, but pigeon peas originated in Africa at least five millenniums ago. They have been found in the tombs of Egyptian pharaohs.

Fresh pigeon pea colors range from red to deep purple, brown to black, even to white. Fresh peas should be crisp and snap when twisted apart. Caribbean people or those in foreign countries like England or Canada can also find pigeon peas in markets, canned, dried, or frozen. I just love the self-relaxation therapy of shelling fresh peas in front of the television.

Growing pigeon peas is much easier than picking the crop. First select good peas and dry them to save the seeds. Peas are fairly easy to grow in most soils, providing the planting area drains in excessive rains. The best areas to plant are slopes or rises. Fork the soil and break all clumps of dirt until it is fine and soft down at least ten inches. The bed should be further raised at least six inches to provide excellent drainage. Make rows at least three feet apart. Plant the seeds one inch deep and at least three feet apart. Before the seeds sprout spray the soil with Banrot.

Water is both the enemy and savior of these peas. Of course, water is necessary for the tree to sprout and grow. Once the pea tree gets big and weighty, it doesn't need much moisture. If torrential rains occur, then the soil loosens and the tree can collapse. Because of the bushy branches, pea trees don't take well to being staked. Roots not only provide stability, but also take available nutrients from the soil.

Moisture also makes insects and fungus thrive. A good spray with a light pesticide like Pestac or Fastac weekly will keep most bugs away. (A light pesticide is one that wears off in about a week when used at the recommended dosage.) Ants seem to love eating pea trees and can cut the trunk to the heart. One type of small black wasp drills the trunk and lays eggs. Fungus is another villain that will ruin a pea crop. There are various types of fungus and it takes a qualified person to define what type is humbugging your peas. The problem with pigeon peas is they take four to five months to mature, much longer than other beans. This gives every parasite a chance to attack.

Picking the ripe pods is the next phase and very labor intensive. You have to select only those pods that have the inside peas almost poking through. You have to feel the peas as hard and firm. By the end of a days' harvest your neck and back ache,

> ## DID YOU KNOW?
>
> Pigeon peas' botanical name is *Cajanus cajan*. They are also called alverja, Bengal bean, Congo pea, dhal, gandul, goongoo pea, gray pea, gungo pea, Indian dhal, Indian pea, noeye pea, pois cajun, pois d'Angole, red gram, yellow dhal. Pigeon pea varieties are classified as tree type, tall varieties, and dwarf.

and you are almost cross-eyed from checking the hanging peas. A nice sized tree can produce ten pounds of peas. Multiply that times two to three hundred trees (the size of a good garden) and decide if you want to grow and sell, or just buy and shell.

For vegetarians and everybody, peas are an excellent source of protein. To get the most protein from peas or beans, eat them with unrefined rice or wheat. All peas and beans are great sources of B vitamins, iron, zinc, and calcium. These peas also have Vitamin C, but this vitamin is more prevalent if the peas are consumed as sprouts. Sprouts can be cooked in stir fry or added to sandwiches. Tender young beans may also be added still in the pod to stir fry, soups and stews.

One cup of cooked peas has about seven hundred calories, but half are from carbohydrates with only twenty-five calories from fat. Pigeon peas are an excellent of protein, potassium, calcium, iron, and fiber.

Shrimped Seim and Peas

Ingredients: half pound of cleaned medium shrimp, one pound of seim beans, half pound of shelled pigeon peas, half TS curry powder, one medium onion chopped small, three cloves of garlic minced, one TBS cooking oil, half TS ground cumin, quarter TS salt or more to taste

Method: In a skillet sauté the onion and garlic with the curry powder. Add two TBS water to open the curry. When mixture has thickened add shrimp, seim, and peas. Add salt, mix well and cover. Simmer on low for about ten minutes. Uncover and add a half cup of water and bring to a boil. Reduce heat, and cover and cook for twenty minutes until peas and seim are tender. In the final minutes sprinkle with cumin as you stir. Remove from heat, cover, and let sit a few minutes before serving with rice or roti.

Goghani

Ingredients: two pounds of very full peas (almost yellow), quarter pound salt fish-boiled, cleaned and mashed, two medium onions sliced thin, five cloves of garlic grated, two TBS cooking oil, salt and spice to taste

Method: In a pot boil peas till tender with salt and drain. In a frying pan heat oil and fry salt fish, then add peas and all other ingredients. Stir well and eat with rice and or sada roti.

Vegetables

Coconut and Pigeon Peas

Ingredients: one pound of fresh peas boiled until soft - drained and rinsed, one TBS olive oil, one small onion quartered, one clove garlic minced, quarter TS oregano, half TS thyme, one TS chadon benee, one TS salt, one chicken bouillon cube, three cups water, two cups coconut milk

Method: Heat olive oil in a pot. Add the onion, garlic, oregano, thyme, salt, and chadon benee. Sauté for one minute. Add the boiled pigeon peas and cook over medium heat for a minute. Add the chicken bouillon and three cups of water. Stir and bring to a boil over medium heat. Mash some of the pigeon peas with a potato masher. Allow to boil about 15 minutes until about half of the water is gone. Add coconut milk and simmer about twenty minutes until the mixture reaches a creamy consistency. Serve with rice.

HEALTH NOTE

A poultice can be made of the young leaves of pigeon peas and applied to sores. Chinese claim powdered leaves help expel kidney stones. Chinese shops also sell dried roots as an anti toxin, to expel parasite worms, expectorant, sedative, and vulnerary. Salted leaf juice is taken for jaundice. Argentines use a pigeon pea leaf decoction for genital and other skin irritations, especially for females. Leaves are also used for toothache, mouthwash, sore gums, child-delivery, and dysentery. Pigeon pea blossom decoctions are used for bronchitis, coughs, and pneumonia. Scorched seed when added to coffee alleviates headache and vertigo. Fresh seeds are said to help incontinence in males, while immature fruits are believed of use in liver and kidney ailments.

To forget how to dig the earth and tend the soil is to forget ourselves.

Mahatma Gandhi

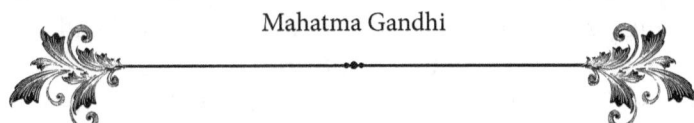

PIMENTO-THE SEASONING PEPPER

Where would Caribbean cooks be without the pimento pepper? The pepper we call 'pimento' is a relatively new comer to our island gardens. It is not really a pimento pepper because that is what is used as the sweet red pepper piece stuffing pitted olives. Pimento is also what the Jamaicans call allspice. What we grow as a seasoning, I believe is close to the pepper internationally named 'pepperoncini'. Our pimentos are also known as Tuscan peppers, sweet Italian peppers, or golden Greek peppers. They are a slightly bitter wrinkled pepper that grows two to three inches long and can be picked from light green, or orange, to bright red. Depending on the seed and if hot peppers are grown close by, our pimentos can be mild to bitter hot.

As I researched our pimento I realized how little is written about this versatile pepper. First, we take it for granted as it grows almost effortlessly and the peppers are inexpensive if we have to purchase. I found a unique web site for pepper lovers that shed some information *http://www.chileplants.com* from Cross Country Nurseries. If you want a specific pepper type, this is the site for you. Some info pointed our pimento was of the *Capsicum Chinese* family, but those peppers are seriously hot and grow straight up like the powerfully hot Thai. The only type called pimento was the 'Pimento Pardon' of the *Capsicum annuum* family. Then I found what I knew had to be it 'The Trinidad Seasoning Pepper'. It was listed as mild; 2.5 to 3 inches long by 0.75 to 1 inches wide; medium thick flesh; matures from green to red; pendant pods; green leaves; 24 to 30 inches tall; Late Season; Uses: Seasoning Pepper; from Trinidad; fruity flavor with no heat; of the *Capsicum Chinese* family. It is also called the Tobago pepper.

Pimento is a great addition to every garden and can be used as a decorative pepper plant even in flower gardens. These pepper trees can grow up to a meter tall and with proper care can produce for more than a year. It usually is not too difficult to grow, but over watering is its biggest enemy. I recommend forking the soil and mixing in some well-rotted chicken manure and about an eighth cup of lime per plant. Mix, breaking down any clumps of dirt, and make a slight mound that will drain. You can raise pimento from seeds of a type you found tasty. First dry the seeds and put one or two in a small styrotex cup with growing medium, or fine soil, or just buy seedlings. Don't go overboard as a family can only use about two pimento trees. At first water every other day, but never drench the plants. The main pests of pimento are mites and any garden shop can recommend a miticide. If there is a considerable rainy, damp period just sprinkle a bit of limestone, less than a quarter cup, around the base of your pimento tree to fight off bacteria that will thrive in the damp conditions and spray with Banrot. Feed the trees every two weeks with about a soda bottle cap of 12-12-17-2 blue fertilizer and you should enjoy these tasty cooking peppers for quite awhile. I replant every three months to have a constant supply.

Four pimento peppers have about ten calories with little food value except they add necessary Caribbean zest to most kitchen creations.

Pimento Beer Beef

Ingredients: six pimento peppers chopped, two pounds beef clod / steak chopped into small pieces, two cups vegetable broth, one medium onion chopped, three cloves of garlic minced, two TBS olive oil, one cup of beer, one TS dried oregano, two bay leaves, half TS dried thyme, salt and spices to taste

Method: In a deep frying pan brown the beef in the olive oil. Add the broth, beer, peppers, garlic, onion, oregano, and spices. Bring to a boil then simmer on low heat, covered, for at least 2 hours. Serve with toasted garlic bread.

Pimento Chicken

Ingredients: a dozen pimento peppers of various colors cut lengthwise into halves, one chicken chunked, one pound fresh mushrooms sliced, two cups bread crumbs, three large eggs, one cup olive oil, two large onions chopped, quarter freshly grated cheese (prefer Romano, but Parmesan or even cheddar could be substituted), quarter TS salt and spice to taste.

DID YOU KNOW?

Asia is the largest producer of peppers and next to salt, chilies are the world's most popular seasoning. Here are some peppers, their pungency and uses: *Aji* - Very hot to fiery ~ condiment, salsa, sauce. *Anaheim* - Mild to very hot ~ soup, stew, rellenos. *Ancho/Poblano* - Mild to fairly hot ~ beans, soup, stews; ground in moles. *Bell* - Sweet to mild ~ salads, casseroles, stuffed, stir-fry. *Banana/Hungarian* - Mild to hot ~ salsa, sauce, pickled. *Cascabel* - Medium hot to hot ~ soup, stew, sauce, sausage. *Cayenne* - Hot to fiery ~ soup, stew, sauce. *Cherry* - Medium to very hot ~ pickled, relish, jelly. *De Arbol* - Very hot ~ soup, stew, beans. *Fresno* - Slightly hot to very hot ~ pickled, salsa. *Habanero* - Fiery to incendiary ~ fresh with lime juice. *Jalapeño* - Very hot to fiery ~ salsa, sauce, beans, escabeche. *Pasilla/Chile Negro* - Mild to fairly hot ~ sauce, soup, stew; dried in moles. *Pepperoncini* - Mild/sweet to fairly hot ~ salads, stew, sandwiches. *Piquin/Tepin* - Very hot to fiery ~ soup, stew, beans; dried as flakes. *Rocotillo* - Mild to fairly hot ~ condiment, salsa, sautéed vegetable. *Serrano* - Very hot to fiery ~ beans, soup, sauce, salsa. *Tabasco* - Very hot to fiery ~ pepper sauce; pack in vinegar. *Thai* - very hot to fiery ~ soup, sauce, stew, stir-fry.

Method: Combine the eggs, salt, spices, and chicken chunks in a large mixing bowl. Heat oil in a large frying pan. Put breadcrumbs on a plate and try to fully cover chicken pieces with the crumbs before dropping them into a frying pan with hot oil until they brown or about ten minutes a side. After cooking all of the chicken remove from frying pan. In the same pan brown the onion and mushroom pieces in the remaining oil on medium heat. Add the pimento peppers and cook for five minutes. Add the fried chicken pieces and cheese. After about fifteen minutes shut off the heat and cover for about ten minutes. Serve on a bed of rice or pasta noodles.

Simple Garlic-Pimento Beef Roast

Ingredients: one nice beef roast 3-4 pounds, six cloves of garlic minced, two medium onions minced, twelve pimento peppers of various colors chopped into pieces, one cup beef broth, salt and spices to your taste

Method: Make several slices across the width of the roast of beef, but do not cut through the piece of meat and put equal portions of the minced garlic and onions into each cut. Place beef in a covered pot or a slow cooker and cover with pimento pieces and broth. Cook on lowest setting for at least six hours to obtain the best flavor.

HEALTH NOTE

As a medicinal plant, spicy peppers have been used to reduce indigestion and gas, improves the stomach's functions and appetite, stimulant, increase the circulation of blood, and as an overall tonic. The plants have also been used as folk remedies for dropsy, colic, diarrhea, asthma, arthritis, muscle cramps, and toothache. This same seasoning peppers are been reported to have hypoglycemic properties.

A gardener learns more in the mistakes than in the successes.

Barbara Borland

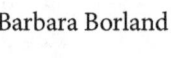

RED SORREL

Auntie Rose taught me to make sorrel drink. I was about eight or nine when she brought sorrel pods for me to peel. I wanted to be outside playing until I tasted the red juice we cooked. Most sorrel is grown in the Caribbean for the Christmas markets. These flowers are actually the leaves surrounding the seedpods of the red sorrel. Red sorrel is a type of hibiscus, sabdariffa. It is called sorrel because its flavor is quite similar to another herb, French sorrel, a member of the 'dock' family, used for flavoring soups and omelets. Our sorrel's reddish stems stand straight, and give the plant the appearance of a strong hedge. It makes a great border for a vegetable or flower garden. Fresh or dried, red sorrel makes a nice addition to flower arrangements.

Caribbean red sorrel is a bush that will grow to eight feet tall. It is cultivated only for the dark-red seedpods surrounding the fruit. These are the basis of the popular red non-alcoholic drink. The funnel-shaped flower petals usually are yellow with deep red blotches near the base, and grow up to five inches wide. Caribbean sorrel leaves can also be eaten steamed, as they have a citrus-like taste when added to salads or curries. The seeds can be roasted and eaten, or ground into flour. Throughout Africa red sorrel seeds are used to make a coffee substitute or fermented to make a simple meat substitute called 'furundu'. Sorrel seeds are a great chicken feed.

Caribbean sorrel is very nutritional, high in calcium, niacin, riboflavin, and iron. Sorrel is growing in popularity with food and beverage manufacturers. Pharmaceutical companies are exploring its potential as a natural coloring to replacing some artificial dyes.

Native to Malaysia, sorrel has traveled the world. It is widely cultivated in Asia, Africa, throughout the Caribbean, and Central America. African slaves carried sorrel seeds to the Western Hemisphere. By 1700 sorrel was cultivated in both Brazil and Jamaica. By the late 1800's sorrel was growing in Florida. Red sorrel has many names such as sour-sour, Florida cranberry, zuring, and roselle.

Sorrel will grow in almost any soil, but likes rich sandy soil. First find a kind farmer who will share some seeds with you. Plant the seeds about a foot apart in mounded rows. Space the rows about two feet apart. Sorrel grows easily and needs little fertilizer. Weeding is necessary until the plants reach two feet tall. More flowers will be produced if the plants are pruned. A fertilizer mix of 4-6-7 is satisfactory. The root-knot nematode is sorrel's main pest, and the mealybug may cause problems. Sorrel is usually a five to six month crop. It is ready to harvest when the buds are still tender and easily snapped off by hand. It is easier to snap off the flowers in the morning than in the evening. The flowers must be harvested quickly as either the flowers will fall off or get too hard for use.

The main use of red sorrel is to make a tea beverage. Sorrel is also used in salads, jellies (such as Jamaica's famous rosella jam), sauces, soups, beverages, chutneys, pickles, tarts, puddings, syrups, and wine. Powdered dried red sorrel is used to flavor and color commercial herbal teas. Most tasters can't discern sorrel drink from cranberry juice in flavor and appearance.

In Africa sorrel is steamed and eaten with ground peanuts. For stewing as sauce or filling for tarts or pies, tender pods are cooked with sugar. To prepare a smooth sorrel sauce, jam, or chutney; the outer leaves should be passed through a food processor. Another method is after cooking press the mixture through a sieve. Some cooks steam the sorrel with a little water until soft before adding the sugar, then boil for 15 minutes. Sweet sorrel sauce is a great addition to custards, cakes, or ice cream. Since sorrel contains 3% pectin it is not necessary to add additional pectin to make sorrel jelly.

Sorrel is an ingredient in many bush medicine remedies. Drinking the tea will help relieve hypertension, coughs, and hangovers. A paste of the leaves and seeds is used in Egypt as an antibiotic on wounds. Leaves warmed in hot water can be used to draw out boils.

Jamaican Christmas Sorrel Punch

Ingredients: half pound sorrel, one cinnamon stick, ten whole cloves, one strip of dried orange peel, one gallon boiling water, one pound of sugar, one TS ground cinnamon, half TS ground cloves, one cup clear rum (optional)

Method: Put the dried sorrel, orange peel, cinnamon stick, and whole cloves in a gallon jar. Fill with hot water. When cool, cover and leave the mixture to steep for 2 days. Then strain off the liquid, add enough sugar to sweeten, add rum, powdered or ground spices, and let it stand for another 2 days before serving chilled, or with crushed ice. This is a popular drink at Christmas time when sorrel is in season. Dried sorrel will last for months if stored in a cool, dry place.

Sorrel Drink

Ingredients: two pints dried sorrel, six pints water, sugar to taste, two TS nutmeg, one TS mace

Method: Cut red petals from sorrel and dry in the sun for about 3 days. Measure 2 pints of the dried sorrel petals and put in a large container. Mix sugar and water to taste and pour over dried sorrel. Then mix in the mace. Cover jar and let stand for one day or longer. Strain, bottle, store in refrigerator

Simple Sorrel Juice

It is not necessary to remove the seedpod to make sorrel juice. Wash sorrel and place in a large pot, cover with water, and boil for fifteen minutes. Strain and add sugar and spices to your taste.

Sorrel Jelly

Bring three cups of sorrel juice to a boil and add two and a half cups of sugar. Heat to 200 degrees. Without an intricate thermometer this will be difficult. Test if the sorrel has jellied by spooning a few drops of the sorrel into a glass of tap water. If the sorrel remains firm and doesn't dissolve, it is jelly. Sterilize empty jelly jars by boiling to avoid contamination. Then after filling and capping, put the jars in a pot, and boil for another ten minutes.

Sour Sorrel Soup

Ingredients: one cup sorrel leaves, one chicken leg with thigh or breast, one lean pork chop, quarter cup small shrimp shelled and deveined, one fillet of fish salmon or king, the following chopped - one onion, one bunch chadon benee, one bunch celery, one ochro, one medium ripe tomato, one clove of garlic minced, salt and spice to taste

Method: In a suitable pot cook chicken and pork in a quart of water. Remove, debone, and shred the meat, saving the water. In the same water cook the shrimp and the fish. Debone the fish and return to the water. Add the sorrel leaves, all vegetables, salt, and spices. Cook fifteen minutes. Add shredded chicken and pork. Serve hot.

Fried Sorrel Leaves

Ingredients: Two cups 'tender' sorrel leaves, one cup small shrimp cleaned, one cup bamboo shoots (canned) sliced, half hot pepper seeded and minced, one onion chopped small, two cloves of garlic minced, two TBS canola oil, half TS turmeric powder, one TS chili powder, salt to taste

Method: In a large frying pan heat oil add turmeric powder, hot pepper, onion, and garlic. Add sorrel leaves and shrimp with one tablespoon of water stirring constantly. Add bamboo shoot slices and cover. Cook at medium heat for fifteen minutes or until the sorrel leaves become dry and give off some oil. Turn off heat and cover for ten minutes before serving on a bed or rice or noodles.

SWEET GREEN PEPPERS

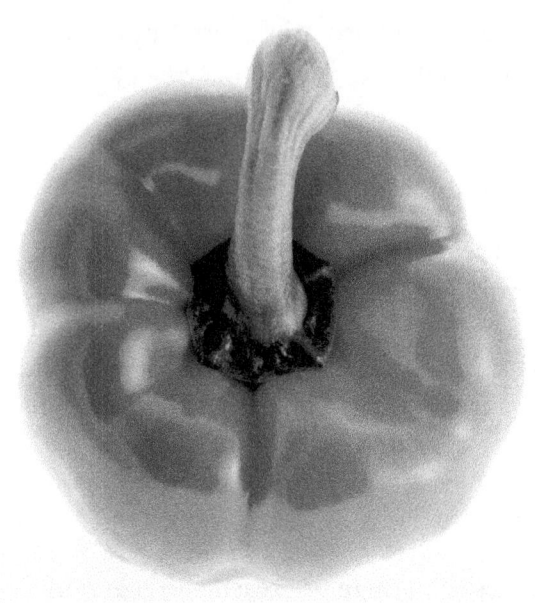

My grandfather didn't farm sweet green pepper, so as a boy all I knew about cooking with sweet pepper was to chop it for fried rice and stewed chicken. Maturing, I experimented in my own kitchen, and now use sweet pepper in many dishes.

Columbus sought the well-known spices of the East, especially pungent black pepper. Instead he discovered sweet and hot (capsicum) peppers. As vegetables and condiments both peppers now dominate the world's spices. Scientists believe both hot and sweet peppers were first cultivated in Bolivia, South America. Wherever explorers landed in the American tropics they encountered native Indians growing peppers. By 1600, Spanish, French, and Portuguese explorers had spread peppers through Europe, England, Asia, and India where they became known as chilis.

Sweet peppers are called bell peppers due to their shape. In some parts of the Caribbean the sweet pepper is called 'the mango pepper' or the 'bull nose pepper'. The bell pepper may be colored green, red, yellow, purple, or brown; and be as big as six inches long. Sweet peppers aren't difficult to grow in the Caribbean. In fact all types of peppers thrive in our hot dry season, but our rainy season doesn't mix with most peppers. If you start your plants from seeds, they should sprout in about two weeks. They are ready for transplanting when at least four inches tall. To prepare your garden for transplanting work well rotted chicken manure into the rows. Soil pH should be 6. Sweet peppers should be spaced at least a foot apart. As seedlings the biggest pest your peppers will encounter is the mole cricket. A ring of newspaper, half buried around each plant will deter them. Put just a pinch of starter fertilizer in each hole and cover with at least an inch of soil before you plant the seedling. Always avoid getting water onto the pepper plant leaves, as this will encourage disease.

Peppers need a high phosphorus fertilizer like red 12–24-12 once, when the plants are about three weeks old. After they have blossomed use blue 12-12-17-2 . Peppers are usually very sturdy plants with few pests, but need water every other day in the dry season. Horned tomato worms, garden snails, or white flies can do severe damage to your plants. Check your leaves. If they are getting eaten, inspect them at night with torchlight to find and destroy the villain. White flies will lay eggs on the underside of the leaves. Mites, in all their many varieties, are mature sweet peppers biggest enemy in Trinidad. Proper insecticide properly applied can stop white fly and mite infestation if caught early.

Most pepper will bear in about seventy days. Do not pull or twist, but cut the fruit so not to damage the stems. One cup of raw green pepper is only twenty-four calories and has three times the daily requirement for vitamin C (four times an orange) and the complete requirement of vitamin A. These two vitamins plus B-6 and folic acid protect against high cholesterol and heart disease. Peppers are also rich in vitamins A, B6, B1, folic acid, manganese, and potassium.

Roasted Peppers

Ingredients: four sweet bell peppers preferably of different colors, one red onion sliced thin, two TBS dried basil or six fresh basil leaves, one clove of garlic minced, six TBS olive oil, two TS balsamic vinegar (or garlic flavored vinegar), salt and seasonings to taste

Method: Coat peppers with the olive oil. Place peppers on a cookie sheet in a 300-degree oven until the skin begins to blister. Remove from oven and place in a bowl of ice water. When the peppers are cool, peel and remove seeds. Slice into one-inch strips. Peel and slice onion as thin as possible. Place peppers, onions, garlic, olive oil, vinegar, and seasonings in a bowl and toss. This may be served warm or cold, or may be stored in a jar in the fridge.

Sweet Pepper Sauce

Ingredients: three bell peppers - clean of seeds and membranes - roasted and cut lengthwise into half inch strips, three TBS olive oil, one red onion sliced, one clove garlic minced, two nice size tomatoes chopped, salt and spices to taste.

DID YOU KNOW?

The sweet pepper is botanically known as *Capsicum annuum*. It is the best known domesticated pepper species in the world. Bell pepper is a member of the nightshade (*Solanaceae*) family, which includes eggplant, tomatoes, and white potatoes. Since the time of Columbus it has spread to every part of the globe. Bell peppers are very adaptable, grown in tropical and temperature climates, and are very versatile foods. Their cultivation and adoption into varying cultures is because they have a long shelf life and travel well. Green peppers are, in fact, the pepper's first stage. If left unpicked, they proceed through various shades of yellow-green on to bright red. Originally sweet peppers were elongated, wrinkled, and much smaller than today, eventually bred into their current marketable size and shapes. The Dutch have produced attractive deep-purple pepper that is green inside and turns green outside when cooked. Other color choices include white, salmon, red, yellow, and chocolate-brown. Sweet peppers are found in all the world's tables from Middle Eastern lamb dishes, Cantonese stir-fries with shrimp and ginger, Tex Mex chili, and Hungarian goulash. A warning though, because of the demand for sweet peppers they are usually pushed and sprayed in cultivation. Bell peppers are among a dozen foods pesticide residue is most frequently detected. Before cutting the pepper, wash it under running water. If the pepper has been waxed, you should also scrub it well.

Method: On low heat in a saucepan sauté the onion and garlic in the olive oil. Add pepper strips and cover. Cook for twenty minutes. Add the tomatoes and seasonings and cook for another five minutes. Put mixture in a blender and pulse about twenty-five times, but do not fully blend it. This can be a side dish or a topping for pasta or a sauce marinade. If you add beef, chicken, or pork this pepper sauce will become a soup base.

Stuffed Peppers

Ingredients: four large sweet green or red peppers, one pound minced beef, one garlic clove minced, one can tomatoes with liquid chopped, half cup ketchup, one cup cooked rice, salt and seasoning to taste

Method: Neatly slice the tops off the peppers (save) and remove the seeds and membranes. Place peppers in a sauce pan of boiling water for four minutes. (Raw peppers may also be used.) In a frying pan brown the minced beef, onions, and seasonings. Add rice and tomatoes to this mixture. Place peppers in a baking dish and fill with the minced beef/rice mix. Mix the ketchup with a quarter cup of water and pour over the filled peppers. Replace the pepper tops and bake for a half hour at 300 degrees. Serves four.

HEALTH NOTE

Due to vitamin C and beta carotene content, capsaicin, and flavonoids, bell peppers seem to aid in preventing cataracts, prevent blood clot formation, and reduce the risk of heart attacks and strokes. Red bell peppers have significantly higher levels of nutrients than green, and also contain lycopene, which helps to protect against cancer and heart disease.

There are no gardening mistakes, only experiments.
Janet Kilburn Phillips

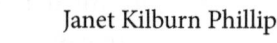

TOMATOES

We always had tomatoes growing in our yard. I never enjoyed raw tomatoes in salads, yet roast tomato choka was one of my favorite dinners as a child.

Central and South American Indian tribes, such as the Incas and Aztecs cultivated tomatoes since 700 AD. The Spanish explorers carried the fruit to Europe where tomatoes became popular in Spain, Portugal and Italy. The French called it 'the apple of love', while the Germans named it 'the apple of paradise'. Botanically the tomato is *lycopersicon esculentum*.

Tomatoes are one of the easiest vegetables to grow in the Caribbean and perfect for a small backyard garden. Trinidad produces almost two million kilograms of tomatoes every year. Tomatoes need sun, and soil that doesn't stay moist. Plants should be sprouted from seeds in trays and kept until they are four to six inches tall. Transplant to rows separated three feet apart, as tomatoes vines will spread out. The plants should be spaced a foot and a half apart. A 5-10-5 fertilizer should be used sparingly, only once or twice throughout the plants' life. Water twice a week. Too much water or fertilizer will harm tomatoes. Ripe fruits will easily pull off the vine. Stake the plants to get the maximum use of garden space.

The biggest pest to young plants is the mole cricket. If you have a small garden make rings from old newspapers and put around the young plants at a dept of one inch. This will keep out the crickets. To reduce the use of pesticide, plant scented herbs such as basil or dill around the edge of the garden. French marigolds are great also and brighten a garden while chasing pests. Shiny strips of foil flashing in the breeze should keep corn birds from pecking the fruit.

The British originally believed the tomato to be poisonous, but this vegetable is really good for you. Tomatoes contain an anti oxidant, lycopene, that reduces the risk of prostrate cancer if eaten almost daily. Tomatoes contain vitamin C, potassium, folacin, and beta-carotene. A diet containing tomatoes may help reduce cancer, heart disease, and premature aging. A medium tomato has only 25 calories.

Caribbean Islanders love tomatoes in salads, sauces, or chokas. Tomatoes are used extensively in Spanish, Italian, and Mexican cuisine. Don't store ripe tomatoes in the fridge. Cold temperatures lessen the flavor in tomatoes.

The tomato is the world's most popular fruit. A fruit is defined as the edible part of the plant that contains seeds. A vegetable is the edible stems, leaves, and roots of the plant. More than sixty million tons of tomatoes are produced per year, 16 million tons more than the second most popular fruit, the banana. Apples are the third most popular at 36 million tons, then oranges at 34 million tons, and watermelons with 22 million tons.

Shriley's Easy Tomato Sauce

Great with pasta for any Italian favorite as spaghetti, lasagna, or can be used over rice.

Ingredients: three cups chopped tomatoes, four TBS olive oil, half cup chopped onion, two cloves garlic sliced as thin as possible, one TBS oregano, three leaves fresh basil or one TBS dried, salt and pepper to taste.

Method: Bring a large frying pan to medium heat and sauté the onion and garlic in the olive oil until the onion is clear, but not browned. Add tomatoes and cook until it becomes thick. Add spices, while reducing the temperature. Stir constantly to avoid burning. Simmer for fifteen minutes. To remove excess liquid and thicken the sauce, remove lid from skillet.

DID YOU KNOW?

The US government classified the tomato as a vegetable for trade purposes in 1893. Tomatoes picked green eventually turn red, but will not have good flavor. A vine ripened tomato tastes best. Tomatoes should never be placed to ripen in direct sunlight, as they will lose most of their vitamin C. Green tomatoes ripen faster stored in a cool place wrapped loosely in newspapers. This method may take a week or two. They will last longer stored stem down. Tomato salsa has replaced ketchup as the top selling condiment in the United States. A salsa/ketchup combination is now available. In the late 1600's ketchup began as ke-tsiap, a Chinese sauce of spicy pickled fish. The tomato variety was reciped in 1800. Heinz started bottling tomato ketchup in 1876.

Easy Oven Tomato Casserole

Ingredients: three cups of tomatoes sliced into wedges, one cup cheddar cheese shredded, one cup bread crumbs, one cup green sweet pepper chopped, one onion chopped, two cloves garlic chopped, quarter cup butter or margarine melted, salt and pepper to taste (corn, okra, bodi may be added)

Method: Combine all ingredients in a large greased oven casserole dish. Bake at 300 degrees for forty-five minutes. Serves four.

Fried Green Tomatoes

Makes a great side dish for fish or chicken. Use green tomatoes only after at least one has ripened on that vine.

Ingredients: five large green tomatoes sliced a half inch thick, one cup flour, one egg beaten into a cup of milk, one cup cornmeal, salt and pepper to taste

Method: Put the egg and milk mixture in a shallow bowl. Sprinkle the flour on a plate or a piece of waxed paper. Adding spices you desire to the cornmeal spread it also like the flour. Flip each tomato in flour and then dip in the egg-milk mix. Coat each slice with cornmeal mix and place on a plate. Heat oil in a frying pan over medium heat and add the slices. Do not crowd the skillet. Cook until golden brown on each side. Drain on a paper towel and serve hot. Serves six.

Salsa

A Mexican specialty that can be eaten as a side with chips or as a condiment on sandwiches. You can chop ingredients either fine or chunky and make it as spicy hot as you prefer.

Ingredients: three large ripe tomatoes chopped, one onion chopped, one whole bunch of chives chopped, one or more hot peppers chopped depending on your taste, quarter cup chadon benee, juice of one or two limes, and a TS of salt.

Method: Toss all chopped ingredients in a bowl, shake the salt, and squeeze the limes over it. Let sit for st least an hour for the flavors to combine.

HEALTH NOTE

Tomatoes' color is what makes them so good for your health. The color is actually lycopene, an incredible antioxidant. Antioxidants block the effect of oxygen free radicals in the cells. This blocks the damage they can do to cells, which causes cancer in the right circumstances. This is why tomatoes appear to have cancer-fighting properties. The amazing thing about lycopene is that it is about twice a good as other antioxidants in foods. It has been studied to be effective in preventing breast cancer, lung cancer, and prostate cancer. Lycopene is effective against aging as well. When choosing tomatoes, get the reddest and the ripest because they have the highest amounts of lycopene as well as beta carotene, another healthful ingredient. The good news is cooking a tomato with a bit of oil, such as olive oil, helps bring out the effectiveness of the lycopene. When you cook tomatoes with a bit of olive oil, the nutrient aspects of the tomato are effectively absorbed.

*It's difficult to think anything but pleasant thoughts
while eating a homegrown tomato.*

Lewis Grizzard

NOTES

28

Leafy Vegetables

Leafy vegetables are also referred to as greens, or leafy greens. They are plant leaves cooked, or eaten raw as a vegetable. Although they come from a variety of plant families, most have nutrition, eating, and cooking methods in common. Leafy vegetables usually mean shortlived herbaceous plants such as lettuce and spinach that grow full cycle in a few months. However, almost one thousand species of plants have edible leaves. Anthropologists believe prehistoric humans consumed five pounds of leaves every day. Leafy vegetables were a major food source.

Lettuce is considered among salad greens usually eaten uncooked, added fresh to tossed salads, providing color and great flavor. Leaf vegetables are among the most nutritious of vegetables when compared by fresh weight. They are also among the most productive garden plants relative to nutrition value per square foot of garden space. They are also dollar valuable because they grow rapidly, allowing several crops during a year.

Leaf vegetables are low in calories, low in fat, high in protein relative to calories, high in dietary fiber, iron, calcium, and very high in vitamin C, carotenoids, and folic acid as well as vitamin K. Darker leaves have more vitamins A, C, and calcium. Leafy vegetables are ideal for weight loss and to manage weight on the long-term. Adding more green vegetables to a balanced diet increases the intake of dietary fiber which in turn regulates the digestive system and aids in bowel health. The fiber cleanses the intestines and removes many dangerous toxins.

Greens have very little carbohydrates in them, and what is there are packed in layers of fiber, which make them very slow to digest. That is why leafy greens have very little impact on blood glucose. Eating green leafy vegetables may lower the risk for type 2 diabetes. The US Department of Agriculture recommends eating three cups of dark green leafy vegetables per week.

Green leafy vegetables also serve to maintain eye health, aid in digestive regulation, increase bone strength, and boost the immune system. Age-related eye / retina problems is a leading cause of blindness among individuals over the age of 50. A research study in Massachusetts found that people who ate spinach, and other dark green, leafy vegetables five or six times a week had about a half the risk of the disease than those who ate it less than once a month.

The typical shelf life for most leaf vegetables is one to two weeks.

The garden is a ground plot for the mind.
Thomas Hill, 1577

CABBAGE

Cabbage is one of the world's oldest edible greens. It is a hardy vegetable that grows especially well in fertile soils. It is believed cabbage originated along the shores of the Mediterranean. Three thousand years ago, Homer wrote of the Greek hero Achilles having cabbage.

Cabbage botanically is *brassica maritime*, from the family known as *cruciferae* or cross bearers. There are many members including cauliflower, bok (pak) choy, broccoli, kale, collards, Brussels sprouts, and kohlrabi. All members of this group have succulent, hairless leaves covered with a waxy coating. This waxy coating often gives the leaf surface a greenish gray, or bluegreen color. Head cabbage is the most familiar through out the Caribbean, but red and purple varieties are available. All cabbage types are low in calories and excellent sources of minerals and vitamins, especially vitamin C. Cabbage may reduce the risk of some forms of cancer including colon or rectal cancers. Cabbage is also high in beta-carotene, and fiber. One cup of cooked chopped cabbage (about 90 grams) has only 22 calories.

Cultivation requires a cool wet growing season and fertile soil. Hot dry weather, on the other hand, stunts the growth and quality of cabbage. The three types of cabbage are: Green - the outside leaves are darker green while the inside leaves are smooth and pale green. Savoy cabbage has blue-green,- purple crinkly leaves. Red cabbage is usually smaller and denser than heads of green cabbage. The flavor of red cabbage is slightly peppery.

Cabbage may be transplanted or seeded directly in the garden. Transplants are the better way. If not start you own nursery bed. Space transplants 12 to 18 inches apart in the row. Close spacing produces smaller heads. Five days after transplanting use starter fertilizer. When the plants are half grown use a high nitrogen fertilizer. Keep down weeds. It is necessary to water cabbage throughout the entire growing season to help it survive the intense sun. Gentle spray from a hose will keep a cool head. Mature cabbage heads may split open if hit with a heavy rain after a a long hot dry period. It takes about seventy to eighty days for the heads to grow to about nine inches or more in width they should be harvested. The most common diseases that attack cabbage are yellow wilt and black rot. Both diseases are transmitted by seed, transplants, and insects. This can be reduced by using hot water treated seeds. Worms hatched from white or brown butterflies cause extensive damage by eating holes in the leaves. Local Caribbean grown cabbage tends to have extreme pesticide residue. It is good practice to discard outer leaves.

Leafy Vegetables

Cabbage is a great food because it stores well. One medium head (three pounds) of green cabbage yields nine cups shredded raw and seven cups cooked. The upper half of the cabbage head is more tender and shreds easier than the bottom. Raw cabbage must be eaten within a few days. Cabbage you plan to cook can be stored in the refrigerator for about two weeks. Fermented, shredded cabbage is called sauerkraut. Koreans ferment spiced cabbage for kim chee.

DID YOU KNOW?

Research shows that one half head of cabbage a day may help to prevent certain types of cancer. The chemical indole may prove to prevent breast cancer. Cabbage odors can be contained if you place a piece of bread on top of the cabbage when cooking in a covered pot. When you need cabbage leaves for cabbage rolls, freeze the whole cabbage first, let it thaw, and the leaves will come apart easier. To keep red cabbage red, try adding a tablespoon of white vinegar to the cooking water.

Cabbage Rolls

Ingredients: One head of cabbage about two pounds - separate leaves and wash thoroughly, two onions, one bell pepper, four cloves of garlic - all chopped small, two pounds of minced meat (beef or chicken), pepper to taste, one cup tomato sauce or ketchup, two TBS oil, and one half cup water.

Method: Remove whole leaves from head and wash. Place leaves in pot of boiling water to wilt. This makes the leaves more flexible. Fry the minced meat in a pan until brown. Pour off any excess liquid. Add garlic, onions, and pepper to the meat. Spoon meat onto the wilted leaves. Roll the leaves, tucking in the ends to retain the minced meat mixture. You may need toothpicks to keep the cabbage rolls closed. Place finished rolls into a baking dish and cover with mixture of tomato sauce, or ketchup and water. Cover and bake for one hour at 300 degrees. Serves four.

Stir Fried Cabbage with Veggies

Ingredients: Half head green cabbage (about two and a half lbs), shredded, one onion chopped, one medium bell pepper chopped, half hot pepper (optional), two chopped cloves of garlic, two TBS olive oil, one cup water, salt to taste

Method: Wash cabbage; remove core, and shred cabbage thinly. Heat a large stainless steel pan with lid over medium high heat until hot. Immediately add oil, onions, and bell peppers and stir for about one minute. Add shredded cabbage and stir for another 30 seconds. Add hot pepper and garlic; continue to stir for fifteen seconds. Do not allow garlic to brown. Add water, cover and cook for ten minutes. Stir occasionally to keep from sticking. Add more water if necessary. When cabbage is done, almost all of the liquid will have cooked away. Makes six servings.

Slaw with Buttermilk Dressing

This slaw can be made using all green cabbage or any combination of green, red and Savoy. Use nine cups Savoy cabbage, thinly shredded, half cup grated carrots two scallions, chopped include green tops

Buttermilk Dressing – Use quarter cup milk, half cup mayonnaise, two TBS vinegar, one TBS sugar, two TS grainy mustard, quarter TS celery seed (optional)

Combine all ingredients in a jar or small bowl and refrigerate. Mix vegetables together in a large bowl. Toss with hands. Add dressing, toss using two spoons, refrigerate. Makes six servings.

Apple Cabbage

Ingredients: One two pound head red cabbage, four large apples - cored and sliced, one cup raisins, two TBS vinegar (prefer apple), two TBS butter, half TS salt, sugar to taste

Method: Slice or grate red cabbage coarsely. Combine cabbage, apples, raisins, vinegar, butter, and salt in a sizable pot. Cover with water. Stir in sugar. Cook until cabbage is tender, stirring occasionally. Add more water if needed. Add small amount of vinegar at a time to increase sour flavor, as desired. Liquid should boil off when done.

HEALTH NOTE

Since cabbage is in high carotene content, regular eating reduces the risk of some cancers. Sulfur in cabbage reduces the growth of tumors, removes toxins, and strengthens our immune systems. Cabbage is rich in vitamins and minerals and reduces the 'bad' cholesterol that hardens arteries. Eating cabbage first will prepare the stomach for a heavy meal and drinks. Crush a raw cabbage leaf in a mortar and use it as a poultice on a cut. To fight acne, drink a cupful of the water cabbage is boiled in, or crush a raw leaf and use it as a poultice on oily facial areas for about 20 minutes. A boiled cabbage leaf, applied while still very hot to the abdomen will cure a stomach ache.

Anybody who wants to rule the world should try to rule a garden first.
Gardening Saying

LETTUCE

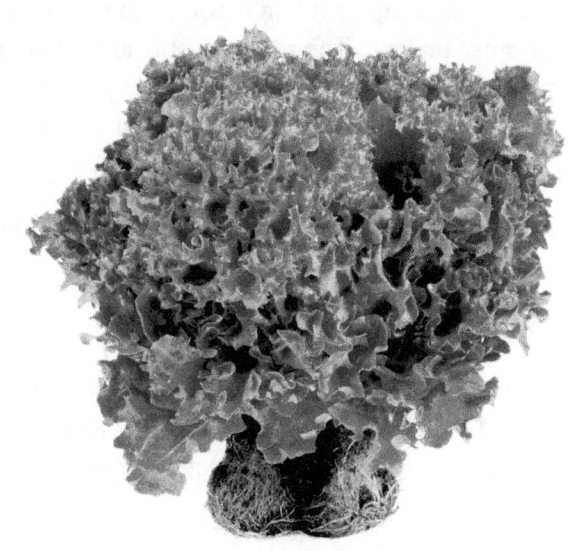

Lettuce was rare at our house while I was growing up because cabbage was the salad vegetable of choice. A few years ago we began growing lettuce in boxes. Now a few fresh crunchy green leaves make my sandwiches and salads taste much better.

Lettuce is becoming more popular throughout the Caribbean both in gardens and in salads. It can be a big moneymaking crop if grown properly with cooperation from the weather. Lettuce is a relatively new crop in the tropics since it does not flourish in the brutal sun, or during dry spells.

Researchers believe lettuce, lactuca sativa, was first grown in the Golden Triangle of the Middle East at least five thousand years ago originally cultivated for royalty. Hieroglyphics in tombs of ancient Egyptians depict long leaf lettuce as food to travel with to the world of the afterlife. Romans and Greeks produced lettuce for salads for the nobility. Lettuce is recorded grown in China by 700 AD. In 1520, England's King Henry VIII gave an estate to a farmer who combined lettuce and cherries in a salad.

There are different types of lettuce; loose heading lettuce is the most common in the Caribbean. This type of lettuce, such as bronze miganette, is sweet, has a loose leafs bushing out from a center stalk. Romaine grows a longer leafed loose head and is slightly bitter. Loose leaf lettuce is the easiest to grow. Loose leaf and loose heading lettuce are more nutritional, because they have more leaves exposed to sunlight, which produces more vitamins. All lettuce is sensitive to heat and needs water. Gardeners must be certain they are using water from an uncontaminated source.

If you are a salad lover, your garden should have at least two rows of lettuce. Plant a row every two weeks. Work the soil with a fork until it is very loose. To develop properly, lettuce roots need soft soil. Local lettuce producers prefer to create a soil mix of bagasse and sharp sand. Lettuce can be planted in a partially shaded area, or in the shade of taller crops. In your seedling bed plant ten lettuce seeds per foot a half-inch deep. Space the garden rows at least a foot apart. Once the lettuce has sprouted, thin to eight inches between plants. It is wise to plant an additional row of lettuce every two weeks. That way you will always have a supply of fresh lettuce. Lettuce needs to be weeded regularly. Light watering daily will cause the leaves to grow faster. Too much water may cause a disease. Lightly fertilize with a nitrogen rich mix once.

Under perfect, controlled conditions, such as in grow boxes, loose leaf head lettuce can grow to harvest in twenty-one days. Usually lettuce is ready to harvest in thirty days. For home use, cut every other head in the row so the remaining heads will expand. Because lettuce is a tender vegetable, it is also a very fragile crop. A change in the watering schedule will cause big problems. Too little water causes leaf tips burn, and too much water will cause leaf rot. The rows must drain adequately to reduce this problem. Aphids are a problem that can be cured with the proper insecticide. As lettuce is eaten raw, be very careful what pesticides are used, what strength, and when the poison wears off. Fungus is an enemy during the rainy season.

Lettuce is best stored in the coolest part of the refrigerator. Never keep lettuce close to

apples, pears or bananas. These fruits emit a natural ripening gas that will cause lettuce to quickly decay. Always wash lettuce thoroughly.

A friend says lettuce is only crunchy water. He's right because lettuce is ninety-five per cent water! Lettuce provides vitamins A and C, and minerals such as potassium, iron, and calcium. One cup of leaf lettuce has only ten calories with one-gram fiber, protein and carbohydrates each.

Eating lettuce is good for the nervous system. It is a good food for diabetics or anyone suffering from anemia since it is low in carbohydrates and with high iron content. Lettuce juice or lettuce cooked as soup is a natural remedy for insomnia.

Lettuce has few recipes other than salads. However lettuce soup is very tasty.

Lettuce Soup

This is an excellent way to use old lettuce, but it may make you sleepy

Ingredients: One head of lettuce chopped in one inch pieces, one medium onion chopped small, one carrot chopped small, one clove of garlic minced, one quart of water, salt and seasonings to taste.

Method: In a large pot combine all ingredients and bring to a boil. Then simmer for ten minutes. Add seasonings. Serves four.

Citrus Salad Dressing

Ingredients: Juice of one orange and one lemon, two TBS olive oil, salt, seasonings to taste.

Method: Combine all ingredients and either hand whisk or use a blender. Seal in a suitable container and this dressing will keep for a week in the refrigerator. If you want to warm this dressing, just place the jar in a pot of warm water for five minutes.

Honey Mustard Dressing

Ingredients: one TBS Dijon mustard, quarter cup fresh chives chopped small, two TBS clear vinegar, two TBS honey, four TBS olive oil, salt and seasonings to taste

Method: In a blender combine all ingredients and pour over your favorite lettuce salad.

Braised Lettuce

Ingredients: quarter cup olive oil, one head lettuce, two TBS minced onion (or chives), two TBS minced garlic, one TBS ground coriander, one cup water, two TBS white vinegar (prefer wine vinegar), salt and spices to taste

Method: wash lettuce and trim off any undesirable spots, then slice the head in half - across the root. Heat olive oil in a skillet and add the lettuce. Cook until golden on both sides. Add garlic, onions, spices, water and vinegar. Place skillet in a 350 degree oven for 15 minutes. Remove and let lettuce cool on a plate. Before serving reheat the liquid and pour sauce over the lettuce.

Grilled Lettuce

Ingredients: two heads of lettuce washed and cut lengthwise, two TBS soy sauce, two TBS brown sugar, four TBS white wine, two TBS olive oil

Method: Blend soy, wine, sugar and oil. Brush the lettuce halves with the mixture and place on a grill for two or three minutes. Turn the lettuce halves and brush again grilling for three more minutes. Serve four warm.

Peas and Lettuce

Ingredients: one head lettuce, two TBS chopped chives, one TBS butter or margarine, one cup boiled pigeon peas, salt and spice to taste

Method: Wash and cut lettuce into inch strips. In a skillet stir fry chives and lettuce in butter for a minute, add boiled peas, spices and cover the skillet. Cook for two minutes until peas are heated.

HEALTH NOTE

Eating lettuce has a tranquilizing effect. Try eating a lettuce salad with a tablespoon of olive oil before going to bed. Sweet dreams. Lettuce tea made from a half cup of lettuce to a cup of boiling water relieves stress and is a good body tonic fighting cold viruses, and works against asthma.

The best fertilizer is the gardener's shadow.
Unknown

PAK CHOY

As a child, I never liked leafy green vegetables as pak choy. Then my Aunt Rose fried it with shrimp and I thought it tasted heavenly. Today I pick it fresh and prepare it with chicken breasts, gizzard, or chipped beef to make great dinners.

Pak choy, *brassica chinensis*, is a member of the cabbage family that forms a small, elongated head with plump white stalks, dark green leaves with a slightly bitter taste. This leafy vegetable has many names. Cantonese Chinese call it pak choi or bok choy; the Mandarin Chinese call it pe-tsai. It is also called choi sum, celery cabbage, white cabbage, Chinese cabbage, or Chinese leaves. Pak choy originated in China, but migrated with the Chinese workers sent to Europe, Australia, and the Americas to mine gold and construct the railroads in the 1800's. When the workers completed the jobs the oriental workers began their own gardens and markets.

Pak choy is easy to grow from either seeds or tray started transplants. The best soil pH is between 6 and 7 and definitely not lower than 5. Fork the soil soft, mix in some well-rotted manure (to help retain moisture), and prepare mounded rows. The raised mounds are necessary for drainage, but not higher than six inches so the soil doesn't become too warm. Use about a cup of limestone per row to combat bacteria and fungus. Place plants every six to eight inches. It grows best in direct sun if it is watered once or twice a day. The sun's heat is its biggest enemy causing it to wilt and die. We keep it under a shade cloth for the first ten days. A higher nitrogen fertilizer mix can be applied lightly once a week. Cabbageworms and flea beetles are the biggest pests. Because the soil is always moist, fungus can be a problem. Pak choy should be ready to pick after a month. It is best to cut it with a knife, and used fresh, but can last in the fridge for a week. When purchasing, check for leaves with no black or slimy spots.

Pak choy is rich in vitamin C, fiber, and folic acid. All reduce the risk of various types of cancer. Pak choy has more beta-carotene than other cabbages with more potassium and calcium. A perfect food for dieters, one cup of cooked pak choy has only 20 calories, with no fat, but 3 grams of carbs and 3 grams of protein.

To prepare pak choy, first rinse thoroughly and shake or pat dry. Young pak choy has a mild flavor and can be eaten raw while mature stalks are slightly bitter. This bitterness is transformed into a sweet creamy taste by cooking. It can be cooked whole, steamed or braised. If the vegetable is mature, separate the leaf from the stalk as the stalks should cook longer. After about two minutes the stalks soften from the heat, then add the leaves.

Pak choy is a necessary ingredient in many Chinese recipes and almost any stir-fry. The stalks can be shredded and lightly sautéed. It is a great addition to soups or stews.

> **DID YOU KNOW?**
>
> Pak choy has been cultivated for over six thousand years. Seeds have been found in jars in an excavated New Stone Age settlement. Other names are bok choy, celery mustard, Chinese mustard, Chinese cabbage, spoon cabbage, and Taisai. Its botanical name is *Brassica rapa ssp. Chinensis*. Asian markets may have as many as twenty different varieties.

Pak Choy Salad

Ingredients: one bunch pak choy chopped into three inch strips, two TBS vinegar (preferably rice vinegar), one TBS soy sauce, one well minced garlic clove, half TS of each sesame oil, canola oil, and dry mustard powder (yellow mustard can be substituted)

Method: Steam pak choy rinse, and allow cooling. In a jar that seals mix all ingredients and shake well. Coat while tossing pak choy. Serves four.

Green Stir Fry

Ingredients: one bunch pak choy sliced to one inch strips, one TBS sesame oil, one TBS canola oil, one cup bean sprouts, one cup seim beans green or fresh bodi cut into one inch pieces, one small onion chopped small, two cloves of garlic minced, one TS cornstarch, one chicken bullion cube, quarter TS soy sauce, half TS sugar, half cup water, salt and spices to taste.

Method: Heat oils in a large skillet; add soy sauce, garlic, onion, and pak choy, sprouts and seim/bodi. Stir for five minutes. Mix together cornstarch, sugar, and chicken bouillon. Pour over vegetables stirring constantly. Serves four.

Pak Choy and Chadon Benee

Ingredients: half cup tomato sauce mixed with an equal amount of water (ketchup may be substituted), two cloves of garlic minced, one TS minced ginger root, four cups pak choy sliced into one inch strips, one small green sweet pepper chopped, quarter cup green onions chopped, two TBS fresh chadon benee, two TBS fresh lime juice, one TS soy sauce

Method: In a large skillet mix half the tomato sauce, the garlic, and ginger over medium heat for two minutes. Then add the remaining ingredients. Cook until pak choy is wilted. Salt and pepper to taste. Serves six.

Pak Choy and Beef

Ingredients: two heads pak choy washed and chopped into one inch strips, one pound beef clod/steak sliced into thin strips (approx half by one inch or smaller), quarter cup soy sauce, quarter cup white wine, two TBS cornstarch, two TBS sesame oil, two TBS canola oil, one chicken bouillon cube dissolved in quarter cup of water, one TBS minced ginger root, two TBS garlic chopped fine, chives chopped fine, salt and spices to taste.

Method: Mix wine, soy sauce, and cornstarch and cover beef strips. Marinate for at least two hours in refrigerator. Over medium heat, heat the oil in a large skillet and brown beef strips. Add ginger, garlic, chives, and stir for half a minute. Add pak choy strips and fry for one more minute. Serves six.

Fried Pak Choy

Easy and delicious

Ingredients: two bunches of pak choy, quarter cup toasted almonds, two cups oil for deep-frying, one TS white sugar, salt and spices to taste

Method: Separate pak choy leaves and wash thoroughly. It is very important to pat very dry – otherwise it will splatter when fried. Roll individual leaves like a cigar and then slice into shreds. Heat oil and test temperature with one shred. Carefully drop in a large spoonful of shredded pak choy. Fry for only a few seconds, do not let leaves brown. Remove to drain on paper Finish frying and put pak choy in a bowl and stir in sugar and almonds.

HEALTH NOTE

Pak Choy is high in vitamins A, B6 and C, beta-carotene, calcium, and dietary fiber and also contains potassium, and iron. It is low in fat, calories, and carbohydrates. The high amount of beta-carotene in pak choy helps to reduce the risk of certain cancers and reduce the risk of cataracts. Pak choy is an excellent source of folic acid.

The greatest fine art of the future will be the making of a comfortable living from a small piece of land.

Abraham Lincoln

SPINACH

Like most kids I never enjoyed cooked spinach. Today it still isn't very interesting unless I add a few leaves of dasheen bush, or have it raw in a salad. I eat spinach because it is one of the world's most nutritional foods. Spinach belongs to the same family as beetroot. It was first cultivated in southwestern Asia over two thousand years ago. Arab traders carried spinach to Persia, now Iran. Irrigation was necessary to grow this green leafy vegetable in a hot dry climate. Centuries later Arab traders spread spinach to Europe and to China where the name still translates as 'Persian green'. The Italians take some credit for civilizing spinach. When an Italian countess, Catherine de Medici, (who was from Florence, Italy) was married to the King of France, she came with her own cooks who prepared spinach 'her way'. Since then spinach dishes have been referred to as 'a la Florentine'. The botanic name is *spinacia oleracea*.

In the cartoons Popeye gets extra strength by consuming spinach. In reality spinach protects against heart disease, arthritis, and types of cancer. One cup of fresh spinach has only forty calories and over twice the daily requirement of vitamin K. This vitamin is essential to keep human bones healthy. Spinach is also a great source for vitamins A, C, magnesium, and folate. Eating this green prevents cholesterol from blocking arteries causing heart attacks or strokes, and reduces high blood pressure. Spinach may be a rival with carrots for benefiting eyesight by keeping the eye muscles strong and reducing the incidence of cataracts. One cup of boiled spinach provides a third of the daily requirement of iron. Iron is necessary for bone growth.

DID YOU KNOW?

The myth of the high iron content of spinach is wrong. Spinach has an undeserved reputation for being high in iron. In 1870, Dr. E von Wolf measured the iron content of spinach, but placed the decimal point in the wrong position so the iron content of spinach was overstated ten-fold. Sixty-seven years later the mistake was discovered, again by German chemists. Iron and calcium in vegetables are not usually fully absorbed by the human body. Spinach contains a chemical called oxalic acid, which binds with iron and calcium and further reduces the absorption of these minerals. To improve iron absorption, spinach should be eaten with vitamin C-rich foods such as orange juice, tomatoes, or citrus fruit.

Spinach grows in most climates where there is sufficient water, especially in sandy soil. Fork a row about ten inches deep and six inches wide to make a four-inch mound. Plant the seeds a half inch deep. Thin the sprouts to six inches apart. Keep watered so the soil remains damp and spinach should mature in three to four weeks. Spray with a mild insecticide such as Pestac or Malathion every two weeks. Fertilize with a high nitrogen mixture every ten days.

Always wash leafy greens well before using then in the kitchen.

Garlic Spinach

Ingredients: one and a half pound spinach-cleaned and trimmed, ten cloves garlic minced, two TBS olive oil, one TBS, butter, two TBS fresh lemon juice, salt and spice to taste

Method: Mix minced garlic and olive oil. In a large skillet, melt the butter and heat this mixture adding spinach until it is just beginning to wilt (four to five minutes). Place spinach in a bowl and mix with salt, spices, and lemon juice.

Curry Spinach

Ingredients: one pound fresh spinach, six cloves garlic minced, quarter cup tomato paste (ketchup may be used), half TS turmeric, one TS coriander powder, half TS cumin powder, quarter cup water, salt and spices to taste

Method: In a large skillet heat oil add garlic and tomato paste, stir over medium heat for two minutes. Add spinach and seasonings, stir well, cover. Add water and reduce heat to low. Cook for five minutes. Serve warm.

Spinach Pie

Ingredients: two pounds fresh spinach (or pak choy), two cloves of garlic minced, one medium onion chopped, two TBS olive oil, four eggs, one TS lemon juice, half pound feta cheese, half pound grated cheddar, three quarters cup whole milk, salt and spice to taste, one pie crust

Method: In a large skillet cook onion and garlic in oil until just browning. Add spinach until it wilts. Blend in all ingredients except cheddar cheese. Pour into pie shell. Bake at 350 degrees for half an hour. Cover with grated cheddar and return to oven for five minutes.

Spinach Rockefeller

Ingredients: two pounds fresh spinach, three quarters cup bread crumbs, two TBS olive oil, half cup butter or margarine, half cup grated Parmesan (cheddar may be substituted) two eggs beaten, two cloves of garlic minced, two small onions minced, one small hot pepper seeded and minced, one large firm tomato sliced, salt and spice to taste

Method: In a large frying pan sauté spinach in oil until it wilts, add bread crumbs, butter, garlic, quarter cup cheese, onions, pepper and spices. Stir to keep mixture from sticking. Cook for half an hour before removing from heat. Arrange tomato slices in a large baking dish. Spoon spinach mixture on each slice. Cover with remaining cheese and bake for five minutes at 350 degrees. Serve immediately.

Spinach Potato Tort

Ingredients: half cup breadcrumbs, two large potatoes, two pounds fresh spinach, two TBS butter or margarine, one TBS olive oil, one medium onion chopped, two cloves of garlic minced, two eggs, half cup grated Parmesan cheese (cheddar may be substituted), two sweet peppers-cored and sliced, two packages sliced turkey breast, half cup grated Mozzarella cheese (or cheddar cheese), salt and spice to taste

Method: In a pot boil potatoes until tender. In a large skillet sauté onions and garlic. Add spinach until wilted. Drain all excess liquid before adding beaten eggs, cheese, and quarter cup bread crumbs. Grease a large baking dish with butter and dust with remaining breadcrumbs. Slice the potatoes and cover the baking dish's bottom. Spread half the spinach mixture evenly over the slices. Then spread half of the peppers, turkey, and cheese. Repeat again beginning with potato slices, spinach, peppers, and turkey. Top with a layer of potatoes brushed with olive oil and seasonings. Bake at 400 degrees for half an hour.

HEALTH NOTE

Eat more spinach to reduce your risk of age-related health problems as muscular degeneration, cancer, heart disease, and neural tube defects. Lutein and zeaxantin are two carotenoids supplied by spinach that help keep your eyes healthy. Carotenoids and the antioxidant vitamins C and E in spinach are also believed to reduce the risk of cancer, heart disease, stroke, and cataracts. And the healthy dose of potassium and calcium found in spinach can help regulate your blood pressure. Spinach and other leafy greens also provide folic acid, which is known to reduce the risk heart disease. Spinach may even improve your memory.

When the world wearies and society fails to satisfy, there is always the garden.

Minnie Aumonier

NOTES

29

Bulb and Stem Vegetables

Bulb vegetables are eaten for the aromatic flavor they add to simple food. Bulbs can be considered storage organs. At the bottom of a bulb is a thin, flat disc called the basal plate. Fine roots grow from this plate. The body of a bulb is made up of layers of fleshy scales, which can be considered a type of modified leaves. It is here these plants store food, mostly sugars. Bulbs are usually biennials grown as annuals. In the center of the bulb is the bud for the next year's plant. Leaves arise from underground stems with long sheathing bases, or straws. Most of the edible bulbs are of the *allium* family – onions, chives garlic, leeks.

If not able to grow your own and are forced to buy, always select firm bulb vegetables that are unblemished, absent of mold or dark spots. The green part of the chive, spring onion, and leek should be firm, bright, and shiny, not withered. Bulb vegetables can be stored for long periods of time and are not only delicious, but very good for you. Some bulb vegetables, garlic, chives, and onions, are also well known for their medicinal qualities.

Celery is the most common stem vegetable in the Caribbean. It is very tasty, used mostly for flavoring along with the bulb vegetables. Actually all parts of the local Caribbean variety of celery are consumed. In most vegetables stems support the entire plant and have buds, leaves, flowers, and fruits. They are also a vital connection between leaves and roots to transfer water and mineral nutrients from roots upward, and organic compounds and some mineral nutrients in any direction within the plant. Bulb plant stems of chives, garlic, onion, and leeks, are usually called straws. They are also used for flavoring.

The man who has planted a garden feels that he has done something for the good of the world.

Charles Dudley Warner

CELERY

I'd be lost cooking without celery. Part of our garden is dedicated to kitchen herbs with chives, chadon benee, sage, thyme, parsley, and of course celery. Celery is a Caribbean kitchen requirement along with carrots, onions, and potatoes. Its distinctive flavor makes it a great addition to many cooked dishes. Our local variety is smaller and stronger tasting than the imported type with larger stalks. Leafy celery stalks grow to a foot tall joined at the base. It belongs to the same family as carrots. Trinidadians consume the stalks, but the leaves, roots and seeds can also be used as a food and seasoning, as well as a natural medicinal remedy.

Celery originated around the Mediterranean Sea and North Africa more than three thousand years ago. The Greeks at the time of Troy considered celery a religious plant and used celery and parsley without any difference. The Romans gave it a name meaning 'strong smelling' and used celery as an herb for cooking, but also considered it a superstitious bad omen. The Chinese recognized celery could reduce blood pressure. Modern varieties of celery have varying bitterness. Eating celery did not become popular until the 1700's.

Celery is not easy to grow under the tropical sun, because it needs plenty of water and some shade. After deep forking a bed and raising it about six inches, it is best to purchase transplants. Seeds are available, but are tiny and newly sprouted seedlings are very fragile to the sun. Transplants should be three to four inches tall and some what hardened to the sun before moving to their specific spot in your garden. Place the shoots four to six inches apart. Water at least twice a day and use a high nitrogen fertilizer mix sparingly every two weeks. First spray with a fungicide such as Ban rot and then spray every two weeks with a pesticide such as Fastac or Pestac. Do not use strong pesticides as the poison will not wear off by harvest. Researchers have listed celery as one of twenty vegetables usually sold with residual garden chemicals. Celery is best grown at home so you know what you are eating!

Celery is a heart friendly vegetable. It contains compounds that can relax the artery muscles, which regulate blood pressure. It also causes blood vessels to constrict. Juice from 4 stalks can cause about a 15% reduction in blood pressure. A cup of celery contains only 20 calories and has a good dose of vitamins C and B-6, folic acid, and fiber. Celery also has minerals such as manganese and calcium. The leaves are valuable as they contain the most vitamins. Always wash celery and keep it in the fridge until ready to use. Since celery has high water content, room temperature will cause it to wilt.

Chopped celery can be added to tuna or chicken salad, and the leaves can be used in salads, stirfry, and soups. If you are a juice lover, mix some celery with carrots.

Broiled or Grilled Celery

Unique side dish.

Ingredients: ten stalks of celery - better to use the big imported stalks, one small onion chopped, two cloves of garlic minced, three quarter cup grated cheddar cheese, salt and spice to taste.

Method: Cut celery stalks four inches long. Put in a baking dish and under the broiler or on foil on the grill or coal pot. Once both sides are slightly brown, turn celery so that the indented part is up. Fill with onions and garlic. Cover with cheese. Return to cooking until cheese melts.

> **DID YOU KNOW?**
> King Tut's tomb contained a shroud adorned with garlands of wild celery, olive leaves, willow, lotus petals, and cornflowers. Ancient Romans, considered celery an aphrodisiac. Scientists now know celery contains a pheromone, androsterone, that attracts females. Casanova, the famous Italian lover ate celery to keep up his stamina. One ounce of celery seeds will grow an acre of celery. Celery's botanical name is *apion graveolens*, a member of the *Umbelliferae* family with carrots, parsley, dill, cilantro, caraway, cumin, and the poisonous hemlock. Portage, Michigan has a celery museum called the Celery Flats Interpretive Center.

Baked Celery

Ingredients: twelve celery stalks with leaves, two TBS butter, one quarter cup grated cheddar cheese, salt and spices to taste

Method: Wash celery and trim the root end. Put into boiling water for ten minutes. (If you prefer more crunch- don't boil.) Chop celery into two inch pieces and place in a greased baking dish. Cover with grated cheddar cheese, spices (add a topping of bread crumbs or chopped nuts). Bake at 200 degrees for 15 minutes.

Celery-Banana Soup

Ingredients: quarter cup celery chopped small, three bananas green to just ripe any type- peeled and chunked, three cups boiling water, one TBS butter or margarine, one cup condensed milk, salt and seasoning to taste

Method: In an appropriate pot with a cover combine bananas, celery, water and seasonings. Bring to a boil for ten minutes. Add milk and butter. Simmer covered stirring infrequently for ten minutes. Serve warm.

Orange-Celery Kingfish

Ingredients: six nice kingfish steaks, half cup celery chopped small, one medium onion chopped small, two oranges - peeled, seeded, and chunked, half hot pepper seeded and minced (optional), three TBS butter or margarine, third cup water, salt and seasonings to taste

Method: place fish steaks in a baking dish. Cover with all remaining ingredients. Cover with foil and bake at 350 for twenty minutes. Uncover and continue to bake for tem more minutes.

Sweet and Sour Celery

Ingredients: one bunch imported celery-leaves removed and chopped into two inch pieces, two cups water, three TBS lemon juice, half hot pepper-seeded and minced (optional), quarter cup vegetable oil, one TBS brown sugar, one TS salt,

Method: Remove leaves from celery and chop into two inch pieces. In suitable deep frying pan combine all ingredients except celery and bring to a boil stirring. Add celery, cover and simmer about 20 minutes. Remove from heat and keep covered until celery cools. Chill and serve as a cutter.

HEALTH NOTE

Celery consumption fights arthritis, rheumatism, and gout. Its anti-inflammatory properties reduces swelling and pain around the joints. Celery assists in removing uric acid crystals that build around joints. This 'stalk/stem' vegetable contains vitamin C; strengthens the immune system, so eat celery to relieve a cold. Eating celery daily may reduce artery-clogging cholesterol. It contains a chemical that can lower levels of stress hormones in your blood, permitting blood vessels to expand, reducing pressure. Celery has about six calories per stalk. Supposedly it takes more calories to eat and digest celery than there is in the celery. It is high in dietary fiber with vitamins A, B2, B5, B6, C, K, calcium, magnesium, phosphorus, magnesium, and potassium. It is low in saturated fat and cholesterol.

CHIVES

Chives are smallest member of the onion family prized for their flavor. Chives are one of the rare vegetables believed to be native to the northern hemispheres of both America and Euro-Asia. Chives are grown almost anywhere and everywhere for their delicate flavor.

Fresh chives are available in local markets all year, but it is easy to grow your own. Chives can be grown in clumps or singly. The dark green, hollow, thin leaves or straws reach twenty inches. Since no large underground bulb forms like regular onions, the leaves are the flavor. Chives are perfect for the kitchen garden because it is a perennial – it just keeps growing.

Chives can be grown from seed, but it takes weeks for the tiny seeds to sprout and it is easy for them to be damaged by the severe sun. It is quicker and easier to start with seedlings. Chives want moist, well drained, very loose soil with a pH of 6-7. Chives grow best in full sun, yet will tolerate partial shade, and most soil types. Plant chives along edges of your garden to keep the plants free from insects; and its flowers attract bees, important for pollination.

Leaves can be harvested after chives are six inches tall. When you are cooking, simply cut or use scissors to snip the leaves two inches above the ground. The plant will continually regenerate leaves, allowing for a continuous harvest. Do not cut off all the leaves of one plant clump at one time. This will permit the plant to rejuvenate and permit that same clump of plants to be cut over and over.

Chives are high in vitamins A and C, potassium, and calcium. Consuming chives can lower blood pressure, but it takes more than the few usually in a meal. The usual amount will improve digestion and stimulate appetite. Chives can reduce fluid retention. Researchers discovered eating a lot of chives may help reduce the risk of prostate cancer, by as much as 50 percent.

The Romans believed chives reduced the pain of sunburn, and a sore throat. It was believed that bunches of dried chives hung around a house would ward off disease and evil.

Chives are usually used fresh and are a common addition to baked potatoes, cream soups, eggs and many other dishes.

Quick Gourmet Coconut Crab Soup

Ingredients: three TBS fresh chopped chives, one stalk celery chopped small, one small onion and one carrot chopped small, two cups coconut milk, two cans cream of asparagus soup (cream of tomato or celery can be substituted), three quarter cup water, one TBS curry powder, one TBS soy sauce, one TS fresh lemon juice, one half pound fresh crab meat, salt and pepper to taste

Method: Combine coconut milk, soup, one TBS chives, onion, celery, carrot, water, curry powder, soy sauce, and lemon juice in a large pot. Simmer, constantly stirring. Add crab and simmer until crab is cooked through. Add salt and spice to your taste and sprinkle with chives before serving with roast bake or sada roti.

> **DID YOU KNOW?**
>
> Chives are an herb with a mild onion flavor that grow in clumps like grass. They are referred to only in the plural, because they grow in clumps rather than as individual plants. Only the leaves, also known as straws, have the flavor. Fresh chives can be stored in the fridge in a plastic bag for up to a week. Do not wash until ready to use them, as excessive moisture will promote decay. Chives botanical name is *Allium schoenoprasum* and is also the only species of *Allium* (onions) native to both the New and Old World. Its species name is from the Greek 'skhoinos sedgeand prason' (onion). Its English name, chive, is from the French word cive, which was derived from cepa, the Latin word for onion.

High-Life Mashed Potatoes

Ingredients: two TBS chives chopped, five pounds potatoes-peeled, cut into chunks and boiled, three quarter cup heavy cream, one quarter pound of butter, one cup sour cream, one cup grated cheddar cheese, three slices cooked bacon, crumbled, salt, spices, and pepper to taste

Method: In a two quart pot warm the cream and butter until hot, yet not boiling. Remove from heat. Add sour cream, salt, spices, pepper, and the cooked potatoes. Mash until smooth. Add cheddar cheese, bacon, and chives. Serve warm.

Shepherd's Pie Americana

Ingredients: four TBS chopped chives, one pound minced beef, one small can mushroom pieces, one half cup beef broth, one medium onion chopped, one carrot chopped small, two cloves garlic minced, salt, spice, and pepper to taste, one TBS English (Worcestershire) Sauce, one TBS flour, one half cup heavy cream, two cups mashed potatoes, two cups cheddar cheese grated

Method: Divide mashed potatoes in half. Push one cup of potatoes in the bottom of a ten inch square three inch deep greased baking dish. (Almost any size including a pie dish will work.) In a large heavy skillet sauté minced beef, mushrooms, onion, carrot, garlic, salt, and pepper until it is almost dry. Stir constantly to break the beef into small pieces. Add English sauce and flour and stir for about a minute. Pour in beef broth. Then stir in the heavy cream. Simmer until everything thickens. Pour over the potatoes in baking dish. Combine the remaining mashed potatoes with chives, one cup of grated cheese, and spices; and spread evenly on top of minced beef layer. Sprinkle one cup of grated cheese on top. Bake for forty-five minutes at 375 degrees, until cheese has melted and is slightly burnt.

Papaya-Pineapple Salsa

Ingredients: two bunches chives chopped small, one cup ripe papaya seeded and chopped, one cup fresh pineapple chopped, quarter cup red onion chopped small, one hot pepper seeded and minced, one clove of garlic minced, one bunch of chadon benee chopped small, two TBS lime juice, one TBS vinegar, pinch of salt Method: Combine all ingredients in a suitable bowl and cover. Chill before serving.

Crab Puffs

Ingredients: two TBS chopped chives, one cup crabmeat, picked clean-fresh or canned, half cup shredded cheddar cheese, one TBS English/Worcestershire sauce, one TS dry mustard, one TS lemon juice, one TBS dill weed, half cup butter, one cup beer, quarter TS pepper, one cup allpurpose flour, four large eggs, one TS baking powder, half TS salt.

Method: Combine crabmeat, cheese, chives, English sauce, dry mustard, lemon juice, and dill in a bowl. In a large pan over medium heat melt butter, add beer, salt and pepper. Remove from heat and stir in flour. Return to heat and add eggs one at a time. Add baking powder and crab. Whip until a nice dough forms. Put spoonfuls on a baking sheet and bake at 400 for half an hour or until golden brown.

Gardening simply does not allow one to be mentally old, because too many hopes and dreams are yet to be realized.

Allan Armitage

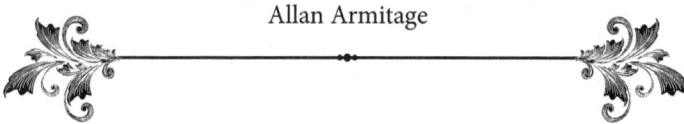

GARLIC

I would be lost cooking without garlic. I'll sit through a few hours of television peeling cloves and put them in a jar in the fridge to have them ready.

Garlic is believed to have originated in the hot dry Kirgiz Desert region of Siberia in Russia. In this region the summers are dry and hot, and there is very little rain. That climate made garlic a very tough plant that can flourish in any soil, and climate with little care. Garlic was cultivated by almost every civilization in history including at the gardens of Babylon. The Egyptians worshiped the garlic herb as a god. They also used garlic as currency. A slave could be bought for fifteen pounds of this bulb. Garlic was spread to Europe by returning crusaders after the Holy Wars. Warrior Vikings carried supplies of garlic in their boats. By 1000 A.D. garlic was grown in virtually the entire known world, and was universally recognized as a valuable plant.

Garlic is valued for its taste, but also for its medicinal benefits. No one knows how much garlic must be ingested to improve health, but experts feel the best results come from using raw garlic. Louis Pasteur discovered garlic kills bacteria. It was used as an antiseptic in World War II when sulfa drugs were scarce. Scientists have found that when raw garlic is cut or crushed it creates a compound, which kills at least twenty-three types of bacteria. Yet when garlic is heated it forms a different compound that reduces blood pressure and cholesterol. Garlic contains vitamins A, B, and C and stimulates the immune system. It may reduce the risk of stomach cancer and be a treatment for AIDS. Sixty kinds of fungi are also killed by garlic, including athlete's foot and vaginitis. If you fear garlic breath will end a romantic moment, eat parsley or fennel seeds.

Growing garlic is easy. First take two or three heads of nice fresh garlic and wrap them in a damp paper towel or paper bag. Place in the vegetable drawer of your refrigerator. The cloves inside the head will soon sprout. In your garden fork a row ten inches deep and break the clods. Plant the sprouted individual cloves every three inches with the sprouted side pointing to the surface. With enough water and light potassium rich fertilizer, each clove will become a head.

While growing carefully snip a few of the garlic's green stalks (not all) and use in dishes. The paper like skin can be saved in a jar with water to sprinkle as a natural insecticide in your garden. Peeled garlic cloves can be soaked in vinegar for two days. When the vinegar is drained off you have garlic-flavored vinegar. Cover the same garlic cloves with cooking oil and refrigerate creating garlic-flavored oil. Both vinegar and oil should be used within three months.

To make garlic salt put three pressed cloves in a half of cup of salt in a sealed jar. Let stand in the fridge for a few days. Use the garlic in cooking and the salt for flavoring. Smashing six cloves and whipping them into a quarter pound of butter or margarine makes potent garlic butter for tasty garlic bread or a base for cooking anything.

Whole heads of garlic may be baked as a spread for bread on crackers. Remove as much outer skin as possible, but leave the head intact. Expose the cloves by cutting the top of the head. After placing the heads in a covered dish, pour olive oil on the heads and add your own seasoning and pepper. Bake in the oven at 350 degrees for an hour. The cloves should be soft enough to squeeze out. To make a roasted garlic salad dressing, roast six crushed cloves with four tablespoons olive oil. Put in a 300-degree oven until the oil crackles. Mix with vinegar and spices of your choice to make flavorful vinaigrette.

One cup of garlic, almost a quarter pound, has only two hundred calories with plenty of calcium, vitamin C, and iron.

> ### DID YOU KNOW?
> April 19, is National Garlic Day in the USA. Garlic is sometimes called the 'stinking rose'. The smell of garlic can be removed by running your hands under cold water while rubbing a stainless steel object. According to Christian mythology, after Satan vanished from the Garden of Eden, garlic grew from his left footprint and onion grew from his right. The botanical reference is *allium sativum*.

Brushetta - Garlic Bread

Ingredients: one loaf of French bread or local butter bread cut into one inch thick slices, two TBS olive oil, four cloves garlic minced, three ripe tomatoes diced, ten fresh basil leaves (or two TBS Italian seasoning), salt and spice to taste

Method: On a cookie sheet or an oven pan, grill bread on both sides either under the broiler or on a tawah. Mix all other ingredients together and coat one side of the bread. Return to broiler for two minutes. For variety add cheese or chopped hot peppers.

Garlic Roast Peppers

Ingredients: six sweet peppers (prefer red), one tomato chopped, three large onions, six cloves garlic chopped, two TBS olive oil, two TBS fresh or dried thyme, and salt and pepper to taste

Method: Slice onions into long strips, mix with tomato and garlic. Slice the top off the bell peppers and brush insides with olive oil. Fill peppers with onion-garlic-tomato mixture, and sprinkle each with thyme. Place in a covered oven dish and bake at 350 for 40 minutes. Uncover and place under broiler for three minutes or until edges of peppers just begin turn brown.

Garlic Shrimp

Ingredients: a quarter pound sweet butter or margarine, four cloves garlic minced, two pounds cleaned medium or large shrimp, three TBS olive oil, one TBS basil, quarter cup white wine, salt and spice to taste, the juice of a fresh lemon or lime

Method: In a large frying pan, melt butter adding garlic, basil, olive oil and wine. Add shrimp and sauté until they turn slightly pink. Squeeze the lemon over the skillet. Serve with rice or pasta.

Garlic Cold Remedy

Crush a few garlic cloves. Put them in a bowl, and cover with olive oil. Let sit at least half an hour. Rub the oil on your feet and wear socks to bed. Sleep well as the garlic enters your system and clears your lungs of any cold.

Garlic Press.

HEALTH NOTE

Eating garlic fights heart disease, cancer, and colds, lowers blood cholesterol levels while reducing plaque in the arteries. Garlic is also known to be an aphrodisiac. Garlic has more germanium than any other herb. Germanium is an anti-cancer agent. Eating garlic may make you less allergic. Eating a clove of garlic every morning will fight asthma. During the World Wars British medics used garlic to treat wounds when the supply of sulfur drugs ran out. Throughout history garlic has been used as a strong antiseptic and also as a strong antibacterial, antifungal, antiviral and anti-parasitic herb. These properties have been verified in countless studies.

LEEKS

We started growing leeks because we couldn't grow onions. Go figure! We can grow great chives, but never a white, red, or yellow onion survives more than a few weeks in our garden. I knew about how tasty leeks were from friends in the UK and got some seeds and had success. Soups may be the most popular use of leeks. I've seen them for sale in various Caribbean supermarkets. You should try the faint, delectable tasty leek.

Leeks are of the lily family same as the onion, but sweeter than the standard onion. They have been grown for more than three thousand years around the Mediterranean. When the Israelites fled Egypt leeks are mentioned in the Bible as one of the foods the Israelites missed. The Romans brought leeks to Great Britain. Although big leeks don't taste the best, there is a yearly competition in England and the winners can range from 4 to 5 inches in diameter.

Better tasting leeks are slim, not fat, with clean white bulbs, and firm tightly rolled dark green tops that are definitely not be yellowed or wilted. The base should be at least a half inch in diameter. The younger the leek, the more delicate the flavor and texture. If the leek is limp at all, don't waste your money. Leeks can be an onion substitute in recipes, yet onions will never replace the unique flavor in leek recipes. Depending on freshness, leeks can keep in the fridge for up to a week. Leeks must be wrapped tightly to store in a fridge or other foods will begin to have a 'leeky' taste. Uncooked leeks can be sliced thin and added to salads.

We grew our leeks from seed in a seedling tray and transplanted them after three months (about chive size) into a grow box. They take a lot of patience, but you can grow a lot of leeks in a small space. The leek routine is to fertilize once about four months after transplanting with 12-24-12 and mold every month to make the white onion-like base grow longer. The higher you mold leeks by pulling the soil up, will reduce tough green outer casing giving you a much tender white stem. They take about six months to mature, but remain good in the bed for at least another year. Leeks grow to about a foot in length and one to two inches in diameter, and when cut they have a mild onion aroma without tears.

Before cooking, always wash leeks and peel off the outer skin layers. Leeks are a good source of fiber and have folic acid, calcium, iron, potassium, manganese, vitamins B6 and C. For many, leeks are easier to digest than onions. Eating leeks helps the bowels, fights arthritis, and reduces the risk of prostate and colon cancer. Eating leeks is also reputed to keep your voice from becoming hoarse.

DID YOU KNOW?

Leeks appear as a giant scallion, with wide, flattened leaves, and a thick white stalk. Hippocrates, the father of medicine, prescribed the leek as a cure for nosebleeds. Leeks were part of the diet of those who built the Egyptian pyramids. Emperor Nero of Rome regularly ate leeks to improve his singing voice. Welsh soldiers wore pieces of leeks in their helmets in 640 AD to distinguish themselves from their Saxon foes in battle. The leek is worn today as the national flower of Wales on St. David's day. The botanical name of leeks is *allium porrum*.

Add chopped leeks to salads, egg dishes, and soups for a new flavor. Potatoes are tasty when cooked with leeks. Remember not to over add other ingredients such as seasonings, garlic, or strong onions that will overwhelm or hide the subtle leek flavor.

The highest reward for man's toil in the garden is not what he gets for it, but what he becomes by it.
    John Ruskin

Potato-Leek Cakes

Ingredients: one large potato peeled and grated, two pounds leeks sliced thin, four eggs beaten, half cup bread crumbs, quarter cup grated cheese, one TS salt, half cup cooking oil (canola)

Method: Combine everything and chill in fridge for at least an hour. Shape into small hand sized cakes. Fry in hot oil until brown on both sides. If cakes do not hold together add one-third cup of flour. Serve with chutney or sour cream.

Curried Leeks

Ingredients: two pounds leeks cleaned and trimmed, two TBS curry powder, one bay leaf, four TBS cooking oil (olive or canola), quarter cup sultana yellow raisins, one apple peeled and sliced thin, half cup white wine (non alcoholic may be substituted), salt and spice to taste

Method: Make a layer of cleaned leeks in a frying pan. Cover with curry powder, bay leaf, oil, raisins, and apple. Add wine (grape juice) and boil. Cover and cook for about twenty minutes. Uncover and simmer until no liquid remains. Serve hot with rice.

Leek Casserole

Ingredients: eight nice cleaned leeks, one small onion chopped, third cup butter, ghee, or margarine, one cup tomato juice (or four TBS ketchup mixed with water), half cup grated cheese, one TBS lemon juice, quarter TS English Sauce, quarter TS sugar, salt and spices to taste

Method: In the butter, fry the whole leeks and chopped onion until the onion is transparent. Spoon this into a greased casserole dish and cover with mixture of remaining ingredients. Cover the top of mixture with pads of butter and grated cheese. Bake at 350 one hour. Uncover for the last ten minutes to brown the top and thicken the liquid.

Bulb and Stem Vegetables

Leek Eggs

Ingredients: four small leeks, quarter cup butter, one clove of garlic minced, quarter cup grated cheese, four eggs beaten, half cup condensed milk, two TBS flour, one TBS baking powder, salt and seasonings to taste

Method: Mix all ingredients in a greased baking dish or bread pan. Bake at 350 for half an hour. Let cool before serving so it holds its shape.

Leek Potato Soup

Ingredients: two to four cleaned leeks, four medium potatoes peeled and diced, one TBS olive oil, two cups water, four cubes vegetable bouillon, one cup milk, two TBS chopped parsley, salt and seasonings to taste

Method: Sauté potatoes and leeks in olive oil for five minutes, Add bouillon, water and seasonings, bring to a boil and then simmer for half an hour, stirring add milk and simmer. Serve warm.

HEALTH NOTE

Leeks are ideal in sauces, dressed vegetable dishes, soups, casseroles and stir-fries. Leeks are a great source of fiber in your diet, and may actually help lower cholesterol. They are low in saturated fat, sodium, and cholesterol while high in vitamins A, B6,C, K, folate, manganese, iron, and magnesium. One cup of raw chopped leeks contains 57 calories.

Who loves a garden still his Eden keeps;
Perennial pleasures plants, and wholesome harvest reaps.

A. Bronson Alcott

ONION

In the Caribbean we grew up with onions and garlic in our foods. I still find it hard to believe some people can't take the taste of onions.

Onions, botanically *allium cepa*, can be grown successfully throughout the Caribbean with care. The onion may be considered an herb, spice, or a vegetable. Most cooks consider onions the most important ingredient. Onion comes from the Latin word 'unio' for one since it produces a single bulb. The onion family is has many members: chives, scallions, leeks, shallots, garlic, red onions, yellow onions, and white onions. The origin of the onion is unknown, but is believed to be the Steppes of Central Asia, or Iran and Pakistan. In Europe, onions were known since the Bronze Age. With garlic, onion is mentioned in the oldest part of the Bible, desired by the Israelites after leaving Egypt for the Promised Land. Onions were found in the Egyptian tomb of King Tut. Columbus carried onions to the Western Hemisphere and their popularity spread among Amerindians.

Some people shy away from onions because they make you cry. When you cut into an onion, it releases a sulfur compound into the air. When it comes in contact with water it is converted to sulfuric acid that stings your eyes. To stop the tears, before chopping chill peeled onions in the refrigerator. To get the onion smell off your hands, rub with lemon juice or vinegar.

Chives are abundant in gardens throughout the Caribbean, although onion growers are scarce. Onions will grow in most soils as long as it is deeply forked with some shade from the heated afternoons. Forking softens the soil so the onion bulb can develop. Build up the row about six inches higher than the garden and soak the soil. With your finger create an inch deep groove in the center of the mounded row. Sprinkle the tiny onion seed in that groove sparingly. Onion seeds are smaller than a pencil point. The best way to plant is to work the seeds through your fingers, dropping as few as possible. Beware of 'dumping' too many seeds in one part of the row. Once the seeds hit the dirt they are almost invisible. Cover the groove and a few days later lightly sprinkle the rows with water. Do not water heavily as the seeds will wash out. Within ten days sprouts should show. Thin the sprouts to two inches apart. Weeds will kill the onions so gently pull any unwelcome visitors to the row. Using a hoe, pull dirt up onto the onions. Water lightly three times a week, but more if it is extremely hot. Heat will burn out the stems. Use a 12 – 24 – 12 fertilizer sparingly every other week, then after six weeks switch to 12 – 12 – 17 – 2. Too much fertilizer will hurt the onions. Once the green stem begins to wither and turn brown, the onions are ready for harvest. Pull the onions and dry in a shaded area. Bright sun may discolor the onions. Onions may need more than a week to fully dry.

Onions can be chopped and dried in the oven. Use the lowest setting and remove when thoroughly dry, yet not brown. Store at room temperature in airtight containers. Onions also can be frozen. Chop and place on a tray in the freezer. When frozen, remove and place in freezer containers or bags, and seal. This way they freeze evenly. This allows you to chop many onions at one time and then remove the amount you want when you need it. Frozen onions should be used for cooking only. Whole frozen onions can also be baked. Onions may be eaten raw, broiled, boiled, baked, creamed, steamed, fried, French fried, or pickled.

Baked Onions

Ingredients: Two large white or yellow onions peeled, two TBS ketchup, two TBS honey, one TBS margarine, salt and pepper to taste

Method: Slice the entire onion in half and place on a baking dish cut side up. Mix ketchup, honey, margarine, and seasonings in a small saucepan on low heat until the margarine is melted. Pour the mixture over the onions and bake at 350 degrees for forty-five minutes.

Shirley's Onion Casserole

Ingredients: Two pounds onions sliced a quarter inch thick and separated into rings, one half cup sweet green pepper chopped, one cup evaporated milk, Two cups cooked rice, one TBS cornstarch, two egg whites, one cup cheddar cheese, salt and pepper to taste.

Method: Combine milk, cornstarch, egg whites, stir until cornstarch is dissolved. Add seasonings. Cover the bottom of a greased baking dish with the onions rings. Then cover the onions with an inch of rice. Cover the rice with a layer of onions and cheddar. Repeat until the dish is filled. Then pour the milk mixture into the dish. Cover the top with onions and cheese. Bake at 350 degrees for half an hour.

Fried Onion Rings

This is a favorite cutter and easy to make once you learn the secret.

Ingredients: Four large white or yellow onions, one cup flour, one cup Carib beer, four cups frying oil, three TBS sugar, salt and pepper to taste.

Method: Blend the flour and beer thoroughly in a large bowl. The batter then must sit covered at room temperature for at least three hours. The batter can be adjusted to be thick or thin by adding more flour or beer. When ready to use stir in the sugar and seasonings. Slice the onions at least a quarter inch thick and separate into rings. Heat oil in a deep pot. The oil must be hot enough that when a battered piece of onion is dropped into it, it immediately sizzles. Dip the onions rings in the batter and drop into the oil. Do not crowd the pot, as the rings will stick together. The onion rings will rise to the top of the oil when they are cooked. Fry them until golden brown. This can also be done as a 'Blooming Onion'. Slice a whole onion almost crossways all the way through in both directions leaving about a quarter inch to hold it together. Put the entire onion in the batter and fry. Then slice and eat.

Two Day Onion Soup

Ingredients: three pounds peeled sweet onions, half cup butter or ghee, two TBS paprika, a bay leaf, three quarters cup flour, three quarts beef bouillon, one cup white wine, two TBS browning sauce, salt and pepper to taste, half pound grated Swiss or cheddar cheese. French bread.

Method: Slice onion a quarter inch thick, place in a large soup pot and sauté slowly in melted butter. Add spices. Cook for ten minutes longer before adding bouillon and wine and browning sauce. Simmer for two hours. Cool and refrigerate over night. Pour into ovenproof bowls topped with a slice of French bread and grated cheese. Place in pre-heated 350 degree oven for twenty to thirty minutes. Serves six.

HEALTH NOTE

Eating onions gives some protection against heart disease and colon cancer. They may also reduce the frequency and strength of asthma attacks. It seems the more pungent onions, especially yellow, are better for you as they have more antioxidants. Chives and green onions contain vitamin A and per half cup only 13 calories with one gram fiber, and one gram protein. Chopped raw, mature onions have sixty calories per cup, 2 grams fiber, and one-gram protein, with six grams carbohydrates. Onions are a good source of vitamin C, chromium, manganese, potassium and phosphorus.

My green thumb came only as a result of the mistakes I made while learning to see things from the plant's point of view.

H. Fred Dale

30

Vines

Vines refer to any climbing or trailing plant. They may be dense, airy, bushy, shiny, colorful, attractive, vertical, and productive. A vine is basically a long stem that uses energy, seeking sunlight to produce a fruit. Vine vegetables are considered 'small space' vegetables because they need just a bit of soil and lots of vertical growing room to climb. One of the best ways to make efficient use of space in a home garden is to use vertical space. You will get more production per square foot by using vines trained to climb instead of allowing them to sprawl. Keeping vines off the ground can be healthier, fighting soil bacteria, fungus, and dampness that could damage the plant before it produces.

Fences can support climbing fruits and vegetables. All that's needed is to plant some vining vegetables at the base of the fence, water, and fertilize as needed. Nature will take care of the rest. Allow vines as cucumbers, squash, melons, and bodi that usually sprawl on the ground to climb. Building supports for climbing vegetable plants adds character to your garden. A tall tripod made of bamboo is a beautiful and easy support for vining plants. Push bamboo posts deeply into the ground, and wrap at the top with garden twine or wire. Wrap wire around the legs of the tripod to add additional support to the structure, and provide additional surface area for the cucumbers or bodi to cling on. Sow seeds directly around the base of each pole, encouraging them to climb as soon as they emerge.

Tie trailing cucumbers, squash, and pumpkins to a sturdy frame or tripod. The vine will be able to support the fruit, in most cases. If you have a very heavy squash or pumpkin developing, a sling made from tying the sleeves of an old shirt and using the trunk of the shirt will make it extra secure.

So, yes, I do experience a type of reverie as a gardener.
But it is not something I control or strive for. When I find spirituality in my garden, it seems to go hand in hand with hard work and diligence.
Like a burst of sunshine on a cloudy day, a feeling of peace will come over me and grab me by surprise. I don't really know why or how it happens.
But then again, I wouldn't want it any other way.

Fran Sorin

BARBADINE

Barbadine is the sweet, good tasting fruit of a climbing vine perfect for growing on a fence. The flesh of the barbadine can be cooked as a vegetable, a dessert, or strained for the juice. This fruit is native to tropical Central and South America. Trinidad and Barbados have grown barbadine since the mid 1700's. Trinidad sent the first barbadine seeds to the United States in 1909. It survived only in southern Florida's warm climate.

Barbadine's blossoms are beautiful reddish-green on the outside with white, pink, and purple inside. The fruit sprouts from the blossoms like a weird shaped, pale green barbell. It will grow to a light yellowish-green, foot long fruit weighing up to a kilo. It is easily grown from seeds, which sprout in two weeks. Seeds from one mature fruit should produce at least ten plants. First fork a hole a foot square and deep to produce fine dirt. If available, mix in some well rotted chicken manure and bagasse into the hole to keep the soil porous. Plant four seeds about an inch from the surface. A distance of ten feet is necessary between vines. Keep the plant watered daily. Drought is one of barbadine's biggest enemies. As it matures weave the vine into a fence or a trellis (jamrah). Use a tablespoon of a fertilizer mixture high in nitrogen at the roots once a month. Every two weeks spray the vine with a mild insecticide as Malathion. When the blossoms open, spray the entire vine with a soluble 20-20-20 fertilizer every other week. A barbadine vine will climb trees to fifty feet if permitted. That is out of easy picking range. On the island Java one vine was reported to have grown to one hundred and fifty feet.

Barbadine's enemies, birds and boring insects, will appear with the fruit. It is wise to protect the hanging fruit by putting them (while on the vine) into plastic or brown paper bags until they mature. Do this carefully so not to pull or damage the immature fruit on the vine. One vine properly watered and fertilized can produce two to three fruits every month. It takes approximately two months for the fruits to ripen after the appearance of blossoms.

Vine growth and fruit production, quality, and size benefits by yearly pruning. This produces young branches, with more flowers. Barbadine should not be permitted to grow on any tree since it will compete aggressively for sunlight, and it can damage or kill the support tree. The fruit is melon-like, has a delicate skin with a thick layer of white flesh, which tastes similar to a pear. It is ready to harvest when the skin becomes translucent and glossy, and turns slightly yellow. Barbadine needs careful handling to prevent bruising.

Barbadine is a good source of calcium and phosphorous and a hundred grams has only sixty calories. Immature fruit can be boiled, breaded, then fried as a vegetable, or cubed and stir fried. Its juice is great chilled, or as a flavoring for shaved ice. Boiling the unpeeled flesh and the pulp separately is the first step in making barbadine jelly. The juice is strained from both and combined with sugar and lemon juice. Boil the combined juices again until it jells. Australians make barbadine wine by crushing the entire fruits with sugar and warm water and permitting it to ferment for three weeks. The Aussies fortify the mix with a quart of brandy and hide it in a dark place for a year. Jamaicans bake the roots of old vines as a survival food, a substitute for yam.

> **DID YOU KNOW?**
>
> Barbadine's botanical name is *passiflora quadrangularis*. It is called this because the root appears square. Barbadine is the French name. It is also known as grande granadilla in Spanish, groote in Suriname, giant tumbo/tambo in Peru, or Badea granadilla or parcha. in Venezuela. Barbadine is the largest of the passion fruits.

Barbadine Colada

Ingredients: one barbadine, one can condensed sweetened milk

Method: Peel the barbadine and cut away the pulp. Force seeds and pulp through a strainer. Add the condensed milk and blend. If it is too thick add water or regular milk. Add sugar, cinnamon, and nutmeg to your taste. This may also be made with chilled water and ice. Use two cups water and two trays of ice. Add sugar and other juices as orange or passion fruit to your taste. Put everything in a blender and push the 'chop' mode. Hit the button about four times until the ice is grainy.

Barbadine Easy Cake

Ingredients: half a barbadine fruit, one yellow cake mix, three eggs, third cup cooking oil or margarine, cinnamon or nutmeg to taste

Method: Peel barbadine and put in blender to get juice. Strain to remove pulp and blend all ingredients. Pour into a greased cake pan. Bake for ten minutes at 350 degrees. Then lower temperature to 300 for half an hour. Check center with a toothpick. Allow cake to cool before slicing.

Barbadine Ice Cream

Ingredients: half barbadine fruit, one tin evaporated milk, one tin sweetened condensed milk, cinnamon and or nutmeg to taste

Method: Crush or blend barbadine to get the juice. Strain to remove pulp. Blend all ingredients and put in suitable container for freezing. The refrigerator cube tray may be used to make delicious ice blocks.

Barbadine Tart

Ingredients: one barbadine skinned and seeded, about two dozen sweet biscuits or cookies of your choice. Four TBS orange marmalade, two TBS sugar, one cup full whipping cream (this must be chilled at least over night), one cup hot water, one cup cold water

Method: Combine two TBS marmalade first with hot water and then cold water, chill in fridge. Whisk cream until thick adding barbadine pulp. Add sugar and marmalade water. Crush cookies/biscuits with a rolling pin. Cover the bottom of a cake or pie pan. Add a layer of barbadine pulp mixture and then another layer of crushed biscuits. Refrigerate until thoroughly set.

HEALTH NOTE

The fruit is valued in the tropics an appetite enhancer. In Brazil, the flesh is used as a tranquilizer to relieve nervous headache, asthma, diarrhea, dysentery, neurasthenia, and insomnia. The seeds are reported to have a narcotic effect in large doses. The leaves boiled in water are used for bathing skin eruptions. Poultices made from the leaves are applied to liver ailments.

No occupation is so delightful to me as the culture of the earth, and no culture comparable to that of the garden.

Thomas Jefferson

CANTALOUPE

Cantaloupe is always a treat whenever I find them in the market. These sweet orange melons may cost a bit more, but we owe ourselves a sweet taste. Cantaloupes are better recognized in the Caribbean as muskmelon and a member of the same vine family of pumpkin, cucumber, and squash. Typically cantaloupe is round with a mesh looking gray skin, sweet tasty orange flesh with a very unique pleasant smell. All cantaloupes are muskmelons, but not all muskmelons are cantaloupes. Honey dews, casaba, and Persians are other types of muskmelons. It is believed cantaloupes originated in Persia, between Iran and Turkey, thousands of years ago. This melon was well known by the Greeks and Romans 2000 years before Christ. On his second voyage in 1494, Columbus brought seeds for cultivation on Hispaniola and before 1650 it was a cash crop of Brazil. The modern, true variety of cantaloupe was first cultivated in Cantaloupe, Italy around 1700 AD, thus the name.

Cantaloupes should be planted in mounds about six inches high to permit drainage. They love the full sun, and rich moist soil. Till the soil with a fork and place some rotted manure at the base before building the mound. Plant four to six seeds per mound about four inches apart and a half-inch deep with about six feet between mounds. Insects like the cucumber beetle, and the vine borer love cantaloupe. Use various recommended insecticides. Fertilize these melon plants regularly and give water once or twice a week. The main killer of this type of muskmelon is powdery mildew fungus. It is wise to give your plants a good drenching of an appropriate fungicide every two weeks until they blossom. Cantaloupes will not cross pollinate with watermelon, cucumber, pumpkin, or squash. Keep the vines from tangling each other. It is time to harvest when the stem end of the fruit dries out. That end of the cantaloupe should be soft when you press it with your finger. It is over ripe if the entire melon is soft. Do not purchase any cantaloupe that still has part of the stem attached as it was picked before it was fully ripe. The skin, underneath the mesh, should be a yellow or cream color when ripe.

A tasty cantaloupe will not spoil your diet as a cup of cantaloupe has only 50 calories. Eating a half a cantaloupe will provide the daily requirement of vitamins A and C, folic acid, and potassium. Cantaloupe has no fat or cholesterol and provides necessary fiber.

Some interesting ways to use cantaloupes are to make a refreshing drink by mixing some sparkling soda water with fresh squeezed cantaloupe juice or pureed flesh. Another is to blend cantaloupe with mango slices and add lemon juice to prepare a unique cold soup. Cut a cantaloupe in half and remove the seeds before filling the cavity with ice cream or vanilla yogurt or fruit salad.

Cantaloupe Pie

Pie Ingredients: one medium cantaloupe - peeled, seeded and cubed, half cup sugar, three TBS cornstarch, three eggs separated - three yolks for pie and the whites for the topping, four TBS butter or margarine, one TBS vanilla extract, pinch salt, one store bought pie shell - graham cracker preferred

Meringue ingredients: three egg whites, quarter cup sugar, half TS vanilla extract

Method: Pie – blend cantaloupe slices until smooth, which should make at least two cups of puree. Pour into a large mixing bowl and add sugar, egg yolks, vanilla and melted butter. Use a mixer or hand whisk. Pour mixture into pie shell and bake for 45 minutes at 350 degrees. To top with meringue beat egg whites until soft peaks form. Then slowly add sugar then vanilla. If this is too time consuming, top pie with Dream Whip.

> **DID YOU KNOW?**
>
> Cantaloupes' botanical name is *cucumis melo*. Its sweet smell makes them actually muskmelons. True 'cantaloupe' (cucumis cantalupensis) from Cantaloupe, Italy, is actually a hard-shelled melon not grown much outside the Mediterranean countries. It is believed the first 'true' cantaloupe grew in the Pope's garden. Muskmelons with soft rinds and netted surface markings are popular worldwide. In some parts of the world, it is also known as the rock melon, for its rough skin looks like a rock. Leaving an uncut cantaloupe at room temperature for two or three days will make the fruit softer and juicier.

Cantaloupe Sorbet

Ingredients: One cantaloupe - peeled, seeded, and chunked, quarter cup fresh orange juice, half cup sugar - optional, half TS salt

Method: Start with about two cups of cantaloupe in a blender with remaining ingredients. Blend until everything is smooth and sugar has dissolved. Pour into shallow dishes with covers and freeze. This will be smoother if you remove from freezer after three hours, blend again, and refreeze.

Cantaloup Chicken

Ingredients: half cantaloupe - peeled seeded and diced, one julie mango - peeled, seeded and chopped, two cooked chicken breasts steamed, grilled, or baked (six thighs may be used) remove bones from chicken, quarter cup sour cream, one bunch chives chopped, jumbo pasta tube shells like manicotti or cannelloni, two TBS fresh lime juice, one TBS mustard – Dijon type preferred, salt and spice to taste

Method: Marinade chicken to your taste before cooking, cool, remove bones, and chunk. Cook pasta, rinse, and cool. Combine diced cantaloupe, mango, sour cream, chives, and spices; then stuff the shells. Serve cool to chilled.

HEALTH NOTE

One serving of a quarter of a medium melon provides more than 400 percent of your daily vitamin A, and it also provides nearly 100 percent of your daily vitamin C! Cantaloupe has high levels of beta-carotene, folic acid, potassium, and dietary fiber. It is also one of the very few fruits that has a high level of vitamin B complex, B1 thiamine, B3 niacin, B5 pantothenic acid, and B6 pyridoxine. Cantaloupe has no fat or cholesterol, and provides fiber in the diet.

Cantaloupe is rich in anti-oxidants that can help prevent cancer and heart diseases. Potassium in cantaloupe helps excrete sodium, reducing high blood pressure especially in those with salt-sensitive hypertension. Cantaloupe juice with potassium can reduce muscular cramps. A special compound in this muskmelon relieves the nerves, calms anxieties, and helps against insomnia. When going through a stressful period, drink this melon's juice regularly. The potassium content helps to rebalance and normalize the heartbeat. This in turn sends oxygen to the brain, and regulates the body's water balance. The natural nutrients and minerals found in cantaloupe juice provide a unique combination to help the body recover from nicotine withdrawal when trying to quit smoking. Smoking also quickly depletes the vitamin A, but cantaloupe juice can help replace it with its betacarotene.

*When the world wearies and society fails to satisfy,
there is always the garden.*

Minnie Aumonier

CARAILLI, THE MYSTERY VINE

Carailli is one vegetable I didn't really know how to cook, but when a neighbor brought over some carialli talkarie, I found it uniquely delicious. This bumpy skinned fruit of a vine is the strangest and bitterest member of the melon family. Carialli is considered a 'strange' food because it is seldom sweet. Caribbean people seem to love a bitter-hot taste. In fact, we equate hot as bitter. Carialli fruit is for all those who love a true bitter taste. A mature fruit should first be sliced and salted, then squeezed to remove the bitter juice before cooking. However, small young fruit are almost sweet.

I call it the mystery vine because it is one of the healthiest foods you could ever 'learn' to eat. You must learn how to cook it to enjoy its weird taste and health benefits. The mystery is why so few people grow it, and so few people know how good it is for you. Try and enjoy the bitter taste for all its healthful virtues!

Carailli, or bitter melon, is a tropical fruit not a vegetable. This fruit has a distinct looking exterior with warts and an oblong shape. When cut in half it shows a relatively thin layer of flesh surrounding a central seed-pith filled cavity with large flat seeds. Seeds and pith appear white in unripe fruits, ripening to red. The flesh is crunchy and watery similar to cucumber or christophene. Carailli is usually eaten before it fully ripens. It can be eaten when ripe and turns yellowish, but it becomes more bitter as it ripens. The fully ripe fruit turns orange and mushy, and is too bitter to eat. It uniquely splits into segments that curl to expose seeds covered in bright red pulp.

Carailli is easy to grow from seeds. It is best planted along a fence or anywhere the vine can climb. Because carialli seeds are scarce, first visit the market and search for an over ripe fruit. Set the fruit out until it softens and then remove the seeds to dry. Dig several small holes along a fence line. Plant about four seeds per hole. Water regularly and in a few days bright green sprouts will appear. As the vine grows carefully weave it onto the fence. Carialli is a natural climber. Spray occasionally with a mild pesticide and water-soluble fertilizer. In a few weeks yellow blossoms will appear. Water every other day and once a month sparingly use a high nitrogen fertilizer mix at the roots. Birds will be the biggest pests to your carialli.

Carialli is nutritional. The bitter juice can be helpful to diabetics. A tea of the leaves and blossoms provides natural relief for high blood pressure. Carailli can be added to soups, stews, and stir fry. This fruit can also be pickled.

The best and traditional East Indian way to prepare carailli to cook is to peel the skin off and cut into thin slices. Salt the pieces and set out where it can get full sun for few hours to reduce its bitterness. After a few hours, squeeze out the excess salty bitter water by hand. Then rinse with water a few times. Now it is ready for any recipe.

> **DID YOU KNOW?**
>
> Carailli's botanical name is *momordica charantia*. It is also known as bitter melon, balsam pear, bitter cucumber, bitter gourd, karolla, African cucumber, balsam pear, bitter apple, bitter gourd, bitter pear melon, cindeamor, carilla plant, concombre (African), karela (Korea), ku gua (China), kuguzai (China), margose, wild cucumber, and ampalaya (Philippines).

Carialli Stuffed with Curried Shrimp

Ingredients: four large carialli, two TBS chadon benee, one hot pepper, two onions, four cloves of garlic, one TS cumin/geera, one pound of cleaned and deveined medium shrimp chopped, one cup coconut milk, three TBS curry massala, two TBS canola oil, salt to taste.

Method: Slice carialli along one side so the other side's shin acts as a hinge. Remove all seeds creating a small pocket. Drop carialli in boiling water for five minutes. Drain on a clean kitchen towel and allow to cool. Put all ingredients except shrimp in a blender to produce a fine consistency. Heat oil in a large frying pan and add blended ingredients for two or three minutes. Add chopped shrimp. Stuff the carialli with the shrimp-spice mixture and place in a covered baking dish. Pour in coconut milk. Bake for thirty minutes at 350 degrees. Serves four to six.

Fried Carialli

Ingredients: one large carialli, four onions chopped, one large tomato chopped, two pimento peppers chopped, four cloves of garlic minced, two TBS canola oil, salt and hot pepper to taste.

Method: Remove seeds and then slice carialli into half inch thick pieces. Salt and let sit for half an hour. Then squeeze and rinse the pieces. In a large skillet, heat the oil adding onions, garlic, peppers, then add carialli pieces. Cover and add two TBS water. Cook for fifteen minutes. Serves four.

Carialli Salad

Ingredients: one whole carailli, cleaned and sliced, one medium onion, sliced thin, one medium tomato sliced, one TS olive oil, half cup vinegar (balsamic vinegar preferred), pinch of sugar to balance the tang of the vinegar, salt and pepper to taste

Method: Combine vinegar, olive oil, salt, and pepper in a bowl. Taste the mixture, and add a pinch more of sugar if desired. Arrange the onion, tomato, and carialli on a shallow salad server. Cover with mixture, and serve without stirring.

HEALTH NOTE

In 1999, a Bangladeshi clinical trial was conducted to examine the effect of carailli on a hundred patients with Type 2 Diabetes. The researchers recorded the patients' sugar levels both without food intake for 12-24 hours and after taking 75g of glucose. They then administered a bitter melon pulp suspension to diabetic patients and 86 out of the 100 responded to the vegetable intake, showing a significant fifteen per cent reduction in fasting and post-meal serum glucose levels.

Carailli is an excellent source of vitamins B1, B2, and B3, C, magnesium, folic acid, zinc, phosphorus, manganese, and has high dietary fiber. It is rich in iron, contains twice the beta-carotene of broccoli, twice the calcium of spinach, and twice the potassium of a banana. Regular consumption of bitter gourd juice has been proven to improve energy and stamina level. Eating it will even improve your sleep. The high beta-carotene and other properties in bitter gourd makes it one of the finest vegetable-fruits that help alleviate eye problems and improves eyesight. Carailli roots are used to treat eye related diseases. Bitter melon juice may be beneficial in the treatment of a hangover for its alcohol detoxification properties. It also helps cleanse, repair, and nourish liver problems due to alcohol consumption. This bitter juice can also help to build your immune system and increase your body's resistance against infection. Take two ounces of fresh bitter melon juice and mix with a cup of honey diluted in water. Drink daily to improve asthma, bronchitis, and laryngitis. Regular consumption of this bitter juice has also been known to improve psoriasis condition and other fungal infections like ring-worm and athletes feet. The fruit is a coolant, aids digestion, a laxative, increases appetite, cures gas pains, blood diseases, anemia, urinary discharges, asthma, ulcers, and bronchitis.

Gardening is the purest of human pleasures.
Francis Bacon

CHRISTOPHENE

We eat a lot of crunchy christophene in stirfry. My wife calls it the 'West Indian mushroom' since it will acquire the taste of whatever it is cooked with. Christophene is a pearshaped member of the squash family, which originated in Central America cultivated by the Mayan and Aztec Amerindians. Christophene is now cultivated in the world's tropics from Australia and Madagascar, to China and Algeria. It has many names, Christophene to the French, chayote in Spanish, custard marrow to the Brits, and vegetable pear or mirliton to the US. The flavor is similar to a zucchini summer squash, but christophene has only a single seed. There are two basic varieties, smooth or prickly; green or white.

Christophene grows as an attractive vine, but it needs a lot of attention. Perhaps you have seen the christophene plantation in Trinidad on the road from Arima to Blanchisseuse, or around Lopinot. This vine loves the sun, but also needs plenty of water and humidity, and a fence or a jammrah (trellis). The easiest method to grow this vegetable is to locate a farmer and beg a plant. Failing that, select two christophene at the market. Ask the vendor if they have any that are over ripe and budding. If not, set the christophene in a warm window, but not in direct sun. In a few days it will start to shrivel and wrinkle, and soon sprout a bud. Plant the seed bud upwards in a clay pot with sandy soil. Lightly fertilize with 12-24-12. Once the plant catches move it outdoors where the vine can climb. Provide it with some shade as a banana leaf or a board. Do not fully cover it. Water regularly and use 12-12-17-2 mix when it begins to blossom. Christophene tends to produce better the second season. Although christophene is self-pollinating, it seems to like having brothers or sisters around. You'll probably get more fruit if you plant a second vine on a close fence.

Christophene requires a good bit of water. It especially likes cooled down in the heat of the day with a light spray. I have successfully grown it in the extreme heat of the dry season by spraying it with a hose every afternoon. The christophene was on a fence overhanging my grow box kitchen garden so both benefited from the water. The christophene also provided some shade for the ground level plants.

One cup of christophene has only twenty-five calories with almost no fat or carbohydrates. It has some fiber and Vitamin C. However it is a source of sodium (salt). A tea made from christophene leaves is a bush treatment for hypertension and is reported to dissolve kidney stones. Christophene is very versatile and can be eaten raw, grated, or sliced, boiled, and mashed, fried – especially good in stir fry, or baked. Christophene takes on the taste of the spices used with it.

Baked Christophene

Ingredients: four christophene, halved and seeded, two TBS olive oil, one bunch chadon benee chopped, salt and spice to taste

Method: Wash, but do not peel christophene halves. Place in baking dish on the cut side. Brush with olive oil or melted butter and sprinkle with the chadon benee, salt and spices. Bake at 350 degrees for 40 minutes.

Christophene Soup

Ingredients: two christophene peeled, seeded and cubed, one large onion (red preferred) chopped, four large ripe tomatoes chopped, two cloves of garlic sliced thin, one bunch chadon benee chopped, four TBS olive oil, half cup water, half hot pepper seeded and minced (optional)

> **DID YOU KNOW?**
>
> Christophene's botanical name is *sechium edule* a member of the *cucurbitaceae* family, a subtropical member of the squash family. It is a pear shaped fruit, has a single seed and a taste similar to zucchini. Somehow we got the French name christophene. It is also known in English as chayote, Madeira marrow, vegetable pear, custard marrow, chouchoute in Madagascar and Polynesia, brione in the French West Indies. Other names include vegetable pear, cho-cho, soussous, chuchu, choko, pipinella, xuxu, mirliton mango squash, and huisquil, sayote, tayota, choko, chocho, chow-chow, fence grown squash, and alligator pear. For all these exotic names this fruit of a vine is simply eaten as a vegetable. The young root tubers are also eaten.

Method: In a large skillet heat the oil before adding the garlic and onion. Then add tomatoes, chadon benee, salt, spices, and water. Simmer for half an hour. Top with grated cheese, and or bread crumbs.

Christophene Onion Quiche

Ingredients: three christophene - peeled, seeded and cubed, one large onion, one medium red sweet pepper sliced into rings, one firm tomato chopped, quarter cup butter, two eggs beaten, quarter cup milk, half cup grated cheddar cheese, one unbaked pie shell, salt and spice to taste.

Method: Sauté onions and christophene in butter until cooked but still firm. Mix in the tomato. Add half of the cheese, salt, and spices and pour into the unbaked pie shell. Mix the eggs with the milk and pour into shell. Cover with remaining cheese and pepper rings. Bake at 350 degrees for 45 minutes, or until the eggs are cooked. This can be changed into an omelet by omitting the pie shell.

Christophene Sweet Pepper Salad

Ingredients: two christophene peeled, seeded and sliced thin, one large sweet pepper (preferably red) - cored, seeded and cut into match sticks, one TS olive oil, two limes for juice, salt and spices to taste

Method: In a bowl, well mix the christophene and sweet pepper pieces with the oil, limejuice and seasonings. Let stand for at least twenty minutes before serving.

Christophene Casserole

Ingredients: two cups christophene - peeled, seeded, and cubed, half pound minced beef (or chicken), one medium onion chopped, two cloves garlic minced, half sweet bell pepper chopped, quarter cup tomato sauce or ketchup, twobutter or margarine, two TBS canola oil, one leaf chadon benee chopped, quarter cup breadcrumbs TBS , salt and spice to taste

Method: In a frying pan brown the onion and garlic with the minced meat in the oil adding sweet pepper and christophene pieces. Mix in tomato sauce, chadon benee, salt and spices before dumping into a casserole dish greased with butter. Cover with breadcrumbs before baking at 350 degrees for 45 minutes.

HEALTH NOTE

Christophene also has medicinal uses such as, infusions of the leaves are used to dissolve kidney stones, cure other kidney diseases, and treat arteriosclerosis and hypertension. Infusions made from the fruit are used to relieve urine retention.

Nevertheless, what a man needs in gardening is a cast-iron back, with a hinge in it.

Francis Bacon

CUCUMBER

Cucumber picked from the vine, sliced and seasoned into chow is one of my favorite garden treats. The phrase 'cool as a cucumber' is an apt one. Growing in a field on a hot summer day, the interior flesh of a 'cuke' is many degrees cooler than the outside air temperature. Cool and moist due to their high water content, cucumbers belong to the same family as pumpkins, zucchini, watermelon, and other squashes. The botanical name is *cucumis sativus*.

Cucumbers are one of the oldest cultivated vegetables, farmed since 8,000 B.C. and probably native to India. Aristotle praised the healing effects of cured cucumbers eight centuries before Christ. Cucumbers spread to China about 200 B.C., and showed up in Europe in Roman times. One Roman emperor is reported to have eaten fresh cucumbers every day of the year, grown by artificial methods in the off-season. Columbus brought cucumbers to the New World on one of his voyages, and the vegetable soon spread to English and Spanish colonies, and to the Native Americans. Cucumbers come in a variety of sizes, some up to two feet long. Pickles are cucumbers that have been cured in a brine or vinegar solution.

Although Caribbean islanders usually have a hot mouth ready for anchar mango or another sour, like plums; cucumber pickles are difficult to locate. Yet last year in the United States over five million pounds of pickles were consumed; nine pounds per person per year! Cucumbers brought from their native India helped begin a tradition of pickling in the Tigris Valley over four thousand years ago. Ancient sources not only refer to the nutritional benefits of pickles, but they have long been considered a beauty aid. Cleopatra attributed her good looks to a hearty diet of pickles. Julius Caesar, among other Roman emperors, fed pickles to their troops in the belief that they lent physical and spiritual strength.

Pickles were brought to the New World by Christopher Columbus. The great navigator grew cucumbers for the purpose of pickling on the island of Haiti. Before Amerigo Vespucci set out to explore the New World (Amerigo is who the Americas are really named after) he was a pickle peddler in Seville, Spain. Since food spoilage and the lack of healthy meals were such concerns on long voyages, he loaded up barrels of pickled vegetables onto explorer ships. Hundreds of sailors were spared the ravages of scurvy because of Vespucci's understanding of the nutritional benefits of pickles. The French explorer Cartier found cucumbers growing in Canada in 1535. In the seventeenth century, Dutch fine food fanciers cultivated pickles as one of their prized delicacies. The area, now New York City, was home to the largest concentration of commercial picklers at the time.

Vines

Cucumbers will grow and produce with just a little care, and require attention about twice a week, even in small garden plots. Trinidad grows more than two and a half million kilos of cucumbers every year. Cucumbers grow best on slightly acid soils - or pH 5.8 to 6.5. Lime should be applied if soil test shows pH 5.5 or less. Rows should be 3 to 4 feet apart. Plant seeds 1/2 to 1 inch deep and thin the seedlings to one plant every 12 inches in the row or to three plants every 36 inches in the hill or mound system. Make cuke vines climb to save garden space.

Cucumbers add a crisp snap to salads and sandwiches, however they are not a very good source of nutrients. The most abundant nutrient in cucumbers is water. A four-inch cucumber has 20 calories, one-gram fiber, one-gram carbohydrates, calcium, vitamins A and C. A small amount of beta-carotene is found in the green peel, but once peeled the level drops to nearly zero. Fiber and vitamin A are also lost by peeling. Cucumbers are mild laxatives.

Depending on variety and time of year grown, cucumbers usually take 40 to 55 days from seeding to first picking. Pick cucumbers while they are still tender, crisp and green. Remove large fruits from the vine so that new fruits are encouraged to grow. Cucumber plants have shallow roots and require ample soil moisture at all stages of growth. When fruit begins setting and maturing, adequate moisture becomes especially critical. For best yields, incorporate compost or well-rotted manure before planting. You should side-dress plants with nitrogen fertilizer when they begin to vine. Cucumber beetles should be controlled from the time young seedlings emerge from the soil. In small gardens, the vines may be trained on a trellis or fence. Do not handle, harvest, or work with the plants when they are wet. Keep weeds a foot or more from each plant's roots. Do not use herbicides/weed killer cheicals. Watch for aphids, leaf miners, beetles, and fruit worms. If insects become a severe problem, spray or dust with an approved insecticide, but always wait until after 10 A.M. to spray so

DID YOU KNOW?

For a quick pick me up, cucumbers are a good source of B vitamins and carbohydrates and can provide a energy burst that can last for hours. Take a cucumber slice and rub it along a hinge, to remove a problem squeak. Rub a freshly cut cucumber over the shoe, its chemicals will provide a quick and durable shine that not only looks great, but also repels water. To avoid a hangover eat a few cucumber slices before going to bed, wake up refreshed and headache free. Cucumbers contain enough sugar, B vitamins, and electrolytes to replenish essential nutrients the body lost, keeping everything in equilibrium. A fast and easy way to remove cellulite, rub a slice or two of cucumbers along your problem area for a few minutes, the phytochemicals in the cucumber cause the collagen in your skin to tighten, firming up the outer layer and reducing the visibility of cellulite. Works great on wrinkles too!!! To keep a bathroom mirror from fogging up after a shower, rub a cucumber slice along the mirror. It will eliminate the fog and provide a soothing, spa-like fragrance.

pollinating bees are not killed.

Refrigerated Dill Chips

The secret to the crisp texture is the sugar; so do not reduce the sugar in the recipe.

Ingredients: two quarts of cucumbers sliced an eighth to a quarter inch thick, one medium onion again sliced thin, one TBS salt, one and a half cups sugar, half cup white distilled vinegar.

Method: First mix the cucumbers, onion, and salt in a large bowl, cover tightly and permit it to rest for at least two hours at room temperature. Then drain any water from the mixture. Completely dissolve the sugar in the vinegar and pour over the cucumbers. Pack into tight sealing containers, or use zip-lock bags. Immediately put into the freezer. Pickles will be ready to eat in one week and will keep in the freezer for at least a year.

Baked Cucumber Au Gratin

Ingredients: two cucumbers, one cup grated cheese, four TBS butter, salt and pepper to taste.

Method: First peel the cucumbers & cut them into 3 inch pieces. Slice each piece in half and remove the seeds. Cook the cucumber in boiling salted water for 10 minutes, then drain and pat dry. Put a layer of cucumber slices in the base of a buttered ovenproof dish. Sprinkle with a third of the cheese, and season with salt & pepper. Repeat these layers, finishing with cheese. Dot the top with butter. Bake cucumber gratin in the center of a preheated oven at 400 for 30 minutes.

Easy Cucumber Soup

Ingredients: six cups chicken broth, three large cucumbers - peeled, quartered, and seeded, half pound fresh mushrooms, one bunch chives chopped, and fresh parsley

Method: Using a large saucepan bring chicken broth to a boil. Slice cucumbers into thin slices about quarter inch thick. Wash mushrooms and cut into slices the same as the cukes. Cook cucumbers and mushrooms in broth for eight to ten minutes or until tender. Before serving, add chives to the soup. Use salt and pepper to your taste and then garnish with parsley. Serves six.

Grow what you love. The love will keep it growing.
Emilie Barnes

PASSION FRUIT

Passion fruit is my wife's favorite juice, so much that our fence is now covered with the vines. The tasty and fragrant passion fruit vine is native to southern South America. Early Spanish missionaries in Brazil first witnessed the beauty of the vines' scented blossoms for the duration of Lent and Easter, and named the fruit after the 'Passion of Jesus'.

Passion fruit can be purple, red, but the Caribbean's most common variety is yellow. To start your crop, buy fruit from at least two different sources. The purple-fruited species is supposedly self-fertile and the yellow fruited species despite claims to the contrary is self-sterile, and requires another for pollination. The two types of passion fruit have clearly differing exterior appearances. The bright yellow variety, also known as the Golden Passion Fruit, can grow up to the size of a big orange and has a smooth, glossy skin. The dark purple (mauve) passion fruit is usually smaller than a lemon, but the purple passion fruit also has a higher flesh proportion, a richer taste and aroma, and is less acidic than the yellow.

Plant the seeds while they are fresh. Remember two different fruits are necessary for future pollination. The vine is fast growing and perfect to provide privacy on the fence, especially in direct sun. Soil pH should be from 6.5 to 7.5. If the soil is too acid, lime must be applied. And good drainage is essential. Beautiful passion fruit blossoms can appear after the first year. The fruit ripens slowly taking almost three months. The vines will grow best in sandy soil, yet can adapt to almost any soil that drains well. The roots do not penetrate the soil very deep so they should be molded with some rotted manure. The most important part of successfully growing passion fruit is keeping it regularly watered. With constant water and monthly fertilizing with 10-5-20, the vines can almost constantly bear fruit. Pruning is necessary to keep the vines from getting out of control. This plant is a vine with great clinging and climbing capabilities. It binds to almost any support it can find. It can grow twenty feet a year.

Passion fruit usually only lives a from five to seven years. The main pest is nematodes. Passion fruit is easily picked as when it ripens it drops. Hopefully you won't have passion fruit loving dogs as we do. Ten pounds of fruit per vine is a good harvest. Each fruit makes a small amount of very pungent, concentrated juice. The flavor of the passion fruit is sweet-tart, guavalike, and musky.

The fruit should stay good in the fridge for two weeks while you organize enough to make the tasty juice. A half-cup of juice has fifty calories with one gram of protein and eleven grams carbohydrates. It is a good source of vitamins A and C.

Passionate Ice

Ingredients: two cups milk, half cup strained passion fruit juice, half cup sugar, quarter cup fresh lime juice. Sugar content can be adjusted to taste.

Method: In a small skillet on low heat, stir the sugar into the milk until it completely dissolves. Permit to cool before adding the juices. Pour into a suitable container and freeze for three hours. Remove from freezer and place in blender until smooth. Return to container and freeze. This blending removes some of the ice crystals. Rum or vodka may be added to this before blending and refreezing.

Passion and Cashew Salad Dressing

Ingredients: quarter cup passion fruit juice, third cup olive oil, two TBS clear vinegar, quarter TS minced ginger, quarter TS mustard, half TS pepper sauce, quarter cup chopped cashews (peanuts may be substituted), salt and spices to taste

DID YOU KNOW?

The passion fruit has had a religious association as reflected by the name 'passion' given to it by Catholic missionaries who thought certain parts of the fruit bore some religious connections. These missionaries used the fruit to illustrate the crucifixion to the local Amerindians. Botanically it is *passiflora edulis*. Other names for this fruit are granadilla (granadilla means little pomegranate because of the numerous seeds), parcha, parchita, parchita maracuyá - Spanish; in Portuguese- maracuja peroba; in French - grenadille, or couzou; in Hawaiian- lilikoi; and in Jamaica - mountain sweet cup. The purple form may be called purple, red, or black granadilla. The yellow fruit is widely known as yellow passion fruit. The seeds are edible and you can eat the orange pulp straight from the shell.

Method: In a container that will seal, mix passion juice, pepper sauce, cashews, ginger, spices and oil. Shake vigorously and use over a salad of greens or watercress.

Passionate Fish from the Coal Pot

Ingredients: one cup passion fruit juice, half cup soy sauce, two TBS sugar, one medium three to five pound salmon cut in four pieces - or pieces of king or carite, one cup finely sliced onions, half cup chopped chives, quarter cup sliced celery, half cup sliced carrots, two TBS minced garlic, half TS pepper sauce salt and spice to taste, eight nice banana leaves

Method: Light your barbecue grill or coal pot. In a small skillet on medium heat mix the soy sauce with sugar stirring for three minutes. Lay out a banana leaf and place the fish on it. Coat the fish with the soy sauce and cover with onions, carrots, ginger, and garlic. Using only half a cup, sprinkle each piece of fish with passion fruit juice. Completely wrap the fish with the banana leaf and then wrap it in a second leaf to seal in the flavor. If the grill is very hot, give each side ten minutes. Uncover and sprinkle the remaining passion fruit juice on the cooked fish. Serve on a bed of rice.

Lovers Cheesecake

Ingredients: one cup crushed passion fruit skinned with seeds removed, one pie shell – made or store bought, one and a half pound cream cheese, one cup sugar, two TBS corn starch, one TS real vanilla essence, three eggs, three quarters cup sour cream,

Method: Blend cream cheese with the sugar until it is velvety. Thoroughly blend in cornstarch and eggs. Mix in the sour cream and vanilla before adding the crushed passion fruit. Pour mixture into the pie shell and bake for ninety minutes. Cool before refrigerating. This must be well chilled, best overnight. Cover so it does not acquire tastes or smells from the fridge.

Romance Cake

Ingredients: one package cake yellow or white follow directions, but add one TS vanilla extract, three passion fruit seeded, skinned and crushed.

Method: Combine all ingredients and bake per box directions. Test with a toothpick or knife to be certain it is thoroughly baked.

HEALTH NOTE

In Madeira, the juice of passion fruits is used to stimulate appetites and as treatment for gastric cancer. In Puerto Rico, where the fruit is known as 'parcha', it is widely believed to lower blood pressure. Fresh passion fruit is high in beta carotene, potassium, vitamin C, and dietary fiber.

Gardening is cheaper than therapy and you get tomatoes.
Author Unknown

PUMPKIN

Pumpkin is the Caribbean's most popular member of the squash family. Last year Trinidad produced almost five million kilos of pumpkin. Pumpkins are grown all continents except Antarctica. They are even grown in Alaska and Siberia. Pumpkins originated in Central America. Seeds from related plants have been found in Mexico, dating back over 7000 years.

Native Amerindians used pumpkin centuries before the Europeans arrived. Pumpkins soon became a staple in the explorers' diets. They returned to Europe, where they became a new foodstuff. Early settlers used pumpkins for stews, soups, and desserts. In addition to cooking, the New World Europeans also dried the shells and cut strips to weave into floor mats. The settlers learned from the natives to make pumpkin pie by filling a hollowed out shell with milk, honey and spices; then baking it.

Pumpkins should be planted on mounds about a foot high to increase drainage from the roots. Because pumpkins vine, they require a minimum of fifteen square feet per seed mound. Plant three to four seeds per mound seeds one inch deep (four or five seeds per hill). Allow 5 to 6 feet between hills, spaced in rows six feet apart. When the young plants are well established, thin each hill to the best two or three plants, and kept free from weeds by hoeing and shallow cultivation. Irrigate if an extended dry period occurs in early summer. Pumpkins will tolerate short periods of hot, dry weather. A long dry period will cause small fruits, however a hard rain after a dry period will cause the fruit to split open. A long wet period will cause the fruit to rot.

Bees are necessary for pollinating squash and pumpkins, and may be killed by insecticides. When insecticides are used, they should be applied only in late afternoon or early evening when the blossoms have closed for the day and bees are no longer visiting the blossoms. As new blossoms open each day and bees land only inside the open blossoms, these pollinating insects should be safe from contact with any potentially deadly sprays. Cut pumpkins from the vines carefully, using pruning shears or a sharp knife and leave 3 to 4 inches of stem attached. Snapping the stems from the vines results in many broken or missing 'handles'. Pumpkins without stems usually do not keep well. Wear gloves when harvesting fruit because many varieties have sharp prickles on their stems.

One cup of cooked pumpkin has 24 calories, with one gram of protein. The orange-flesh is a dead giveaway that pumpkin is a source of beta-carotene, which is a powerful antioxidant. Beta-carotene is converted to vitamin A in the body. Vitamin A is essential for healthy skin, vision, bone development, and many other functions. Pumpkin is also a tasty source of carbohydrates and potassium. They are also high in fiber. Eating pumpkin seeds helps men avoid prostrate cancer. They were once recommended as a cure for freckles and a cure for snakebites. Pumpkins are used to make pumpkin butter, pies, custard, bread, cookies, and soup.

Pumpkin Seeds

A great healthy snack.

Ingredients – Pumpkin seeds, salt, and spice to taste.

Method: Wash seeds. In a pot of water dissolve two TBS salt and spices – hot pepper, curry or geera (cumin) - whatever is your taste. Bring to a boil and add seeds. Simmer for fifteen minutes. Drain, add more salt/spice if desired, and bake in a 350 oven for ten minutes. Eat them as a great snack. (Use less salt or add sugar).

DID YOU KNOW?

The world's largest pumpkin was 1,725 pounds grown in the US in 2009. The U.S. grew 1.1 billion pounds of pumpkin production in 2007, and 99% of all those pumpkins were sold for decorations. Americans don't eat, but rather carve faces in pumpkins for All Hallows Eve. (Halloween). The tradition originally started with the carving of turnips by Irish immigrants. They found pumpkins easier to carve for the ancient holiday. Pumpkins are about 90% water. Its name is from the medieval French word 'pompom', meaning 'cooked by the sun.' Pumpkins belong to the *cucurbitaceae* family and most tropical versions are *cucurbita mixta*.

Pumpkin Broccoli Chowder

Ingredients: three cups fresh pumpkin puree, three TBS olive oil, one large onion chopped, one TBS soy sauce, one ripe tomato diced, one large potato diced, four cups chicken stock - canned or fresh, one bunch broccoli - tops cut into small florets - stems into thin strips, , one TBS syrup or honey, half cup canned evaporated skim milk

Method: In a skillet, heat olive oil over medium-low heat. Add onions and sauté slowly for three minutes. Add soy sauce and diced tomatoes, and cook stirring often until tomato's juice has evaporated - about 5 minutes. Transfer sauté to a soup pot. Deglaze the skillet with a little stock, add to pot, and add remaining stock and pumpkin puree. Heat, stirring often. In a separate pot cook diced potato in half cup boiling water until tender. When done, using a slotted spoon, transfer to soup pot. Add the broccoli to potato cooking liquid and blanch for 4 minutes, covered. Add broccoli and cooking liquid to soup pot. Then stir in enough milk to desired consistency. Season with salt and pepper to taste. Let soup cook over low heat, stirring occasionally, until hot and the flavors have blended, 8 to 10 minutes. Do not let soup boil. Serve hot. As an entree, serves four.

Curried Pumpkin Soup

Ingredients: one cup grated pumpkin, one medium onion chopped, three cloves garlic minced, one TBS Madras curry powder, two TBS butter or margarine, two cups chicken broth, one TBS cornstarch, one and a half cups milk, one bay leaf, salt and spice to taste

Method: In a large soup pot sauté onion and garlic in butter, add curry powder for three minutes. Add pumpkin, bay leaf, salt and spices, add broth and boil. Reduce heat and simmer for ten minutes. In a next small pot add cornstarch to the mix and heat until cornstarch is dissolved. Add to pumpkin mixture and cook until mixture has thickened and is bubbling. Remove bay leaf. Serves 4. (Add whatever garden veggies you may enjoy.)

Pumpkin Bread

Ingredients: two cups cooked pumpkin mashed, half cup canola oil, two cups sugar (half if you desire), one egg, one TBS cinnamon, one TS salt, two TS baking soda (not powder), two and a half cup bakers flour, (Optional – half cup raisins, peanuts, or coconut)

Method: Mix all ingredients until batter is smooth. Fill greased bread pans. Bake at 350 degrees for 90 minutes. Watch after an hour as small baking pans will cook faster.

Pumpkin Pancakes (Fritters)

Ingredients: one cup bakers flour, one cup boiled mashed pumpkin, one TBS sugar, one cup milk, two eggs, two TBS baking soda, two TBS oil, one TS cinnamon, salt to taste

Method: Combine all dry ingredients in a good-sized bowl. In another bowl mix wet ingredients. Then mix dry and wet together. An electric mixer will save effort. Spoon batter on a greased griddle or skillet and cook both sides until golden brown. Top with stewed pumpkin.

HEALTH NOTE

Pumpkin has alpha-carotene and beta-carotene, which are potent antioxidants and the body converts them to vitamin A. Vitamin A promotes healthy vision and ensures proper immune system function. The beta-carotene in pumpkin may also reverse skin damage caused by the sun and act as an anti-inflammatory for sore muscles and joints.

SUMMER SQUASH / ZUCCHINI

My family never grew squash so I didn't get the chance to enjoy it until I was a teenager. My aunt bought two and fried them the same as pumpkin. The squash cooked firmer and I liked it better than its orange cousin.

Squash is separated into summer and winter types. Caribbean islanders are accustomed to winter squash such as the butternut. The long season, odd-shaped, hard skinned squash that store well are usually referred to as winter squash. Smaller, short season types, which are eaten before the skin and seeds begin to thicken are the summer squashes. They have a mild somewhat nutty taste that resembles corn.

The most common summer squash is zucchini squash that usually has smooth, thin dark green skin and creamy white flesh. Crooknecks with yellow skin and white flesh and white saucer-shaped patty pan or scalloped squash are other common varieties of summer squash, but seldom seen in Trinidad. Botanically summer squash are *c. pepo*.

Modern day squash developed from the wild squash, which originated 10,000 years ago in an area of southern Mexico. Squash developed varieties and a better taste as it spread throughout the Western Hemisphere. Squash comes from the Massachuset Indian word askutasquash, which means, „eaten raw or uncooked". Christopher Columbus brought squash back to Europe, and Portuguese and Spanish explorers took squash to the rest of the world. Presently China and Japan are the largest squash growers in the world.

Zucchini is a member of the cucumber and melon family. Although zucchini has been grown in Central America for thousands of years modern zucchini was developed in Italy.

Squash will grow in almost any well-drained garden. One or two plants should be enough to supply any family. Be certain you have first generation seeds as cross pollination of last year's crop may give you a surprise this year. Second generation squash seeds may produce pumpkins. Since squash has shallow roots, prepare six inch high mounds about three feet apart by forking the soil. Place a shovel of rotted manure in the base. Plant four seeds about one inch below the surface. Use a fungicide every two weeks for the first six weeks to prevent powdery mildew. Just as the squash begins to vine, carefully pull dirt and mould the roots. Cucumber beetles and white fly are common pests that must be treated with chemicals. Water regularly and use a high nitrogen fertilizer mix every other week.

DID YOU KNOW?

The word zucchini comes from "zucca" the Italian word for squash. A zucchini has more potassium than a banana. Summer squash's magnesium has been shown to be helpful for reducing the risk of heart attack and stroke. Together with the potassium in summer squash, magnesium is also helpful for reducing high blood pressure.

Summer squash grow rapidly and should be ready to pick in ten days or les after flowering. These squash should be picked when they are immature and tender. It is best to use a knife to remove the fruit to not damage the vine.

Squash male blossoms can be eaten raw or cooked by dipping in a batter and frying. If you don't want to fry the male blossoms they are a delicious addition to any salad. Summer squash can be prepared on the barbecue grill, steamed, boiled, sautéed, fried, or stir fried. Squash combines excellently with onions, tomatoes, and okra in vegetable stews. Summer squash such as zucchini are low in calories with only 16 to a cup. Zucchini and crookneck squash are an excellent source for vitamins A and C, potassium, calcium, folate, and magnesium.

Handle summer squash delicately as small cuts in the skin can easily cause decay. Zucchini will keep about a week in the fridge. It can be frozen, but the flesh will get soft. Spices that go well with summer squash are marjoram, cumin seeds, parsley, dill, rosemary, chadon benee, and savory. Use them sparingly otherwise they will hide the real flavor of the squash.

Shredded or diced summer squash can be added to salads or sandwiches. They can also be steamed, boiled, baked, fried, and stuffed. Because squash are mostly water little is necessary to steam them in a covered pot.

Baked Zucchini

Ingredients: two medium zucchini (or other squash) washed and sliced, one medium onion chopped, two carrots shredded, one sweet pepper cored and chopped, two medium tomatoes chopped, two leaves or one TBS of sweet basil (or processed Italian seasoning), half hot pepper seeded and minced, two cloves of garlic minced, half cup cheddar cheese shredded (optional), salt and other spices to taste

Method: Mix all the vegetables and spices and pour into a casserole dish. Cover with cheese and bake at 350 degrees for 45 minutes. This same recipe can be used by splitting the zucchini or other squash lengthwise and coring the centers of seeds. Pour the vegetable mix into the cavity and cover with cheese. Depending on the size of the squash you may have to increase cooking time to one hour.

Cool Zucchini Soup

Ingredients: four medium zucchinis sliced a quarter inch thick, one large onion chopped, three cups water, half ripe avocado diced, one bunch chadon benee chopped, four TS lemon juice, half hot pepper seeded and minced, four cloves of garlic minced, half TS English/Worcestershire sauce, salt and spices to taste

Method: Place zucchini pieces, chopped onions, garlic, hot pepper, water and salt into a large – 6 quart pot and bring to a boil. Then simmer for 8 minutes. Cool before pouring into a blender. Blend until smooth. Add English sauce and the lemon juice and blend again. Chill for 3 hours before serving. Garnish each bowl with a few pieces of avocado and a pinch of chadon benee.

Zucchini and Banana Loafs

Ingredients: two cups grated zucchini, two cups mashed bananas, three eggs beaten, one cup brown sugar, four cups bakers flour, one TS cinnamon, one cup vegetable oil (canola preferred), one TS vanilla extract, one cup grated coconut

Method: Combine eggs, sugar, oil and vanilla in a large bowl. After this is mixed add zucchini, then slowly add the flour. Next add cinnamon, coconut, and bananas. After thoroughly mixing everything into a smooth batter, spoon into two greased bread pans and bake at 350 for at least 50 minutes. Cool, but zucchini bread is best served warm.

Zucchini and Lentils

Ingredients: one medium zucchini chopped, half cup lentils, two cups of water, half TS turmeric, three TBS butter or ghee, two cloves of garlic minced, half hot pepper seeded and minced, one TS ginger minced, half TS curry masala, salt and other spices to taste

Method: In a four quart pot place the washed lentils in the water with the turmeric and bring to a boil. Simmer for half an hour until the lentils are tender. In a large skillet heat the butter and brown the onion with the garlic. Add the pepper, ginger, and zucchini and cook for 5 minutes. Add the cooked lentils to the skillet stirring in the curry masala. Cook for 15 more minutes.

WATERMELON

Grandfather grew the sweetest watermelon only for the family and friends to enjoy. My cousins and I collected the seeds, and sewed them in cloth bags to play scooch. Scooch was just the local name for pelting each other with these bags. The watermelon seeds would sting ya!

Watermelon originated in the deserts of Southern Africa. Egyptian hieroglyphics depict the earliest watermelon harvest on tomb walls dating back 5000 years. Watermelons were left in tombs as food to nourish the dearly departed in the afterlife. Merchant ships spread watermelons throughout countries along the Mediterranean Sea. African slaves brought watermelon to the Caribbean.

Watermelons, *citrullus lanatus*, require a good sandy soil and should be planted at least four feet apart in rows six feet apart, in beds raised six to twelve inches to allow for drainage. Watering should be done by soaking, not sprinkling, which damages the leaves. The vine of the watermelon plant branches in many directions, with numerous large leaves. The watermelon flower is not very showy and must be pollinated by honeybees, to produce fruit. Use a 20-10-10 fertilizer mix when they begin to vine, and 12-12-17-2 when flowering. It takes the watermelon plant eighty to ninety-five days to become full grown, and it is ready for harvest when the part of the rind touching the ground changes from white to pale yellow.

Watermelon is one of the best taste treats your garden can produce and it is nutritionally good for you. Watermelons are 92% water and are low in calories and very nutritious. Related to cucumbers, pumpkins, and squash, there are over 1,200 varieties of watermelon grown worldwide. Every part of a watermelon is edible, even the seeds and rinds. By weight, watermelon is the most-consumed melon in the world. Last year the United States grew and consumed over 2 billion kilos of watermelon. The leading commercial growers of watermelon include Russia, China, Turkey, Iran, and the United States. Trinidad produces over a million kilos of watermelon yearly. In 1990, Bill Carson, of Arrington, Tennessee, grew the largest watermelon at 262 pounds. That is still the record of the Guinness Book.

Watermelon is practically a multi-vitamin unto itself. Watermelon contains about 10% of the daily requirement of potassium, which helps regulate heart functions and normalize blood pressure. One wedge, or a quarter of a small melon, has 90 calories, 2 grams protein, 20 grams of carbohydrates, 1.5 grams of fiber, potassium, vitamins C and A. Watermelon is also high in disease fighting beta-carotene. Lycopene and beta-carotene work with plant chemicals, which are not found in vitamin/mineral supplements. Watermelon is the leader in lycopene among fresh fruits and vegetables. Watermelon contains such high concentrations of lycopene that regular consumption may help reduce the risks of prostate cancer.

Watermelon seeds contain 'cucurbocitrin' to aid in lowering blood pressure and improve kidney function. The sweet watermelon surprisingly has only half the sugar content (5 percent) of an apple. It tastes sweeter because the sugar is its main taste-producing agent.

> **DID YOU KNOW?**
>
> Watermelon is grown in over 96 countries worldwide. Watermelons are very fragile and cannot be harvested by machines. Instead they are carefully tossed by workers on a relay that runs between the fields and the truck. Every part of the watermelon, including the seeds and the rind are edible. Watermelons are ideal for the health as they do not contain any fat or cholesterol, are high in fiber content and vitamins A and C, and are also a good source of potassium. Eating watermelon will reduce inflammation that contributes to conditions like asthma, atherosclerosis, diabetes, colon cancer, and arthritis.

Watermelon Slush

All you need is a blender.

Ingredients: five cups watermelon with the seeds removed, one cup sugar syrup optional - boil one half cups water with one cup sugar for one minute and cool, two TBS fresh lime juice

Method: Put watermelon into a blender. Pour into a suitable sized baking dish 12 x 12. Stir in lime juice and syrup. Freeze until solid. Makes four servings. This slush will keep while covered in your freezer for three months.

Fried Watermelon

For those who don't count calories!

Ingredients: three cups of watermelon - seeded, and cut from the rind. The red flesh should be cut into squares or circles about an inch thick. One cup flour, quarter cup cornstarch, two egg whites beaten, and three cups oil for frying, powdered sugar.

Method: Coat watermelon shapes with flour. Mix egg whites and cornstarch with just enough water to make a thick batter. Heat the oil in a deep saucepan. Coat the watermelon pieces with the egg cornstarch batter and put into oil. Fry pieces until light brown. Remove and drain the melon pieces on a paper towel. Sprinkle with powdered sugar.

Three Day Pickled Watermelon Rind

Ingredients: two pounds watermelon rind cleaned of seeds and red flesh, two TBS pickling spice, two cups brown sugar, four cups distilled white vinegar, five cups water, one

TBS allspice, one TBS whole cloves, two TBS cinnamon

Method: Cut rind into one inch cubes. Mix pickling spice, cinnamon, cloves, allspice, and sugar with 4 cups water and one cup vinegar. Boil for five minutes. Then cover and soak rind pieces for a day. Drain liquid mixture from rind and reheat it. Then pour it over the rind again and let stand for another day and cover with two cups water mixed with one cup vinegar. Let stand overnight. Then boil all together for five minutes and allow to cool. Put into clean sealing bottles and refrigerate. If you want spicy pickles add half of a hot pepper minced to the initial mix.

Watermelon Colada

Ingredients: four cups watermelon - seeded and cubed, half cup water, two TBS brown sugar, one lime sliced, two TBS fresh mint, ice

Method: Combine watermelon, ice, and sugar in a blender and blend to the consistency you desire - smooth or chunky. Put a lime slice and a TS of mint leaves into every glass and squash with a spoon to release the flavors. Cover with the watermelon liquid and enjoy.

Tropical Salad

Ingredients: two cups watermelon seeded and chopped into half inch cubes, two ripe mangos chopped into half inch pieces, two ripe avocados chopped into half inch cubes, one small red onion chopped, one lime sliced thin, two TBS vinegar, half cup fresh orange juice, one TBS chadon benee minced, one TBS fresh lime juice, two TS olive oil, one TBS grated orange zest, quarter TS salt and black pepper to taste

Method: Pour orange juice into a large bowl. Stir in the olive oil and orange zest; season with pinch of teaspoon salt, and black pepper. Toss the watermelon, and mango in the dressing. Stir in the onions and chadon benee. Sprinkle avocado cubes with lime juice, and season another pinch of salt. Stir and cover with melon – mango combination. Garnish with lime slices.

When one has tasted watermelon he knows what the angels eat.
Mark Twain

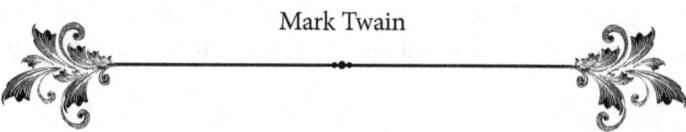

WINTER SQUASH

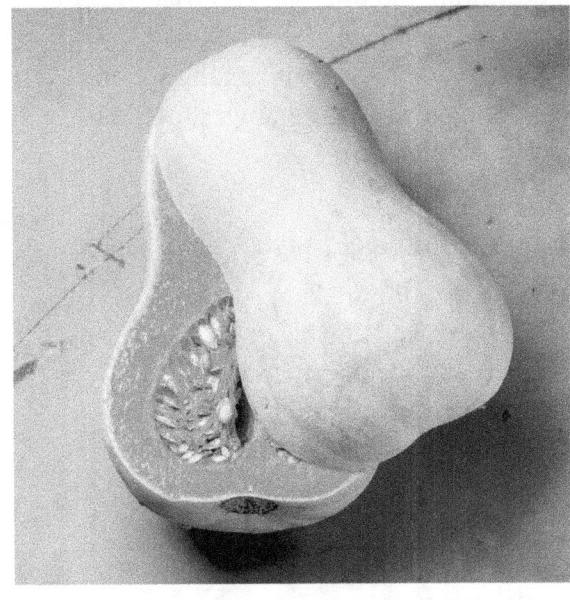

Caribbean farmers produce squash, yet few realize squash has summer and winter varieties. Two varieties of winter squash known and enjoyed in Trinidad are the cream-colored, sweet butternut, and the green skinned acorn. Botanists feel squash has grown in Central American for ten thousand years. The first squash were small and bitter, cultivated for only to the seeds. Over centuries the flesh fattened and sweetened until Columbus brought squash to Europe. Winter squash could be stored for months aboard ships, Portuguese and Spanish explorers introduced the world to the tasty squash. Today the world's largest producers of squash are China and Japan.

The hardest part of growing squash is locating the seeds. If you dry the seeds from local squash you may end up with pumpkins. This is because of cross-pollination. Otherwise growing squash is easy except for Trinidad's rain. Squash takes well to sandy soil. It is recommended to create rows of mounds, which are about two feet in diameter and six to ten inches high. This will permit excess water to drain from the root system. Too much water will cause the roots to rot. Plant four seeds per mound, each about an inch deep. It is wise to mark the center of the mound with a stake so the roots can be watered after the plant begins to vine because after the plant matures, water should not touch the leaves. Too much water will make the squash look as if it has melted. Slight fertilizer mix high in nitrogen should be used infrequently. Spray a pesticide as Pestac or Fastac every two weeks, but after ten AM as not to kill the pollinating bees.

Squash is ready to harvest when you can pierce the skin with your thumbnail and see the orange flesh. Stored properly in a cool dark place, squash should keep for three to four months. Consuming squash prevents against men's prostrate gland problems and reduces the risk of some types of cancers especially lung cancer and cancer of the colon. Squash has such high vitamin A content it may prevent emphysema.

One cup of cooked squash has one hundred and fifty per cent of the daily requirement of vitamin A, a third of the vitamin C necessary daily, and a quarter of the potassium needed. A cup of cooked squash has only eighty calories, plenty of fiber, plenty of manganese, folic acid, vitamin B1, and even copper. Winter squash, such as the butternut, can be stored in your fridge's vegetable drawer for months, but eating it fresh from the garden is best.

Squash is an easy vegetable to prepare. Washing is always necessary; yet peeling depends on the recipe. It can be boiled, or baked. Squash is an excellent addition to soups. It can also be peeled, grated, mixed with a little flour and one egg, and fried as cakes. Squash can be cubed and steamed then mixed with a tablespoon each of olive oil, grated ginger root and soy sauce.

Easiest Baked Squash

Wash acorn or butternut squash. Cut off the stem end and clean out cavity of seeds and membrane. Rub interior with spices as cinnamon and nutmeg – perhaps maple syrup or brown sugar, or salt and pepper depending on your taste. Wrap in foil and put in a 350 degree oven for 45 minutes. Serve one squash per person.

Pineapple Squash

Ingredients: one large butternut or acorn squash - peeled, seeded, and cubed, two TS cinnamon, one TS nutmeg, half TS allspice, half TS fresh grated ginger, half cup crushed pineapple

DID YOU KNOW?

The word "squash" comes from "askutasquash," which literally means "a green thing eaten raw" in the language of the native Americans in present-day Rhode Island, portions of Connecticut, and Massachusetts. Types of winter squash include: acorn, amber cup, autumn cup, Australian blue squash, baby boo pumpkin, banana, butternut, buttercup, calabash, calabaza or West Indian squash, carnival, delicate, cheese wheels or cheese pumpkin, crookneck, cucuzza – louki or Italian squash, eight-ball squash, fairytale pumpkin, gold ball squash, gold nugget, gooseneck squash, hubbard, kabocha, lumina squash, pattypan or sunburst squash, pebbled or warty, red kuri squash or uchiki kuri squash, spaghetti, sweet dumpling, sweet potato squash, and turban.

Method: Boil squash until soft. In a bowl mix all ingredients. Place in a baking dish and put in a 350 degree oven for five minutes. Serve hot.

Squash and Oats

Ingredients: two large butternut squash - peeled, seeded, and cubed, half cup butter or margarine, two cups oats, quarter cup brown sugar, quarter cup grated coconut, half cup water

Method: Boil squash until tender. Put squash in a baking dish. In a bowl mix all other ingredients and cover squash. Put squash mix in a 350 degree oven for 30 minutes.

Baked Squash Italian Style

Ingredients: two nice sized squash - washed and halved, one cup cheddar cheese grated, two TBS butter or margarine, two TBS olive oil, one medium sweet green pepper seeded and chopped, three bunches chives chopped, two cloves garlic minced, two leaves fresh oregano and sweet basil chopped fine or two TBS dried Italian spice mix, quarter cup tomato sauce (ketchup may be substituted), four tomatoes chopped, quarter hot pepper

minced, salt and spices to taste

Method: Remove seeds and membrane from squash halves. In a large pot boil halves for fifteen minutes. Allow cooling before handling. Smear butter around the cavity. Then sprinkle half of the oregano-basil or Italian spice into the squash halves. Place haves in a baking dish. In a skillet heat oil and sauté garlic, chives, and peppers until just browning. Mix in tomatoes and fill squash. Pour tomato sauce over them and cover with cheese. Bake at 375 degrees for 30 minutes. Raise heat to 425 and bake for 10 additional minutes until cheese browns.

Squash and Chicken Soup

Ingredients: two chicken breasts or six thighs chopped, one and a half pounds squash (or pumpkin) peeled and sliced, half hot pepper seeded and minced (optional), two TBS canola oil, two TBS fresh lime juice, one onion chopped, two cloves of garlic, two tomatoes chopped, half packet of coconut milk, one quart of water, salt and spice to taste

Method: In a large pot, heat oil and sauté onions and garlic before adding chicken chunks. Cook over medium heat for ten minutes. Pour in water, limejuice, salt, and spices. Boil, then simmer for fifteen minutes. Add tomatoes, squash, coconut, and stir to a boil. Serve hot.

HEALTH NOTE

Most winter squash varieties, *c. pepo, c. maxima* & *c. moschata*, have beta-carotene content to rival the content of mangoes and cantaloupe. That helps fight against cancer, heart disease, and cataracts. Generally, the richer the color, the richer the beta-carotene concentration. Beta-carotene may also reduce lung inflammation and emphysema. Winter squash also contain beneficial amounts of vitamin C, potassium, and fiber, which fills you up, not out. All squash are technically fruit because they contains seeds. Low in fat, winter squash deliver a good dose of dietary fiber, making it an exceptionally heart-friendly choice. It provides significant amounts of potassium, important for bone health, and vitamin B6, essential for the proper functioning of both the nervous and immune systems. Winter squash is not known to have any negative effects. It does not have any allergic effects. It is not even found to contain pesticide residues.

The glory of gardening: hands in the dirt, head in the sun, heart with nature. To nurture a garden is to feed not just on the body, but the soul.

Alfred Austin

NOTES

Nuts

The term 'nut' is applied to many seeds that are not botanically true nuts. Any large, oily kernel found within a shell and used in food may be considered a nut. While a wide variety of dried seeds and fruits are called nuts, only a certain number are considered truly nuts. Nuts are an important source of nutrients for both humans and wildlife. All nuts are seeds, but not all seeds are nuts. Nuts are both the seed and the fruit, and cannot be separated. Seeds come from fruit, and can be removed from the fruit, like almonds, cashews, walnuts, and pistachios, which were once inside fruit.

Because nuts generally have high oil content, they are a highly prized food and energy source. A large number of seeds are edible by humans and used in cooking, eaten raw, sprouted, or roasted as a snack food, or pressed for edible oils and cosmetics. Nuts or seeds are also a significant source of nutrition for wildlife.

Nuts are cholesterol-free. Unless salt is added to nuts, they naturally contain, at most, just a trace of sodium. Nuts can be used in many ways. Whole, flaked, and ground nuts and nut butters are widely available. Nuts can be added to sweet dishes, cakes, and biscuits. Nut butters can be added to soups and stews to thicken them. Nuts, including both tree nuts and peanuts, are among the most common food allergies.

Consumption of various nuts such as almonds and walnuts can lower serum LDL or 'bad' cholesterol. One study found that people who eat nuts live two to three years longer than those who do not. However, this may be because people who eat nuts tend to eat less junk food and be more conscious of their weight. Nuts may be enjoyed simply, eaten out of hand. You don't have to get out your cookbook to enjoy nuts. The essence of eating healthy with nuts is not to over indulge.

The home gardener is part scientist, part artist, part philosopher, part plowman. He modifies the climate around his home.

John R. Whiting

ALMONDS

Almonds grow throughout the Caribbean. When we go to the beach, I gather a bucket of the sweet nut to shell later. Throughout the world almonds are the most widely-grown and eaten tree nut, cultivated for thousands of years before they acquired their original name of, 'the Greek nut'. Botanists consider almonds a fruit, and part of the plum family originally native to the area surrounding the Mediterranean. Primitive man prized these tasty nuts as a food staple since it kept well. According to anthropologists early nomads created a trail mix of ground almonds, chopped dates, rolled with sesame oil into little balls. By 4,000 B.C., humans learned to cultivate almonds and grown by almost every ancient civilization. Several handfuls of almonds were found in King Tut's tomb, to nourish him on his journey into the here after.

To grow almonds, first decide if you have enough space for a sizeable tree far away from your septic tank. Search around a mature tree, usually near the beaches, for a sprouted nut. The almond is extremely adaptable. Because it has a deep root system the almond can withstand severe drought, and poor soils, but the roots will seek a constant water source like your septic or soak-away. Always put bat chat (ant) bait close to young trees. Those big ants will eat all the new leaves, and kill, or stunt the new tree. To gain the maximum yield from your almond tree spray every other month with a soluble 20-20-20 fertilizer mixed with a light pesticide. Monthly broadcast a cup of 12-12-17-2 blue fertilizer around the base of the tree. In the dry season water the tree soaking the ground every other week. To try and contain the size of the tree you might cut (or top) the center stem of the tree after about three years. It is best to top trees on the full moon. This will make the lower branches grow out, but it should not get any taller.

Almonds contain the most dietary fiber of any nut or seed, with 3 grams of fiber per ounce; and are a good source of protein. One ounce of almonds contains about 10 percent of the recommended daily allowance of calcium, a great non-dairy source for vegetarians. Almonds are rich in vitamin E, with just a handful (30g, about 20 nuts) providing 85% of the Recommended Daily Intake (RDI). Vitamin E is a fat-soluble vitamin and antioxidant. One ounce of almonds has 160 calories with 15 grams of fat, 3 grams of fiber, 6 grams of protein, and 6 grams of carbohydrates, yet amazingly no cholesterol. Almonds are good eating nuts, high in monounsaturated fatty acids, and actually lower your cholesterol level, reducing risk of heart disease. Almonds contain significant amounts of magnesium, vitamin E, fiber, and potassium, all of which are beneficial to a healthy heart. Almonds are loaded with flavoids in the nut's skin and they are antioxidants linked to improving breathing. In fact, scientists believe these chemicals may even prevent found in almonds and certain other protects smokers from respiratory diseases such as asthma, emphysema, and chronic bronchitis. Almonds are also a significant source of magnesium and potassium, which contributes to strong bones.

Almonds are sold raw or natural, roasted, or dry-roasted. Almonds are roasted (deep fried) in oil usually (bad) highly saturated coconut oil. The process adds about ten calories per ounce of nuts, or a little more than a gram of fat (mostly saturated fat, if coconut oil is used). Dry -roasted almonds are not cooked in oil and better for your health, but they may be salted or contain other ingredients, such as corn syrup, sugar, starch, MSG, and preservatives. I've found that the best way to 'patch' raw almonds, is to toast them in a dry skillet over low heat, stirring frequently, until golden and fragrant, about five minutes. Remember, remove the almonds immediately from the skillet or they're likely to scorch with a burnt taste. You can also toast almonds in a baking pan in a 350°F oven for 10 minutes. Slivered and sliced almonds will take less time than whole almonds. Blanched almonds are briefly heated in boiling water and then shocked in cold water to stop the cooking, which kills enzymes that would cause them to deteriorate.

> **DID YOU KNOW?**
>
> Almonds are actually stone fruits related to cherries, plums, and peaches. California produces almost a billion pounds of almonds yearly. It takes more than 1.2 million bee hives to pollinate California's almond crop (over 550,000 acres). Chocolate manufacturers currently use 40 percent of the world's almonds. The botanical name for almonds is *prunus amygdalus*.

Almonds are a tasty addition to any curried dish and can be mixed with chilled, cooked rice and raisins to make an easy and tasty salad. To make delicious almond flavoured 'milk' place one-cup fresh roasted almonds with 4 cups water in a jar. Tightly screw on the lid and refrigerate for one or two days, but no longer as it may begin to ferment. Blend until smooth.

Almond One Pot Nutritious Stir Fry

Ingredients: half cup blanched almonds, six cups assorted vegetables (bodi, carrots, onions, cabbage, cauliflower, etc) chopped small and thin, two TBS fresh ginger root minced, two garlic cloves chopped, third cup water, two TBS cornstarch, one TS sesame oil, three TBS soy sauce, three cups cooked rice (prefer brown), three TBS cooking oil, salt and spices to taste

Method: In a large skillet, wok, or frying pan heat half of the canola oil – one and a half TBS - on medium heat, add almonds and garlic and cook for five minutes. Remove almonds and garlic carefully with a spoon and set aside. Add rest of the canola oil, increase the heat to high, and then add ginger and vegetables. Stir fry for five minutes and reduce heat to medium. Mix the cornstarch, soy sauce, and water in a bowl and pour over vegetables. Toss for two minutes over medium heat. Mix in seasonings, sesame oil, almonds, and rice.

Almond Shark

Ingredients: half cup slivered almonds, one pound shark or firm fish fillets - cut into nice size pieces, two TBS butter or margarine, two TBS parsley chopped, two TBS lemon juice, salt and seasonings to taste

Method: In a frying pan lightly brown the almonds in the heated butter and remove. Combine parsley, lemon juice, your seasonings, and rub shark pieces. Fry shark. As it cooks spoon the remaining mixture over the pieces. Do not overcook. Sprinkle the cooked shark with the almonds. Serve with rice or pasta.

Coconut and Almond Rice

Ingredients: one ounce crushed almonds, two cups low fat milk, two cups uncooked rice, half cup coconut milk, quarter TS salt, and seasonings to your taste

Method: Put almonds in a plastic bag and crush with a spoon. In a medium pot bring milk and salt to a boil before adding rice. Reduce heat, cover and cook till rice is done. Add coconut milk, remove cover and simmer for five minutes. Stir in almonds with a for to fluff the rice.

Hot Almond Chicken (or Fish)

Ingredients: half chicken cut up skin removed, quarter cup slivered almonds, quarter cup sesame seeds, two cups cornflakes, two TBS brown sugar, one cup milk, six TBS butter or margarine, half hot pepper seeded and minced. two eggs, salt and seasoning to taste

Method: In a heated frying pan toast the sesame seeds and almond slivers. Remove and cool before mix in a plastic bag with cornflakes, hot pepper, sugar, salt and seasonings. Close the bag forcing out all of the air. Crush contents with a spoon or rolling pin. In a bowl stir milk and eggs together to make a wash. Have crushed cornflake mixture in a flat dish. Dip chicken first in the egg and then roll in the crushed flakes. In a large frying pan heat butter and gently put in the coated chicken, careful not to lose some of the flakes coating. Fry each side for five minutes or less, until it is golden brown and crunchy.

BRAZIL NUTS

I first encountered Brazil nuts (islanders call walnuts), on a trip to Biche. 'Take a right turn at the huge walnut tree' was the main direction to a tract of land in wild eastern part of Trinidad. We found several of the big pods and smashed one open to enjoy the raw nuts. Researching the Brazil (walnut) nut provided some insight of the importance wilderness is to this tree.

Big, reaching a hundred and fifty feet tree and up to six feet in diameter, a Brazil nut tree isn't exactly perfect for every backyard because of its size and long root system. Instead it is perfect for an estate, or even better just to know where one is at and visit when the seeds are ripe. Planting a Brazil (walnut) tree could become a time capsule as they can live for more than five hundred years. (Some trees in remote Brazilian highlands are estimated to have existed for a thousand years!) A seed picking picnic under its shading branches would be an excellent day.

Brazil nuts aren't considered a true nut, but instead the seed of the Bertholletia excels species. They're called Brazil nuts because they're from the Amazon non-flooding rain forest. Amazingly these trees do not take to easy cultivation. Brazil nuts come almost entirely from collectors in the wild. There are very few Brazil nut tree plantations. In fact more Brazil nuts come from Bolivia than Brazil. More than twenty thousand tons of these nuts are harvested each year. Bolivia collects about half, Brazil forty per cent, and Peru ten per cent.

The Brazil nut produces better in the wild than cultivated because they depend on the complexity of nature more than other trees. Their pale white blossoms have very sweet nectar, but it is protected by a cover flap on the blossom. This must be pollinated by large bodied bees with very long tongues. All these circumstances and necessities are only available in the wilderness. Small, long-tongues male bees use the scent of the sweet nectar to attract large bodied, long -tongued orchid bees, which eventually pollinates the Brazil nut blossoms. This is Mother Nature at her best. Without the blossoms, the bees do not mate. A lack of bees means the trees won't get pollinated and no Brazil nuts. The pods take more than a year to mature after pollination. This 'natural' system is a bit too complex for many cultivators.

The Brazil nut tree is actually grown from one of the seeds inside the nuts. Again Mother Nature is at her best as these trees occur naturally in the wilderness. The huge pod drops under the shade tree, and is often chewed open by an animal like the agouti to eat some of the rich nuts. Some of the remaining nut / seeds germinate in the shade and actually

> ### DID YOU KNOW?
> Brazil nuts are so rich in oil they will burn like a candle when lit. The oil is often used in shampoos, soaps, hair conditioners. These nuts are also called para nut, walnut, butternut, cream nut, or castanea. Brazil is named after a tree, but not this nut tree.

sprout and never develop until a tree falls and provides the necessary exposure to sunlight for growth. This wait could be a decade. Once the conditions are right after six years, the trees begin to produce fruit. Brazil nut oil is also used to oil clocks, an ingredient in artists' paints, and in the cosmetics industry.

Cutting of Brazil nut trees is prohibited by law in Brazil, Bolivia and Peru. Because of the length of time these trees survive and their unique station in nature, Brazil nut trees should be protected everywhere. Illegal cutting of timber and slash and burn clearing of land is a continual threat.

Eight Brazil nuts equal a whopping hundred and eighty calories with 18 grams of fat, 4 grams of protein, 3 grams of carbohydrates, and very significant amounts of magnesium and thiamine. Brazil nuts are an excellent source of selenium, a vital mineral and antioxidant that may help prevent heart disease. Two Brazil nuts can provide your entire daily intake of selenium. Brazil nuts are particularly healthy because selenium makes their protein content 'complete'. This means that, unlike most plant proteins from beans etc, the proteins contained in Brazil nuts have all the necessary amino acids for optimal growth in humans just like meat and fish. Brazil nuts also contain small amounts of radioactive radium. This is not because of elevated levels of radium in the soil, but due to the incredibly developed roots of the tree. The radium is not dangerous. There are high amounts of fat in brazil nuts. The fats are unsaturated, and healthy when eaten in moderation. Eight medium Brazil nuts count as one serving, an ounce. Since these nuts are relatively high in fat, you shouldn't eat them more than three times per week. Buy and crack open a pod of fresh Brazil / walnuts and roast them yourself on a baking tray at 350 for a five minutes. Once you have the roasted nuts you must try some recipes.

Brazil Nut Bread Pudding

Ingredients: six slices toasted bread buttered, cut into inch long strips, half cup Brazil nuts sliced or chopped very small (crushed almonds may be substituted), two large eggs, quarter cup sugar, pinch of salt, one TS vanilla essence, two cups whole milk

Method: Arrange bread pieces in layers in buttered baking dish, sprinkling each layer with Brazil nuts. Beat eggs slightly, add sugar, salt, vanilla, and milk. Mix well and pour over bread. Sprinkle top with Brazil nuts and bake in a 325 degree oven for one hour.

Brazil Nut and Brown Rice Salad

Ingredients : Salad - one pound cooked brown long grain rice, one pound Brazil nuts or almondsroasted and chopped, one cup spinach, one cup watercress, one large purple

Spanish onion chopped small, quarter raisins, one crisp apple chopped small, quarter cup parsley chopped, two bunches chives chopped., two TBS basil. Dressing - two TBS fresh lemon juice, quarter cup olive oil, two TBS white vinegar, juice of one orange, one TBS lemon zest

Method: In a large bowl add the spinach and water cress to the rice. add the onion, currants, apple, chopped nuts and herbs and mix well with the rice mixture. Whisk dressing ingredients together and pour over the rice and mix well.

Roasted Broccoli with Brazil Nut Pesto

Ingredients: quarter cup Brazil nuts chopped, half cup chopped parsley, two TBS water, one large clove of garlic minced, half cup fresh basil chopped, half TS lemon zest, quarter cup olive oil, four TBS Parmesan cheese grated, pinch of salt, two heads of broccoli cut into four inchlong florets, spices to your taste

Method: Mix the parsley, Brazil nuts, water, basil, garlic and lemon zest in a food processor and pulse to a coarse paste. Add the three quarters of the olive oil, salt, and the Parmesan and process to a slightly smooth paste. In an oven preheated to 450 degrees toss the broccoli with the remaining olive oil and spread in an even layer on rimmed baking sheets. Roast broccoli until the broccoli is browned and crisp-tender. Put the broccoli on a serving dish, pour the pesto on top, mix, and serve.

Quick Brazil Nut Soup

Ingredients: one cup Brazil nuts chopped into big pieces, one large onion chopped, four cups water, three quarter TS salt, eight medium tomatoes diced, vegetable/canola oil for frying.

Method: Sauté onion until tender. In medium pot add water, onion, and salt. Bring to a boil, reduce to simmer, before adding tomatoes and Brazil nut pieces. Simmer ten minutes and serve.

*People who will not sustain trees will soon live in
a world which cannot sustain people.*

Bryce Nelson

CASHEW

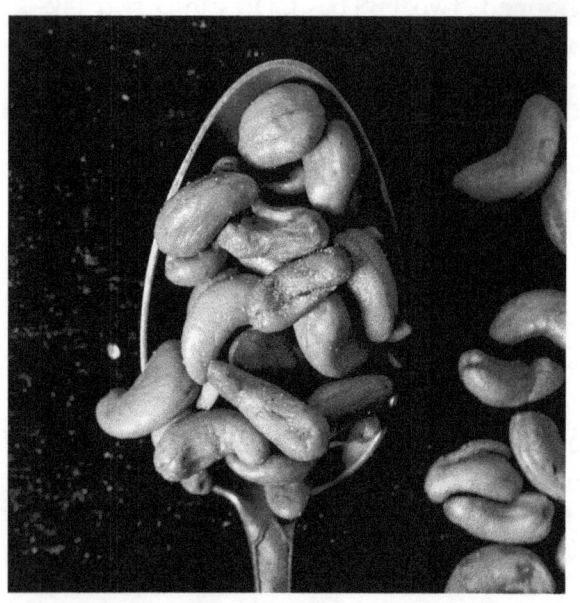

My wife thinks cashews are one of God's practical jokes and one of nature's strangest creations. It is an egg shaped brilliant yellow, orange, or red fruit atop a brown wrinkly attached nut; as if it were an afterthought. Related to the mango, this soft, juicy fruit is incredibly sweet, but the raw nut is severely bitter. Portuguese explorers discovered the trees, which they called 'caju', in northeastern Brazil and transported the original cashews to Africa's east coast shortly after Columbus. Africans cultivated the trees for the nuts, which they sold back to the Portuguese. They shipped the nuts to India to be shelled and roasted. India soon took over cashew cultivation and now is the world's largest exporter of the delicious nuts with Brazil second, and Africa third. Together they produce 200,000,000 pounds a year.

The cashew fruit or 'apple' is really a false fruit that develops from the blossom. The nut is really the cashew seed. You will never see cashews sold in the shell. The nut is surrounded by a double shell that contains a caustic resin, which is a potent skin irritant and toxin also found in poison ivy. The delicious apple is seldom sold since they are too fragile to market spoiling within a day. The apples contain tannin and begin to ferment immediately. East Indians prepare the fruit into liquor they call 'fenny'. Juice of the cashew fruit will badly stain clothes.

Cashew makes a beautiful garden tree usually growing to less than twenty feet tall. Find a tree vendor, or visit with an owner of a cashew estate. You can try to sprout a tree from a raw nut; good luck. With regular watering and monthly doses of high nitrogen fertilizer mix, trees should bear in five years. Cashews have a good local market, however getting the nuts are not easy. First you have to pick and twist the nut from the usually discarded fruit. Try to avoid staining your clothes from the fruit juice. Then the nuts must be shelled, and parched or roasted. The fruit can be prepared into a marmalade jelly, or canned whole. To roast cashews at home, place nuts in a preheated oven at 175 degrees for twenty minutes. At room temperature cashew nuts spoil quickly since they contain much oil. Refrigerated nuts can remain for half a year.

Large-commercial cashew operations use the nutshells to make varnish, insecticide, paint, and even rocket lubricant. For this primary reason, cashews are never sold in the shell. Cashew Nutshell Liquid (CNSL) has been processed similar to petroleum since the 1930's. The solids are used to make automobile brake shoes, while the liquid is used in resins and epoxy coatings.

One ounce of cashew nuts has one hundred and fifty calories with twelve grams of fat, no cholesterol, and nine grams of carbs. Cashews have less total fat than peanuts or almonds, and more than half of their fat is unsaturated fatty acids. This unsaturated fatty acid is oleic acid, the same healthy mono-unsaturated fat found in olive oil. Oleic acid is good for the heart, even in diabetics. If you are health conscious, dry-roasted cashews have a lower fat content. Iron, copper, zinc, and magnesium are obtained from cashews. Count 15 cashews as a handful. For recipes, one pound of shelled cashews equals three cups.

It is easy to prepare a cashew version of peanut butter by just placing a pound of roasted nuts in food processor until you get the desired consistency of crunchy or creamy style. Cashews are a great addition to vegetable rices, salads, stir-fries, pastas, or steamed vegetable dishes. Always add the cashew nut after the cooking process is complete, as heat will cause the nuts to soften and dissolve. This softening is why other nuts are preferred to use for baking recipes rather than cashews.

DID YOU KNOW?

Cashews are one of the best-tasting nuts on earth and now rank #1 among nut crops in the world with 4.1 billion pounds. Also known as 'Wilberts', or the blister nut because it is related to poison ivy. The leaves, bark and cashew apple are antiseptic, stop diarrhea, reduce fever, lower blood sugar, blood pressure and body temperature. Cashew tree products have long been alleged to be effective anti-inflammatory agents, counter high blood sugar and prevent insulin resistance among diabetics. Cashew seed extract stimulates blood sugar absorption by muscle cells. Botanically cashew is *anacardium occidentale*.

Spirited Pine-Nut Soup

Ingredients: half pound cashew nuts chopped, one oz. salted butter or margarine, one red Spanish onion minced, one cup pineapple pieces without juice, two cloves of garlic chopped, four red potatoes peeled and diced, two cups vegetable bouillon, quarter cup dark rum (optional), two TBS cornstarch with four TBS water, two cups water, salt and spices to taste

Method: In a large skillet fry onion and garlic until soft. Add cashews, pineapple, rum, water, bouillon, and spices. Bring to a boil. Simmer on very low heat for thirty minutes. Stir cornstarch into the four TBS of water until smooth. Add to soup stirring constantly until mixture thickens.

Cashew Rice Special

Ingredients: quarter cup chopped cashews, one and a half cups brown rice, three cups water, quarter cup raisins, four cloves, one TS cinnamon, two TBS soft butter or margarine, two bay leaves, salt and other spices to taste

Method: Always rinse rice before cooking until the water is clear. In a suitable pot combine rice, water, cinnamon, cloves, bay leaf, and salt. Cover pot and bring to a boil, then cook on low for twenty minutes. Remove from heat, but keep covered for fifteen minutes. With a fork blend in butter, cashews, and raisins.

Cashew Chicken Casserole

Ingredients: one cup cashews, two cups chicken cooked and cubed, quarter cup chopped red Spanish onion, one cup celery chopped, one TBS butter or margarine, half cup chicken broth, four TBS soy sauce, two cups cooked chow mien noodles or brown rice, half hot pepper-seeded and minced (optional), half cup mushroom sliced, two TBS cornstarch, four TBS olive oil, one TS brown sugar, half bunch of pak choy shredded, salt and spice to taste

Method: This recipe is to be cooked in a wok as stirfry, stirring constantly over high heat. If you do not have a wok a large frying pan will be adequate. Place chopped chicken in a medium sized bowl and cover with two TBS soy and one TBS cornstarch mixture and refrigerate for half an hour. Heat two TBS oil in a large skillet, add chicken and fry for five minutes. Add chopped onion, hot pepper, and mushrooms and cook another three minutes. Empty the skillet to a bowl. Refresh skillet with two TBS oil, pak choy strips, and sugar. Cook for four minutes. Return chicken -onion mixture to the heated skillet with the pak choy. Stir one TBS of cornstarch into two remaining TBS soy sauce. Pour over chicken veggie mix. Add cashews and cover for one minute. Uncover and stir until sauce thickens. Pour mixture over chow mien noodles or cooked rice.

Nutty Tomato Sauce

Ingredients: four pounds diced plum tomatoes, one large onion chopped, one cup water, five cloves of minced garlic, one TS each fresh or dried marjoram, rosemary, and oregano leaves, one cup cashews chopped as small as possible, salt and spice to taste

Method: Bring water to boil in a large skillet. Add all ingredients. Cook on high, but stir frequently so it does not stick. After twenty minutes pour or spoon off excess liquid. Stir cashew pieces into sauce. Serve over noodles, rice, or vegetables.

No shade tree? Blame not the sun, but yourself.
Chinese proverb

COCONUTS

What would Caribbean cuisine be without coconuts? Peleau, and oil dong would be bland, pastries usual, and our rum strong. The coconut is one of nature's most useful trees. What would shade our beaches; where would we tie our hammocks; how would we make kalaloo without coconuts? Ocean currents have distributed floating nuts throughout the world and coconuts grow everywhere that has a true tropical climate. The nuts will only grow between 28 degrees north or south latitude, the closer to the equator the better. All the hundreds of varieties of coconuts belong to the same species.

Trees can grow to eighty feet or bear as short as six feet. The nuts can be red, yellow, orange, green, brown, or double.

The coconut's origin is a mystery. Scientists believe it was first grown over three thousand years ago in South East Asia, or northwestern South America. In ancient Sanskrit tablets the coconut is named 'kalpa vriksha', which means 'the tree that provides everything necessary for life'. Spanish explorers gave the common name, 'coco', which means monkey face, because of the three dark spots at the dry nuts' base look like a wide-eyed face. Botanically coconut is referenced *cocos nucifera*.

Coconuts may be harvested at different ages for different purposes. A young, six months old, nut has jelly inside, as the white meat has not yet formed. Since coconut water is sterile, it has been used intravenously as a substitute for glucose. Mature nuts are processed for their oil, a saturated fat, used for cooking, religious ceremonies, or soap. Pressing the meat of mature nuts makes coconut milk. Grating the mature meat also produces the world's most familiar type of coconut slivers used in cooking, baking, and candy. Coconut flesh can be dried, grated, powdered, flaked, toasted, frozen, or reconstituted. Processed coconut has less than 3% moisture, but is 68% oil. The coconut palm leaves can be woven into hats, or stripped to make simple brooms. The husks can be stripped into a fiber called 'coir' and woven into mats, fishnets, paintbrushes and rope. Islands in the Indian Ocean used discs carved from coconuts as currency until 1910.

To grow a tree, simply find the type of nuts you enjoy. Scan the area to find any nuts, which may have already sprouted. If none are growing, select three or four mature nuts. I find the easiest way to sprout a nut is to place it in a drain. Be watchful a heavy rain doesn't wash them away. Nuts kept damp usually sprout a stalk in three to four months, and should bear five to six years after planting. It is recommended to plant dwarf coconut palms at least twenty feet apart, from fence lines, or structures. Certain trees can bloom ten times a year so nuts will be continuously available. It takes ten to twelve

DID YOU KNOW?

More than 20 billion coconuts are produced each year. A third of the world's population depends on coconut for their either food or their economy. Coconut oil was the leading vegetable oil until soybean oil. Falling coconuts kill 150 people every year - 10 times the people killed by sharks.

months for a nut to mature on the palm. Yearly a tree usually will produce forty or more nuts. Fresh nuts can be stored up to three months.

The almost clear liquid in a coconut is not coconut milk, but coconut water. To make true coconut milk boil equal parts of shredded coconut and water, simmer, and strain it. 'Coco Loco' or other varieties of sweetened cream of coconut used in pina coladas are not canned coconut milk. One regular sized coconut should yield three cups grated and one cup of liquid. If your grated coconut dries it can be reconstituted by adding milk to it for half an hour. Drain off the milk and let the coconut dry on paper towels.

Eighty grams or three ounces of coconut has 280 calories, but 220 are from fat. It has some dietary fiber, minimal protein with some iron, calcium, and vitamin C. One cup of coconut water has forty-five calories with four from fat.

Spicy Saltfish Avocado Guacamole

Ingredients: quarter pound salt fish without the bones, one medium ripe avocado, half hot pepper minced as fine as possible, half cup canola oil, quarter cup vegetable oil, quarter cup lemon juice, one clove of garlic minced, one TBS fresh parsley, half cup bread crumbs, quarter cup coconut milk, salt and spice to taste

Method: Soak saltfish over night, drain and rinse. In a skillet, first brown fish on both sides, and then shred with a fork. In a bowl mash avocado with the salt fish and then mix with remaining ingredients. Chill before serving with biscuits or sada roti.

Easy Coconut Pie

Ingredients: four eggs beaten, one cup sugar, half cup bakers flour, four TBS melted butter or margarine, two cups grated coconut, one TBS vanilla extract

Method: Mix all ingredients together preferably in the above order. Pour into a greased baking dish or pie pan. Bake at 350 degrees for forty minutes.

Coconut Rice Pudding

Ingredients: half cup uncooked rice, one cup grated coconut, one cinnamon stick (or one TBS ground cinnamon), two cups coconut milk, quarter cup sugar (prefer brown)

Method: In a medium sauce pot place rice and cinnamon stick, cover with water and bring to a boil. Reduce heat and simmer until water is absorbed. Remove cinnamon stick before adding coconut milk vanilla and sugar. Simmer until rice is creamy. Stir in on half cup grated coconut. Remove from heat and allow to cool. Cover with half cup grated coconut. Sliced mango or pineapple pieces may be added before serving.

Coco-Lentil Soup

Ingredients: one cup lentils, two TBS fresh grated ginger, one medium onion chopped, two cloves of garlic minced, one TBS canola oil, one TS turmeric powder, two cups chicken broth, half cup grated coconut, one cup coconut milk, half cup chopped sweet green pepper, half cup chopped ripe tomatoes, hot pepper whole (can be removed before serving), salt and spices to taste

Method: In a large soup pot heat the oil and add the onion, ginger and garlic. Add turmeric powder, chicken broth, hot pepper, and lentils (wash first). Bring to a boil and then simmer for twenty minutes. Add tomatoes, sweet pepper, grated coconut, and coconut milk. Simmer for ten more minutes. Serve hot.

HEALTH NOTE

Coconut is attributed with the following healthful benefits. Kills bacteria that cause ulcers, throat infections, urinary tract infections, gum disease, pneumonia, and other diseases. Kills fungi and yeasts that cause ringworm, athlete's foot, thrush, diaper rash, and other infections. Expels or kills tapeworms, lice, and other parasites. Helps reduce health risks associated with diabetes. Improves calcium and magnesium absorption and supports the development of strong bones and teeth. Improves digestion and bowel function. Relieves pain and irritation caused by hemorrhoids. Is heart healthy; improves cholesterol ratio reducing risk of heart disease. Helps prevent liver disease, protect against kidney disease and bladder infections and dissolves kidney stones.

He who plants a coconut tree plants food and drink, vessels and clothing, a home for himself and a heritage for his children.

South Seas saying

PEANUTS

A bottle of roasted ground nuts doesn't last long in our household. Salted nuts are a basic for a nice lime. Peanuts are not really nuts, but a type of bean that forms under ground. These tasty 'nuts' have a variety of names including ground nuts, ground peas, monkey nuts, and goobers. Peanuts originated on the slopes of the Andes Mountains in South America at least 3500 years ago. Caribbean Indians called peanuts 'mandi or mani'. Botanically they are arachis hypogaea. Spanish and Portuguese explorers brought the peanut to Europe, Africa, and Asia. Peanuts were used as a basic food aboard early sailing ships because of their high nutritional value and low cost. Virginia, in the United States, harvested the first crop for sale in 1840. Roasted peanuts began at Barnum's Circus in 1870. Peanut butter was created in 1890 as a paste for elderly patients who couldn't chew. Really, the ancient Incas created peanut butter and flavored it with ground cocoa beans. The Aztecs used mashed peanut paste to cure fevers. Today, over half of the peanuts grown in the USA are used to make peanut butter.

Some African tribes believed peanuts had souls, so they cast gold replicas of the groundnuts. Very little, if any of the peanut plant is wasted. Peanut oil is used for lubrication, cosmetics, paint, soap, and lamp oil. Cattle farmers use the peanut as a food source to fatten their livestock. Peanut shells are compressed into artificial fireplace logs, kitty litter, and particleboard for home construction. The skins are processed into paper.

The Caribbean grows peanuts in backyards and on a small scale for personal consumption. Peanuts are a big money crop through out the world today bringing in over four billion US dollars a year. The peanut market expanded with George Washington Carver in 1903. Carver developed over 300 uses for the peanut including soap, cheese, medicine, grease, ink, and bleach. It only takes 720 peanuts to produce a one-pound jar, and twenty-six million tons of peanuts are harvested every year!

The peanut is not a 'usual' plant since it has blossoms above the ground, yet the fruit (the peanut) grows beneath the soil like a potato. Each peanut is actually a seed. There are two basic types of peanut plants, runners and bush. The runner spreads out like a watermelon with nuts growing from the main branches. The bush type is similar to a typical bean plant growing more than two feet tall. Once the small yellow flowers are self-pollinated, the bud of the nut begins to grow below the surface. One plant can produce forty nuts. Peanuts are a 'long crop' taking about five to six months to mature. They are great for the soil as they enrich it with the nitrogen they produce while forming the nuts. Raw nuts (not salted, baked, or otherwise processed) are easily found at most supermarkets.

Nuts

Soak the raw nut in a damp cloth for two days. Work the soil at least a foot deep with a fork and pull up into a mound six inches high and wide. Plant two nuts together about two inches deep, and space plantings about six inches. Sprouts should appear in eight days. Blossoms should appear a month and a half later. Use a 12-12-17-2 fertilizer mix every two weeks for six weeks then switch to 7-11-27 once a month. Water regularly. Using a fork carefully harvest the plants. Each plant should produce twenty to forty nuts. Determining when to harvest is a problem. Most farmers pull a bush and check. If the pod breaks from the root easily they are ripe. If the nuts are pale pink and watery, the plant needs more time to mature. Raw nuts are forty per cent water so they must be dried to prevent spoilage.

> *No man in the world has more courage than the man who can stop after eating one peanut.*
> Channing Pollock

Peanuts are a very 'fatty food'. Every ounce of raw peanuts provides seven grams of protein, seven grams of fat, and three grams of fiber. A cup has over six hundred calories, because they are over seventy-five per cent oil. However, it is a healthy oil; monounsaturated, not polyunsaturated. Researchers in Great Britain discovered women who ate five ounces of peanuts weekly reduced heart attacks by a third. Peanuts nutritional value includes protein, fiber, calcium, potassium, iron, copper, and vitamins E and B complex especially B-3.

Peanuts can be eaten raw. Raw nuts may be added to soups, salads, or stirfry. Placing them in a baking pan in a 350-degree oven for half an hour can roast nuts.

Peanut Stew

Ingredients: two medium onions chopped, five medium tomatoes chopped, six cloves of garlic minced, one cup ochro, three cups potatoes cubed, two TBS olive oil, five cups water, half cup tomato sauce (or ketchup), one TBS ground cumin, one TBS chili powder, one hot pepper (remove before serving), two cups spinach or pak choy chopped, quarter cup fresh mint leaves chopped, three quarters cup chunky peanut butter, half cup chopped roasted peanuts. Salt and spices to taste

Method: In a large stockpot, mix onions, garlic, potatoes, tomatoes, and olive oil. Sauté about five minutes then simmer. Add water, tomato sauce, spices and mint leaves. Continue to simmer for ten minutes. Add ochro, spinach or pak choy and peanut butter. Cook for five minutes until stew begins to thicken. Serve bowls garnished with chopped nuts.

Peanut Spicy Sauce

Ingredients: one cup chunky peanut butter, three cloves garlic minced, one large hot pepper chopped fine, two TBS fresh ginger peeled and chopped, three TBS brown sugar, four cups coconut milk, three TBS soy sauce, one TBS molasses, one TBS fresh lime juice

Method: In a suitable pot over very low heat, whisk together all ingredients until well combined.

Boiled Peanut Bread

Ingredients: half pound crushed peanuts, one pound cassava peeled and grated, half pound pumpkin peeled and grated, three TBS milk powder, sugar, spices, and salt to taste

Method: In a large bowl combine all ingredients and divide into six equal portions. Place each portion on a piece of greased aluminium foil. (Traditionally banana leaves were used as packets.) Boil packets in a suitable pot for one hour.

HEALTH NOTE

If you eat one ounce of peanuts every day the unsaturated fats in peanut butter will reduce the risk of heart disease by 25%. Rich in folate and niacin (vitamin B3) will increase the HDL, good cholesterol, by as much as 30%. Twenty-five percent of peanuts consists of proteins and dietary fiber. The most unique property of peanut butter is its high content in resveratrol, a substance that's been shown to have very strong anti-cancer properties.

As many as one-and-a-half million Americans are allergic to peanuts. This allergy accounts for over three-fourths of all deaths related to food allergies each year.

Man cannot live by bread alone; he must have peanut butter.
James A. Garfield

Grasses

For lack of a better term these four plants are lumped together as 'grasses'. Rice is a domesticated grass that produces a grain that feeds half the world's population. Sugar cane is a type of perennial grass that satisfies most of the world's sweet tooth. Tobacco and marijuana are not food, spices, or herbs, but just agricultural plants. Marijuana, rice, and sugar cane originated in Asia; while the world has the Amerindian to thank for tobacco. All are extremely profitable to produce. A third of the world's population uses tobacco every day, while five percent enjoys marijuana.

All of the 'grasses' in this classification are easy to grow. Once they begin to grow they dominate and grow like weeds. One tobacco plant can produce enough seeds to plant an acre. Rice, the whole grain brown variety, is extremely nutritious, while sugar cane, tobacco, and marijuana consumption may lead to health hazards. According to my Net research, the world produces one and three quarter billion tons of sugar annually and consumes 175,000 tons every minute! Every resident of Cuba, Trinidad and Tobago, Costa Rica, Brazil, and St. Kitts and Nevis all consume more than fifty kilos of sugar each year.

Tobacco companies produce five and a half trillion cigarettes every year. That's almost a thousand cigarettes for every man, woman, and child in the world. Asia, Australia, and the Far East are the largest consumers. One and a half billion cigarettes are smoked daily!

Brown rice, especially when accompanied with beans, is the perfect food. To create white rice, the germ and the inner husk or bran is removed. Then the grain is then polished, usually with glucose or talc. Brown rice has 349% more fiber, 203% more Vitamin E, 185% more B6, and 219% more magnesium. With 19% more protein, brown rice is a more balanced food. White rice does include 21% more thiamin, B1, which is added in the enrichment process. Brown rice has a low Glycemic Index, 55 compared to white rice's 70, or even more with additional processing, such as parboiling, which posts at 87. For reference, a donut is 76. The development of diabetes later in life has been linked to the consumption of foods with a high Glycemic Index. The same type of thing happens in brown bread vs. white bread scenario.

Bet you didn't know that if white rice is not 'fortified or enriched' with vitamin B1 it causes the deadly disease beriberi.

Gardening is medicine that does not need a prescription...
And with no limit on dosage.

Author unknown

MARIJUANA – CANNABIS

Marijuana, cannabis, ganja, weed is probably one of the biggest cash crops among the islands and the mainland. It is absolutely illegal to use, possess, cultivate, transfer, or trade in most countries including every island in the Caribbean. If caught with this lucrative vegetable contraband, the Caribbean poses severe penalties including confiscation of any vehicle or boat used in its transport. Yet, if an American or European tourist were asked to identify a prevalent island culture it would probably be a dark-skinned West Indian with long dreadlocks smoking marijuana. I do not use, nor do I condone the use of this drug.

Actually marijuana is the innocent hemp plant used around the world for tens of thousands of years. The first fabric is believed to have been woven from dried hemp weed. Another shocker is that Europeans brought marijuana/hemp to the western hemisphere for their own purposes. Cannabis is indigenous to Central and South Asia. Evidence of the inhalation of cannabis smoke can be found as far back as 3000 BCE. It is also known to have been used by the ancient Hindus of India and Nepal thousands of years ago. That was the origin of cannabis indica. The herb was called ganjika in Sanskrit, shortened to ganja in the modern Indic language. Hemp quickly adapted to thrive in the pre-latrine soils around man's early settlements, which quickly led to its domestication. It was first grown in Chile - South America in 1545, and in North America at Virginia in 1606. From the end of the Civil War until 1912, virtually all hemp in the US was produced in Kentucky. Until the beginning of the 19th century, hemp was the leading cordage fiber and rivaled flax as the chief textile fiber of vegetable origin. Hemp was described as 'the king of fiber-bearing plants',—the standard by which all other fibers are measured.

As 'hemp', cannabis sativa is valued for how easy it grows, and the many uses. Hemp can be made into are textiles, rope, or oils for fuel or to create food products high in potassium. The waste product from manufacturing these items can be used to make paper.

Everything about marijuana – except writing about it I hope – is currently illegal. I won't tell you how to grow it except it grows easily like its name, a weed. It is dangerous and illegal to get or possess the seeds. However marijuana seeds are a huge business worldwide going for five to twenty-five US dollars a piece from the internet! If that shocks you then get ready. An eighth of an ounce - three and a half grams - of good tasting, illegal hemp in New York or Los Angeles can go for fifty US or more, and a pound is upwards of five thousand dollars! Is there any wonder why ganja is now the world's biggest cash crop? Many analysts contend the market value of ganja produced in the

United States alone exceeds $35 billion - far more than the crop value of such staples as corn, soybeans, and hay. The value of the yearly marijuana crop of the world is beyond a trillion dollars. California grows more than one-third of the US national harvest, worth an estimated $14 billion, exceeding the value of that state's grapes, vegetables, and hay combined. Marijuana is the largest revenue producing crop in Alabama, California, Colorado, Hawaii, Kentucky, Maine, Rhode Island, Tennessee, Virginia, and West Virginia, and one of the top five cash crops in 29 other states.

Around 7000 - 8000 BCE, the first fabric is believed to have been woven from dried hemp weed. Supposedly Christopher Columbus brought cannabis sativa to the Americas on his first voyage. In 1619 the Virginia Assembly passed legislation requiring every farmer to grow hemp. Hemp was allowed to be exchanged as legal tender or money in Pennsylvania, Virginia, and Maryland. The US Declaration of Independence was written on hemp paper!

Cannabis was criminalized in South Africa in1911, 1913 in Jamaica, and during the 1920s in the United Kingdom and New Zealand. Canada criminalized marijuana in the Opium and Drug Act of 1923, and the United States outlawed it with the Marihuana Tax Act of 1937. This was after the Mexican Revolution of 1910, when Mexican immigrants flooded into the U.S., introducing to American culture the recreational use of ganja. Marijuana has shown positive effects on cancer, AIDS, and glaucoma. Its use is effective on AIDS patients from its ability to increase a person's appetite as well as relieving nausea allowing a patient to regain weight. Marijuana reportedly helps glaucoma patients by reducing ocular pressure, which can cause damage to the eye. It is the most effective treatment for chronic nausea. It is not physically addictive, but is psychologically addictive. Warnings: coughing, asthma, upper respiratory problems, difficulty with short term memory loss, racing heart, agitation, laziness, confusion, paranoia, and possible psychological dependence can occur with use.

Smoking marijuana is bad for your health. The carcinogenic by-products of combusted plant matter inhaled into the lungs should be avoided whenever possible. It is currently held that there are no known carcinogens in marijuana when not smoked. Therefore this drug should be taken orally and absorbed into the body through the digestive system by means of capsules, medicinal teas, and various forms of edibles.

Although no country in the world has actually fully legalized the drug for personal use, more than ten countries have decriminalized its use and/or its cultivation in limited quantities. Medicinal use of the plant is already legal in a growing list of countries, including Australia, Belgium, Canada, the Netherlands, Israel, and 14 states of the USA. Dealing and trafficking are still illegal. Medical marijuana centers now appear like syndicated coffee shops on streets in American cities.

The marijuana 'high' comes from tetrahydrocannabinol (THC), concentrated in the flowers. The minimum amount of THC required to have a perceptible effect is about ten micrograms per kilo of body weight. Aside from a subjective change in perception - most notably enhanced mood, effects include increased heart rate, lowered blood pressure, impairment of short-term memory, working memory, coordination, and concentration.

There are basically two types of ganja. Cannabis indica differs from cannabis sativa in that it is a shorter plant with broader leaves with less of a euphoric high. Sativa is found practically everywhere around the world, excluding Antarctica. Indica is chosen for its medicinal properties, in particular the anti-epileptic, anti-inflammatory, and stimulant properties.

As the world wide economy withers, and taxes climb, illegal/contraband products like marijuana that relieve stress while making an enormous profit are more desirable. Everyone knows that you can get a nice safe high in an Amsterdam coffee shop. In the Netherlands the term coffee shop has come to mean a place where hashish and marijuana are available. In 1998 they began the ACD or Amsterdam Coffeeshop Directory. It lists cool places to smoke. Above all, the ACD is about unashamed cannabis tourism.

What island will be the first to realize the value of Caribbean cannabis tourism? Most knowledgeable people realize that Jamaica and St. Vincent are the centers of cannabis cultivation in the Caribbean. Yet look at what has happened recently to Jamaica's tourism product due to unregulated drug dealers in Kingston. It has died along with seventy plus people defending an illegal culture. Thousands of people are imprisoned and warded at the expense of every nation for marijuana offenses.

If you were inclined to enjoy a vacation swinging in a hammock while smoking ganja with no fear of persecution or prosecution would that attract you as a tourist to a lenient island? Would the leniency contribute positively or negatively to that island's revenue compared with legalized gambling?

Suppose the world economy slips further and drastic methods must be taken to attract tourist dollars. The island could issue a grower's license at a substantial fee on an identified plot of owned or leased land. The crop and growing methods would be inspected. The island would tax the product or buy it from the grower like nutmeg or coffee, and distribute it through legal, comfortable, safe shops. Of course just like the visitor's drivers license there would be a paid permit for use, but the welcomed tourists would no longer fear arrest or theft when purchasing the contraband. Locals would have also have to buy a permit for use. Terminally ill patients could spend their last days enjoying the tropical climate using medicinal marijuana in hospices to ease their pain. Every aspect of inhalation would be cordoned off from impressionable youths.

The small island economy no longer benefits by having to police, judge, penalize, and incarcerate mostly those who are committing a victimless crime. Time, funds, and resources could be better spent dealing with violent acts that further destroy the tourism product.

The US federal and state governments combined spend over $27 billion dollars annually to enforce marijuana laws, try cases, and incarcerate prisoners. California, presently strapped for cash, is proposing legalization and licensing which would bring in an expected $1.3 billion in revenue. It would be treated essentially the same as alcohol. Users would have to be 21 years old. Smoking would still be banned in public, and operating a vehicle under the influence would be a crime.

Remember all the logical, realistic complaints against legalized gambling? Has that positively increased tourism while helping the public domain? What island will be the first to explode ganja tourism? Hemp stalks could be used for cordage and paper products setting a world example. Envision the expansion of the usual tourist buying T-shits made by Irie Hemp Garments, or their postcards to back home from Jah-Maken paper products.

Is it time for a government to increase—not the enforcement—but the economic revenues from the Caribbean's most marketable agricultural product, ganja? How much money does a local farmer make from the bananas tourists eat? This is not a pro marijuana article, only food for thought.

Why is marijuana against the law? It grows naturally upon our planet.
Doesn't the idea of making nature against the law
seem to you a bit . . . unnatural?

Bill Hicks

When I was a kid I inhaled frequently. That was the point.

Barack Obama

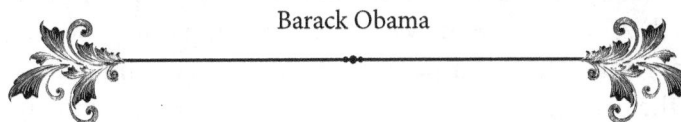

RICE

Rice is one of the Caribbean's favorite foods and in past years it was one of Trinidad's major crops. Various nationalities seem to have their own brand of starches. Those from North America love wheat. Central Americans love corn, and Asians love rice. Trinidadians fall into a middle ground loving wheat roti, chewing on roasted corn, while eating plenty rice. It wasn't very many years ago when families had their own rice fields and a box of rice under the house.

Actually rice is a domesticated version of a type of grass. Just like wheat, barley, or rye; its seeds or grains of rice are consumed as a major food staple. Rice is source of carbohydrates and has fed more people longer than any other grain; for at least ten thousand years! The first cultivation is believed to have been from wild Asian rice from the area around the Yangtze River. Chinese legends tell rice is a gift of survival given to man from the animals after the great flood. The 'great flood' destroyed all plants and everyone was starving. A dog appeared to the people with rice seeds tangled in its tail. They planted the seeds, the rice grew, and mankind survived.

Rice cultivation moved through Sri Lanka to India. About 3500 years ago rice came to Africa in the Niger River delta. Around 10 AD Southern Europe began farming rice. Portuguese explorers brought rice to Brazil, and Spain spread it to Central and South America. Rice is second only to corn in world cultivation. More than half of the world's population depends on rice as a staple food.

Rice cultivation is usually identified with the flooded rice plains or paddies of Southeast Asia. Rice has developed a unique versatility enabling it to grow even in the desert conditions of Saudi Arabia. Rice is now cultivated on every continent except Antarctica. Ninety percent of the world's rice is grown and eaten in Asia. Asian countries, including India, consume an average of a half pound a day per person, or 180 pounds a year. Americans only eat about twenty-five pounds of rice a year. Rice increased in cost since April 2008. Rice producing countries like China and India reduced exports to feed their own people. China produces 180 million tons a year and eats only 135 million tons, India grows 135 million tons and eats 85 million tons, the USA grows only 8 million and eats only 3.5 million tons.

Trinidad now imports almost all of its rice. In the early nineties rice farmers produced more than twenty thousand tons. Today barely thirty-five hundred tons are locally grown. As of March 2009 the price of locally grown rice increased more than thirty percent.

Long-grain varieties such as basmati and jasmine are suited for hot, humid climates. Medium and short-grain rice was developed for temperate and mountainous regions. Non mechanized rice cultivation has previously been ideal for countries with high rainfall and cheap labor. Modern technology makes rice cultivation less labor intensive, but still requires irrigation.

Most rice lovers have tried a few of the many different types such as arborio, basmati, Bhutanese red rice, black forbidden, black japonica, calrose, carnaroli, glutinous, jasmine, kalijira, koshihikari, poha, shahi, vialone nano, and others. Many of these types also have versions that are aromatic, brown, wild, converted, instant, and bleached white. Any variety of rice with different spices, nuts, vegetables, beans, meats, or seafood makes a belly filling, nutritious meal.

Brown rice retains its outer brown shell, which contains the proteins and minerals, and is much more nutritious than refined white, which is mainly just carbohydrate. Compared to corn and wheat, rice is lower in fat and protein. Agro scientists have developed strains of 'miracle rice' with more protein. It is still wise to compliment rice with soy, animal, or fish protein. Rice cannot be used to make bread because it does not usually contain gluten.

DID YOU KNOW?

Long grain rice is light and fluffy because the grains do not stick together. The taste of white long grain rice is quite subtle. On the other hand, the brown variety has a somewhat nutty flavor. Medium grain rice is shorter than long grain and a little plumper. It is more sticky than long, but not as much as the short grain. It's used for creamy dishes, like risotto or paella and perhaps even certain desserts. Short grain rice is almost round and is featured in many Oriental and Caribbean specialty foods. It is an especially popular for Japanese sushi as it sticks together quite easily. "Converted" or "parboiled" rice means it is steamed under pressure before it is milled. This makes the grain harder, preventing overcooking. It also helps maintain several important vitamins and minerals, and provides a slightly different flavor. Instant rice or pre-cooked is pre-boiled dehydrated, and packaged. It only needs to boil a few minutes before it's ready to eat. The dehydration removes a lot of the flavor from the rice, making this the least desirable form. It also tends to be rather costly as the consumer is paying for convenience.

Grow rice at home as an experiment in a clean, solid plastic bucket with no cracks or holes. Purchase long-grain brown rice, unrefined, and chemical free. White rice will not work because it has been processed. Put about ten inches of dirt or potting medium in the bucket. Fill with water to about two inches higher than the soil. Then throw a handful of the brown rice. It will sink to the soil. Keep the bucket in the sun and the water level about two inches above dirt until the rice sprouts. When your plants (look like lawn grass) have grown to six inches add more water to about four inches deep. Add no more water. In the coming weeks evaporation will lower the water in the bucket. The bucket should not have any standing water when the rice plants are ready to harvest. If you keep the bucket warm, it usually takes four months for rice to mature. The green stalks will dry and whither to gold in color when they are ready. Cut your stalks with scissors. Wrap in a brown paper bag and put in a warm breezy place for about three weeks. Roast the rice in your oven at about 150 degrees for an hour. Husk it by rubbing it between your hands. Every bucket should grow enough for a meal, a small meal.

Traditional rice farming is hard work, planting seedlings by hand in wet fields. Modern techniques include laser leveling the fields before shallow plowing, and flooding to five inches deep. Now fast airplanes sow the seeds. The seedlings get nutrients from the water, which also repels weeds. It usually takes four months for the green seedlings to mature to three foot tall golden brown stalks topped with grains of rice. Rice is usually harvested about a month after the rice plants have flowered. The fields are drained and the plants are cut halfway up the stalk. Brown rice is sheathed in the bran, which is removed by rubbing the grains against each other to produce white rice. The rice must be dried and milled. One acre can yield 8,000 pounds of rice.

My grandfather had eighteen acres he would bank to grow rice. He would cut the mature rice with a grass knife (sickle) and bundle it. Then they would beat the bundles and collect the paddies. Once dried the rice would be stored in big wooden storage boxes. We would take a month's supply and have it milled.

The botanical name for rice is *Oryza sativa L.* of the Gramineae family. There are three main rice types. Indica has long slender grains, japonica is a shorter, plumper medium-grain rice, and javanica lies between the other two. Each type of rice has long, medium and short-grained varieties. Brown rice is naturally better for you compared to white rice because it has more fiber. This is better than white rice fortified with vitamins. If you experience diarrhea eat a hand full of uncooked rice. As you digest it, the rice will scrape your intestines and the runs will be over. A bush medicine remedy is to boil rice in excess water and strain. Mix with hot pepper and apply externally for gout. Natural brown rice has about a calorie a gram and is low in saturated fat, cholesterol, and sodium. It is also a good source of selenium, and manganese.

Cooking rice is easy. First wash and rinse the rice before cooking. Look for stones and impurities. For every cup of rice add two cups of water. Choose a pot with a lid that seals. Bring the rice and water to a boil uncovered. Once it boils reduce heat to a simmer and cover. You might want to put a piece of foil under the lid to make a good seal. Do not open for half an hour unless you smell it burning. Add spices and enjoy.

> *To you who eat a lot of rice because you're lonely,*
> *To you who sleep a lot because you're bored,*
> *To you who cry a lot because you are sad, I write this down.*
> *Chew on your feelings that are cornerned like you would chew on rice.*
> *Anyway, life is something that you need to digest.*
>
> Chun Yang Hee

SUGAR CANE

Most of the Caribbean knows sugar cane intimately. Almost everybody knew someone who either grew, harvested, or processed sugar. We all sucked cane as children and adults. Until the last few years, cane was everywhere. The sap from the thick stalk stores energy as sucrose. From this juice, sugar is extracted by evaporating the water. Crop over was signaled by the smell of burning sugar when the fields were readied for the cutlass.

Most people don't realize that sugar cane is a type of perennial grass. Sugar cane is native to southern Asia. Agronomists believe a specific type of cane developed in India while others types could have developed independently in Indonesia. Sugar cane's botanical name is *saccharum officinarum*. Crystallized sugar was reported 5000 years ago in India.

Around 700 AD, Arab merchants carried sugar to most of the countries surrounding the Mediterranean Sea. By the tenth century there wasn't a village from Syria to Spain that didn't grow sugar cane. On the second voyage Christopher Columbus brought sugar cane to the Caribbean. The desire for profitable sugar delivered African slaves to these islands as well as indentured Indians and Chinese. The Caribbean's history is a sugar dominated story of this cultural, racial, and religious mix.

When was the last time you chewed on some cane? Sugar cane is eaten raw, crushed to make cane juice, and of course processed into white rum. Cane first is burned in the field to remove the dead leaves, or trash. After cutting, juice is extracted by crushing or mashing the stalks. These mashed stalks are termed bagasse.

The juice is boiled into a concentrate and the sugar crystallizes. Sugar processing was done through to the 1800's with a boiling house. At the top of each furnace were up to seven large metal basins called coppers. Each copper was smaller and much hotter than the preceding one. The cane juice was placed in the first copper kettle and heated with some limestone added to remove impurities. The juice was skimmed, then channeled to the other copper kettles.

The result of this first boiling and removal of the sugar crystals produces first molasses, which has the highest sugar content since only a small percentage of the sugar has been removed. A second boiling creates second molasses with a slight bitter taste. Blackstrap molasses is produced after a third boiling of the original cane juice. Unlike refined sugars with zero health benefits, blackstrap molasses contains significant amounts of

DID YOU KNOW?

Sugar is a carbohydrate that occurs naturally in fruits and vegetables. Of all known plants, sugar is most highly concentrated in sugar beets and sugar cane. Lemons contain more sugar than strawberries. In the late 1500's a teaspoon of sugar (4.5 grams) cost the equivalent of five dollars in London. A can of Coke has 39 grams of sugar and a can of Pepsi has 41 grams of sugar. That is about seven teaspoons, or 13 cubes of sugar per can. (28 grams are an ounce!) Sugar hardens asphalt. It slows the setting of ready-mixed concrete and glue. Chemical manufacturers use sugar to grow penicillin. Cane juice can cure a sore throat, and prevents a cold or flu. It also helps in curing jaundice as it gives strength to liver.

vitamins and minerals especially calcium, magnesium, potassium, and iron. Today mills located in sugar plantations extract raw sugar from sugarcane. Raw sugar is a yellowish tan. Refineries purify raw sugar by bubbling sulfur dioxide through the cane juice. This bleaches all impurities transparent creating refined white sugar, almost pure sucrose.

Today Brazil, India, and China are the world's largest producers of sugar. Brazil produces about thirty tons of raw sugar cane per acre. Every ton separates into 1500 pounds of juice, which is 300 pounds of sucrose, 1,200 pounds of water, and 500 pounds of bagasse. Beyond a food sweetener, one acre of sugar cane can be used to produce 420 gallons of ethanol fuel.

Growing sugar cane is easy, all you need in the necessary space and some cane. The latter might be hard as it seems to be disappearing from our culture. A line of planted cane makes a sweet hedge line, but must be constantly trimmed or it can take over. Cane likes an slightly acidic soil around pH 6.5, but will grow in soils from 5 to 8.5. Fork your area so the dirt is loose.

Next check out the stalks of cane you are about to plant. Near every joints in the stem is a little pointed leaf, which will take root. Chop the stalk two inches after this joint and before the next joint. Stick the cane in the loose dirt so the joint is covered. If you keep the soil moist, a shoot should develop in about two weeks. In about six months you should have sizeable cane. Keep it trimmed and enjoy the trimmings.

Products made from sugar cane include molasses and rum. Cane sugar syrup was the traditional sweetener in soft drinks for many years, but was replaced by less expensive, and less sweet, corn syrup. Rock candy is enjoyed by people everywhere.

Cane juice can be purchased from several roadside vendors. It is a natural high energy drink that is a great mix for fresh fruit juices, and especially rum. Fresh sugarcane juice is a good source of riboflavin, calcium, and magnesium. Cane juice provides the glucose and renews energy. One tablespoon of cane juice has 45 calories. One tablespoon of white granulated sugar has 46 calories, and brown has 34.

Sugarcane Roti

Cane juice is substituted for water.

Ingredients: two cups rice flour, (or one cup rice flour and one cup baker's flour), one cup cane juice, one TBS butter or ghee, one TS salt

Method: In an appropriate heavy frying pan heat the sugarcane juice until it boils. Stir in butter, flours, and salt. Stir until all the flours are fully combined with the cane juice. Remove from the heat and allow to cool. Then work the dough with your hands until there are no lumps. Form dough into balls and roll on wax paper into roti. Roast as any roti and serve. These roti will be stiffer than usual roti because of the cane juice.

Caned Rice

Ingredients: four cups cane juice, two cups white rice (Basmati preferred)

Method: In a two quart pot heat the cane juice. After washing the rice combine it with the cane juice. Cook over low heat stirring constantly until mixture becomes smooth. When mixture is very thick remove from heat and refrigerate. Serve with chopped mint.

Sugar Cane Seafood

Ingredients: two pounds peeled deveined medium to large shrimp (two pounds of fish fillets can be substituted), two one foot lengths of mature sugar cane, one bunch of chives chopped, one half cup water, one TS fresh mint chopped, one TS salt

Method: Wash sugar cane and carefully cut lengthwise pieces that will fit into a baking dish, the smaller the pieces, the better. Line the dish with the cane pieces. Lay the washed shrimp on top of the cane, pour in the water. Sprinkle shrimp with the salt and chives. Cover tightly and bake at 300 for thirty minutes. Uncover and bake for five minutes. Serve with rice. Garnish with mint. Use the remaining liquid as a sauce.

Be not like the sugarcane -
do not hold your sweetness inside.
Be like the fruit tree -
be generous with your best.

Jonathan Lockwood Huie

TOBACCO

Tobacco is a true West Indian plant. It is believed tobacco began growing in the Americas about 6,000 B.C. Early Amerindians used it in religious and medicinal practices. Tobacco was believed to be a cure-all; to dress wounds, as well as a pain killer. Chewing tobacco was believed to relieve the pain of a toothache.

The Spanish word '*tabaco*' originated in the Arawak - Taino language of the Caribbean. In Taino, it referred to a roll of tobacco leaves—like a cigar. It may also have resulted from Tobago - a kind of Y shaped pipe that covered both nostrils to sniff tobacco smoke. Amerindians smoked the crushed leaves of the plant. On Columbus' first landing at San Salvador natives brought fruit, wooden spears, and certain dried leaves that had a distinct fragrance. Each item seemed prized by the natives. Columbus accepted the gifts and ordered them brought back to the ship. The fruit was eaten, but the pungent 'dried leaves' were discarded.

When Columbus landed at Cuba, natives wrapped dried tobacco leaves in palm or maize leaves and lit one end. The natives commenced 'drinking' the smoke from the other end. A sailor, Rodrigo de Jerez, became the first confirmed European smoker. He returned to Spain with the habit, but the smoke billowing from his mouth and nose frightened his neighbors. He was imprisoned for seven years. When he was released smoking was a Spanish craze.

A few decades ago tobacco was king, the most popular of all herbs, botanically *nicotiana rustica*. This plant has lately acquired an unsavory reputation. Indoors it smells horrible, and when over used it has been proven to cause many deadly diseases. The Caribes and Arawaks used tobacco at infrequent ceremonies, and certainly not twenty times a day. The major reason for tobacco's growing popularity in Europe was its supposed healing properties. It was believed tobacco could cure almost anything, from bad breath to cancer. In 1571, A Spanish doctor named Nicolas Monardes wrote a book about the history of medicinal plants of the new world where he claimed tobacco could cure 36 health problems. In 1588, A Virginian named Thomas Harriet promoted smoking as a viable way to get one's daily dose of tobacco. Unfortunately, he died of nose cancer because it was popular then to exhale smoke out through the nose.

During the 1600's tobacco was so popular that it was frequently used as money, literally 'as good as gold'! It wasn't until the 1900's that the cigarette became the major tobacco product. By 1901 three billion cigarettes and six billion cigars were sold. In 1902, the British Phillip Morris built a New York headquarters to market its cigarettes, including a now famous Marlboro brand. Today about 840 packs of cigarettes are sold every second in the U.S. That's more than one million every hour!

Most tobacco is grown commercially today, but it is attractive and can be grown in the backyard garden as an ornamental, or for personal consumption. Tobacco is a member of the nightshade family that includes tomatoes, peppers, and eggplants. Growing it is very similar to growing tomatoes. Getting the seed or a starter plant is the first hurdle. We got ours from a friend who has it growing wild. Even though family members were smokers they did not grow their own. Seeds of various varieties can be bought inexpensively from the Internet. Get ready, the seeds are miniscule. It is said a teaspoon of tobacco seeds will grow six acres of tobacco.

The second hurdle is to plant the seeds. Tobacco seeds are not much larger than a pin prick and care should be taken when sowing seed as to not sow to thickly. An easy way to spread the seed evenly is to mix it two parts sand to one part seeds. The best method is to start the seeds in cups or trays. Use moistened commercial potting soil mix. Tobacco plants feed heavily on nitrogen and potash, but sprouted seeds can be burnt by nutrients. Commercial potting soil mix has no nutrients. DO NOT cover the seed with any soil as they need light for germination. If covered too deeply the seed won't germinate at all. Tobacco seed has three requirements for germination: light, moisture, and a temperature of at least 65 degrees F.

Tobacco seeds should germinate in about a week to ten days. Although these seeds need to be kept moist, don't hit them with a heavy spray that can wash them into the soil. It is best to use a hand spray bottle adjusted to a fine mist. Your plants should never dry completely. Cover the starter containers with sheets of white paper so the seedlings don't get burned by the hot sun.

As a start try about six to ten plants. Tobacco seedlings should be hardened before you transplant into your field or garden. A week in partial sun should be adequate, but two weeks is better. The seedlings are ready to transplant into your garden or bigger containers when they are about six inches tall. Once repotted, water with a starter fertilizer. The tobacco plant needs full sun to grow broad leaves. If you plan to grow tobacco in your garden plot space the tobacco plants two feet apart in the row, and space rows three feet apart. Keep transplants from drying out by transplanting either on a cloudy day, or in the evening. Water the plants thoroughly once transplanted. During dry weather water each evening till plants become established.

Mold the base of each plant and keep the plot weeded. Tobacco roots grow quickly with thousands of small hair-like feeder roots close to the soil surface. Care should be taken when hand weeding to not damage the roots. Fertilize each plant with a pinch of 12-12-17-2 bearing salt. Molding will give support to these plants, which can grow taller than six feet. Tobacco likes full sun. Plants grown in partial shade will produce slender leaves. When growing tobacco for harvesting, remove both flowers and suckers from your plants to enable the plant to devote its energy to growing large leaves. Your tobacco will be ready to harvest and cure about three months after germination.

Around the time flower-heads start to form (if you haven't chopped them off) the plants are full grown and the bottom leaves will be ready to pick. Pick them when they show signs of yellowing. Cut a slit near the butt end of the center rib of each leaf, feed a thin wire or cord through these slits to hang them. The leaves should be hung about an inch apart, somewhere dry, out of the way and preferably warm - like garage rafters. You can make acceptable smoke by drying the leaves, slicing them thinly, rolling them in cigarette paper, and setting them alight, or put that in your pipe and smoke it!

Insect bites and dog bites are relieved after applying a paste powdered tobacco leaves and water. Tobacco when eaten, if your stomach can handle it, will supposedly relieve gas. A hair rinse or body wash of tobacco leaves boiled in water will clean the hair while killing lice.

I am a light smoker and have tinkered with a few recipes that were passed on to me. I tried a dreadful tea made by steeping a cured tobacco leaf in water. Even honey didn't help it. Another was to reduce a pint of water with a tobacco leaf in it to about a quarter. It was then recommended to stir in chocolate powder until it thickens. Add honey and condensed milk. This was supposed to be a dessert. It wasn't tasty, and my kitchen reeked.

Trees

Most of our fruit grows on trees, and even spices as nutmeg, cinnamon, and cloves. The trees of this section are unique. Noni bears a fruit, although definitely not sweet and certainly having an unusual smell. Nevertheless, Tahitian Noni does a have a billion in sales every year dealing with seventy countries.

Roucou and mauby are virtually unknown beyond the Caribbean. Roucou could be considered a spice since it makes a food coloring with a hint of taste. Mauby makes a distinctive, tasty drink, but is not used to flavor any other dish. The calabash tree grows containers, and is definitely in a class by itself.

Coffee is undoubtedly the most important, most transported, most valuable of any producing tree. A few well spaced coffee trees in the back yard and you are on your way to caffeine self sufficiency. Coffee is big business worldwide. Independent coffee shops in the USA do more than $12 billion in sales every year. After petroleum, coffee is the world's most traded commodity, yet most of the world's coffee is still grown by small-scale coffee farming families. Coffee is grown in over fifty countries, all of them located in the tropics. Brazil produces thirty per cent of total coffee and Colombia ranks second. More than seven million tons of green coffee beans are hand-picked every year. For every pound of gourmet coffee sold, small-coffee farmers earn and average of just one eighth of a US dollar! Americans consume 400 million cups of coffee per day and 4 million espresso coffees are daily in Italy. Coffee, cocoa, and spices could provide a national income alternative to fossil fuels.

The best time to plant a tree was 20 years ago. The next best time is now.

Chinese Proverb

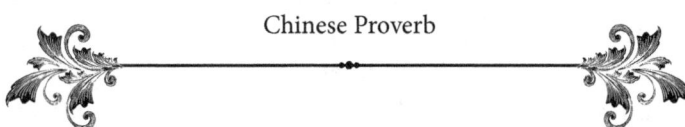

CALABASH – BOLLE

Most of us 'old timers' know a calabash tree produces large round gourds. Calabash isn't used functionally in the current Caribbean, yet instead this gourd is more decorative. You might remember a Caribbean television program called Calabash Alley? It is shameful the calabash tree has almost vanished. It is a totally unique tree that has made considerable contributions to Caribbean Island cultures.

Native Amerindians planted useful calabash trees throughout the Caribbean, Mexico, Central and South America centuries before Columbus. It is uncertain where the tree originated. This tree was priceless to those Indians. Fibers from the bark were twisted into twine and woven into ropes. The hard branches and trunk made tools and tool handles. The wood has an elasticity and can be shaved into strips like the apple tree, and woven into baskets. The gourd-like fruit was indispensable for cups and water containers, made into musical instruments, and storage containers. This tree's wood was used later by Europeans for cattle yokes, tool handles, wooden wagon wheels, and ribs for building boats.

The calabash is now considered a unique tropical tree that produces gourds or 'calabashes'. It is a great backyard tree because it doesn't get really big, usually about thirty feet and can be pruned to a desirable height and shape. The fruit can be made into artful gifts.

Botanists classify the calabash as Crescentia cujete. This tree can be grown from the small flat seeds of a dried fruit, cuttings, or from root suckers. Calabash can take most soils from fine to course, as long as it is well drained. The calabash can survive salty sea blast. Most calabash develop at least two trunks with a few strong branches that seem to twist with a natural sag. For some strange reason, orchids love to nest in a calabash tree.

Water the tree during the dry season and fertilize with a cup of 12-12-17-2 bearing fertilizer every two months for superior calabash development. The calabash will bloom and bear at the same time. The large light green bell shaped blossoms hang directly on the large branches and trunk. The branches are long, and spread outward with almost no secondary branches. They will produce fruit that can grow to a foot or more in diameter. The blossoms usually bloom at night. The only downside to this tree is that the blossoms are fertilized by bats. The fruit matures in about seven months.

A Benedictine monk in the 1500's reported the Caribbean Taíno Indians (in Puerto Rico) cut eye holes in large calabashes to pull over their heads. This was camouflage when they hunted river and lake birds. The Indians wore the calabash and waded into the water. The floating calabash didn't frighten the birds and they could easily grab the birds' legs from underwater.

The Taíno gave the musical world two percussion instruments made from the calabash, the maracas and the güiro. Maracas are still made from small dried calabash filled with a few pebbles or hard seeds. The traditional güiro (also called the fish) is made out of a hollowed out calabash. The outside of the calabash is carved with grooves. A set of flexible wood sticks, a pua, are banded together and either scraped or rubbed up, down, or across the ridges, with a fast or slow tempo. That creates fine harmonious clicks that blend into the infamous 'cha-cha' sound.

> **DID YOU KNOW?**
> The unusual calabash blossoms develop from buds that literally grow out of the main trunk and limbs, a condition termed cauliflory. Like many other large-flowered cauliflorous species, calabash trees are commonly pollinated by small bats when the pollen on the upper side of the blossom is placed on the head and shoulders of the bat. In Central America the seeds of the calabash are toasted and ground with other ingredients including rice, cinnamon, and allspice to make the drink horchata.

The calabash güiro isn't only recognized as a Caribbean percussion instrument. It is used in musical pieces ranging from Igor Stravinsky's ultra classical *The Rite of Spring*; to the famous rock and roll band REM. Listen for it in the back in times music of The Drifters' *Under the Boardwalk*.

I've never known anyone to try and eat a calabash and thought all were considered poisonous. However bush medicine uses the pulp to make a decoction for severe diarrhea, and respiratory ailments such as colds, bronchitis, cough, and especially asthma. A tea made from this tree's leaves is used to treat high blood pressure.

Today calabash art has bypassed the calabash as a utensil. With a bit of carving, a splash of paint, and a coat of varnish; the calabash can be transformed into a unique container, purse, or wall art.

Calabash Art

Ingredients: One calabash, one bucket water, rough scrub brush, a Scotch scrub pad, sandpaper, paint (to your taste) and varnish (optional)

Method: First the freshly picked calabash is prepared by cutting (and keeping) an access and removing the seedy pulp. Then soak the shell in water and scrub with a rough brush and then finish with a green Scotch pad. Put it somewhere in partial shade, but breezy, to dry. Once dried the calabash will appear carved from wood. Rub both the exterior and interior with sandpaper until smooth. Create whatever you want a güiro, or maracas, a vase for potted plants, or a bowl to hold your keys. Paint as the spirit moves you.

Enjoy for years.

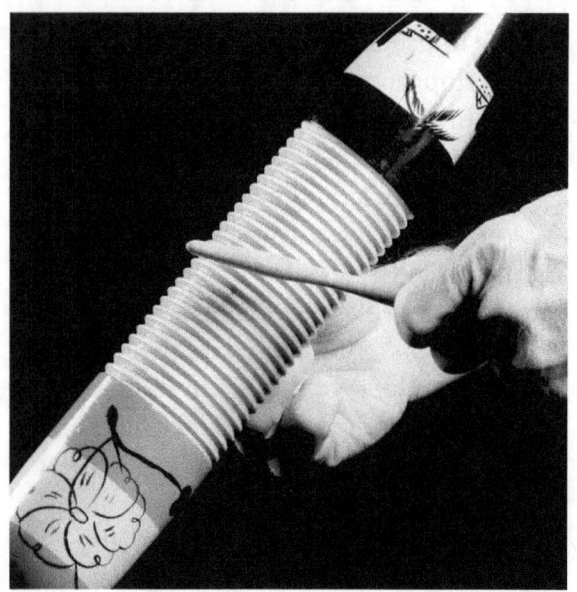

Güiro

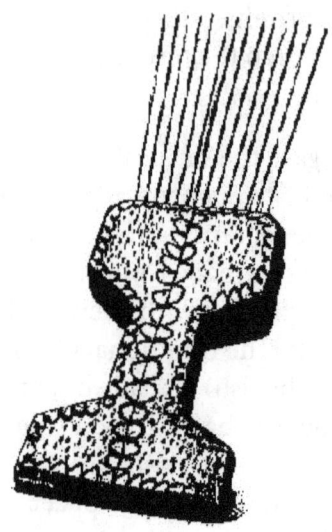

A güiro pick is called a pua.

Maracas

COFFEE

History

Coffee is the popular beverage prepared from the roasted seeds of the coffee bush. Known as cafe, java, mud, Joe, or Nescafe; the drink contains caffeine, the most prevalent stimulant in the world. Usually served hot, also enjoyed chilled, one cup of coffee contains 80 to 120 mgs of the stimulant caffeine, depending on the method of preparation. Coffee is the world's sixth largest agricultural export in terms of value, behind wheat, corn, soybeans, palm oil, and sugar. Coffee is also second only to oil as the world's most heavily traded commodity.

Although today there are as many as sixty different types of coffee, only two are produced in great amounts. Arabica coffee is believed to be the oldest variety, and considered to have the better taste and aroma. Arabica is believed to have originated in Ethiopia in prehistoric times. While the other main type, Robusta, contains forty per cent more caffeine, is less desirable on the world market. Robusta was first discovered in Uganda and is cultivated where Arabica is less likely to grow.

Coffee is one of Africa's gifts to the world. Supposedly, the bush was first discovered by accident in the Ethiopian highlands. There is more than one legend of coffee's origin. A thousand years before Christ two tribes, the Oromos and Bongas, were at war in the Ethiopia region of Kefa (cafe). The Oromos warriors ate a stimulant made from crushed coffee beans rolled in animal fat. However, the Bongas won and enslaved the Oromos marching them to Congo Highlands of Harrar to be sold. The slaves who ate the harsh tasting Robusta version coffee planted a few seeds. Their effort took roots in the highlands' rich soil and transformed into the more flavorful Arabica, which is today's most common type of coffee.

Another origin story begins twelve hundred years ago with a shepherd named Kaldi. Supposedly Kaldi watched his goats prancing among the coffee bushes eating red berries containing the beans. The shepherd ate a few berries and proceeded to romp with his flock. Kaldi related this experience to his Imam. After the holy man watched the shepherd and the goats' bizarre energy, he picked some berries to share with the herder. That night the holy man and his monks were extremely energetic for the teachings. As this legend reports, when they finally slept, the prophet Mohammed revealed to the Imam the berries enhanced wakefulness and wakefulness promoted prayer, and prayer was better than sleep.

That Imam and his monastery became famous throughout Arabia for the spirited praying of its brethren, known as dervishes, who chewed on the berries during sermons. Even today, Sufi's start the whirling dervish ceremonies after drinking a brew made from coffee beans. Coffee drinking spread with Islam through northern Africa and through the eastern Mediterranean into India.

In the 10th century an Arabian physician wrote the earliest comments about coffee. By chewing the leaves or berries, coffee use became a religious event. Around a 1000 A.D. the first coffee was brewed from the leaves of the coffee plant. In a few years many people sought caffeine exhilaration from the drink. A legend of Yemen, famous for Mocha coffee, tells of an exiled sheik brewed bitter coffee from green berries. The energy from caffeine probably aided in his surviving his exile.

The method of preparing coffee still in use today, first boiling then roasting the beans, started a thousand years ago in Arabia. However, by parching or boiling coffee export beans (a roasted bean can't grow) production remained only in Arabia until 1500. The coffee trees belonged to the King. It was punishable by death to possess either a living tree or a living coffee seed, which are usually misnamed as beans.

The popularity of the drink spread as methods of preparing coffee were continually refined. For three centuries coffee grounds were consumed with the hot water. Then, patient settling left the grounds at the bottom of the cup. The first public coffeehouse opened around 1475 in Constantinople. In the home, coffee was only consumed after elaborate ceremonies. Coffee became such an integral part of Arab life that Turkish men had to provide the beverage to their wives or face divorce. When it first appeared in Africa and Yemen, coffee was a religious intoxicant. This usage in religious rites among the Sufi branch of Islam led to it being put on trial in Mecca for being a 'heretic' substance much as wine. The caffeine effects of coffee made it forbidden among orthodox and conservative Imams in Mecca in 1510 and in Cairo in 1530.

Italian merchants from Venice traded coffee with other spices through out the Mediterranean. The first coffee imported into Europe was known as 'qhaweh', or 'Arabia wine'. An Indian pilgrim smuggled fertile seeds strapped to his belly from Mecca and brought coffee trees to Italy in the 1500's. The Dutch founded the first coffee estate in Indonesia in 1696. Around 1715,the Dutch gifted several coffee trees to the French Royal Botanical Garden. From this garden sprung the Caribbean brand of coffee. The first coffee tree in the Western Hemisphere was brought from France to the Island of Martinique in the 1720's. Gabriel Mathieu de Clieu, a naval officer, raided some coffee sprouts from the Royal Botanical Garden at night. He sailed for Martinique where those sprouts fathered at least 18 million coffee trees during the next half-century throughout suitable French colonies. Brazil lured their coffee industry with romance. In 1727, a Brazilian colonel sweet-talked the wife of the governor of French Guiana for seedlings.

Coffee became an important part of many cultures throughout the world today as both a stimulant and a cure for digestive disorders. It was found to stimulate conversations. During themid -1600s coffee gained acceptance in New York. Within a quarter century, coffeehouses became popular throughout all New England. Before 1600 the favorite drink at breakfast was beer!

The coffee houses in France, England, and the American colonies proved to aid the spread of political opinions. In 1675 King Charles II tried to close London coffee houses in order to stop the discussion of liberal ideas. The desire for coffee made the king bow; eleven days later the coffee houses reopened. The French opened the first coffee cart 325 years ago at the St. Germaine Fair in Paris. This was the beginning of door-to-door delivery of coffee heated by charcoal urns in Paris. During the 1700s, some coffeehouses served as barbershops and casinos.

In 1773, the Boston Tea Party beginning the American Revolution was planned in the Green Dragon coffee house. The Merchants' coffee house in New York was the site of US Government headquarters just after the beginning of the American Revolution. The New York Stock Exchange started as a coffee house. Lloyd's Coffeehouse became Lloyds of London. The Baltic Coffeehouse became the London Shipping Exchange. The Jerusalem Cafe evolved into the East India Company. Until recently the runners at the British Stock Exchange were called waiters because it began as a coffee house. A cup of coffee cost a penny in the first English coffeehouses. Coffeehouse life was addictive for those wanting to discuss ideas. Due to the penny charge, coffee houses were called 'penny universities'.

> ## DID YOU KNOW?
> Coffee as a beverage has taken about 1,000 years to evolve to its current presentation in specialty coffee shops. In the 1400's the first coffee shop opened in Constantinople, where the Turks thought the drink was an aphrodisiac. The first coffee house in Europe opened in Venice in 1683, while coffee was available in Europe as early as 1608, mostly for the rich. In the year 1763, there were over 200 coffee shops in Venice. Italy now has over 200,000 coffee bars. The first commercial espresso machine was manufactured in Italy in 1906. Southern Europe enjoys the flavor of dark roasted coffee. A coffee tree can be harvested during its fifth year and many times throughout every year. Coffee cherries usually contain two beans. Cherries with three beans is considered a sign good of luck. Brazil, is responsible for 30 to 40 % of total world output. Approximately 2,200 ships just haul coffee beans each year. In December 2001 Brazil produced a scented postage stamp to promote its coffee - the smell should last between 3 and 5 years.

Twenty-five years ago most American coffee was made from percolators. This is a bad way to make coffee since the coffee continually boils, but sounds and smells nice. Ninety years ago the drip coffeemaker was created when a German housewife, Melitta Bentz used a coffee filter of blotting paper from her son's notebook. The introduction of the Melita version with cone-shaped drip units improved the taste.

Caffeine belongs to a group of drugs called xanthines, central nervous system stimulants. The effects of caffeine are physical, not psychological. Physicians regard one cup of coffee with 150 milligrams of caffeine as a therapeutic dose. Caffeine invigorates, quickens and clarifies thought, and expands idea association. Coffee was accidentally decaffeinated in 1903. Seawater damaged a shipment and removed most of the caffeine from the beans. Using this method, German coffee importer Ludwig Roselius began extracting caffeine from coffee beans. His creation was 'Sanka', French for sans caffeine or 'without caffeine'.

The coffee table replaced the tea table in most American living rooms in the 1920's. Coffee breaks began during World War II when employers reasoned coffee increased the productivity of their workers.

Coffee Consumption

Plain black coffee is a natural beverage with no added sugar or preservative, and does not contain any calories. It is the world's second most popular drink after water. North America and Europe drink coffee an average of about one cup of coffee to three glasses of water. Last year coffee was drank in the USA at 22.1 gallons per person and is the world's most popular beverage with over 400 billion cups consumed each year, or 1.4 billion cups every day. More than half of the US adult population daily drinks some type of coffee beverage, averaging about three cups.

By 1960 coffee had become the beverage of choice for teenagers, who went to modern coffee houses to hear the new folk music. In 1965 Nescafe introduced freeze-dried soluble coffee, and two years later invented a way to capture more aroma and flavor from every single coffee bean. Today every corner of the World treats itself to a cup of Nescafe.

Coffee is grown commercially in over 70 countries throughout the world. In Brazil over 5 million people work in the coffee trade. Most of those are involved with the cultivation and harvesting of more than 3 billion coffee plants. Only 20% of all harvested coffee beans are considered to be high quality premium beans. The quality of a cup of coffee does not only depend on the bean blend, but also on the ratio of the amount of water and coffee used when brewed.

Nine out of ten of coffee drinkers have coffee at breakfast. Work is the second most prominent location. Americans drink an estimated 350 million cups of coffee a day. Coffee is second only to oil as the world's most valuable commodity.

Coffee travelled a long journey from the end of the first millennium when Arabs soaked green coffee beans in cold water to make the first coffee. James Mason patented the first American coffee percolator in 1865. A German housewife introduced cone-shaped drip units that improved coffee's quality. Ironically it was George Washington, not the first American president, but a Belgian living in Guatemala who created the first instant coffee in 1906 before he immigrated to the United States. In 1930 the Brazilian government approached the Swiss company Nestlé to produce a quality cup of naturally flavorful coffee by only adding water. Nestle experimented for seven years before creating Nescafé in 1938. During World War II, American forces launched Nescafé in

Europe, because it was included in their food rations. Coffee was first called 'a cup of Joe' during WWII, when American servicemen (G.I. Joes) became big coffee drinkers.

The number of cups of gourmet coffee beverages consumed per drinker per day is 2.5 cups. The average American adult consumes 10.2 pounds of coffee beans per year. The largest gourmet coffee purveyor, Starbucks, had net earnings of $564 million, compared to $494 million in fiscal year 2005. Starbucks opened in 1971 in Seattle named after the first mate in Moby Dick. The chain now has 30 blends and at its height in 2007 opened three new stores every day. Gourmet coffee lovers will spend as much as 45 hours a year waiting in line. The average person who buys gourmet coffee spends the equivalent value of a round trip plane ticket to Florida every year.

Coffee Producers and Growing

Coffee is one of the world's most important commodities with seven million tons produced every year. A good coffee tree can produce up two pounds of raw coffee per year. One acre of coffee trees will produce up to five tons of coffee cherries, which reduces to one ton of beans after hulling and milling. Coffee increases in volume by twenty per cent during roasting. Daily, Americans consume 300 million cups of coffee. Four thousand coffee beans are necessary to produce one pound of roasted coffee, or fifty beans for each cup. Coffee grows only in fifty-six tropical countries around the world. Annually it is worth 45 billion USD to the growers.

Worldwide approximately 20 million people work in the coffee industry. Small farmers grow most of the world's coffee, and rarely share in the huge profits. The mostly third world governments, facing huge international debts, must sell their coffee crop regardless of price. These coffee producers compete against each other, often resulting in an over-supply, which drives prices down. The world's largest coffee producer is Brazil with over four billion coffee trees. Colombia comes in second with nearly two thirds of Brazil's production. Recently Vietnam has flooded the market with large quantities of green beans.

A few giant manufacturers and retailers control the international coffee market, which wildly fluctuates. When the price of coffee rises, estates plant more trees. When these trees start producing, it causes a glut and the price falls. Then, new bushes are not planted, there is a shortage, and the price rises. Small producers often have to sell when their harvest is ready with little or no choice of who buys. In the UK where ninety per cent of the coffee sold as 'instant' - just two multinational food companies, Nestlé and Kraft, account for seventy per cent of all retail coffee sales.

Coffee is of the botanical family *rubiaceae*, with more than sixty different varieties. Only two have any economic significance, *Arabica* and *Robusta*. Three-quarters of world production is of the milder, higher-quality Arabica produced largely in Latin America. Arabica has been known from prehistoric times and is believed to originate in southwest Ethiopia, specifically from Kaffa; thus its name. There are 900 different flavors of Arabica. While more susceptible to disease, it is considered to taste better than Robusta. It takes a coffee tree three to four years to produce berries. The Arabica species self-pollinates, whereas the Robusta uses cross-pollination.

Robusta, with forty percent more caffeine, probably originated in Uganda and is grown where Arabica will not thrive. Many commercial coffee blends use as Robusta as an inexpensive substitute for Arabica. Robusta tastes bitter with little flavor compared to Arabica. However superior Robusta beans are used in some espresso blends to provide the foamy head while reducing the ingredient cost.

Another type, Liberica from Western Africa, has no great importance in coffee trade. Two more bean types are Mocha from Yemen, and Java from Indonesia. The modern coffee trade is much more specific about origin, labelling coffees by country, region, and sometimes even the estate where the beans were grown.

Coffee means subsistence to more than 100 million people. Each year some 7 million tons of green beans are produced worldwide. Most of which is hand picked, dried, sorted, (and some aged) before coffee is transformed into the familiar roasted coffee. Roasting coaxes golden flavor from a bland bean. All coffee is roasted before being consumed either by the supplier, or roasted at your home. It takes heat to turn coffee's carbohydrates and fats into aromatic oils, burn off moisture and carbon dioxide, and alternately break down and build up acids, unlocking the characteristic coffee flavor.

How to Grow

It's easy to grow coffee at home either in soil or large containers. Since coffee is a variety of tropical evergreen, trees can be used to landscape as shrubs. The trees begin full yield when five or six years old and continue top harvest for another decade. Coffee plants may live for 60 years. Trees are kept trimmed to six feet to get the best yield and to make picking easier. If not pruned, a coffee tree can reach 40 feet.

A coffee tree starts with a fresh picked coffee cherry that should germinate in three months. Soak the cherry in water for a day before planting flat side down about one and a half inch deep in fast draining potting soil. The soil should be moist, never soggy, and should be watered daily.

After about a year and the tree is a few feet tall fertilize with 10-10-10 every month. The plants will grow to about 10 feet if given ample root room, but a mature root system can extend six feet. Simple pinching of branches produces a bushier plant. The coffee cherries turn from yellow to orange and then bright red, about six months after blossoming. While in bloom, the coffee tree is covered with 30,000 white flowers that develop into fruit after a day.

Each ripe red cherry has two beans. Coffee cherries do not ripen at the same time. In fact it will have blossoms and berries in various stages of ripening. Only the ripe berries can be picked and should be washed with water, and fermented in a small container until the pulp falls off. Wash again with fresh water. Any coffee beans that float at any stage of washing should be discarded. Spread out the harvested cherries to dry in the hot sun on a concrete slab. Turn periodically for a week, until the outer shell of the cherries turns brown and the beans rattle around inside.

To make home grown coffee you need to be self taught on roasting; and that can be done in your oven. The smell of this process may fill your home as you burn off the chaff. Your beans should be placed in something perforated, a steel strainer or veggie steamer, so all sides get evenly heated at 250 degree F. for about seven minutes. Increase the oven temperature to 450 degrees. Within ten minutes the beans should crackle. Then, stir them so they roast consistently. About every two minutes check them until they have achieved a color slightly lighter than what you desire. As the beans cool, they will continue to roast. Mill, brew, drink and savour the flavor of your personal plantation coffee!

Among the numerous luxuries of the table…
coffee may be considered as one of the most valuable. It excites cheerfulness without intoxication; and the pleasing flow of spirits which it occasions …is never followed by sadness, languor or debility.

Ben Franklin

MAUBY

Mauby, like sorrel, was always a special holiday drink at our home. The drink is made from the dried bark of a small tree native to the northern Caribbean and Central America. West Indians call the tree mauby, but the botanical name is *colubrina ellipticain*, a member of the buckthorn family. Most Caribbean people don't know the tree, but the refreshing drink. Some claim it as an aphrodisiac, others say it helps for arthritis, but everyone knows it is a great coolant on a hot day.

The mauby is a hardwood and a nice functional backyard tree. The sapwood is light brown, while the heartwood is much darker brown. The wood is hard and heavy, strong and durable commonly used for posts. It grows to about twenty feet. The orange-brown bark is smooth on young small trees, but as the tree matures it becomes scaly. The inner bark is light brown and bitter. The tree will be shrouded in attractive purplish green leaves at the height of the rainy season. This is when the bark should be harvested. During the dry season it will shed most of its leaves as the sap drains to the roots.

This is another virtually effortless tree since it only needs direct sunlight a few hours a day, shelter-to be staked when hard winds blow, and well drained soil. Every month during the dry season, I recommend giving it a five gallon bucket of water. As the wet season ends, broadcast two cups of starter (12-24-12) fertilizer around the roots. Small green blossoms appear usually in July and the berries come on from September to March. Then switch to a bearing fertilizer such as 12-12-17-2. Molding with mulch after broadcasting the fertilizer will help it to feed and not wash away. Molding will give support to the young roots and help the soil conserve nutrients and water. This tree has few enemies except for fungus which can be protected with occasional spraying of appropriate fungicides. This tree not only drops its leaves, as it matures it will have a multitude of small berries that have three seeds. I would not recommend this tree if you have a swimming pool. Some mauby trees are evergreen, but you won't know until after planting.

All the mauby I've made and drank has only been prepared from the bark and other herbs. My research found sources that also use the leaves and berries. Unsweetened and tangy, which is very seldom, the refreshing bark decoction is used as a bitter tonic for diabetes – lowering blood sugar, hypertension- lowering blood pressure and cholesterol, and stomach disorders. According to the University of the West Indies, mauby combined with coconut milk, may lower blood pressure.

People love mauby! Trinidad locally produces more than one and a half million gallons a year of mauby concentrate. Due to the lack of local bark, it is imported from Haiti and the Dominican Republic. We are lucky to have a choice of either the real bark, the distilled concentrate, or Mauby Fizz—the ready drink.

Often the drink is fermented using a portion of the previous batch, while sometimes it is consumed unfermented. Mauby can be bought as a pre-made syrup and mixed with water or soda. To the mauby novice the first taste is sweet, but changes to a bitter aftertaste and may give you a dose of the trots (diarrhea). Many find it an acquired taste.

DID YOU KNOW?

This bitter bark is known by more than one name, depending on the island where it is grown or consumed. Mabi or mavi in Puerto Rico, Haiti, and the Dominican Republic. Cuba names it jayajabico, in the US it is soldier wood, while in the Bahamas it is called smooth snake bark, and in the French Caribbean it is bois mambee. Other names are black velvet, coffee colubrina, corazon de paloma, mawbie, and snakewood. Botanically it is *colubrina arborescens*.

Mauby Island Total Refresher

Enough for a party or for gifts

Ingredients: six pieces of mauby bark, one gallon of fresh water, four sprigs of marjoram, one bunch anise (optional), one stem of rosemary, a half cup of peeled ginger root sliced thin, one stick of cinnamon, one TS ground nutmeg, a dozen cloves, two TBS Angostura bitters, three cups brown sugar (more or less to taste), one TS dry yeast

Method: Boil the mauby bark alone in one quart of water and let sit covered for at least an hour. Then add everything except the yeast. Bring up the heat and simmer for an hour before letting it cool preferably overnight. Add the one TS of yeast to a tablespoon of water and combine with batch. Then carefully bottle filling each to the neck. Let sit in a shaded place again overnight. Chill and enjoy. Using white or brown sugar will contribute to the darkness of this drink. The bitters will buffer the slightly bitter aftertaste.

Look at the trees, look at the birds, look at the clouds, look at the stars... and if you have eyes you will be able to see that the whole existence is joyful. Everything is simply happy. Trees are happy for no reason; they are not going to become prime ministers or presidents and they are not going to become rich and they will never have any bank balance. Look at the flowers - for no reason. It is simply unbelievable how happy flowers are.

Osho

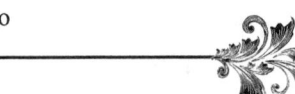

NONI

Noni is a strange plant that grows easily in the tropics. The fruit looks like a pineapple that has been shaved. I first encountered noni when a friend into natural health foods offered the fruit to me. Noni has a varied reputation of being a cure all, or a fake. Like aloe vera it is a very different plant, is very bitter, but noni also smells, perhaps stinks.

Botanically noni is *morinda citrifolia*, and is known by a variety of names like nono, nonu, great morinda, Indian mulberry, nunaakai in India, dog dumpling in Barbados, mengkudu in Malaysia, beach mulberry, and cheese fruit. The name noni is derived from Hawaiian. This weird fruit is a tree related to coffee family; native to areas ranging from Southeast Asia to Australia, including Polynesia.

Historically the noni plant was known in Sanskrit as 'ach' and attributed special properties by ancient physicians. It has been known and used in northwest India in ayurveda, the practice of holistic medicine, for thousands of years. East Indians use powdered extracts from roots, leaves, and the fruit of the plant as a sedative and for other medicinal purposes.

First, find someone that has noni and will give you a branch to plant. Noni will grow almost anywhere in almost any condition, but the better the soil, the better it will grow. It will thrive in full sun, or partial shade, and in a variety of soil conditions. The best approach is to start your plant in a pot. Transplant once the plant seems hardy and is about a foot tall. First fork the soil and break all clumps. Keep the area weeded to reduce competition for water and sun. Fertilize after three months with 12-24-12. Use a bearing fertilizer as 12-12-17-2 when noni begins sprouting fruits in a year and a half. Water regularly during dry spell. Every month this tree should have about fifteen pounds of fruit. Keep it trimmed to the size of a shrub, because it can reach to fifteen feet.

Not an overly attractive plant, it doesn't take up much space in the backyard. Noni has large, dark green, deeply veined leaves, and should continuously have flowers and fruits. The noni fruit is a multiple fruit like a pineapple. Multiple fruits are bunches of simple fruits, each from its own flower with a single pistil. The simple fruits grow together to form the multiple fruit. Noni begins to stink as it ripens. This smell has gained it the names 'cheese fruit' or even 'vomit fruit'. It is oval in shape and reaches four inches. This fruit is at first green, then yellow and almost white as it ripens.

Noni has many seeds. Despite its strong smell and bitter taste, the fruit is categorized as a starvation food to be eaten if nothing else is available. However, it is a staple in some Pacific islands, eaten raw or cooked. Southeast Asians and Australian Aborigines consume the fruit raw with salt, or cook it with curry. The seeds are edible when roasted.

Traditionally, the leaves of the noni tree were used topically for healing wounds. In herbal Polynesian medicine, noni has been used for many health conditions, such as constipation, diarrhea, skin inflammation, infection, and mouth sores. Today noni is adverted to cure everything from arthritis, atherosclerosis, bladder infections, boils, bowel conditions, burns, cancer, chronic fatigue syndrome, circulatory weakness, colds, cold sores, constipation, diabetes, drug addiction, eye inflammation, fever, fractures, gastric ulcers, gingivitis, headaches, heart disease, hypertension, improved digestion, immune weakness, indigestion, kidney disease, malaria, menstrual cramps, menstrual disorders, mouth sores, respiratory disorders, ringworm, sinusitis, skin inflammation, sprains, strokes, thrush, and wounds. There is no real evidence, however, that noni is effective for any of these conditions.

Studies evaluating the effects of noni suggest that it may have anti-cancer, pain relieving, and immune system-enhancing effects. However, these studies used extremely high doses that would be difficult to obtain from taking the juice. More importantly, there's no reliable evidence about the safety, or effectiveness of noni for any health condition in humans. Noni juice is high in potassium, and should be avoided by people with kidney disease.

Noni was virtually unknown outside the Pacific Islands until the 1990's. Hawaiian noni was first marketed as a health supplement in powdered capsule form and later as noni juice. Recently organic noni fruit has become popular. Today noni is big business. Tahitian Noni International is the largest noni product manufacturer that markets and sells the reputed health benefits in the form of noni juice, noni cosmetics, and pet care products. Three hundred other companies sell noni health supplements, which is a multi-billion dollar industry. Noni is one of the chief agricultural exports of Polynesia. Some noni juice has water added despite claims of 100% pure noni juice. Manufacturers also sweeten this juice to improve the taste. Lack of regulation means you must carefully research all noni products.

Noni fruit are ripe when yellow to pale white. Once picked they can be placed in glass jars and kept lightly capped until they soften and release their juices; or ripen the fruit until they split by setting in the sun. Some recommend keeping noni in jars six weeks until fermentation begins. Noni should be crushed over a bucket that has a sieve incorporated, so the juice can be strained. The juice should be stored in a cool place or refrigerated. Noni often has a bitter taste. Mix it with water, sugar, or additional fruit juices. Pure noni juice has only ten calories per cup.

Cranberry Noni

Two ounces noni juice, half cup cranberry juice, quarter cup orange juice, fill glass with club soda

Grape Noni

Two ounces noni juice, half cup grape juice, one TS fresh lemon or lime juice,

fill glass with lemon lime soda

Noni Fruit Salad

Ingredients: quarter cup noni juice, grapefruit slices, crushed pineapple, bananas, cherries, orange pieces, grapes, mangoes, and papaya pieces. Combine, chill, and serve.

Curried Noni

Ingredients, three small green noni fruit - sliced thin, one TBS sesame oil, one sweet pepper, cauliflower, broccoli, and carrot - all chopped, one cup coconut milk, one TBS curry powder

Method: Heat oil and add curry powder for one minute, add noni and veggies. Add coconut milk and bring to a boil. Reduce heat and simmer for ten minutes. Serve with pasta or rice.

There can be no other occupation like gardening in which, if you were to creep up behind someone at their work, you would find them smiling.

Mirabel Osler

ROUCOU TREE

Years ago Caribbean islanders utilized a lot of roucou to color and flavor foods. Now, as with many traditions, it is seldom seen unless at vending stands along less traveled roads. We call it roucou while others say oucou. It comes from the fruit of the achiote, botanically the *bixa orellana* tree. Roucou is native to Central and South America.

I was lucky to get a starter bush from Tanty Dorothy in Cunupia. Ours was started from a cutting, but roucou can be grown from seeds. It will grow almost anywhere as long as the soil is well drained. Start this shrub in a sizeable container and keep the growing medium slightly damp until it catches when new leaves appear. It needs the usual starter fertilizer until it begins to show pods. Then switch to a bearing salt. Transplant when it is too big for your container. These shrubs make nice ornamental bushes at the entrance to driveways, sidewalks, or paths.

This is usually a short, attractive evergreen shrub, but it can grow to over twenty feet with shiny heart-shaped leaves, sometimes with red veins. The three inch pale pink blossoms bear a strange, hairy fruit that is heart-shaped with red prickly spines. It may be yellow, red, or maroon. Red is the most common variety. When ripe, the pod splits in half to reveal about fifty seeds encased in a red pulp.

After the explorers encountered Amerindians as the Mayans, Incas, and Aztecs colored in brilliant red, roucou seeds and pulp were imported to Europe in the 1500's. Commercial cultivation began in India two centuries later. The dye was supposedly used by the Amerindians as an antidote to poisoning caused by eating the wild / bitter version of cassava (that had not been properly processed to remove the natural cyanide poison). In the past few years banana growing islands like St. Lucia were preparing a banana version of ketchup using roucou for the red color. It was difficult to discern the banana variety from the traditional tomato ketchup.

We used the roucou to color and flavor special dishes. The pulp is termed bixin and Amerindians used it as the original war paint and to give a startlingly attractive color their bodies while protecting from the sun and insects. Amerindians supposedly used the seeds as an aphrodisiac. The pulp is processed to produce a commercial dye and the seeds are dried to make a rust colored paste used for coloring foods such as rice, smoked fish, oil, or cheese. It is also used as a fabric dye. Roucou seeds 'supposedly' are given to bulls to make them more aggressive for bullfighters.

Roucou seed pod

As an herbal remedy a mixture of roucou pulp and seeds boiled in oil makes a salve that helps heal small cuts and burns, preventing scarring and blistering. A decoction of the leaves and pulp relieves stomach disorders like indigestion, and will help relieve asthma. Roucou leaves in a bath will be refreshing. Leaves heated in oil will reduce the pain of a headache when pressed to the forehead.

Roucou Seasoning

Pick at least a gallon of roucou pods, cut and scrape out the seeds. From personal experience wear rubber gloves and do this procedure on a piece of plastic to ease clean up. Do this carefully with a teaspoon because it really stains! Place everything in a clean bucket and cover with clean fresh water. Allow to soak for at least a day. Strain the water into a next bucket. Rub the seeds between the palms of your hands to remove any remaining pulp. I recommend wearing latex gloves and not getting too splashy. Strain again and repeat until the seeds fail to give off any color. In a cast iron or stainless pot (It may stain aluminum.) bring the strained roucou liquid to a boil and simmer for ten minutes. Add salt and any herbs you desire for your personal taste. Cover and let sit for a few hours. Allow to cool before pouring in bottles. If you were neat – as few roucouians are- clean up is easy. If not use diluted bleach to clean surfaces and hands. I suggest keeping this in the refrigerator.

Roucou Oil

Ingredients: a half cup cooking oil, two TBS roucou seeds Method: In an appropriate frying pan heat the oil over medium heat for three minutes. Add the seeds continuously stirring. Heat for one more minute. Allow to cool. Strain or not depending on the intended use. Refrigerate.

Red Fish Recipe

This takes some time to prepare but is worth it!

Ingredients: two pounds / four fish fillets or steaks – grouper or king, one TBS roucou seeds, two TBS orange juice, two TBS vinegar, two cloves garlic minced, one hot pepper seeded and minced, one TS ground cumin, half TS ground allspice, pinch of salt, one cup boiling water, oil for frying

Method: Combine boiling water and roucou seeds in a cup and let stand overnight to soften the seeds. When ready to prepare this meal drain away the water from the seeds and combine the softened seeds with orange juice, vinegar, garlic, chili, cumin, allspice, salt, and pepper in blender container. Process until it forms a smooth paste. Cover both sides of fish pieces with roucou paste and place in a well oiled baking dish. Spread paste over fish to coat both sides. Refrigerate covered, to blend flavors for at least two hours. Bake fish covered at 350 for twenty minutes. Uncover and bake another ten to fifteen minutes.

Gardening is a matter of your enthusiasm holding up until your back gets used to it.

Author Unknown

NOTES

Calorie and Nutrition Guide

ACEROLA CHERRY–WEST INDIAN CHERRY
One hundred grams has 32 calories high in vitamin C, potassium, and iron.

ALLSPICE
A teaspoon of ground allspice has only six calories with some vitamin C and calcium.

ALMONDS
One ounce of almonds has 160 calories with 15 grams of fat, 3 grams of fiber, 6 grams of protein, and 6 grams of carbohydrates, yet amazingly no cholesterol.

AVACADO
One cup of avocado has 236 calories, but is also rich in vitamins K, B-6, C, and copper. They contain oleic acid, which helps lower cholesterol, potassium to lower blood pressure, and folate to lower the risk of heart attacks. Avocado contains a high percentage of lutein, an important nutrient for healthy eyes.

BALATA
A hundred grams of balatas, about a big handful, have sixty-two calories with two and a half grams of protein and ten grams of fat.

BANANAS
Bananas not only taste good, but also are a healthy quick energy food packed with vitamins with 2 grams of protein and 4 grams of fiber. Bananas are rich in potassium, vitamins B complex, A, and C. One banana is about 99.5% fat free with about 90 calories comprised of 75 percent water, 20% starch and 1% sugar. Compared to apples, bananas have less water, fifty percent more food energy, four times the protein, half the fat, twice the carbohydrate, almost three times the phosphorus, nearly five times the vitamin A and iron, at least twice the other vitamins and minerals.

BARBADINE
Barbadine is a good source of calcium and phosphorous, and a hundred grams has only sixty calories.

BASIL
Basil has very few calories and is a good source of vitamins A, C and K, magnesium and potassium.

BEET ROOT
Beets are rich in folic acid, which fights heart disease and anemia. Beets are high

in fiber. Fiber is good for the intestines and helps regulate blood sugar and cholesterol. One cup of fresh cooked beets has only seventy - five calories of which one and a half grams are fiber and the same amount of protein with eight grams of carbohydrates. Beets also contains vitamin A, potassium, and phosphorus.

BLACK PEPPER
One tablespoon of black pepper has only sixteen calories with a bit of calcium and iron.

BRAZIL NUTS
Eight Brazil nuts equal a whopping hundred and eighty calories with 18 grams of fat and thiamine. Brazil nuts are an excellent source of selenium, a vital mineral and antioxidant that may help prevent heart disease. Two Brazil nuts can provide your entire daily intake of selenium. Brazil nuts are particularly healthy because selenium makes their protein content 'complete'. This means that, unlike most plant proteins from beans etc, proteins contained in Brazil nuts have all the necessary amino acids for optimal growth in humans just as meat or fish.

BREADFRUIT
Nutritionally a breadfruit has about a hundred calories of which two grams are protein with less than one gram of fat. It has twenty-five grams of carbs. Breadfruit is a good source of vitamin B, and there is more vitamin C in the riper fruits. It contains calcium, phosphorus, and iron.

BROCCOLI
A half cup of steamed or boiled broccoli has twenty-two calories, two and a half grams of both protein and fiber with a tiny bit of fat, and no cholesterol. The same small portion of broccoli has one and a half times the daily amount of vitamin C, plus vitamin A, niacin, thiamin, iron, folate, selenium, phosphorus, potassium, zinc, and magnesium.

CABBAGE
All cabbage types are low in calories and excellent sources of minerals and vitamins; especially C. Cabbage may reduce the risk of some forms of cancer including colon or rectal cancers. Cabbage is also high in beta-carotene, vitamin C, and fiber. A half cup cooked cabbage has 16 calories, 3 grams fiber, 3 grams carbohydrates, and 18 milligrams of vitamin C.

CAIMATE
A hundred grams of caimate has sixty calories with calcium and phosphorous.

CANNISTEL
A hundred grams of canistels has 140 calories, with 35 grams of carbs, 1 gram of protein and plenty of calcium, phosphorus, iron, niacin, carotene, and vitamin C.

CANTALOUPE
A tasty cantaloupe will not spoil your diet as a cup has only 50 calories. Eating a half a cantaloupe will provide the daily requirement of vitamins A and C, folic acid, and potassium. Cantaloupe has no fat or cholesterol and provides necessary fiber.

CARDAMOM
Nutritionally per hundred grams cardamom has three hundred calories, seventy grams of carbohydrates, ten grams of protein, and seven grams of fat, with twelve grams of fiber. It is high in calcium, iron, magnesium, phosphorus, and potassium. It also has vitamins C, B, thiamin, niacin, and folate.

CARROTS
A half cup serving of cooked carrots contains four times the recommended daily intake of vitamin A, with 35 calories, 1 gram protein, 8 grams of carbohydrates, 2 grams fiber.

CASHEW
One ounce of cashew nuts has one hundred and fifty calories with twelve grams of fat, no cholesterol, and nine grams of carbs. Cashews have less total fat than peanuts or almonds, and more than half of their fat is unsaturated fatty acids. This unsaturated fatty acid is oleic acid, the same healthy monounsaturated fat found in olive oil. Oleic acid is good for the heart, even in diabetics. If you are health conscious, dry-roasted cashews have a lower fat content.

CASSAVA
Cassava is such an important food because it is high in starch, which produces energy. A half pound of cassava has 215 calories, of which a quarter is carbohydrates, with one gram of fat, and three grams of protein. It also has Vitamin C.

CAULIFLOWER
One cup of raw cauliflower has only twenty-five calories. It is very rich in vitamin K, and C. One cup has more than the daily requirement of vitamins B6, B5, B3, folate, biotin, magnesium, iron, manganese, and molybdenum.

CAYENNE PEPPER
Two teaspoons of cayenne pepper has about ten calories. It is a good source of vitamins A and C, has the complete B complexes, and is very rich in calcium, manganese, and potassium.

CELERY
A cup of celery contains only 20 calories and has a good dose of vitamin C and B-6, folic acid, and fiber. Celery also has minerals such as manganese and calcium. The leaves are valuable as they contain the most vitamins.

CHADON BENEE
Other than taste, chadon benee has slight food value. A quarter cup of leaves has only 4 calories, with virtually no fat, fiber, cholesterol, or carbohydrates and only one mg. of vitamin C.

CHALTA
Chalta or wood apple It is a source of slight protein, calcium, and phosphorus. One apple has about a hundred calories.

CHATAIGNE
One ounce of chataigne fruit has about 100 calories, of which 5% is protein, 1% fat, 45% carbs, 17% fiber, with vitamins C, B6, thiamin, folate, and niacin

CHENETS/GENIPS
Chenets have about sixty calories per quarter pound with some calcium, phosphorus, and iron.

CHIVES
One tablespoon of chives has only one calorie. Chives are high in vitamins A and C, potassium, and calcium.

CHOCOLATE
Cocoa powder is actually good for you! It has nearly twice the antioxidants of red wine, and up to three times the antioxidants found in green tea. Cocoa also contains magnesium, iron, chromium, vitamin C, zinc, and others minerals at twelve calories a tablespoon.

CHRISTOPHENE
One cup of christophene has only twenty-five calories with almost no fat or carbohydrates. It has some fiber and vitamin C. However it is a source of sodium (salt).

COCONUT
Eighty grams or three ounces of coconut has 280 calories, with 220 are from fat. It has some dietary fiber, minimal protein with some iron, calcium, and vitamin C. One cup of coconut water has 45 calories with 4 from fat.

CORN
One ear yellow corn has only 80 calories, 2.5 grams protein, 20 grams carbohydrates, 2 grams dietary fiber, potassium, vitamin A, niacin, and folate.

CORRIANDER
Four grams has only one calorie with some vitamin A and C.

CUCUMBER
A four-inch cucumber has 20 calories, one-gram fiber, one-gram carbohydrates, calcium, vitamins A, and C.

CUMIN
Six grams of cumin has about twenty calories of which half are from fat. It also has some iron and calcium

CUSTARD APPLE
Custard apples are a well-balanced food having protein, fiber, minerals, vitamins, energy, and little fat. They are an excellent source of vitamin C, a good source of dietary fiber, vitamin B6, magnesium, potassium, with some B2, and complex carbohydrate. One hundred grams of custard apple flesh has a hundred calories. A small custard apple will weigh around 250grams and will provide your entire daily intake of vitamin C.

DASHEEN
Dasheen is a belly filling starch with 250 calories to a cup full. It has low fat, no cholesterol, one gram of fiber, but 60 grams of carbohydrates with healthy Palmitic, oleic and linoleic acids and adequate levels of the other essential amino acids. Dasheen is low in protein, but contain moderate quantities of calcium, phosphorus, and magnesium.

DILL
One gram of dill has no calories It is rich in vitamin C and one tablespoon contains more calcium than in a third cup of milk.

DUNKS
Dunks have more vitamin A and vitamin C than apples. 100 grams have 80 calories.

EDDOES
Eddoes provide a good dietary fiber at 110 calories per adult serving with no cholesterol, but two grams of protein.

EGGPLANT
Eating eggplant is good for you. It can reduce high cholesterol. One cup of cooked eggplant has 27 calories, 1 gram of protein, 6 grams of carbohydrates (two grams of fiber if eaten with the skin), phosphorus, potassium, and folate.

FAT PORK
These fruits are so rich a quarter pound has fifty calories with some calcium and phosphorus.

FENNEL
Three grams of fennel have about three calories. Fennel contains manganese, calcium, potassium, magnesium, phosphorus, and vitamin C.

GARLIC
One cup of garlic, almost a quarter pound, has only two hundred calories with plenty of calcium, vitamin C, and iron.

GINGER
Two grams of ginger have eight calories, only thirty milligrams of carbs, four milligrams of fiber, and just three milligrams of protein, with no noticeable vitamins or minerals.

GOVERNOR PLUMS
Governor plums are a good source of vitamins A and C and potassium. They have very little protein and only a trace of fat, but they do contain more antioxidants than many other fruit.

GRAPEFRUIT
One grapefruit has 80 calories with one gram of protein, eighteen grams of carbohydrates, and three grams of fiber. It is an excellent source for vitamins A and C, most B vitamins with folic acid, pectin, calcium, potassium, and magnesium.

GREEN BEANS
Green beans, have only 45 calories per cup, yet are loaded with many potent nutrients. They are an great source of vitamins A, C, and K. green beans are a good source of dietary fiber, potassium, folate, iron, magnesium, manganese, thiamin, riboflavin, copper, calcium, phosphorous, protein, omega-3 fatty acids, and niacin.

GUAVAS
Guavas are high in vitamins A and C, phosphorus, and niacin. Some guavas have four times the vitamin C of an orange. A quarter pound of guavas has only 60 calories.

HOG PLUM
A quarter pound of hog plums has about forty calories with a lot of carotene, calcium, and thiamine.

HORSERADISH
Horseradish has only two calories per teaspoon. High in fiber, vitamin C, folate, pantothenic acid, magnesium, potassium, manganese, riboflavin, vitamin B6, phosphorus and copper.

JACKFRUIT / KATAHAR
One cup of raw jackfruit has about one hundred and fifty calories, with four grams of fat and two grams of protein. It provides a tenth the daily requirement of vitamin A and twenty per cent of vitamin C with calcium, iron, zinc, and phosphorus.

JALAPENO PEPPER
One of these hot spicy peppers has only twenty calories with plenty of vitamins A and C.

LEEKS
Leeks are a good source of fiber, leeks folic acid, calcium, iron, potassium, manganese, vitamins B6 and C. For many, leeks are easier to digest than onions. A cup of raw leeks has 60 calories, but a half-cup of boiled leeks has only sixteen calories.

LEMON
A lemon has only 25 calories with one gram of protein, eight grams of carbs with calcium, iron, potassium, and phosphorous. One hundred ml of lemon juice has 50 ml of vitamin C (ascorbic acid).

LETTUCE
Lettuce provides vitamins A and C, and minerals such as potassium, iron, and calcium. A cup of lettuce is ten calories with one-gram each of fiber, protein, and carbohydrates.

LIME
One lime has only twenty calories with absolutely no fat, sugar, or cholesterol. Citrate of lime and citric acid are also derived from this fruit. One lime contains a third of the daily requirement of vitamin C as ascorbic acid. Limes also have some fiber and potassium.

MACE
Five grams of mace has about twenty five calories. It is high in calcium, phosphorus, and magnesium.

MAMEY APPLE
A hundred grams of mamey apple pulp has only 45 calories with some calcium, phosphorus, iron, vitamins A & B, and thiamine.

MANGOS
Mangos not only make you feel good, they are great health wise because they contain plenty of fiber, vitamins A and C, and potassium. One large mango has about a hundred calories with no cholesterol, and half of the necessary daily fiber.

MANGOSTEEN
Mangosteen have sixty calories per hundred grams of flesh with calcium, phosphorus, and iron.

MARJORAM
One tablespoon has five calories with some vitamin A and C, calcium, and iron.

MINT
Two leaves of mint have hardly any calories with some calcium and potassium.

MUSTARD
A cup of cooked mustard greens has only twenty calories with vitamins K, A, E, and C, potassium, calcium, and iron.

NUTMEG
Nutritionally nutmeg is high in calories, twelve calories a teaspoon, two thirds of which come from fat. It has no vitamins and only some iron and calcium.

OCHRO / OKRA
A half-cup of cooked ochro has only 25 calories; 2 grams of fiber, 1.5 grams protein, vitamins A and C, calcium, potassium, and manganese. Nearly 10% of the recommended levels of vitamin B6 and folic acid are also present.

ONIONS
Chopped raw, mature onions have sixty calories per cup, 2 grams fiber, and one-gram protein, with six grams carbohydrates. Onions are a good source of vitamin C, chromium, manganese, potassium, and phosphorus.

ORANGES
Each orange has about sixty calories packed with vitamins C and B-1, fiber, and folate. One orange contains about 50mg. vitamin C; or two-thirds of our daily need.

OREGANO
Oregano's pungent taste is reduced by cooking, so it is beast best added to any dish just shortly before serving it. Oregano has five calories per tablespoon with some protein. It is high in vitamins A, C, E, and K, and minerals as calcium, iron, magnesium,

phosphorus, and potassium.

PAK CHOY / CHINESE CABBAGE
A perfect food for dieters, one cup of cooked pak choy has only 20 calories, with no fat, but 3 grams of carbs and 3 grams of protein.

PAPAYA
A cup of papaya has 120 calories with good doses of vitamins A, E, and C, folic acid, potassium, and fiber.

PAPRIKA
Paprika has only six calories per teaspoon with a good bit of calcium and potassium.

PARSLEY
One ounce of fresh parsley has only ten calories with two thirds of the daily requirement of vitamin C while rich in minerals as calcium and potassium. Parsley contains antioxidants such as vitamin C, beta-carotene, and folic acid. These antioxidants fight many diseases such as arthritis, asthma, diabetes, colon cancer, heart attacks, and strokes.

PASSION FRUIT
A half-cup of juice has fifty calories with one gram of protein and eleven grams carbohydrates. It is a good source of vitamins A and C.

PEANUTS
Every ounce of raw peanuts provides seven grams of protein, seven grams of fat, and 3 grams of fiber. A cup has over six hundred calories, because they are over seventy-five per cent oil. However, it is healthy oil, monounsaturated, not polyunsaturated.

PEWA / PEACH PALM
Pewa fruit contain carotene, calcium, phosphorus, ascorbic acid, vitamin A, and nicotinic acid. Fruit should be boiled within 2 to 4 days of picking.

PIMENTO SEASONING PEPPERS
Four pimento peppers have about ten calories with little food value.

PINEAPPLE
Two slices of a regular sized pineapple should be about a hundred grams and has sixty calories with no fat or cholesterol. Pineapple is a good source of vitamin C.

PLANTAINS
Plantains are belly fillers, not for the dieters, as they are mostly carbohydrate, approximately 40 grams per half, with180 calories, very high in potassium approximately 500 milligrams per serving. Plantains are a very healthy fruit to eat. This is because they do not contain any cholesterol or sodium, and are low in fat. They also contain traces of calcium, iron, and potassium, and are high in vitamin A.

POMMECYTHERE
Pommecythere fruit have 160 calories for 100 grams because 10 per cent is sugar, 85% is water, which is why it is great for juice. The fruit is good source of vitamin C. potassium,

carbohydrates and fiber.

POMMEGRANATE
Pomegranate A hundred 100 grams of pomegranate has seventy calories with plenty of potassium, vitamins C and B5

POMMELO / SHADDOCK
A cup of shaddock has seventy calories and is high in potassium.

PUMPKIN
One cup of cooked pumpkin has 24 calories, one gram of protein. Pumpkin is a good source of thiamin, niacin, vitamin A, C, E, B6, folate, pantothenic acid, iron, magnesium, phosphorus, riboflavin, potassium, copper, and manganese.

RADISH
Morai is considered a 'winter radish' while the red 'globe' (seldom found in the Caribbean unless at an upscale grocery) is a summer type. All radishes are very flavorful and low in calories. A half cup has only 12 calories with a good balance of fiber, potassium, and folate.

RED BANANAS
Every red banana has about 115 calories with 400 mg potassium and 15% of your daily requirements for vitamin C and B6, with one gram of protein. Red bananas have more vitamin C than the usual yellow types. The redder the fruit the more nutritious. Eat at least one banana a day and it comes in truly germ proof packaging because its thick peel is an excellent protection against bacteria and other contamination.

RICE
White, long-grain, regular, not enriched, cooked, without salt 205 calories—one cup brown medium grain 218. Natural brown rice has about a calorie a gram and is low in saturated fat, cholesterol, and sodium. It is also a good source of selenium, and manganese.

ROSEMARY
Rosemary has about three calories per teaspoon with some calcium and iron.

SAFFRON
One teaspoon has four calories with some potassium.

SAGE
Sage contains six calories in two grams with some calcium and iron. Sage is a good source of vitamins A and C

SAPODILLA
A raw sapodilla has about 120 calories with calcium, potassium, vitamins A, C, and folate.

SEIM BEANS
Seim is an excellent of low calorie protein as one cup of the boiled beans has 6 grams of

protein with only 65 calories with vitamin A, potassium, calcium, with plenty of fiber. Seim is an excellent source of the amino acid lysine.

SOURSOP
A hundred grams of soursop has sixty calories with good amounts of calcium, phosphorus and amino acids. The fruit also contains significant amounts of vitamins C, B1, and B2.

SPINACH
One cup of fresh spinach has only forty calories and over twice the daily requirement of vitamin K. This vitamin is essential to keep human bones healthy. Spinach is also a great source for vitamins A, C, magnesium, and folate.

STARFRUIT / CARAMBOLA / FIVE FINGER
One nice star fruit has about twenty calories and is high in carbohydrates, calcium, phosphorus, vitamins A, B, and C, plus amino acids. Starfruit is a good source of dietary fiber, and can help to reduce blood pressure and cholesterol.

SUMMER SQUASH
Summer squash such as zucchini are low in calories with only 16 to a cup. Zucchini and crookneck squash are an excellent source for vitamins A and C, and minerals such as potassium, calcium, folate, and magnesium.

SWEET PEPPER
One cup of raw sweet green pepper has only twenty-four calories and has three times the daily requirement for vitamin C (four times an orange), and the complete requirement of vitamin A. These two vitamins plus B-6 and folic acid protect against high cholesterol and heart disease. Peppers are also rich in vitamins B6, B1, folic acid, manganese, and potassium.

SUGAR APPLE
A medium sized fruit is about eighty calories with a little protein, but one gram of fat. They contain good amounts of phosphorous and calcium.

SUGAR CANE
Sugar cane juice provides glucose and renews energy. One tablespoon of cane juice has 45 calories. One tablespoon white granulated sugar has 46 calories, and brown has 34.

SWEET POTATOES
The sweet potato is very nutritious. A half-cup of cooked sweet potato supplies 2 grams of protein, four grams of fiber, vitamins A and C, calcium, beta-carotene, manganese, and folic acid. One ounce steamed sweet potato has 24 calories.

TAMARIND
Tamarind pulp has only fifty calories in two ounces with some protein and fiber. Tamarind is high in calcium, phosphorus, and potassium.

TANGELOS
Tangelos have about a hundred calories per fruit with plenty of potassium, and of course

vitamin C.

TANNIA
One cup of cooked tannia has about a hundred calories, mostly water and carbohydrates with a little protein, and virtually no fat. Tannia is a great source of calcium, phosphorous, and iron. These roots also supply vitamin A, thiamin, and riboflavin.

TARRAGON
One teaspoon of ground tarragon has 14 calories with plenty of potassium. A half ounce of fresh tarragon equals a third of a cup. One tablespoon of fresh tarragon equals one teaspoon of dried.

THYME
One gram of thyme has three calories with calcium, vitamin A and iron.

TONKA BEANS
There is no accurate calorie counter for tonka beans, but they are a quarter fat with a larger percentage of starch.

TOMATOES
Tomatoes contain vitamin C, potassium, folacin, and beta-carotene. A diet containing tomatoes may help reduce cancer, heart disease, and premature aging. A medium tomato has only 25 calories.

TOPPEETAMBU
Nutritionally toppee tambu is actually more than a starchy, belly filler. Per 100 grams nutrition the roots have sixty calories, nine grams of carbs, a half gram of protein, with calcium, phosphorus, and some vitamin C.

TURMERIC
This root has eight calories per teaspoon with manganese, iron, vitamin B-6 and potassium.

WATERMELON
Watermelon is practically a multi-vitamin itself. Watermelon contains about 10% of the daily requirement of potassium, which helps regulate heart functions and normalize blood pressure. One wedge, or a quarter of a small melon, has 90 calories, 2 grams protein, 20 grams of carbohydrates, 1.5 grams of fiber, potassium, and vitamins A and C.

YAM
Yam flesh is poisonous raw, but cooking make sit safe and edible. One cup of cooked yam contains 150 calories with five grams of fiber, vitamins C and B6, potassium, and manganese.

He that takes medicine and neglects diet wastes the skills of the physician.
Chinese proverb

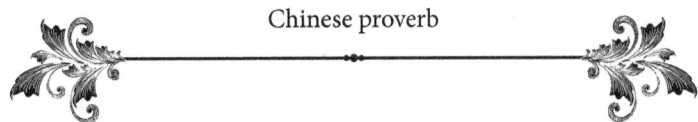

NOTES

Food Remedies

Please note: The use and dosage of herbs and foods vary with circumstances as climate, whether it is hot or cold, the person's health and age, and the manner the dose is administered. Herbs and foodstuffs should be used for medical purposes only with proper medical advice.

*The way you think, the way you behave, the way you eat,
can influence your life by 30 to 50 years.*

Deepak Chopra

ACEROLA - WEST INDIAN CHERRY
Historically, acerola cherry has been used to treat dysentery and fever. Research suggests that the cherry possesses anti-inflammatory and astringent properties. It is rich in vitamin C and over 150 phytonutrients have been found in the acerola cherry. This cherry contains vitamin C, potassium, magnesium, and other minerals.

ALLSPICE
In the past, allspice was used to treat indigestion and gas. It was eaten as treatment for stomachaches, vomiting, diarrhea, fever, and colds. It has been used to flavor toothpastes.

ALMONDS
Almonds are good eating nuts, high in monounsaturated fatty acids, and actually lower your cholesterol level, reducing risk of heart disease. Almonds contain significant amounts of magnesium, vitamin E, fiber, and potassium, all of which are beneficial to a healthy heart. Almonds are loaded with vitamin E and flavonoids in the nut's skin. Both are antioxidants linked to improving breathing. In fact, scientists believe these chemicals may even prevent respiratory diseases such as asthma, emphysema, and chronic bronchitis.

ALOE
For centuries aloe vera has been used medicinal purposes. The secret is its concentrations of nutrients and vital substances that include water, vitamins A, B, C, and E, more than 20 minerals, and both fatty and amino acids. It seems scientists didn't believe aloe actually cured burns, so it was tested. Aloe is now proven to heal first and second degree burns, but it has not been proven to protect from sunburn. Drinking aloe juice improves blood glucose levels for diabetics, and helps patients with liver disease. Aloe juice may reduce symptoms and inflammation of stomach ulcers. It will also reduce gum disease

and dental plaque. Aloe vera extracts are antibiotic and fight fungus. Aloe Vera is used to treat skin ailments as insect bites, acne, sunburns, rashes, scars, blemishes, sores, eczema, and psoriasis. It is drunk to treat blood pressure, hypoglycemia, arthritis, ulcers, constipation, poor appetite, digestive disorders, diarrhea, and hemorrhoids. Aloe should be simply patted on the skin once a day as sufficient for the desired results.

BALATA
Legends report the sap is so creamy it could be substituted for cow milk. However, over indulging the sap will 'bind', or constipate you.

BANANA
The New England Journal of Medicine reported a banana a day can decrease the risk of death from strokes by as much as 40 percent in certain cases. Bananas have many medicinal uses. Because they are very high in iron they are great for treating anemia. The high potassium and low salt help reduce blood pressure. The high fiber can overcome constipation. Bananas naturally contain tryptophan, which the body converts into serotonin – known improve your mood and generally make you feel happier, fighting depression. The banana neutralizes burning stomach acid and reduces irritation by coating the lining of the stomach. Bananas keep blood sugar levels up and help to avoid morning sickness. Banana skin rubbed on a mosquito bite will reduce swelling and irritation. B vitamins in bananas can calm jittery nerves while potassium helps normalize the heartbeat. If you are trying to quit smoking, bananas help the body recover from the effects of nicotine withdrawal and are a great snack to assist in weight loss. Supposedly unsightly warts can be removed by covering with a piece of banana skin, yellow side out.

BASIL
A basil leaf will relieve the pain of a mouth ulcer and basil tea will soothe sore gums. Basil tea is also a good soothing remedy for arthritis or rheumatism. This herb improves blood circulation by fighting bad cholesterol, while reducing the chance of irregular heartbeats.

BAY LEAVES
Put bay leaves in a damp washcloth to alleviate the pain of headaches, especially migraines. Bathing in a bath with bay leaves can treat skin rashes and pain from over sore muscles or arthritis. These same leaves hung in a wardrobe can protect your clothes from moths. Bay oil (if you can find it) increases blood circulation and is reported to prevent baldness. Bay leaf helps the body process insulin more efficiently, which lowers blood sugar levels. It has also been used to treat stomach ulcers. Bay leaf has anti-inflammatory, anti-oxidant properties, antifungal and anti-bacterial. Bay also treats rheumatism, and colic.

BLACK PEPPER
Medicinally black pepper is considered good for the digestive system and fights bacteria. Pepper sooths nausea and increases body temperature to fight fevers and chills. Its spicy hot flavor makes the nose and throat produce (water) a lubricating secretion, and assists anyone who needs to cough up and clear their lungs. Pepper was also used ointment to relieve skin afflictions and hives. However, coarsely ground black pepper does irritate

the intestines.

BEET ROOT
Beet juice is considered as one of the best vegetable juices. It is a rich source of natural sugar. It contains sodium, potassium, phosphorus, calcium, sulfur, chlorine, iodine, iron, copper, vitamins B1, B2, C, and P. This juice is rich in easily digestible carbohydrates, but the calorie content is low. Red beet juice is high in iron, and it regenerates and reactivates the red blood cells, supplies fresh oxygen to the body. It is useful in treating anemia. Beet juice is a good treatment for jaundice, hepatitis, and nausea. Add a teaspoonful of lime juice to increase its medicinal value. Fresh beet juice mixed with a tablespoonful of honey taken every morning before breakfast will help heal a gastric ulcer. Beet juice combined with the carrot and cucumber juices is one of the finest cleansers for kidneys and gall bladder. Beet juice acts as a natural tonic for the dry tired skin. Blend one beet root with a half cup of cabbage, set some juice aside. Add a tablespoon of mayonnaise or olive oil with beets and cabbage, apply to your face. Mix beet juice with water and freeze the ice cubes. Use a cube to cleanse and tone your skin every morning and evening.

BRAZIL NUTS
Brazil nuts health benefits are known to the world, due to the fact that the nuts are the richest source of the mineral selenium. An ounce of Brazil nuts contains 544 mcg. Selenium found in Brazil nuts is also effective in reducing the risk of breast cancer, prostate cancer, and other cancers. It also helps to maintain the proper functioning of the thyroid and is good for building the immune system.

BROCCOLI
Researchers have discovered a compound in broccoli that fights the bacteria that cause peptic ulcers much better modern antibiotic drugs. This same broccoli compound protects against stomach cancer, currently the second most common type of cancer. Broccoli has been found to lower the risk of prostrate and lung cancers.

CABBAGE
Cabbage may reduce the risk of some forms of cancer including colon or rectal cancers. Since cabbage is in high carotene content, regular eating reduces the risk of some cancers. Sulfur in cabbage reduces the growth of tumors, removes toxins, and strengthens our immune systems. Cabbage is rich in vitamins and minerals and reduces the 'bad' cholesterol that hardens arteries Eating cabbage first will prepares the stomach for a heavy meal and drinks. Crush a raw cabbage leaf in a mortar and use it as a poultice on a cut. To fight acne drink a cupful of the water cabbage is boiled in, or crush a raw leaf and use it as a poultice on oily facial areas for about 20 minutes. A boiled cabbage leaf applied while still very hot to the abdomen will cure a stomach ache.

CAIMATE
Caimate bark is rich in tannin used to tan leather and is thought to fight cancer. A drink made from the boiled bark is used as a stimulant tonic. Cooked caimate is used to reduce a fever. The leaves are grated and applied to cuts to reduce infection. The leaves may be boiled and the resulting liquid drank to combat hypoglycemia.

CANNISTEL
A decoction of the astringent bark is taken to lower a fever in Mexico and applied on skin eruptions in Cuba. A preparation of the seeds is used as a remedy for ulcers

CARIALLI
Carialli is nutritional. The bitter juice can be helpful to diabetics. A tea of the leaves and blossoms provides natural relief for high blood pressure.

CARDAMOM
A medicinal, perhaps aphrodisiac, drink can be made by steeping seeds in hot water, or you can just suck a cardamom seed. This is good for the throat, respiratory tract, teeth, breath, and stomach. Green cardamom is used to treat tooth and gum infections (just like cloves), treat throat problems, lung congestion, and also digestive disorders.

CARROTS
Eating carrots may protect against strokes, and heart disease. Carrots are rich in beta-carotene, which the human body converts to vitamin A in. Beta-carotene fights some forms of cancer, especially lung cancer. Carrot is rich in alkaline elements that cleanse and rejuvenate the blood. Carrots also supply the human body with vitamin C, calcium, phosphorus, sodium, sulfur, chlorine, and contain traces of iodine. The mineral contents in carrots lie very close to the skin and should not be peeled or scrapped off. A good washing is always necessary. Carrot juice strengthens the eyes and is a great treatment when rubbed on dry skin. Carrot juice drank daily may cure colic, colitis, and peptic ulcer. Raw carrots are good for fertility. Eaten after a meal, a raw carrot destroys germs in the mouth and prevents bleeding of the gums and tooth decay. Carrots speed up digestion. Carrots eaten regularly prevent gastric ulcer and other digestive disorders. Carrot soup is a natural remedy for diarrhea. Carrots fight all body parasites including intestinal worms.

CASSAVA
Cassava leaves and roots have been a folk remedy for tumors and cancers, which may be due to the B17 content, also known as laetrile. Vitamin B17 is also found in some seeds like apricots, peaches, and apples. B17 stimulates hemoglobin red blood cell count. The bitter cassava variety is used to treat diarrhea and malaria. The leaves are used to treat hypertension, headache, and pain. Cubans commonly use cassava to treat irritable bowel syndrome, the paste eaten in excess during treatment.

CAULIFLOWER
Cauliflower has compounds that activate enzymes that may disable and eliminate cancer-causing agents. Cauliflower also helps the liver neutralize poisons.

CAYENNE PEPPER
Cayenne is a food spice, but it also has been used as a miracle herb for the digestive and circulatory system. Peppers like cayenne have reputation for causing stomach problems including ulcers. That is unfounded because hot peppers actually may help prevent problems by killing bacteria you may have eaten, and stimulates the stomach to secrete a natural protective coating that prevents ulcers. Cayenne also helps the body secrete

hydrochloric acid necessary for digestion. Once you have good digestion all the other organs of the body get the proper nutrients. Consumed as a tea or in a capsule, cayenne pepper lowers the effects of asthma, and clears congestion. Rubbed on the skin, mixed with a skin cream as a paste, will reduce the pain of arthritis or stop an itch. Studies have demonstrated if you consume a lot of 'pepper' you chances of having a heart attack or stroke are lowered. It is a good source of vitamins A and C, has the complete B complexes, and is very rich in calcium and potassium. Gargling with cayenne pepper tea will help relieve a sore throat.

CAYENNE OINTMENT
Good for aches and sore muscles

Ingredients: one cayenne pepper chopped very fine, half cup vegetable oil, two TBS natural beeswax grated. (Get this from a beekeeper or a hair dresser who waxes).

Method: Heat oil on medium heat in a small sauce pan. Add minced pepper. Cook without boiling for five minutes. Remove from heat and pour through a strainer to remove pepper and seeds. Add beeswax and reheat until wax melts. Pour into suitable container or small jar and cool. Try on your next muscle ache.

CAYENNE JUMP UP JUICE
More spike than coffee without caffeine.

Ingredients: two TBS apple cider vinegar, eighth TS (a pinch) of baking soda, quarter TS cayenne pepper powder, one glass of hot water

Method: First, turn your head away as you add the cayenne powder to the vinegar and water so you don't inhale as the vinegar (acid) bubbles with the baking soda (alkaline). Sip slowly. It is a real energy boost, especially when I am over hungry and tired in the afternoon.

CELERY
Celery is a heart friendly vegetable. It contains compounds that can relax the artery muscles, which regulate blood pressure. It also causes blood vessels to constrict. Juice from 4 stalks can cause blood pressure to reduce 15%.

CHADON BENEE
Chadon benee and coriander are regarded as a drug. It is thought to be an aphrodisiac. If a large quantity is eaten, it acts as a narcotic. The seeds are a common remedy for gas pains and are chewed to ease the pains of birth labor.

CHALTA
The fruit is much used in India as a liver and cardiac tonic, and, when unripe, as an astringent means of halting diarrhea and dysentery and effective treatment for hiccough, sore throat and diseases of the gums. The pulp is used in poultices on bites and stings of venomous insects, as is the powdered rind. Juice of young leaves is mixed with milk and sugar candy and given as a remedy for biliousness and intestinal troubles of children. The powdered gum, mixed with honey, is given to overcome dysentery and diarrhea in

children. Oil derived from the crushed leaves is applied to relieve an itch, and the leaf decoction is given to children as an aid to digestion. Leaves, bark, roots, and fruit pulp are all used against snakebite.

CHANNA
Unlike hard to digest meat, channa is low in calories and virtually fat-free. However channa contains 'purine' and individuals with kidney problems or gout may want to avoid these beans. Research has found that a seven day diet (one meal a day) of channa cooked with onions and turmeric powder will drastically reduce your overall cholesterol.

CHATAIGNE
Tea made of young chataigne leaves lowers blood pressure and fights diabetes.

CHOCOLATE
In moderation chocolate actually reduces blood pressure. Men over fifty who eat a small bit of dark unsweetened chocolate every day live longer! Chocolate contains many health benefits from flavonoids, which act as antioxidants that protect the body from aging caused by free radicals, which can cause damage that leads to heart disease. Dark chocolate contains a large number of antioxidants. Studies show consuming a small bar of dark chocolate everyday can reduce blood pressure in individuals with high blood pressure. Dark chocolate has also been shown to reduce LDL cholesterol (bad cholesterol) up to 10 percent. Chocolate tastes good and stimulates endorphin production, which gives a feeling of pleasure. It also contains caffeine and other substances which are stimulants. Dark chocolate has 65 percent cocoa content.

CHRISTOPHENE
A tea made from christophene leaves is a bush treatment for hypertension and is reported to dissolve kidney stones.

CINNAMON
Medicinally cinnamon is considered a mild tranquilizer and relieves nausea and gas. It is an antibiotic that fights some fungi and bacteria better than over the counter medication. One-half teaspoon of cinnamon each day may reduce blood sugar and cholesterol in Type II diabetes sufferers. A tea of cinnamon and ginger is great for fighting a cold or flu, and indigestion.

COCONUT
Since coconut water is sterile, it has been used intravenously as a substitute for glucose. Coconut water kills bacteria that cause ulcers, throat infections, urinary tract infections, gum disease, cavities, pneumonia, and other diseases. Kills fungi and yeasts that cause ringworm, athlete's foot, thrush, diaper rash, and other infections. Expels or kills tapeworms, lice, and other parasites. Helps reduce health risks associated with diabetes. Improves calcium and magnesium absorption and supports the development of strong bones and teeth. Improves digestion and bowel function. Relieves pain and irritation caused by hemorrhoids. Is heart healthy; improves cholesterol ratio reducing risk of heart disease. Helps prevent liver disease, protect against kidney disease, bladder

infections, and dissolves kidney stones.

COFFEE

Coffee is one of the most heavily researched commodities in the world today and the general conclusion is coffee drinking is perfectly safe. There is no conclusive evidence to suggest a moderate amount of coffee is bad for you. Research has shown caffeine consumption may have a small effect on blood pressure, however scientists do not consider coffee drinking to be an important risk factor for hypertension. The key risk factors are known to be a low potassium intake, high sodium (salt) intake, slack lifestyle, and obesity. However, if you drink three to four cups - at a sitting - several times a day, coffee can slow pulse rate, raise blood pressure, contract blood vessels under the skin, and dilate blood vessels of the kidneys, muscles, skin, and heart. Finally, caffeine in large amounts makes the heart contract harder while it's pumping. Caffeine is a stimulant. It increases alertness and concentration, intensifies muscle responses, quickens heartbeat, and elevates mood. Its effects derive from the fact that its molecular structure is similar to that of adenosine, a natural chemical by-product of normal cell activity. Adenosine is a regular chemical that keeps nerve cell activity within safe limits. When caffeine molecules hook up to sites in the brain where adenosine molecules normally dock, nerve cells continue to fire indiscriminately, producing a jingly feeling sometimes associated with drinking coffee, tea, and other caffeine products. A remarkable remedy for rheumatism and gout is said to be; a pint of hot, strong, black coffee, which must be perfectly pure, and seasoned with a teaspoonful of pure black pepper, thoroughly mixed before drinking, and the preparation taken just before retiring.

CORRIANDER

Recent studies have supported its use as a stomach soother for both adults and colicky babies. Coriander contains an antioxidant that helps prevent animal fats from turning rancid, killing meat-spoiling bacteria and fungi. These same substances in cilantro also prevent infection in wounds. Coriander has been shown to improve tummy troubles of all kinds, from indigestion to flatulence to diarrhea. Weak coriander tea may be given to children under age two for colic. It's safe for infants and may relieve their pain and help you get some much-needed sleep. Cilantro and coriander contain substances that kill certain bacteria and fungi, thereby preventing infections from developing in wounds. Sprinkle some coriander seed on minor cuts and scrapes after thoroughly washing the injured area with soap and water. Intriguing new studies suggest that coriander has anti-inflammatory effects. Since the pain of arthritis is caused by inflammation coriander oil may help.

CORN

Eating corn is good for you. Corn is high in fiber, niacin, folate and some vitamin A. Folate has been found to prevent some birth defects and to reduce the risk of heart disease and stroke. Fiber keeps the intestinal track running smoothly.

CUCUMBERS

Cucumbers are mild laxatives. Cucumbers are a good source of B vitamins and carbohydrates and can provide a energy burst that can last for hours. To avoid a hangover eat a few cucumber slices before going to bed, wake up refreshed, and headache free. Cucumbers contain enough sugar, B vitamins, and electrolytes to replenish essential nutrients the body lost, keeping everything in equilibrium. A fast and easy way to remove cellulite, rub a slice or two of cucumbers along your problem area for a few minutes, the phytochemicals in the cucumber cause the collagen in your skin to tighten, firming up the outer layer and reducing the visibility of cellulite. Works great on wrinkles.

CUMIN

Cumin stimulates your appetite while helping the stomach to relieve gas. It will reduce nausea during pregnancy. Cumin could be called the 'breast spice' because it supposedly increases both lactation and size.

DILL

Dill weed contains carvone, which has a calming effect and aids digestion by relieving intestinal gas. Dill seeds are high in calcium; one tablespoon equals a quarter cup of milk. Dill is believed to increase lactation in nursing mothers and is used in a weak tea for babies to ease colic, encourage sleep, and get rid of hiccups. Crushed dill seeds, mixed with water, is used to strengthen fingernails. Chewed dill seeds can cure bad breath.

DUNKS

Dunks cure stomach-aches and calm intestinal irritations. They were used in past times in the treatment of syphilis, Dunks were used for the treatment of respiratory, throat, intestinal, urinary inflammation, and very helpful in liver troubles. They were also used to fight asthma. It has sedative properties. The bark is an effective astringent in dysentery and diarrhea; the fruit is a mild laxative and expectorant. The phytochemical betulinic acid, present in this plant, may be helpful against melanoma cells. Betulinic acid inhibits the growth of cancer cells.

EDDOES

Eddoes are very high in starch, and are a good source of dietary fiber. Oxalic acid may be present in the corm and especially in the leaf, and these foods should be eaten with milk or other foods rich in calcium in order to remove the oxalate in the digestive tract. Absorbing a large quantity of the oxalate ion into the blood stream poses health risks, especially for people with kidney disorders, gout, or rheumatoid arthritis. Calcium in the body reacts with the oxalate to form calcium oxalate, which is highly insoluble and is suspected to cause kidney stones. Food allergies most frequently afflict children, with cow's milk being the most common allergenic food for infants, followed by eggs, peanuts, tree nuts, and soybeans. Poi, eddoes mashed to liquid, is considered a substitute for soy milk in infants allergic to both soy and cow's milk. In addition, the easy digestibility and other characteristics of poi might make it a nutritional supplement for weight gain in patients with conditions

EGGPLANT

Eating eggplant is good for you. It can reduce high cholesterol. One cup of cooked eggplant has 27 calories, 1 gram of protein, 6 grams of carbohydrates (two grams of fiber if eaten with the skin), phosphorus, potassium, and folate. An ingredient in common eggplant has been shown to cure cancer. The eggplant extract is a phytochemical called solasodine glycoside, or BEC5. The types of cancer treated by eggplant are both invasive and non-invasive nonmelanoma skin cancers. In every case the cancers went into remission and did not return. Australians have been curing their skin cancers using these phytochemicals for decades.BEC5 acts by killing cancer cells without harming any other healthy cells in the human body. BEC5 can also be used to treat actinic keratose, the precursor to cancer, as well as age or sunspots on the skin. Skin cancer is now reported to be the most common illness in men over the age of 50.

FENNEL

Fennel is used as an eyewash and was thought to increase breast milk. Fennel is believed to curb eating and great for dieters. It will reduce gas and stomach cramps. In medieval times this herb was hung over doors to ward off evil spirits. It is reputed to stimulate strength and courage, and increase the eater's life span. Fennel is in mouth fresheners, toothpastes, desserts, antacids. It fights anemia, indigestion, flatulence, constipation, colic, diarrhea, respiratory disorders, menstrual disorders, and eye care. With carrot juice, fennel is a very good treatment for night blindness, or to strengthen the optic nerve. Add beet juice to make a remedy for anemia resulting from menstruation. Fennel juice assists convalescence. The French use it for migraine and dizziness. Boiling fennel leaves and inhaling the steam can relieve asthma and bronchitis. Fennel is used after cancer radiation and chemotherapy treatments to help rebuild the digestive system. Ground fennel seed tea is believed to be good for snake bites, insect bites, or food poisoning. It increases the flow of urine.

GARLIC

Garlic is valued as a spice, but also for its medicinal benefits. No one knows how much garlic must be ingested to improve health, but experts feel the best results come from using raw garlic. Louis Pasteur discovered garlic kills bacteria. It was used as an antiseptic in World War II when sulfa drugs were scarce. Scientists have found that when raw garlic is cut or crushed it creates a compound, which kills at least twenty-three types of bacteria. Yet when garlic is heated it forms a different compound that reduces blood pressure and cholesterol. Garlic contains vitamins A, B, and C and stimulates the immune system. It may reduce the risk of stomach cancer and be a treatment for AIDS. Sixty kinds of fungi are also killed by garlic, including athlete's foot and vaginitis.

GINGER

Ginger is an excellent natural remedy for nausea, motion sickness, morning sickness, and general stomach upset due to its carminative effect that helps break up and expel intestinal gas. Ginger tea has been recommended to alleviate nausea in chemotherapy patients primarily because its natural properties do not interact in a negative way with other medications. It is a safe remedy for morning sickness, since it will not harm the fetus. Some studies show ginger may also help prevent certain forms of cancer. Ginger is used medicinally because it stimulates and strengthens the stomach, breaks colds and coughs, diarrhea, rheumatism, and especially for nausea. The root can be boiled and pounded into a paste applied to the forehead to ease headaches or made into a poultice to sooth arthritis. To make ginger tea, slice some ginger root, put it in a tea ball and place in a teapot. Pour boiling water over the tea ball and let it sit for ten minutes. Sweeten with honey or drink it straight. In spite of it being a natural remedy, it's important that any medicinal use of ginger be discussed with a physician, as it must be taken in moderation to avoid gastric irritation.

GRAPEFRUIT
Grapefruit lowers some cholesterol, helps digestion, and reduces gas. It is a treatment for water retention, urinary, liver, kidney, and gall bladder problems. Grapefruit is rubbed directly on the skin to fight pimples and greasiness. The leaves have antibiotic properties.

GREEN BEANS
Eating these delicious beans helps lower high blood pressure, and their fiber may also help prevent colon cancer. Green beans reduce the severity of diseases such as asthma, arthritis, and rheumatoid arthritis. These beans are a good source of riboflavin, which has been shown to help reduce the frequency of migraine attacks. Green beans are a very good source of iron. In comparison to red meat green beans provide iron for a lot less calories and are totally fat free. Iron is an integral component of hemoglobin, which transports oxygen from the lungs to all body cells, and is also part of key enzyme systems for energy production and metabolism.

GUAVA
The guava tree leaves are also a natural astringent that are used to stop diarrhea. They can be pounded into a poultice for wounds, boils, and aches. In fact, guava leaves can be chewed to relieve a toothache. Amazon Indians use a tea of the leaves as a remedy for sore throats, nausea, and to regulate menstrual periods. Tender leaves are chewed for bleeding gums and bad breath. If chewed before drinking alcohol, it is said to prevent hangovers. A poultice of guava blossoms is reported to relieve sun strain, conjunctivitis, or eye injuries.

HORSERADISH
Horseradish is a gastric stimulant that will helps digest rich foods. It is richer in vitamin C than an orange, and works as an antiseptic. It is valued for its medicinal properties to relieve respiratory congestion. A poultice reduce aches from arthritis or rheumatism.

JACKFRUIT/ KATAHAR
A one-cup serving of raw jackfruit has about one hundred and fifty calories, with four grams of fat and two grams of protein. It provides one-tenth the daily requirement of vitamin A and twenty per cent of vitamin C with calcium, iron, zinc, and phosphorus. The benefits of the antioxidant seeds fights cancer, hypertension, ageing, and ulcers. Powder ground from the seeds relieves indigestion.

JALAPENO PEPPERS
Jalapeños contain a substance called capsaicin that has shown to have anti cancer effects. However, the amount needed to achieve this effect is relatively high, up to eight habanero peppers per week (roughly equivalent to 24 jalapeños). Capsaicin in jalapenos not only causes the tongue to burn, it also drives prostate cancer cells to kill themselves.

Appendix B: Food Remedies

These peppers are naturally high in vitamins A and C, and also bioflavinoids, help strengthen blood vessels, and makes them more elastic to adjust to blood pressure fluctuations. All hot peppers make us sweat causing fluid loss, temporarily reducing overall blood volume.

LEMONS
Lemons, rich in vitamin C, strengthen the body's immune system as an antioxidant, protecting cells from damage. For a cough, sore throat, or cold, make a syrup by blending one tablespoon lemon juice with two tablespoons honey. You can also try lemon juice mixed with salt and ginger as a tonic for a cold. The aroma of lemon oil has been tested to reduce stress in aromatherapy. Lemon juice mixed with water will aid digestion, and pat an insect bite with raw lemon to stop the itch and reduce swelling. Lemons help cleanse the body through perspiration and as a natural diuretic. Lemon juice is believed to actually cleanse the liver of toxins.

LEEKS
Eating leeks helps the bowels, fights arthritis, and reduces the risk of prostate and colon cancer. Eating leeks is also reputed to keep your voice from becoming hoarse.

LETTUCE
Eating lettuce is good for the nervous system. Since it is low in carbohydrates it is a good food for diabetics and with high iron content it is good for anyone suffering from anemia. Lettuce juice or lettuce cooked as soup is a natural remedy for insomnia. Eating lettuce has a tranquilizing effect. Try eating a lettuce salad with a TBS olive oil before going to bed for sweet dreams. Lettuce tea made from a half cup of lettuce to a cup of boiling water relieves stress and is a good body tonic fighting cold viruses, and against asthma.

LIMES
Ancients used the lime for medicinal purposes. During the Middle Ages fragrant limes were used to ward moths from hanging clothes just as mothballs do today. Sailors loved the lime since it prevented the weakening disease of scurvy.

MACE
Mace and nutmeg are very similar in culinary and medicinal properties. Both spices are efficient in treating digestive and stomach problems, relive intestinal gas and flatulence. It can reduce vomiting, nausea, and general stomach uneasiness.

MANGOS
Mango contains a stomach-soothing enzyme. The skin of the unripe fruit is an astrigent, and a stimulant tonic. The bark is also astringent and will dry a runny nose. Mango pickles preserved in an oil and salted solution are used throughout India. However, these pickles (anchar), if extremely sour, spicy, and oily, are not good for health and should be specially avoided by those suffering from arthritis, rheumatism, sinusitis, sore throat and hyperacidity. The ripe mango is anti-scorbutic, diuretic, laxative, invigorating, fattening, and astringent. It tones up the heart muscle, improves complexion, and stimulates appetite. The fruit is beneficial in liver disorders, loss of weight, and other

physical disturbances. The unripe mango protects men from the adverse effects of hot, scorching winds. A drink, prepared from the unripe mango by cooking it in hot ashes and mixing the pith with sugar and water, is an effective remedy for heat exhaustion and heat stroke. Eating raw mango with salt quenches thirst, and prevents the excessive loss of sodium chloride and iron due to excessive sweating.

MARJORAM
A tea brewed from marjoram leaves may help with indigestion, headache, or stress. Externally dried leaves flowers may be applied as poultices to reduce the pain of rheumatism. Marjoram is considered the most fragrant essential oil among all herbs used in aromatherapy. It is also a warming and soothing message oil for muscle aches. It fights asthma, headaches, and soothes digestion. Marjoram is used to loosen phlegm, and is a decongestant used to fight bronchitis, and sinus headaches. It is useful as a tonic for the nervous system. Marjoram may be more calming than oregano, to soothe the nerves, reduce tension and stress. One component in marjoram is flavonoids, which relieve insomnia, tension headaches, and migraines.

MAUBY
Unsweetened and tangy, which is very seldom, the refreshing bark decoction is used as a bitter tonic for diabetes – lowering blood sugar, hypertension- lowering blood pressure, and cholesterol, and combating stomach disorders. According to the University of the West Indies, mauby combined with coconut milk may lower blood pressure.

MINT
Peppermint is one of the oldest and best tasting home remedies for indigestion, headache, and rheumatism. After dinner mints are used to improve bad breath, ease gas, and aid digestion. Peppermint lessens the amount of time food spends in the stomach by stimulating the gastric lining to produce enzymes which aid digestion. It relaxes muscles lessening stress, has antiviral and bactericidal qualities, clears congestion related to colds and allergies, and eases intestinal cramping. Regular use of mint is very beneficial for asthma patients, as it is a good relaxant, and gives relief in congestion. But, over dosage may irritate as well. Mint juice is an excellent skin cleanser. It soothes skin, cures infections, itching, and is also good for pimples.

MUSTARD
Mustard was always important in medicine. Mustard oil can be so irritable that it can burn the skin. It is used diluted as a liniment for sore muscles. Powdered mustard is used in mustard plasters to fight bad coughs and colds. Various peoples have used mustard for snake bites, bruises, stiff neck, rheumatism, and respiratory troubles. It is delightful in bath water or as a foot bath to ease aches and pains.

NUTMEG
Nutmeg was so important because of the purported medicinal properties of its seeds. It is an astringent and stimulant, as well as an aphrodisiac. At the height of its value in Europe, nutmeg was carried to demonstrate wealth. Ground nutmeg is also smoked in India and used for asthma, fever, and heart disease. Nutmeg oil is used in perfume, toothpastes, and cough medicines, and in pharmaceutical drugs. The oil is used

externally for rheumatism, and gargled for bad breath and toothaches. Nutmeg oil contains myristicine, which somewhat controls stomach gases, and if consumed in large doses causes hallucinations. Nutmeg oil stimulates the brain reducing mental exhaustion and stress. It improves the quality of your dreams, making them more intense and colorful. It is a good remedy for anxiety as well as depression. Nutmeg oil treats muscular and joint pain and it is an excellent sedative. Nutmeg's relaxing aroma comforts the body, and increases blood circulation.

OCHRO-OKRA
Ochro has many valuable nutrients. It is a prime source of soluble fiber in the form of gums and pectins. Soluble fiber lowers cholesterol and reduces the risk of heart disease. The other half is insoluble fiber, which keeps the intestinal tract healthy, decreasing the risk of some forms of cancer, especially colon-rectal cancer.

ONIONS
Eating onions gives some protection against heart disease and colon cancer. Onions may also reduce the frequency and strength of asthma attacks. Onions in soups are especially good to help ward off flues. It seems the more pungent onions, especially yellow, are better for you as they have more antioxidants.

ORANGES
Each orange has about sixty calories packed with vitamins C and B-1, fiber, and folate. One orange contains about 50mg. vitamin C; or two-thirds of our daily need. Vitamin C is necessary to fight colds and infections, helps reduce asthma attacks, and rheumatoid arthritis while decreasing the chance of colon cancer. It also helps heal wounds and broken bones. Pregnant women need more vitamin C because it helps form collagen, a protein that helps form bones, and makes the expectant mother's body easily absorb iron. Remember how our grannies had dried orange peels hanging for use in flavoring tea? Seems they knew more then than we do today. Orange peels contain compounds known as 'polymethoxylates (PMF)', which has been tested to lower cholesterol significantly – as much as some prescription drugs! Just dry the peel and add to tea or boiling water.

OREGANO
The ancient Greeks applied poultices of oregano leaves to treat sores, and muscle aches. Chinese herbal doctors use oregano to lower fevers, fight vomiting, diarrhea, jaundice, and itchy skin. Europeans use this herb for improved digestion, and to soothe coughs. Germans produce oregano based cough syrups. Oregano fights the common bacterial disease known as giardia amoeba, common throughout the world. It can cause serious illness and oregano proved to be more effective as treatment than the prescription drug. Oregano is very good for you, helping with digestion by increasing the flow of bile. Studies have shown oregano fights viruses, fungus, bacteria. The French oregano soaps may have been the first to really be antibacterial. This is a great herb to drink as a tea whenever you have a cold or fever.

PAK CHOY or CHINESE CABBAGE
Pak Choy is rich in vitamin C, fiber, and folic acid. All reduce the risk of various types of

cancer. Pak choy has more beta-carotene than other cabbages, and more potassium and calcium.

PAPAYAS

Eating papayas helps prevent diabetic heart disease. Nutrients in papayas prevent cholesterol from clogging arteries reducing the possibility of strokes. Papaya may lower cholesterol, prevent against colon cancer, and reduce inflammation caused by rheumatoid arthritis. Researchers believe papaya may be great for your sense of sight. The high vitamin A (300 percent of the daily need) content of papaya will help smokers prevent emphysema, or lung inflammation from second hand smoke.

PAPRIKA

Red peppers, from which paprika is ground, have much more vitamin C than oranges. The high heat of commercial processing destroys much of the vitamin C in paprika so look for the sun dried variety. Paprika is a good source for beta carotene, and is considered both a stimulant, and a blood pressure regulator. It fights bacteria, and aids digestion. Try substituting at least part of the salt you use on cooked food with paprika, and you will be pleasantly surprised. As an antibacterial agent and stimulant, paprika can help normalize blood pressure, improve circulation, and increase the production of saliva and stomach acids to aid digestion.

PARSLEY

Parsley is a natural diuretic and can be used by women to alleviate irregular menstrual cycles. Parsley eaten raw or as tea may ease the bloating that occurs during the time of the month. Chewing parsley will help with bad breath from food odors such as garlic or onions. A tea made from parsley will stimulate as much as a cup of coffee, but watch out as parsley has been reported to be an aphrodisiac. A poultice of its leaves can be used for insect bites or stings.

PEANUTS

Researchers in Great Britain discovered women who ate five ounces of peanuts weekly reduced heart attacks by a third. If you eat one ounce of peanuts every day the unsaturated fats in peanut butter will reduce the risk of heart disease by 25%. Rich in folate and niacin (vitamin B3) will increase the HDL, good cholesterol, by as much as 30%. Twenty-five percent of peanuts consists of proteins and dietary fiber. The most unique property of peanut butter is its high content in resveratrol, a substance that's been shown to have very strong anti-cancer properties. As many as one per cent of the world's population are allergic to peanuts. This allergy accounts for over three-fourths of all deaths related to food allergies each year.

PINEAPPLE

Pineapple is another fruit that not only tastes good, but also is good for you. Pineapple juice is close to our stomach juices. Consumed moderately, pineapple aids digestion. It has plenty of fiber and helps the body relieve fluids especially mucus from nasal passages. Never consume an unripe pineapple, as it can be poisonous causing throat irritations and diarrhea.

PLANTAIN
Young plantain leaves are a survival food raw in salad or cooked. They are very rich in vitamin B1 and riboflavin. The herb has a long history of use as an alternative medicine dating back to ancient times. A traditional healing salve can be made by placing one large whole plantain chopped (skin too) in large non-metallic pan (ceramic or Corning ware), with one cup vegetable oil or lard; cover and simmer on low heat till all is mushy and green. Strain while hot. Once cool put in a container that seals tight. It is good for burns, insect bites, rashes, all sores, and used as night cream for wrinkles.

POMMECYTHERE
Pommecythere leaves smell great, but are slightly sour and are used for flavoring, particularly curries. Indonesians make a dish with steamed leaves, salt fish, and rice. Tree sap can be used for medicinal poultices. A tea made from the bark is a supposed remedy for diarrhea. The fruit is good source of vitamin C, and the juice can be used for a remedy for diabetes, heart ailments, and urinary problems.

POMMERAC
Pommerac has many medicinal uses. An extract of the bark is used as an astringent to fight infections. The bark is pounded into a mix with sea salt, filtered through coconut husks, and poured into deep wounds. The root is used to sooth itches, and is effective against dysentery, and as a diuretic. Brazilians used pommerac as a remedy for diabetes and constipation. The juice of crushed leaves can be used as a skin treatment, and can be steeped into baths.

PUMPKIN
Eating pumpkin seeds helps men avoid prostrate cancer. They were once recommended as a cure for freckles and a cure for snakebites. The orange-flesh is a dead giveaway that pumpkin is a source of beta-carotene, which is a powerful antioxidant. Beta-carotene is converted to vitamin A in the body. Vitamin A is essential for healthy skin, vision, bone development, and many other functions.

RADISH
Radishes and their green tops are an excellent source of vitamin C. The leaves contain six times the vitamin C content of their root, and are also a good source of calcium. Red radishes provide the trace mineral molybdenum, and a good source of potassium. Morai provide a very good source of copper. Historically radishes used as a medicinal food for liver disorders. They contain a variety of sulfur-based chemicals to increase the flow of bile, which helps to maintain a healthy gallbladder and liver, and improve digestion. Morai aids in digestion of fatty fried foods. A half cup of morai daily will prevent kidney or gall stones.

ROSEMARY
Rosemary stimulates the circulatory and nervous systems while it also calms indigestion. It will help fight severe headaches. Rosemary's essential oil will ease muscle strains and aches. It is a usual ingredient in shampoos and hair conditioners that fights dandruff and (if you believe it) hair loss. Boil ten sprigs fresh rosemary in two cups water for thirty minutes. Cool and store in a tightly sealed container. Refrigerate. Once a

week combine one half cup of this rosemary water with a cup of warm water and work through hair after shampooing. It is thought that adding rosemary to your diet may reduce the chances of having a stroke, or contracting Alzheimer's. Rosemary is a good herb to use as a mouth wash because it soothes sore throats and freshens breath. Chinese combine it with borax to treat baldness. Rub your pets with powdered rosemary leaves as a natural flea and tick repellent due to its antimicrobial properties.

ROU KOU
Roucou pulp and seeds boiled in oil makes a salve that helps heal small cuts and burns, preventing scarring, and blistering. A decoction of the leaves and pulp relieves stomach disorders like indigestion, and will help asthma. Roucou leaves in a bath will be refreshing. Leaves heated in oil will reduce a headache when pressed to the forehead.

SAFFRON
Large dosages of saffron can be fatal. It is considered an excellent stomach tonic and helps digestion and increases appetite. It is also relieves tension and fights depression. It is a fact since antiquity, crocus was attributed to have aphrodisiac properties. Rubbing a salve made from saffron into achy joints is an old folk remedy for gout. Because of saffron's high price, it is unlikely that you will find it ready made in health food stores. You can make your own, however, by blending a few threads of saffron into petroleum jelly. Spread a thin layer of the salve on the affected areas in the morning and evening. Use the salve until the joint pain abates. Saffron alleviates fatigue and exhaustion, primarily because it works to strengthen the heart and nervous system. It aids digestion, by increasing appetite and gastric juice production. When added to some homeopathic preparations, it also relieves nosebleeds. Saffron milk is a tasty, soothing drink that can be helpful in relieving cardiac problems. To make it, bring one cup of milk just to boil, add a pinch of saffron. Reduce the heat and simmer the mixture for two minutes. Sweeten with honey to taste, and drink it once a day.

SAGE
Medicinally smoking sage helps relieve asthma, and sage tea will help fight a fever, or a sore throat. To hide gray hair put one half cup of dried sage in two cups of water and simmer for half an hour. Cover and allow the sage water to steep overnight. Over a basin, pour the rinse on your hair at least ten times reusing the same sage water. On the last rinsing, leave the sage water dry on the hair before rinsing with fresh water. Repeat every week until your hair is the desired shade. Then rinse every month to retain your hair color. For sore throats, try mixing a sage tea with apple cider vinegar, and salt for gargling. Sage is reported to have moisture-drying properties, and can be used as an antiperspirant. It can also be used as a compress on cuts and wounds. Clinical studies have also shown that it can lower blood sugar in cases of diabetes. Pour boiling water over two teaspoons of sage leaves. Let mixture steep for ten minutes. Strain, then drink one to two cups per day to relieve symptoms of coughs, tonsillitis, and respiratory infections. Because sage has a powerful antiseptic effect, combine sage with your toothpaste. This will help remove plaque, and will strengthen bleeding gums.

Appendix B: Food Remedies

SAPODILLA
Medicinally young sapodilla fruits can be boiled and eaten as a bush remedy for diarrhea. A tea made from the old, yellowed leaves is a reputed remedy for coughs and colds. Eating crushed seeds are claimed to expel bladder and kidney stones, while the liquid essence of the crushed seeds is used throughout the Yucatan as a tranquillizer. The seeds can be crushed into a paste to sooth insect bites. Chicle is used in Central America as a primitive dental filling.

SEIM BEANS
Eating seim can help reduce water retention and possibly cure a severely upset stomach and diarrhea.

SORREL
Sorrel has many bush medicine remedies. Drinking the tea will relieve hypertension, coughs, and is a cure for hangovers. A paste of the leaves and seeds is used in Egypt as an antibiotic on wounds. Leaves that have been warmed in hot water can be used on the skin to draw out boils or ulcers.

SOURSOP
Ripe fruit juice is said to be diuretic, and a remedy for blood in the urine and urethritis. Taken when fasting, it is believed to relieve liver ailments, and leprosy. Pulverized immature fruits, which are very astringent, are decocted as a dysentery remedy. To draw out chiggers and speed healing, apply the flesh of an acid soursop as a poultice unchanged for three days. In the Materia Medica of British Guiana, it is recommended to break soursop leaves in water, "squeeze a couple of limes therein, get a drunken man and rub his head well with the leaves and water and give him a little of the water to drink, and he gets as sober as a judge in no time." This sobering or tranquilizing formula may not have been widely tested, but soursop leaves are regarded throughout the West Indies as having sedative or properties. In the Dutch Antilles, the leaves are put into one's pillowslip or strewn on the bed to promote a good night's sleep. An infusion of the leaves is commonly taken internally for the same purpose. It is taken as an analgesic and antispasmodic in Esmeraldas Province, Ecuador. In Africa, it is given to children with fever and they are also bathed lightly with it. A decoction of the young shoots or leaves is regarded in the West Indies as a remedy for gall bladder trouble, as well as coughs, catarrh, diarrhea, dysentery and indigestion. It is said to 'cool the blood', and to be able to stop vomiting, and aid delivery in childbirth. The decoction is also employed in wet compresses on inflammations and swollen feet. The chewed leaves, mixed with saliva, are applied to incisions after surgery, causing the incision to disappear without leaving a scar. Mashed leaves are used as a poultice to alleviate eczema and other skin afflictions and rheumatism, and the sap of young leaves is put on skin eruptions. Research suggests a connection may exist between eating soursop and atypical forms of Parkinson's disease because of the high content of annonacin present in soursop. What a shame because annonacin is also supposed to cure cancer!

SPINACH
Spinach protects against heart disease, arthritis, and types of cancer. Eating this green

prevents cholesterol from blocking arteries causing heart attacks or strokes, and reduces high blood pressure. Spinach may be a rival with carrots for benefiting eyesight by keeping the eye muscles strong and reducing the incidence of cataracts.

STARFRUIT

Star fruit juice will clean brass and silver. It will also remove rust stains from white clothes. East Indians use this five-finger fruit widely for many medicinal purposes. The juice will help reduce a fever and quench the associated thirst. Boiled fruit will relieve diarrhea or a hangover. A salve made by continuously boiling the fruit to almost nothing is good for eye infections. Eating the ripe fruit is said to reduce hemorrhoids. A poultice of crushed leaves will fight ringworm. The powdered seeds are said to have a sedative effect, and are useful in fighting children's colic. In bush medicine, the starfruit tree is a virtual pharmacy. In India, ripe starfruit is used to halt hemorrhages and to relieve bleeding hemorrhoids. Starfruit is used by Brazilians to fight kidney and bladder problems. It is also used to treat eczema. A decoction made from the fruit will overcome severe nausea and vomiting. Starfruit tree leaves can be plastered on the temples to soothe headaches. Beware hydrocyanic acid has been detected in the leaves, stems, and roots. Powdered seeds serve as a sedative in cases of asthma and colic.

SUGAR APPLE

A tea made of sugar apple leaves is considered an excellent tonic, especially for colds and diarrhea. A bath in the leaves relieves severe arthritis and rheumatism.

SUGAR CANE JUICE

Sugarcane juice is believed to have many medicinal properties. It supposedly strengthens the stomach, kidneys, heart, eyes, brain, and sex organs. Cane juice is beneficial to drink to break fevers. Sugarcane juice has been found to be very beneficial for preventing as well as treating sore throat, cold and flu. Being alkaline in nature, sugarcane juice helps the body in fighting against cancer, especially prostate and breast cancer. Sugarcane provides glucose to the body, which is stored as glycogen and burned by the muscles, whenever they require energy. Therefore, it is considered to be one of the best sources of energy. If you have been exposed to heat and physical activity for too long, drink sugarcane juice. It will help rehydrate the body quickly. Mixing sugarcane juice with lime juice, ginger juice, and coconut water will give good results for enlarged prostrate gland. Sugarcane juice is said to speed up the recovery process after jaundice, especially when mixed with lime juice. The juice sucked from the sugarcane can prove highly valuable in case of weak teeth due to lack of proper exercise resulting from excessive use of soft foods. It gives a form of exercise to the teeth and makes them strong. It also keeps the teeth clean and increases their life. Sugarcane juice is a fattening food. It is thus an effective remedy for thinness. Rapid gain in weight can be achieved by its regular use. The dew which collects on the long leaves of sugarcane is useful in several eye disorders. When instilled in the eyes, it is an effective medicine in defective vision, cataract, conjunctivitis, burning of the eyes, and eye-strain after excessive reading.

Appendix B: Food Remedies

SWEET POTATO

Sweet potato is believed by Chinese medicine to be supplementing and warming to the stomach. However, patients suffering from indigestion, or heat-dampness should not eat too much sweet potatoes as it can cause swelling of the stomach and abdominal pain. The leaves of sweet potato are bitter in taste, and are anti-diabetic. They are helpful in lowering blood sugar. These roots are extremely useful in treating asthma. Sweet potato contains phytoestrogens helpful for women's reproductive systems. Sweet potato on your regular diet will fight colon, kidney, prostrate, and intestinal cancer. They help prevent acid stomach and ulcers. Use the water the potatoes are boiled in for muscle and joint aches and arthritis.

TAMARIND— Tamarind pulp can be applied directly on inflammations, and used as a rinse for a sore throat. Pets infested with fleas or ticks can be washed, then rinsed with strong tamarind water, and let dry on them. Boiled tamarind leaves and flowers can be used as poultices for sprains and arthritis. A tea from the tree's bark makes an excellent tonic. Hard tamarind heart wood makes the best hoe handles, and mortars and pestles.

TANNIA

As a kitchen remedy, tannia may be used to regulate energy, support digestion, and disperse congestion.

TARRAGON

Tarragon increases appetite, improves circulation of blood, and helps in the proper distribution of nutrients, oxygen, hormones and enzymes throughout the body. It stimulates the brain, nervous system, digestive system, circulatory system, and the endocrinal system. This in turn stimulates the whole metabolic system and as a result, growth and immunity are stimulated.

> *He who has so little knowledge of human nature as to*
> *seek happiness by changing anything but his own disposition*
> *will waste his life in fruitless efforts.*
> Samuel Johnson

THYME

Thyme's best use medicinally is as an antiseptic, but it also has expectorant, antispasmodic, and deodorant properties. It aids in digestion, and as such, is excellent when combined with fatty meats that often cause gastrointestinal problems such as duck, lamb, and pork. Herbalists use thyme in infusions, extracts, teas, compresses, bath preparations, and gargles. Recent studies indicate that thyme strengthens the immune system. Nightmares were treated with thyme tea. Thyme oil was used during World War I to treat infection and to help relieve pain. Small amounts of this herb are sedative, but larger amounts are stimulant. Thyme is used against hookworm, roundworms, and threadworms. Thyme also warms and stimulates the lungs, expels mucus, and relieves congestion such as asthma. It also helps deter bacterial, fungal, and viral infections. Thyme has always been used as a poultice for wounds, insect bites and stings. It is a good wash for sore eyes, and a hair rinse to fight dandruff.

TOMATO

The British originally believed the tomato to be poisonous, but this vegetable is really good for you. Tomatoes contain an anti oxidant, lycopene that reduces the risk of prostrate cancer if eaten almost daily. Tomato is excellent for purifying and rejuvenating your skin, removing acne scars, and healing sunburn. Rub tomato slices directly onto your clean skin, focus on pimply areas. Tomatoes contain Vitamin C which has healing powers, and an acid which eliminates dead skin and opens pores, making skin soft and radiant. Tomatoes are rich in Vitamin A that prevents overproduction of sebum that causes acne. To remove dark circles under your eyes make a paste using one tablespoon tomato juice with a half teaspoon of lemon juice, a pinch of turmeric powder and a pinch of gram flour. Keep the paste under your eyes for 10 minutes. Dark circles will disappear after several treatments.

TONKA BEANS

The bark is prepared as a decoction to bathe fever patients. The seeds are fermented in rum and used for snakebites, cuts, contusions, coughs, rheumatism, and as a shampoo. The seed oil is dropped into the ears for earaches and ear infections. They are used in local supernatural potions to bolster courage, attract good luck with money, and in finding love. In fact it is known as the love wishing bean. Supposedly if you wish and throw seven tonka beans into a river, your wish will come true.

TOPPEETAMBU

It is good food for a non-irritating recuperation diet, and for infants as a replacement of breast milk. It can eaten in the form of jelly seasoned with sugar, lemon-juice, or fruit jellies. Medicinally the leaves are used in broth as a diuretic, and in the treatment of cystitis.

TURMERIC

Occasionally shredded and used fresh, turmeric is more often dried and powdered for use. The roots are boiled for hours, dried for days or weeks, then ground into powder. Turmeric removes accumulation of cholesterol in the liver and promotes a healthy circulatory system. It is also a great stomach tonic for gas, or indigestion. East Indian women with lovely, velvety skin often attribute it to consuming turmeric. It contains manganese, vitamin B6, and iron with about four calories to a gram. To make a tea from turmeric, pour 8 ounces of boiling water over a half-teaspoon and let sit covered for five minutes, then strain, if necessary. Drink two or three cups daily, as desired. Mix turmeric powder with cooking oil to make a thick paste. Put on the skin over wounds, bites, bruises, etc. Cover with bandage and leave on several hours. It washes off and color disappears quickly. If you have a toothache, paint this on your face over the toothache.

WATERMELON

Watermelon is high in disease fighting beta-carotene. Research also suggests that red-pigmented foods provide this protection. Lycopene and beta-carotene work with plant chemicals, which are not found in vitamin/mineral supplements. Watermelon is the leader in lycopene among fresh fruits and vegetables. Watermelon contains such high concentrations of lycopene that may help reduce the risks of prostate cancer.

Appendix B: Food Remedies

Watermelon seeds contain 'cucurbocitrin' to aid in lowering blood pressure and improve kidney function. The sweet watermelon surprisingly has only half the sugar content of an apple. It tastes sweeter because the sugar is its main taste-producing agent.

YAM

Yam flesh is poisonous raw, but cooking make sit safe and edible. Wild Asian yam has traditionally been used in herbal medicine to treat organ system function, especially the kidneys and the female endocrine system. Diosgenin, a natural occurring steroid, in yam makes it an herbal remedy for arthritis, asthma, eczema, carbuncles, diarrhea, menstrual disorders, and certain inflammatory conditions and may help reduce the risk of osteoporosis. Yam extracts are used as a natural alternative to hormonal replacement in women who have reached the age of menopause. Yams' vitamin B6 has been used as a natural herbal supplement for premenstrual syndrome (PMS) in women, especially with the accompanied depression.

Of all the home remedies, a good wife is best.
Unanimous

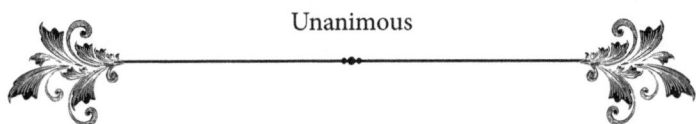

NOTES

Appendix C: Illness and Natural Remedies

Illness and Natural Remedies

The home remedies mentioned in the following text are meant to be informative and of historical value. These natural remedies have been derived from various sources. Every remedy has not been tested or verified. Any natural medicine guide does not replace the advice of your doctor. Never use any home remedy or other self treatment without being advised to do so by a physician. Please be careful when anything is combined with prescription drugs. Always store any herbal preparations away from children and pets.

ACNE
Cabbage, mint, grapefruit, mint, soursop leaves

Apply affected acne areas with a paste made from pounding dried orange peel with a tablespoon of pure (boiled) water. Apply cucumber leaves or grated pieces of cuke to acne areas. Rub the affected acne area with a fresh cut clove of garlic. Drink at least a quart of pure water every day to keep your skin free of impurities that cause acne and pimples. Grapefruit can be rubbed directly on the skin to alleviate pimples and greasiness. Mint juice is an excellent skin cleanser. The sap of young soursop leaves is put on skin eruptions.

ANEMIA
Bananas, beets, cassava

APHRODISIAC/SEXUAL IMPOTENCE
Carrot, garlic, ginger, onion, nutmeg, parsley, saffron

Sex is a basic instinct like hunger. Sexual activity, however, demands complete concentration and relaxation. It cannot be performed in haste and tension. Many persons, therefore, suffer from sexual dysfunctions. The most common male sexual dysfunction is impotence. The main problem of secondary impotence is the apprehension created by an earlier failure, which generates a good deal of anxiety for the next time. Impotence takes three forms. There is primary impotence when the man's erectile dysfunction is there from the very beginning of sexual activity and he simply cannot have an erection. Secondary impotence is the commonest and this implies that the man can normally attain an erection, yet fails on one or more occasions in between normal activity. The third form is advancing age. Garlic is one of the most remarkable home remedies found beneficial in the treatment of sexual impotence. It is a natural and harmless aphrodisiac. According to an eminent sexologist of the United States, garlic has a pronounced aphrodisiac effect. It is a tonic for loss of sexual power due to any cause, and for sexual debility and impotency resulting from sexual overindulgence and nervous exhaustion. Two to three cloves of raw garlic should be chewed daily. Onion is another important aphrodisiac food, second only to garlic. It increases libido and strengthens the reproduction organs. The white variety of onion is, however, more useful for this purpose. Carrot be taken with a halfboiled egg, dipped in a tablespoon of honey, once daily for a month or two. This recipe increases sexual stamina. The juice extracted from ginger is a valuable aphrodisiac, and beneficial in the treatment of sexual weakness. For better results, half a teaspoon of ginger juice should be taken with a half-boiled egg and honey, once daily at night, for a month. It is said to relieve impotency, premature ejaculation, and increase sperm.

ARTHRITIS

Apples, basil leaf, ginger, green beans, horseradish, leeks, spinach, sugar apple leaves, tamarind blossoms, yam

Drinking raw vegetable juices is beneficial, especially a mixture of carrot, beet, and cucumber. Green salad with lemon juice, cooked vegetables like pumpkin, spices like ginger, coriander, and turmeric all help to keep body joints painless. Apples, oranges, grapes, and papayas should be eaten frequently. Tomatoes, potatoes, and some peppers can hinder body joint actions. If these cause a problem they need to be excluded from your diet. Allergic foods may cause joint pain as a symptom. Identify any problem causing foods and stop eating them. Consume less tea, sugar, yogurt, chocolate, or fried foods. Change your eating habits for better joint health. Raw potato juice may be a successful treatment for arthritis. Slice a potato thin, without peeling. Place the slices in a bowl filled with cold water overnight. Drink the water the following morning on an empty stomach. Fresh juice can also be extracted from potatoes. A medium-sized potato juiced diluted with a cup of water should be drank first thing in the morning. Extract a cup of juice from any fresh green leafy vegetable, mixed in equal proportions with carrot, celery, and red beet juices for arthritis. After a regimen this should dissolve any deposits around the joints. Every day drink a cup of fresh pineapple juice and it will help reduce swelling and inflammation. A diet of only eight or nine bananas daily for three or four days is advised in the treatment of arthritis. The juice of one lime diluted with water taken first thing in the morning is a remedy for arthritis. The natural iodine in sea water may relieve arthritis pain. If sea bathing is not possible, the patient should relax for thirty minutes every night in a tub of warm water, in which a cup of common salt has been mixed. Blend a few threads of saffron into petroleum jelly and spread a thin layer of the salve on the affected areas in the morning and evening. Use the salve until the joint pain abates. A bath in sugar apple leaves relieves severe arthritis. Boiled tamarind leaves and flowers can be used as poultices for sprains and arthritis.

ASTHMA

Almonds, carrot, coffee, dunks, fennel, green beans, lemon, lettuce, marjoram, mint, nutmeg, onions, oranges, spinach, starfruit, yam.

Various remedies include: Add fifteen drops of fresh garlic juice in warm water and drink for asthma relief. Combine a quarter cup of onion juice with one tablespoon water and a pinch of black pepper and drink. Consume three cups of a combination of fresh carrot and spinach juice daily. Add 30-40 leaves of basil to a liter of water, strain the leaves, and drink the water throughout the day effective for asthma. For quick relief from asthma breathe the vapors from a jar of fresh honey. At every meal drink a glass of water with the juice of one lemon. Lettuce tea made from a half cup of lettuce to a cup of boiling water relieves stress and is a good body tonic fighting colds, viruses, and against asthma. Ground nutmeg is also smoked in India for asthma. A couple of cups of strong, regular black coffee will have a beneficial effect on asthma. Powdered starfruit seeds serve as a sedative in cases of asthma.

BAD BREATH
Cumin, fennel, mint, nutmeg, rosemary

BALDNESS/ HAIR
Bay leaf oil, black pepper, lime seeds, onions, rosemary, sage, thyme, tonka beans

Varoius remedies include: Massage one tablespoon on the bald patches daily of one cup mustard oil boiled with four tablespoon henna leaf. Apply to bald patches daily a mixture of ground lime seeds and black pepper corns in equal proportions. Scrub the bald area with onions until it becomes red. Then apply honey. Rub scalp daily with one teaspoon of vegetable oil in which raw mangoes have been preserved for over a year. The Chinese combine rosemary and borax to treat baldness. To make a rosemary hair rinse boil ten sprigs fresh rosemary in two cups water for thirty minutes. Cool and store in a tightly sealed container. Refrigerate. Once a week combine one half cup of this rosemary water with a cup of warm water and work through your hair after shampooing. You will be amazed at the luster. To hide gray hair put one half cup of dried sage in two cups of water and simmer for half an hour. Cover and allow the sage water to steep overnight. Over a basin, rinse hair at least ten times reusing the same sage water. On the last rinsing, leave the sage water dry on the hair before rinsing with fresh water. Repeat every week until your hair is the desired shade. Then rinse every month to retain your hair color. Thyme is a good hair rinse to fight dandruff. Tonka bean seeds are fermented in rum and used as a shampoo.

BLOATING
Cumin, ginger

The most effective home remedies for bloating are herbal teas. You can brew chamomile, ginger, peppermint, or basil tea. Another natural remedy is to boil one tea spoon of ground cinnamon with water, add some honey.

BLOOD CLEANSERS
Aloe vera, carrots

BLOOD PRESSURE/ HYPERTENSDION (lower)
Beetroot, carailli leaf tea, bananas, celery, chataigne leaves, chocolate, christophene, garlic, green beans, jackfruit/katahar, mauby bark, nutmeg, onion, papaya, paprika, sorrel, soursop, sour tamarind leaves, spinach, watermelon seeds

Reducing intake of salt/sodium, while increasing potassium and magnesium may lower blood pressure. Consume bananas, melons, grapefruit, oranges, cabbage, cauliflower, and other fresh vegetables and fruits rich in potassium. Magnesium is present in nuts, rice, wheat germ, beans, soy, and also in bananas. Supplementing with oral calcium will also help. Celery assists the dilation of the muscles that regulate blood pressure. Celery juice, carrot juice, and water may lower your BP. Garlic helps to lower cholesterol and increase circulation of blood. Drink a glass of raw beetroot juice twice a day for at least a week. Prepare a bottle of equal proportions onion juice and honey, and drink two tablespoons daily for a month. Eat a papaya on an empty stomach daily for a month, and do not eat anything else for about two hours. Drinking sorrel tea will relieve hypertension. Watermelon seeds contain 'cucurbocitrin' to aid in lowering blood pressure. Slice immature soursop fruit and soak in water overnight in the fridge and drink daily. Drink a cup of tea made with sour tamarind leaves or mauby bark daily.

BOILS
Cashew bark, garlic, guava leaves, onion, parsley, sorrel, turmeric

Boils are mainly caused by bacteria staphylococcus germs that enter pores or hair follicles. Cleanse your system thoroughly for treatment of boils. Begin the fast with a glass equal proportions orange juice and water for three to four days, or eat only fresh fruits for a week. Onion juice or garlic juice may be applied on boils externally to ripen, break, and evacuate pus. Boil parsley in water till it becomes soft and apply it on the boils as a poultice. Cover with a fresh, dry wash cloth. Roast a few roots of turmeric. Then dissolve the ashes in a cupful of water and apply to boils. This solution will cause the boil to burst. Sorrel leaves that have been warmed in hot water can be used on the skin to draw out boils. Make a tea of guava and cashew bark and drink a cup three times a day.

CANCERS
Brazil nuts, broccoli, cabbage, cassava , dunks, garlic, ginger, green beans, jalapeno peppers, jackfruit/katahar, leeks, ochro/okra, onions, oranges, pak choy, papayas, peanuts, pumpkin, spinach, sugar cane juice, tomato, wasabi, watermelon

Tomatoes reduces the risk of prostrate cancer if eaten almost daily. Watermelon contains such high concentrations of lycopene that may help reduce the risks of prostate cancer. Eggplant in an poultice may help against skin cancer.

CATARACTS
Almonds are valuable in cataract prevention. To help strengthen the eyes grind seven almonds finely and combine with half a teaspoon black pepper in half a cup of water, and sweeten with honey. Drink daily. An ancient Egyptian remedy for cataracts is to put a few drops of unprocessed pure honey in the eyes. Extract the juice of pumpkin flowers and apply externally on the eyelids twice a day. This is purported to stop further clouding of the eye lens.

CHOLESTEROL (lower)
Almonds, cabbage, onions, garlic, chana, dark chocolate, eggplant, ochro/okra, dry oranges peel tea, papayas, peanuts, turmeric

Cholesterol, a yellowish fatty substance, is one of the essential ingredients of the body.

Appendix C: Illness and Natural Remedies

Although it is essential to life, it has a bad reputation, being a major villain in heart disease. Every person with high blood cholesterol is regarded as a potential candidate for heart attack or a stroke. Most of the cholesterol found in the body is produced in the liver. However, about twenty to thirty per cent generally comes from the food we eat. Cholesterol is measured in milligrams per 100 millimeters of blood. The normal level of cholesterol varies between 150 - 200 mg per 100 ml. It is also caused by taking rich foods and fried foods; excessive consumption of milk and its products like clarified butter, butter, and cream; white flour, sugar, cakes, pastries, biscuits, cheese, and ice cream; and non-vegetarian foods like meat, fish, and eggs. Other causes of cholesterol increase are smoking and drinking alcohol. Stress has also been found to be a major cause of high cholesterol. Lecithin is a fatty food substance that breaks up cholesterol into small particles easily handled by the system. With sufficient intake of lecithin, cholesterol cannot build up against the walls of the arteries and veins. Lecithin also increases the production of bile acids made from cholesterol, thereby reducing its amount in the blood. Egg yolk, vegetable oils, wholegrain cereals, soybeans, and unpasteurized milk are good sources of lecithin. It can also be taken in powder or capsules. HDL cholesterol, or 'good' cholesterol, appears to scour the walls of blood vessels, cleaning out excess cholesterol. It carries the excess cholesterol - which otherwise might cause coronary artery (heart) disease - back to the liver for processing. Measure a person's HDL cholesterol level, is measuring how their blood vessels are being 'scrubbed' free of cholesterol. HDL levels below 40 mg/dL result in an increased risk of coronary artery disease, even in people whose total cholesterol and LDL cholesterol levels are normal. HDL levels between 40 and 60 mg/dL are considered 'normal'. However, HDL levels greater than 60 mg/dL may actually protect people from heart disease. LDL cholesterol is called 'bad' cholesterol, because elevated levels of LDL cholesterol (lipoprotein deposits) increase the risk of coronary heart disease by forming a hard, thick substance called cholesterol plaque. Over time, cholesterol plaque causes thickening of the artery walls and narrowing of the arteries, a process called atherosclerosis. To reduce the risk of heart disease, it is essential to lower the level of LDL and increase the level of HDL. This can be achieved by a change in diet and lifestyle. As a first step, foods rich in cholesterol and saturated fats, which lead to an increase in the LDL level, such as eggs, meats, cheese, butter, bacon, beef, and whole milk, should be eaten minimally. Virtually all foods from animals, and coconut and palm vegetable oils are high in saturated fats. These should be replaced by polyunsaturated fats such as corn, safflower, and soy bean, and sesame oils which can lower the level of LDL. Persons with high blood cholesterol level should drink at least eight to ten glasses of water every day, to eliminate excess cholesterol from the system. Regular physical exercise promotes circulation and helps maintain the blood flow to every part of the body. Gardening, jogging, swimming, bicycling, are excellent forms of exercise. Onion juice reduces cholesterol and works as a tonic for nervous system. It cleans blood, helps digestive system, cures insomnia, and regulates the heart action. Regular drinking of a decoction of coriander seeds helps lower blood cholesterol. It is a good diuretic and helps stimulate the kidneys. It is prepared by boiling two tablespoons of dry seeds in a glass of water and straining the decoction after cooling. This decoction should be taken twice daily.

COLDS
Garlic, ginger, lemon, mustard powder, onion, orange, oregano, pineapple, sapodilla, sugar apple leaves

Lemon is an important home remedy for common cold. It is beneficial in all types of colds with fever. Vitamin C rich lemon juice increases body resistance, decreases toxicity, and reduces the duration of the illness. One lemon should be squeezed and diluted in a glass of warm water, and a teaspoon of honey should be added. This should be taken once or twice daily. Garlic soup of four cloves of chopped garlic boiled in a cup of water is an old remedy to reduce the severity of a cold, and should be taken once daily. Garlic contains antiseptic and antispasmodic properties, besides several other medicinal virtues. The oil contained in this vegetable helps to open up the respiratory passages. In soup form, it flushes out all toxins from the system and thus helps bring down fever. Another effective treatment for the common cold is five drops of garlic juice combined with a teaspoon of onion juice diluted in a cup of water; drunk two to three times a day. Ginger is another excellent remedy for colds and coughs. A small piece of ginger should be cut into small pieces and boiled in a cup of water, strained, and combined with a half a teaspoon of honey or sugar. This decoction should be drunk hot. Ginger tea or a teaspoonful of ginger juice taken with equal quantity of honey brings relief. Lettuce tea made from a half cup of lettuce to a cup of boiling water relieves stress and is a good body tonic fighting cold viruses and against asthma. A tea made from old, yellowed sapodilla leaves is a reputed remedy for coughs and colds.

CONSTIPATION
Bananas, turmeric, coriander, cucumbers, dunk, pommerac

Use spices such as cumin powder, turmeric powder, and coriander while cooking to make food easily digestible.

COUGH
Almonds, ginger, lemon, mustard powder, nutmeg, oregano, sage, sapodilla, sorrel, tonka beans, wasabi

Soak almonds overnight. Remove their skin. Make a paste of these almonds with a little butter and sugar. Very useful for a dry cough. This paste should be taken in the morning and evening. Mix 2 tablespoons of pure aloe vera gel into a glass of apple juice or cranberry juice. Drink this once a day for 5 days, either in the morning or before going to bed. Pour boiling water over two teaspoons of sage leaves. Let mixture steep for ten minutes. Strain, then drink one to two cups per day to relieve symptoms of coughs, tonsillitis, and respiratory infections. Raw onion is should be juiced. One teaspoon of onion juice should be mixed with one teaspoon of honey and be taken twice daily. Onions are also useful in removing phlegm. One medium onion should be crushed and combined with the juice of one lemon, and one cup of boiling water. Add a teaspoon of honey for taste. This remedy should be taken two or three times a day. Turmeric root should be roasted and powdered. This powder should be taken in tablespoon doses twice daily, in the morning and evening. A tea made from the old, yellowed sapodilla leaves is a reputed remedy for coughs and colds. Drinking sorrel tea will relieve coughs.

Appendix C: Illness and Natural Remedies

CUTS
Cabbage leaf raw in a poultice, coriander, garlic, guava leaves, mint, oranges, pommerac bark, sage, sorrel, thyme, tonka beans, turmeric

A paste of sorrel leaves and seeds is used in Egypt as an antibiotic on wounds. Thyme has always been used as a poultice for wounds. Mix turmeric powder with cooking oil to make a thick paste. Put on the skin over wounds, bites, or bruises.

DEPRESSION and IMPROVE MOOD
Apples, bananas, cardamom, cashew nuts, nutmeg, saffron

The symptoms of depression are a feeling of loss, inexplicable sadness, loss of energy, lack of interest in the world around, and fatigue. A disturbed sleep is a frequent symptom. The diet of a depressed person should completely exclude tea, coffee, alcohol, chocolate, colas, all white flour products, sugar, food colorings, chemical additives, white rice, and strong condiments. Eating apples is a good remedy for mental depression. Substances present in apples such as vitamin B, phosphorus, and potassium help the synthesis of glutamic acid, which controls the wear and tear of nerve cells. The fruit should be taken with milk and honey. This remedy will act as a very effective nerve tonic and recharge the nerves with new energy and life. Cashew nuts are another valuable remedy for general depression and nervousness. It is rich in vitamins of the B group, especially thiamine, and useful in stimulating the appetite and the nervous system. It is also rich in riboflavin which keeps the body active, cheerful, and energetic. The use of cardamom has proved valuable in depression. Powdered seeds should be boiled in water and tea prepared in the usual way.

DIABETES
Carailli juice, cinnamon tea, mango leaves, chataigne leaves, mauby bark, pommecythere, pommerac, rou kou roots, sage

Diabetes mellitus (commonly referred to as just diabetes) is a blood sugar disease in which the body either does not produce, or does not properly utilize insulin. Insulin is a hormone that is needed to convert sugar, starches and other food into energy needed for daily life. Because diabetics have a problem with insulin, their body's can't use glucose (blood sugar) for energy, which results in elevated blood glucose levels (hyperglycemia) and the eventual urination of sugar out of their bodies. As a result diabetics can literally starve themselves to death. Diabetes is now being found at younger ages and is even being diagnosed among children and teens. Every cell of our body is surrounded by an oily membrane that separates it from the surrounding extra cellular fluid. This oily membrane is designed to allow nutrients and oxygen to flow in, and carbon dioxide and waste products to be removed. The consumption of fats / oils causes a hardening of the oils / fats in our cells' membrane, preventing hormones and nutrients from passing into them. This is not only a cause of Type 2 Diabetes, but also may also cause many other chronic diseases and health problems. It is caused almost entirely by the replacement of traditional fats and oils by modern fats and oils that harden in the body. Each body cell, for reasons which are becoming clearer, finds itself unable to accept glucose from the bloodstream. The glucose then remains in the bloodstream, or is stored as body fat or as glycogen, or is passed in urine. The pancreas compensates in early stages of insulin resistance, by producing more and more insulin. This stress of excessive insulin production eventually wears out the pancreas. The most common causes of type 2 diabetes are poor diet and/or lack of exercise; both of which can result in insulin resistance, a condition where the cells in our bodies aren't sensitive enough to react to the insulin produced by our pancreas. To fight the incidence of diabetes it is considered best to eliminate almost all vegetable, seed, bean, and nut oils obtained by heat extraction. The only ones that are considered safe state 'cold pressed/unheated' on the label and most usually are obtained at a health shop. Cooking –fired, roasted, or grilled - the higher the temperature, and reused are even more dangerous to the body. To regain a soft oily membrane around the billions of cells in our body virgin olive, canola, and sunflower oils may be used. These will gradually dissolve hardened fats and oils and expel out of the body. Iodine as a supplement has many benefits, with just a few drops a day added to a drink. This is a convenient, cost effective way to become healthier and contribute to normalizing blood sugar levels. North American ginseng may improve blood sugar control. Magnesium is a mineral found naturally in foods such as green leafy vegetables, nuts, seeds, whole grains, and in nutritional supplements. Magnesium helps regulate blood sugar levels, and is needed for normal muscle and nerve function, heart rhythm, immune function, blood pressure, and for bone health. The mineral zinc plays an important role in the production and storage of insulin. Zinc is found in fresh oysters, ginger root, lamb, split peas, egg yolk, rye, beef liver, lima beans, almonds, walnuts, sardines, chicken, and buckwheat. Some research has discovered cinnamon improves blood glucose control in people with type 2 diabetes. Aloe vera gel, a home remedy for minor burns and other skin conditions, may help people with diabetes. Carailli is the best reputed home remedy for diabetes. Eat this vine vegetable or drink at least one tablespoon of the juice daily. Ten fresh mango leaves soaked in a pint of water overnight, squeezed, then filter the water through a cloth, and drink every morning to control early diabetes. Clinical studies have also shown that it can lower blood sugar in cases of diabetes. Boil roukou roots or mauby bark in water and drink a cup daily for a week.

Let thy food be thy medicine and thy medicine be thy food.
Hippocrates

DIARRHEA

acerola cherry, allspice, carrot soup, chalta, coriander, dunk bark, ginger, pomegranate, guava leaves, oregano, pommecythere bark, sapodilla, seim beans, soursop leaves, starfruit, yam

Diarrhea occurs due to over indulgence in food and or alcohol, incomplete digestion causing food to rot in the intestines, nervous stress, some antibiotic drugs, and laxatives. Parasites, germs, virus, bacteria, poisons, and allergies can also attribute to this inconstancy of the bowels. Carrot soup is an effective remedy. It supplies water to rehydrate; replenishes sodium, potassium, phosphorus, calcium, sulfur, and magnesium; supplies pectin; and coats the intestine to allay inflammation. It also checks the growth of harmful intestinal bacteria and prevents vomiting. Boil a pound of carrots in a quart of water until soft. Add a tablespoon of salt and give in small amounts to the patient every half an hour. Ginger in a tea, being carminative, aids digestion by stimulating the gastrointestinal tract and will assist the nausea of diarrhea. Another treatment is combining teaspoons of fresh mint juice, lime juice, and honey: given three times daily. Drinking pomegranate juice will fight diarrhea. Mango seeds should be dried in the shade and powdered, and a dose of about one and a half to two grams with or without honey, should be administered twice daily. Young sapodilla fruits can be boiled and eaten as a remedy for diarrhea. Boiled starfruit will relieve diarrhea.

DYSENTERY
acerola cherry, dunk bark, oregano, pommerac root

Dysentery is an inflammatory disorder of the intestine, especially of the colon, that results in severe diarrhea. Basically the same remedies as diarrhea apply.

EYE WASH
The liquid squeezed from heated plantain leaves dropped into the eyes, or use cooled green tea water.

FERTILITY
carrots

FEVERS
basil, cardamom, grapefruit, honey and ginger, potato slices, onions, lemon, oregano, sage, starfruit juice, sugar cane juice, tonka bean tree bark

Fever is when the body's temperature exceeds 37.5 C, or 98.6 F. Drinking plenty of water helps to lower body temperature. Sleep under a warm blanket. Permit the body to sweat through the night, and in the morning the fever should be gone. A decoction made of about forty holy basil leaves boiled in a pint of water combined with a half cup of milk, one teaspoon of sugar, and a quarter teaspoon of powdered cardamom drank twice daily should lower the temperature. The juice of grapefruit mixed equally with water quenches thirst and removes the burning sensation produced by the fever. Combine three drops of ginger juice with a teaspoonful of honey to help break the fever. Slice potatoes and place the slices on your head, chest, and stomach to help reduce the fever. Drink a tea of lemon juice and honey several times daily. To lower the body temperature tie or tape half onion to the sole of each bare foot as long as possible. Cane juice is beneficial to drink to break fevers. Bathe in a decoction of tonka bean tree bark.

GAS / FLAUTENCE
Ginger and lime juice, peppermint, chalta, coriander, cumin, dill, fennel, hot pepper seeds, nutmeg, starfruit, turmeric

Stomach gas can be caused by the presence of excessive bacteria in the intestines, drinking too much beer, eating too much fibrous food like cabbage, broccoli, or cauliflower, or yeasty foods such as breads and cheeses. Carbonated drinks produce gas. After meals chew fresh ginger slices soaked in lime juice. Chewing peppermint fights flatulence, bloating, and abdominal pain that accompanies gas. A cup of tea daily from hot pepper leaves and seeds may help.

GENERAL CURE ALL
Combine two TBS aloe vera gel, one TBS medicinal charcoal, one TS molasses, and one egg white, and drink.

HEALTHY HEART
Almonds, bananas, carrots, chalta, peanuts, pommecythere, saffron, and plenty of exercise.

HEADACHES/ MIGRAINES
Apples, basil, bay leaves, grapes, cinnamon, ginger, green beans, lemon, marjoram, mint, mustard seeds, starfruit leaves

Headaches may be caused by allergies, emotional stress, eye strain, high blood pressure, a hangover, infection, low blood sugar, nutritional deficiency, tension, and or the presence of poisons and toxins in the body. Make a decoction of half a teaspoon mustard seed powder and three teaspoons water and snort into the nostrils to fight migraines. The juice of ripe grapes will fight a migraine. Eating apples, peeled and cored, with a little salt every morning on an empty stomach for about a week fights all types of headaches. Crush a few cabbage leaves, place in a cloth and apply on the forehead for extended period of time. Use fresh leaves when the compressed leaves dry. Also try bay leaves in a damp wash cloth resting on the eyes. For a sinus headache, eat a jalapeno pepper as soon as possible. Combine a teaspoon of ground cinnamon in a teaspoon water and apply on the forehead. Make a paste of dry ginger with a little water or milk, and apply to the forehead for sinus. Grind a dozen basil leaves with four cloves and a teaspoon dried ginger into a paste and apply to forehead for sinus. The juice of three or four slices of lemon in a cup of tea gives immediate relief. Cinnamon should be mixed with water and applied to the temples and forehead to obtain relief. An infusion of the leaves of the herb marjoram drank as a tea is a treatment of a nervous headache.

> *A man's health can be judged by which he takes two at a time - pills or stairs.*
> Joan Welsh

HEART DESEASE
Corn, peanuts, pommecythere, spinach, tarragon, turmeric

Many diseases are related to the heart, arteriosclerosis and atherosclerosis, angina, heart attack, heart failure, arrhythmias, heart murmurs, rheumatic heart disease, and high blood pressure or hypertension. The heart is a muscle and needs the blood to supply oxygen and nutrients. If coronary arteries become narrowed or clogged, and cannot supply enough blood to the heart, the result is coronary heart disease.

HICCCUPS
Peanut butter, sugar, chalta, dill

Hiccups start from the diaphragm, a dome shaped muscle in the chest that pulls and pushes air in and out of the lungs. Hiccups are caused when the diaphragm is irritated. Generally hiccups last for a few minutes, yet sometimes they may last for days or weeks.

Appendix C: Illness and Natural Remedies

This may be a sign of some other medical problems in the body. There is no special diet recommended for hiccups. However, it is advisable to avoid hot and spicy food because they can irritate the lining of the esophagus. Some natural remedies are to hold your breath, gargle with water, sip ice water quickly, close your eyes and gently press your eye balls, drink a glass of soda water quickly, eat some sugar, or eat one tablespoon either peanut butter or mustard.

HIGH BLOOD PRESSURE
Garlic, grapefruit, lemon, parsley, potatoes, rice, watermelon seeds

Hypertension or high blood pressure is a disease of the modern age. Blood pressure is measured with an instrument called sphygmomanometer in millimeters of mercury. The highest pressure reached during each heart beat is called systolic pressure, and the lowest between two beats is known as diastolic pressure. Most young adults have blood pressure around 120/80. It increases normally with age, even going to 160/90. The main causes of high blood pressure are stress and a faulty style of living. Hardening of the arteries (atherosclerosis), obesity, and diabetes cause hypertension. Persons with high blood pressure should always follow a well-balanced routine of a proper diet, exercise, and rest. The pressure can be lowered by eating fruits, and a vegetarian diet consisting of fresh fruits and vegetables. Salt should be avoided. Persons suffering from hypertension must get at least eight hours of good sleep, because proper rest is a vital treatment. Most important of all, the patient must avoid overstrain, worries, tension, and anger and create a calm, cheerful attitude, and contented state of mind. Garlic is regarded as an effective means of lowering blood pressure. It slows down the pulse rate and modifies the heart rhythm, besides relieving the symptoms of dizziness, numbness, shortness of breath, and the formation of gas within the digestive tract. It may be taken in the form of two raw cloves daily. Lemon is essential for preventing capillary fragility. Grapefruit is helpful in toning up the arteries. Watermelon seeds, dried, and roasted, should be taken in liberal quantities to lower the blood pressure. Natural brown rice is perfect food for hypertensive people who have been advised to a salt-restricted diets because it has low-fat, low-cholesterol, and low-salt content. Calcium in brown rice, in particular, soothes and relaxes the nervous system, and helps relieve the symptoms of high blood pressure. Potatoes are rich in potassium, but not in sodium salts. The magnesium in potatoes has beneficial effects in lowering blood pressure when boiled with their skin. Parsley tea made with a handful of fresh leaves boiled in a liter of water for three minutes, drunk several times daily will reduce high blood pressure and keeps the arterial system healthy.

IMMUNE SYSTEM (strengthen)
Broccoli, cabbage, carrots, cauliflower, greens (bagghi), jackfruit/katahar seeds, radish (morai), red peppers, sweet potatoes, tarragon, yams

Emotional stress, lifestyle, dietary habits can affect the immune system. To strengthen the immune system eat fruits, vegetables, beans, seeds, whole grains, and nuts; especially foods high in carotenes such as yellow and orange squash, dark greens, carrots, yams, sweet potatoes, red peppers, tomatoes, and cabbage family foods as brussel sprouts, cauliflower, broccoli, radish, and turnip help prevent low immunity. Eat adequate amounts of protein, keep the diet low in fats and refined sugars.

INDIGESTION
Allspice, aloe vera, almonds, bananas, cabbage leaf (boiled), cinnamon, cloves, coriander, lemon, cumin, dill, dunks, ginger, mace, mango, marjoram, mint, nutmeg, pineapple, radish, rosemary, saffron, seim beans, soursop leaves, tarragon, thyme, turmeric

Indigestion, also known as dyspepsia, is a stomach problem. Indigestion can cause heartburn due to stomach acid reflux. Following are the causes of indigestion eating without chewing properly, heavy food, excess alcohol, smoking, pregnancy, and stress. Improve eating habits to reduce acidity, heartburn, and gastritis. Avoid drinking liquids during meals, and wait at least for fifteen minutes to drink after you have eaten. Avoid large meals, take small and frequent meals. Abstain from smoking and alcoholic beverages. Avoid tea, coffee, and other drinks that contain caffeine. Avoid hot spicy and fatty foods. Restrict intake of chocolates. Take at least 30 minutes walk daily. Decrease your stress level by relaxing. Regular exercise is good for digestive system. Eat your meals on time and chew them properly. Lemon juice or cider vinegar in a glass of water drank before a meal will help prevent acid indigestion. Take one piece of clove and suck on it slowly for relief from acidity. Eat a cup of vanilla ice cream, or drink a glass of cold milk to get heartburn and acidity relief within minutes. Eat several almonds when heartburn symptoms persist. Cut a lemon into thin strips and dip in salt and eat before meals to prevent heartburn. Mix equal parts of baking soda and water in a glass. Drink as soon as you feel indigestion coming. The gel of aloe vera can also help improve digestion.

INSECT BITES
Reduce irritation and swelling: banana skin, chalta, fennel, lemon, lime juice, papaya, plantain, thyme, turmeric

Hundreds of insects that can bite or sting, from mosquitoes to spiders, can cause serious reactions in the body. The problem is not the injury, but what the insect leaves behind - the venom. The area becomes swollen, red, extremely painful, or burning. If the symptoms are, hard to breath or swallow, disorientation, swelling of eyes and mouth seek a doctor as fast as possible because and in some cases, especially allergic reactions, stings can cause unconsciousness or death. Remove the stinger. Do not squeeze it, this will inject more of the venom in the patient. Clean the area. Crush plantain leaves extracting the juice and applying it on the injured area. Apply toothpaste on the sting. For mosquito bites apply lime juice diluted with water over the bite, or rub dry soap over the mosquito bite. For wasp or jep stings make a poultice of ripe or green papaya. Try a mud pack of fresh dirt (clay if possible) and water. Sapodilla seeds can be crushed into a paste to sooth insect bites. Thyme has always been used as a poultice for insect bites. Mix turmeric powder with cooking oil to make a thick paste. Put on the skin over wounds, bites, bruises.

INSOMNIA
Calabash leaves, honey, lettuce, marjoram, nutmeg

Often worrying about falling asleep is enough to keep one awake. The most common cause of sleeplessness is mental tension brought about by anxiety, worries, overwork, suppressed resentment, anger, bitterness, or over excitement. It is also caused by constipation, overeating, excessive tea/coffee/smoking. A balanced diet with simple modifications in the eating pattern will go a long way in the treatment of insomnia. Avoid white flour products, sugar products, tea, coffee, cola drinks, alcohol, fatty foods, and fried foods. Two teaspoons of honey in a glass of water taken before bedtime induces a sound sleep. Babies generally fall asleep after taking honey. Lettuce soup is also useful in insomnia. Drink tea made from calabash leaves.

JAUNDICE

Beet root, lemons, lime, pigeon peas, radish (morai), sugarcane juice, tomatoes, rou kou seeds sugar cane juice, watermelon, yam

The symptoms of jaundice are extreme weakness, headache, fever, loss of appetite, severe constipation, nausea, and yellow discoloration of the eyes, tongue, skin, and urine, and or a dull pain in the liver region. Obstructive jaundice may be associated with intense itching. Jaundice may be caused by an obstruction of the bile ducts which normally discharge bile salts and pigment into the intestine. The bile gets mixed with blood and this gives a yellow pigmentation to the skin. The obstruction of the bile ducts could be due to gallstones or inflammation of the liver, which is known as hepatitis caused by a virus. The green leaves of radish, such as morai, should be pounded and their juice extracted through cloth. Drink a pint of this juice daily for adults. It induces a healthy appetite and proper evacuation of bowels, and this results in gradual decrease of the trouble within eight or ten days. A glass of fresh tomato juice, mixed with a pinch of salt and pepper, taken early in the morning, is considered an effective remedy. The juice from the green leaves of pigeon pea taken in two tablespoons daily fights jaundice. One glass of pure sugar cane juice combined with the juice of half a lime taken twice daily will help recovery. Drink a half cup of fresh lemon juice mixed with water several times a day to regenerate damaged liver cells. Sugar cane juice is said to speed up the recovery process after jaundice especially when mixed with lime juice. Watermelon seeds contain 'cucurbocitrin' to improve kidney function. Boil rou kou seeds and drink three cups daily.

KIDNEY STONES

Apples, basil, celery, grapes, pomegranate, watermelon, christophene leaves, coconut, grapefruit, radish (morai), starfruit,

Stones in the kidneys or urinary tract are formed from the chemicals usually found in the urine such as uric acid, phosphorus, calcium, and oxalic acid. Stones grow because a substance in the urine exceeds its solubility. Most kidney stones are composed either of calcium oxalate or phosphate. A patient with kidney stones should avoid foods, which irritate the kidneys, such as alcoholic beverages, condiments and pickles, cucumber, radish, tomato, spinach, onion, beans, cabbage, and cauliflower; meat and gravies; and carbonated waters. The patient should take a lowprotein diet. Try to drink a gallon of water daily to flush the system. A half cup of morai daily will prevent kidney or gall stones.

DO NOT EAT EDDOES IF YOU HAVE A PROBLEM WITH KIDNEY STONES.

One teaspoon basil juice and honey taken daily for six months may expel stones. Eating apples and celery prevents stone formation. Grapes or grape juice is an excellent cure for kidney stones. A tablespoon of the seeds from either sour or sweet pomegranates ground into a fine paste, with a cup of hot water and two tablespoons cooked mung or udri beans will help dissolve stones. Watermelon is one of the safest and best diuretics which can be used to fight kidney stones because it has plenty of water and potassium. Eating crushed sapodilla seeds are claimed to expel bladder and kidney stones.

In order to change we must be sick and tired of being sick and tired.
Unknown

LEG CRAMPS
bananas

Leg cramps are an painful and extremely discomforting involuntary contraction of a single muscle or a group of muscles, the calf muscle, the hamstring, or the quadriceps in the leg. The duration ranges from less than a minute to several minutes at times. Increase water consumption to stay well hydrated throughout the day. Potassium and calcium rich foods will help to prevent muscle cramps. Increase your intake of calcium rich foods to about 1,200 milligrams of calcium a day. Concentrate on fresh yogurts and soy and tofu. Stretch the sore muscle, follow your instinct, your body will automatically guide you in the correct manner. Eat one or two bananas a day, drink plenty of fluids, and stretches help relax muscles.

LIVER AILMENTS
beetroot, carrot juice, dunks, grapes, grapefruit, lemon, papaya, lime, chalta, radish, roucou roots and seeds, soursop, sour tamarind

The liver may become damaged or diseased due to bacterial infection or an injury. Gall stones often obstruct the normal flow of bile, causing an unnecessary accumulation and infection and/or cholesterol and triglycerides may also begin to accumulate in the liver. This is one of the major causes of infection and liver damage. Chemicals or an

over consumption of minerals may also cause the liver cells to get damaged. Excessive use of alcohol over a long period is the most potent cause of cirrhosis of the liver in adults. The black seeds of papaya have been found beneficial in the treatment of cirrhosis of the liver caused by alcoholism or malnutrition. A tablespoon of juice obtained by grinding the seeds, mixed with ten drops of fresh lime juice, should be given once or twice daily for about a month as treatment while abstaining from alcohol in any form. The liver can be cleansed with a juice fast for seven days. Use red beetroot, lemon, papaya, and grapes. A diet rich in vitamins A and C is the best for keeping your liver healthy. However, if the liver is diseased, a qualified doctor should prepare a diet. Carrot juice can help detoxify the liver on a regular basis. Taken when fasting, soursop juice is believed to relieve liver ailments. Boil the seeds and roots of the rou kou tree into a tea and drink three times a day as a liver purifier. Soak sour tamarind in hot water overnight and drink.

MENSTRUAL PROBLEMS
Beetroot, carrot, cucumber, fennel, ginger, green beans, guava leaves, papaya, parsley, yam

The two major female sex hormones in the body are estrogen and progesterone. They are produced in a pair of organs in the abdomen, known as the ovaries. Begin with an all-fruit diet for about five days, taking three meals a day of fresh, juicy fruits. Adding a glass of milk to each fruit meal is recommended if this causes weight loss. Parsley is most effective in treatment of menstrual disorders. It increases menstruation and assists in the regularization of the monthly cycle. Cramps are relieved and frequently corrected entirely by the regular use of parsley juice, with beetroot juice; or with beet, carrot, and cucumber juices. The recommended quantity is 75 ml of each of the four juices. A piece of fresh ginger pounded and boiled in a cup of water for a few minutes sweetened with sugar, should be used three times a day after meals. Unripe papaya helps a proper menstrual flow. Papaya is especially helpful when menstruation ceases due to stress or fright in young unmarried girls.

MORNING SICKNESS
Bananas, cumin, soursop leaves

Morning sickness causes nausea and in many cases vomiting in women who are in the early stages of pregnancy. It usually restricts itself to the first trimester of pregnancy. Try eating smaller meals more often, so that you are never too hungry or too full at one time. Avoid fatty or fried foods. Keep crackers, bread or toast, cereal, or other bland foods handy. Try eating a few crackers before getting out of bed in the morning. Drink enough fluids, especially if you have been vomiting. Try drinking in between meals rather than with meals. Make a tea from grated root ginger. Steep this in boiled water, leave it to cool and sip it throughout the day. Try sipping peppermint or spearmint tea.

MOUTH ULCER
Basil leaf, coconut milk, turmeric, coriander seeds, tomatoes

Mouth ulcers are small white spot on the inside of the cheek, the tongue, or clustered on the inner side of the lip. They are also known as canker sores. Mouth ulcers may be caused by nutritional deficiencies such as iron, vitamins, especially B12 and C, poor dental hygiene, food allergies, stress, infections - particularly herpes simplex, biting the cheek, or an hormonal imbalance. Apply peppermint oil, or mix coconut milk with honey and massage the gums 3 times a day. Mix a pinch of turmeric powder to one teaspoon glycerin and apply on ulcers. Take one teaspoon of coriander seeds in one cup of water and boil to make slightly warm. Gargle 3-4 times a day. Eating raw tomatoes helps mouth ulcers. Also gargle with tomato juice four times a day.

MUSCLE ACHES
Aloe vera, bay leaf bath, basil, cayenne pepper, peppermint, ginger, guava leaves, mustard oil, turmeric, nutmeg oil, oregano

Many things can cause muscle soreness. Overdoing it at work or sports can cause small tears in your muscles that can cause extreme discomfort. Dehydration can cause the agonizing pain of a muscle spasm. Muscle cramps can occur from being deficient in certain vitamins. Using a heating pad or hot water bottle may feel good, but it's the worst thing for sore muscles because it dilates blood vessels and increases circulation to the area, which in turn leads to more swelling. Heat can actually increases muscle soreness and stiffness, especially if applied during the first 24 hours after the strenuous activity. As long as it's gentle, massage can help ease muscle soreness and stiffness. Menthol, a component of peppermint, can be of great benefit when added to a hot, steamy bath. Squeeze the juice of fresh, grated ginger and combine with equal parts of olive or sesame oil to massage into the skin for relief of muscle pain. You can also try bay leaves in a little olive oil to help with pain as well as swelling and sprains. The active compound of cayenne is capsaicin; it can reduce pain at skin level as well as possibly help with deeper pain. It increases blood flow and warms the area. Turmeric, a common spice used in India, can be taken internally and externally for pain and inflammation. Heat aloe vera in the oven and apply warm to sore area.

NAUSEA
beets, allspice, black pepper, ginger, guava leaves, mace, mango, mint, nutmeg, oregano, soursop leaves

Nausea is the symptom for various other conditions. If you are not suffering from upset stomach there are other illnesses that can cause this problem. Nausea is basically a reaction to the presence of some illness in your body. You can treat it by having two capsules of ginger root. It will give you a quick relief and depending how severe is your nausea. Smaller amounts of food are always good for you diet. Once you start feeling better, have a fiber rich diet such as banana, rice, apple sauce and toast. Mint is a soothing herb which is useful in helping to calm and settle the stomach. Eat half a teaspoon powdered cumin seed to relieve nausea and vomiting. Another natural remedy for nausea is lemon. Simply smelling a freshly cut lemon can stop nausea, or drink a bit of lemon juice in water.

NERVOUSNESS
Almonds, bananas, marjoram, orange, onions, celery, nutmeg, sapodilla, soursop leaves, tarragon

Nervousness is a feeling of restlessness, apprehension, and worry. Inhale the fragrance while peeling an orange, or drop an orange in a pot of boiling water and inhale the vapor. Drink the mixture of two tablespoons of honey with one teaspoon nutmeg in a cup of orange juice. Add dried rosemary herb to boiling hot water and let it steep for 15 minutes. Drain the decoction and sip it when it cools. Grate two onions and add two cups celery as a salad to relieve restlessness. Soak ten raw almonds in water overnight. Peel and pound them adding just enough water to form a paste. Add one teaspoon nutmeg, with a pinch of ginger. Eat paste at bedtime. Crushed sapodilla seeds are used throughout the Yucatan as a tranquillizer. Soursop leaves are regarded throughout the West Indies as having sedative or soporific properties. In the Netherlands Antilles, the leaves are put into one's pillowslip or strewn on the bed to promote a good night's sleep. An infusion of the leaves is commonly taken internally for the same purpose. Slice lacatan banana thin, dry in an oven at low heat, and pound into powder. Add two tablespoons of powder to boiling water and drink three time a day.

PARASITES AND WORMS
Carrots, carailli seeds, coconut, papaya, pumpkin seeds, starfruit

Parasites are organisms that depend on other living organisms (host) for nourishment and protection. There are more than a hundred types of parasitic worms that live in human bodies. They enter the human body through food and water. Eat two grated carrots with an empty stomach in the morning every day to remove worms. Fry ten carailli seeds in a little ghee or butter and take 2-3 times in a day. Drinking of coconut water daily and chewing coconut continuously for three days removes worms. Combine one tablespoon raw papaya juice with one teaspoon of honey and take on empty stomach in morning followed by a glass full of warm milk with one teaspoon castor oil. This treatment should be done for two to three days. A poultice of crushed starfruit leaves will fight ringworm. Eat raw pumpkin seeds to expel worms.

QUIT SMOKING
Bananas, cayenne pepper, ginger, orange juice

Every cigarette contains nicotine which is very addictive and causes many problems to the body. Nicotine stimulates different parts of the brain producing a feeling of pleasure, causes adrenaline production to increase, accelerates the heart rate, and increases blood pressure. It also affects the level of some hormones, and the body's temperature. These sudden changes produced by smoking tobacco causes a feeling of pleasure, and is the principal fact that makes quitting smoking so hard. For cravings take powdered cayenne pepper because it desensitizes the respiratory linings to tobacco. It's an antioxidant that stabilizes lung membranes preventing damage. The warm peppery taste reduces cigarette cravings. Ginger prevents nausea and helps quitting, reducing anxiety. Ginger also produces perspiration to flush toxins generated from smoking. Oats reduce or eliminate tobacco cravings, and also reduce the number of cigarettes desired even in those people not trying to quit. Orange juice is acidic in nature and the first step in quitting smoking is to eliminate the nicotine from the body. Drinking orange juice twice a day will be useful.

RESPIRATORY DISEASES / BRONCHITIS
Almonds, thyme, cayenne pepper, dunks, fennel, horseradish, garlic, ginger, marjoram, mustard powder, oranges, papayas

Signs and symptoms of respiratory disease include shortness of breath after mild physical activity, wheezing and coughing especially at night, blood in cough, drowsiness, loss of appetite, unexplained weight loss, and mild to severe chest pain. Acute bronchitis is most often caused by a virus. Stop smoking and avoid second hand smoke. Get plenty of rest. Avoid any kind of stress. One of the best home remedies for cold and cough is salt water gargles as it can soothe the throat and get rid of mucous. Drink a cup of thyme tea four times a day. For severe bronchitis combine one small cayenne pepper chopped, one clove garlic chopped, one tablespoon crushed horseradish root, one teaspoon mustard powder, one large onion, a pinch of ground ginger, and a pinch of turmeric. Place the cayenne pepper, garlic, ginger, horseradish, mustard, onion, and turmeric in a medium sized saucepan and cover with water. Bring to the boil and then reduce the heat and simmer for twenty minutes. Strain the mixture and allow to cool a little before drinking.

RHEUMATISM
Basil leaf tea, carailli, coffee, green beans, horseradish, marjoram, mint, mustard powder, potato, onions, oranges, papayas, soursop leaves, sugar apple leaves, tonka beans

Rheumatism is painful state muscles, ligaments, tendons, and joints. It is an acute and chronic illness that affects people of all ages and both the sexes. The juice of raw potato is regarded as an excellent remedy for rheumatism. One or two teaspoons of the juice, taken out by pressing mashed raw potatoes, should be taken before meals. This will help to eliminate the toxic condition and relieve rheumatism. The potato skin is exceptionally rich in vital mineral salts, and the water in which the peelings are boiled is one of the best medicines for ailments caused by excess toxic matter in the system. About two big handfuls of potato peelings should be thoroughly washed and boiled in a pint of water until half boils away. Strain this decoction and take four times a day. A cup of carailli juice mixed with a teaspoon of honey can be taken daily as treatment for at least three months to provide relief. Take the juice of two or three lemons each day. Thoroughly chew six walnuts daily to relieve this pain. A remarkable remedy for rheumatism and gout is said to be as follows :—A pint of hot, strong, black coffee, which must be perfectly pure, and seasoned with a teaspoonful of pure black pepper, thoroughly mixed before drinking, and the preparation taken just before retiring. (If you can sleep!) Mashed soursop leaves are used as a poultice to alleviate rheumatism. A bath in sugar apple leaves relieves severe rheumatism. Tonka bean seeds are fermented in rum and used for rheumatism.

SKIN RASHES / DRY SKIN
Bay leaves in a bath, beet juice, canistel bark, carrot juice, black pepper, mint, oregano, plantain, pommerac leaves, soursop leaves, turmeric, yam

Dry skin is primarily caused due to a lack of natural oils (sebum) being secreted by the pores of the skin. It may also be caused due to an insufficient intake of water and other fluids. Prolonged exposure to extreme temperatures or harsh chemicals can also result in dry skin. An improper or insufficient diet may also lead to dry skin. Prolonged exposure to the sun or prolonged submersion in water, especially sea water, can also dry out your skin. Drink plenty of water and fluids. This is the best thing you can do to keep dry skin at bay. The juice of crushed pommerac leaves can be used as a skin treatment steeped into baths. Mashed soursop leaves are used as a poultice to alleviate eczema and other skin afflictions. East Indian women with lovely, velvety skin often attribute it to consuming turmeric. Aloe vera plant, cut open a leaf and rub the moist insides directly onto the affected skin. This will act as an anti-septic bandage as well as an anti-bacterial, anti-fungal, anti-inflammatory ointment.

SNAKE BITES
Plantain, pumpkin

One can also use plantain poultice on a snake or venomous insect bite.

GO TO THE HOSPITAL OR CLINIC IMMEDIATELY

SORE GUMS
Basil leaf tea, carrots, basil, coconut, sage

Combine sage with your toothpaste. This will help to remove plaque and will strengthen bleeding gums.

SORE THROAT
lemon, leeks, sage, sugar cane juice, tamarind

For sore throats, try mixing a sage tea with apple cider vinegar and salt for gargling. Eating leeks is also reputed to keep your voice from becoming hoarse. Tamarind pulp can be used as a rinse for a sore throat.

STOMACH ULCERS
Broccoli, canistel seeds, carrots, basil, coconut, jackfruit

WARTS
Banana skin, marigolds, onion

Warts refer to hard growths on the skin. They are common both in children and adults. Warts are capable of spreading, but they are usually harmless. The main cause of warts is a virus infection of the skin. Plantar warts on the soles are usually contracted in swimming pools. Constitutional factors, however, appear to be at the root of the trouble. These factors lead to some defects in the proper development of the skin surface in certain areas. Marigold is another herb found beneficial in the treatment of warts. The juice of the leaves of this plant can be applied beneficially over warts. The sap from the stem has also been found beneficial in the removal of warts. Raw potatoes are beneficial in the treatment of warts. They should be cut and rubbed on the affected area several times daily, for at least two weeks. This will bring about good results. Onions are also valuable in fighting warts. They are irritating to the skin and stimulate the circulation of the blood. Warts sometimes disappear when rubbed with cut onions.

> *We have finally started to notice that there is real curative value in local herbs and remedies. In fact, we are also becoming aware that there are little or no side effects to most natural remedies, and that they are often more effective than Western medicine.*
>
> Anne Wilson Schaef

NOTES

Appendix D: Glossary

D

Glossary

This glossary defines terms within the previous text.

The home remedies mentioned in the following text are meant to be informative and of historical value. The natural remedies here have been derived from various sources. Every remedy has not been tested or verified. Any natural medicine guide does not replace the advice of your doctor. Never use any home remedy or other self treatment without being advised to do so by a physician. Please be careful when anything is combined with prescription drugs. Always store any herbal preparations away from children and pets.

NOTE: Any vitamin or mineral essential to the body's healthy operation has a recommended daily allowance or RDA measured in mg –milligrams or mcg - micrograms.

AMINO ACIDS
There are twenty-two amino acids, but the human body can only produce thirteen naturally. The other nine amino acids are acquired by eating protein-rich foods. They are termed 'the essential amino acids' because your body needs to acquire them from the foods you eat. They are the building blocks of protein.

ANTI-INFLAMATORY
Anything that helps to reduce inflammation, which is the body's reaction to harm, such as infections from germs, damaged cells, or irritants. Inflammation is the body's effort to fight, remove, and heal the tissue. Inflammation does not mean infection, and is necessary for a wound to heal. Eating a variety of anti -inflammatory foods such as olive oil, walnuts, and pumpkin seeds will reduce inflammation. Avoid refined oils and sugars.

ANTIOXIDANT
In much the same way as oxidation weakens iron and steel with rust, causing an eventual breakdown, oxidation inside the body causes a breakdown of cells. An antioxidant helps slow or prevent oxidation of other molecules. Antioxidants are substances that may protect your cells against the effects of free radicals. Within the human body, millions of processes are occurring at all times. These processes require oxygen. Unfortunately, that same life giving oxygen can create harmful side effects, or oxidant substances, which cause cell damage and lead to chronic disease. Free radicals are molecules produced when your body breaks down food, or caused by stress, alcohol, or by exposures to chemicals, tobacco smoke, and radiation. Free radicals can damage cells, and may play a role in heart disease, cancer, and other diseases. Any substance thought

to protect body cells from the damaging effects of oxidation, such as vitamin E, vitamin C, or beta carotene, and beans are some of the best antioxidants.

AROMATIC OILS
Natural essential oils or blended synthetic compounds used in perfumes and aromatherapy.

ASTRINGENT PROPERTIES
An astringent substance tends to shrink or constrict body tissues, usually locally after topical application. Astringent medicines cause shrinkage of mucous membranes. This can happen with a sore throat, diarrhea, or with peptic ulcers. Externally applied astringents dry, harden, and protect the skin. Acne sufferers use astringents if they have oily skin. Astringents also help heal stretch marks and other scars. Apples, pomegranate, pears, beans, and lentils are very astringent foods. To make a basic astringent to clean skin slice a half a lemon thin, do the same with half an orange (or a lime), and combine with three quarters cup of rubbing alcohol. Stain though a cloth and keep refrigerated. Apply to skin with a cotton ball or gauze pad. Rinse with cool water.

ANTI-SPASMODIC
Prevent spasms of the stomach, intestine, or bladder. Peppermint oil has been traditionally used as an antispasmodic, also yam.

B COMPLEX VITAMINS
All B vitamins help the body to convert carbohydrates into fuel / glucose, to produce energy. B vitamins also help the body metabolize fats and protein. B complex vitamins are necessary for healthy skin, hair, eyes, and liver. They also help the nervous system function properly.

BATH PREPARATIONS
For a herbal bath place a handful of herbs into a teapot or suitable vessel and cover with boiled water. Leave for at least fifteen minutes and strain when pouring into bath water. You may add a handful of natural sea salt to the bath. Another method is to place the herbs in a muslin pouch, or tie them in a piece of natural, thin material, and leave to soak in the bath while the hot water is running. The pouch can also be used as a gentle exfoliating rub over the skin after soaking. Use rolled oats to soften the water and soothe irritated skin, particularly eczema. A handful of rose petals makes a romantic bathing experience and may ease rheumatic aches and pains. Rosemary soothes aches and pains and stimulates the mind. Soaking with thyme and marjoram will help soothe aches and pains. Stimulating bath herbs include basil, bay, fennel, lavender flowers, mint, rosemary, sage, savory, and thyme. Soothing bath herbs include catnip, chamomile flowers, comfrey, jasmine flowers, lemon balm, and rose flowers. Bath tonic herbs include comfrey, ginseng root, orange, and raspberry leaves. Bath herbs for muscles and joints include bay, oregano, and sage. Antiseptic bath herbs are eucalyptus and sandalwood. Astringent bath herbs include bay, comfrey, lemongrass, nasturtium flowers, raspberry leaves, rose flowers, rosemary, and witch hazel.

Appendix D: Glossary

BETA CAROTENE
Beta-carotene is the main source of vitamin A, essential for normal growth and development, immune system function, and vision. Beta-carotene is one of a group of natural chemicals known as carotenes responsible for the red-orange color in many fruits and vegetables as carrots, pumpkins, and sweet potatoes. Beta carotene is converted by the body to vitamin A. It is an antioxidant, like vitamins E and C. Good sources of betacarotene include carrots, sweet potatoes, squash, spinach, broccoli, romaine lettuce, apricots, and green peppers. It helps to prevent cancer and heart disease, slow the progression of cataracts, boost immunity, protect the skin against sunburn, asthma, depression, arthritis, and high blood pressure. No RDA

BIOTIN
Biotin is vitamin B7 needed to produce fatty acids and glucose for energy. It helps metabolize carbohydrates, fats, and proteins. It is found naturally in food as brewer's yeast, liver, cauliflower, salmon, bananas, carrots, egg yolks, sardines, beans, and mushrooms. Excessive alcohol consumption may increase a person's requirement for biotin. A deficiency may cause skin rash, hair loss, cholesterol and heart problems. 300 mcg RDA

BOTANY
The scientific study of plant life. Scientific efforts to identify edible, medicinal, and poisonous plants make botany one of the oldest sciences. Today botanists study over half a million species of living organisms.

CALCIUM
This is a dietary mineral needed for healthy bones, and proper function of muscles and nerves. It even helps your blood clot. Calcium is the most abundant mineral in the body. Milk, yogurt, and cheese are rich sources of calcium, and vegetables, such as pak choy, kale, and broccoli. When blood calcium levels drop too low, the vital mineral is 'borrowed' from the bones. It is returned to the bones from calcium supplied through the diet. The average person loses 400 mg of calcium every day. 2500 mg RDA

CALORIE
Calories are usually associated with food, but they apply to anything containing energy. For example, a gallon of gasoline contains about 31,000,000 calories. When you hear something contains 100 calories, it's a way of describing how much energy your body could get from eating or drinking it. The body needs calories for energy. Eating too many calories and not burning enough of them off through activity can lead to weight gain. Processed food should have a nutrition fact label describing the components of the food. An easy way to remember calorie content is that every gram of carbohydrates has four calories. Every gram of protein has four calories while a gram of fat has nine calories. So a ten gram baked potato with a gram of butter is forty-nine calories. Your body needs some calories just to operate, to keep your heart beating and your lungs breathing. A youthful body also needs calories to grow and develop. To lose weight women should consume 1200 calories per day and men 1600.

CARBOHYDRATES

When you eat carbs, the body breaks them down into simple sugars, which are absorbed into the bloodstream. As the sugar level rises in the body, the pancreas release a hormone called insulin. Insulin is needed to move sugar from the blood into the cells, where the sugar can be used as a source of energy. Simple carbohydrates, also called simple sugars, are found in refined sugars, fruit, and milk. It's better to get your simple sugars from the latter since they contain vitamins, fiber, and important nutrients like calcium. Complex carbohydrates are also called starches like grain products, bread, biscuits, pasta, and rice. Processing grains removes nutrients and fiber, yet unrefined grains still contain these valuable food stuffs with vitamins and minerals..

CARMATIVE

A substance that stops the formation of intestinal gas and helps expel gas that has already formed.

CAROTENE

See beta carotene

CATARRH

It consists of inflammation of the mucous membrane of the nose, sinuses, or cavities. It is a very common affliction, arising from repeated colds, damp living conditions, wet feet, insufficient clothing, or hot rooms. The symptoms are weariness, pains in the back and limbs, frontal headache, increased discharge from the nose, hoarseness, sore throat, impaired vision, fever, constant hawking, and cough. If the disease continues, partial or complete deafness may result. Constant dripping of the secretions into the throat, the catarrhal inflammation will extend to the mucous membrane of the throat and larynx, causing gastritis, tonsillitis, laryngitis, and bronchitis.

CATHARTIC

A substance which accelerates bowel movement.

CHOLESTEROL

This is a yellowish fatty substance and one of the essential ingredients of the body with a bad reputation of being the major cause of heart disease. Every person with high blood cholesterol is regarded as a potential candidate for heart attack or a stroke. Most of the cholesterol found in the body is produced in the liver. LDL cholesterol is called 'bad' cholesterol because it forms a hard, thick substance called cholesterol plaque. HDL cholesterol, or 'good' cholesterol, appears to scour the walls of blood vessels, cleaning out excess cholesterol. However, about twenty to thirty per cent generally comes from the food we eat. Cholesterol is measured in milligrams per hundred millimeters of blood. The normal level of cholesterol varies between 150 - 200 mg per 100 ml. It is also caused by eating rich foods and fried foods, excessive consumption of milk and milk products like butter, and cheese. It is also raised by consuming white flour, sugar, cakes, pastries, biscuits; and non-vegetarian foods like meat, fish, and eggs. Cholesterol increases with smoking and drinking alcohol. Stress has also been found to be a major cause of high cholesterol. Lecithin is a fatty food substance that breaks up cholesterol into small particles easily handled by the body's system. With sufficient intake of lecithin, cholesterol cannot build up against the walls of the arteries and veins. Lecithin also increases the production of bile acids made from cholesterol, thereby reducing its amount in the blood, Egg yolk, vegetable oils, wholegrain cereals, soybeans, and unpasteurized milk are good sources of lecithin. It can also be taken in powder or capsules. It carries that excess cholesterol, which might cause heart disease back to the liver for processing. Over time, cholesterol plaque causes thickening of the artery walls and narrowing of the arteries, a process called atherosclerosis. To reduce the risk of heart disease, it is essential to lower the level of LDL and increase the level of HDL. This can be achieved by a change in diet and lifestyle. Virtually all foods from animals and coconut and palm vegetable oils, are high in saturated fats. These should be replaced by polyunsaturated fats such as corn, safflower, soy bean, and sesame oils which can lower the level of LDL. Persons with high blood cholesterol should drink at least eight to ten glasses of water every day, to eliminate excess cholesterol from the system. Regular physical exercise promotes circulation and helps maintain blood flow to every part of the body. Gardening, jogging, swimming, bicycling are excellent forms of exercise.

COLLAGEN
A type of fibrous protein, which connects and supports other bodily tissues as skin, bone, tendons, muscles, and cartilage. It also supports the internal organs and is even in teeth. There are more than 25 types of collagens that naturally occur in the body and makes up about a quarter of the total amount of proteins in the body. Some people refer to collagen as the glue that holds the body together. Without it, the body would, literally, fall apart.

COMPRESS
A compress is a cloth soaked in a water-based herbal infusion, decoction, or diluted tincture which can be held against the skin to relieve swelling, bruising and pain, or to soothe headaches and cool fevers. Soak a towel in a hot herbal tea and lay it on the affected area. Be careful not to burn yourself when you wring out the towel thoroughly, or the 'patient' when you lay it on the area to be treated. Cover the compress with a dry towel. Leave it in place until it no longer feels warm, and then replace it with another. Keep the area under compresses for up to 30 minutes, depending on the condition and the herb used. Stop the application when the skin becomes uniformly flushed, a tingling sensation begins, or feels better. Stop if the patient feels discomfort. Some herbs are stimulating and warming as cayenne pepper or ginger root. They will increase circulation and energize areas of the body. Other herbs sooth, cool, and reduce fevers or swelling from sprains or bruises.

CONSERVE
A conserve is cooked mixture of fruit, or nuts heated until they become thick and heavy textured. To make a simple conserve put a handful of dried herbs in a small jar and cover the herbs with two inches of apple juice or cider. Add two cinnamon sticks to the jar and steep the mixture in the refrigerator overnight. By morning the herbs should have absorbed the liquid. Remove the cinnamon and add honey to your taste. Spread some on your toast or biscuits, and enjoy right away. Store the remaining conserve in the

refrigerator.

CONSTIPATION: Constipation is defined as having a bowel movement fewer than three times per week. With constipation stools are usually hard, dry, small in size, and difficult to eliminate. Some people who are constipated find it painful to have a bowel movement and often experience straining, bloating, and the sensation of a full bowel.

DAHL, DAL, DAAL or DHAL
A preparation of dried lentils, peas, or beans stripped of their outer hulls and split. It also refers to the thick stew prepared from these.

DECOCTION
A standard quantity to make a four dose concoction is add twenty grams of dried or forty grams fresh herbs to a pint and a half cold water. Crush, chop, or bruise the herbs and place in a pan. Cover with cold water, bring to the boil and simmer for half an hour, or until the liquid is reduced by about a third. Strain into a clean container, cover, and store in a cool place until required. It is best used fresh that day. A decoction is made by boiling the hard and woody parts of herbs. Be sure to break up the bark or roots into small pieces; the smaller the better. More heat is needed in making decoctions than infusions because these parts of herbs are more difficult to extract active constituents and be absorbed by water.

DIETARY FIBER
Dietary fiber, or simply fiber, refers to plant components not digestible by the body's digestive enzymes. Dietary fiber is classified into soluble dietary fiber and insoluble dietary fiber. Food sources rich in soluble dietary fiber beans, lentils, brussel sprouts, cabbage, apples, berries, and oat bran. Insoluble dietary fiber can be found in whole grain breakfast cereals, celery, and carrots. The rate and extent of fermentation of insoluble fiber in the colon is slower than soluble fiber. The body needs an average of about 35 grams a day.

DIURETICS
Diuretics are natural foods or herbs that increase the flow of urine, and remove fluids from the body. It may also remove important vitamins and minerals. Foods like salt and sugar cause the body to retain considerable fluids, and may cause water retention. Natural foods with high water content such as watermelons and cucumbers help increase urination and better flush out toxins. Cucumbers are rich in sulfur and silicon that stimulate the kidneys into better removal of uric acid. Watercress is a natural diuretic. Asparagus contains asparigine - a chemical alkaloid that boosts kidney performance, thereby improving waste removal from the body. Brussel spouts help in stimulating the kidneys and pancreas. Beets are natural diuretic foods that attack floating body fats and fatty deposits. Oats contain silica, which is a natural diuretic. Eating cabbage is known to breakdown fatty deposits, especially around the abdominal region. Carrots are a rich source of carotene that speeds the metabolic rate of the body and removes fat deposits and waste. Lettuce aids better metabolism and flushing of toxins. Tomatoes are rich in vitamin C and assist the release of water from the kidneys flush out waste. Garlic is a natural diuretic food that aids breakage of fat. Horseradish, raw onions, and radish

speed up your metabolism.

DYSENTERY
A disease that inflames the intestines, especially the colon (large intestine), accompanied by fever, pain in the abdomen, low volume of diarrhea, and possible blood in the stool.

ECZEMA
Inflammation of the skin, characterized by redness, itching, and lesions.

EMETIC
Induce vomiting. Controlling nausea and vomiting is anti-emetic. Peppermints or peppermint tea, ginger biscuits or ginger beer may help some people.

EXFOLIATE
To remove old dead skin cells from skins surface by chemical or mechanical means.

EXPECTORANT
A medication that helps bring up mucus and other material from the lungs, bronchi, and trachea.

Gardening is the purest of all human pleasures.
Francis Bacon

EXTRACT
Extracts and tinctures are more potent than decoctions or infusions, so smaller doses are necessary, in drops, not cups. To make an extract combine three ounces of fresh herbs with hundred proof alcohol, preferably vodka, in an air tight bottle. Shake the extract twice a day to maintain the blend. It takes time for the active ingredients of the herb to be released into the alcohol. This should be good up to six weeks depending on the herb, but can last for over a year because alcohol acts as a preservative. If you prefer not to use alcohol, use vinegar

FAMILY
A botanical category of groups of similar genus. Families may represent the highest natural grouping.

FAT
This is one of the three nutrients used as energy sources by the body. The energy produced by fats is nine calories per gram. Proteins and carbohydrates each provide four calories per gram. Total fat is the sum of saturated, monounsaturated, and polyunsaturated fats. Intake of monounsaturated and polyunsaturated fats can help reduce blood cholesterol when substituted for saturated fats in the diet.

FREE RADICALS
Free radicals are molecules produced when your body breaks down food, but can be caused by stress, alcohol, or by exposures to chemicals, tobacco smoke, and radiation. Free radicals can damage cells, and may play a role in heart disease, cancer, and other diseases. Substances such as vitamin E, vitamin C, or beta carotene, thought to protect

body cells from the damaging effects of oxidation.

FLATUENCE
Excess gas in the intestinal tract.

FLAVANOIDS
Together with carotenes, flavanoids are responsible for the colors of fruits, vegetables, and herbs. They are found in most plant material especially fruits, tea, and soybeans. Green and black tea are a quarter flavanoids. They are known for their antioxidant activity in prevention of cancers and cardiovascular diseases.

FOLIC ACID / FOLATE
Folic acid is a vitamin B9. It helps the body make healthy new cells. Everyone needs folic acid, but it is really important for pregnant women. Folic acid may reduce the risk of stroke. It can be found in leafy green vegetables, fruits, dried beans, peas, nuts, enriched breads, cereals, and other grain products.

GARGLES
Gargling with herbal preparations is one way to soothe a sore throat, gum pain, and mouth sores such as ulcers. They are inexpensive and easy to prepare. Gargles made from herbal tinctures are one part herbal tincture to five parts clean water used four or more times daily as long as the condition persists. Sage tea is particularly good for mouth health. A pinch of salt provides a soothing element to herbal gargles.

GENUS
Classification of biological of living and fossil organisms above species and below family.

HERB BATH
Herbal baths include the use of various herbal additives to enhance the natural healing power of the water. They are baths to which plant decoctions or infusions have been added. There are full and partial herbal baths. For a full bath some of the medicinal plant parts should be sewn into a cloth bag and then boiled in a quart of water; the strained mixture is then added to the bath. Sometimes you can put the bag right into the tub for a more thorough extraction of the herbal properties.

HERBAL POWDER
Grind dried plant parts to a powder. The powder can be taken with water, milk, or soup.

HERBAL TEAS:
To make a cup of herbal tea, for drinking or as a face wash, boil ten ounces of water and pour over one tablespoon dried herbs or a large pinch of fresh herbs. Add honey, cover and steep for five minutes. Strain and drink.

INFUSION or TISANE
To make an infusion, fill a teapot with one quart of boiling water. Then throw in a large handful of fresh herbs, or an ounce or more of dried herbs. Add some honey, if desired, and let the mixture steep for ten to twenty minutes. Now strain and drink. Another easy way to make an herbal remedy is to bruise one ounce of dried flowers, leaves, or petals of the herb of your choice in a clean cloth. If you are using multiple herbs, the total

amount used should equal one ounce. Then, pour three cups of boiling water over the herb. Cover and let steep for at least half an hour. Strain and drink at room temperature or cold. Infusions generally will last in the refrigerator for three days. Dosage is in cups per day. Herb infused water preparations can be used in a number of ways; as a natural herbal bath infusion, skin rinse, hair rinse, mouthwash and gargle, herbal cleaning infusion, flea wash for cats and dogs, or as an ingredient in a more complex preparation. Use a glass or ceramic container. Aluminum, iron, tin or other metals will leach into the tea. Although copper and stainless steel may be okay, herbalists recommend you use clean glass, ceramic, pottery, or enameled pot. Use pure water. Fresh spring water or distilled water is best. Strain the finished tea before capping and storing. Refrigerate if kept for more than a few hours.

IRON

A dietary mineral needed for transportation of oxygen throughout the body. Iron is essential for the regulation of cell growth and differentiation. Iron deficiency results in fatigue, poor work performance, and low immunity. There are two forms of dietary iron: heme and nonheme. Heme iron is derived from hemoglobin, the protein in red blood cells that delivers oxygen to cells. Heme iron is in animal foods that originally contained hemoglobin, such as red meats, fish, and poultry. Iron in plant foods such as lentils and beans is arranged in a chemical structure called nonheme iron This is the form of iron added to iron-enriched and iron-fortified foods. Heme iron is absorbed better than non-heme iron, but most dietary iron is nonheme iron. Rich sources of dietary iron include red meat, fish, poultry, lentils, beans, leaf vegetables, tofu, chickpeas, black-eyed peas, fortified bread, and breakfast cereals. 8 mg RDA

LYCOPENE

Lycopene is a carotinoid found in red fruits as tomatoes and watermelons. Carotinoids are natural pigments that act as antioxidants for the body. Antioxidants serve to lessen the effects of free radicals, blamed by some in the scientific community for damage to cells. Lycopene gets its name from the species classification of the tomato. Numerous studies have shown that eating foods high in lycopene is beneficial in warding off heart disease and several types of cancer such as lung, prostate, cervical, digestive tract, and breast. Good sources of lycopene are pink grapefruit, guava, watermelon, and rosehips, but the most common and perhaps most powerful is the tomato.

Mg

Milligram measurement

Mcg

Microgram measurement

MAGNESIUM

A dietary mineral needed for healthy muscle function and other processes in the body. Magnesium is the fourth most abundant mineral in the body. Approximately 50% of total body magnesium is found in bones. The other half is found predominantly inside cells of body tissues and organs. Only 1% of magnesium is found in blood, but the body works very hard to keep blood levels of magnesium constant. It helps maintain normal muscle and nerve function, keeps heart rhythm steady, supports a healthy immune system, and keeps bones strong. Magnesium also helps regulate blood sugar levels, promotes normal blood pressure, and is known to be involved in energy metabolism and protein synthesis. Eating a wide variety of beans, nuts (especially peanut butter), whole grains, bananas, and vegetables will help you meet your daily dietary need for magnesium. 400 mg RDA

MANGANESE: Manganese is a mineral element that is nutritionally essential in the breakdown of amino acids and the production of energy. It is necessary for the metabolism of vitamin B-1 and vitamin E, and it activates various enzymes important for proper digestion & utilization of foods. Manganese is a catalyst in the breakdown of fats and cholesterol. It helps nourish the nerves and brain, is necessary for normal skeletal development, helps maintain sex hormone production, and to regulate blood sugar levels. Manganese plays an important role in a number of physiological processes as a constituent of some enzymes and an activator of other enzymes. A manganese deficiency may cause joint pain, high blood sugar, bone and spinal disc problems, and or poor memory. Excellent sources of manganese include mustard greens, kale, chard, raspberries, pineapple, romaine lettuce, spinach, collard greens, turnip greens, kale, maple syrup, molasses, garlic, grapes, summer squash, strawberries, oats, green beans, brown rice, chana/garbanzo beans, ground cloves, cinnamon, thyme, peppermint, and turmeric. 2.5 to 5 mg RDA

METABOLISM

Our bodies' chemical reactions to convert fuel from food into the energy needed to do everything. Specific proteins in the body control the chemical reactions of metabolism, and each chemical reaction is coordinated with other body functions. In fact, thousands of metabolic reactions happen at the same time — all regulated by the body — to keep our cells healthy and working. To increase your metabolism, do not skip any meals. Eat six small meals daily. Starving will slow down your metabolism. Exercise daily and build your muscles. Avoid alcohol and sugar. Drink ten glasses of water daily. Eat only nutritious food. Drink a mixture of one ounce of vinegar, honey with two crushed garlic cloves three times a day.

MINERALS

Dietary minerals are the chemical elements required by living organisms. In nutrition minerals are elements which the body requires at least 100 mg per day, and trace minerals are needed in smaller amounts. Dietary minerals are derived from the earth's crust when plants extract the minerals from the soil, and humans eat the plants. There are seven major minerals. Calcium occurs mainly in the teeth and bones, but a small amount is found in blood plasma and other body fluids where it influences nerve transmission, blood clotting, and muscle contraction. Dairy products and green leafy vegetables are dietary sources of calcium, and an adequate intake of vitamin D is required for calcium absorption. Phosphorus is closely allied to calcium in bone and tooth formation and its association with vitamin D. It is present in every cell and is also found in dairy products. Magnesium is necessary for carbohydrate and protein metabolism, cell reproduction, and smooth muscle action. Food sources include nuts, soy beans, and cocoa. Sodium is in the skeleton and extracellular fluids and is necessary for fluid and acid -base balance, cell permeability, and muscle function. It's main source is table salt, milk, and spinach. Potassium is found in intra - and extracellular fluid, plays a major role in fluid and electrolyte balance and in heart muscle activity, and is also required for carbohydrate metabolism and protein synthesis. Its sources include beans, whole grains, and bananas. Chlorine helps maintain normal fluid-electrolyte and acid-base balance, and in the stomach it provides the acidic environment necessary for digestion. Table salt is its main dietary source. Sulfur is important to the structure of proteins, is also necessary for energy metabolism, enzyme function, and detoxification. Sulfur is obtained from protein foods, such as meat, eggs, and beans. Some trace minerals are considered 'essential' in human nutrition and include iron, which is a constituent of hemoglobin; iodine, which is necessary for the thyroid gland, and cobalt, which is a component of vitamin B 12. Other essential trace minerals are chromium, copper, fluorine, manganese, molybdenum, selenium, and zinc.

> **DID YOU KNOW?**
> One pound of fat burns only two calories a day, but one pound of muscle burns fifty calories a day. Themore muscle you build, your metabolism increases, and the more calories will burn while at rest. When muscle mass decreases, the metabolic rate also drops.

MONOUNSATURATED
Monounsaturated fat is considered to be probably the healthiest type of general fat, and may assist in reducing heart disease. Oils high in mono-unsaturates are better oils for cooking. Monounsaturated fat is believed to lower cholesterol and essential fatty acids for healthy skin and the development of body cells. Monounsaturated fat is also believed to offer protection against certain cancers, like breast and colon cancer. Olive oil is considered the best because it has none of the adverse effects associated with saturated fats, trans-fats, or omega-6 polyunsaturated vegetable oils. Like polyunsaturated fat it provides remains stable at higher temperatures and does not easily become hydrogenated or saturated. Olive oil, hazelnuts, almonds, Brazil nuts, cashews, avocado, sesame seeds, and pumpkin seeds are the best sources.

NAICIN
Niacin (nicotinic acid) is a B3 vitamin that's used by your body to turn carbohydrates into energy. Niacin also helps keep your nervous system, digestive system, skin, hair, and eyes healthy. Niacin can be found in chicken, liver, eggs, and milk. It is also available in nuts, seeds, beans, fruits, and vegetables as broccoli. Fish is one of the best sources. 35 mg RDA

OINTMENT / SALVE
An ointment, unguent, or salve is made by combining a decoction of a herb with olive oil and simmering it until the water has completely evaporated. A little beeswax is then added to get a firm consistency. An alternate way to make an ointment or salve is to add crushed dried herbs to the olive oil and cook in very low heat in the oven for 3-4 hours.

Then, strain into melted beeswax and quickly add to containers before the beeswax sets. For ointments, add one to one and a half ounces of melted beeswax (or tallow) to any herb oil.

OMEGA

Two important polyunsaturated fatty acids are linoleic acid and alpha-linolenic acid. Linoleic acid is used to build omega-6 fatty acids and alpha-linolenic acid is used to build omega-3 fatty acids. These fatty acids cannot be synthesized in the body and must be supplied by the diet. They are called essential fatty acids. Omega-3 and omega-6 fatty acids are important in the normal functioning of all tissues of the body. You should include good sources of omega-3 and omega-6 each day. Pregnant women have an increased need for omega-3 and omega-6 fatty acids. They are needed for the fetal growth, brain development, learning, and behavior. Lactating women should also increase their fatty acids intake, since infants receive their essential fatty acids through the breast milk. Omega-6 fatty acids can be found in leafy vegetables, seeds, nuts, grains, and vegetable oils (corn, safflower, soybean, cottonseed, sesame, sunflower). Most diets provide adequate amounts of omega-6. Unless you eat a diet that is extremely low in fat, it is very easy to get more than enough omega-6. Supplementation of omega-6 is usually not necessary. It is obtained in oils as canola oil, walnut oil, wheat germ oil, soybean oil, green leafy vegetables as lettuce, broccoli, kale, and spinach, beans as mung, kidney, navy, pinto, lima, peas and split peas, and citrus fruits, melons, and cherries. Omega-3s are damaged by heat, so the oils should not be cooked. They are also damaged by oxidation; that's why you should store the oils in dark bottles in the refrigerator or freezer. The absolute best source of omega-3 are flaxseeds. One tablespoon of ground flaxseed will supply the daily requirement of omega-3. Flaxseeds need to be ground for your body to be able to absorb the omega-3 from them. You can grind flaxseeds in a spice grinder. Once flaxseeds are ground, the shells don't protect them from oxidation anymore and you will need to store them in the refrigerator or freezer, just like the oils.

PARASITES

The major groups of parasites include one cell organisms and parasitic worms such as hookworms. Parasites can get into the intestine through the mouth from uncooked or unwashed food, or contaminated water, or by skin contact with larva from infected soil. When the organisms are swallowed, they move into the intestine, where they can reproduce and cause symptoms. Children are particularly susceptible if they are not thoroughly sterilized after coming into contact with infected soil that is present in environments that they may frequently visit such as sandboxes and school playgrounds. People in developing countries are also at particular risk due to drinking water from sources that may be contaminated with parasites that colonize the gastrointestinal tract. Extreme temperatures kill parasites and their eggs. Avoid drinking from natural waters without boiling. Always wash and peel fruits carefully. If there are any splits or flaws, get rid of the bad parts. Sushi and other raw foods should be put in the freezer for a few days before eating. Salting might also help because it dries the parasite's body. Educate yourself about common parasites in your area. Avoid known parasite carriers such as mosquitoes.

PHOSPHORUS: Phosphorus is the second most-abundant mineral found in the human body, next only to calcium. It is very involved with bone and teeth formation as well as most metabolic actions in the body, including kidney functioning, cell growth, and the contraction of the heart muscle. It plays an important role in the body's utilization of carbohydrates and fats and in the synthesis of protein for the growth, maintenance, and repair of cells and tissues. It is also crucial for the production of ATP, a molecule the body uses to store energy. The main food sources are the protein food groups of meat and milk. A meal plan that provides adequate amounts of calcium and protein also provides an adequate amount of phosphorus. Meat, poultry and fish, as well as eggs, nuts, seeds, milk, carbonated soft drinks, broccoli, almonds, apples, carrots, asparagus, bran, brewer's yeast, and corn contain a good source of phosphorus. 700 mg RDA

PHYTONUTRIENTS

A substance derived from plants, such as a pigment, that is beneficial to health, especially one that is neither a vitamin, nor a mineral. Chemicals in plants apart from vitamins, minerals, and macronutrients that have a beneficial effect the body. There are hundreds, if not thousands of them, and they have effects such as antioxidants, boosting the immune system, anti-inflammatory, antiviral, antibacterial, and cellular repair. Highly colored vegetables and fruits tend to be highest in these chemicals, but tea, chocolate, nuts, and flax seeds are all excellent sources as well.

PLASTER

Make an herb paste as described in 'Poultice' and place within folds of cheesecloth or muslin. Apply to the injured area. Cayenne and mustard powder are best applied as plasters rather than poultices so they don't touch the skin. Other herbs work well as plasters when you want an antiseptic and healing effect on an injury.

POLYUNSATURATED

Polyunsaturated and monounsaturated fats are the two unsaturated fats. Some examples of foods that contain these fats include fish, avocados, olives, walnuts, and liquid vegetable oils such as soybean, corn, safflower, canola, olive, and sunflower. Both polyunsaturated and monounsaturated fats may help lower your blood cholesterol level when you use them in place of saturated and trans fats. Keep total fat intake to only a quarter of your total calories. They also include essential fats that your body needs, but can't produce itself as omega-6 and omega-3, which are crucial to brain function and normal growth and development of the body. Polyunsaturated fats – like all fats – contain nine calories per gram. All fats are equally high in calories.

POTASSIUM

A dietary mineral needed for water balance and healthy muscle function in the body. 3500 mg RDA

POULTICE

To make a poultice crush the medicinal parts of the plant to a pulpy mass and heat. Mix with a hot, sticky substance such as moist flour or corn meal. Apply the pasty mixture directly to the skin. Wrap a hot towel around and moisten the towel periodically. A poultice will draw impurities from the body. Some poultices require the herbs to be simmered first for roughly two minutes. If you want a paste like mixture, add flour or oatmeal. Then the excess liquid is squeezed out and the herbs applied to the area, bandaging them in place for up to three hours. To prevent the mixture from sticking to the skin apply a little oil such as olive oil to the area before applying the poultice. Alternatively fold crushed herbs in a surgical gauze or muslin to make a pack, place in a dish and pour on just enough boiling water to cover the pack. Soak for 3-5 minutes, drain off the water, allow the poultice to cool to a comfortable temperature and place on the affected area. To make a cold poultice crush and bruise fresh herbs to make a paste which is then spread on a piece of gauze and placed in the freezer for ten minutes. Remove and place on affected area.

PROTEIN: The protein in our food contributes essential amino acids. Amino acids are used by cells to build new proteins and repair muscles. Protein food is not a high source of energy, however protein is essential in the right amount for proper functioning of our bodies. The amino acids then can be reused to make the proteins your body needs to maintain muscles, bones, blood, and body organs. Protein from animal sources, such as meat and milk, is called complete, because it contains all nine of the essential amino acids. Most vegetable protein is considered incomplete because it lacks one or more of the essential amino acids. This can be a concern for someone who doesn't eat meat or dairy products. But people who eat a vegetarian diet can still get all their essential amino acids by eating a wide variety of protein-rich vegetable foods. For instance, you can't get all the amino acids you need from peanuts alone, but if you have peanut butter on whole-grain bread you're set. Likewise, red beans won't give you everything you need, but red beans and brown - unrefined rice will do the trick. The good news is that you don't have to eat all the essential amino acids in every meal. As long as you have a variety of protein sources throughout the day, your body will grab what it needs from each meal. Good sources of protein are meat, pumpkin seeds, peanuts, cheese, almonds, cashews, eggs, milk, beans, and brown rice. About 50 grams a day RDA

RECOMMENDED DAILY ALLOWANCE (RDA)
The daily dietary intake level of a nutrient considered sufficient by the Food and Nutrition Board to meet the requirements of nearly all (97–98%) healthy individuals in each life-stage and gender group.

RIBOFLAVIN
Also known as vitamin B2 is an easily absorbed micronutrient with a key role in maintaining health in humans. Riboflavin is yellow or yellow-orange in color and in addition to being used as a food coloring, it is also used to fortify some foods. It is a member of the water-soluble family of B-complex vitamins required for glucose metabolism so the body can produce energy from carbohydrates, normal red blood cell production, and general body growth. It prevents skin lesions and weight loss, and is necessary for the maintenance of good vision, skin, nails, and hair; alleviates eye fatigue; promotes general health. Exposure to light destroys riboflavin. Milk, cheese, leafy green vegetables, liver, kidneys, legumes, tomatoes, yeast, mushrooms, and almonds are good sources of vitamin B 2.

Appendix D: Glossary

SASHIMI
A delicacy consisting of very fresh raw fish or seafood sliced into thin pieces. Traditionally it's served with just soy sauce, wasabi paste, and ginger slices, but other simple garnishes are also popular.

SATURATED FATS
Saturated fat is the main dietary cause of high blood cholesterol. Saturated fat is found mostly in foods from animals and some plants. Foods from animals include beef, beef fat, veal, lamb, pork, lard, poultry fat, butter, cream, milk, cheeses, and other dairy products made from whole and two percent milk. All of these foods also contain dietary cholesterol. Foods from plants that contain saturated fat include coconut, coconut oil, palm oil, palm kernel oil, and cocoa butter.

SELENIUM
Selenium is a trace mineral essential to good health, but only in small amounts. It makes special proteins, antioxidant enzymes, which play a role in preventing cell damage. Some medical information suggests that selenium may help prevent certain cancers. Selenium may boost fertility, especially among men as it has been shown to improve the production of sperm and sperm movement. Brazil nuts are the best source of selenium. Fish, shellfish, red meat, grains, eggs, chicken, liver, and garlic are all good sources of selenium. Too much selenium in the blood can cause loss of hair, nail problems, nausea, irritability, fatigue, and mild nerve damage. 50 IU RDA

SPECIES
A group of plants or animals having similar appearance; A rank in the classification of organisms, below genus. A group of organisms which resemble each other and can interbreed with each other

STEAMS AND INHALATIONS
For a facial steam place a handful of herbs in a wide bowl, pour on freshly boiled water and using a towel draped over the back of your head, sit with your face at a comfortable distance from the water and steam for at least ten minutes, or as long as is comfortable. Do not put your face too close to the water to begin with or the steam may scald you.

STEEP
It is important to cover your pot while steeping to prevent the aromatic oils from evaporating into the air. A lid will cause the steam to condense back into the water. Boil the water first, then remove it from the heat and add the herb, or pour over the herb. Any herb left sitting in water.

SUSHI
Rice with raw fish wrapped in seaweed

SYRUPS
Syrups are made using equal proportions of herbal infusions or decoctions with honey or unrefined sugar. Herbal infusions or decoctions used in syrups need to be brewed or simmered for longer than normal. Place the infusion or decoction in a saucepan together with the honey or sugar and gently heat, stirring until the honey or sugar has

dissolved and the mixture has a syrupy consistency. Remove from the heat and leave to cool. Once cooled pour into a sterile glass bottle, seal with a cork, and store in a cool, dark place. The cork seal is important because syrups are prone to ferment and may explode if kept in a screw-lid topped bottle. A regular dose for syrups is one to two teaspoons taken three times daily.

SECOND METHOD
Honey-based syrups preserve the healing qualities of some herbs and can be used to soothe sore throats and provide relief from coughs and colds. To make an herbal syrup, combine two ounces of dried herbs with one quart of water in a large pot. Boil down until it is reduced to one pint. Add one to two tablespoons of honey. Store all herbal syrups in the refrigerator for up to one month.

TEA
The standard quantity for a cup of herb 'tea' is one teaspoon dried, or two teaspoons fresh herbs per cup of freshly boiled water. If you are making your herbal brew in a teapot warm the teapot first with water from the kettle just before it boils, add the appropriate quantity of herbs and pour on freshly boiled water. Put the lid on the teapot and leave to infuse for about five minutes, then strain into a cup and add honey, lemon, or spices to taste as desired. For medicinal brews use twice the standard amount depending on your chosen herb or remedy, and leave to infuse for longer, generally at least ten minutes.

TBS
Tablespoon

TS
Teaspoon

THIAMIN
It is also known as vitamin B1 and is an energy building vitamin which helps you to digest carbohydrates. It also keeps your heart and muscles stable. Assists in production of blood formation, carbohydrate metabolism, and affects energy levels in the body. 1.2 mg RDA

TINCTURES
Use eight ounces dried or twelve ounces of fresh herbs to a quart of high proof alcohol - vodka, whiskey, brandy, or rum. A regular dose is a teaspoon diluted in water or fruit juice, taken three times daily. Place the herbs in a clean glass jar, pour on alcohol ensuring all the herb is covered, put the lid on and shake. Leave in a cool dark place for at least two weeks shaking every day. It takes time for the active ingredients of the herb to be released into the alcohol. Strain and pour into clean glass bottles and store in a cool, dark place. Use a small, sterile, leak - proof, air tight bottle or jar. Tinctures can last for over a year. The alcohol acts as a preservative. If you prefer not to use alcohol use vinegar instead; or add the tincture when finished as above to one cup of warm water, which will cause most of the alcohol to evaporate. This will also dilute the bitter taste. However, the strength is also changed.

Appendix D: Glossary

TONICS
Tonic wines are like a tincture. The herbs are used to fill a clean jar over which wine is poured so that the herb is completely covered and the level of the wine is above the top of the herbs. Close securely and leave to mature for at least one month. Regularly top up the jar to ensure the herbs remain covered, replacing with a new batch of herbs as required. Lasts for about four months. Discard the mixture if any mold occurs. A quicker method is to add the herbs and wine / port to a saucepan roughly six ounces of herbs to a quart of liquid. Cover with a lid and heat gently until the wine begins to simmer. Do not allow the mixture to boil unless you wish to eliminate the alcohol content. Remove from the heat and leave covered for a day. Strain and bottle.

TOPICAL
Topical medicinal agent is applied to a certain area of the skin intended to affect only the area to which it is applied. Whether its effects are indeed limited to that area depends upon whether the agent stays where it is put or is absorbed into the blood stream.

ULCERS
An open sore of the skin, eyes, or mucous membranes in the nose or mouth, often caused by an initial abrasion and maintained by an inflammation and/or an infection. Germs can enter an ulcer and make difficult to heal. Sores that develop in the mucous membrane of the stomach—more frequent among women, or in the duodenum, which is the beginning portion of the small intestine—more frequent in men. An ulcer develops when the area's ability to resist acid in gastric juice is reduced. It causes a burning ache and hunger-like pain. Ulcers can bleed, perforate the abdominal wall, or block the gastrointestinal tract. Stress and diet were blamed until a specific type of bacteria was discovered. This type of ulcer can be treated with combination drug therapy. Long-term use of aspirin and similar drugs were shown to be the two major causes and the best therapy is stop using those drugs. Cigarette smoking and alcohol consumption slows healing and promotes recurrence.

VITAMINS
A lot of the vitamins in fruits and vegetables are lost between the garden and your plate. The longer the foods are stored before you eat them, the more nutrients are lost. Heat, light, and exposure to air all reduce the amount of vitamins, especially vitamin C, thiamin, and folic acid. Many people do not eat balanced meals that meet the requirements the body needs in digesting enough nutrients to sustain the body's health and fuel factors. Research demonstrates almost all varieties of disease can be produced by the deficiency of vitamins, minerals, amino acids, and other nutrients. Vitamins are vital for your skin. The most important factor of nutritional deficiencies is the intense processing and refining of foods like cereals and sugar. The human body uses food to manufacture all its building blocks as well as to provide fuel. To do this, it performs several thousand different chemical reactions. Water soluble vitamins, B-complex vitamins and vitamin C, are vitamins not stored in the body and must be replaced each day. These vitamins are easily destroyed or washed out during food storage and preparations. Fat soluble vitamins are foods with these vitamins will not lose them when cooked and the body does not need these every day and stores them in the liver when not used.

VITAMIN A
Vitamin A is referred to as retinol or carotene, and is a vitamin for growth and body repair. It is very vital in the formation of bone and tissues, and also keeps your skin smooth. And if you are night blind, the cure is having more vitamin A. This is a fat soluble vitamin. Vitamin A works together with vitamins D, B, E, zinc, phosphorus, and calcium. It also acts as an antioxidant essential in pregnancy and lactation, which may help protect against cancer and other diseases, and night blindness —if deficient. Good sources are liver, carrots, mangos, papayas, spinach, eggs, dairy products, and sweet potatoes. 800 mcg RDA

VITAMIN B-1
Also named thiamin, it is a water-soluble vitamin of the B complex, which converts food to energy, promotes healthy nerve function, muscle tone, and growth. It helps digest carbohydrates and keeps your heart and muscles stable. Good sources are baked potatoes, beef kidney and liver, pork, rye and whole grain flour, beans, oranges, oysters, peanuts, peas, raisins, wheat germ, and brown rice. 1.2 mg RDA

VITAMIN B-2
Also called riboflavin, it is yellow or yellow-orange in color. In addition to being used as a food coloring, it is used to fortify some foods. Aids in formation of red blood cells and antibodies, essential for carbohydrate, protein, and fat metabolism, promotes general health, necessary for the maintenance of good skin, nails, hair and good vision, and maintains cell respiration. If deficient painful tongue and fissures occur at the corners of the mouth, and/or chapped lips. Good food sources are liver, eggs, whole grains, soybeans, and green leafy vegetables. 1.3 mg RDA

VITAMIN B-3
Also referred as niacin, helps the body transform carbohydrates into energy and maintains nervous and digestive systems, skin, hair and eyes healthy, reduces high blood pressure, improves circulation, lowers cholesterol levels while increasing energy. If deficient pellagra - scaly skin sores appear. Good sources are meat, fish, whole grains, beans, nuts, and peas. 15 mg RDA

VITAMIN B-5
Also called pantothenic acid, is an essential nutrient, a water-soluble vitamin required to sustain life, needed to form coenzyme-A, and is critical in the metabolism and synthesis of carbohydrates, proteins, and fats. Aids in the utilization of vitamins, helps in cell building, development of the central nervous system, fights infections, and helps release energy from carbohydrates. If deficient paresthesia develops, which is abnormal skin sensations as tingling, tickling, itching, or burning usually associated with nerve damage. Good sources are liver, eggs, peanuts, mushrooms, split peas, beans—especially soy beans, and whole grains. 5 IU MG RDA

VITAMIN B-6
Also called pyridoxine is necessary for production of antibodies, building blocks of protein, necessary for synthesis and breakdown of amino acids, promotes healthy skin, reduces muscle spasms and leg cramps, and helps the body maintain a proper balance of

phosphorous and sodium. If deficient anemia and fatigue develop. Good sources are fish –especially tuna, bananas, poultry, lean meat, whole grains, and potatoes. 1.5 mg RDA

VITAMIN B-9

Also called folic acid and very important to the growth and reproduction of all body cells, including red blood cells. It is a water-soluble vitamin. Folic acid helps digestion, and the nervous system, improving mental as well as emotional health, and can be used to treat depression and anxiety. Deficiency may cause fatigue, acne, a sore tongue, and cracking at the corners of mouth while a severe deficiency may cause infertility or even sterility. Deficiency during pregnancy is associated with birth defects. Good sources are green leafy vegetables, dried beans, poultry, fortified cereals, whole grains, oranges, and nuts. 400 mcg RDA

VITAMIN B-12

Also called cobalamin, is required for carbohydrate and fat metabolism. This is a water soluble vitamin. This is a must for children's growth, needed to make red blood cells and DNA, which is the genetic material in cells, and to keep nerve cells healthy. Prevents anemia by helping in formation and regeneration of red blood cells, Necessary for fat, carbohydrate and protein metabolism, and increases energy. Good food sources are beef, fish, poultry, eggs, and dairy products. 2.4 mcg RDA

VITAMIN C

Also known as ascorbic acid is a water soluble vitamin very essential as it protects your bones, teeth and gums. It is the ultimate medicine for curing scurvy and also fights any body infection. Without its support collagen cannot be synthesized in the body. Aids in absorption of iron. Good sources are citrus fruits, guava, cherries, tomatoes, melons, berries, sweet and hot peppers, and broccoli. 80 mg RDA

VITAMIN D

Vitamin D is also called cholecalciferol, a fat soluble vitamin and very important for children. The common disease seen in kids suffering from malnutrition is rickets, which is actually caused by the deficiency of vitamin D. Bones cannot grow in a normal way if there is a lack of this vitamin. In adults osteoporosis is caused due to lack of vitamin D. It is necessary for the reproduction of new skin cells. It is one of only three vitamins that are absorbed by the skin, as are vitamins A and E. It plays a key role in ensuring the absorption of calcium and phosphorus from the intestines. Maintains a stable nervous system. Direct sunlight is a natural source of vitamins apart from spinach and vegetables. Good sources are egg yolks, fatty fish like herring and mackerel, milk. This vitamin is also made in skin when exposed to sunlight. 10 mcg RDA

VITAMIN E

Also known as alpha-tocopherol, vitamin E is fat soluble, and good to treat cuts and wounds. It helps protect against aging and damage that may lead to cancer by supplying oxygen to the cells. It is an antioxidant vitamin that prevents cell damage by inhibiting the oxidation of LDL cholesterol. Vitamin E may reduce the risk of heart disease. It is essential to prevent sterility. Prevents and dissolves blood clots. Good sources are vegetable oil, wheat germ, nuts, dark green vegetables, pumpkin, whole grains, and beans. 1000 mg RDA

VITAMIN H

Also named biotin is a water soluble B complex vitamin essential for metabolic reactions to synthesize fatty acids. The body needs biotin to metabolize carbohydrates, fats, and amino acids. Biotin is often recommended to strengthen hair and nails, and it's found in many cosmetic products for hair and skin. Good sources are egg yolk, meat, dairy products, dark green vegetables, nuts, and bananas.. It is also formed by microorganisms inside intestinal tract. Deficiency causes hair loss, dry skin, dermatitis, and fungal infections. 30 mcg RDA

VITAMIN K

This is also referred as phytonadione, is fat soluble and is known as the clotting vitamin, because without it blood would not clot. Some studies indicate that it helps in maintaining strong bones in the elderly. It accomplishes this by helping the body transport calcium. Vitamin K plays an important role in the intestines and aids in converting glucose into glycogen for long term energy storage in the liver, promoting healthy liver function. Deficiency causes delayed clotting and hemorrhaging, bruising easily,, and nosebleeds. Good sources are green leafy vegetables – spinach, avocados, meat –especially liver, cheese, asparagus, coffee, and green tea. Vitamin K is also made by the bacteria that line the gastrointestinal tract. 35 mcg RDA

VITAMIN P

This is also called bioflavonoids or phytochemicals and is water soluble. It enhances the use of vitamin C by improving absorption and protecting it from oxidation. Promotes blood vessel health, including improving capillary strength, Prevents accumulation of cholesterol plaque. Great sources of this vitamin are found in the edible pulp of fruits, green pepper, broccoli, and red wine. There are no daily recommended allowances for this vitamin.

WATER

The most important nutrient for the human body is water. An average person can live for about forty to forty-five days without food, yet only three to five days without water. Our body's about seventy-five per cent water. The average-sized person requires three quarts of water a day or 96 ounces. A good rule to follow is divide your body weight in half, and that's the number of ounces of water you should be drinking daily. If you are eating adequate amounts of fresh fruits and vegetables daily, you're getting about one quart of water already. Water is the major ingredient of all fluids in the body including saliva, gastric juice, bile, pancreatic juices, and intestinal secretions. Water is necessary for almost every bodily function. It helps carry essential nutrients to all our cells, aids in circulation, digestion, and helps remove waste products. Drink at least one 8-ounce glass of water thirty minutes before each meal and then another 8-ounce glass about two hours after each meal. Before your largest meal of the day, drink at least 16 ounces of water and you will decrease your appetite and greatly help your digestion. Stay away from drinks with caffeine, such as coffee, tea, and sodas. Caffeine is a diuretic and actually causes you to lose water, so it does more harm than good. Drink filtered water. There are three basic types of filters you can purchase, distillation, carbon filtration and reverse osmosis. Carbon filters are the most common and least expensive. Change filters regularly.

ZINC

Zinc is needed for the body's immune system to properly work. It plays a role in cell division, cell growth, healing wounds, and the break down of carbohydrates. Zinc is also needed for the senses of smell and taste. Deficiency causes hair loss, poor appetite, reduced sense of taste and smell. High-protein foods contain high amounts of zinc. Beef, pork, and lamb contain more zinc than fish. The dark meat of a chicken has more zinc than the light meat. Other good sources of zinc are peanuts, peanut butter, and legumes. Fruits and vegetables are not good sources, because zinc in plant proteins is not as available for use by the body as the zinc from animal proteins. Therefore, low-protein diets and vegetarian diets tend to be low in zinc. 40 mg RDA

You are what you eat, so don't be fast, cheap, easy, or fake.
Every time you eat is an opportunity to nourish your body.

Author unknown

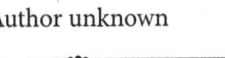

NOTES

Sources and References

Books that helped and I heartily recommend are:

Back To Eden by Jethro Kloss - Healing Herbs, Home Remedies, Diet and Health 1971 USA.

The Folk Remedy Encyclopedia: Olive Oil, Vinegar, Honey and 1,001 Other Home Remedies By Frank K. Wood and the Members of FC&A Medical Publishing 2003 USA

Treatment and Cures With Local Herbs by Albertina Pavy 1988 Trinidad

www.nalis.gov.tt/Biography%5Cbio_AlbertinaPavy_herbalist.htm

ralphtrout@hotmail.com

A garden fork will serve better than a silver fork to eat good food.
Ralph Trout

www.ingramcontent.com/pod-product-compliance
Lightning Source LLC
Chambersburg PA
CBHW080402300426
44113CB00015B/2380